TRAVELER'S
TOOL KIT

SECOND EDITION

TRAVELER'S TOOL KIT

Second Edition

How to Travel
Absolutely
Anywhere

ROBERT
POWELL
SANGSTER

Menasha
Ridge
Press
1999

All photographs by Rob Sangster except the following:
back cover, Sheila Macdonald; page 6, Sally Sears; page
157, Scott Sangster; page 284, Tom Gettlefinger; page
381, Rutledge Forney; page 396 and back cover, C. J.
Pinnel; 406, Ritchie Smith; and page 451, Jack Kenner.

Web page at http://www.travelers-tool-kit.com
designed by Scott Sangster

Manufactured in the United States of America
Text design by Barbara E. Williams
Cover design by Grant Tatum

Published by
Menasha Ridge Press
P.O. Box 43673
Birmingham, AL 35243

Library of Congress
Cataloging-in-Publication Data:
The traveler's tool kit : how
to travel absolutely anywhere /
by Rob Sangster. — 2nd ed.
p.   cm.
Includes bibliographical
references (p. –   )
and index.
ISBN 0-89732-300-9
1. Travel   I. Title.
G151.S185   1996
S10'.2'02—dc20
95-39406
CIP

I loved writing *Traveler's Tool Kit* and hope it enables every reader to board his or her personal magic carpet.

I am deeply grateful to all those who provided personal and professional support while I was writing this book. My warmest thanks to Lisa C. Turner, gifted writer and traveler of the mind for her loving inspiration. As travel partners, I've had three of the finest: Dr. V. Rutledge Forney, who said, "That's a great idea" one late afternoon at a campsite in Botswana's Okavango Delta and stuck with the project from there on; Sally J. Sears, an intrepid adventurer who kept an eye on the breaking news from Ladakh to the Australian Gold Coast; and my son and best friend, Scott Sangster, explorer of the present and future. Jo Frances Powell Sangster and Robert Francis Sangster, my parents, showed me that experiencing the whole world should be a priority, and Kathy Lowry, my sister, made everything easier through her friendship.

ACKNOWLEDGMENTS

The manuscript of *Traveler's Tool Kit* benefited greatly from the generous attention of Betty Goff Cartwright, septuagenarian traveler of the century; Dr. Ann Livingstone, international political scientist; Dr. Emily McClure, tropical medical consultant; Ms. Ellen Rolfes, generous advisor; Bud Zehmer, for his astute editing; and Bob Sehlinger, for his continuing enthusiasm and counsel.

And finally, I salute all the kindred spirits with whom I've shared the wonders of the road.

CONTENTS

Part Four: The Finish Line ("And the Winner Is . . . !")

Introduction

Whatever you can do, or dream you can, begin it.
Boldness has genius and magic in it.
— Johann Wolfgang von Goethe

The sun was high as we glided into Picton Harbor aboard the *Arahua*, a white-hulled ferry that sails between the north and south islands of New Zealand. Gulls hung suspended against the wind, casting dark shadows on the teak decks. The moment the lines were fast, I bounded down the gangway. No one held up a chalkboard with my name written on it; no tour bus waited for me at the end of the wharf. Backpack over my shoulder, I was on my own. Time and direction were mine to command. I was free!

During the next few weeks, I strolled through tranquil rain forests, puffed across alpine passes, jammed spiked crampons into the flank of a glacier, and hung on with all my strength in a jet boat as it careened along the flinty wall of a river canyon. After skiing at Coronet Peak, I drifted into Queenstown beneath a parasail rainbow. Along the way, I read some wonderful books and listened to rugby boasts in local pubs. For better or worse, each one of those choices was my own.

In other words, I was a traveler. And the fact is that every one of us is already a traveler—in a big way. After all, we're passengers aboard a giant rock speeding through space at more than sixty-six thousand miles per hour. As explorers of the universe, doesn't it make sense to get to know our home planet better?

Traveler's Tool Kit is a practical "how to" book that will help you break free from ruts and visit the places of your dreams. There's an abundance of beauty in this world and you can bring much more of it into your life.

The information in this book prepares you for travel experiences that far surpass those of a mere vacation. Too many vacations consist of lying down,

Water seller.
Marrakesh, Morocco.

dressing up, and paying someone else a lot of money; too many vacations are limited to seeing in "life" what you've already seen dozens of times in travel posters and school books. Too often, sights are collected as trophies to be displayed during dinner party conversations by collectors who never know how much they missed.

Rather than offering opinions about where to eat in Paris, *Traveler's Tool Kit* shows you how to find delicious, affordable meals anywhere in the world. Instead of rating the world's "best" hotels (usually meaning the most expensive), this book shows you how to locate comfortable, affordable lodging anywhere in the world. You'll learn how to travel happily by train throughout Europe, negotiate successfully with cab drivers in New Delhi, and dramatically cut the costs of travel to any destination. You will be convinced you can afford to travel—and that you can't afford not to.

Hundreds of books recount daring adventures at altitudes or depths most of us will never reach. While I couldn't resist describing some remarkable places and including a few adventure stories, the goal of this book is to help you discover where *you* really want to go and show you how to plan your own adventures.

This book is for you if

- you are *curious about the rest of the world;*
- you are contemplating your *first foreign travel;*
- you want to *travel farther and more independently;*
- you choose to *travel on a budget;*
- you are a *business traveler;*
- you feel *inhibited by the unknowns of international travel;*
- you are interested in *personal safety and avoiding illness;*
- you have the *time and desire to travel;*
- you know that *life offers more than a two-week vacation once a year.*

Planning a trip is like running a whitewater rapid—preparation determines success. Scout the rapid carefully, evaluate alternative routes, then plot your course. As you begin your run through the whitewater, you will know what to expect and will be in the right state of mind. After that, it's mostly a matter of hanging on for an exciting ride. If, on the other hand, you enter a rapid without a good plan, you may get a chilly surprise. In the same way, planning a trip to a foreign destination can initially seem mystifying, but learning a simple process will enable you to avoid costly, frustrating, and possibly dangerous mistakes.

Assuming that money is an issue for you, as it is for most of us, *Traveler's Tool Kit* shows you dozens of ways to SAVE MONEY without detracting from the quality of your trip. Here's a quick example. A friend wanted to visit Moldavia, one of the republics of the former Soviet Union. When her travel agent quoted a round-trip ticket price of $1,850, she decided she couldn't afford to go. Using a telephone number I gave her, one of many in this book, she purchased the same ticket for only $875. That savings convinced her to make the trip—and to stay an extra week!

With respect to money, I hope to persuade you that sometimes spending less gets you more. By avoiding high-priced tourist circuits, you meet more local people and learn about their hopes and values. You get the *feel* of a place; you experience the essence of travel.

You'll learn how to connect with a network of travelers who will help you find the most enjoyable things to do and provide guidance on how much to pay for them. You'll even learn how to earn money from your travels after returning home.

Common sense tells you a lot about what kind of travel clothing and equipment you'll need—but not everything. You can learn the rest the hard way, on the road, or the easy way, right here in *Traveler's Tool Kit.* Take the wrong kind of mosquito protection to Africa and you'll see what I mean.

Travel provides an opportunity to think of beginnings and endings.

Travel provides an opportunity to think of beginnings and endings, to spend time alone, to challenge fears and inhibitions, to experience freedom and joy. The traveler becomes a treasure-house filled with images of the Sistine Chapel, of a cheetah bounding across the African savannah, the Li River flowing like liquid jade between ebony peaks, and the lights of Hong Kong harbor sparkling like stars in never-never land.

I know international travel may seem overwhelming to someone who's never tried it. Before traveling abroad, most people have little reason to know the difference between a passport and a visa. Add issues of language, currency, customs, transportation, food, and lodging, and there's a lot to think about. Even a short trip to Mexico may be intimidating, never mind a trek in Nepal.

Nobody says you have to fling yourself into the water as if you're an Olympic swimmer. If you're more comfortable testing the water with a toe, do it that way. Start slowly. Build confidence by limiting challenges, keeping the number of unknowns manageable.

For example, a trip from the United States to Canada or vice versa will introduce you to crossing a border, and possibly changing currency, but won't require a passport or dealing with a foreign language. As confidence builds, catch a spur-of-the-moment package deal to Acapulco. Get the feel of being in a place where English isn't the mother tongue and experience unfamiliar food and standards of sanitation somewhat different from those to which you're accustomed. You might also engage gently in the virtually worldwide practice of bargaining. At the same time, you'll be in a culture used to dealing with travelers beginning their careers in international travel. In short, no big surprises. With a taste of Canada and Mexico as a warm-up, you're ready to range farther afield.

What about testing your wings next in London? Rely on a travel agent's helping hand, sign up for one of the many tour packages available, or plan your own itinerary. The local language is surprisingly recognizable, the streets are safe, and the people are friendly. Like many of the great cities of the world, London has an extensive, efficient mass transit system. The assurance you develop from mastering the London "tube" enables you to look forward with confidence to using mass transit in Budapest, Moscow, Paris, Rome, Tokyo—anywhere you like.

By this point, you'll notice that it's not so difficult to travel in foreign countries and the so-called language barrier is really made of papier-mâché. Having experienced crossing borders, exchanging currency, and hopping aboard public transport, you're ready for independent travel wherever you choose.

Organizing a trip is one of the ways to take charge of your life. Shakespeare's Caesar said it well: "Men at some time are masters of their fates. The fault, dear Brutus, is not with our stars, but in ourselves, that we are underlings." On the same subject, Tom Robbins said, in *Jitterbug Perfume*, "If you insist on leaving your fate to the gods, the gods will repay your weakness by having a grin or two at your expense." If you believe, as I do, that travel is essential to a fulfilling life, it's up to you to make it happen. The starting bell rang for each of us at birth and there's all too little time to get through the gate and down the track.

Carpe Diem!

Above all else, you must make the decision to overcome inertia. Here's a parable to illustrate what I mean. Two couples, the Browns and the Greens, were midwestern neighbors in their youth. The Greens moved away but stayed in touch. One day, Mrs. Green called Mrs. Brown to say the Greens were planning a trip to Europe and to invite the Browns to come along. Well, Mr. Brown said he was just too busy, couldn't get away from his job right then. That evening he told his wife he didn't much like the idea of going someplace where people didn't speak English. The Greens made that trip and invited the Browns on a couple of others, but the answer was always about the same. After all, said Mr. Brown, "We'll have plenty of time to travel after I retire." The Greens kept traveling and the Browns couldn't figure out how the Greens could afford it, much less where they got the courage to go to such exotic places. After Mrs. Green started an importing business and Mr. Green joined the board of directors of the World Wildlife Fund, the couples fell out of touch.

Mr. Brown finally did retire, but by then he didn't feel much like traveling; in fact, those foreign places seemed even more intimidating. Before long, Mr. Brown died—and Mrs. Brown just didn't have the energy to go anywhere.

One sunny afternoon, years later, Mrs. Green thought, "I wonder whatever happened to the Browns?" Glancing up, she waved at her husband as he jogged toward her on the beach in Bora Bora.

ABOUT THE AUTHOR

You'll receive the greatest benefit from the following pages if you feel you can rely on what I say. I hope my words will establish that trust as we go along. Still, when I'm reading a book, especially one offering advice, I want to know a little about the author. In case you're like me, here's a sketch of the person behind these words.

As I grew up in Boston, my parents often used nice weekends to visit New England's nooks and crannies such as the Old North Church in Boston and the stone fences of Lexington from behind which farmers struck blows for independence. We vacationed in New Hampshire's apple orchards and the deep, cool woods of Maine. Later, living in Houston, the family traveled from the eerie bayous of Louisiana to the bone-dry canyons of Big Bend National Park. In other words, travel, even of limited scope, was established as a value in my mind.

Author (far right) with travel partners. Ladakh, India.

Since the Navy paid most of the costs of my college education, at graduation I received a formal invitation to board an aircraft carrier for a three-year guided and catered tour (conducted by the biggest tour operator of them all). Fortunately, the tour took place during a period when no one was shooting at anyone, so I had the opportunity to read books I'd missed along the way and, as recruiting posters promised, "see the world"—well, at least the part of the world visited by the Seventh Fleet. But it kept the travel bug well nourished.

After the Navy, I went to Stanford Law School to prepare for what could have been a fairly conventional life. As it turned out though, after practicing corporate law for a few years, I switched to the public sector for jobs in finance and housing policy in Washington, D.C. Then I returned to the private sector as a real estate developer with some interesting entrepreneurial adventures thrown in (including a natural foods restaurant, an importing company, and a foundation which donates, to Third World villages, equipment that disinfects contaminated water).

For a number of those years I did a little domestic travel, such as river trips, skiing, and hiking, but limited myself to the standard one- or two-week vacation. Then I had an unexpected opportunity to join a group running 277 miles of Colorado River whitewater in the Grand Canyon in 14-foot wooden dories. As it happened, the chance to take the three-week trip came at a time when I thought I was too busy to get away. Wrestling my left brain to the ground, I went anyway.

The length of the trip gave me enough time to separate myself from home and business and to synchronize myself completely with where I was; time to appreciate the geological evidence of more than a billion years of earth cycles, the tales of the ancient Anasazi recorded in their artifacts, and the profound night silence. Above all, I learned how important it is to be on the road long enough at a stretch for a magic "click" to occur in my psyche. That was my first glimmer of the potential rewards of travel. It was a turning point.

When I returned from that trip, everything was under control. My office was only days away from issuing $80 million in bonds but everyone had done his or her job beautifully. That was the day I gave up the fantasy of being indispensable—and was emancipated. I was also a sitting duck for an article in *National Geographic* a few months later that described New Zealand's Milford Track as "the finest walk in the world." I realized I was ready to see the rest of the world—and bought an airline ticket the next day.

Living fully is infinitely more important to me than earning the last possible dollar. Besides, learning about people and experiencing the physical majesty of our planet are like money in the bank. I think of the priest who reportedly said, "In all my years, I've never once heard a man on his deathbed say, 'My only regret in life is that I didn't spend more time in the office.' " I'll never say that either.

At the time I write this, I've traveled in India, China, other Asian and Southeast Asian countries, Central America, about half of the countries in Africa and South America, a fair number of the Pacific Islands, most of Western and Eastern Europe, the former Soviet Union, Australia, New Zealand, Antarctica, and throughout the United States. I've visited favorite places more than once. India and New Zealand are at the top of the list, but then there's Peru, Botswana, Namibia, Egypt, Chile, and . . . We'll talk more about special places as we go along.

Literary Housekeeping

This is a good place for a little literary housekeeping. I place an asterisk (*) or one of a series of symbols after a place name that may be unfamiliar, then describe its location and say a few words about it in a footnote. I've included many such place names because, as they enter your vocabulary, they become keys to the rest of the world. From the first time you see the name of some exotic place, you begin to make it yours. Perhaps my brief mention will strike a spark, igniting a desire to take a look for yourself.

It is difficult to find pronouns that automatically include both genders and it is tedious to use the phrase "he and she" repeatedly. Grammar and common usage in our language haven't caught up with social consciousness. I have, as appropriate, alternated male and

Literary Housekeeping (continued)

female references. My heart is in the right place even if my pen is grammar-tied on occasion.

Finally, a comment about the term "Third World." I use it reluctantly because it's often used carelessly as a catchall for countries characterized by poverty and political instability. Through such usage, the term has gained an undertone of disapproval or condescension. Historically, the phrase gained popularity at the 1955 Conference of Non-Aligned Nations in Bandung, Indonesia. Participants described NATO countries as the First World and the Warsaw Pact countries as the Second World. Choosing nonalignment with either, conference participants referred to themselves as the Third World. I suppose the demise of the Warsaw Pact technically took the Second World out of the lineup. I wonder if that means the Third World is moving up a step?

Plowshares Institute substitutes the term "Two-Thirds World" as a reminder that we're referring to countries that include more than two-thirds of the people, resources, and land mass of this planet—not inconsiderable factors in our future. I could refer to the "rest of the world," but that's a little confusing. In *Africa: Dispatches from a Fragile Continent*, Blaine Harden called Africa the "Nth World" to convey the sense of conditions far inferior even to the rest of the Third World. His term reminds us that Third World countries exist across a very broad spectrum. Standards of living in Hong Kong and Singapore have little in common with those in Bolivia, Madagascar, and Zaire.

Countries constituting the Third World can be described as diversified, fascinating, intriguing, and spellbinding, but, since none of those words carries enough recognition, we're left with "Third World." When I use the term, it is as a shorthand geographical description and I intend no negative connotation.

Both the Index and the Bibliography are extensive, and I urge you to take advantage of them. The Index is a road map to help direct you to all references in the book on a particular topic or place. The Bibliography is a fine collection, and I've annotated it to make it easier for you to make selections.

1

The Most Powerful Reasons to Travel

> The world is a book, and those who
> do not travel read only a page.
> — St. Augustine

Penny Hardaway slashes to the hoop for a reverse lay-up. Five seconds left in the game, Orlando Magic up by two. Shaquille O'Neal brings the ball in, firing a long pass to Kobe Bryant. Kobe spins at the three-point line and goes up to shoot his trademark jumper. . . . Sure, it's exciting, but whichever team you root for you're still only a spectator, not a participant—and life is meant to be lived, not watched. It takes more effort to travel than it does to sit in front of the tube. So what makes it worthwhile? Most people say they take a vacation to relax, perhaps fish, play golf or tennis, or lie on the beach. Given the amount of stress in daily life, it's no surprise that relaxation is the first thing that comes to mind. However, the rewards of travel are many. Here are some that seem most compelling:

Perspective. Freed from the cocoon of familiar places, the traveler learns how people elsewhere live and what they care about. Perspective expands. After you've been there, you own a bit of London, know something of the people of Bangkok, and begin to understand the emotions in Jerusalem. When expressions of artists in a dozen cultures have enriched your mind, you develop true appreciation for the immense breadth of human creativity. A small article reporting that an earthquake has devastated a village high in the Peruvian Andes will escape the scanning eye of most readers, but if you've met those villagers and listened to their music, that article leaps off the page. Having been to India, you no longer skim past an article describing a violent clash between Hindus and Muslims; you read it and your heart aches.

Travelers develop a deeper understanding of the strivings of billions of humans, of lives filled with achievement as well as lives filled from dawn to dusk with hard work, disease, and hopelessness. Learning about the religions,

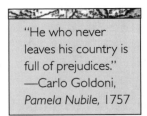

politics, customs, and attitudes of very different cultures helps us understand our own culture better. We come to realize that much of what we accept as true reflects the values of the country, even the neighborhood, in which each of us grew up.

Do you remember the fable of the blind men and the elephant? One blind man puts his arms around the elephant's sturdy front leg and says the animal resembles a tree. Another grasps the trunk and insists the elephant is like a snake. A third runs his hand along the great flank and declares that an elephant is very like a wall. None got it right. In other words, it's hard to have an accurate perspective on humankind when your experience is limited to a single culture.

Beauty. The greatest beauty devised by humans and nature awaits you: music, landscapes, and sunsets; the architectural brilliance of cathedrals and palaces; the breathtaking majesty of the Himalayas and the redwood forests. Beauty surrounds you when you're gliding silently in a dugout through the papyrus-bordered waterways of the Okavango Delta, strolling in the south of France, or listening to the roar of the lion or the roar of the sea.

Special Places. You may be compelled to travel by the lure of a specific place, a vision with a mysterious resonance. It may be Kathmandu, a cavern, a carnival, or an entire culture; any image reinforced until it becomes a command. It may be a yearning, ingrained by childhood tales, to return to the "old country" to see how your ancestors lived.

Special Interests. Sail to Madagascar to seek rare orchids, trek along Peru's Tambopata River in search of nearly extinct birds, or dive among exotic tropical fish at the Great Barrier Reef. Learn that language you've always wanted to master. Whether it's art, wine, food, architecture, Siberian tigers, or just better weather, travel can gratify your special interests.

Personal Growth. A person would have to be almost brain-dead to wander about the world for weeks or months without growing from the experience. On the road, there's no phone ringing and no lawn to be mowed. Instead, there's plenty of time for contemplation, even solitude. Personal growth may take years to be recognized, or it may become evident with dramatic suddenness.

Personal Challenges. Trekking, diving, and climbing stretch physical capabilities and awaken what someone called the "adrenaline angel." Other activities challenge the mind. Surely, some of the finest moments of our lives are those when we're stretched the most.

Self-Esteem. Planning a complicated trip, say to a half-dozen Asian countries, is no easy task. When you return, having successfully solved every problem that came up along the way, your feelings of competence and confidence are strengthened. For example, after riding a bicycle solo from Ireland to India, the writer Dervla Murphy probably felt little need to conform to the conventional Irish view of a "woman's role."

New Priorities. Travel provides the opportunity to set new priorities and decide how to reallocate your time. If you write down your insights as you travel, they won't be swept away by the familiar routines of home.

Renewed Energy. After the exercise, daily mental stimulation, constant variety, and excitement of travel, you return home full of plans, eager to re-energize your life and get into action.

Escape. Some people travel not to get to some place as much as to get away from some place. From beaches to bar stools, people talk about travel as an escape—from a weak economy, a lost job, an unhappy relationship, or the daily treadmill. Some travelers are recent graduates, perhaps waiting for a new job to start. Others, looking ahead to careers and family, feel it might be now or never for travel. Some, dissatisfied, tired of responsibility, or newly retired, hope that travel will stimulate changes in their lives.

> "Most of us abandoned the idea of a life full of adventure and travel sometime between puberty and our first job. Our dreams die under the dark weight of responsibility. Occasionally the old urge surfaces, and we label it with names that suggest psychological aberrations: the big chill, a mid-life crisis."
> —Tim Cahill, *Jaguars Ripped My Flesh*, 1987

Curiosity. Travel satisfies, at least in part, our curiosity about the other side of the mountain. It enables us to see beyond the horizon, to learn about people in faraway places. In the big picture, the earth is no more than a tiny mass, not really the center of anything. At the very least, we should learn as much about it as we can.

Business Expertise. Knowledge of the world can be a major asset in business. Western nations continue to increase their trade with the three billion people who live in the less-developed world. When you've traveled in a country and understand its politics and business practices, and have a sense of the place not revealed by statistics, you're a valuable resource when decisions are made about doing business in that country. On a résumé, visits to less-traveled places imply independence, confidence, energy, and intellectual curiosity.

Awakened Emotions. Travel evokes not only positive emotions such as excitement and awe, but other emotions as well. You'll sometimes be in the midst of people whose living conditions are *wretched*. Not quaint, or merely lower than those of Western societies, but wretched. In some countries, many people can't afford education or even nutritious food. They're chronically ill with diseases that could easily be prevented or cured in the developed world.

They can't earn a living because there's no longer a market for the products of their labor. After seeing people as individual human beings rather than electronic images on a screen, you may find yourself emotionally kidnapped, compelled by compassion to do something to improve their conditions. It doesn't happen to all travelers, but it could happen to you.

Memories. Can it be better said than Hemingway said it? "If you are lucky enough to have lived in Paris as a young man, then wherever you go for the rest of your life, it stays with you, for Paris is a moveable feast." Memories of travel experiences are a treasure.

Memories of travel experiences are a treasure.

Friendship. For the fortunate traveler, memories of people last the longest. As we travel, we luxuriate in trading life stories, speaking our minds, breaking free from familiar roles. Friendships made on the road, with local people as well as other travelers, are one of life's deepest pleasures.

Romance. More than a few people hit the road with romance on their minds. They hear about the allure of men or women in foreign lands and decide to see for themselves. Some relationships pass with the sunset, some remain vivid for years, and a few last a lifetime.

Firsthand Information. Traveling frees you from having to rely on what's reported on television or in newspapers. You become able to interpret and respond to international events on your own. Relations among nations are affected by how well people in different cultures know one another as individuals rather than as stereotypes.

Reward. Many people finally figure out that they deserve a treat. They've worked hard and want to reward themselves. Travel is that reward.

Freedom. In the end, travel is freedom. Freedom from the weight of possessions and from ruts, freedom to be the person you think of yourself as being.

Evan Connell said something to the effect that "Some people do not travel the way most of us travel. Not only do they sometimes choose odd vehicles, they take dangerous and unusual trips for incomprehensible reasons." If you understand the reasons for your desire to travel, that's good. If not, "incomprehensible reasons" do fine. Someone suggested, perhaps with tongue in cheek, that the desire to travel may be genetically programmed into some people. If so, I have that gene. I can't *not* travel.

HOW WE TALK OURSELVES OUT OF TRAVELING

Since the reasons to travel are so compelling, why do people stay at home? I put that question to quite a few people and came up with the answers I've summarized below. Most people said travel was a high priority—even though they weren't doing it. However, as you'll see, the reasons given for not traveling can all be overcome by knowledge and motivation. That's what this book provides.

Lack of Knowledge. Jean thought about traveling, but she had no idea how to choose a destination. She hadn't seen a geography book since fourth grade and had dropped out of her only world history course. Where should she go? What should she take? Would she find decent places to stay? Would the bathrooms be clean? Until she knows what to expect, Jean will never leave home.

Money. The prices listed in tour brochures persuaded Vicki she couldn't afford to travel abroad. The photographs were beautiful and the hotels appealing, but the prices were stratospheric. The Kenya safari she liked best cost over $300 a day and that didn't even include airfare from home (she couldn't believe what the travel agent told her that would cost). When her neighbor said a glass of orange juice costs $5 in Rome, Vicki concluded that foreign destinations were for jet-setters only.

Vicki has no idea that the actual costs of travel are far lower than she believes them to be. She tossed the safari brochure away without realizing she could contact a local safari operator directly and cut the cost by 75 percent. She didn't know she could cut 30 percent off the quoted air fare and she would have scoffed at the idea that good food and lodging are available in most of the world for one-fourth of what she routinely pays at home. Of course, her attitude about money also needs adjustment; if she changes her spending habits at home, she can easily free more money for travel.

> Actual costs of travel are far lower than you think.

Lack of Time. William said, "I just can't get away." He feels harried—not just one day, but every day. He thinks he's indispensable at work and doesn't want to hear otherwise. The idea that he could organize his life so that everything would carry on successfully in his absence has never occurred to him. Secretly, he feels best when his nose is jammed to the grindstone. He can't conceive of taking a two-month sabbatical. He'll die sooner than he should— or maybe he'll read this book!

Barbara, on the other hand, said, "*They* won't let me get away." Her employer's manual says she's entitled to only one week of paid vacation a year—and she's never questioned it. She doesn't realize how many options she has that could free more of her time for living a full life.

> "And don't let the feeble excuse of work keep you back; remember the Haitian proverb: If work is such a good thing, how come the rich haven't grabbed it all for themselves."
> —John Hatt, *The Tropical Traveler,* 1982

Traditional-style Thai house. Bangkok, Thailand.

Language. The only foreign words Jeannine knows came from menus in Mexican restaurants. That never bothered her until she began thinking about taking a trip overseas. As far as she knows, English is spoken in only England and Australia and she's not about to go any place where "they" don't speak English. She has no idea that the English language has spread throughout large parts of the world and she could communicate easily even where no English is spoken.

Inertia. For Harold, the primary obstacle is plain old inertia; the beer-and-TV barrier. His homebound rut is too comfortable. When he considers forcing himself out of the house for a vacation, he doesn't see any reason not to return to the same old places. To him, "remote" means the instrument he uses to flick from channel to channel. Although he uses television primarily to fall asleep, he sometimes stumbles onto an exciting National Geographic program. Someone else might see the same program and start planning—but not Harold. Why make the effort to go to Athens when he can bring a pale electronic image of it into his home with his index finger?

Control. Dupont sees himself as being in control of his little world and that's the way he likes it. When he thinks of traveling abroad, he feels uneasy. Even in France, let alone someplace like China, he's afraid he wouldn't know what was going on and couldn't possibly be in charge. Besides, at home everyone knows who he is; over there, he'd be just another guy. He doesn't like that feeling at all.

Safety. Jo Ann heard of a woman who went to Costa del Sol in Spain and had her purse stolen "right there on the beach the very first night." So Jo Ann decided to stay put. She'll never find out how mistaken she is about safety abroad and how easily she could protect herself.

Health. Michael figured that if people get sick in Mexico, he'd be crazy to go someplace like India. He has never bothered to learn anything about the actual likelihood of health problems or how to prevent or cure anything he might encounter. He doesn't know that it's easy to keep yourself healthy on the road if you know how.

Most of these reasons for staying at home are understandable. Travel *can* be expensive if you don't learn how to spend money wisely. Health and safety *can* be at risk unless you understand the risks and guard against them. You have to know what to expect and have the knowledge to make the right choices. By the time you reach the end of *Traveler's Tool Kit*, you'll find that every reason not to travel was written on the wind.

PART ONE

Planning Your Trip ("On Your Mark . . .")

2

How to Choose Where to Go

All journeys have secret destinations of which
the traveler is unaware.
— Martin Buber

Where do you most want to go in this fascinating world? Since identifying your favorite destinations is essential to a fulfilling trip, first look inside, not out. Forget about self-imposed limitations and answer two questions: What kinds of experiences do you want, and what do you want to gain from the trip?

What would you like to be doing? Would the days be peaceful or would they be full of activities? Would you be alone or meeting lots of other people? Do you lust for fine food, sensuous beaches, wildlife, spectacular landscapes, physical challenges—or do you seek insights and internal change, perhaps a new direction for your life? Choosing a purpose for your trip and writing it down helps you get in touch with your feelings and gives you something to review when you get back. Your answers enable you to think about where to go without being influenced by the popularity of a destination or a desire to impress people.

The moment you've made up your mind to go somewhere, the most difficult part of the trip is behind you. You've overcome inertia and the risk of doing nothing.

CHOOSING WHERE *YOU* REALLY WANT TO GO

Many people choose destinations on the basis of beautiful scenery, climate, and available activities. Or they've been to a place before and liked it, or they have a friend or spouse who wants to go there. They're concerned about affordability, health, and personal safety and want to avoid unsanitary hotels, attempts by "locals" to rip them off, bad weather, extreme poverty, high costs, and tourist traps. No surprises there.

These are reasonable criteria—but I urge you not to settle for some destination just because it meets them. Make your choice of destination more personal. Close your eyes and conjure up the names of places that make your heart beat fast. Brainstorm. Think of cultures that appeal to you, parts of the world with a history that fascinates you, less-traveled places that have beckoned since childhood. What places offer the adventures, weather, or scenery you most enjoy? Whose art and music do you love? List every one of these places without worrying about practicality.

Think of cultures that appeal to you.

Next, prompt your memory with a world map. Continent by continent, country by country, add new places to your list. Read travel books to stimulate your imagination. Skim back copies of *National Geographic, Outside, International Travel News,* and *Condé Nast Traveler.* Attend local travelogues. Watch the Travel Channel, the Discovery Channel, and "National Geographic Explorer." Seek out travel tales from friends and travel agents.

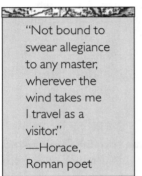

"Not bound to swear allegiance to any master, wherever the wind takes me I travel as a visitor."
—Horace, Roman poet

Make a list of destinations, then group your choices by continent or geographic region. Post this list on the refrigerator or bathroom mirror, anywhere that will keep it in your consciousness. After you've lived with this list for a while, cut it to a dozen or so magic places. With your original objectives clearly in mind, rank them and let the following factors influence your decision.

Factors to Consider

At this point, practical considerations should begin to affect your choice of destinations: Would you prefer to survey many countries or to focus on a single country or region? Are political conditions a problem at any of the destinations on your list? Would a certain destination present more of a mental or physical challenge than you want? Would local language seem to be a deterrent?

One Country—or Many?

The differences between a survey trip through many countries and a trip that focuses on a single country or region are substantial. If you have just a week or two, a tightly focused trip, dealing with only one language, one transportation system, and one culture, may be ideal. In general, your daily costs of transportation, lodging, and food are lower when you spend more time in one place. On the other hand, a multicountry trip is like a buffet table loaded with rich and varied dishes, many of which will be new to your palate. It requires more effort and a faster pace to sample everything on the table.

A tightly focused choice might be a trip to London with side trips to Cambridge and the Cotswolds, or a trip to Cuzco that includes hiking the Inca Trail and wandering in the sacred valley of the Urubamba.* A multi-country trip might take you cross-country from Amsterdam to Athens, or overland from London to Lagos,† or maybe from Kathmandu to Kalimantan.§

Either type of trip can be rewarding but, to make an informed choice, understand that they differ.

Political Conditions

Research the political situation at destinations you're considering. It was risky to visit Chile during the decades in which the Pinochet military dictatorship governed. However, Chile had its second modern democratic election in 1994 and is again one of the world's most rewarding—and safe—destinations. While conditions in Kashmir, Colombia, and Mozambique may not be as dangerous for travelers as media reports suggest, it's better to defer trips to places like these until things quiet down. Sri Lanka is wonderful, but I'm not going back until the Tamils and the Sinhalese decide they want to live in harmony. When the welcome mat has blood on it, think twice about crossing the threshold.

Mental and Physical Fitness

There are times on the road when you won't know exactly what's happening, or why, or what will happen next. Ask yourself how much input you can handle from cultures very different from your own, and for how long. If your tolerance for ambiguity is low, you may prefer traveling in Western-style cultures until you're a more seasoned traveler.

Physical fitness should also affect your decisions. For some, the rigors of walking the halls of art museums and galleries in Paris for a week can be substantial, let alone visiting dozens of Egyptian temples and tombs. Where heat, altitude, or exertion will be factors, be honest with yourself about the physical condition required. If you're considering trekking in the Zanskar

---

* *Sacred valley of the Urubamba.* This lovely valley near Cuzco in southern Peru is the site of several towns built on and out of Inca stones. Don't miss Ollantaytambo and Machu Picchu.

† *Lagos.* The capital of Nigeria, this city is located on the southern border on the Bight of Benin. Think of noise, pollution, dense traffic, greed, corruption, and incredibly high prices, and you'll appreciate Lagos's reputation as a "hell hole."

§ *Kalimantan.* The name of the Indonesian part of the Island of Borneo (the northern part is Malaysian). Straight south of Hong Kong, it is the third largest island in the world.

Valley* or to the summit of Kilimanjaro,† don't think in terms of how fit you were when you were eighteen, or how fit you could be if you worked out for three months. Think of how fit you actually will be when you board the plane.

Decide how much exertion you want to handle. For some, making a strenuous effort is part of the reward; achieving a goal and the ensuing fitness are worth a little pain. Others prefer a more languorous trip. At the beginning of your international travel life, err on the side of caution and stay well within your capacity. After a trip or two, you'll know much more about what you can, and choose to, handle. At that point, you may want to test yourself a bit.

As departure date approaches, step up your physical conditioning a notch or two. Unless you're already fit, consider walking a brisk three miles a day three times a week for six or eight weeks before you go. Like preparing for the ski season it's mostly a matter of building up your legs and stamina. No need to let sore muscles take you out of action.

To the extent it's connected to fitness, age is a consideration but need not be a deterrent. I've met many travelers well beyond their mid-sixties. Aboard a bus in steamy Tamil Nadu,§ I leaned across the aisle and struck up a conversation with a sturdy, white-haired woman who looked to be about sixty-five years old. As we got off the bus, I swung my backpack down from the overhead rack and asked if I might help with hers. She thanked me and suggested we have tea. I wasn't surprised when she said she'd been a British civil servant for more than forty years, but I was amazed when she told me the rest of her story. She'd just completed a solo bicycle ride the entire length of India and, several years earlier, had ridden more or less around the world. She exemplifies the point that age need not be a disqualification when the flame is burning brightly. Ben Franklin said that "Travel is one way of lengthening life." Few activities keep a person feeling as young as does independent travel.

> Age need not be a deterrent to travel.

The more remote reaches of the world are not very accommodating to people with physical handicaps. Nevertheless, I've met people traveling successfully with what seem to be fairly severe physical handicaps. It can be done; it's just more of a hassle. In the Bibliography I've listed several publications that provide information on traveling with various disabilities.

---

* *Zanskar Valley.* This remote valley in the far north of India was opened only recently to hardy trekkers.

† *Kilimanjaro.* Over 19,000 feet, this snowcapped volcano on the Kenya/Tanzania border is a popular five- or six-day trek. Because of fees and mandatory guides, it's a somewhat expensive trip.

§ *Tamil Nadu.* Located in the southeast corner of the Indian subcontinent, this state is sometimes called the most Indian part of India. It's a Hindu showplace in terms of architecture (particularly ornate temples), dance, and food. It also offers wildlife preserves, hundreds of miles of beaches, and comparatively cool hill stations.

Local Languages

Since we humans use more than 5,800 different languages and dialects, some prospective travelers may worry about inability to communicate. They needn't. First, English is rapidly becoming a global language. Second, where English is not spoken there's plenty of help available in the form of pocket-size dictionaries and phrase books with functional sections containing words for shopping, asking directions, ordering meals, and changing money. Third, language training courses on cassettes and accelerated language classes in community colleges can bring you up to speed quickly. Fourth, even when you have absolutely no language in common, it's amazing how much can be communicated nonverbally. Sure, it's sometimes more difficult than talking across the back fence, but lack of familiarity with a foreign language should not deter you from going somewhere you really want to go.

If you take a cross-country trek out of Iquitos, Peru, with several Aymara Indians, your inability to speak Spanish or Quechua won't matter much, though you will miss out on stories told around the campfire. In more populated areas, say Portugal or Germany, lack of knowledge of the local language can make handling daily details a bit difficult, but a few phrases and a couple dozen words will get you by anywhere. You need not avoid non-English-speaking destinations.

We'll talk more about language in Chapter 14. I mention it here only to signal that it is a factor to consider as you choose destinations.

A few final thoughts about destinations. If your interests are in less-developed countries, expect to invest more effort than if you travel to places such as England, France, or Sweden. Rather than staring passively at marble sculptures and cracked paintings, your trip is likely to be more active, focusing on wild animals, magnificent landscapes, and the people of unique cultures.

Also, be aware that some places on your list may bear little relationship today to the romantic images established in literature from an earlier age. For me, such places include Buenos Aires, Cairo, Casablanca, Papeete, Singapore, and Timbuktu. Ladakh (in northern India), Nepal, Sri Lanka, and Thailand are still jewels, but they've lost a little of their luster in recent decades as they've become more widely known. Up-to-date information will help you make the best choices.

Lastly, if this is your first overseas experience, the turmoil of India or the travails of Zaire may be a bit much. Or maybe not. Just be clear about how big a bite you want to take the first time out. If you feel uncertain, take an easier trial run. After all, you have a lifetime of trips coming up.

Timing

If you feel locked into taking a trip during a specified period—by an employer, kids, school, or whatever—the following factors may also influence your choice of destinations. If you've already chosen a destination, they'll help you know what to expect. If you have flexibility as to when you go, these factors should definitely affect where you go.

Weather. In a world where climatic temperatures range from above 130 degrees to below minus 130 degrees Fahrenheit, and monsoons and drought are common, weather always matters to some degree. It may determine your timing, especially for activities such as skiing, trekking, and hanging out on a beach. If it's not possible to go someplace when the weather there is ideal, at least avoid extremes in temperature and rainfall. If you can travel only at a certain time of year, find out what weather to expect so you'll be prepared.

Does continuous rain get you down? A rousing thunderstorm may be exciting, but dark skies day after day dampen most spirits. In many countries, heavy rains close the roads and transform trails into slick, muddy chutes.

Altitude affects local weather. As you slowly melt into a puddle in the steamy Kenyan port of Mombasa,* people are cool in nearby Nairobi on its high plateau. Even in tropical countries, temperatures can be very cold at high altitudes.

Continents tend not to have a single, predictable climate. For example, Europe has three distinct climate zones, north to south. In Africa, dry deserts in the north and south flank hot, wet tropics in between. On high plateaus, where nature preserves such as Masai Mara are located, temperatures are moderate, even during summer, because of the altitude. Also keep in mind that seasons in the Southern Hemisphere are the reverse of those in the Northern Hemisphere.

Asia ranges from a severely cold, dry arctic climate in the far north to excruciatingly hot summers in the southwest and monsoons in India. If generalizations hold, expect greater extremes of temperature inland and more rainfall on coastal areas. November to March is a relatively cooler period in Southeast Asia, while the rest of the year is likely to be rainy and humid. Monsoons are more common in June and July. Find out when they occur at your destination and avoid them.

In South America, the summer season comes during winter in the Northern Hemisphere. Summer in the lowlands is extremely hot and humid, but destinations at high altitudes, such as much of Peru, almost never experience extreme heat.

A hard-core traveler with a passion for a certain place will go when the opportunity arises, even if that may mean hell *and* high water; after all, people living there get through it. But why suffer if you have a choice? Tamil Nadu is renowned for friendly people, unique dance performances, and spectacular temples, but why visit in May when heat and humidity will muddle your

---

* *Mombasa.* This Kenyan port, the largest on Africa's east coast, was formerly an Arab trading post and retains much of that aura today. Of 600,000 inhabitants, 30 percent are Asian.

brain? Go to countries on the Mediterranean Sea in May when weather there is at its best. Why walk the beautiful trails in Nepal in March when pouring rain quenches your spirit and mists conceal the great peaks? Go in September when it rains least and visibility is best.

In the wet season, when they can find drinking water anywhere, wild animals scatter all over the African landscape. That means you can spend hours searching for them. In the dry season, animals must go to the few remaining waterholes—where you wait with your camera.

Since the timing of wet and dry seasons, as well as the temperature, differs region by region, you need specific information. The following are useful resources:

- The U.S. Department of Commerce *Climates of the World* booklet, available from the Government Printing Office (GPO), reports average precipitation by month in cities around the world. However, average temperature and rainfall reports are not as helpful as they appear. What you need are highs and lows.
- The GPO publishes National Weather Service reports on international climates.
- Some guidebooks have good information on weather.
- Use the Web. See www.weather.com and www.weatherpost.com.
- Good travel agents and tour operators are familiar with international weather.
- The Current Conditions section in the back of *Condé Nast Traveler* magazine provides information on the climate (temperature highs and lows, humidity, rain, and so on) in different destinations.
- Call The Weather Channel Connection at (900) WEATHER (932-8437). The cost is 95 cents a minute.
- Local newspapers give daily high and low temperatures for 50 or so cities around the world.
- Call American Express at (800) 554-2639 for worldwide weather reports and forecasts.
- National tourist offices can be good sources, but, because they promote tourism, it's wise to be a little skeptical of their reports. For example, the tourist office in Panama denies the existence of a rainy season. It admits only to a "Green Season." Oh, sure.
- *Traveler's Weather Guide* by Ten Speed Press provides a detailed overview of what weather to expect in many regions.

Tourist Seasons. Because crowds of tourists rank with monsoons as things to avoid, know when the tourist high season begins and ends at a potential destination. In general, it's June through September in the Northern Hemisphere, including Europe, and November through February in the Southern Hemisphere, but there are exceptions. The tourist high season may not always coincide with the best weather. Instead, it may reflect the time of year when most people are free to travel.

Crowds change every travel experience—almost always for the worse. Limited facilities become crowded in high season and local people become noticeably less congenial. Prices go up, sometimes tripling. Avoiding tourist high season should be a major factor in planning.

When your ferry ties up to the wharf in Lamu,* Kenya, in May, a swarm of young men compete to guide you to a fine hotel room overlooking the water or take you out in their sailing dhows. Prices are rock bottom. If you arrive in December, you'll find the tiny hotels packed and you'll have to pay whatever is demanded. Now, I ask you . . . ?

If you can't avoid high season, keep your sanity by visiting popular tourist sights very early in the morning or as late as permitted in the evening. Take a leisurely stroll while tourists are still wolfing down heavy breakfasts, then hole up in a museum during the heat of the day. Shoulder seasons, on either side of high and low, are often the best times to visit.

Local Holidays, School Recesses, and Special Events. Local holidays and school recesses create their own high season, with the majority of travelers being local people. The moment school is out, young people and families hit the road. Since local people know those dates, they book transportation and accommodations far in advance.

If you're committed to participating in the running of the bulls or watching the World Cup, make preparations well in advance. Watch for major events like these so you can incorporate them into your planning, one way or the other. Find out about special events through tour brochures, guide books, national tourist offices, travel agents, and Culturegrams (discussed later in this chapter).

The first time I tried to get to the Island of Zanzibar from Tanzania, I forgot that religious restrictions of the Islamic period of Ramadan were ending and joyful celebrations beginning. The few planes and cross-channel boats were packed with people seeking pleasure after an ascetic month. I never did get to Zanzibar, but I could have if I'd left a couple of days earlier.

DECIDING HOW MUCH TIME TO TAKE

The typical vacation is usually not long enough to fully disengage from work, friends, and habits and become immersed in where you are. And a trip

---

Lamu. This tiny island off the coast of Kenya was nicknamed the "Kathmandu of Africa" as it became a haven for travelers. Its cool, narrow streets are traveled by Abyssinian asses (and only one motor car). The traditional Arab architecture and intricate carvings are unchanged from centuries past. It's a perfect place to take a break: lie on Shela Beach, sail a dhow out to the reef to snorkel, and enjoy the camaraderie and a cool Tusker at Petley's Inn in the evening.

Street food in one
of the free markets.
Xi'an, China.

of short duration means other limitations. The countdown to return begins almost as soon as you walk out the door. You may wind up spending most of your time in big cities, seeing only the most well-known sites. You travel at a hectic pace, always on the move, struggling to absorb what's around you. When you're rushed, it's hard to be flexible, to change your route with your mood or fall in with other travelers for a side trip.

As you think about allotting time for your trip, don't accept the idea of a two-week vacation as natural or inevitable. Would it surprise you that working people in most other developed countries routinely take more than two weeks away from their jobs? Swedes get up to eight weeks a year; Germans, the French, and Finns get six weeks. Other Europeans expect no less than five weeks. On average, a European takes three times as much time away from work as an American does. As Europeans put it: *we work to live while Americans live to work.* European employers believe, and there is evidence to back them, that time off improves efficiency and productivity and is undoubtedly related to morale.

Try negotiating with your employer. Can you get more time off if part of it is unpaid? Can you trade some overtime work for time off? Or can you take an unpaid leave of absence? Life is too short to limit ourselves to two-week bursts of interaction with the rest of the world. Do everything you can, including loosening restrictions you place on yourself, to take long trips—the ultimate trip being open-ended.

Having said all that, if time or money or other constraints mean that you can absolutely get away for only fourteen days, or ten, or five—do it! Every bit of the world you see will motivate you to experience more next time. Draw as much juice from those days as you can. Just don't accept two weeks quietly if you can have more.

HOW MUCH DO YOU WANT TO SPEND?

There are at two ways to go about deciding how much you want to spend:

1. Review your resources and competing priorities and *choose an amount of money you're comfortable spending on a trip.* In other words, set a maximum and then select destinations. When choosing the amount, don't forget to consider all the money you *won't* be spending at home for food, entertainment, utilities, and so on. If this is your approach, and it's a rational one, I'll wager that you'll increasingly raise the figure as you come to recognize that travel is an investment that pays rich dividends.

   Obviously, the amount you set influences your choice of destinations. If a destination is far away and the cost of living there is high, you won't be able to stay very long. Suppose you choose $2,500. Subtract from $2,500 the approximate costs of getting to a potential destination and back. Let's say that leaves a balance of $1,700. Use the Checklist in Chapter 6 to estimate local daily costs of traveling. Dividing that daily cost into $1,700 reveals how long—or short—your trip can be. If it's too short, and you want to stay within your maximum, you may have to go somewhere else.

2. *Choose your favorite destination,* and make it your highest priority. Then figure out how many days it will take to experience everything you want to. Next, use the Checklist in Chapter 6 to calculate how much that many days will cost. Now all you have to do is persuade yourself to spend that amount. If you absolutely can't make the case, or the cupboard is too bare for the grandest scheme, cut back on the level of accommodations, class of tickets, or even time, until you have a match. The main point is this: don't persuade yourself that you can't afford to do what you really want to do. *Traveler's Tool Kit* will help empower you to go wherever you want.

Obviously, choice of destinations greatly affects the cost of the trip. Tokyo (more than twice as expensive as New York City), Hong Kong, Paris, Oslo,

Copenhagen, Geneva, Frankfurt, and Brussels are among the most expensive cities. Notice a pattern? Most are European and all are Northern Hemisphere. The least expensive cities include Bogotá, Colombo, Johannesburg, Karachi, Lima, Lusaka, New Delhi, and Tunis. Notice a pattern?

Traveling in South America, Africa, India, and Southeast Asia can be moderately expensive if you stay in international hotel chains, eat at tourist restaurants, and hire private transportation. But for savvy travelers, these places can be *very inexpensive.* You can travel comfortably in Peru or Indonesia for six months on what you would spend in Norway or Japan in a month or two.

Expect higher costs in tourist areas.

However, be wary about making generalizations about an entire continent. For example, in sub-Saharan Africa, Kenya is inexpensive, neighboring Rwanda is moderate, and South Africa is comparatively expensive. In Southeast Asia, Thailand and Indonesia are inexpensive, but costs are sharply higher in neighboring Cambodia and Myanmar (that's the historic name; Burma was a more recent name used by the British). Nepal is cheap, but in nearby Bhutan you're likely to have to spend at least $250 per day. Expect high travel costs wherever governments channel tourists through expensive hotels, restaurants, and transportation.

By the way, if someone says that the cost of living in a certain place is inexpensive, be certain you and that person agree on what inexpensive means— and the information is current. When I say inexpensive, I'm thinking of a private room with two beds, and sometimes a private bath, for $8 to $20 a night.

The cost of travel in a given country also depends in part on the strength of your currency in relation to that country's. Years ago, when the U.S. dollar was strong and European currencies were weak, *Europe on $5 a Day* was the book carried by students and it was possible to travel for that. How world economics have changed. Today, the cost of buying a Coca-Cola in Holland may not seem extraordinary to someone paying with marks, francs, or guilders, but if you're using U.S. currency, that Coke could cost you three or four dollars. Imagine what you'd spend for a night on the town. A haircut that costs $4 in Caracas costs $43 in Tokyo. For a fast food meal that costs $2.50 in Bangkok, you'd pay $6.75 in Paris. These things add up fast on a long trip.

In some countries, costs to travelers are artificially high because the government doesn't permit its currency to "float." That is, it doesn't allow world market forces to establish the true value of its currency. Instead, the government simply announces what their currency is worth as you convert yours to theirs. The former Soviet Union was an example. As the ruble is now slowly being allowed to float, it is valued at far less than the government always asserted it was worth. Theoretically, that should give your currency much more buying power. Ah, if only life were that simple. Sometimes when a government devalues its currency, prices for goods and services are increased at the same time, offsetting your advantage.

The existence of a black market (euphemistically referred to by economists as a "parallel" or "alternative" market) and the extent to which you participate in it also influence the cost of travel. Exchanging your money for local currency on the black market can lower costs by 15 to 50 percent in some countries. We'll discuss black markets in Chapter 6.

THE CHANGING WORLD

I want to comment on one other factor that I hope will influence your decisions concerning destinations and timing: the relentless rate at which the world is changing.

In Keoladeo National Park outside Bharatpur, India, I sat motionless in a rowboat, resting my hands on palm-worn oars, watching majestic Siberian cranes sweep into sight like a flight of snow-white arrows. They dropped gracefully from 15,000 feet to nest at the end of a 3,000-mile migration. Hovering on seven-foot wings above the marsh, they settled as softly as giant snowflakes, seeming to radiate rather than reflect light from their breasts. That sight will always remain in my memory. In 1980, more than 200 Siberian cranes made the annual migration to India that their ancestors have flown for millennia. In 1992, only five cranes arrived.

As recently as 1994, millions of flamingoes, with striking pink, black, and scarlet plumages, brightened Lake Nakurur in Kenya. Deforestation, pollution, and a sinking water level have so battered the lake and ecosystem that fewer than 10,000 flamingoes remain.

Wildness is disappearing from our world; distinct cultures are blending together into a shapeless mass. Diversity is sacrificed to unimaginable increases in population. Where millions of people must plant crops and burn forests to survive, elephants, lemurs, and gorillas are inevitably condemned to extinction. Where multinational greed rapes forests, turns mountains inside out, and spews toxic chemicals across the earth, can any species survive in the long run?

It's too late for us to share with Stanley and Livingstone, or Burton and Speke, the experience of forging trails across an Africa never before traversed. In fact, it wouldn't surprise me today to find a new Pizza Hut at one of their old campsites. We can no longer follow Thesiger across harsh Arabian deserts and encounter the nomadic cultures about which he wrote with such respect and affection. Those same deserts are now, only a few decades later, crisscrossed by oily black ribbons of asphalt. Camels, the ships of the desert, have been replaced by Aramco tankers.

Paradoxically, television documentaries both reveal and mask what is happening. By bringing the Serengeti migration, the mountain gorillas, and the Papua New Guinea "sing-sing" to our armchairs, they imply that parts of the world remain as they were, that nature is thriving. Behind the scenes, however, directors take care to shield the camera lens from evidence of the encroachment of modernization. They are well-intentioned in focusing on what remains but, in doing so, lead us to underestimate the ferocious pace of change.

We'll probably manage to keep a few exotic specimens, but the leopard in a cage is not the leopard of the jungle any more than a river "turned on" for a few hours by the keeper of the dam is a wild river. Further, when we experience specimens in a tame environment, our response is not the same as when we meet them in their natural setting. A pygmy chieftain in London has even less stature than when at home in Zaire. And what is our sense of accomplishment when the price of meeting him is no greater than crosstown bus fare?

In other words, fine-tune your timing—but do not delay. Whatever we've missed, the world is still rich with marvels. The message is simple: go now!

DRAFTING AN ITINERARY

An itinerary, which simply means a proposed route, is the foundation for your trip, and you can't draft a good one without doing your homework. When you know where you want to go, what you want to experience, how much time you have, and how much money you're willing to spend, link it all together to create an itinerary.

To a spontaneous person, the idea of a detailed itinerary may seem restrictive. Believe me, it's not. Once you're out the door with a thoughtful itinerary in hand, you're free to indulge whatever spontaneous urges arise. Having done the research, you understand the costs and benefits of each change you consider making on the road. If you were winging it, you could easily underestimate the chaos a spontaneous side trip might cause later on in the trip. Drafting an itinerary also uncovers opportunities to explore along the way. People who pride themselves on winging it miss a lot.

Here are five principles that apply to drafting an itinerary:

1. If you have a choice, schedule destinations most like your own country early in your trip so culture shock will be minimal. Having grown "salty" by the time you reach more exotic destinations, you'll cope with them easily.

2. Schedule countries with higher health risks toward the end of your trip. The odds are greatly against your getting sick but, if it happens, it's convenient for home to be on the horizon.

3. If you can handle the crowds, include music, art, and religious festivals in your plan.

4. If traveling in Canada, Europe, Australia, New Zealand, or the United States, you'll probably meet few unforeseeable obstacles. In most of the

rest of the world, however, expect delays. Obstacles come in unlimited variety: a train ticket you can't get; a border closed because of a flare-up between neighboring countries; stolen travelers checks; anything. Then there are serendipitous obstacles: scuba diving so great you can't tear yourself away; the friend's friend you called who insists on taking you on a five-day trip to Bariloche;* tickets to the Bolshoi Ballet that came through—for next week. In other words, after calculating the time your trip should take, add 10 to 20 percent, depending on your destination, as a "fudge factor" to cover unexpected events, good and bad.

5. When scheduling connecting flights, leave enough time between them to keep a minor delay along the way from toppling your entire flight plan. Avoid changing planes and airlines if you have a choice and try to avoid routing yourself through airports notorious for foul-weather shutdowns (for example, Chicago or Boston).

When you've come up with an itinerary that works, calculate how many days it will take, including obstacles and rest days, and compare that with how much time you have.

Learning to create an itinerary will help you SAVE MONEY for a new reason. Some travel agents are suggesting that, to offset commission caps (discussed later), they may charge from $50 to $500 to draft a detailed itinerary for a client. In addition to the fee, you wind up with their ideas, not yours. Do it yourself and spend that money on some faraway adventure.

To summarize:

1. On a good map, circle your intended stops and choose the cities abroad where your travels will start and end. Review the options with your travel agent. Make the most commonsense connections among your circled destinations, avoiding doubling back when possible.

2. Once you've selected a preliminary route, adjust it to take into account factors such as available transport, tourist seasons, temperatures, rain, festivals, national holidays, costs, and accomplishing your objectives. Having made adjustments based on these factors, you have your basic itinerary.

3. Decide how you'll get from place to place and determine approximately how long each trip will take. A good guidebook and/or travel agent makes this easy. If you must estimate time when you know the distance involved but have no further guidance, err on the generous side.

---

* *Bariloche.* This is a Swiss-style ski resort in the Lake District of southwest Argentina. Located at the foot of the Andes, it's also the entrance to a spectacular national park.

4. List things you want to do or see along the way and attach time values to each. This needn't be tedious; in fact, it brings your trip to life. *Be realistic.* Don't plan a supertight trip. Rushing every day just to squeeze in an extra country, or even one more city, is seldom worth it. Remind yourself of your reasons for traveling and build in time for rest, a missed connection, or a little longer stay in some wonderful place.

If you add up the days and are over your time budget, think first about granting yourself more time. When you've stretched that as far as you can, make your route more efficient and cut some destinations. But leave time to enjoy each place rather than rush, rush, rush. You have a lifetime for travel.

Drafting an itinerary motivates you to assemble information you ought to have anyway. Having an itinerary enables you to stay within your time and money budgets and to get the most from your trip. It is a servant, not a master.

RESOURCES

No one plans a trip wholly out of his or her head; we all draw on other resources. Most of us have dealt with travel agents and some of us have already used guidebooks. However, in this section we'll discuss what to ask to ensure that you find the best travel agent for your needs, identify the best guidebook for your trip while avoiding the turkeys, and take advantage of the vast amount of information available, often free, for your use.

How to Choose and Work with a Travel Agent

A volcano erupted in the world of travel agencies in 1995 and the dust is still settling. In this changing environment, travelers who don't educate themselves and learn to do their own research may pay dearly.

For decades, travel agents provided their services without direct charge to the consumer. They were compensated by receiving commissions from those whose services they sold (including airlines, tour operators, car rental agencies, and hotels). Thus, using a travel agent cost you nothing extra unless the agent was not competent or not objective in choosing among providers. To the contrary, a good travel agent could save you money and time and provide valuable advice.

However, in early 1995 many airlines changed the way they compensate travel agencies for distributing *domestic* tickets. In place of the common 10 percent commission, airlines set a maximum dollar amount they would pay (no matter how high the price of the ticket). The immediate result was loss of income to travel agencies. The American Society of Travel Agents (ASTA) estimated that 50,000 travel agents would lose their jobs and 5,000 to 10,000 agencies (of about 33,600) would close. As it turned out, only about 500 more agencies voluntarily folded in 1995 than in 1994, and more agencies came into business in 1997 than left it. Nevertheless, commission caps changed the nature of the relationship between airlines and travel agents, creating a certain, shall we say, distance.

Less obvious, but no less real, is the resulting change in the relationship between travel agents and consumers like you and me. The warm fuzzy days are cooling and travelers should be prepared for changes. Remember when owners started paying baseball players astronomical salaries? Before long the public had to pay more to attend games. Well, because airlines capped the amount of commissions they pay travel agencies, you and I are feeling the pinch.

Travel agencies are necessarily becoming more aware of the cost to them of each service they provide, and some are compensating for lost income by charging the consumer for certain services. By 1996, almost 30 percent of all travel agencies had begun charging service fees and another 30 percent were considering them. Although consumers can avoid these fees by dealing directly with the airlines, no one yet knows how much energy will be vented by exasperated travelers fuming at tied-up phone lines. Services that consumers won't pay for may simply disappear.

Complex, customized itineraries provided without charge by your travel agency may be a thing of the past. At present, AmEx charges for reissuing a ticket, making a refund, and retrieving records of past travel. AmEx tried to charge a $20 fee for booking air tickets that cost $300 or less, but consumer resentment was so great that AmEx decided the fee "didn't meet business objectives." However, certain other agencies have retained similar fees so far.

If you ask for a service for which an agency charges a fee, the agent should advise you in advance. However, it's worth asking about fees to avoid a misunderstanding. In practice, the situation is flexible. Many agencies don't charge fees to established customers, particularly if the customer objects. Other agencies are committed to charging no one. Shop around.

Some agents have hinted publicly that they'll make less effort to find the least expensive flights for clients. Their rationale is that small commissions on cheap flights are below the agency's cost of providing the service. Agencies handled cheap loss-leaders in the past since large commissions (at 10 percent) on expensive flights made up for the cheapies. With some of the fat commissions gone, time spent finding the cheapest flights is harder to recoup. Certain agencies might even be tempted to steer consumers to providers paying the highest commissions. In short, travelers must be more alert than in the past.

If you plan your journeys with the help of a travel agent, keep in mind that information from that agent will affect your biggest travel expenditures (airfare, fees to tour operators, and so on). A good travel agent can find the best (cheapest, if that's what you ask for) airline tickets, negotiate upgrades, get a ticket on a supposedly sold-out flight, locate discounts, and provide reliable advice. A poor agent can cost you time and money.

Since it's so important to find the best travel agency and agent for your trip, let's consider how to do that. First, seek recommendations from friends, then look in the Yellow Pages and newspapers for advertisements that suggest a good fit with your travel plans.

Evaluating Travel Agencies

To make an informed choice of a travel agency, ask questions (this seems obvious but few travelers take the time):

- Are the agency's personnel knowledgeable about the kind of travel that interests you? This is especially important if you're considering adventure travel.
- Does the agency charge fees for its services? Some do, some don't. For example, one national agency charges $75 for preparing a complicated domestic itinerary and $150 for a complicated international itinerary.
- Does the agency use consolidators? It is essential that it does (see Chapter 6).
- Does the agency have International Air Transport Association (IATA) approval? To get it, the agency must be bonded. If it is, funds from you that are held by the agency are protected. Be cautious about making payments directly to an agency to prepay hotels, car rentals, and so on. If an agency asks you to make payments directly to it, see if the money will be held in an escrow account (and where). If you pay a deposit, get a receipt. Protect yourself by paying with a credit card. Although ASTA (800-ASK-ASTA) keeps records of complaints filed against travel agencies that are ASTA members, ASTA considers an agency's reputation to be clean as soon as a complaint is satisfied. That means you won't be told how many complaints there have been in the past.
- Does the agency belong to a consortium of travel agencies? If so, it may be able to offer certain services that a small, independent agency can't. For example, it might be able to transmit your travel plans to overseas consortium members that can assist you while you're in their area.
- Does the agency have a staff person who understands complicated international fares? If not, it may send your itinerary to an airline's rate desk for pricing and the result may reflect that airline's interests more than yours.
- Does the agency have a toll-free number you can call from abroad? Can you reach it by fax?
- What materials (for example, lists of things to do and information on holidays) will the agency provide?

- Does it have a library of guidebooks, brochures, and videos from which you can borrow? Does it have the *Official Airline Guide*, Star Service, the Specialty Travel Index, and other resource materials?
- Will it maintain a file on you so you won't have to repeat your seating, eating, and other preferences every time you book a trip?
- Will it keep track of your frequent flyer miles?

Evaluating Travel Agents

Finding a reliable travel agency is only the first step. Next you must choose the most appropriate travel agent in that firm. Again, ask questions:

- Is the travel agent a traveler? If this sounds like a silly question, remember that there are desk-bound members of every business. You want someone who thinks like a traveler.
- How much traveling has the agent done to the areas in which you're interested?
- Does he or she seem bright and well organized? Seek someone who listens and pays attention to details, is excited by travel, and is willing to make an extra effort on your behalf.
- Does the agent try to learn what you like and don't like?
- Do your personalities seem compatible?
- How much experience does the agent have? Is he or she a Certified Travel Counselor (meaning someone with at least five years' experience and a regular participant in professional training)?
- Can the agent give you relevant information about the recent experiences of other clients?
- Is the agent knowledgeable about obtaining free travelers checks, exchanging money, choosing travel insurance, and ordering visas?
- Is the agent paid a salary or paid by commission?
- Does the agent seek fare quotes directly or does someone else supply this information? Some simply use one airline to provide fares for all segments of your trip, including those on other airlines. For you to get the best deal, it's better if your agent looks up published routes and tariffs before checking with the airlines. You want an agent willing to keep digging, willing to look for fares not on the computer, willing to shop relentlessly for the best deal for you.
- Does the agent work with "preferred" suppliers? If so, he or she may receive additional compensation by steering business to those airlines, tour operators, hotels, etc. That may be okay if it's the most desirable product and the supplier is reliable. If not, you may wind up with inferior and/or more expensive travel arrangements.
- Will the agent give you the names of other clients as references?

Just because a person is not the right agent for you doesn't mean they are not right for someone else. The idea is to find the right match for you.

What Else Can You Expect from a Travel Agent?

A good, full-service travel agent can do many things:

- reserve the seat you want
- identify the airport you'll use if there is more than one in a city
- tell you about penalties associated with your tickets
- ask the airline to accommodate your dietary preferences (although getting you a really good-tasting meal may be beyond anyone's influence)
- advise you of any maximum baggage weight or size limits
- find discounted lodging for stopover passengers (something that is especially useful when you'll be stuck with an overnight layover in high-priced places like Honolulu)
- list airport departure taxes charged along the way
- give you information about weather at your destinations
- tell you about frequent flyer procedures before you fly
- let you know when and how your tickets will arrive

When you've given instructions to your agent, it's up to you to follow through to make sure everything is done to get your trip under way smoothly. Remember the squeaky wheel.

It's unrealistic to expect travel agents to get the same pleasure from planning your trip as you do. When an agent provides service, he or she expects a commission from suppliers of products sold to you. No sale, no commission. Therefore, the amount you ask an agent to do should be proportional to the likelihood of your buying something. If you're only going to purchase a plane ticket or air pass (no hotel or rental car reservations, no expensive safaris, etc.), there's a practical limit on how much time he or she can devote to you. If that's the case, offer to go to their office and look up information yourself.

Sources of Information

Travel agents have access to details, and you need lots of details. They work from sources such as the following:

- *Fairchild's Travel Industry Personnel Directory* provides information on airlines, shipping lines, railroads, tour operators, government agencies, hotels, and special travel services.
- The *Official Tour Directory* (OTD) lists tour operators and world-wide destinations. Whether your special interest is botany, Buddhism, camel safaris, gorillas, panning for gold, rafting, whale watching, or wine tasting, the OTD can help you connect.

- The *Worldwide Services Manual* lists tours available around the world.
- The *Official Airline Guide* (OAG) includes information on regulations and requirements in various countries. By the way, the familiar OAG in book form is quickly being replaced by an electronic version.
- Flight schedules for most of the major airlines around the world, as well as fairly extensive information on train, bus, and boat schedules.
- Services that provide information on every country, including special tour and package deals.

Later in this chapter, we will review the wealth of information available on the Internet and online services pertaining to airline, hotel, car rental reservations, and virtually every other aspect of travel.

Explore the Options

What you want from your agent is the full range of options so you can choose the ones you want. Be clear about what you want and press to get it. Don't passively accept the first offer. If you're willing to endure some inconve-

---

Rebaters

There are agencies known as "rebaters" that give clients varying percentages of the commission the agency receives from suppliers. Like discount stock brokers, they provide little substantive assistance. If you know exactly what reservations you want to make, you can use a rebater and save yourself part of the commission (which you won't save if you book directly with the airline). The following is a partial list of rebaters and a brief summary of their terms:

- All-American Travel Club (800-451-8747). Annual fee of $29.95, deducted from the first rebate. Rebates are 10 percent of the cost of the ticket you purchase, minus a fee of $24.95 per ticket (or 6 percent rebate on cheaper tickets, with no fee).
- Pennsylvania Travel (800-331-0947). No membership fee. Rebate of entire commission minus a booking fee of $35 (the fee increases with the price of the ticket).
- The Smart Traveller (800-448-3338). No fee. Rebate of 6 percent on packages. Higher on international air. None on domestic.
- Travel Avenue (800-333-3335). No membership fee. Rebate of 7 percent minus $15 processing fee. Consolidator tickets sold at a net price.

nience in return for lower fares, say so. Ask whether the fare would be lower if you flew on a different day of the week. Or at a different time of day. Or if you moved the departure date a few days one way or the other (which might move you into a less expensive "season"). Ask whether there any special promotional deals available (or coming up).

Here's the bottom line as I see it. Travel agencies are caught in a changing, somewhat threatening, business environment. They must figure out how to survive in a world of commission caps, ticketless travel, and online bookings. Some feel they have to charge for previously free services or cut back on services. Some may be tempted to steer travelers to use suppliers who pay the highest commissions. At the same time, because of the weak dollar, international travel is increasingly expensive.

With all this going on, it's essential that a smart traveler choose a travel agency and agent carefully. Do your research, ask questions, and insist on getting what you need. As a prepared, enthusiastic traveler, you'll be a joy to a good travel agent.

How to Choose a Guidebook

A good guidebook can become a trusted friend. It saves time, money, and frustration, building your confidence by arming you with information. In contrast, it can also become a silken cord that binds without being noticed, inhibiting you from experimenting. The trick is to benefit from a guidebook without being constrained by it. Ensure that your feet find their own path or you'll find yourself too often in the midst of familiar faces.

Since most new guidebooks cost $14 to $35, it makes sense, while still in the early planning stage of a trip, to borrow guidebooks from friends or the library. Even out-of-date books are helpful at that point. See what various guidebooks have to say about countries that seem attractive to you. Learn what each country has to offer, whether travel there is difficult or easy, whether costs are **Buy the most updated guidebook for your trip.** high or low, which are the best and worst seasons for visiting. In the beginning, don't waste time figuring out where you'll spend the night in Edinburgh or eat dinner in Puerto Montt.* Review enough general information to decide whether a country appeals to you.

When you have an idea of your rough itinerary, buy the most current edition of the best guidebook. Despite everyone's best efforts, most guidebooks lose some accuracy quickly due to changing prices, political machinations, currency revaluations, and so on. You need current information. While there's no guarantee that the most expensive book is best for you, choosing a book because it costs the least could be very expensive.

---

* *Puerto Montt.* This Southern Chilean port is excellent for boat trips to Chilean fiords and glaciers.

Evaluating Guidebooks

A traveler needs facts, not fluff—solid information on how a country works. By "works," I mean prices, locations, and recommendations concerning transportation, lodging, and restaurants—but more than that. I also mean opinions on whether local public transportation is reliable, what to expect at border crossings, whether bureaucrats are a problem, and the details of daily life. You need to know that the steamboat across Lake Titicaca* leaves only on Tuesday mornings and if you miss it you'll have to wait a week in bitter cold. You want to know current scams being pulled on careless travelers, whether there's a safe black market, and what behavior would offend local customs. Are the prices of places recommended by a guidebook in the range of your budget? Is the index extensive enough to enable you to look things up quickly?

Finally, listen to the author's tone to see if it pleases your ear. If the author is a spectator, rushing from sight to sight (rather than insight), return the book to the shelf. There's a Swahili saying: *Mwenye pupa hadriki kula tamu*, or, "A hasty person misses the sweet things" (referring to one who doesn't wait for the fruit to ripen).

The Guidebooks

Quite a few series of guidebooks have developed a reputation for offering reliable, useful information. These include Baedeker, Berlitz, Birnbaum, Cadogan, Thomas Cook, Fielding, Fodor, Frommer, Hildebrand, Knopf, Michelin, and the *Unofficial Guide* series, among others. However, some of these are written for somewhat affluent travelers, those unlikely to hike independently into the deep outback.

The *Michelin Red Guides* provide detailed information about European hotels and restaurants, while the *Michelin Green Guides* focus more on European history, art, and places of interest. Michelin recommendations of accommodations and restaurants might please your aesthetic sense, but consider carefully whether they please your wallet. Michelin has recently added an *In Your Pocket* series that focuses on walking tours, culture, and sight-seeing tips.

Fielding is very candid and well written and seems to have changed course in recent years to include more information about off-beat destinations.

Fodor's Travel Guides has celebrated its sixtieth anniversary, and there are now almost one hundred titles in its Gold Guide series (including *Affordable Guides, Exploring Guides,* etc.). Although emphasizing the West, Fodor's Guides cover countries throughout the world. They provide historical and

---

* *Lake Titicaca.* Often called the world's highest navigable lake, this body of water lies on the Peru/Bolivia border. These waters are honored as the birthplace of the first Inca.

cultural information about interesting places to visit, as well as practical recommendations for restaurants and hotels. These are longtime best-sellers
designed to keep travelers in the middle of the road.

The *Frommer* series now numbers more than one hundred volumes counting the basic Guides (to a specific country), $-A-Day (the original *Europe on
$5 a Day* has become *Europe on $40 a Day,* and that only covers basic costs),
Touring Guides (walking tours), City Guides, and Special Editions (home
exchanges, bed & breakfasts in North America, etc.). Frommer emphasizes
Europe and the United States and is at its best when describing restaurants,
hotels, and nightlife.

Baedeker's guides and maps are good for European sightseeing but of
minimal help as far as providing practical information for daily use.
Hildebrand's Travel Guides are similar in format to Baedecker, but they
cover Asia and Africa. Both of these are more helpful for people on a tour than
for independent travelers.

Berlitz Pocket Guides publishes pocket-size (four-by-six-inch) guidebooks
helpful to people on tour, while the Berlitz Traveller's Phrase Books (25 languages) are helpful to any traveler. There is also a *Berlitz Complete Guide to
Cruising and Cruise Ships.*

The *Unofficial Guide* series includes more than 20 titles. Independent
and irreverent in tone, it is very professional in execution. It includes some
specialty subjects such as cruises and skiing.

Illustrated Travel Guides from Thomas Cook cover more than 40 cities and
countries.

Several series of books are well designed specifically for travelers with low
to moderate budgets. Some of the more popular include *Lonely Planet Guides,
Moon Travel Handbooks, Through the Back Door, Let's Go, Berkeley Guides,
South American Handbook, Maverick Guide,* and *The Rough Guides.*

The *Lonely Planet* series, colloquially referred to as the LP, has earned a
fine reputation in the realm of worldwide budget/independent travel. Born
in Australia, the U.S. address is Lonely Planet Publications, 155 Filbert Street,
Oakland, CA 94607 (call 800-275-8555). Books in the LP series cover Africa,
Asia, Australia, the Middle East, New Zealand, the Pacific, South and Central
America. It is now expanding coverage of North America and Europe. There
are five series: *Travel Survival Kits,* covering a specific country for a range of
budgets; *On a Shoestring* guides, covering anything from a region to a
continent for the low-budget traveler; *City Guides; Walking Guides* (on
hiking and trekking in a dozen or so countries); and *PhraseBooks* (for about
50 languages). The LP series now includes the former Soviet Union, and it has
recently published *Central Asia* and *Romania & Moldova.* Enormous
numbers of travelers with moderate to lower budgets—especially student,
independent, and adventure travelers—carry the LP. It even shows up on tour
buses. I consider it the first choice for virtually every country it covers, except

Shopper in famous market of Chichicastenango, Guatemala.

that it may fall to second place for India, Indonesia, and the South American continent.

LP books are written in a personal, opinionated tone. In fact, authors of some editions have opined on local politics with sufficient candor that the book has been temporarily banned in the country covered. One caution: LP updates individual books in the LP series only every few years, so check the publication date.

The *Travel Handbook* series of more than 50 books published by *Moon Publications* (722 Wall Street, Chico, CA 95928; 800-345-5473) is comprehensive and accurate (because it's updated annually). Its tone is fairly dry and reportorial. The books themselves are durable and compact. About half pertain to North America, but I like Moon best in Asia—especially India—and the Pacific. For Indonesia, the first choice is Bill Dalton's *Indonesia Handbook* in the Moon series. Dalton's obvious affection for the islands gives his commentary an appealing flavor. Although one of its newest titles is *Antarctica*, the book that really puts Moon in the vanguard is the *Moon Handbook*, an account of lunar explorations and a fantasy excursion to a hypothetical city on the moon.

Independent travelers to Europe enjoy the relaxed tone of Rick Steves' commentary in *Europe through the Back Door*. His long-running series of *2 to 22 Days in . . .* (a certain country) has been retired, replaced by *Rick Steves' Best of . . . .* Each proposes an itinerary and "must see" sights for limited European trips.

The *Harvard Student Association's Let's Go* series of over 20 guidebooks is said to be the best-selling series in the world (it's certainly under a lot of students' arms in Europe). *Let's Go* focuses on the United States, Mexico, the Middle East, Europe, and the Confederation of Independent States. Contact *Let's Go* at 1 Story Street, Cambridge, MA 02138.

A new challenger to *Let's Go* is the *Berkeley Guides on the Loose* series written by University of California students. The first four books covered Mexico, California, the Pacific Northwest and Alaska, and Eastern Europe. Those were followed by France, Germany, Britain/Ireland, and Central America. Contact them c/o Fodor's Travel Publications (owned by Random House), 201 East 50th Street, NY, NY 10022 or at 505 Eshleman Hall, University of California, Berkeley, CA 94720. An *Atlanta Constitution* review referred to this series as intended for travelers who belong to the "Order of the Translucent Wallet."

For South America, the *South American Handbook* (Trade & Travel Publications, Ltd., 6 Riverside Court, Riverside Road, Bath BA2 3DZ, United Kingdom) is casually referred to as "the bible." To reduce its size, sections on Central America and Mexico have been published as a separate volume. The series now includes fine handbooks entitled *Caribbean Islands*, *South Asia*, *Thailand*, *Indo-china and Burma*, *Indonesia*, and *Malaysia and Singapore*. Even though comparatively expensive, these books are good investments.

Other reliable guidebook series carried by budget-conscious travelers include *The Rough Guides*, focused on college-age travelers in Europe, with some of the flavor of the Lonely Planet series (c/o Penguin Books, Ltd., Bath Road, Harmondsworth, West Drayton, Middlesex, UB7 ODA, United Kingdom); *Maverick Guides*, but some of these books are not current so check the publication date (c/o Pelican Publishing Copany, 1101 Monroe Street, Gretna, LA 70053); and *NTC Passport Books' Handbooks of the World* (some of the newest cover Sri Lanka, Nepal and Tibet, and Pakistan), *Essential Travel Guides* to more than 54 cities and countries, and *Trip Planners* for several European countries (4255 West Touhy Avenue, Lincolnwood, IL 60646). *The Insight Guide to . . .* series is international in scope with a strong budget travel orientation. They present masses of information in a very handsome format.

Among guidebooks with a narrower focus are Linda White's *Independent Woman's Travel Guide to Europe*, of special interest to female travelers; *People's*

Guide to Mexico, by Karl Franz, a venerable, humorous, practical guide for travel in Mexico; and *Traveler's Guide to Asian Customs and Manners*, by E. Devine, a guide to good behavior in Asia. *The Active Travel Resource Guide* (Ultimate Ventures, $19.95) provides detailed annual information on over 3,300 trips and the more than 400 tour operators who offer them. This guide offers helpful information on a terrific variety of adventures. At the very least, it stimulates your imagination.

A good guidebook makes travel *vastly* easier. It's one of the differences between you and Columbus. But there's a downside to guidebooks. After you've been on the road for a while, you realize that many people are carrying the same guidebook you are and, therefore, going to the same places. Since some of your most powerful memories are likely to come from your time away from the tourist trail, don't let a guidebook become a tether. Get off the bus or train on impulse at a village which has no temple that rates a mention in

More Tips

- *Lonely Planet* and some of the other guidebooks solicit your comments, corrections, and criticisms of their books. If accepted, they send you a free copy of your choice of their books. Earning a free book, even on your first trip, is a slam dunk if you take the time to gather a few pages of substantive information. I make notes in the margin of the book I'm using—about price changes, attitudes, services, people, new experiences, and discoveries—and summarize them in a letter when I return. They'll even accept your marked-up book if you want to send that in. Sure, you're providing cheap labor for the publisher, but you're also helping other travelers and saving yourself $25 or so. Besides, having a new guidebook near at hand is a great stimulus to putting it to use.
- Unfortunately, the best guidebooks are not always the lightest or smallest. After a moment of solemn hesitation, cut out any sections of a guidebook that cover areas where you won't be traveling and leave them at home for another trip.
- If you lose a guidebook or become unhappy with the one you have, it's not hard to find another on the road. You may be able to buy one "used" from a departing traveler or in a book shop or street stall along your route.
- Away from the "tourist trail," guidebooks are hard to find, are expensive, or both.
- If trying to get psyched or inspire a potential partner, try a travel video. International Video Network sells 60-minute Videovisits, and Rand McNally has a series of inexpensive 30-minute videos covering many countries.

anyone's guidebook. Take local transport, rent a bike, walk. Get into the interior of the country, into the small places where village life is still unaffected by clicking cameras or streams of gringos. Use the guidebook as a guide—not as a crutch.

Internet Travel Resources

I'll begin with a few words about the Internet for those to whom it remains a mystery. The Internet is simply an electronic means of communication. The most popular uses of the Internet include exchange of messages (e-mail or in real time), access to vast sources of information, and the buying or selling of goods and services. All you need is a computer, a relatively high speed modem, appropriate software, and an Internet service provider (ISP) or a commercial online service (such as AOL, MSN, etc.).

The Internet is the single most powerful information-gathering tool available for travelers. Instead of repeated visits to the library and lots of telephone calls, you can find answers to many travel questions on the Internet—at your convenience 24 hours a day. And most Internet resources are free! It's easy to learn what temperatures to expect in the Peruvian highlands, review a photo of a seaside cottage on some exotic Indonesian island, or log on to a travel forum or a chat room where travelers exchange tips and answer one another's questions.

Another important benefit of using the Internet is that the information is likely to be more current than that distributed in hard copy. On the other hand, there's no guarantee that it's always accurate. After all, a fool can publish on the Internet as easily as a sage can. It's all waiting for you in cyberspace. The Internet has become an important supplement to traditional travel resources.

Take a look at the Internet for electronic editions of travel magazines and guides, information about prospective destinations, weather reports, and lists of restaurants and hotels. You can make airline, hotel, and car rental reservations. A real bonus is the input from people around the world who have visited destinations you are considering. Ask for comments on your proposed itinerary, view videos and photographs of destinations around the world, and even meet potential travel partners.

New sites appear on the Web like daisies in the spring—and many curl up and die just about as quickly. That's why some published lists of Web-based travel-related sites and other resources may be less useful than they appear. For that reason, learning "how to fish" for information on the Internet is more helpful than remaining dependent on someone else to feed you. The goal is to learn to find sites that are relevant, accurate, current, and comprehensive.

Explaining how to "surf" the Internet is tricky. If you are starting from scratch, check out a book or two, make full use of the trusty "Help" button, and follow your intuition. Almost everyone has a knowledgeable friend who will help him or her get started. Don't be intimidated; it's easier than you may think to get up to speed.

In the beginning, it's hard to know where to start to find what you're looking for. For the novice, seeking information on the Web can be like wandering in the desert; you don't know where you are and you can't find your way back. As you catch on, you develop skills that prevent wasting a lot of time.

Fortunately, everyone who establishes a resource (a Web site or home page) wants you to find it to show you the way. They scatter its address (known as an URL) around the Internet like breadcrumbs . All you have to do is recognize and follow that trail. You do that with the help of a "search engine" or "portal." Search engines and portals attempt to organize the resources of the Web into a logical index and provide a user-friendly interface to search for information. Think of a search engine as an index listing some portion of the information on the Internet. Some search engines organize Web sites into categories while others ask you to enter a topic you want it to find.

Here are addresses of some very popular search engines (se) and portals (p):

- AltaVista (se)   http://www.altavista.com/
- Cnet (se, p)   http://www.search.com/
- Excite (se, p)   http://www.excite.com/
- HotBot (se)   http://www.hotbot.com/
- InfoSeek (se, p)   http://wwwinfoseek.com/
- Microsoft (se)   http://www.microsoft.com/access/allinone.asp
- Yahoo! (p)   http://www.yahoo.com/

Which is best for you? If you're just beginning the information-gathering process (e.g., selecting a destination), choose a portal that groups Web sites into logical categories. For example, Yahoo! guides you through a series of options to help find the best Web sites for your needs. However, if you're ready to gather more specific details, consider a search engine that bases searches on keywords. Want the name of a 3-star hotel in Paris or a scuba outfitter in Belize? Try AltaVisa or InfoSeek. These are mammoth databases that automatically update themselves by tirelessly roaming the Web looking for new information to gobble up and store. If the keyword you use is in its database, it presents you with the address of the original Web site. Impressive, isn't it?

To locate the information you want, be clear on what you're looking for. However, as soon as you begin your quest, you'll discover unexpected information along the way. Record addresses (URLs) of intriguing Web sites (using a "bookmark") for later perusal.

One key to effective use of a search engine is to put yourself in the mind of the person who originally posted the information on the Internet. That person wants your search to succeed. What words would he or she think you would use to look for the information? Use those words in your search and their Web site should appear. This may sound a little like becoming a Jedi, but it works. To avoid being overwhelmed with barely relevant information, choose keywords that describe the information you want with as much specificity as you can.

When using a search engine, it's helpful to know a few rules of the road. For example, if you're looking for **trekking guides** and enter those keywords, you may be presented with a list of all sites containing either the word **trekking** or the word **guides**—more than you want and off the mark as well. The solution? Well, rules differ among search engines, but putting quotation marks around the phrase will usually limit the results to sites containing the exact phrase.

Internet Service Providers

Use either an online service or an ISP to gain access to the Web. Whether a monthly or hourly fee is more to your advantage depends on the amount of time you're on the Web. There are already more than 5,000 ISPs in operation, most of which are very small businesses. You want reliable service, speedy Web surfing, and expert customer technical support. If the ISP you choose doesn't come through for you, move to another. To avoid frustration, spend the money necessary for good service.

Online services

If you decide to use a full-feature online service, just call one of them and request a membership kit. You'll receive a local access telephone number—and will quickly develop a lust for a faster modem.

Online Services

- America Online (800-827-6364)
- MSN (800-386-5550)
- CompuServe (800-848-8990)
- Prodigy (800-776-0836)

Internet travel databases

I've found some Web sites so helpful to travelers that I can't resist sharing them with you. They emphasize destinations and practical information on the mechanics of successful travel. I've included only a few addresses for airlines, travel agencies, and other services and products. Since it was impractical to evaluate the quality of all the companies that post "book here" signs or offer "pay-to-play" services on the Internet, I've left most of them out. Besides, I still prefer to buy most of my books from a human bookseller and buy my tickets through a human travel agent.

Some of the following sites are beautifully presented and provide so much information it's hard to absorb. The price of admission is usually only a little of your time.

- AccuWeather (www.accuweather.com/web/welcome).
- Adventure Travel Society (www.adventuretravel.com/ats). Lists reliable operators by destination and activity.
- American Airlines (www.americanair.com). Look for Net SAAver. Great prices for last-minute travel.
- America's Best Online (www.americasbestonline.com/train.htm). Links to train tours throughout North America.
- Amtrak (www.amtrak.com). For routes and special promotions.
- Banana Travel (www.bananatravel.com). Cheap airfares.
- Bean, L.L. (www.llbean.com). You know what to expect.
- Best Fare Finder (www.previewtravel.com).
- Best Fares Discount Travel (www.bestfares.com).
- Budget Travel (www.budgettravel.com). Special airfares.
- Canadian Rocky Mountain train trips (www.colibritours.com/emount.html).
- Castaways Travel (www.CastawaysTravel.com). Clothing optional travel opportunities.
- Centers for Disease Control (www.cdc.gov/travel/). Travel vaccines, food and water precautions, etc.
- City Net (www.citynet.com). Valuable travel resource—links to favorite destinations—and much more.
- Climbing Archive (www.dtek.chalmers.se/Climbing/index.html).
- Condé Nast Traveler (www.cntraveler.com).
- Country Info Online (www.countries.com).
- Currency conversion (www.oanda.com). More than 160 currencies.
- Cyberlinks Travel (www.cyberlinks.com). Site contains links to many travel sites on the web.
- DisABILITY Travel and Recreation Resources (www.eskimo.com/~jlubin/disabled/travel.htm). Information for travelers with disabilities.
- Elderhostel (www.elderhostel.org). Educational adventures for older adults.

- Embassy Network (www.emb.com). Great for visa research and links to embassies throughout the world.
- Epicurious Travel (travel.epicurious.com). Conde Nast.
- European Rail Travel (www.starnetinc.com/eurorail/home.htm).
- Exchanging Money (www.cnn.com/TRAVEL/). Conversion rates worldwide.
- ExpressNet. Travel info and reservations on AOL. Keywords Expressnet and Travel Form.
- Flyte Comm (www.flytecomm.com). Tracks and reports on every plane in flight in the continental United States.
- Fodor's (www.fodors.com). Offers resources for travel and forums to receive advice from fellow travlers.
- Foreign Languages for Travelers (www.travlang.com/languages).
- Frommer's City Guides (www.frommers.com). On AOL, keyword Frommer's.
- Geographic Maps Online (wwwipl.org/ref/). This site has political, cultural, environmental, economic, and historical maps as well as many links for further data collection.
- Global Online Travel (www.got.com). Airfares.
- GreenNet (www.gn.apc.org). Contributions from environmental, peace, and human rights groups.
- Health (www.moon.com/travel_matters/index.html). A good site for comprehensive information on travel.
- Himalayan Travel–World Adventures (www.gorp.com/himtravel). Offering trips to rugged destinations.
- Homestays (www.commerce.com/homestays). American International Homestay.
- Hospitality Net (www.hospitalitynet.nl/index/chain). Links to many conventional hotels.
- Hostelling International and American Youth Hostels (www.youthhostel.com/home.html and www.hiayh.org). Information on hosteling and other travel links.
- HotBot (www.hotbot.com/travel). Comprehensive and user friendly, this site has links all over the place for books, lodging, destinations, maps, etc.
- Hotel Reservation Service (www.hrs.de).
- IBM Travel (www01.ny.us.ibm.net/channels/travel/travel.html). Contains links to various travel resources.

- India (www.manesn.com/india). Travel information.
- InfoHub Travel Guides (www.infohub.com).
- Inns and Outs (www.innsandouts.com). More than 15,000 bed & breakfast accommodations.
- International Travel News (www.intltravelnews.com).
- Internet Sleuth (www.isleuth.com/trav.html). 450 indexes and databases, including travel.
- Internet Travel Network (www.itn.net).
- Internet Travel Solutions (www.travel-library.com).
- Latin American Information (www.latinworld.com).
- Learning Vacations (www.learningvactions.com).
- Le Web Louvre (www.sunsite.unc.edu/louvre). Visit a great art museum.
- Lonely Planet (www.lonelyplanet.com). Fact sheets, newsletter, travel tips, and destination comments.
- Lycos (www.lycos.com). Popular free directory of home pages.
- MapQuest Map Maker (www.mapquest.com). Enter an address and print out a map.
- MasterCard International (www.mastercard.com). Includes a currency converter.
- Microsoft–Expedia Travel Service (expedia.msn.com/daily/home/default.hts?). For a version of its Automap Road Atlas, see (www.expediamaps.com).
- Moon Publications (www.moon.com). Complement to its guidebooks.
- Mountain Travel/Sobek (www.MTSobek.com). Adventure travel company.
- National Geographic Traveler (www.nationalgeographic.com).
- NetGuide Travel Directory (www.netguide.com/Travel/Independent).
- Northwest Airlines (www.nwa.com). Look for "cybersaver."
- Orbit Global Travel (www.pi.se/~orbit/welcome.html). Info on Australia, New Zealand, and the Pacific.
- Outside Magazine (outside.starwave.com). Stories, guidebooks, environmental news, reviews, and adventure travel locations.
- Outtahere (www.outtahere.com).
- Pathfinder Travel (pathfinder.com/Travel). Travel deals, travel the world.
- Priceline (www.priceline.com). Bid for cheap air fares.
- Rail Europe (www.raileurope.com).
- Rail Rides in North America (www.castles.com/vs/usa/train.html).
- Rough Guides (www.roughguides.com).

St. Basil's Russian Orthodox Church, Red Square. Moscow, Russia.

- SABLE (www.travel.sable.com). Massive amounts of information for world travelers, including lists of travel agencies, travel suppliers, and much more.
- Shoestring Travel (stratpub.com/). For budget travelers.
- Specialty Travel Index (www.spectrav.com). Lists more than 600 special interest tour operators by destination and activity.
- Student Travel—STA Travel (www.sta-travel.com), Council Travel (www.counciltravel.com), and International Student Travel Confederation (www.istc.org).
- Subway Navigator (metro.ratp.fr:10001/bin/cities/english). Plot your course on subways around the world.
- The Trip (www.thetrip.com). For cheap tickets.
- Trans World Airlines (www.twa.com). Look for "ways."

- Travel Agents Directory (www.ten10.com/tad). Listing of more than 30,000 travel agencies.
- TravelASSIST (www.travelassist.com/mag/mag_home.html). For adventure stories and photographs.
- Travel Channel Online Network (www.travelchannel.com). Places, events, cuisine, Travel Talk forum.
- Travel Club Adventures (www.travelclubadv.com/page28.html). Offers train trips and other unique travel experiences.
- Travel.com (www.travel.com). Another great, comprehensive with plenty of links to airlines, cruises, etc.
- Traveler (www.traveler.com). Airfares.
- Traveler's Tool Kit (www.travelers-tool-kit.com/links.html). Includes this entire list of Internet sites so you don't have to type them in.
- Travelocity (www.travelocity.com). 3 million pages of air bookings, chat rooms, destination info, maps, parks, travel info, and weather.
- Travelon (www.travelon.com). Extensive list of interesting tours.
- Travel Source travel links (www.travelsource.com).
- Travel Web (www.travelweb.com). Allows travel agents to post home pages with information that allows searchers to choose among them.
- Traveler Net (www.traveler.net). Covers every mayor category of travel.
- Travel Weekly's Crossroads (www.twcrossroads.com). Information on travel agents.
- Travel Wiz (www.travelwiz.com/connection/car) Offers information on car rental agencies and hotel chains (www.travelwiz.com/connection/hotel/index.html).
- Tripod (www.tripod.com/explore/travel/). Collection of travel information for students on the road.
- USA Today–travel (www.usatoday.com/life/travel/ltfront.htm). Overall good site for travel information.
- USA Today–weather (www.usatoday.com/weather/wfront). Weather forecasts.
- US Airlines (www.usair.com).
- U.S. Department of State (www.state.gov).
- U.S. Department of State Travel Advisories and Background Notes (travel.state.gov/travel_warnings.html).
- VIA Rail Canada (www.viarail.ca).
- VISA ATM locations worldwide (www.visa.com/pd/atm/main.htm).
- Weather (weatherpost.com). Reports on 3,400 cities.

- Weather (www.intellicast.com). Reports, forecasts, links.
- Weather Channel (www.weather.com). Local and international forecasts.
- Web Travel Review (web-travel.org/webtravel/). Travelogue and photos.
- World Fact Book (www.odci.gov/cia/publications/factbook/). Immense amount of information about destinations.
- World Maps (www.parc.xerox.com/istl/projects/mapdocs). Available for downloading.
- World Travel Guide (www.wtgonline.com).
- Worldwide Brochures (www.wwb.com). More than 10,000 maps, guides, and brochures.
- WorldPages (www.worldpages.com). Directories of phone numbers and addresses.
- Yahoo (www.yahoo.com). Enormous free directory of home pages and newsgroups; country-specific resource listing (www.yahoo.com/Regional/Countries); airline travel guide (netscape.yahoo.com/guide/travel/air.html); also see www.biztravel.com and yahoo.com/Recreation/Travel/ as well as travel.yahoo.com.

Traveler's Tool Kit Web Site

To provide continuing travel information, I maintain an updated list of ever-evolving travel resources on my Web site (http://www.travelers-tool-kit.com). I invite you to visit and I look forward to your comments. If you leave travel tips and comments on your favorite destinations, they'll be shared with other travelers.

Other Sources of Information

Commercial Tour Operators

Some tour operators are experienced travelers who entered the business to put their happily acquired knowledge to profitable use. Others are desk-bound managers who spent years assembling mountains of information. And, as with any business, a few operators are simply unqualified, relying on untested local contractors and shipping people to any destination for which they'll pay. Overall, though, tour operators are an excellent source of information about destinations.

So, how do you find them? Look for advertisements in the travel section of major newspapers, in travel magazines, and in special interest magazines (scuba diving, photography, and so on). Call their toll-free telephone numbers for brochures covering destinations of interest. Their brochures are helpful, even if sometimes filled with wildly enthusiastic descriptions.

There are good reasons why tour operators take groups where they do and follow certain routes. You may dislike the crowds that congregate at popular sites, but do you really want to skip the Temple of Karnak,* the Vatican Museum,† or the Taj Mahal?§ Even if many tour itineraries skip small, memorable places, overall they provide, as you will see in Chapter 4, very helpful information.

National Tourist Offices

National tourist offices are an excellent resource. Call the embassies of the countries that you plan to visit and ask for the tourist information office. They'll be delighted to send you information presenting their country in its best light. Ask about late-breaking information or permit requirements. Many countries also have an extensive network of tourist offices in-country that can make your travels much easier. Networks in India and New Zealand, for example, are two of the best.

Conversations

Bring up pending travel plans in conversation. You may be surprised at how frequently you'll find people who've been where you're thinking of going or know someone who's been there. Even small scraps of information can change and enrich your trip. Naturally, evaluate the information in terms of how current it is and the personality of the person who gave it to you. Ask for names of people to contact abroad, no matter how tenuous the relationship. You can make great acquaintances by calling friends of friends.

Public Library

Check out books and videotapes on possible destinations. A catalogue entitled Destinations on Tape lists more than 250 international travel videos (call 800-822-4604 to order a free copy).

---

* *Karnak.* The Temple of Karnak, one of the most impressive of all ancient Egyptian sites, is located in Luxor (called Thebes in the days of the Pharaohs).

† *Vatican Museum.* The museum is located in Vatican City, a sovereign region within Rome. In addition to one of the world's greatest art collections, it contains the Sistine Chapel, built in 1473, with its famous ceiling fresco by Michelangelo.

§ *Taj Mahal.* Located in Agra, the Taj is a national symbol of India. It was built by Shah Jahan to express his heartbreak at the death of his wife in 1629. The Shah intended to build a similar tomb for himself, but he was imprisoned by his ungrateful son, Aurangzeb, before he could do so.

Travel Bookstores

Bookstores that specialize in travel books and maps usually have experienced travelers on staff who will gladly talk with you about trip planning and destinations. An example of the next generation of travel resource stores opened in 1994 in Austin, Texas, in the form of a chain of superstores named TravelFest (800-343-3378 or 800-590-3378). They offer thousands of travel books, maps, videos, a full range of travel equipment (luggage, first aid kits, etc.), plus travel agents knowledgeable about international travel.

The Adventurous Traveler Bookstore, carrying more than 3,000 guidebooks on travel in remote areas, operates by mail. For a free catalogue call (800) 282-3963.

International Video Network offers 60- to 90-minute videos ($25 to $30) of sites around the world. These videos were produced by Reader's Digest, Video Visits, Fodor's, and Rand McNally, among others. Call (800) 669-4486 for information.

State Department

The State Department issues Travel Warnings and Consular Information Sheets to advise against travel or describe circumstances in specific countries. Call the automated answering system at (202) 647-5225 for information on countries in which you have an interest. Alternatively, you can log onto the Consular Affairs Bulletin Board at (202) 647-9225 for warnings and information on topics including terrorism, crime rates, political disturbances, epidemics, and road conditions. Communicate by fax at (202) 657-3000.

Subscribers to online services can connect with OAG Electronic Edition Travel Service at (800) 323-4000 for the text of Travel Warnings and Consular Information Sheets.

The State Department has several other useful travel-related publications, including *Your Trip Abroad*, with basic advice for travelers ($1.25), *Safe Trip Abroad* ($1), and *Travel Tips for Older Americans* ($1).

Periodicals

Members of the Globetrotters Club (c/o BCM Roving, London WC1N 3XX, United Kingdom; membership $14) receive *The Globe*, a bimonthly newsletter as well as *The Globetrotters Directory*. The former is packed with reports written by travelers returning from exotic trips. The latter lists the names of members, along with offers of free accommodations and tidbits of advice. Locally, you can subscribe to *National Geographic* (800-647-5463), *International Travel News* (916-457-3643), *South American Explorer* (303-320-0388), *Transitions Abroad* (413-256-0373), or *Outside* (800-678-1131). Then there are the glossies: *Traveler, Travel Holiday,* and *Travel & Leisure.*

The Travel Alert Bulletin is a four-page synopsis of news and reviews for international business travelers. Its companion publications, *Personal Travel*

Bulletin and *Fax Travel Bulletin*, are written for recreational travelers. Contact Nationwide Intelligence, P.O. Box 1922, Saginaw, MI 48605. See the Bibliography for further suggestions.

Literature

Understand the people of a country by reading its literature, both fiction and nonfiction. With that in mind, I hope you'll take advantage of the Bibliography at the end of the book. It lists some of the most authentic, well-written travel literature available.

Consider CD-ROMs such as *The Traveler* offered by Magellan Interactive Media. Compatible with IBM and Macintosh, it offers presentations on more than 100 destinations and 25 activities (along with promotions by airlines, tour operators, adventure travel companies, tourist boards, hotel chains, and travel gear retailers). The disc is free, but there is a $4.50 shipping fee. Call (800) 561-3114.

Maps

There's no reason to plan a trip using only a small map when there are fine maps available from AAA, *National Geographic*, travel bookstores, and even some regular bookstores. A good 11-by-15-inch map atlas is a great investment.

If appropriate for your destinations, call Best Western International (800-528-1234) and ask for their free *North American Travel Guide* (which covers Mexico, Canada, the Caribbean, and the United States) or *European Travel Guide* (which covers 15 countries).

If you don't have immediate access to a good source for maps, consider these: Magellan (800-929-4627), Map Link (805-965-4402), Maps Plus (800-221-3389), Map Store (800-862-7626), Powell's Travel Store (800-546-5025), Rand McNally (800-333-0136), TravelFest (800-343-3378), and Wide World of Maps (800-279-7654).

Check out *Expert Map for Windows* (about $15), which contains more than 200 country and regional maps. Check a local computer store or call (305) 567-1516. This program is packed with useful information.

If maps inspire you, Worldwide Uniques (call 800-938-7623) offers an eight-color, 8'8" by 13' world map for your wall. It can be trimmed to fit your space and you can write on it with a dry-erase marker to plan your itinerary. It costs $95 to $135.

A final thought about research. After you've gathered masses of information, cut, extract, and summarize it. Take with you only what is essential. Don't overload yourself with all the data you might conceivably need as you travel.

3

How to Decide Whether to Travel Solo— or with a Partner

> There ain't no surer way to find out whether you like
> people or you hate them than to travel with them.
> —Mark Twain

Some people instinctively prefer to travel alone, while others wouldn't consider leaving home without a partner. All those who are undecided should be aware that traveling with someone—anyone—results in a trip very different from traveling by yourself. It's not that one way is necessarily better than the other, just that they are different. In other words, don't think first about who to travel with; think first about *whether* to travel with anyone.

Even traveling with someone you think you know pretty well may reveal how superficial your relationship has been. Years ago, I had a travel partner who flaked out just before we were to leave on a long trip. I chose a replacement at the last moment and wound up traveling with Godzilla for three months. A careless choice is a mistake I'll never make again!

Traveling with a partner is like paddling a canoe together. If you're not synchronized, paddles are likely to clash and you might even capsize. I strongly recommend a short trip before tackling heavy whitewater.

WHY TRAVEL ALONE?

- Traveling solo is the ultimate freedom. You set the itinerary and make all the decisions. No arguments, no second-guessing, no compromises. Cornelia Parker, a very wise woman, wrote, "Traveling with anyone is a very ticklish business. What is your thrill may be my bore. I cannot imagine what fire and pillage I would commit if someone were in a position to keep me looking at things longer than I wanted to look."

- Traveling alone is a confidence-builder. You learn that you can solve problems, get over the blues, and find hidden treasures all by yourself.

- When you're on your own, people are more willing to start a conversation with you and you may feel more like taking the initiative yourself. Local people seem more likely to extend invitations for a meal, a trip, or a stay in their home. In contrast, many people keep a slight distance from couples, romantic or otherwise.

- You have abundant time for contemplating, vegetating, or anything you want. Thomas Jefferson said, "One travels more usefully when alone because he reflects more."

- You needn't deal with someone else's mood swings, nor they with yours.

- You learn languages faster because you must.

- Then there's romance. On your own, you're free to meet someone who might turn out to be very important in your life.

- Your own personality may be the deciding factor. A person who is exceptionally independent and who has little tolerance for the idiosyncrasies of others might be happier traveling alone.

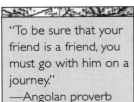

"To be sure that your friend is a friend, you must go with him on a journey."
—Angolan proverb

Traveling alone can be wonderful, but there are also reasons for traveling with a good partner. Of course, if you have an eager spouse, relative, friend, or lover, it may be a moot question.

WHY TRAVEL WITH A PARTNER?

- Travel almost always costs less when you travel with a partner. Since a single room usually costs at least 80 percent of the price of a double room, your lodging costs drop when you split room rent fifty-fifty. The same is true for expenses such as taxis, guidebooks, medicine, film, and reading material. If you're on a tour, having a partner avoids a stiff single supplement charge.

- It can be a relief to divide daily chores, such as changing money, buying tickets, finding a room, or figuring out how to get across town to see Chinese acrobats perform.

- You're probably safer if you travel with someone. Having a partner is especially helpful to women for minimizing unwanted advances.

- A companion keeps the lonesome, homesick blues at bay. If your partner has a down day, you can be a cheerful presence, and vice versa.

- Traveling with someone who speaks the local language makes daily life a little easier.

- Brainstorming with a partner sometimes leads to better choices than you get with solo decisions; even the best fantasy can benefit from a reality check.

- If a traveler becomes ill, a partner assumes the attributes of an angel.

- When the trip is history, you have a person with whom to reminisce.

Handling Money

If you travel with a partner, the last thing you need is conflict over money. Do you want to account for every cent spent? Do you prefer to split restaurant checks evenly or to pay for exactly what you ordered? Does one of you prefer to keep track of all expenditures?

Having each person pay for only his or her own expenses every day is one way to avoid the problem—but it's also tedious. If you assume that from time to time you'll pay for one another and there will also be mutually beneficial expenditures, agree in advance how you'll keep track.

> Discuss how you and your partner will handle money.

You'll both be consuming medical supplies, film, meals, groceries, and, possibly, liquor, but you probably won't be consuming them in equal quantities. If, for example, one of you typically has a couple of cold beers with meals and the other doesn't, it adds up over the course of a long trip.

One approach is to pool enough money for meals and incidentals for a week or so and pay joint expenses from this common wallet. To share the burden, alternate who carries these funds.

Another approach is to keep a running tally, keeping expenditures fairly even on a daily basis. Or note expenditures in a journal and settle up every country or two. Or settle up after returning home. Whichever of you is most comfortable with record-keeping can keep track of partnership finances. Whatever you agree on is fine so long as both of you are satisfied. Keep who owes whom from becoming a matter of importance or irritation. There are stresses in independent travel, but this need not be one of them. Talk it over in advance. Adjust as you go.

Traveling with a Group

Since it's not unusual to fall in with several other travelers for a few days, perhaps to share costs renting a car or hiring a guide, I'll offer a few words about traveling with a group. Given all the decisions that must be made in the course of a day, trying to reach consensus every time can be time-consuming. Further, the possibility of jealousy or misunderstanding in an ad hoc group is quite real. If there's a burr anywhere in the interpersonal relationships, it can become the size of a bowling ball within a few days. Try not to become locked-in to staying with the group. If a problem develops, don't suffer. Bail out.

CHARACTERISTICS OF THE IDEAL TRAVEL PARTNER

If you've decided to travel solo, that's the end of that. But if you prefer a partner, think very carefully about what kind of person you want. Finding the ideal travel partner is easier than finding the source of the Nile or safe passage around Cape Horn—but not much. The prize is definitely worth the effort and it's a lot easier to succeed if you know what you're looking for.

The ideal travel partner is:

- *Someone you like.*

- *Someone who visualizes the trip approximately the same way you do.* Do you agree on destinations? Is one of you thinking of an active, adventure-seeking trip while the other dreams of long afternoons lying on the beach? Does one of you have a vision that includes a curling iron, a hair dryer, and panty hose while the other is thinking about campgrounds and hostels? Does one of you love to hike, while the other looks for a taxi if the restaurant is more than two blocks away? Are you likely to want to keep finding new places, while your partner would rather return every day to a known place? It's not a question of who's right. It's a matter of being certain the trip has the same shape for both of you or, if there are differences, that you identify and reconcile them before you leave home.

- *Someone who shares your feelings about taking risks.* How do you both feel about riding on top of the bus, hiking without a guide, spending the night at the top of the pyramid, or visiting areas that may not be completely safe?

- *Someone who shares your feelings about the budget.* Reasonable people can become very weird when it comes to money. Do you both have the same ideas about your budget? Are you thinking of paying $12 a night for a hotel room, but your prospective partner won't be comfortable for less than $112? How do you feel about splurging when hit by an urge? If you anticipate different standards of living on the road, it may signal differences in your respective views of the whole trip.

On the easygoing tropical island of Gili Trawangan,* I met a couple from Sydney who were barely into their first vacation together. They had just moved into a clean bungalow with a bathroom, decent beds, a fan, and only fifty feet from the water—all for $5 a night. He was obviously delighted by the place and the price. A few hours later, they stood on the front porch heatedly discussing her desire to return to the main-

---

*Gili Trawangan. A tiny island off the coast of Lombok, Indonesia, offering sunny days, snorkeling, and magic moonlight.

Fierce rapids on the Rio Futaleufú. Chile.

land and the comforts of the Sengiggi Beach Hotel* at $70 per night. I have a feeling that was not the last of their disputes.

That couple is a reminder that there are risks in traveling with a significant other, especially when romance is in first bloom. The occasional stresses of long-term travel can exert a little pressure on even an intimate relationship. Small irritants, if not acknowledged and dealt with, can grow to overwhelm romantic illusions.

- *Someone who operates on a similar clock.* As Thoreau put it, "The man who goes alone can start today; but he who travels with another must wait till that other is ready." The day person/night person issue has plagued more than a few travelers. If one partner dedicates himself to late-night partying and the other prefers visiting local markets at dawn, there's a problem on the horizon. Partners can also fall out over the timing of meals. Do you wake ravenous, or prefer to wait until mid-morning? Do you want three meals a day, or is catch-as-catch-can fine? Would one of you become crazed if the other were late for a meeting? A stickler for punctuality and orderliness could find the occasional chaos of the Third World rather trying. Be certain you understand one another and can adjust accordingly.

- *Someone whose energy level is similar to your own.* Be sure you and your prospective partner seek a similar pace of travel. If you don't have compatible degrees of fitness, you may not be able to travel well as a team. An upbeat, peppy partner is a real joy.

---

* *Sengiggi Beach Hotel.* This is an upscale hotel on the island of Lombok, Indonesia. Lombok is said to resemble Bali of fifty years ago, but that's a bit of exaggeration.

- *Someone who doesn't have health problems that would interfere.* On an easygoing trip, health is probably not an issue. For a long or arduous trip, allergies or potentially serious afflictions should be considered carefully in advance. The important thing is that both partners share the same expectations.

- *Someone who has a flexible, easygoing personality.* There are bumps in the road that will jostle anyone's cart. Travel requires solving problems and resolving uncertainties. The more remote from your own culture, the greater the challenges. Choose a partner who blows up easily, and you'll be very unhappy. Look for a partner who has a sense of humor and understands that most frustrations arise from the very differences in culture that make a place worth visiting.

- *Someone who has personal habits compatible with your own.* Do you have similar feelings about alcohol? Cigarettes? Illegal drugs? If one partner spreads his gear over every available surface, will the other flip out? If one of you snores like a chainsaw . . . well, then what? No judgments, just a reality check before the plane rolls down the runway.

- *Someone who understands how a partnership works.* Travel with someone who will share the load and keep agreements; someone you can count on; and someone who will respect your privacy.

- *Someone who recognizes the need for "quiet time."* Everyone enjoys a good conversationalist, but anyone who doesn't get enough quiet time, or time alone, to maintain equilibrium may get cranky. Many of us are simply not used to spending 24 hours a day within 50 feet of the same person. Unless you're into non-stop conversation, it helps if both of you are comfortable with silence. When you need quiet time, don't suffer: ask for it. Writing in your journal and reading are two ways to create quiet time. Reach agreement that the need for time alone is not a rejection of the other person. If you need an occasional meal alone, a solitary walk, a breakfast-to-dinner solo day, or some parallel travel, can your partner recognize that need without feeling rejected?

- *Someone who feels the same way you do about intimacy.* Is romance on the agenda? Do you feel okay about sharing a room, or a bed? Don't make assumptions about this one.

- *Someone who is willing to communicate and solve problems.* If there's a problem, a molehill can become volcanic if not dealt with when it arises. Agree not to store up small resentments; to express, calmly and contemporaneously, your feelings about your partner's behavior, the dynamics of the trip, or whatever the issue is.

There must be a mutual commitment to solving problems in creative ways. If you can't find a mutually satisfactory solution, or a practical compromise, consider a trade-off. Your partner prevails this time, you get your way next time. There is no point in silently compiling a list that demonstrates, to your own satisfaction at least, that your partner is Jack the Ripper.

> "I learned one thing."
> "What?" "Never go on trips with anyone you do not love."
> —Ernest Hemingway, *A Moveable Feast,* 1964

Choose some regular time, like Sunday breakfast, to discuss candidly how you both think the trip is going. Are you spending money at about the right rate? Are you traveling at a pace that makes you both happy? Is it time to change the itinerary or make any other changes? Are you having fun?

- *Someone you like!* Nothing is more important.

Don't decide lightly whether to travel solo or with a partner. If you'll be happier with a partner, choose that person with great care. And don't expect someone to change just because he or she is on a trip. If you're considering traveling with a non-stop talker who criticizes and complains, take a cold shower.

HOW TO FIND YOUR TRAVEL PARTNER

You've decided to travel with someone and you have a good idea of what your ideal person would be like. Now what? If you're not married to or romantically involved with a potential traveling partner, and neither family nor friends are suitable, check bulletin boards at colleges and bookstores. Review *International Travel News, International Living, South American Explorer*, and other travel periodicals in which travelers seeking partners list where they'd like to go and when.

The richest resource I know of is the Travel Companion Exchange (TCE) at (800) 392-1256 or (516) 454-0880. This reputable, 15-year-old service is one of the largest in the country. Its well-written, bimonthly newsletter, full of useful travel information, lists more than 500 males and females eagerly looking for partners with whom to hit the road. Whether you want to avoid the single supplement charge on a tour in the south of France or seek someone to join you for a yearlong stroll from Capetown to Cairo, you have a good chance of finding likely candidates through TCE. The newsletter costs $48, a membership, including the newsletter, costs $198 for six months.

Other organizations that I am not personally familiar with but that advertise in reputable places include the following:

- Partners-in-Travel (310-476-4869), which publishes a Traveler's Directory of about 500 singles looking for travel partners, plus a list of about 150 tour operators offering package tours that accommodate singles. There's no charge for listing yourself in the directory, but only members ($25) receive a copy of it.
- Golden Age Travelers Club (800-258-8880), a travel club for people over age 50, which will either find you a roommate for a tour or cruise or waive the single supplement fee ($10 membership, quarterly catalogue of trips).
- Partners for Travel (800-866-5565), which charges $120 per year to help find traveling companions for those over age 50 and single. However, the charge is refunded if you take one of their educational or adventure trips.
- Connecting (800-557-1757), which publishes an annual *Single-Friendly Travel Directory* listing tour operators, outfitters, resorts, cruise lines, and singles clubs whose services and pricing policies are directed toward the solo traveler. The directory is free with a subscription to *News for Solo Travelers* (bimonthly, $25 per year). Travel tips in the newsletter are oriented toward solo travelers. In addition to listing travel companions, *Connecting* lists persons willing to host traveling singles.

You can also leave home alone, planning to find one or more partners along the way. While you can't be sure you'll meet someone compatible who's going your direction, it's easy to meet travelers in museums, on city bus trips, on trains, on the trail, at the beach, in hostels and restaurants, even just walking along the street. You can't count on it, but you may find potential partners on Bencoolen Street in Singapore, at the Iqbal Hotel in Nairobi, around the language schools in Antigua, on the Spanish Steps in Rome—all over the world.

If one of these spur-of-the-moment partnerships doesn't work out, it's easy to dissolve. In other words, if you prefer traveling with a partner but don't find one at home, don't let that ground you.

Wherever you find a potential partner, run through the "ideal partner" checklist to make sure you're compatible. And when you find a great travel partner, treasure her or him. Partners who finish a long trip on a friendly basis are a good bet to be friends for life.

HOW TO AVOID LOSING YOUR TRAVEL PARTNER

Most travelers never stop to think what they would do if they and their partner were separated. As a result, the next time they meet, after considerable inconvenience and anxiety, might be back in their hometown. It's worth creating a contingency plan to get back together if you're separated. It doesn't matter much what your plan is so long as you've agreed on one before you're unexpectedly in different places. Each partner must know what the other will do in a missing-person situation. With a contingency plan it may take a while to get together, but at least you will.

For example, you might agree that if separated while walking around town, each of you will return to your hotel. Alternatively, you can agree on a time and place to look for one another. That's easy.

It's more likely you'll become separated just as the train you were about to catch is pulling out. My agreement with my partner is that if I'm not *certain* she's aboard, I'll get off. If I don't find her after looking around, I'll wait a while hoping she'll find me. If still no luck, I'll return to our last hotel and wait. If my partner was aboard the train that pulled out without me, she'll get off at some reasonable place and try to reach me at the hotel. If that doesn't work, she'll head back.

If there's a language barrier at your hotel, you might specify that you'll meet at one of the major tourist hotels. English will be spoken and the manager should be able to help.

Some people agree to reconnect through the appropriate consulate or embassy or the central police station.

As a fail-safe back-up, keep a telephone number in your money belts that each of you will call (usually a number at home likely to be answered).

If you come up with a more fool-proof contingency plan than the ones I've suggested, I'd like to hear about it.

A final comment about travel partners. The man who holds the *Guinness Book of Records* title as the World's Most Traveled Man has been married and divorced six times. His explanation: "My wives all said they loved travel, but they were thinking the QE II and the Ritz, not riding some dirty boat from one godforsaken island to another." I wonder if this chapter would have helped.

4

The Organized Tour

Tourists capture the image of a well-known place in a
photo but miss its essence; the anti-tourist dismisses
the place as a cliché and misses the whole thing;
while the traveler grasps its majesty.
— John Thorn

I've often heard people discuss theoretical distinctions between "tourist" and "traveler." Naturally, those who think of themselves as travelers insist on the distinction, while even those who see the world on organized tours are reluctant to categorize themselves as tourists. Certainly, effortless mass tourism has inspired satire, especially in the case of tourists who think they are intrepid travelers as they're shepherded safely to places previously accessible only to daring adventurers.

Paul Fussell opined, "An explorer seeks the undiscovered; a traveler seeks that which has been discovered by the mind working in history; and the tourist seeks that which has been discovered by entrepreneurship and prepared for him by the arts of mass publicity." Another critic described tourists as people who travel primarily to raise their social status at home, to realize fantasies of freedom, or to pose as members of a social class above their own. Doesn't make you want to be categorized as a tourist, does it?

In my opinion, the distinction between traveler and tourist goes beyond destination, means of transport, length of time on the road—and even whether someone else takes your luggage down to a bus each morning. It's based on your objectives and state of mind. A traveler intends to merge with a place and its people in a way that a tourist does not wish to.

To me, the word "tourist" has a connotation different from merely describing people who travel on an organized tour. It identifies people who see the well-known sights but leave a place understanding the culture only superficially. They have few friendly contacts with local people and are little changed by their trip. A tourist is a person who, whether with a tour group or not, is primarily along for the ride and doesn't get actively involved.

From that perspective, it would be inaccurate to categorize everyone on an organized tour as a tourist. Tour participants can be far more than tourists if they educate themselves about what they will experience, interact with local people as meaningfully as possible—and choose their tour operator wisely.

Independent travel requires endurance, a measure of self-confidence, the ability to organize, adequate health, and some control over your business and personal responsibilities. Uncertain about meeting these requirements, many people hook up with a tour, especially for their first major trip, and have a great time. If anxiety about coping with distant parts of the world might cause you to stay home, you'd be doing yourself a disservice to dismiss tours. It's far better to explore the world in whatever vehicle feels comfortable than to mildew in an armchair at home.

If taking a tour seems like a good way to get under way, the trick is to select the tour that will meet the objectives you set. That's what this chapter is about. Even if you are not interested in tours today, it's possible you'll travel with an organized tour group in the future.

REASONS TO TRAVEL WITH A TOUR OPERATOR

- *Someone else does the thinking and makes the arrangements.* Decide to travel with a tour group and that's one of the last decisions required. Before long, the mailman delivers a glossy brochure bulging with superlatives, an itinerary, a list of what to bring, an orange plastic luggage tag, and detailed instructions. Under way, courteous guides answer every question, adequate hotels and restaurants appear when wanted, and scenic vistas flow by without misadventure. If there are hassles, you probably won't even hear about them, much less have to deal with them. Participating in a tour, by the way, can teach you a lot about planning your own itinerary the next time out.

  Some people sign up for tours because they lust for luxury. For example, one banking tycoon engaged a tour operator to lease a swanky private train to take his party deep into the Gobi Desert for a sumptuous banquet brought in by camel caravan. Another client wanted to "rough it" on the Salmon River, with silver, china, crystal, and violins at night. One tour operator makes a living providing suites on the QE II that cost over $37,000 for the five-day Atlantic crossing.

- *Some countries require that visitors travel with a tour group.* For many years that was the only way outsiders were permitted to travel in China. That requirement has been generally abandoned, although permission to travel independently in places such as Bhutan, Myanmar, and North Korea phases in and out. Countries with limited tourist facilities want to be sure that big spenders are given priority. It's also easier for an inquisitive government to keep tabs on groups than on independent travelers.

  In several countries, traveling with a tour group is not mandatory, but logistics can be daunting for an independent traveler. For example, consider a group if you want to travel hassle-free in Mongolia.

- *Some tour operators include considerable educational value in their trips.* If so, you're likely to be accompanied by an art historian, a geologist, or some other appropriate expert to help satisfy your curious mind.

- *A tour can be an efficient way of moving from place to place.* Since independent travel, especially in the Third World, can be very time-consuming, a tour may be a good fit for a traveler with limited time. If you don't want company, an "air and accommodations only" tour package may be useful.

- *Some people prize the company of others.* In fact, meeting like-minded people may be part of the reason for the trip. It is not unusual to travel repeatedly with people with whom you've formed friendships on a tour.

- *Tours may increase opportunities to meet local people.* Although many tours tend to insulate tour members from local contact, some are organized specifically to permit participants to talk with educated and well-traveled local people, perhaps when they give lectures to the group.

- *Some tours actually SAVE MONEY.* For example, joining a budget safari group after arriving in Kenya will cost you much less than organizing a safari for yourself. If you don't mind staying in the places, eating the type of food, and seeing the sights that tour groups do, you can save money by joining tours and taking advantage of group rates. In fact, if you book an off-season tour not long before departure, you should get an extremely good price.

- *A tour may be ideal for persons with less than robust health.* The availability of assistance may enable someone to travel who doesn't have the reasonably robust health required for independent travel.

- *Tours free you from handling the logistics of a trip.* Running the Colorado River through the Grand Canyon or the Rio Bio Bio in Chile on your own would require acquiring and transporting quite a bit of specialized equipment and supplies. It's a lot easier to leave that to others.

- *A tour provides the opportunity to combine high adventure with low risk.* The expertise of experienced guides enables people to make difficult trips in comparative safety.

After reading a stack of tour brochures, you will realize that tourist trails around the world are deeply worn. On the other hand, if you read brochures put out by a few companies such as Geographic Expeditions, Mountain Travel/Sobek, and Turtle Tours, you may be amazed at how many remote corners of the world still await your visit. Companies like these have sought out nearly inaccessible hideaways from Mongolia to Indochina, from the sub-Sahara to Antarctica. They'll take you to Lunana in northern Bhutan, to the fabled Inner Dolpo region of northwest Nepal, across the Himalayas from Manali to Ladakh, or on an icebreaker out of Cape Town bound for the far side of Antarctica. Yes, you could arrange almost all of these trips on your own, but you'd have to do extensive research and overcome formidable logistical problems to do so. Even if you're prepared to make the rigorous effort, choosing whether to do it on your own or with a tour operator is not always an easy call.

REASONS *NOT* TO TRAVEL WITH A TOUR OPERATOR

It's interesting that some of the reasons that persuade people to sign on with a tour group are the very reasons that persuade other people *not* to. Tours come with trade-offs. Many tour operators work hard to combat the disadvantages I mention below but, to some extent, they are inherent in tours.

- *Many tours are expensive when compared to the costs of independent travel.* For single travelers, part of the extra expense of a tour is the dreaded single supplement. This is a substantial charge often added to cruise, hotel, or tour prices for people traveling alone. After all, the single traveler takes up a space which would otherwise accommodate two fare-paying people. SAVE MONEY by seeking out tour operators who don't impose this charge or who waive it if you're willing to accept an assigned roommate. Negotiate. Tell the tour operator you'll sign up only if the charge is waived. As departure date approaches, the operator may see it your way. If not, consider finding a partner (see Chapter 3).

  Because many tours are very expensive even without the single supplement, you may be interested in knowing why they cost you more than independent travel. It's because the tour operator, trying to anticipate the preferences of prospective clients, often builds upscale amenities into trips. They usually lodge you in expensive hotels all the way, or at least before and after a trek, and furnish a sociable, educated, English-speaking guide. On your own, you might stay in less expensive lodgings and get along without a guide (or with one whose English is only somewhat better than your command of his language). Beyond that, the operator pays for other helpers, local permits, fuel, equipment, food, transportation, and insurance. On your own, you might eat more simply and rely on public transportation.

Then there's overhead. The tour operator maintains a staff to provide all those pretrip services to you. Remember that gorgeous brochure? To the high cost of producing it, add what it cost the operator to find you and mail it to you. On top of all that, at least 10 percent of the trip price is paid by the tour operator to the travel agency and another 3 percent goes to your credit card company.

The operator spends extra money to ensure that the trip is flawless—because that's what people seem to expect on tour. The independent traveler, on the other hand, is prepared to accept a glitch or two (after all, he's his own tour operator). It's up to you to understand and choose what you want.

- *Regimentation is the rule.* On a typical tour, you board the daily transportation at a prescribed time, travel a fixed path selected by others, and eat as a group when the bell rings. The tour operator sets the pace. If it's significantly different from your natural pace, you can go bananas. There is seldom any "down time." You're expected to eat, and enjoy, everything on the plate. You can struggle against the routine by skipping some of the planned activities, substituting your own and hitting the streets every time there's a free period on the schedule. In the end, however, you're still aboard a guided missile.

- *Being with a tour group changes the nature of any experience.* A cloud-wrapped monastery, a memorable experience when seen alone, changes when twenty-five people pile through the low door and the monks scramble to peddle their crafts (and they do).

- *Unprofessional tour guides can drive anyone crazy.* Unprofessionalism ranges from not knowing the subject to paying no attention to group preferences to hitting on the clients.

> "Most travelers content themselves with what they may chance to see from car-windows, hotel verandahs, or the deck of a steamer . . . clinging to the battered highways like drowning sailors to a life raft."
> —John Muir, American naturalist

- *Your companions can make or break the tour, and possibly you in the bargain.* Noel Coward referred to tourists as " . . . monumental bores who travel in groups, herds and troupes." As a generalization that's unfair, but bores are not nearly the worst human peril you encounter on tour. A mysterious metamorphosis lies dormant in some people, seemingly triggered by paying a lot of money to a tour operator. Failing to ask the tour operator in advance for an honest profile of the group could be a serious error.

Richard Bangs, founding partner of Mountain Travel/Sobek, listed some of the clients his guides dread: The Stud—who's out to conquer the landscape and anything else available; The Ignoramus—who learned nothing about the tour destinations ahead of time and didn't bring the proper gear; The Inflexible Retentive—who has memorized the brochure and explodes when local conditions force the slightest deviation (even an otherwise understanding person may cast her cape aside and emerge as a chronic complainer); The Peacock—whose primary pleasure is parading around in the most expensive clothing available; The Snipe—who snarfs up far more than his share of whatever goodies are available; and The Grunge—who violates all rules of hygiene, endangering everyone else's health.

- *Food and hotels selected by tour operators are typically Westernized.* You could wind up missing much of the flavor of the country.

- *You meet few local people.* Those you encounter are lecturers very familiar with Westerners, or hardened traders whose primary goal is to sell you as much as possible during the brief moments you are together. They're very good at it but it's not what you would call a fulfilling experience for you.

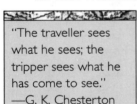
"The traveller sees what he sees; the tripper sees what he has come to see."
—G. K. Chesterton

People on tour see restaurant workers, taxi drivers, and beggars who gather outside their hotel (who are there precisely because it is a tourist hotel), but have little interaction with the general populace. They don't hang out with local artists, musicians, soldiers, store keepers, politicians—or even travelers. An invisible cocoon forms around a tour, difficult to penetrate in either direction.

- *You're likely to become dependent on the lifeline of bus and guide.* Travel becomes too easy. Someone else has the answers and you become timid about venturing out on your own.

Some independent travelers may be tempted to look down their noses a bit as they see a tour bus pulling up in front of yet another temple. However, there's another way to look at it. First, that tour bus is taking people to places to which they would not, or could not, otherwise go—and that's good. Second, tour groups pay in hard currency, vitally needed by the host country—and that's good. Third, I remember standing in a blazing hot, dusty, chaotic bus yard, trying to figure out what the name of my destination might look like in Hindi. Overwhelmed by noxious fumes and the sound of roaring engines, my eye was caught by an air-conditioned luxury tour bus gliding by, stereo playing, hostess already pouring ice-cold beers. I promise you, I wasn't looking down my nose at tour groups at that moment. And that's good.

If you're feeling uncertain about what you'll encounter in some faraway land, you're not quite as fit as you'd like to be, don't want to take the time to organize a trip on your own, or just want to be coddled, consider a tour. If going on a tour will initiate a lifetime of traveling, give it a try. If you decide to take a tour, hit the road with optimism and a cheerful spirit. Make it your trip—and don't sweat the small stuff.

TOURS—HIGH COST TO LOW COST

Tours don't come just in vanilla. They vary widely in cost, services provided, and objectives. Itineraries, multiplying like a computer network, are now a great spider web covering the globe. To make wise choices, you need to understand what is available.

Upscale. On some fully escorted tours, you never lift a hand; in fact, your feet may barely touch the ground. The accommodations are five-star and the food is gourmet (although being served Chicken Cordon Bleu in Beijing may strike you as a little weird). An imported expert guides you through the sights of the day and lectures to you at night. After a nightcap, you tuck yourself into a crisp, clean bed (yes, you generally have to do that yourself).

Standard. On the majority of tours, you're accompanied by an escort, stay in good hotels, eat well, and listen to local guides reel off a galaxy of details. Every morning, you're rousted out early to line up your bags in the hall, ready for the next lap. These tours generally last between ten and thirty days, and prices vary accordingly.

Locally hosted packages. A guide meets you or your group as you arrive at a destination, takes care of you for a few days, then sees you safely onto transport to your next destination—where you meet your next guide-for-a-day.

Special focus. Some tours distinguish themselves with a special focus, such as Chinese celadon, butterflies along the Tambopata,* French wines, or the Namibian system of jurisprudence. Special focus tours are often organized by zoological societies, museums, cultural groups, and the like.

Adventure travel. The popularity of this type of special interest tour is rapidly expanding. I'll discuss them at greater length in the next section.

Affinity groups. These groups can be composed of anything from accountants to zydeco musicians to redheaded people named Smith. Shoppers, feeding wildly in country after country, are a common affinity group.

---

*Tambopata. This river in eastern Peru joins the Madre de Dios to flow into the Amazon. It is noted for spectacular bird life and nature preserves.

Package. You initiate a package tour by stepping into a travel agency with a general idea of where you'd like to go. You leave the agency with a package of airline/hotel/overland transport reservations and travel on your own within that framework. No escorts are provided. Hotels, airlines, and rental car companies sell blocks of space to package operators (sometimes called wholesalers) at a discount, so the cost to you can be significantly less than if you bought the individual components separately. You get the group discount without the group; not a bad deal. The accommodations will be somewhat upscale and Westernized, but at least you're on your own. A Foreign Independent Tour (FIT) is similar, usually unescorted but with occasional guide service.

Disability groups. Since international travel can be difficult for persons with significant disabilities, it's worth getting advice and assistance in advance. The Society for the Advancement of Travel for the Handicapped (212-447-7284) has a list of tour operators who make special efforts to assist travelers with disabilities. Gersten and Freedman have written a helpful book titled *Traveling Like Everybody Else: A Practical Guide for Disabled Travelers* (Adama Books, Bellmore, NY).

Not specifically fitting in the standard concept of a tour are two other situations in which you employ someone else to show you the sights. Although local tours and local guides are passed up by many travelers, each has merits worth considering.

Local Tours

Inexpensive local tours are offered by a unit of government or by private tour operators. Most commonly, they are bus trips around a city or region lasting for one long day, although some continue for a week or more. There's usually no problem boarding just before departure, but it's safer to sign up a day ahead of time. A local day tour saves you from having to figure out how to get to and from a dozen remote sites in a city new to you. The driver or guide explains what you're seeing and is usually willing to answer questions having little to do with the tour. By the end of the day, you've identified places to which you want to return and you may have met interesting people in the bargain. I often take a local tour on my first day in a large city new to me.

It would be logical to assume that everyone on the bus paid the same for the local tour—and it would be wrong. Those who asked their hotel or a local travel agency to book them almost certainly paid much more than those who booked directly with the tour operator. If you book through your hotel, ask for a discount. If someone tries to switch you from a tour you requested to a different one, it's probably because they get a higher commission from the latter.

Local Guides

Wherever your elbow is in the world, a would-be guide will touch it to commend himself to your attention. He may dress in a shiny suit and speak a melodic upper-school English, or he may be a 14-year-old in a scruffy *djellaba*. Whichever, he is certain to be tenacious. He will also probably be knowledgeable, which he'll attempt to demonstrate by bombarding you with arcane info-bits before you can say, "No, thank you." He'll offer to guide you safely through the maze of the *souks* of Marrakech, protect you from being cheated by merchants, and shield you from his "not honest" competitors who are also seeking your attention.

After several experiences with guides who told me much more than I wanted to know and always seemed to have an uncle whose carpet shop just happened to be on our route, I responded by turning away every applicant. I remember one guide I turned down in a Prague museum who ran ahead of me and turned all the lights off. Before long, I learned better. In addition to what they've programmed themselves to tell me, guides provide answers that help satisfy my curiosity as no guidebook can. With encouragement, they take me to remote corners I would otherwise miss. As a bonus, beneath the routine patter, many guides are interesting—proud of their knowledge and their fluency in foreign languages.

If you think a person would expect to be compensated for performing such services, you would be right. The question is, how much? Starting off without an agreement almost assures that one or both parties will be unhappy at the end. However, before discussing price, agree on exactly what services the guide will provide. That done, if he's failed to state a price, raise the subject yourself. He's likely to respond, "Nothing, sir. Nothing at all. If you do not like my services, you pay me nothing. If I am helpful, you pay whatever you decide." Sounds fair, eh? Yes, it does—but it's a trap. Your conscience will never permit "nothing" and the guide knows it. If you pay anything less than a year's income, the guide will protest that it is too little. His protest may be quiet and courteous, as if embarrassed that you don't know any better, or he may feign shock or grief. You are vastly better off reaching agreement in advance. If you wish, talk with several prospective guides, comparing their merits and their asking prices. Or decide what a guide's services would be worth to you and offer a take-it-or-leave-it price. The price of a guide is, to put it mildly, highly elastic, reflecting how many guides there are and how many prospective clients. Only if the trip involves some strenuous activity such as climbing with you to the top of the four highest pyramids at Tikal is there likely to be an irreducible minimum price.

You often see a little knot of tourists being towed passively through a site by a fast-talking guide. Within minutes a few become hostile, but most lapse into glassy-eyed boredom. In contrast, when I set off with a guide I immediately try to engage him as a person and get him to see me as an individual traveler. I let him know my special interests in the site. As we walk, I ensure that we proceed at my pace, so I can understand what I'm seeing, take photographs if I choose, and ask questions. If the guide makes a special effort, he is paid a bit more than we agreed on—and we're both happy.

HOW TO CHOOSE THE BEST TOUR OPERATOR

Before investigating any particular tour, decide where you want to go, how long you want to travel, what time of year you prefer, how much you want to spend, and the kind of people with whom you want to travel. In other words, set the initial agenda yourself. If you choose to make adjustments later to meet the specifics of available tours, at least you're following your own path.

Resources

Read travel magazine ads. If you have a special interest, such as scuba diving, bicycling, or historic preservation, review ads in magazines that concentrate on your interest. Send for every brochure that tweaks your interest.

You seldom get a discount if you book directly with the tour operator, so you lose nothing if you deal with a good travel agent. However, the travel agent is paid by tour operators, not by you, so there is some potential for a conflict of interest. Travel agents have access to thousands of brochures which they'll order for you on request. Take a look at their *Official Tour Directory*. See Chapter 2 on how to choose the best agent for your trip.

Write to the U.S. Tour Operators Association (211 E. 51st Street, Suite 12-B, New York, NY 10022) for a free copy of its *Smart Travelers Planning Kit*. This USTOA guide lists all member companies and the areas of the world in which each specializes.

Local and national business and philanthropic organizations promote tours all over the globe, as do many universities. Watch for their ads.

The American Association of Retired Persons (AARP) and other "seniors" organizations (such as the Golden Age Travelers Club, Grand Circle Travel, National Alliance of Senior Citizens, and the National Association of Retired Federal Employees) sponsor tours, as well enabling members to obtain discounts of 10 to 50 percent on many hotel and tour rates.

Tourspeak

One of the most helpful foreign languages to learn is "tourspeak." Here are some samples: If an agent (or brochure) says you will "visit" someplace, it means that the bus will stop and you'll have time to get off and look around. If the word is "view," however, there will be only a brief opportunity to take a photo or two, while "see" means that the bus might slow down as it whizzes by the attraction. If a brochure says that you "can" play golf or "will be able" to visit an amusement park, these activities are probably not included in the price. Another tricky word is "near," as in "your little cottage is near the beach." It may be near only in a taxi. Listen and read with care so you'll know what to expect.

"Options galore" means not much is included in the price. "Spacious quarters" may mean sparsely furnished, while "airy" means no air conditioning. "Carefree natives" may be a euphemism for terrible service while "no extra fees" probably means no extras at all.

Check Out the Tour Operator

Evaluating tour operators is a good way to avoid aggravation and yet an amazing number of people don't bother. A man was recently indicted in Alexandria, Virginia, for ripping off more than 2,000 people in 43 states. He used telemarketing to sell cheap vacation packages (e.g., $199 for two people to the Caribbean and Cancun). Requiring the would-be traveler to pay in full in advance, he would then deliver "promotional vouchers" with so many restrictions that virtually no one could use the trips. Here's the kicker. Among the aliases he used were Dusty Rhodes and Skip Town! It must be true; it was reported in *Travel Weekly*.

Several magazines, such as *International Travel News* and *Consumer Reports* (see the Bibliography), periodically publish ratings of major tour operators. Call the American Society of Travel Agents (ASTA, 800-ASK-ASTA) or the USTOA (212-750-7371) to check credentials of travel agents and tour operators.

What to Ask the Travel Agent or Tour Operator

1. *Firsthand experience.* Has anybody in the travel agent's office traveled with this tour operator? If so, were they OK? Have any clients of the travel agency traveled with the operator? Were they satisfied? Get the names of some with whom can you speak (you'll get good advice about the trip as well as inside information on the tour operator).

2. *Operator's experience.* How long has the tour operator been in business? How many tours does it handle annually? How many trips has it sponsored to the area that interests you?

3. *Protection.* Since you'll want your money back if the tour operator cancels the trip or goes bankrupt, is it financially responsible? Does it have liability insurance? Is it bonded? Does it belong to the consumer protection program (a $5 million fund available to reimburse consumers in the event of bankruptcy) of the USTOA? Details on that program are provided in a free brochure, *The Standard for Confident Travel* (call USTOA at 212-750-7371). Does your payment go into a trust account or

escrow held by a third party? Can you pay by credit card? What penalties are there if you cancel? Have any complaints been filed with the state consumer affairs office against the tour operator? Naturally, you won't pay any tour operator until you've carefully read all the terms of the contract.

4. *Price.* Exactly what does the price of the tour include? If meals are referred to as European Plan, no meals are included in the price. If it is American Plan, three meals a day are included, whether you are hungry or not. Modified American Plan (MAP) means that breakfast and lunch or dinner are included. If it's Continental Plan, you'll get a bread and beverage breakfast that may leave an echo in your stomach. Is the price firm—or does the tour operator retain the right to increase the fare after you've signed the contract? An increase of more than 10 percent or a significant change in departure date should entitle you to a refund. Are there any extra charges, such as side trips, taxes, and so on, not included in the price? Will they provide other single travelers so you don't have to pay a single supplement? To compare prices of various trips, take the total price, subtract your estimate of the airfare if it is included, then divide that figure by the number of *nights* included. That will give you a uniform price/day figure for each trip.

5. *Cancellation.* What are the cancellation penalties? Are there situations in which either you or the tour operator may cancel without penalty?

6. *Trip difficulty.* Many tour brochures grade the trips they offer in terms of physical difficulty. Seek a match with your own energy level. Don't hesitate to ask; you're in this for fun. An active person could be climbing the walls after two weeks of sitting on a bus. On the other hand, if a trip is billed as "strenuous trekking" or "high altitude," don't sign up without understanding what that means.

7. *Guides.* Who will accompany the tour group? Who *exactly* will be the guide? There's nothing wrong with using local subcontractors if they're well-trained and reliable. When they're not . . . well, that's when the glossy brochure turns into toilet paper. What is the ratio of guides to group members? How long have the guides been with the company?

8. *Accommodations.* What is the quality of the scheduled accommodations? Lodging differs considerably, so ask for specifics. Where is the lodging located? If it's frequently far from the center of towns, you'll waste time commuting.

9. *Group demographics.* What are the maximum and minimum number of persons in the group? Ask about the demographics of people who have

already signed up. If you have an interest in romance, find out if there are appropriate singles on the manifest.

10. *Pace.* What will the pace of the trip be?

11. *Independence.* Will there be time to explore on your own during the tour?

12. *Contacts.* Will there be opportunities to connect with local people?

13. *Materials.* What materials will the tour operator provide in advance (gear lists, maps, readings, and so on)?

14. *Extensions.* Are there side trips or extensions you can take rather than returning home with the group?

15. *Diet.* Will dietary, religious, nonsmoking, and other personal preferences be accommodated?

16. *Free trip.* If you deliver a certain number of other people who sign up for a tour, will the tour operator give you a free trip, including air fare, room and board? If so, how many people would it take?

17. *Payoff.* What is there about this trip that will make it a "trip of a life-time"?

Choosing the tour operator who can best meet your objectives is as important as deciding whether to travel with a tour group at all. It's worth doing your homework.

ECOLOGICAL RESPONSIBILITY

In the real world, few travelers are likely to select a tour operator solely or even primarily because it treats the environment gently. However, in choosing from among a group of otherwise qualified firms, ecological responsibility could be the deciding factor. Not surprisingly, you'll have to look beyond mere inclusion of some form of "eco" in a company's title. That word is meant to appeal to the public but may mean little in practice.

When evaluating a tour operator in terms of ecological responsibility, ask questions such as: Do you use wood for fires or do you use alternative fuel sources? How do you dispose of organic and inorganic waste? Are your guides sensitive to local cultures? Are your local support staff members adequately clothed, fed, and housed? Do you provide predeparture information about the ecology of the destination? Do you use low-impact transportation when practical? Do you purchase goods and services locally? Are your local facilities designed to minimize environmental damage? Do you donate money or equipment to help the local environment or protect natural resources?

Since these are like "have you stopped beating your wife" questions, not all tour operators may be candid, but their answers will give you a chance to form an opinion. Further, even a few inquiries may motivate operators to be more ecologically responsible.

Some tour operators, listed in the table on the following page, are well regarded for their efforts to provide travelers with environmentally sensitive experiences.

Other good resources on ecotourism include the Ecotourism Society (703-549-8979); the Center for Responsible Tourism (415-258-6594); the *Alternative Tourism Resource Guide,* published by the Center for Socially Responsible Travel (415-258-6594); *Handle with Care: A Guide to Responsible Travel in Developing Countries* (800-486-7737); *Archaeological Field Work Opportunities,* which lists hundreds of sites where you can assist with archaeological work (call the Archaeological Institute of America, 800-338-5578); *EcoTraveler* magazine (see the Bibliography); and *Earth Trips: A Guide to Nature Travel on a Fragile Planet,* by Dwight Holing, which offers a lengthy list of nature tour operators.

The Ecumenical Coalition on Third World Tourism has published some considerations for travelers to keep in mind. Among them are the following: travel with a genuine desire to learn more about people and be aware of their feelings; listen and observe; realize that your personal time concepts and thought patterns are not universal; learn local customs; ask questions; don't expect special privileges; don't make promises you can't or won't keep; and, reflect on the experiences of each day.

Environmentally Responsible Tour Operators

Above the Clouds Trekking	800-233-4499
Actif International (British Columbia)	800-822-8438
Amazonia Expeditions	800-262-9669
Capirona (Ecuador)	011-593-6-886-614
Center for Global Education (Minneapolis, MN)	612-330-1159
Center for Socially Responsible Travel	415-258-6594
Costa Rica Expeditions (Costa Rica)	011-506-222-0333
Earth River Expeditions	800-643-2784
Earthwatch (Watertown, MA)	617-926-8200
International Expeditions	800-633-4734
Inuit Adventures (Arctic Quebec)	800-465-9474
Mountain Travel/Sobek (El Cerrito, CA)	800-527-8100
Overseas Adventure Travel (Cambridge, MA)	800-221-0814
Plowshares Institute	203-651-4304
Sierra Club	415-923-5630
Travel Links	800-648-2667
Wildlands Adventures	800-345-4453

> **Code of Ethics for Nature and Culture Travelers**
>
> 1. Aspire to invisibility (observe but do not disturb natural systems);
> 2. Vanish without a trace (minimize your impact on the environment);
> 3. Seize the power of your experience (act directly to accomplish conservation); and
> 4. Reverse missionary zeal (respect local cultures).
>
> (Earth Preservation Fund; 206-365-0686)

EIGHT VERY UNUSUAL TOUR OPPORTUNITIES

Although many tours follow a basic pattern, the creativity of some tour operators has resulted in magnificent exceptions. These exceptions demand a little more of participants, provide contact with local people, and inevitably have a deeper impact on those who choose them.

Political Consciousness/Reality Tours

Dr. Toni Hagen, a long-time trekker in Nepal, expressed the view that mass tourism has even more impact on local cultures than it does on local ecology. Some ecological damage can be reversed, but neither technological advances nor money can restore loss of cultural identity.

With that in mind, several organizations offer tours specifically intended to interact gently with local cultures while enhancing the political consciousness of travelers. *People to People International* (816-531-4701), with chapters in 34 countries, sends American teenagers abroad as student ambassadors. It also has a program that arranges for adults to meet professional peers (scientists, doctors, teachers, and so on) and sit in on speeches and seminars. The idea is to explore common interests through personal contacts.

Friendship Tours (209-576-7775) sends knowledgeable lecturers with its groups and arranges meetings and interviews along the way. *Anniversary Tours* (800-223-1336) shows its guests the nitty-gritty of life in the Confederation of Independent States and Eastern Europe. *Global Awareness through Experience* (GATE; 608-791-0462) attempts to promote change, especially with respect to equality and justice, in countries such as Peru, Nicaragua, and Mexico. Participants meet spokespersons for the poor and attend meetings of reform movements.

Perhaps the most prominent provider of "reality tours" is the *Center for Global Education* (612-330-1159). CGE specializes in trips to the Middle East, Southeast Asia, South Africa, Latin America, and various other parts of the "Two-Thirds World" (which includes two-thirds of the human population, land mass, and resources). Its objective is to expose participants to poverty, injustice, political instability, unequal allocation of resources, and the dynamics of international social change. Participants talk with poor people as well as

> "They shall beat their swords into plowshares, and their spears into pruning hooks; nation shall not lift up sword against nation, neither shall they learn war anymore."
> —Isaiah 2:4

with traditional decision makers. These are intense trips, intended to educate through frequent meetings with everyone from *campesinas* to refugees, clerics to ambassadors. The center calls it "experiential education" and expects you to do some reading before you go. Recent trips have included meetings with refugees returning to El Salvador and Guatemala, acting as election observers in El Salvador, and exploring causes and effects of violence in South Africa.

Plowshares Institute (203-651-4304) offers short-term (e.g., two and a half weeks) "immersion seminars" and cross-cultural experiences to promote greater global understanding on the part of North Americans. Trip members meet religious, business, government, and local leaders in Africa, Asia, Latin America, and Eastern Europe. The institute has held recent seminars in Brazil, Hong Kong, the Czech Republic, Hungary, Germany, and South Africa. They want travelers to listen to as many voices as possible so they can think more deeply about solutions to inequities. Participants must agree to do some reading before the trip and to share their experiences with others after they return. They want trip members to act on what they learn about issues of global peace and justice.

The goals of *Global Exchange* (415-255-7296), a relatively new group with very modest fees, include linking people north and south of the equator who are promoting social justice, democracy, and disarmament. Their trips visit Central America, Cuba, Mexico, Vietnam, Brazil, and southern Africa. Global Exchange is active in efforts such as a literacy project in Honduras, delivering medical supplies to Haiti, and sending books to schools in South Africa. They've published several very good books and will furnish speakers on request.

The *Center for Responsible Tourism* (415-258-6954) is another highly regarded organization whose objectives are similar to those of Global Exchange.

Trips for Women

There is a growing belief that women traveling with other women tend to behave differently from women traveling with men. A friend suggested that when women travel together, each has the opportunity to take responsibility, exercise initiative, compete less, and be herself. To provide these opportunities, some tour operators specialize in trips for women only.

Woodswomen (800-279-0555), founded in 1977, says it is the largest women's travel organization in the world. Its trips include Mount Rainier, Denali Park, Alaska, Minnesota, Nepal, Ecuador, Europe, and Africa. Woodswomen offers bicycle touring, dogsledding, backpacking, mountaineering, canoeing, snorkeling, scuba, rock climbing, horse packing, hiking, safaris, skiing, and more. Typical group size is between five and twelve women. Since one objective is to encourage the spirit of adventure through travel experiences, these are not armchair vacations. Call for a copy of *Woodswomen News.*

Outdoor Vacations for Women over 40 (508-448-3331) specializes in trips for active women over 40. The group visits New Zealand, Guatemala, Belize, and Idaho's Salmon River. *Overseas Adventure Travel* (800-221-0814) offers women's cross-cultural adventures in Bolivia, Tanzania, and Nepal/Tibet (including optional homestays). *Rainbow Adventures* (800-804-8686) organizes almost two dozen exciting international adventure trips for women over 30.

Other women-only tour operators include *Hawk, I Am Your Sister* (505-984-2268), *Women in the Wilderness* (612-227-2284), and *Womanship* (800-342-9295).

Overlanders

Don't mistake an overland adventure trip or expedition for a typical general-purpose tour. The overlander consists of a heavy-duty truck transporting a group of young people who may have little in common other than a bare-bones budget and willingness to absorb hardship in the quest for adventure. These trips travel rough routes, but passengers get to know the rural essence of the countries they traverse. Long days of travel are broken up by camping in some idyllic spots and visits to spectacular attractions.

The typical truck carries 20 to 24 people, usually an amalgam of Aussies, Kiwis, Brits, Yanks, and a few Europeans. The most popular trips traverse South America, Africa, and Asia, using routes such as Bogotá to Patagonia, Tangier to Johannesburg, Cairo to Nairobi, and London to Kathmandu. Hostilities cut some of the traditional routes across Asia from time to time, but there are always plenty of trips taking off from London, or elsewhere in Europe, heading south into Africa. Three to eight months later, the survivors roll into Kenya, Zimbabwe, or South Africa. There are less challenging overland trips in Europe and Australia which use comfortable coaches on trips of four to twelve weeks.

Because these trips cover difficult terrain, people who sign on should be flexible. Some companies even discourage middle-aged travelers unless they're supernaturally young at heart. These aren't trips for people who are disposed to complain or who expect to be pampered. If an overland trip will be one of your first, I recommend signing on for only a limited time (there are plenty of two-week trips). If it suits you, continue with the group. If not, you'll be ready to be on your own.

The overland tour operator furnishes the vehicle, fuel, tents, cooking equipment, and a leader/driver. Some companies throw in a second driver who may also do the shopping and cooking. More often, passengers do both themselves. Lodging may be the back of the truck, tents, or basic local accommodations. The longer trips are priced in the range of $40 to $45 per day (though some are as high as $75), including food and lodging.

Trucks supplied by reputable companies are comfortable, mechanically sound, and staffed by experienced drivers. Nevertheless, I've heard tales about trips on which the truck broke down three days into the Sahara or the axle snapped in one of the monster potholes in central Congo. On occasion, relationships among the passengers make the Middle East look peaceful. On one trip I heard about, the driver and cook disappeared for good during the 14th rainy night in a row. On another, the driver drove off in the truck, sold it, and kept going. Whichever company you choose, get a solid financial guarantee covering cancellations, breakdowns, or other interruptions.

Three heavyweights in the overland business are *Encounter Overland* (EO; 071-370-6845), *Dragoman* (01728-861133), and *Guerba* (0171-938-3939). EO uses trucks with soft tops (the sides roll up, the top rolls back) and tow a gear trailer. Seating faces inward in a row along each side. EO accepts ages 18 to 40. The longest EO trip is 155 days, London to Harare, for about $42 per day, including the kitty that pays for food, campsites, entrance fees, and similar expenses. EO runs dozens of trips of varying lengths in Africa, Asia, and South America.

Dragoman operates in the same areas, plus the Middle East and Central and North America. Its longest trip is 217 days and runs the length of Africa (for about $40 per day, including food). Dragoman uses Mercedes trucks with side windows, a hard top, and forward-facing seats. Dragoman accepts ages 18 to 60.

Guerba concentrates on Africa. Its longest trip covers 27 countries in 231 days and costs $40 per day, including the food kitty. Its Mercedes and Bedford trucks have roll-up sides, a hard roof, and sideways seating. Guerba accepts ages 18 to 65.

In the United States, contact all three companies through the Adventure Center (800-227-8747). This 20-year-old California company, representing overseas tour operators who offer more than 300 trips (safaris, trekking, overlanding, etc.) in 65 countries, deals with individuals as well as travel agents.

Adventure Travel

Adventure travel trips, fairly expensive and often physically demanding, appeal primarily to comparatively affluent people in their late 20s to late 40s. Trips range from "gravity adventures" such as whitewater rafting, bungee jumping, and tandem skydiving, to "soft adventures" that combine the exploration of wilderness with considerable creature comforts. One operator, reflecting the spirit of many, bills itself as a "broker of your dreams."

Adventure travel tour operators, of whom there are now more than 10,000 in the United States alone, offer trips through some areas so remote or undeveloped that arranging a trip on your own would be a logistical nightmare. Some trips involve real danger, but more often guides work hard to convey the feeling of adventure and challenge without placing clients at undue risk.

Most tour operators grade their trips in terms of how physically demanding they are. Since getting in over your head guarantees an unhappy trip, pay attention to these grades. If a trip isn't graded, ask. When considering an adventure trip, get opinions from several people who have taken that specific trip.

From among thousands of adventure travel operators, I'll mention a few that, in my opinion, offer especially high-quality trips. *Mountain Travel/Sobek* (MTS; 800-227-2384) has built a fine reputation for its mountain and river trips (and its brochure is a visual treat). It charges more than most of its competitors, but superior equipment, experience, and services may justify the price. MTS sometimes invites you to join it on an exploratory whitewater expedition (the first descent of a wild river). Of course, you return the compliment by paying a considerable fee. By the time you read this, you may have missed the opportunity to join MTS on its first circumnavigation of Greenland: 25 days on an icebreaker for only $19,900 (I wonder if they thought a flat $20,000 looked like too much?).

A high percentage of organized adventure travel treks take place in Nepal and neighboring Indian states of Kashmir and Ladakh. One of the best and least expensive operators in these areas is *Himalayan Travel* (800-225-2380). However, its trips extend far beyond the Himalayas, including Europe, Latin America, and Africa. *Wilderness Travel*, based in Berkeley, California (800-368-2794), is another highly regarded company, especially for trips in Nepal. It offers over 100 trips on five continents, holding its group size to a maximum of 15.

Above the Clouds Trekking (800-233-4499) was first active in the mountains but has expanded to areas as diverse as Patagonia and Madagascar while maintaining its emphasis on trekking. *Journeys* (800-255-8735) offers more than 300 trips in 35 countries. Several of its trips in eastern Nepal and Burma visit remote Buddhist monasteries and include instruction in meditation. Journeys also sponsors trail clean-up expeditions, monastery restoration, and solar heating projects. *Turtle Tours* (602-488-3688) offers trips from Brazil to Irian Jaya, but its unique expertise is with the cultures of Mali, Niger, and Ethiopia, including up-close experiences with nomadic tribes. *Wildland Adventures* (800-345-4453) established the Earth Preservation Fund, which supports community projects promoting environmental or cultural preservation.

Many other fine companies emphasize a specific geographic or activity niche. For example, *Earth River Expeditions* (800-643-2784) and *Outdoor Adventure River Specialists* (OARS, at 800-346-6277) specialize in highly challenging whitewater river trips and *Marine Expeditions* (800-263-9147) is a leader in trips to Antarctica (see the section on Antarctica later in this chapter).

You can organize many of these trips by yourself, possibly at a lower cost, but doing so requires considerable effort and a high tolerance for ambiguity (since some arrangements can't be made until you're on the ground near where the adventure starts). You can also join local tours. Safaris in Africa are an excellent example. Joining a safari locally is not difficult—and the savings are great. In contrast, whitewater and mountaineering trips are particularly difficult to arrange on your own. In addition to logistic issues, risk goes up greatly in the absence of guides expert in the ways of the river or mountain.

The adventure travel business is generally unregulated, so it's up to you to separate experienced, reliable operators from underfinanced, uninsured companies run out of someone's basement. Ask questions and ask for references. Also take a look at the Adventure Travel Society and Specialty Travel Index Web addresses listed in the Internet section of Chapter 2.

Bicycling

Years ago, most bike trips were pretty hard-core; long days were spent in the saddle and routes demanded serious fitness. More recently, options have expanded considerably. Picture yourself pedaling south on the Carreterra Austral in southern Chile: gravel roads, few motor vehicles, milky-blue glacier-fed streams, snowcapped Andes to the east, deep blue bays to the west, crisp cool air, silence broken only by raptors conversing far overhead. Or pedaling through a landscape of fjords, orchards, alps, and rain forest on New Zealand's South Island. Or surrounded by sculptured rice paddies, Hindu temples, and friendly artisans in Bali. Or visiting cool teak forests and colorful hill tribe villages in northern Thailand. Or pedaling slowly through romantic European countryside.

You needn't spend all your time on the seat of the bike. Many bike trips include short diversions such as whitewater rafting, elephant riding, sailing—you get the picture. Depending on the trip and the outfitter, you may camp on a beach or snuggle up with a down pillow in an elegant country inn.

Backroads (800-462-2848), based in Berkeley, California, is one of the best and largest bicycle tour operators, serving more than 12,000 bicyclists a year. Another sound choice is *Butterfield & Robinson* (800-678-1147 is the U.S. number for this Toronto-based firm). If you prefer a boutique operator and a world of personal attention, try Aspen-based *Adventure Worldwide* (303-925-4371).

Other qualified bicycling trip operators advertise in bicycling magazines. You'll find trips designed for singles, family travel, students, pedalers over age 55, women—and even for those who want to try it tandem.

Work

I haven't set out on the road specifically for a work experience, but thousands of travelers have. An English friend has been traveling for three years, stopping to take jobs once in a while to pay for her trip. She's picked fruit in New Zealand, worked in a restaurant in Hong Kong, and been a nanny in India. She always earns enough to finance her forward progress.

For $10, the Archeological Institute of America (617-353-9361) will send you its *Archeological Fieldwork Opportunities Bulletin,* which lists scores of domestic and overseas digs. Some sites sound exotic, such as Egypt or Sri Lanka, while others are less interesting. Be aware that the location affects your opportunities to meet local people so choose your spot carefully. You may pay something for room and board, but you may also receive a small salary. No experience in archeology is required. Before you sign up, be clear on the nature of the work—and how hot it's likely to be.

Earthwatch (617-926-8200) will, for a fee, volunteer your services to work on a worthwhile project. These projects typically involve hard work, sometimes in challenging surroundings, but require no specialized skills. Trips include helping ornithologists in China survey native birds, analyzing artifacts to learn the role of ceremonial caves in the religion of the Maya, and seeking revelations about Stone Age settlements in Auvergne, France. Go to the Ring of Fire on the Russian Kamchatka Peninsula to find out what triggers massive volcanic eruptions. Visit the Himalayas to study avalanches; dig for woolly mammoth, camel, and giant armadillo fossils in Mexico to learn about migrations between continents; collect rare plants on Mount Cameroon to make the case for establishing a forest reserve. Not long ago, I met Earthwatch volunteers measuring water quality on the island of Roatán off the coast of Honduras. Although the volunteers seemed to be minoring in scuba diving, their valuable work may lead to a reduction in waterborne diseases among the island's population.

The *Educational Travel Directory* ($6.95) is a country-by-country listing of publications and organizations offering thousands of jobs, study/travel programs, special interest travel, and exchange living arrangements abroad.

If you're interested in overseas employment, take copies of your résumé on your travels and plant them where they might mature into a future full-time job. You can get a job overseas while at home, but it's far more effective to introduce yourself as you're passing through. If you're interested in working abroad, review the discussion on work permits in Chapter 5.

Homestays

World Learning, previously known as Experiment in International Living, arranges homestays (802-387-4210). Let them know the dates and country you prefer in Europe, Asia, Latin America, or the South Pacific. The opportunity to stay in a family home, long available to students during the summer, is now available to adults throughout the year. During a homestay of one to four weeks, you gain a depth of understanding quite different from that available to a traveler staying in commercial lodgings or hopping from place to place. There's a fee to the organization (averaging less than $500 for a two-week stay), but little or nothing to the family with whom you stay. They offer their hospitality for the same reasons you would.

Soviet-American Homestays (319-626-2125) arranges homestays in about a dozen Russian cities. The cost, usually for a separate room, is about 20 percent less than for a hotel-based tour. Host families speak English and are eager to learn about Western life. Since escaping the usual tourist routes is a greater achievement in Russia than in most other countries, homestays make a lot of sense.

Servas (212-267-0252) can put you in touch with host families in 80 countries for free homestays of two to fourteen days. In turn, you have an opportunity to act as a host for international travelers under the same program.

The *Friendship Force* (404-522-9490), cofounded by Jimmy and Rosalynn Carter, sends groups of 20 to 80 people to various countries to spend a week with host families (more than 100,000 people have gone to 45 countries since 1977). A second week is spent traveling in-country. The emphasis is on personal contact or, as they put it, "faces, not places."

Other organizations helpful in arranging homestays include *World Learning* (different from the one mentioned above; 802-257-7751), with more than 250 programs in 60 countries, and the *Citizens Exchange Council* (212-643-1985) and *Home Host International* (612-871-0596), both of which specialize in Eastern Europe and Russia.

American-International Homestays (800-876-2048) arranges rooms with families. On a bed and breakfast basis, the price is $49 per day; for bed, meals, and a guide it's $99 per day. It operates in the United Kingdom, Western and Eastern Europe, the Confederation of Independent States, China, and Australasia.

Antarctic Cruises

Since Antarctica is much larger than the United States, even when considerably reduced in size during summer, there is no way to experience all facets of the continent in the course of a one- or two-week trip. The common experience is a cruise during the Antarctic summer, December through March, concentrating on the South Shetland Islands and the Antarctic Peninsula. In these areas, temperatures are tolerable, wildlife abundant, and coastlines accessible. What such cruises miss are the jagged Trans-Antarctic Mountains, vast stretches of ice and snow, the driest deserts on earth, and the frigid interior where temperatures drop to minus 80 degrees Fahrenheit and the wind can howl at more than 150 knots.

Gentoo penguins. Antarctica.

Still, a trip along the coast is incredibly rewarding. Rumpled glaciers squeeze forward imperceptibly, tumbling massive blocks of ice into the ocean with a sound like sonic booms. Crabeater and Weddell seals cruise as first-class passengers on wind-sculpted icebergs whose great bulk glows iridescent blue below the waterline. You stand in the midst of more than 100,000 squawking Adelie penguins, nervously eyeing the 8,000-pound elephant seal basking a dozen meters away in the cold sunlight.

The word "cruise" evokes images along a spectrum from Loveboat to the Queen Elizabeth II. While some of the ships sailing the Southern Ocean resemble those images, there are now alternatives. *Abercrombie & Kent, Explorer Shipping Corporation, International Expeditions, Marine Expeditions, Mountain Travel/Sobek, Quark Expeditions, Society Expeditions, Zegrahm Expeditions*, and several other reputable firms sponsor Antarctica itineraries. These trips vary considerably in terms of ship size, itinerary and, not least, cost. Prices of $6,000 to $15,000 are not uncommon.

In my opinion, the best choices are presently offered by *Marine Expeditions*, a subsidiary of Blyth & Company, based in Toronto. Trips start at about $3,000, *including* airfare from several U.S. gateway cities. It charters excellent ships commissioned by the Russians in the late 1980s as polar research ships. These ships, now available for passenger transport because research funds have dried up, carry between 38 and 78 passengers. They're comfortable, tough enough to power through light pack ice and small bergs, small enough to enter constricted harbors, and staffed with expert naturalists. Marine Expeditions uses versatile Zodiac rafts to visit one or two different on-shore sites every day. You learn about the evolution of Antarctica and its impact on the planet's weather and food chain, as well as how to identify species of whales, seals, penguins, and seabirds as if they were familiar neighbors. The company has also received a major eco-tourism award.

For more information on cruises, see Chapter 16.

PART TWO

Getting
Ready
("Get Set . . .")

5

Going into Action

A journey of a thousand miles must
begin with a single step.
— Lao-tzu
The Way of Lao-tzu

It's time to make it happen! You've decided where you're going, the amount of time you'll take, how much money you'll probably spend, and what time of year you'll leave. Now you're ready to deal with passports, visas, plane tickets, reservations, and other nuts and bolts of travel. At this point more than a few prospective travelers skid to a halt. A process that will soon be familiar and routine can seem like an impenetrable labyrinth the first time around. This chapter will help you solve the puzzle forever.

DOCUMENTS YOU WILL NEED

Passport

What It Is

To become a citizen of the world, you need a passport. Without it, you're tethered to home base. Once you have it, it's like a chocolate bar full of crunchy almonds in your pocket—awfully hard to resist.

A passport is a form of identification issued by a government permitting the holder to enter and leave his or her *own* country. However, if you want to enter almost any foreign country, its government will also require that you carry a valid passport issued by your country. For U.S. citizens, the main exceptions are Mexico, Canada, and many countries in the Caribbean. To be a traveler, you need a passport.

The U.S. passport has undergone significant changes in recent years. There's now special ink and a security thread to reduce forgeries. A new machine-readable code enables immigration officers to determine quickly whether you are an international diamond thief in disguise.

How to Get It

In the United States, the Department of State issues passports through its Passport Agency. To obtain your first passport, if you are age 13 or older, you must apply in person at a Passport Agency office, a state or federal court, or at a post office authorized to accept passport applications.

Passport Agency Offices

Boston	617-565-6990	Chicago	312-353-7155
Honolulu	808-541-1918	Houston	713-653-3153
Los Angeles	310-575-7075	Miami	305-536-4681
New Orleans	504-589-6161	New York	212-399-7710
Philadelphia	215-597-7480	San Francisco	415-744-4010
Seattle	206-220-7788	Stamford	203-325-3538
Washington, DC	202-647-0518		

To obtain your passport:

1. Fill in a Passport Application (Form DSP-11), which you get from a Passport Agency office, post office, or travel agent. This and other passport forms and information are also available at http://travel.state.gov on the Internet.

2. Show proof of U.S. citizenship in the form of a certified copy of your birth certificate, naturalization certificate, or proof that you were a U.S. citizen born abroad. If you can't locate the necessary documents, the Passport Agency will suggest substitutes.

3. Provide proof of identity (such as a driver's license or a government or military ID card).

4. Submit two identical two-by-two-inch photographs (front view, no hat or sunglasses, with a plain light background). Vending machine photos will not be accepted. Since passport photos convey an impression of your status to a foreign official whose cooperation you may need, it's worth dressing nicely.

5. Pay the correct fee (credit cards not accepted). A ten-year passport for persons age 18 and older costs $65; a five-year passport for those under 18 costs $40.

Make certain your paperwork is filled out correctly and all information requested is provided. Otherwise your application will be returned, and you will have to resubmit the forms.

If you were issued a passport within the past 12 years and were older than 18 at that time, you may renew using an Application for Passport by Mail (Form DSP-82), which you obtain from a Passport Agency office, a state or federal court, or any post office. Simply send the application, your old passport, two photos, and the fee ($55 if 18 years or over, $40 if under 18) to the address on the form. Normal time for issuing a passport by mail used to be about two weeks but can now be five weeks or more. If you become worried, call (603) 334-0500 to check on the status of your application. Payment of an extra $30 gets your application processed within three days, but you may have to demonstrate necessity, rather than procrastination, as the reason. If you appear in person, have a ticket showing departure within 48 hours, and have good travel karma, you can even get same-day service. If you have time, send your application in as much as three months prior to your planned departure date. Getting your passport is a big deal; why risk disappointment?

A travel agent can handle the passport application process for you or you can hire a professional service to do it. If you use a service (see the Visa Services section below), the charge would be $35 or more for seven-day service and as much as $100 for same-day service. Plan ahead and spend the extra money on an elephant ride in Thailand instead. If you think those fees are steep, a Russian who uses a service to help obtain a passport to leave his country would pay $280 for two-week delivery and $1,000 for same-day issuance.

Passport pages provide the spaces into which visas are entered, so request a passport with the greatest number of pages allowed (currently 48). It costs no more and you will, hopefully, need every page. When those are filled up, use a Passport Amendment/Validation Application (Form DSP-19) to ask for an accordion page or refill section. Why do you need so many pages? First, a visa for a single country may take up a full page. Second, when you enter most countries, your passport will be vigorously hand-stamped, perhaps more than once. You may collect additional stamp imprints as you travel within a country and the stamp will strike again on your way out. To make it worse, some officials disdain putting their country's stamp anywhere except on a blank page.

Request a passport with the greatest number of pages allowed.

Use Form DSP-19 to have a passport changed to incorporate a legal name change, enclosing a copy of the document that caused the change (adoption, marriage, etc.).

> **Store It in Your Mind**
>
> Memorize your passport number, the city it was issued in, and the dates of issue and expiration. Otherwise, you have to pull out your money belt every time there's an immigration or hotel registration form to fill in.

Expiration

Don't let yourself be surprised by a sharp-eyed immigration officer who discovers that your passport has just expired. If you'll be on the road when your passport expires, renew before you leave. Since some countries require that a passport have at least six months of life remaining at the time of entry, don't take a chance. I've heard of an occasional immigration officer raising this objection, then happily waiving it upon receipt of a small gratuity. If you arrive home with an expired passport, you're subject to a $100 fee.

By the way, the ten or fifteen minutes it often takes to reach the U.S. immigrations officer to show your passport when returning may be greatly reduced in the near future. The Immigration and Naturalization Service Passenger Accelerated Service System (all that just to produce the acronym INSPASS) being tested at JFK and Newark airports should reduce the wait to less than a minute. After enrolling in the program, you insert a plastic card into a machine, then let the machine read your fingerprints. It grinds out a receipt and you're on your way to the customs counter.

For information about passports, order *Your Trip Abroad* by sending $1 to the Superintendent of Documents, U.S. Government Printing Office, Washington, DC 20402 (or call 202-783-3238); alternatively, call the Passport Agency (202-647-0518). You may also call the National Passport Information Center (900-225-5674). This is a 900 number, so charges do apply. The charge for talking to a live operator is three times the charge for automated service (what is this world coming to?).

Visas

What They Are

None of us has an internationally recognized "right" to travel. Thus, a visa is a document issued by a foreign government permitting the holder to enter its country and stay for a limited period of time. A visa usually takes the form of a rubber stamp impression inked on a page of a passport, but may also be a postal-type stamp or a sheet of paper stapled or glued into the passport.

Who Needs Them

At the moment, about 90 countries require nationals of at least some other countries to obtain a visa. It's common for a country to require nationals of some countries to obtain a visa while permitting nationals from other countries to enter without one. That decision is often made on the basis of economics or politics. Citizens from wealthy countries are less likely to be required to obtain visas than are citizens of poor countries.

Generally speaking, Canada, Mexico, Caribbean, and western European countries do not require U.S. citizens to have a visa. About a dozen European countries have eliminated border visa and passport checks altogether. Now, travelers breeze across their borders without slowing down. However, many people are seeking less-expensive destinations and these countries are more likely to require visas. Therefore, every traveler should master the process of obtaining a visa.

It would be a disservice to provide a list of countries that require visas because requirements change frequently and out-of-date information could create serious inconvenience. To find out whether a particular country requires a visa and, if so, what its conditions are

- Order *Foreign Entry Requirements of Foreign Governments* from the Consumer Information Center (719-948-3334; or P.O. Box 100, Pueblo, CO 81009).
- Call the State Department Citizens' Emergency Center (202-647-5225).
- Call the appropriate embassy in Washington, DC.

Ask at the same time whether any special permits are required for internal travel. If you contemplate an extended stay, see if an HIV test is required (it is in more than 40 countries). Foreign embassies and consulates in the United States are listed on the Internet (http://dosfan.lib.uic.edu/dosfan.html). The Automobile Association of America (AAA) is another reliable source of information about visa requirements.

If you ask your travel agent which countries on your itinerary require visas, be sure the answer is based on fact, not assumption. Of course, travelers make assumptions too. An experienced travel agent told me that any time a client of hers bought an airline ticket to a country that required a visa, she would write on the ticket: "Don't forget your visa." That worked until the client who, upon arriving in Taiwan, reached in his wallet and produced— what else?—his Visa credit card.

If you ask other travelers about visa requirements, it's better not to rely 100 percent on their answers. The information may be out of date or involve special circumstances of which you are unaware. You don't want to be standing at the border when you hear the bad news.

At the Border

Even having a visa in hand does not always guarantee entry into a country. Some countries require that you have (a) sufficient funds to pay for your stay and (b) an outbound ticket in hand. These seemingly inhospitable requirements usually are reactions to the impoverished students and joyful hippies who streamed around the world in the 1960s. Only once has a border official asked me for evidence of sufficient funds or an onward ticket. A couple of years ago, guards at a border crossing into Zimbabwe required all foreigners to produce onward tickets. Happening to possess a Zimbabwe-to-Kenya ticket purchased in Nairobi, I lucked out. Half a dozen other travelers were left behind as our bus pulled away from the remote guard station.

Border guard.
Portugal.

Ask your travel agent to check her computer to see whether you will be running into an onward ticket requirement. If so, purchase a fully refundable plane ticket for a short leg out of the country. If you decide not to use it, cash it in later. Alternatively, a few travelers carry a Miscellaneous Change Order (MCO). An MCO is *not* a ticket. It's more like a cashier's check, showing that you have a guaranteed credit in a specified amount which can be used to pay for a plane ticket. An MCO is easily converted back into cash when you return. If you want an MCO, ask your travel agent or get it directly from an airline.

Although immigration officials have discretionary authority to bar a traveler from entry, that happens only rarely. When it does, it's almost always when arriving via an overland border crossing rather than at an airport. For that reason, think of a border crossing as a one-act play. Dress for the part by wearing your most normal clothes. Be as well-groomed as circumstances permit. Approach with a smile, say something courteous, and be patient. On the other hand, anyone with an urge to spend a few hours broiling in the sun outside a crumbling concrete guard shack on the Rwanda-Congo border should challenge the guard's authority, throw in some vulgar language, and assert his importance back home.

Should there be a problem, stay calm and follow any reasonable instruction, such as opening your luggage. If the situation is prolonged or threatens to get out of hand, ask for the guard's superior officer.

At a checkpoint entrance to West Sikkim, a young, smartly uniformed guard sitting at a scarred table pointed out that the visa in my passport permitted travel to Gangtok, the capital of Sikkim, but said nothing about traveling into *West* Sikkim. He was quite right. The Indian consulate official in Washington, DC, had erred and I had overlooked it. The guard had me and we both knew it. After flipping through my passport for a full three minutes, he tossed it aside on his desk without comment and dismissed me with a lackadaisical backhand flip of his wrist. I stayed within sight, but didn't press him. After about twenty minutes, I approached his table again. This time, I mentioned that I was actually *leaving* Sikkim by a circuitous route which only at the moment happened to be going away from the border. Satisfied that he had demonstrated his authority, he stamped my passport vehemently and held it out to me without a glance. We'd played the game and were satisfied.

Different Types of Visas

Visas come in several versions: transit, business, student, resident, and tourist. The three most important to travelers are the transit, business, and tourist. A *transit visa* permits only a short-term visit. Its purpose is to give you time to dash into a principal city, or visit a particular sight, then continue your journey. When you present a transit visa, an immigration official may want to see your onward ticket and enough money to cover your visit. The purpose of a *business visa* speaks for itself. Some countries require that you produce an invitation from a local person or a government ministry official, or be coming for a business purpose, as a prerequisite for issuing a business visa. The *tourist visa* is what most travelers need.

The visa indicates what type it is, its length or dates of validity, and how many times you are permitted to enter the country. Normally, a visa permits a single entry. If you foresee entering, leaving, and returning to the same country, you'll need a multiple-entry visa. If you don't have a multiple-entry visa, you may be able to purchase a new visa at the border. If not, you'll have to backtrack to a major city in another country. The fee for multiple-entry is higher than for single-entry, but less than you would pay if you bought a new visa for repeated entries.

Visas are valid only for a specified length of time, usually between 30 and 90 days, but they can range from a week to a year. For some visas, the period starts on the date you request. However, if the period of validity starts on the date the visa *is issued*, and you won't get to the country for a while, the time limit could pose a problem.

Applying for a Visa

When answering questions on a visa application, keep in mind that the government basically wants some idea why you're entering its country and where you want to go. I recommend against listing your occupation as writer or reporter, or stating affiliation with any military, government, or international organization, or anything else that could be interpreted as meaning you would be inspecting their country. Any remotely prestigious occupation is enough to establish credibility; "teacher" seems to make officials happy.

If forms ask for a local address, officials are satisfied with the name of any moderately upscale hotel (check you guidebook). Even "hotel" is usually sufficient. When it inquires about "religion," the question may be loaded in some countries. You have a choice to make. If answering "none" feels okay, that's probably safest. You could finesse the issue by putting "nondenominational" or leaving it blank. If the question feels like a challenge and you don't want to avoid it, respond as you feel you should. If a form asks about your itinerary, list everywhere you might possibly go. Under "length of stay," ask for the maximum the visa allows. Give yourself the widest latitude in case the official limits you to what you asked for. Have a passport photo handy just in case the form requires it

Don't underestimate how long it may take to obtain visas. While some are issued automatically, obtaining others can be time-consuming. You might get it in a few days or it might take several weeks. If a country is reluctant to admit visitors or is especially bureaucratic, an applicant can be in for a challenging experience. It may reduce your frustration if you realize that the United States is notorious for making it difficult for foreigners to obtain visas to visit. Here's the kicker: when you've sent your passport to one embassy with your visa application, you can't apply for visas from other countries.

If you need a fast turnaround, expect to pay more; for example, if you give a Russian consulate 20 working days to issue a visa, the fee may be $40. However, for ten-day turnaround, it might cost $50. If you want a business visa on a same-day basis, expect to cough up more than $100. Plan ahead and SAVE MONEY.

If you apply in person, a clerk will tell you when to return for the visa. If you apply by mail, the issue date is less certain. Although travel agents and tour operators are usually reliable in obtaining visas, it's your responsibility to follow up relentlessly until the visas are in hand.

In the great majority of cases, it's much easier to obtain a visa *before* leaving home than while on the road. You have plenty of time and don't have to deal with a foreign language. In fact, unless you're certain of the practice, it's risky to arrive at a border without a visa hoping that some official will issue a point-of-entry visa on the spot. It's possible to obtain most visas abroad, but you may have to detour to a city where the visa can be issued—and the office may be closed when you get there. In any case, your forward motion will stop while you wait (and wait and wait) for the visa to be issued. You may even discover that you just can't get the visa you want, or you can get it only by complying with some restriction, such as joining a tour group. If there is a restriction, discover it at home when you have plenty of time to dance the bureaucratic break dance, rather than on the road in the turmoil of a crowded visa office.

It's usually easier to obtain a visa at home than on the road.

By the way, when you give up your passport abroad when applying for a visa or any other reason, always ask for a receipt.

If you decide to get your visas as you travel, find out from the appropriate consulates exactly where to get their visas abroad. Some guidebooks provide this information. Bring along extra photos in case the application requires one.

Fees

Fees for visas vary greatly. Prior to 1994, few countries charged U.S. citizens more than $20 for a single-entry tourist visa. Then in 1994, the United States initiated a $20 surcharge on machine-readable visas issued to foreign travelers wishing to visit the U.S. That provoked reciprocal increases by many other countries. While most fees currently range from $20 to $50, they may soon emulate new car prices. It's important to call ahead to ensure you send the correct fee. If you send the wrong fee, your application may be returned unprocessed.

Visa Services

Another approach in obtaining a visa is to employ a professional service. They know current requirements and ease your mind, but you pay generously for their assistance. They charge from $30 to $100 per visa, plus postage and the cost of the visa itself. These services fill in the forms and hand-carry them, with your photos, International Health Certificate (if required), and passport, from embassy to embassy. Knowing embassy personnel helps them speed up the process.

Tell the service the date you want each visa to become effective. As I mentioned earlier, a visa has a time boundary so don't let it become effective so far in advance of your arrival that you have to cut your visit short. Give the service a date by which you want the visas returned to you. Follow up periodically to monitor their progress. When they return your passport and visas, check to ensure you received all the visas you requested. Don't discover their mistake in a Sierra Leone airport. Yes, it happens.

While many services are listed in the Yellow Pages under "Passport and Visa Services," here are a few to consider:

- Express Visa Service, Washington, DC (202-337-2442)
- Global Visa Service, New York City (212-682-3895)
- Intercontinental Visa Service, Los Angeles (213-625-7175)
- Visa Advisors, Washington, DC (202-797-7976)
- Visa Center, New York (212-986-0924)
- Visa Expediters, Washington, DC (202-387-4789)
- Visa International, Los Angeles (213-850-1192)
- Zierer Visa Service, Washington, DC (800-843-9151)

Expiration

Don't overstay the expiration date of a visa. Pay a fee and get an extension, or, if you must, leave the country and return with a new visa. If you overstay, you become an illegal alien, subject to fine, deportation, and arrest. You might be lucky enough to blow by the border official on the way out without being noticed. However, if they catch you there will probably be a fine; in Thailand it's $100 a day.

Special Permits

Permits are sometimes needed to go certain places or do certain things. For example, because authorities want to keep track of who is wandering where, many treks on Himalayan trails require a permit. If you don't reappear, they know where to look. Sometimes a permit is required to take photographs. The fee is small for 35mm cameras but is often high for video cameras.

Some permits are a bureaucratic way of enforcing an unofficial policy. For example, posters throughout India welcome tourists to the eastern state of Assam. However, during periods when foreigners aren't welcome in Assam, you won't be permitted to enter without a permit, no matter how many posters you point to. And that permit will not be quickly forthcoming. In three tries I've never been willing to stay in Calcutta long enough to see if a permit would eventually pop out of the system.

Permits also are used to protect natural resources. Showing admirable restraint in light of its need for hard currency, the Rwandan government permitted only 24 people a day, split into four groups, to climb the mountainsides to see gorilla families in the wild. Travelers who reached Rwanda without this permit in hand were likely to find all permits sold. Some had to wait a day, others a week or more, depending on how many no-shows there were and how long the line of hopefuls.

To sustain Milford Track's reputation as "the finest walk in the world," New Zealand officials regulate the number of people on trails and in huts. The permit is expensive and months may pass before it's issued. Arrive without a permit and you might be lucky—but you're more likely to be disappointed.

Another type of permit is the requirement in a few countries that you register with the police within 24 hours of arrival. This requirement is noted in guidebooks and is usually brought to your attention by a point-of-entry official. Your hotel clerk will probably take care of it for you. That service should be a freebie, but an appropriate tip is a good investment. To avoid an unpleasant surprise, in the form of a fine, when you're ready to leave the country, follow up to ensure that the registration occurred.

> Some countries require you to register with police on arrival.

Fortunately, permits are seldom required. Many can only be obtained on the spot. Those that can be acquired at home should be.

Work Permits

If you're thinking of getting a job abroad, find out before you leave what is required to get a work permit. It's difficult to get a permit abroad, so it would be unwise to depend on earning money you'll need as you travel. Many countries, especially those in Europe, are flooded by refugees seeking work. Regions with depressed economies often exclude outside labor to protect jobs for their own citizens. Employers can be heavily penalized for hiring people who lack official work permits. If you want a job that would require an extended visa or formal working arrangements, expect obstacles.

Your best chance of getting a work permit is to possess a specialized skill in short supply and high demand in the country where you want to work. In addition, before you arrive you may have to find an employer who will give you a written offer of employment. Not many travelers can pull that off in advance.

How to Find a Job

Once in a country on a tourist visa, you may find temporary jobs "off the books." Although the most frequent employers of passing travelers are restaurants and farmers, many Western travelers have at least two other skills they can market in any economy. Proficiency with English vocabulary and grammar, and knowledge about business at home, are potentially valuable skills to someone wanting to export goods to your home market.

Be alert for opportunities for self-help. English-language menus, brochures, store-window signs, and other forms of advertising often contain incorrect grammar or spelling. Travelers regularly trade meals in return for correcting a restaurant's menu.

Check out trade shows as you travel. Talk with potential employers and other local people. Try to connect with the expatriate community, if there is one. As with so many things in life, success depends on taking the initiative.

Under its Work Abroad program, the *Council on International Education Exchange* (CIEE, Work Abroad, 205 42nd Street, New York, NY 10017; 212-661-1450) negotiated reciprocal agreements with New Zealand, Costa Rica, Germany, France, Ireland, England, Jamaica, and Canada, allowing U.S. students to work in those countries on a temporary basis. To be eligible, you must (a) be at least 18 years old, (b) be taking at least eight hours of classes or begin the program within six months after you were last enrolled, and (c) apply *before* leaving the United States. To work in Germany, France, or Costa Rica, you must also be fairly fluent in the national language. In five of the countries above, the work must take place within a specified four- to seven-month period, usually including summer. For a reasonable fee, CIEE will obtain your work authorization and give you a list of potential employers, general tips on employment, and information on living in the country. An on-site CIEE representative will help with job-hunting and finding lodging. If you're willing to take a subsistence-level job to support yourself and cover costs of some local travel, you should have no problem. If you want a job related to a special interest of yours, contact potential employers before leaving home.

CIEE also sponsors work camps from late June to early September in Europe, North Africa, and a few other places. You work on a local project in return for free room and board. In addition to the merits of the project, you meet people from other countries, learn some foreign language, and experience another culture. Typical projects include restoration of historical sites, well-digging, road building, housing rehabilitation, archeological digs, historic preservation, forestry, and working with children, elderly persons, and people with disabilities. For most countries you must be over 18 but need not be a student.

Many books provide guidance concerning overseas jobs. See, for example, *Teaching English Abroad* and *Work Your Way Around the World* by Susan Griffiths; *Directory to Overseas Employment* from Transitions Abroad (800-562-1973); *The Directory of Jobs and Careers Abroad* by Alex Lepinski; *The Almanac of International Jobs and Careers* by Ronald and Caryl Krannich; and *Jobs for People Who Love to Travel*, Impact Publications (703-361-7300). English-language newspapers published abroad, such as the *International Herald Tribune* and the *South China Post* in Hong Kong, list job opportunities. If you meet the requirements listed for a job, the employer will arrange a work permit.

Be skeptical of ads in U.S. newspapers promising high-paying jobs abroad. They may be legitimate—or may be the first move in a scam intended to extract money from you. If you line up a job through correspondence, satisfy yourself, perhaps through a reconnaissance trip, that you know enough about the foreign country to be sure it's worth making the commitment.

MORE BEFORE YOU GO

Rail Passes

A rail pass may SAVE MONEY, make travel easier, increase your flexibility, and enable you to lock in a major travel cost for budgeting purposes. Or it may be a waste of money. We'll discuss how to figure out if a pass would be a good purchase for your next trip.

Although rail passes are available for use in Canada, Japan, and Australia, among other places, you are most likely to consider them for use in Europe since the rail network there is comprehensive, fast, and comfortable, and the variety of passes is so great.

Think about rail passes before you go. Since rail passes are often intended to be an inducement for tourists, some must be purchased outside the country where they'll be used. For example, a Eurailpass is supposed to be purchased outside Europe—and that's the safest thing to do. However, Eurailpasses are also sold at some major European railway stations at about 20 percent more than the U.S. price. The *Eurail Traveller's Guide* lists a limited number of places where you may be able to purchase a pass in Europe and Euraid Tourist Information offices may also be able to help. Most other types of rail passes can be bought in Europe.

For much more information on determining whether buying a rail pass is a good way to SAVE MONEY for your trip, see Chapter 6.

Airline Tickets

Since airfare is such a major part of travel costs, it's one of the best opportunities to use your knowledge to SAVE MONEY. When flying domestically, most people call a travel agent and buy tickets for their whole itinerary. For international travel, the matter is not so simple since booking everything at home may cost you the opportunity of buying tickets abroad at lower prices. It may also commit you to being at certain airports on certain dates, curtailing flexibility and freedom. Whether to pack that albatross in your luggage deserves serious thought.

There are several situations in which you *should* buy your airline tickets before leaving home:

1. When you're going to an area where flights are infrequent, which means they're often fully booked. One approach is to buy fully refundable tickets in the United States for the entire itinerary, treating the extra cost of refundability as an insurance premium. If you can buy a segment cheaper as you travel, buy it and get a refund on that segment when you get home. If you can't buy a significantly cheaper ticket, you won't be left standing in the airport.
2. When an air pass must be bought before arriving in the country in which you'll use it.
3. When you want to fly as a courier.
4. When you'll be traveling to or from a popular resort area in high season.

For much more information on buying airline tickets, see How to Choose and Work with a Travel Agent (Chapter 2) and SAVING MONEY on Air Fares (Chapter 6).

Travel and Health Insurance

Let's face it, insurance is not a fun topic. Nevertheless, I suggest spending a little time thinking about it because a few people do experience losses while traveling. A camera disappears, there's a bill for medical services in a foreign hospital, or it becomes necessary to cancel a trip after sending in a large deposit. The odds are highly in your favor that none of this will happen, and in later chapters we'll discuss how to make the odds even better. Still, a prudent traveler should at least understand insurance options.

Like other forms of insurance, terms of travel insurance are understood by practically no one, at least not until after a loss. Let's improve our understanding by dividing travel insurance into three types of coverage: personal property, trip interruption or cancellation, and medical.

Personal Property

You may already have some personal property coverage for losses overseas; check your homeowners, renters, or automobile insurance and the fine print in your credit card agreements. Many insurance companies offer a low-cost rider to an existing policy.

If you're not covered, should you buy insurance? The answer depends on how insurance-conscious you are at home, how inherently risky your trip will be, what risks would be covered, and the premium. If you insure everything to the hilt at home, you may be disposed to buy insurance for peace of mind. If you're undecided, consider how much you have at stake and what risks you would be insuring against.

Ask if your policy covers losses overseas.

To provide perspective, the insurance industry reports that half of all claims relate to loss of baggage and personal effects, and, as you'll see in Chapter 13, airlines accept only limited liability for luggage they lose. If you do have coverage, remember that it has a deductible. On balance, insurance that covers lost baggage alone seems disproportionately expensive to me, especially considering the exclusions.

Terms of insurance policies vary widely. Ask *exactly* what would be covered. Lost luggage? Lost cash? What about the loss of specific items, including a camera, jewelry, or other valuables? Would you need a police report to make a claim? What about costs incurred by delays? Would you be covered for harm you cause to others and their possessions, perhaps through use of a motor vehicle? What exclusions are there (if, for example, you travel through certain territories)?

The scope of coverage matters. For example, a standard policy covers luggage only if you can prove it was stolen, while an "all risks" policy covers you whatever the cause of loss. Since no insurance policy will reimburse you for loss of your journal, exposed film, or passport, the best coverage is to stay alert.

Trip Interruption or Cancellation

What are the odds you'll have a claim for trip cancellation or interruption? The National Tour Association says that only 1 in 100,000 individuals who book tours might be affected by failure of the tour company. On the other hand, the U.S. Tour Operators Association estimates those odds are as high as 1 in 20. Figure that out. Travel Guard International, an insurer, reports that approximately 3 percent of people who buy trip cancellation insurance actually cancel a trip.

For most travelers who cancel a trip just before departure, loss might consist of hotel reservation deposits or a nonrefundable airline ticket. The bigger loser would be someone who had made a nonrefundable payment for a cruise or tour. Further, if you have to change your flight schedule midtrip, the extra cost could be substantial. Only you know how likely it is that health or business obligations might interfere with your trip and whether the odds suggest buying cancellation/interruption insurance.

Some policies bury exclusions as if they were land mines, so read the fine print. To do that, you need a copy of the complete policy, not a summary prepared by the marketing department. Take it for granted that an insurer will interpret the policy strictly against you.

Here's what you want to know. If a travel agent can't answer your questions satisfactorily, call the insurance company yourself.

— When would coverage begin and end? Coverage of some policies (especially for cruises) ends 72 hours before the trip starts. If you were forced to cancel after that, you'd be out of luck.

— Under what conditions would the policy reimburse you for penalties and deposits if you canceled after your deposit with the tour operator became nonrefundable? Would a personal or business conflict, or change of heart, qualify? What about missing the trip for work or weather-related reasons? A policy that would reimburse you in case of voluntary cancellation could be extremely expensive.

— Would you be covered if illness, injury, or death (yours or your companion's), or some other major problem at home, caused cancellation or interruption of your trip? Would proof of medical reasons be required? Would you be covered for extra trip costs incurred as a result of disaster striking a close family member?

— Would the policy cover you if a preexisting medical condition forced you to cancel the trip? A typical definition of such a condition is "any ailment for which a person was treated by a doctor, or for which he took prescribed medication, during a specific time period." Some policies will not reimburse you if the preexisting condition that caused the loss existed between 30 and 180 days before you purchased the policy. If you have a preexisting condition, look for a policy that will cover you if that condition has been controlled by medication. Application of the preexisting exclusion has prompted so many complaints that companies are abandoning it (this is discussed below under "Medical").

- Would you be covered if unexpected problems along your route, such as a hurricane, terrorism, or a communicable disease, interfered with the trip?

- Are there other exclusions (e.g., drugs, hazardous activities, war)?

- Would you be required to have a doctor certify your illness before you canceled? After you cancelled?

- Could you extend the policy if you extend your trip?

- What sort of failure by the tour/cruise operator would result in payment to you? Exactly which of your expenses would be covered if the tour operator canceled? You want protection against failure to perform, not merely bankruptcy. By the way, you may get free protection against operator failure simply by paying with a credit card. If the operator fails, the charge can be removed from your account.

If an interruption is caused by the airline (say there's a mechanical problem or a pilot fails to show up sober, that sort of thing), the airline is not required to make any special effort on your behalf but it will usually do its best to speed you on your way—or feed and house you if necessary. If, however, the delay is caused by bad weather or heavy air traffic, airlines uniformly disclaim responsibility.

Some trip cancellation/interruption insurance bundles coverage for accidents, lost or stolen baggage, some medical problems, and evacuation costs. In other policies, these various coverages are treated separately.

Trip cancellation/interruption insurance is not inexpensive. Premiums range from $5.50 to $8 for every $100 of coverage you want. Balance the premium for temporary coverage against what you have at stake in up-front money (e.g., a deposit on a tour, a cancellation fee charged by the tour operator if you drop out, or nonrefundable tickets). Consider health and other factors that might intervene.

I've read letters to travel columnists praising trip cancellation/interruption insurance, but I've also read angry complaints that one policy or another didn't pay off. Some tour operators and travel agents recommend cancellation insurance because it keeps clients off their backs in case of a problem.

You can SAVE MONEY if you use a travel agency that has purchased ASTA's Travel Reimbursement Protection Insurance. In that case, coverage may cost you nothing. Ask your agent or call (800) 285-1779.

There is also *package insurance* available that covers everything for a fee of about 7 percent of your *prepaid* expenses. If there are no tour costs involved, that means air fare, rail or air passes, and not much else. For tours, the premium cost of package insurance may be reasonable.

Tour operators assert that insurance supplied by them is somewhat less expensive and has more generous terms than individually purchased policies. Compare prices.

Medical

Whether overseas health insurance coverage is a good investment is such a personal decision that no general recommendation is possible. The State Department reports that of the 16 million adult U.S. citizens who flew overseas in a recent year, 23,000 were hospitalized abroad. That's 1½ out of each 1,000 travelers. If we assume that a 45-year-old male with no specific threatening health problems is three times as likely to be hospitalized as the average traveler, he's still only likely to be hospitalized 1 out of every 222 trips.

Existing Coverage. If you already have health insurance, call the carrier to see what your policy covers overseas and what it doesn't. Most Blue Cross and Blue Shield plans cover some emergency care overseas and bills are sent directly to them. Medicare, on the other hand, does not cover anyone overseas.

What Is Covered? Travel medical insurance typically pays for treatment of an illness incurred abroad, including prescription drugs. It may or may not pay for dental care. Virtually no one's insurance covers emergency medical evacuation overseas.

If you consider buying coverage for overseas medical expenses, ask first about premiums, deductibles, and copayments, then about possible exclusions of preexisting conditions, sexually-transmitted diseases, injuries arising from civil war, and problems related to illegal drugs, pregnancy, and self-inflicted injuries. Ask whether travel in particular countries is excluded.

If you have what might be considered a preexisting medical condition, discuss the situation with the insurer. Some won't pay if you had a health problem during a specified time period prior to your trip and that condition was responsible for your later claim. Most companies that retain this exclusion use a relatively lenient 60-day period (although some use 90 days or more and some even exclude conditions controlled by medication). Most policies provide coverage for preexisting conditions if there have been neither symptoms nor treatment within the stated period prior to the trip; that is, for conditions that are stable or controlled.

The good news is that an increasing number of companies have recently begun waiving the preexisting medical condition exclusion. However, they often have a requirement that coverage be purchased within 24 hours of payment of the first deposit on your trip. Therefore, if you want insurance coverage, you should identify an insurance company before you book the trip. Keep documentation of the timing in case you later need to make a claim.

Ask the insurer whether you must call home for precertification for an elective or surgical procedure. You probably will, at least for nonemergencies. Ask whether the insurer requires a second opinion. Naturally, if you claim a loss due to health, you'll have to prove that health was the cause.

Does the policy cover risk sports like scuba diving or skiing? Some policies exclude coverage for injuries that arise from sports such as scuba diving, mountain climbing, and skiing. Some will include them if you pay an additional premium. The Diver's Alert Network (DAN; 800-446-2671) was established to cover divers for the costs of transportation/evacuation and treatment for the bends. DAN will also evacuate anyone, regardless of preexisting conditions. The cost is $25 a year for an individual, $35 for a family.

If you decide to buy travel medical insurance, the amount of coverage should depend on whether your primary medical insurance will be in force. If it will, a policy for enough to cover its deductible should be sufficient. If not, premiums run about $3 to $5 per day for coverage of up to $100,000. For a small additional fee, you can usually buy lost luggage and trip cancellation/interruption riders to medical insurance.

Reimbursement or Direct Payment. Payment by an insurance company comes in two forms. In one case, you are reimbursed for expenses you've already paid, while in the other the company pays the medical care provider directly. This is an important distinction because if you incur medical expenses you are likely to be required to pay them on the spot—which will require cash, a direct-payment insurance policy, or possibly a credit card. Carrying evidence of reimbursement insurance may help delay payment, but don't count on it. If you plan to seek reimbursement for expenses, collect receipts for payments and documentation of diagnosis and treatments (these records will also assist your doctor at home).

Other Health-Related Coverage

Emergency Evacuation. If you'll be taking above-average risks, such as climbing peaks in Torres del Paines, consider emergency evacuation coverage. Although most medical care abroad is fairly inexpensive, evacuation is not. From relatively remote areas of the Pacific, Asia, South America, or Africa, air evacuation could cost $30,000 to $50,000.

The Traveler's Emergency Network (TEN; 800-275-4836) will provide and pay for emergency evacuation (up to $45,000), including transport home if necessary, should a member become ill or injured when more than 100 miles from home. They may advance money to cover medical fees, but you'll have to reimburse them. They will also arrange reputable medical assistance, which can be every bit as valuable as airlifting you off the mountain. If you'll be hospitalized abroad for more than a week, TEN will pay round-trip expenses for someone you choose to fly to your side. TEN coverage is provided regardless of preexisting conditions. The fee for these and other services is $35 a year for an individual, $50 for a family. Other major firms in the field include International SOS Assistance (800-523-8930), Worldwide Assistance Services (800-821-2828), and Medex (800-537-2029). Again, trip interruption insurance may include evacuation insurance.

Medical Assistance Overseas. The MedPass program offered by Global Emergency Medical Services (800-860-1111) helps travelers connect with high-quality medical help when needed. Leave a medical history form with them, call their hotline if you need assistance on the road, and they will connect you with a selected English-speaking health care provider and send your records by fax. You pay for any treatment. If evacuation is required, there's no extra charge. At a cost of $95 per year, compare it to what you get from the International Association for Medical Assistance to Travelers (see Chapter 8).

For a registration fee of $60 and an annual fee of $52, the Blood Care Foundation (Box 7, Sevenoaks, Kent TN13 2SZ, England; 44-732-742427) will immediately dispatch a safe supply of blood for transfusion to a traveler in need in any country. This could be of benefit in countries where blood is not safely screened for HIV and other diseases.

By the way, if you have a health problem that's not obvious, consider wearing a Medic Alert tag that signals medical personnel of allergies and special health conditions. The tag includes a telephone number that can be called for additional information about your condition. Call or write the Medic Alert Foundation if you're interested in the $35 tag (800-344-3226; P.O. Box 1009, Turlock, CA 95381).

Where to Buy Insurance

Insurance companies sell travel coverage policies directly, through travel agencies, or through tour/cruise operators (sometimes under the operator's name even though it is not the insurer). Don't make the decision on price alone. Take a close look at the breadth of coverage, the amount of coverage, the terms, and the extras. A good company will let you call collect if you need medical assistance and will provide direction to nearby medical care (and a translator if needed). It will also contact your family if you ask them to. If you decide you want health insurance, ask your travel agent's opinion as to the best carrier. Ask other travelers about their experiences.

The following are some of the better-known travel insurance companies:

- Access America (800-284-8300)
- American Express Travel Protection Plan (800-234-0375)
- Berkeley Care (800-645-2424)
- Carefree Travel Insurance (800-323-3149)
- Corporate Assist (800-756-5900)
- CSA (800-234-0375)
- Global Care (800-779-1017)
- Health Care Abroad (800-237-6615)
- Humana/WorldCare Travel Assistance (800-521-4882)
- International SOS Assistance (800-523-8930)
- Nationwide (800-654-6700)
- Safe Passage International (800-777-7665)
- The Travelers (800-243-3174)
- Travel Assistance International (800-821-2828)
- Travel Guard International (800-826-1300)
- Travel Insured International (800-243-3174)
- TravMed/Medex Assistance (800-732-5309)
- Trip Mate (800-888-0432)

Figuring out what to do about insurance may be a minor hassle the first time around, but from then on it's easy.

On the subject of car rental insurance, please see Chapter 16.

Hotel Reservations

Many travelers venturing for the first time to foreign countries take it for granted they should make hotel reservations before leaving home. Travel agents say many of their clients make reservations for every night of the trip, while others reserve a hotel room for at least their first night out and the night before they fly home. Making reservations is common for travelers heading for an event likely to fill a city, such as Carnival in Rio or Octoberfest in Munich. Others make a reservation because they've heard that a certain hotel is so splendid they're determined to stay there.

The bottom line: most people make reservations to reduce concern about the unknown. A reservation is a security blanket, ensuring there will be a room available in a safe location at an acceptable price. It also eliminates the need to spend time selecting lodgings on arrival, perhaps while struggling with an unfamiliar language.

If you decide to make reservations, consider whether you want a smoke-free room, a view, quiet, a certain floor, proximity to certain services, or whatever. If you're not dealing directly with the hotel desk, the operator may note your request but may not be able to guarantee that it will be met. Remember that you're likely to pay more, perhaps considerably more, for amenities such as a favored view.

Making Reservations

If a standard brand hotel is okay and you don't care much about the cost, it's probably easiest to let your travel agent handle the reservation. If you prefer to have a hand in the process, you need information.

- All of the U.S.-based hotel chains with international operations have *800 numbers*. However, you won't get the best deals by talking to a central 800 operator staring at a computer screen full of standard prices that don't reflect how eager a certain hotel is for your business. Nor is the operator likely to know many of the particulars of the hotel, such as the best rooms or views (let alone the location of noisy ice machines).

  Instead, call 800 information (800-555-1212) for the direct dial number of the hotel location you want. Many of the international chains based in other countries also have 800 numbers in the United States. After the hotel quotes a rate, ask about special package deals, corporate rates, and other discounts. Say you are willing to pay a certain amount and ask what they have available. By the way, listen carefully to whether you are quoted a "double occupancy" rate or a "double room" rate. The former means that *each* of two people pays the quoted amount; the latter is the total price of the room.

- *UTELL International* (800-448-8355) is an international reservation service that has connections with over 6,500 hotels in 140 countries (about 1,100 hotels are in the United States). Its hotels range from small independents to international chains and from tourist class to deluxe. In France you can choose from among 400 UTELL hotels, while in Gambia your only choice is the Atlantic Hotel Banjul (hey, they say it has four stars). There's no separate fee for using this service.

- *The Hotel Restaurant Service* offers 65,000 hotels worldwide (many of which can be reviewed at www.hrs.de.

- *INNterREST* on the Microsoft Network enables users to make reservations for hotels and other travel products around the world. It provides Web site addresses for participating hotels so users can access more information about each hotel chain. It also has a restaurant database.

- Purchase the *Entertainment International Hotel Directory* ($9.95; call 800-445-4137), which offers 50 percent savings on more than 1,800 three-, four-, and five-star hotels in 400 international cities.

- Call the U.S. representative of the *Tourist Board* of the country in which you're interested. Most are associated with their embassies in Washington, D.C. Ask for a list of hotels for personal recommendations and for addresses of local tourist information offices to whom you can write.

- Good *guidebooks* give you information on locally owned hotels and list phone and fax numbers of recommended hotels. However, these numbers are more useful if you're calling Scotland than Shanghai (the language barrier becomes a little more formidable on long distance). If need be, send a letter.
- Check out lodging used by interesting *tour operators* (since they obviously approve of the property and the management). For example, the *Backroads* brochure lists a fine group of European inns at which its bicycle tours stop for the night.
- Travel agencies have *lists of hotels* overseas as well as access to a computer-based service on which thousands of hotels are listed. Fax machines minimize language barriers and let a travel agent exchange information with foreign hotels quickly and easily. Since travel agents may receive a commission from the hotel, be sure their suggestions match your preferences. Any time you make a reservation, get a confirmation.
- Draw from other travelers (including reports in International Travel News and on the Internet).
- In *bookstores* or *libraries,* take a look at books that review international lodging (e.g., *Country Inns and Castles*).
- Using a travel agent at your destination to suggest hotels can sometimes lead to a great result.
- The Internet is the most powerful research tool available to you. However, it's unlikely you'll get the most favorable prices via computer booking (in fact, you may pay a surcharge). Further, computer reservations don't always "take," which you won't discover until you arrive late on a rainy night. Review Chapter 2 for a list of Internet travel resources.
- However you make contact, be clear about what amenities you want—especially in terms of beds and bathroom facilities.

Reasons Not to Make Reservations

Are there reasons not to make reservations? Many travelers suggest four main arguments against doing so.

- If a hotel abroad has spent enough on advertising to be known here and to make a reservation easy, its rates are likely to be pretty high. According to *The Wall Street Journal*, rates at "name" international hotels are setting all-time records. Even U.S. rates seem out of control: a suite at the Ritz-Carlton in San Francisco rents for more than $600 a night, as does the Mark Hotel in Manhattan. It's a cinch that restaurant prices in those hotels average $50 a meal or more. Is that in your budget?

  Don't assume that reasonably priced domestic hotel chains are equally reasonable overseas. For example, the Best Western in Paris was around $200 per night for what the *Journal* described as a "room with chipped paint and no shower curtain." Quality Inn charged $160 a night in Rome and Best Western charged $135 in New Delhi. If you are disposed to stay in a chain hotel, don't make assumptions about the international price.

In the end, you'll spend a lot more on hotel rooms if you make reservations from home.

- Upscale hotels overseas tend to be cocoons for well-heeled tourists, insulating them from the rich texture of local life.
- A reservation is unnecessary except in a few very popular destinations or during some special event.
- If you reserve and do not or cannot show up, you will lose your deposit, and maybe more, if you don't cancel well ahead of scheduled arrival. Similarly, if you check out early, you may have to pay for the entire period reserved. Try to avoid reserving with a credit card number (say you'll be paying cash).
- More important than the other disadvantages, a reservation is a commitment to be at a certain place on a specified date. That may not sound bad before you leave home, but it can become a serious restriction on your freedom once you're traveling.
- If you are quoted a room rate in U.S. dollars, you are about to lose the benefit of the exchange rate and pay far more than you should.

After traveling for a while, the security of having a reservation no longer feels necessary. You know what to expect. You've learned that lodging is easy to find locally through guidebooks, tourist information offices, other travelers, and your own common sense. Throughout the world, hotels, lodges, inns, guest houses, pensions, bungalows, youth hostels, and a dozen other forms of lodging compete vigorously for your business. Something will be available with the amenities and price that suit you. As you reminisce years from now, you'll remember the funky, family-style lodging and its proprietors, not international chains.

Exceptions

There are a few circumstances in which even an experienced traveler might want to make advance reservations:

- If you'll be flying into a city late at night and flying out early the next day, you may prefer to know for sure where you'll lay your head.

- While you don't need reservations to travel happily in Europe, you can, on rare occasions, wind up in a charmless dump without one.

- If your destination is a specific resort.

- A woman arriving solo in some destinations, especially late in the evening, may prefer to be booked into a known destination.

Other than these exceptions, I recommend the freedom of winging it.

To SAVE MONEY when booking rooms, see Chapter 6. If you decide to find lodging as you travel, see Chapter 11 for an extensive discussion of how to find superior, affordable lodging anywhere in the world and how to ensure you get it at a fair price.

Adventures

By adventures, I'm referring to short-term activities such as safaris, white-water river trips, treks, and so on. The decision you must make in the planning phase is whether to make arrangements at home, usually through a travel agent or tour operator, or to do your own research to see whether you can arrange things when you get there. It's probably easier to do it at home, but that will result in a different experience and be more expensive.

People pay higher prices to avoid uncertainty when arriving in a foreign country with limited time, and that's understandable. Time is also a factor. If you make the arrangements at home, you hit the ground running when you get there. Otherwise, you may burn a day or two getting something organized locally. If you want to trek in Thailand, you can set it up in the afternoon and leave with a guide the next morning. For an African safari, you might have to wait several days until the next one leaves. Raft trips in Costa Rica leave on set days of the week. Adventures like these are extremely easy to arrange locally—and considerably less expensive than if done at home.

Arranging an adventure when you're at or near the local site is an excellent way to SAVE MONEY. I've often saved 50 percent or more compared to what I'd have paid for a similar, though probably more luxurious, trip had I booked it at home through a tour operator or travel agent. Yet many people routinely have someone make these arrangements for them, paying dearly for advertising, intermediaries, and upscale amenities.

The time will quickly come when you'll be comfortable arranging mini-adventures while abroad. It requires a little effort, but it's not nearly as difficult as it appears. In foreign countries, outfitters and tour operators seek you out and are often willing to tailor their services to your desires.

If cost is the controlling factor, you're better off making arrangements locally. If time is more important, it may be to your advantage to sign up for an adventure before you leave home. If you see an adventure that appeals to you, say in a guidebook, and you want to book it at home, select a tour operator or outfitter as we discussed in Chapter 4. For a discussion of how to SAVE MONEY when arranging an adventure, see Chapter 6.

The steps necessary to go into action are very manageable. Obtaining a passport and visas is simple when you know the routine. If you want a job abroad, need a permit, or want to buy a rail or bus pass, you now know how to go about it. Making travel and health insurance decisions requires research and attention to details, but doing it once makes the decisions easy for later trips. You know the factors to consider when deciding when to buy airline tickets, whether to make hotel reservations, and when to book adventures.

Checklist: What Needs to Be Done When

12 months before D (Departure) Date
__Start initial planning for your trip.
__Start setting money aside.
__Start collecting information.
__Start interviewing travel agents.
__Start studying languages, if appropriate.
__Start talking with travelers.

6 months before D Date
__Rough out your itinerary and the length and cost of your trip.
__Select your travel agent.
__Research air fares, tour options, and insurance.
__Have passport photos taken and start the process of getting a passport.
__Read literature from and about countries you may visit.
__Review guidebooks.
__Determine what shots you'll want and when the sequence should start (Chapter 8).
__If you're in marginal physical condition, begin increasing your physical activity.

3 months before D Date
__Firm up your itinerary.
__Obtain a credit card and ATM card.
__Start getting visas.
__Make decisions about your gear and begin assembling it.
__Add to your travel information file.
__Collect addresses of people to contact abroad.
__Increase your physical activity; build your stamina.
__Choose someone to look after your affairs while you're away.
__If you have a will, update it if appropriate.

2 months before D Date
__Decide whether you want an International Drivers License, Youth Hostel card, and/or International Student ID card. Get the ones you choose.

__Take medical and dental exams.
__Start inoculations.
__Complete research and make airline reservations.
__Buy any new clothing and equipment you need.
__Decide whether additional insurance is appropriate.
__Test new equipment, especially shoes and camera.
__Set aside a place to pile travel gear; start piling.

1 month before D Date
__Buy airline tickets; get seat assignments.
__Buy film.
__Buy medical supplies.
__Make photocopies of appropriate documents and distribute them.
__Complete inoculations.
__Prepare for closing your house or apartment.
__Make financial arrangements (someone to pay bills, pay credit card charges, etc.).
__Give necessary documents to the person who will be taking care of things.

2 weeks before D Date
__Buy travelers checks.
__Organize gear for packing; see if it will fit in your luggage.
__Schedule suspension of utilities, subscriptions, and other services.
__Arrange for mail to be forwarded.

Final week
__Shut down your home (Chapter 9).
__Send your itinerary to those who should have it.
__Complete packing at least three days before departure.
__Confirm all flights; ensure you have all tickets and other documents.
__Say your good-byes.

6

Money

Not all those who wander are lost.
— J.R.R. Tolkien
Fellowship of the Ring

Would cutting the cost by $1,000 make your dream trip affordable? You'll learn how to save that much and more in this chapter. What we're about to discuss will buy you more time, distance, and adventure—yet not cost you one extra cent! This chapter is filled with suggestions about how to SAVE MONEY, prepare a reliable budget, and manage your money successfully as you travel.

If you assume that it costs a fortune to travel internationally, and money matters, you're likely to conclude that you can't afford to travel. Unless you know what you're doing, you might be right. Unhappily, it's getting ever more expensive for the uninformed to travel. In the United States, according to the Dow Jones Travel Index, business and leisure air fares continue to increase at double-digit rates. In addition, higher occupancy rates made hotel managers more bold about charging domestic travelers close to rack rates. In other words, it's rough out there—at least for the unwary. It takes a well-informed traveler to avoid outrageous prices, both at home and abroad.

I'm going to begin this chapter with three thoughts about saving money:

1. If you have a choice, it would be a mistake to travel in the cheapest way possible. A miserly trip can exact a high price on your health and state of mind.

2. Some people assume that traveling on a low to moderate budget assures a meaningful trip. Not true. It does provide many opportunities for personal contact with local people, but it's up to you to take advantage of those opportunities.

3. When we discuss getting the most for your money, it is always in the context of accomplishing your goals for the trip and having a great time.

HOW TO SAVE MONEY

Saving Money on Air Fare

Let's start with the premise that you need never pay full fare for any ticket to anywhere. It's up to you. You may not believe that now, but I'll bet you will by the time you reach the end of this chapter.

The Internet revolutution has created important opportunities for informed travlers to save money SAVE MONEY in air travel. Most of the airlines have sites offering their standard ticket prices, but why pay those prices when you can so easily find less expensive tickets? Check out the alternative Web sites I listed in Chapter 2, which offer excellent ticket prices. New sites pop up almost daily, Sure, you may have to be flexible enough to fly on short notice, or adjust your schedule a bit—but you may pay only 25 percent of the regular ticket price. It won't work for everyone, but it is a resource to be consulted. Now, let's take a look at what has historically been the biggest money saver of all: consolidators.

Bucket Shops

Elsewhere in the world, savvy travelers buy airline tickets in "bucket shops," a term applied to agencies that sell normal airline tickets at heavily discounted prices. Among cities renowned for bucket shops are Amsterdam, Athens, Bangkok, Calcutta, Hong Kong, London, Nairobi, Penang, and Singapore. When you walk into a bucket shop abroad, you're unlikely to mistake it for the American Express office. The decor is usually spartan and the clerk's manner a bit, shall we say, brisk. They know you're there because of price, not pretty paintings on the wall or small talk.

The bucket shop I used in Calcutta consisted of two desks and a computer set up on a landing halfway up the first flight of stairs in a budget hotel. That seemed a little shaky, but they handed me authentic tickets in return for my money.

By the way, if the ticket available happens to be on an airline you haven't heard of, don't assume there's something wrong with it. For example, the 747s of Air Garuda (Indonesia) and Varig Air (Brazil) can compete in service and reliability with planes used anywhere in the world. If you are concerned, call the FAA to see if an airline is on its "not permitted to land in the United States" list.

Here are a few leads, not endorsements, from among dozens of established bucket shops:

- In Singapore: GASI Travel, 12 Devonshire Road (tel. 65-734-0133)
- In Amsterdam: Malibu Travel, Damrak 30 (tel. 31-20-623-2977)
- In London: Major Travel, 28/34 Fortess Road, Kentish Town (tel. 071-482-4840); Lupus Travel Centre, 93/95 Regent Street (tel. 071-734-9174); Air Travel Advisory Bureau, 320 Regent Street (tel. 071-636-5000)
- In Athens: Inter Trust Travel, 43 Nikis Street (tel. 30-1-322-8181)

Consolidators

Here's the great news: there's a little-known equivalent to the bucket shop in the United States. The domestic versions are called "consolidators" and they have plenty of heavily discounted tickets available. Since you pay 15 to 60 percent less than published air fare prices, buying from a consolidator is a vitally important way to SAVE MONEY. Exactly how much you save depends on your destination, the time of year, and the day of the week on which you want to leave. The deal you get also depends on the research you do, the questions you ask, and your persistence. Consolidator prices may even be somewhat negotiable; some consolidators will give up a little of their profit to close a sale. It's still a good deal for them because they thrive on high volume.

From experience, airlines know when to expect large numbers of empty seats. Since an unfilled seat is worth nothing to them, they allocate blocks of tickets to consolidators to sell at below-market prices. To avoid offending full-fare flyers, airlines don't advertise this practice. Instead, they contract with consolidators to sell tickets for prices they would never publish on the Computer Reservations System (CRS) from which travel agents draw fares. Consolidator tickets aren't sold behind the airlines' backs. They are part of overall yield management by the airlines to maximize their profits. All you have to do to take advantage of these low fares is to know how to find and evaluate them. You're about to find out how to do that.

The airlines allocate tickets to consolidators at very low fares or simply give consolidators a high commission. In the latter case, part of the commission is passed on to you in the form of a lower fare (which is why you may have some negotiating room).

Even though consolidators' prices are consistently excellent, airlines in the midst of a price war or major promotion may temporarily make prices of certain tickets competitive with consolidator prices. However, as we've all learned, tickets available at "price war" prices may be as plentiful as hens' teeth.

Price wars can make consolidator's tickets less appealing.

Unfortunately, a few consolidators follow the same practice. When you ask for the ticket at the price they've advertised, they can't deliver. I understand that they have only a limited number of tickets and may sell out quickly, but if I sense a bait-and-switch, that consolidator never hears from me again.

If you see an ad, call the consolidator or take the ad to a travel agency and ask them to get the ticket for you at the advertised price. The majority of consolidators will deal directly with individuals, while the rest sell only through tour operators or travel agents. In either case, your travel agent can make the purchase for you if you prefer and don't mind paying a small markup. Since the fare isn't in the CRS, travel agents have to do a little more work than with standard tickets, but they get commissions from the consolidator. In the past, many travel agents haven't taken advantage of consolidator tickets even though they would benefit clients because they wanted to maintain their historic relationships with the airlines. With commission caps that may change.

Consolidators are located everywhere from a tiny office in Santa Ana, California, to substantial suites in New York City, Los Angeles, and Washington, DC. Many advertise in newspapers such as *The New York Times, The Washington Post,* and the *Los Angeles Times,* and periodicals such as *Travel Weekly.* Check your bookstore or library. The best resource I know of is *Fly for Less: The Only Complete Guide to Selecting Reliable Consolidators and Wholesalers Who Offer Bargain Airfares,* by Gary Schmidt. It's in some bookstores, or you can call the publisher (800-241-9299). Its publisher will match subscribers with local travel agencies who use consolidators. The Better Business Bureau of New York publishes a booklet entitled *Advisory on Ticket Consolidators* (257 Park Avenue South, New York, NY 10010).

In addition to low prices, another potential advantage in buying a ticket from a consolidator is that its contract with an airline may permit it to waive advance purchase or Saturday night stayover requirements, a real bonus for seize-the-opportunity travelers. These tickets sometimes even count toward frequent flier mileage. The terms of a consolidator's tickets are frequently *less* restrictive with respect to penalties for cancellation or changes than a standard ticket bought from an airline at a higher price. Nevertheless, be sure you understand any restrictions and penalties. For example, it's not unusual for a consolidator to impose a "last minute" (meaning within seven days of departure) booking fee and a penalty if you cancel a ticket just before departure.

If you can't find the discounted tickets you want at home, buy them on the road. For one complicated trip throughout Southeast Asia, I bought a ticket in the United States for only the first leg of the trip. By purchasing the rest of my tickets at bucket shops in Singapore and Bangkok, I saved almost $800 over what I would have paid had I purchased regular tickets in the United States for all segments. For other trips, I've saved thousands by buying consolidator tickets for the entire trip.

Potential Drawbacks to Consolidators

There are several potential drawbacks in dealing with a consolidator:
- Occasionally you don't get frequent flyer mileage credit.
- You may not be able to get an advance seat assignment.
- Your choice of airlines and flight times may be restricted.
- The route you fly may not be the most direct. There may be an overnight stop before you reach your destination.
- Tickets often cannot be transferred or exchanged (at least not without a fee).
- If your flight is canceled, it's unlikely you will be able to transfer easily to another airline.

Here's another tip. You are often much better off buying air tickets abroad, even at standard prices—especially intracountry tickets. For example, a ticket from one Italian city to another might cost $275 in the United States but only $75 in Italy.

You can usually pay for tickets purchased in London's bucket shops or from U.S. consolidators with a credit card. Doing so would enable you to cancel the charge if the ticket didn't arrive or the consolidator went bankrupt. A few U.S. consolidators insist on payment by cash or check. I would be very cautious in such cases. In most of the rest of the world, however, you may have to pay in cash. If so, you're at risk until you have the ticket in hand.

After you've made your reservation with a consolidator, wait a day, then confirm with the airline that it holds a reservation in your name. If it doesn't, call the consolidator at once. Avoid anxiety by insisting on delivery of the ticket comfortably ahead of your departure date. When you receive it, check that flight numbers, times, and dates are correct. Ensure that your status is shown as "OK," which means you have a confirmed seat (rather than being wait listed). Again, confirm directly with the airline.

I haven't had a problem with consolidators or bucket shops nor do I know anyone who has. The few problems I've read about in the United States generally concern a consolidator who went bankrupt, issued a phony ticket, or received payments without issuing the tickets. These situations have been rare. Of course, travel agencies, cruise lines, and airlines go bankrupt from time to time as well. Use common sense, trust your intuition, and ask questions:

- Where is your office located (street address, not a post office box)?
- How long have you been in business?
- With what airlines do you have contracts?
- Whom can I contact at the airlines to vouch for your firm?
- Is your firm accredited with the ARC and IATAN?
- Are you bonded? If so, for how much?

If you still have any doubts, call the Better Business Bureau where the firm is located, or call the American Society of Travel Agents consumer affairs department. If you buy from a consolidator recommened by a travel agency, the consolidator will be of known quality

Consolidators have formed the Airline Consolidators Association, which may become a self-regulating body. They contemplate a default protection program, similar to what some tour operators have, to compensate agents and consumers if a member goes out of business.

There are two types of organizations that could be mistaken for consolidators. The first is a ticket *broker*. Unlike a consolidator, a broker has no contract with the airlines. Instead, a broker locates cheap tickets, often buying from consolidators, and resells them to the public. If a ticket broker is undercapitalized, it may be somewhat risky to deal with it.

The second is a *wholesaler*, who buys low-cost tickets in volume from airlines to serve the wholesaler's tours. Individuals can often purchase tickets from a wholesaler at an excellent price.

There are almost 200 true consolidators (excluding ticket brokers and travel agencies who claim to be consolidators but aren't). All sell to travel agencies, while about 60 percent sell to individuals as well. The following list of consolidators excludes many of the smallest and newest, and those that are neither bonded nor accredited by ARC or IATAN. Consolidators tend to specialize in geographic regions, so seek out ones most suitable for your trip. I'm not endorsing any consolidator by including it on the list below, but I've had successful experiences with every one I've used.

Major Consolidators

Air Brokers International	(800) 883-3273	Around-the-World, South Pacific *#
Alta Tours	(800) 338-4191	Latin America *#
AmeriCorp Travel Professionals	(800) 299-5284	Latin America *#
Asensio Tours	(800) 221-7679	Latin America *#
Campus Connections	(800) 428-3235	Low fares in the United States for ages 12 to 25
Campus Travel Center	(800) 328-3359	Europe, South Pacific *#
Centrav	(800) 874-2033	Europe, Mid-East, Latin America Africa, Asia; agents only *#
Consolidated Tours	(800) 228-0877	Europe; agents only *#
Council Travel	(800) 226-8624	Asia, Latin America, Europe, United States; a travel agency that deals with consolidators; 40 offices
D-FW Tours	(800) 527-2589	Europe, Mid-East, Asia, Africa, Latin America; agents only *#
Diplomat Tours	(800) 727-8687	Europe, Latin America, Asia, North America, Africa; agents only *#
Fare Deals Travel	(800) 347-7006	Africa, Asia, Europe, Latin America, South Pacific #
Getaway Travel	(800) 683-6336	Mid-East, Africa, Asia, Europe, Latin America *#
GIT Travel	(800) 228-1777	Europe, Africa, Russia, Latin America *#
Interworld Travel	(800) 468-3796	Africa, Latin America, Europe *#

Intourist	(800) 556-5305	Russia, CIS, China, Mongolia, Scandinavia *#
J & O Air	(800) 877-8111	Europe, Asia, Latin America, South Pacific; agents only *#
Jetset Tours	(800) 638-3273	Europe, Australia/New Zealand, Asia, Africa, Circle Pacific; agents only *#
Maazda Travel	(310) 273-9100	Specializes in India *#
Magical Holidays	(800) 433-7773	Europe, Africa, Latin America, Asia *#
New Frontiers	(800) 366-6387	Specializes in Europe *
Overseas Express	(800) 343-4873	Europe, Asia, Latin America, Africa *#
Picasso Travel	(800) PICASSO	Europe, Mid-East, Africa, Latin America, South Pacific, Africa *#
Premier Travel Services	(800) 545-1910	Latin America, South Pacific, Africa, Mid-East, Europe #
Skytours	(800) 246-8687	Europe *#
South Pacific Express Travels	(800) 321-7739	South Pacific, North America *#
Student Travel Network (STA)	(800) 825-3001	Europe, Mid-East, Africa, Asia, Latin America, North America, South Pacific; STA offers substantial discounts to anyone under 25 and to students under age 30 (or up to age 34 on some airlines); agents only #
Trans Am Travel	(800) 822-7600	Europe, Mid-East, Africa, Latin America, Asia, South Pacific *#
Travac	(800) 872-8800	Europe, Mid-East, Africa #
Travel 800	(800) FLY-CHEAP	All domestic and international
Travel Center	(800) 419-0960	Africa, India, Europe *#
Travel N Tours	(800) 854-5400	Europe, Africa, Latin America, Asia; agents only *#
Travnet	(800) 359-6388	Asia, South Pacific; agents only *#
UniTravel	(800) 325-2222	Europe, Latin America, North America, Asia, Africa; agents only #
Up & Away Travel	(800) 275-8001	Europe, Mid-East, Latin America, North America, South Pacific *#
Worldwide Travel	(800) 343-0038	Europe, Mid-East, Africa, India, Asia *#

Note: * means the agency has bond coverage, although it may be as low as $30,000, and # means accreditation by ARC and/or IATAN

For names of more consolidators:

- Look in the travel section of major newspapers.
- Call any airline and ask for names of consolidators with whom they have contracts.
- Send $3.50 to Travel Consolidators (Better Business Bureau of Metro New York, 257 Park Avenue South, New York, NY 10010) for its *Advisory on Ticket Consolidators*.
- Read *Fly There for Less: How to Slash the Cost of Air Travel Worldwide* (Bob Martin, Teak Press; $18.95), *Consolidators: Air Travel's Bargain Basement* (Kelly Monaghan, Intrepid Traveler; 800-356-9315; $8.95), or *Fly for Less* (cited above). All three list consolidators and make a variety of money-saving suggestions.
- Take a look at *Best Fares*, a discount air fare magazine (817-261-6114).
- Order *Airline Consolidators Quick Reference Chart* which lists forty consolidators ($8 from On the Go Publishing, P.O. Box 91033 HE6, Columbus, OH 43209).
- Read the regular *Consumer Reports Travel Letter* on domestic and international consolidators.
- Subscribe to *Jax Fax*, which lists current consolidator flights (call 800-952-9329; $15).

Global Discount Travel Services, a relatively new agency, is said to sell TWA domestic and international (Europe and Mexico) tickets at 25 percent less than whatever TWA charges for the same ticket (even during fare wars). There are rumors that this discount, available as a result of a complex legal settlement, may drop to 20 percent. For information, call (800) 497-6678 or write 4052 South Industrial Road, Las Vegas, NV 89103.

Flightpath USA has a database of more than 200,000 airfares offered by more than 30 consolidators, which it makes available to subscribing travel agents. Using this database streamlines the process of finding the best fare, and Flightpath says it weeds out any consolidators with questionable reputations. If your travel agent is not a subscriber, call Flightpath directly (703-812-9500) for a listing of travel agents located near you who do subscribe. This service is worth looking into.

If you deal with a travel agency, remind them as often as necessary to find discounted tickets for you—not merely low published rates, but discounted rates. If your agent doesn't have contacts with consolidators, try elsewhere or buy the tickets yourself. Any traveler who doesn't learn about and utilize consolidator tickets is missing the biggest money saver of all.

APEX Fares

Advance purchase excursions (APEX) are sold by airlines and travel agents. These fares are inexpensive when compared to the cost of regular tickets, but, by definition, tickets must be purchased well ahead of departure date. Procrastinate and you lose the APEX option. The advance-purchase requirement is usually 21 days, but can fluctuate between 7 and 30 days.

The lower price is a trade-off for accepting certain restrictions that vary from airline to airline and month to month. APEX tickets may have minimum and maximum length of stay requirements, plus restrictions on, or penalties for, making schedule changes (in departure date, itinerary, etc.) after you've bought the ticket. If you buy an APEX ticket and don't use it, you may lose the entire purchase price, or at least have to pay a substantial penalty.

An advantage of many APEX tickets is that they are "open jaw." That means the ticket permits you to fly from home to one city and return home from a different city without paying a penalty. For example, if you've flown to Nairobi and traveled overland to southern Africa, you can fly home from Johannesburg rather than returning all the way to Nairobi to leave for home. An open jaw ticket saves considerable travel time and money.

Other Bargain Air Fares

No Frills Carriers. Whether traveling to a domestic destination or connecting with an international flight, SAVE MONEY by using a no frills carrier. Expect a little less leg room and a lunch that consists of a bag of peanuts and a soft drink—in return for saving hundreds of dollars. This is an area in which a travel agent may not be your best friend because the commission for booking a cut-rate flight may not be enticing. Further, tickets for some of these carriers must be filled in by hand rather than by computer, which doesn't thrill many agents. Of course, no frills carriers such as Southwest Airlines are already in the vanguard of ticketless travel.

If your travel agent routinely suggests only the major carriers, ask for information on some of the no frills carriers listed on the following page. If it's not forthcoming, call yourself.

For flights in the United Kingdom and nine European countries, it's difficult to beat the fares of *British Midland Airlines.* However, to get the lowest fare you must purchase your ticket before reaching the United Kingdom or Europe. To learn more about this reputable airline, call (800) 788-0555.

Last-Minute Brokers. Distress situations are another good source of discounts. An airline or cruise ship that has vacancies at the last minute is likely to offer major discounts. To take advantage of them, you have to be flexible regarding your departure date. Here are a few of the many last-minute brokers:

- *Discount Travel International* (800-334-9294): $45 membership; claims discounts of 15 to 60 percent off published rates for international airfare and cruises; 5 percent off domestic air fare rates.

Major No Frills Air Carriers

America West	(800) 235-9292	Coast-to-coast, Mexico, Vancouver, BC
Carnival	(800) 824-7386	New York, California, Florida, Caribbean
Frontier	(800) 432-1359	
Kiwi	(800) 538-5494	Midwest, East Coast
Midway	(800) 446-4392	Midwest, Northeast
Reno Air	(800) 736-6247	West Coast
Southwest Airlines	(800) 435-9792	Coast-to-coast
Spirit Air	(800) 395-7117	Milwaukee, Midwest, coast-to-coast
Sun Jet	(800) 478-6538	Texas, California, Florida
Tower Air	(800) 221-2500	Coast-to-coast, several international destinations
USAir	(800) 428-4322	Coast-to-coast

- *Entertainment Hot Line Travel Club* (313-637-9780): annual fee of $35; claims up to 65 percent off market prices.
- *Last Minute Travel* (800-527-8646): no fee, operates primarily in the Caribbean.
- *Moment's Notice* (212-486-0500): yearly fee of $25; claims discounts of 15 to 50 percent; claims airfare discounts of up to 60 percent.
- *Vacations To Go* (800-338-4962): membership $19.95; good discounts, but mostly on cruises.
- *Worldwide Discount Travel Club* (305-534-2082).

Standby. Standby brokers are similar to distress brokers. I know of the following brokers:

- Access (212-333-7280)
- Airhitch (212-864-2000)
- ANZ Travel (310-379-2483)
- Encore Short Notice (800-638-8976)
- Stand-Buys, Ltd. (800-255-0200)

To take one example, you give Airhitch a period during which you would like to leave for Europe, listing several acceptable destinations. A few days ahead of time, they tell you the date of your flight and where you'll wind up. However, short notice means that finding a cheap connecting flight in the United States could be a problem.

With standbys, you call a hotline to hear details on available trips leaving from your region. Savings average 34 to 62 percent.

Round-the-World. Airlines offer more than 40 separate round-the-world (RTW) packages, most of which must be purchased before you leave home, including Circle Pacific (for the Pacific Rim region), Pacific Air Pass, Polypass (South Pacific), Super Caribbean, Scandinavian, Discover Pacific, and Visit South America. These packages can usually be purchased at prices well below the cost of out-and-back or point-to-point fares. In addition, some ticket brokers specialize in combining one-way tickets at low fares.

Ask about restrictions affecting changes to itinerary, flight dates, doubling back, side trips, minimum stopovers, traveling only during off-season time periods, limits on refunds, and minimum and maximum travel periods. These tickets are usually valid for six months or a year. Expect to pay in the range of $1,200 to $3,000. For a long-term "walkabout," they're hard to beat.

Consolidators who specialize in RTW tickets typically have the best prices. Among them, Air Brokers International (800-883-3273) specializes in Circle-the-Globe and Circle-the-Pacific tickets. Travel Brokers (415-398-2925) features RTW tickets, as does Pan Express Travel (212-719-9292). Consider also Council Travel RTW Desk (617-576-3134), Global Access (800-938-5355), or High Adventure (800-428-8735)

Foreign Airlines. SAVE MONEY by flying on one of the lesser-known foreign flag airlines such as Malev (Hungary), Lot (Poland), or Korean Air. If you're working with a travel agent, you'll probably have to make a specific request. You can do the research by calling embassies of the countries where you'll be traveling. You get lower prices as well as a chance to talk with local people returning home, but you usually won't receive usable frequent flyer miles (although an increasing number of foreign carriers have reciprocal arrangements with American carriers). Just because an airline isn't well known in the United States does not mean it isn't reliable.

Air Passes

Air passes, which you purchase through your travel agent or directly from a foreign airline, can be an excellent way to SAVE MONEY. Passes do have certain restrictions: travel must be taken within a specified time period (typically between two and twelve weeks), sometimes you must circle back through a hub city, you must buy the pass before arriving in the country, and occasionally you must arrive on the sponsoring airline.

While your itinerary is in the planning stage, compare point-to-point airfare with the cost of the pass to see which is the better deal. Because distances are vast and normal tickets are relatively expensive, air passes permitting multiple stops have worked well for me in Brazil, Australia, and Indonesia.

In Europe, take a look at the *Discover Europe Airpass* (British Midland Airlines) that covers the United Kingdom and includes almost a dozen European cities. *Discover Europe* (Lufthansa and Finnair) offers many European routes. Some of the others include *EuroFlyer Pass* (Air France and others), *Europe AirPass* (British Airways and others), *EuroPass* (Iberia), *Passport to Europe* (KLM and Northwest), *Baltic Pass* (SAS), *LeFrance Pass* (Air Inter), *Visit Norway Pass* (Braathens SAFE), and *Visit Spain Airpass* (Iberia). Some of these passes must be bought in conjunction with a transatlantic ticket on the sponsoring airline. In any case, a pass makes sense only if you can use it fully without letting it distort your itinerary.

Air passes are very suitable for Latin America. One of the best is the *Sudameripass* (Aeroperu). You receive six flights, starting from Miami, Mexico City or Cancun to Lima, then on to many other South American cities. Additional international flights are inexpensive and add-ons within Peru are only $25 each. This is a great deal!

Chile, Bolivia, Colombia, Argentina, Venezuela, and Brazil also offer passes. The Brazil air pass permits five flights among 19 cities ($100 each for additional segments). The Argentina pass offers four stops.

One of the best ways to see the South Pacific is with a *Polypass* (Polynesian Airlines) starting from Honolulu. You get unlimited travel among the Cook Islands, Samoa, French Polynesia, Fiji, Tonga, New Caledonia, and Niue, plus one round trip to Auckland, New Zealand, and one round trip to either Sydney or Melbourne, Australia. Even though the pass is valid only for 30 days, it's another great deal. Other passes in the region: *Australia and New Zealand Airpass, Visit Australia New Zealand Airpass, Australia Explorer Pass*, and the *Kiwi Air Pass*.

The concept of 21 days of unlimited travel in India may be a bit daunting, but that's what you get with a *Discover India Fare*. In Indonesia, I've used the *Visit Indonesia Decade Pass*. The Thai Airways pass is good for four domestic flights.

On the *Discover Asia Airpass* offered by SilkAir (based in Singapore), you buy various flight segments at either one of two prices. Also, check the Internet for the All Asia Pass offered by Cathay Pacific (30 days of unlimited travel to 17 destinations).

Similar to an air pass is a ticket for a *fixed* multistop itinerary sold at a price below that of the requisite one-way tickets. In Europe, these tickets may involve more than one participating airline.

Frequent Flyer Coupons

The frequent flyer program is not aging well. Intended as a marketing ploy, it worked so much better than anyone imagined that it's been converted into a house of mirrors. In addition to inspiring brand loyalty, it has set employees against employers, and 38 million frequent flyers against the very airlines that sought their business. Some employees fly odd routes at odd times just to travel on "their" airline, costing employers money in the process. At the same time, airlines set snares for frequent flyers who want to make money by selling the coupons they have earned. On top of all that, after drawing consumers into their programs, airlines restrict frequent flyer seats to an average of only 7 percent of capacity of each flight. As a result, many loyal customers wind up having to fly thousands of miles out of their way or make reservations 12 to 18 months ahead of departure.

How to Earn Credits. The usual way to earn frequent flyer points is by—what else?—flying. However, the nonflying ways in which you can increase your frequent flyer credits are increasing daily. For example, AT&T, feeling the bite of competition, is offering a True Rewards plan (800-773-9273) which credits five frequent flyer miles to one of three airlines for each dollar you spend on long distance calls. In other words, if it takes 25,000 miles to earn a "free" domestic flight, you must spend $5,000 on long distance phone calls to earn it. If you average $100 a month, that's more than four years worth of calls. MCI and Sprint have equivalent plans in partnership with different airlines. Several car rental firms have similar deals. The concept keeps expanding. A grocery chain in Texas awards frequent flyer miles in return for the veggies and bologna you buy.

You can earn frequent flyer miles with some calling cards or credit cards.

If other terms are competitive, consider using credit cards that award frequent flyer miles in proportion to your purchases. Many airlines sponsor MasterCard or Visa credit cards, issued by various banks, that earn frequent flyer mileage credits. Use of Diners Club or American Express cards earns credit with one airline or another.

With the BancOne TravelPlus Visa card ($25), the value of every purchase you make is converted to points that accumulate toward a free ticket on most airlines. When you get enough points, the bank buys the ticket for you. Under this program, you are unaffected by blackouts or limited seat allocations imposed by the airlines. When you take the trip you've earned, it earns additional frequent flyer mileage. The BancOne gold Visa card ($55) also includes car rental collision damage waiver coverage and other benefits (call 800-945-2023). Keep an eye open for other deals that build your frequent flyer credits.

Flying on any of two dozen or more *foreign* airlines earns frequent flyer miles on one of the U.S.-based airlines. For example, flying Chile's Ladeco Airline earns mileage credit on TWA; flying LanChile earns mileage on Continental.

To avoid wasting mileage, join several frequent flyer programs. However, most people need to concentrate their mileage on one, or at most two, airlines to earn the minimum mileage required to earn a "free" flight before their miles start expiring.

If you fly a lot, keep track of your mileage yourself (including miles earned as bonuses from related purchases) rather than relying on the airline to keep an accurate record.

Transfers. Transfering frequent flyer coupons is not against the law, but that doesn't mean airlines don't try to prevent it. On most airlines, a traveler caught trying to use a coupon with someone else's name on it may lose it or be denied boarding (similar to the situation when a person buys a nonrefundable ticket from someone who can't use it). Nevertheless, a market for coupons struggles on. If you haven't accumulated enough frequent flyer miles to earn a trip and can't find a friend who wants to share extra mileage with you, check newspaper classified ads under "ticket swap" for offers from individuals and dealers.

National coupon brokers deal mostly in first and business class tickets. Although that's where the greatest savings are, that's not how most international travelers fly. If you deal with a coupon broker, have the coupon reissued in your name (which may take four to six weeks). Some brokers provide you with a newly issued ticket, not coupons, by handling the coupon transfers in-house. If the coupon won't be in your name, there's probably a reason—and a greater risk that the airline won't accept it (don't get your hopes up). Paying with a credit card gives you and the broker something to discuss if there's a problem.

When offered a coupon, check its terms carefully including the expiration date. Many certificates state: "Void if bartered or sold." However, some airlines permit transfers. Under the Delta Skymiles program, mileage awards may be transferred to anyone you choose but, at least theoretically, not sold or bartered.

For international travel, you must show your passport to the ticket agent when checking in. If the passport doesn't match the frequent flyer coupon and the agent makes an issue of it, the airline could confiscate it and your trip could end on the spot.

Traveling with a *ticket* bearing someone else's name is asking for confiscation. During periods when domestic airport security is tightened, the agent will ask for a photo ID to demonstrate that you're the person to whom the ticket was issued. If they don't match, the agent may either confiscate the ticket—or decide you're a mad bomber. As a result of security checks, airlines have discovered so many "transferred" tickets in use that they may keep checking IDs even after security concerns are reduced. If you're not certain of an airline's policy, ask ahead of time. Coupons SAVE MONEY, but it's "buyer beware" all the way.

Cashing In. You can exchange your frequent flyer miles for a ticket directly with the airline (but they may charge a fee for rush service). If you want your travel agent to handle the exchange, ask first whether there would be a charge for the service. Remember to use frequent flyer mileage credit to buy an expensive ticket, not a cheap one. Assume you spend about $.02 to earn a frequent flyer mile. If you can buy a ticket for cash for significantly less than the value of the mileage credit you've accumulated, hold onto the credit for a later day.

What the airlines promote with one hand, they take away with the other, meaning there are often restrictions on when you can take trips earned with frequent flyer points. In what was perceived by some as a cynical move, Northwest recently offered to let its frequent flyers "buy" their way out of blackouts and various other restrictions by paying additional frequent flyer points. Of course, the restrictions were imposed by Northwest itself.

To avoid being shut out, you may have to avoid "hub cities," fly to cities close to your real destination, pay a big premium in miles, or go where most travelers do not.

Sources of Information. There are so many frequent flyer programs and the rules change so often that the most helpful thing I can do is provide sources of current information on various programs. *InsideFlyer Magazine* ($33 a year) reports on bonuses and new programs and rates the various programs. The annual reference edition of *The Official Frequent Flyer Guidebook* ($14.99) explains all airline, hotel, car rental, and credit card programs, and lists all blackout dates. Both are available by calling (800) 487-8893. Check back issues of *Consumer Reports Travel Letter* for comparisons of the various programs.

A computer program called FTM AirMax helps travelers find the best combination of airline, hotel, car rental, and credit cards to maximize frequent flyer points. Order the $80 software by calling (800) 386-2476. Travel libraries of major online services and many travel bulletins boards offer shareware that will help you keep track of frequent flyer points and let you know when you have earned awards.

Couriers

Even most experienced travelers don't know what a courier is—so they miss a great way to SAVE MONEY. Here's the situation. Air freight companies often have rush shipments but, for security reasons, the FAA won't permit them to be sent as unaccompanied baggage on regular airline flights. To send the shipment air freight would be expensive and clearing customs on the other end could take days. On the other hand, if sent as part of a traveler's personal baggage allowance, it clears customs immediately. That's where you come in. Sending you as a courier costs them less than paying air cargo rates, especially since you partially reimburse them for your ticket.

A courier typically pays only one-third to one-half the unrestricted coach fare, although savings of 85 percent or more are possible. As shipment date approaches, the fare drops. When time is running out, the courier firm may even pick up the whole cost of your flight. As a bonus, you'll probably be entitled to frequent flyer credit for the flight.

More than 30,000 courier flights originate from the United States each year; 90 percent depart from Los Angeles, Miami, New York, and San Francisco, and a few flights leave from Atlanta, Boston, Chicago, Houston, and Washington, DC.

Summer courier fares are higher than at any other time because the balance of supply and demand is working against you.

Who Is Eligible? To become a courier you must be at least 21 years old and have a valid passport. Some courier companies charge a fee (e.g., $35 to $50) the first time you fly with them. Many require a refundable deposit (e.g., $100 to $200) to assure that you'll show up to accompany the return shipment. You also have to pay any airport departure tax (typically, $18 to $28).

How It Works. You leave from a designated city and are probably limited to carry-on luggage, although you're sometimes allowed to check one bag. In some cases, you're a courier on the outbound flight only, leaving you with a full baggage allowance for the return flight.

As a rule, it's better to book a flight one to three months before you'd like to travel. Most popular destinations require at least a two-week advance reservation, and four to six weeks is better during the summer to assure you'll get a ride.

It's normal to wonder, "What's in that baggage anyway?" meaning, "Am I going to wind up in the Saigon slammer?" Courier companies insist that shipments are legitimate: canceled checks, contracts, electronic replacement

Major Courier Brokers

Council Travel	(212) 661-1450	
Courier Travel	(800) 275-2359	to Europe, the Middle East, and South America
Discount Travel International	(212) 362-3636	
Go Travel	(213) 466-1126	
Halbart Travel	(718) 656-8189	to Mexico City, London, and Madrid
IBC	(310) 607-0215	to the Far East and London
Line Haul Service	(305) 477-0651	to Central and South America
Midnite Express	(310) 672-100	to London
Now Voyager	(212) 431-1616	to Europe, South America, and the Far East
Polo Express	(415) 742-9613	to Australia, Asia, London
UTL Travel	(415) 583-5074	to London and Asia
Way to Go Travel	(213) 466-1126	to Australia and the Far East

Why Don't More People Fly as Couriers?

- Almost no one knows the opportunity exists.
- The amount of personal baggage you can take is usually limited to one carry-on.
- You must return home within a comparatively short time. The typical turnaround to Europe is one week, two weeks to Asia, and seven to twenty-one days to South America. However, you can negotiate with some courier companies to get a longer turnaround, even up to six months.
- You may want to fly with a companion and they don't get the courier rate. However, that may not be an obstacle because the company may need two couriers on the same day, or at least on successive days, or it may be willing to sell a ticket to your companion at a discount. Worst case, you fly as a courier and your partner flies on a commercial ticket.

parts, that kind of thing. Fortunately, it doesn't matter. For your protection and theirs, the courier generally never touches the baggage and is not personally liable for it. When you arrive, you hand an envelope containing the manifest and the claim check to the courier company's representatives. They take the baggage from the claim area and clear it through customs while you go off to play.

How to Become a Courier. Look up courier companies in the Yellow Pages under air courier service, courier service, delivery service, or freight forwarding. If your directory has no listings, visit the library and look in directories for the gateway cities listed above. Alternatively, contact a courier broker. However, if you arrange a flight through a broker, you may pay a registration fee to the broker, and the air fare may be slightly higher than if you book the flight directly.

When you've located the flight that goes when and where you want, it's time to ask the courier company or broker a few questions:

- Will I be a courier in both directions?
- What will my baggage allowance be?
- How long will I be allowed to stay?
- Will I need a visa?
- Are there any other restrictions?
- What is the cost of the ticket? Are there any extra costs I'll have to pay?
- How and when do I book a ticket?

An efficient way to find out about hundreds of opportunities is to join the International Association of Air Travel Couriers (IAATC). For $42 a year, you receive bimonthly *Shoestring Traveler* newsletters and the *Air Courier Bulletin* listing what's available. The IAATC provides a no-charge, fax-on-demand service to communicate last-minute opportunities and has a bulletin board that searches for the lowest courier and noncourier air fares. They'll even send a free audiocassette telling you how to become an air courier. For more information, call (407) 582-8320.

A monthly newsletter called *Travel Unlimited* (P.O. Box 1058, Allston, MA 02134; $5 for a single copy, $25 for an annual subscription) used to emphasize courier flights but has now broadened its interest to travel bargains in general.

Several books have been written on the subject, including the *Air Couriers Guide Book* (Owen Publications, Box 16845-A, St. Petersburg, Florida, 33733); *The Insider's Guide to Air Courier Bargains*, by Kelly Monaghan, $17.95 postpaid (Upper Access Publishing, P.O. Box 457, Hinesburg, VT 05461; or call 800-356-9315); and *The Courier Air Travel Handbook,* by Mark Field, $10.70 postpaid (Thunderbird Press, 5390-10 West Greenway Road, Suite 112, Glendale, AZ 85306; or call (800) 345-0096). Check the publication date because courier information is quickly outdated.

Flying courier won't fit the travel plans of all independent travelers, but it's a very economical way to explore the world, especially if you live in or near one of the major gateway cities.

Good Deals and Money-Saving Tips
- Check the ads in the travel sections of *The New York Times, The Washington Post,* the *Los Angeles Times,* and your local paper for *national airline specials.* These airlines often cut prices sharply to encourage travelers to visit. I recently flew from the United States to New Zealand on Air New Zealand for $650 round trip (or "return," as they say in N.Z.), instead of the usual $1,300. That ticket also allowed two additional stopovers (I chose Sydney and Rarotonga*). That's a deal to watch for.

- Ask a travel agent about *air-hotel package deals.* Special promotions offer air fare and several nights lodging for less than you might pay for regular air fare alone. Some packages are priced so low that they're worth it even if you don't stay in their hotel. These deals are common for Jamaica, Cancun, and major cities in Europe, but you may find some for more adventuresome destinations. Most of these packages are legitimate; only a few offer poorly located or maintained facilities. Ask for the names of previous travelers you may call for references.

Rarotonga. Largest of the 15 Cook Islands, Rarotonga is located 3,000 miles due south of Honolulu. It is inhabited by Polynesians who migrated there perhaps as long ago as 500 A.D., along with a sprinkling of New Zealanders who came along considerably later. Some feel you haven't lived until you've spent Saturday night dancing and drinking Leopard Beer in the Banana Court Bar.

- *Senior Airfare Coupons* are available to travelers age 62 and above. You buy a book of four or eight coupons. Each coupon costs from $130 to $150 and is good for a one-way flight anywhere in the contiguous 48 states (note: no international flights). Companions not over age 62 can buy coupons at a higher, but still discounted, fare. There is usually a 14-day advance reservation requirement, but it's possible to fly standby as well. Typically, you must use coupons within a year after purchase, although there's a refund on unused books. These coupons save the most money on long flights.

- Many airlines have *10 to 30 percent discounts for "seniors"* (generally age 62 and up, but sometimes as low as 50). Even bargain-hunting travelers fail to take advantage of this one. There are two reasons. Many of them don't know about it (and the airlines aren't going to mention it). Worse, many travelers who know about the discount so hate the idea of being considered a "senior" that they don't bring it up. Many hotels, including Sheratons, Holiday Inns, and Days Inns, offer 10 to 20 percent discounts to people as young as 50 or 55. National Car Rental gives a 30 percent discount to seniors. In some cases, these discounts are available only to AARP members. If you travel with a companion, the companion may get a 10 percent discount regardless of age. SAVE MONEY.

- You'll get a discount if you have an *International Student Identity Card* and use the network of travel agencies associated with the card. Produce the card overseas, ask for a discount, and you may get one.

- Time on your hands? Book yourself on a busy flight, one likely to be full. When you check in, tell the agent that if they need to bump someone, you're willing to be bumped. If the airline has *overbooked the flight* and you're bumped you may get a cash payment and/or a free flight any-where the airline flies.

- There are various other strategies for saving money on airline tickets, but they're a little complicated and airlines frown on them (not surpris-ing, since the idea is to defeat airline restrictions). If an airline catches a travel agency helping you with one of these, it may penalize the agency severely. Ask about:
  - phantom or *hidden city tickets*. Book a ticket to a cheap hub destination for less than the cost of a ticket to the intermediate, higher-priced stop where you really want to go. Since you get off before the destination shown on your ticket, you have to travel with carry-on luggage only.
  - *back-to-back tickets*. These avoid the requirement that you stay over a Saturday night to get the cheapest air fare. Buy two cheap tickets which include the Saturday night stay, the first from your

home to the destination and back, the second from the destination to your home and back. Use the first portion of each ticket to go and return. Either use the second portion of both tickets for another round trip (which usually must be within 30 days) or throw them away. The back-to-back strategy will SAVE MONEY whenever the cost of the cheapest ticket is less than half as much as the unrestricted (no Saturday night stay) ticket. Savings can be huge if you must fly on short notice.

- To get the cheapest fare you must ask for it. Ask again. Be absolutely clear that you want the least expensive fare and nothing else. Make sure the travel agent knows you are *flexible*. For example, can you

  - leave on any day within a period of several days?
  - stay at your destination over a Saturday night?
  - depart from a nearby airport rather than your hometown?
  - accept an intermediate stop or a change of planes?
  - accept an alternative destination? For example, you may save as much as 70 percent by flying into Louisville instead of Cincinnati, or Colorado Springs instead of Denver, or Toledo instead of Detroit, or Birmingham instead of Atlanta, among others. There is usually public or private transportation between airports.
  - fly during off-peak hours (especially overnight)?
  - fly during off-season (that is, other than June through September)?

  The more "yes" answers, the more likely you'll SAVE MONEY.

- Don't buy tickets on *weekends*. Airlines often raise ticket prices on Saturday and Sunday. If other carriers don't go along immediately, they lower prices on Monday.

- *Fare wars* often follow a major holiday. Be ready.

- Domestic coach-class *fares dip at three predictable times* of the year. Prices start down in March and hit a low from mid-May to mid-June. They rise from mid-June, then dip to a similar low about August 1. For the rest of the year, it's all uphill, except for a dip between Thanksgiving and mid-December.

- When you've tentatively selected an airline, dates, and route, review the *restrictions* carefully:

  - Are you permitted to make changes or cancel the ticket? If so, what is the charge? If not, be certain you're really ready to make the deal final.
  - Does the ticket permit you to add a stopover without charge?
  - Is there a minimum or maximum stay?

- Can you make the whole trip on one airline? If so, it may be cheaper than using several airlines (unless you are buying bucket shop segments abroad).
- Are you entitled to a discount (e.g., as a student or a senior)? If you take a domestic flight to connect with your international flight, remember to seek the best deal on the domestic flight as well.

- Watch the World Wide Web. Airlines are using silent auctions to fill last-minute vacancies at prices 16 to 25 percent off full-fare prices.

Saving Money When Booking Lodging

If you choose to make hotel reservations before leaving home and want to SAVE MONEY, here are some ideas:

- Use *hotel consolidators* for rates 25 to 70 percent off rack rates (the theoretical full price). Hotels Plus (800-235-0909) specializes in Great Britain and Europe but has some locations in Asia, Africa, and the Middle East. It represents everything from cottages to hotels and mansions. Room Exchange (800-846-7000) specializes in upscale hotels in the United States, Mexico, the Caribbean, and several European and Asian cities. The Hotel Reservations Network (800-964-6835) offers discounted rates of up to 50 percent for fairly expensive (up to four star) hotels, mostly in the United States but also in Paris and London. Luxury hotels seldom advertise specials because they don't want to antagonize their less-creative guests, but your travel agent should know about them. You'll beat the rack rate with these services, but you'll still be well above the prices charged by budget hotels. For hotels in the United States, try Accomodations Express (800-444-7666) or Room Finders USA (800-473-7829).

- *"Half-price" discount programs* sound good but (a) you may not be able to reserve a room with that kind of discount on the dates you want it (the same problem as trying to book a frequent flyer ticket), (b) the rate on which the discount is calculated (the rack rate) may be an inflated rate that almost no one actually pays, and (c) the programs have membership fees of $30 to $125.

  When you enroll, you receive a directory and an ID card and make your own reservations (preferably at least 30 days ahead of time). Since the program is designed to fill empty hotel rooms during slack periods, you probably won't get a room when the hotel expects to be able to rent it for a higher price.

  These companies tend to emphasize hotels in the United States, but some lists include hotels in Europe, Canada, Mexico, and the Caribbean, as well as a fair selection in Latin America. Half-price programs are not very active outside of developed countries.

The *Europe Hotel Directory* of Entertainment Publications (800-445-4137; $60 annual fee) seems to have the largest selection, including at least some choices for budget travelers. Their *Ultimate Hotel Directory* ($60) covers the rest of the world. Both include car rental and airline coupons. The International Travel Card (800-342-0558; $49 annual fee) is more useful in Asia and the South Pacific than its competitors. Others worth considering are Carte Royale (800-847-7002; $40 annual fee), and Privilege Card (800-236-9732; $50 annual fee).

- Several *hotel brokers* offer rates at about 30 to 60 percent off rack rate. Of those, Vacationland (800-245-0050) and Travel InterLink (800-477-7172) have the best selection in Asia. The problem with most hotel brokers, from the standpoint of adventurous travelers, is their concentration on a relatively few large cities.

- You may be able to obtain *"preferred" hotel rates* through your travel agent. A preferred rate is one negotiated with a hotel by a travel agency, consortium (e.g., Carlson Wagonlit, American Express, U.S. Travel), or travel club (e.g., International Airline Passengers Association). Even small travel agencies offer a preferred rate program if they have signed up with independent booking services such as Thor 24 or ABC. Discounts range between 10 and 40 percent, averaging about 20 percent. Most of the hotels that participate in preferred rate programs are midscale to expensive. Ask to see your travel agent's preferred rate directory to find hotels available where you want to go, then ask the agent to make the booking. Preferred discounts may be somewhat less than half-price and broker deals, but rooms should be available at any season.

  Ask if your travel agent can get you a preferred hotel rate.

  In evaluating these discount programs, remember that the rack rate may be fictional. The discount may sound large, but the result may be neither as good as you could negotiate on the spot nor anywhere close to the deal you could make with a smaller, independent hotel.

- When making a reservation, SAVE MONEY by asking for a discount on grounds of being a *member of a privileged category*, such as an employee of a specific corporation, a student, a travel writer, a frequent flyer, a senior, or a member of the government/military/clergy or some organization such as AAA, AARP, Encore, or anything else that seems remotely defensible. The hotel may ask for some identification, but a business card is usually sufficient to capture the corporate rate (which may be up to 20 percent off the rack rate).

- If you are a senior, say so. The minimum age for a *senior discount* varies from 50 to 65. In addition, almost a dozen large hotel chains have "clubs" for seniors with discounts clustered in the 10 to 25 percent range (though some go up to 50 percent). Membership in some is free; in others it's $10 to $50 a year. For $10, anyone age 50 or above may join AARP (202-434-2277) and take advantage of its discount arrangements with hotel chains.

- Ask about a hotel's *promotional discounts* for weekends, two-for-breakfast, summer season (July and August are bargain times in Europe), or whatever. Ask what discount they give for making a reservation 30 days in advance (it could be as much as 30 percent). See whether they have a package deal with an airline. Don't ask *whether* the hotel has such a discount; just ask for it. If the hotel clerk expects vacancies, which is often the case, he or she will work with you to find a way to encourage your presence. It may not be as good a deal as you could make in person, but you should get some break.

- Some travel agents sell *vouchers* for hotel rooms. Before starting your trip, you buy as many vouchers as you expect to need, then pay with them as you travel. The incentive is that you're supposed to receive significant discounts by using vouchers. In some cases you do; in others, you wind up paying even more than the rack rate. The hotel chain with the best voucher deals consistently seems to be Holiday Inn (discounts are between 10 and 20 percent), but its rates are still above those of some other chains and many good local hotels. Vouchers are good for travel agents and great for hotels, but not so good for travelers.

- Take advantage of special deals offered on the World Wide Web. Please refer to listings in Chapter 2.

By the way, if you can prove you made a reservation that a hotel doesn't honor, the custom is to give you a free night at a comparable hotel and transport you there. Act as though both you and the clerk take it for granted that that is the least they can do.

Saving Money on Adventures

Part of the exhilaration of travel is doing new things, unusual things, challenging things. In other words, having adventures. For the purposes of this section, I use "adventure" to mean experiences of short duration; part of a trip rather than its entirety. I'm thinking of rafting day-trips, diving, snorkeling, renting a bike, going up in a hot-air balloon, taking a safari, renting a boat or helicopter, and so on.

Assuming you want as many adventures as practical, and that cost is a consideration, let's discuss how to SAVE MONEY on adventures. We know that paying someone at home to make arrangements for you in some faraway place is more expensive than doing it yourself. But there's another cost that's less obvious. The service you can buy for $200 in Greece may be advertised at

$400 in the United States, so that's the base price—before the agent's commission is added on. The message here: SAVE MONEY by doing it yourself.

Here's an example. By arranging my own trip to Rwanda, I paid less than $350 to visit the mountain gorillas. This amount included round-trip air fare from Kenya to Rwanda, the park permit, food, lodging, and local transportation. If a U.S. travel agent had arranged a similar trip, the price could have exceeded $2,000. From home, I called the Kinigi Park Administrative Office in Rwanda (the telephone number was in the Lonely Planet *Africa* guidebook, but I could have gotten it from the embassy) and chose a date on which a permit was available to visit the gorillas. Next, I got a Rwandan visa, specifying the dates I wanted it to be effective. The Rwandan visa is unusual in that you must arrive in the country on the date your visa becomes effective. Because of the time constraints of the visa and the permit, I booked the Kenya to Rwanda flight while still in the United States to avoid any delays in Kenya. I waited until I arrived in Rwanda to arrange for local lodging and transportation. *Hakuna matata*—"no problems."

Another example. In Nairobi, you can sign up for a tent camping safari to Masai Mara, Lake Nakuru, Amboseli, and any of the other game parks, and pay about $40 per day for food, transportation, camping gear, cooks, guide—everything. The safari companies have offices on the main streets and their representatives roam the hotels seeking your business. Guidebooks mention recommended companies. It's worth a little shoe leather to visit several offices to compare destinations, services, prices, and personnel. To avoid this small effort, or for the comfort of certainty, many people book the trip at home and pay $200, $300, even $800 or more per person per day. For the extra money you receive an impressive brochure and stay in upscale accommodations that are considerably less authentic than a simple tent. Either way, the wild game is the same. Sign up for the safari in Kenya and save enough money to travel for an extra month—or bank a down payment for your next trip!

There are two ways to organize your adventure yourself. Do it from home, or do it when you get there. Either way, gather information before you leave. Guidebooks are good at identifying potential adventures and listing reputable operators (other sources of information are listed at the end of Chapter 2).

When you know what adventures appeal to you and have the names of several providers of services, you can contact them from home and you're also prepared to contact them as soon as you arrive.

Saving Money with a Rail Pass

Does a Rail Pass Make Sense for Your Trip?

Since the rail pass is most commonly used in Europe, let's look at the Eurailpass in its various versions. Train travel is fairly expensive in Europe, so a rail pass initially seems like a good investment. However, don't buy any pass without first doing the calculations necessary to see if it makes economic sense for your itinerary. For one thing, the basic Eurailpass may not save you any money unless you travel 1,200 to 1,500 miles within a two-week period—and that's a lot of traveling in Europe. If you travel on five days during that period, that's 240 to 300 miles a day. Another consideration is that a Eurailpass is a better value in northern Europe than in southern Europe since train tickets cost more in the north.

Ask a travel agent how much individual tickets would cost between your destinations or review the point-to-point fares in the Rail Europe brochure or the Rick Steves guide mentioned later in this chapter. Compare those costs with the cost of various rail passes.

If a rail pass makes sense, the next step is to select the one that works best for you. Here are the choices.

The Eurailpass

Of the several rail passes available for use in Europe, the most well known are the various versions of the Eurailpass. This pass, valid in 17 countries, can also be used on ferries from Sweden to Finland, Ireland to France, and Italy to Greece. It is accepted for boats on the Rhine and Danube and on buses in Ireland.

A basic Eurailpass is good for unlimited travel during periods ranging from 15 days to three months. If you are 26 or older on your first travel date, your rail pass must be for first-class space (which costs 50 percent more than second class). If you are under 26, you can buy either first or second class.

Other Versions. The Eurail *Flexipass* works best for people who don't plan to travel frequently. If you can concentrate your travel into a limited number of days, a Flexipass will SAVE MONEY over an unlimited pass. Travel is first class and the pass is valid for travel on a certain number of days within a two-month period.

Anyone under age 26 on the first date of travel may buy a Eurail *Youthpass*, which differs from the regular pass in that it costs less and you travel second class, as do most Europeans.

The Eurail *Youth Flexipass* permits travel on any ten or fifteen days within a two-month period.

The Eurail *Saverpass* is designed for two to five people traveling together. The *Saver Flexipass* allows ten to fifteen days travel within two months. I've seen off-season Saverpass specials in which one person pays full price and all others in the group pay only 50 percent. There's a deal!

To add to the confusion, there is a Eurail *Drive Pass* that combines first-class train travel (four days) with a rental car (three days) within a twenty-one-day period.

The Europass

If those weren't enough choices, there's the Europass, which serves people who plan to take short trips to fewer places than covered by the 17-country Eurail passes. The basic Europass allows you five day's travel in up to five countries (France, Germany, Italy, Spain, and Switzerland). If it takes adding one or more from among Portugal, Belgium, Luxembourg, Greece, Hungary, or Austria to make you happy, you can do that for an additional fee. To give you an idea of prices, the Europass for three countries costs around $325 per person for five days of travel within a two-month period. Extra days cost about $45 each. Europass Youth tickets for persons under 26 cost $210 (plus $29 for each day beyond five). When a traveler buys a first-class Europass, one partner on the same trip can buy an identical Europass for half-price. This deal does not apply to youth Europasses.

The Europass will be 15 to 20 percent more economical than the Eurailpass if your travels will be limited to the Europass countries (rather than the 17 covered by the Eurailpass). In addition, the Europass provides somewhat more flexibility. However, keep two principles in mind. First, if your itinerary is flexible, you may be better off with the Eurailpass so you can travel more widely if you choose. Second, the more you travel by train, the more your savings grow over buying point-to-point tickets.

Country/Regional Passes

If you'll be traveling in only one area, a country or regional pass is a better buy than a Eurailpass. Choices include Austrian Rabbit Card, Benelux Tourrail, BritFrance Rail, Czech Flexipass, European East Pass, Finnrail, Freedom of Scotland Travelpass, Greek Railpass, Hungarian Flexipass, Italian Railpass, Polrailpass, Portuguese Flexipass, Russian Flexipass, Scanrail (extra discounts for persons over age 55), Spanish Flexipass, and the Swiss Pass, among others.

VIA Canrailpass

There are rail passes in many non-European countries, but the *VIA Canrailpass* stands out. It permits 12 days of multistop travel from Nova Scotia to British Columbia within a 30-day period. Between June and September, the price is just over $400. The rest of the time, it's about $300. The price is discounted for students (24 and under) and seniors (60 and over). It even throws in a few bells and whistles such as a free long-distance calling card worth $15, the right to purchase extra travel days separately, and cheap rental car options.

Resources

My choice as the best source for European rail pass information is Rick Steves' *Back Door Guide to European Railpasses* (call 206-771-8303 for a free copy). Match your itinerary with the guide's map, which shows individual fares among European cities, and then determine whether a rail pass is a good deal for your trip. If you buy a rail pass from Steves, there is no handling fee and you receive a video, *How to Get the Most Out of your Railpass*, a free guidebook, and comments on your itinerary. Add a staff that understands the priorities of budget travelers and you have a tough combination to beat.

Call Rail Europe (800-438-7245) for its *Traveler's Guide, Eurail Sales Information* and the excellent brochure *On Track*, which lists current train schedules and fare information. The Council on International Educational Exchange (205 East 42nd Street, New York, NY 10017) is another sound resource for information. You might also consult the following:

- *Traveling Europe's Trains*, Jay Brunhouse. Pelican.
- *Thomas Cook's On the Rails around Europe*. Thomas Cook.
- *Europe by Eurail*, George and LaVerne Ferguson. Globe Pequot.
- *Eurail Guide*. Houghton Mifflin.
- *Let's Go Europe*
- *Europe through the Back Door*
- *Europe by Train*, Katie Wood and George MacDonald. Harper Perennial.

European railway schedules and other information are available on CompuServe (access GO RAILWAY).

Companies in the United States that represent European railroads include Rail Europe (800-438-7145); DER (800-337-8724); CIT (800-248-7245); and BritRail International (800-677-8585). They can also make reservations for the Eurostar Chunnel service, InterCity and EuroCity routes, and the high-speed trains in France and Germany.

A last word on rail passes. It's a lot of fun to be able to hop aboard the train any time you want (more on how to do that in Chapter 16), but it takes time and a bit of study to figure out if a rail pass will SAVE MONEY. The outline above gives you a good foundation, and more information is readily available from the sources I've listed.

Saving Money with a Youth Identity Card

The International Identity Card, issued by the Council on International Education Exchange (CIEE), will help you SAVE MONEY abroad. It's available for $18 by mail from CIEE, ID Department, 205 East 42nd Street, New York, NY 10017; or buy it for less on any of more than 400 college campuses.

Eligibility

To be eligible for the student card, you must (a) demonstrate enrollment in a study program leading to a degree at an accredited school during the year of application, and (b) be at least 12 years old and not over 25. To be eligible for the GO-25 card, which costs $18, you need not be a student but must be under 26. Full-time teachers are eligible regardless of age.

Benefits of the Card

The CIEE card entitles holders to discounts on transportation through Council Travel (800-743-1823), a subsidiary of CIEE. Council Travel, with dozens of offices located on or near college campuses, also offers guidebooks and information on budget travel. With the card, you receive the *International Student Travel Guide,* which contains information on student discounts in 65 countries. The card also entitles you to discounts on selected local transportation abroad (e.g., 35 percent off Italian train fares), as well as on some entrance fees and tickets to events. Most other ID cards are worthless overseas as far as entitling you to discounts.

The CIEE card provides insurance to help pay the expenses of accidents and injuries (up to $3,000), sickness (up to $100 per day for inpatient confinement for a maximum of 60 days), and emergency medical evacuation (up to $10,000). Card holders have access to a toll-free hotline to ask for help with a medical, financial, or legal emergency while abroad.

If all that isn't enough, CIEE sells many useful travel publications, including *Work, Study, Travel Abroad* and *Volunteer.*

Even if you don't have the CIEE card, or any card at all, ask whether there's a student discount before handing over your money.

HOW TO PREPARE A RELIABLE BUDGET

Most people are about as fond of figuring budgets as they are of figuring their taxes. As with taxes, you may pay a penalty if you fail to learn how to construct a reliable budget. Until you know how, you're flying blind, likely to run out of money in the middle of your trip. With a sound budget, you can plan well and stretch your trip to the limit. In other words, budgeting is a liberating experience.

Some travelers initially think in terms of a bare-bones trip, spending as little as they can. What that requires is some hitchhiking, cooking a number of your own meals, eating on the margins of nutrition and hygiene, living occasionally in barely habitable accommodations, and foregoing most treats. Sound like fun? Aren't your time, health, and safety worth a lot more to you than a few rupees? After all, one reason to travel is pleasure. If you make informed choices, bargain, do without a private bathroom some of the time, and skip overpriced tourist frills, you can easily have a great trip within a reasonably tight budget.

One thing is certain: the amount of money you have available to spend is a major factor in choosing destinations. Think New York City is expensive? It ranked only 56th on a list of the world's most expensive cities. Heading the list: Tokyo (more than twice as expensive as New York City), Osaka, Zurich, Geneva, Oslo, Copenhagen, Vienna, Moscow, Helsinki, and Libreville (Gabon). Other high-priced destinations: Singapore, London,

Berlin, Rome, and Paris. One hundred dollars admits you and a friend to an opera in Sydney, pays for a couple of hours on a Venetian gondola, or just gets you through the door of a geisha show in Tokyo. Some other examples: Gas costs $4.54 in Oslo, $0.40 in Caracas. A fast food meal that costs $3.60 in Mexico City costs $7.60 in Tokyo and $13 in Oslo. A haircut is $7 in Mexico City, $66 in Tokyo.

Europe is no longer the inexpensive paradise it was in the 1960s. Traveling very economically in one of the least expensive countries, such as Portugal, you might scrape by for around $20 a day (including lodging, food, and public transportation). Budgeting carefully, expect to spend $25 to $50 a day in less expensive countries and around $75 in the higher-cost countries. With a few exceptions, it's easy to live reasonably for $25 to $30 a day in the rest of the world.

Constructing the Budget

Put together a budget by listing all the *types* of things you expect to spend money on, then plug in *times* and local *cost* estimates. With a little practice and decent information to work from, there's nothing to it.

Let's practice by assuming certain expenses for a hypothetical 30-day trip in Asia, departing from San Francisco:

1. *Predeparture expenses.* These include the cost of visas, film and other photographic equipment, medical protection (e.g., shots, prescription medicines, over-the-counter medicines), guidebooks, information-seeking long-distance calls, clothing, and other gear. Let's estimate predeparture expenses for this trip at $350.

2. *Air fare.* To estimate air fare, first decide whether to buy all tickets at home or to take advantage of lower prices in bucket shops along the way. For a first trip, we'll budget the higher figure, as if you were using tickets purchased at home (you'll get a bonus refund if you buy cheaper air tickets abroad). Assume a net cost for air fare (getting to Asia, traveling around, and returning home) of $1,000.

3. *Other types of transportation.* This includes trains, local buses, taxis, and other non-air transport. Your itinerary shows the segments for which you'll be buying tickets and guidebooks give you a reasonable idea of the costs. Estimate $100.

4. *Lodging and meal expenses.* Since bed and board consume a large part of your budget, it's fortunate they're costs you can control. The best cost estimates come from current guidebooks and from people who've recently returned from your destinations. Of course, before you're actually there, it's hard to know exactly how much you have to spend to buy the type of meals and lodging that make you happy. Ten dollars

will rent a charming room in Thailand while a $90 room in Paris may be a dump. Nevertheless, since you have to make an estimate, here's the process:

Regarding lodging: For our 30-day trip, subtract the number of days when you'll pay no separate charge for lodging, such as when you'll be trekking or on an overnight plane or train. Let's say there are eight of those days, leaving twenty-two days. An average cost of $15 per day (this is Asia) times 22 gives you $330. Adjust that upward by 15 percent to cover price escalation and an occasional splurge and budget $380 for lodging.

Regarding meals: An average cost of $12 per day for meals times 30 gives you $360. Adjust that upward 15 percent and budget $415. If that seems like a lot, compare it with what you'd spend in 30 days at home.

5. *Special experiences.* If you don't plan for them, paying for special experiences can wreck your budget. I'm referring to things like the cost of a safari, scuba diving, a helicopter flight over the Franz Josef Glacier,[*] sailing along the fjordland coast of Norway, trekking among the hill tribe villages in Thailand,[†] climbing Mount Kilimanjaro, or chartering a plane into the Okavango Delta.[§] Most of these opportunities will surface during your research but you won't recognize some as "musts" until you get there. Include as many as you can in your budget.

How much do these special experiences cost? Check guidebooks, call the embassy, ask a knowledgeable travel agent, ask someone who's been there recently. If you can't turn up anything, take a guess. I suggest three rules of thumb: (a) special experiences in *developed* countries cost more than you might expect; (b) if modern technology is involved, such as a helicopter, they'll be fairly expensive even in a Third World country; and (c) prices quoted by a travel agent for special experiences will almost certainly be higher than you'll pay if you make your own arrangements abroad.

For our hypothetical trip, assume four days of scuba diving off the coast of Indonesia and a four-day trek in Thailand with a locally hired guide. Estimate $350.

---

[*] *Franz Josef Glacier.* Located on the west coast of the South Island of New Zealand, this glacier was named for the Austrian emperor. Hike alongside the glacier, climb up its face, fly over it, or even land on it.

[†] *Hill tribe villages.* Located in northern Thailand, these villages are home to several groups of people who immigrated from Burma and Cambodia and have retained their distinctive dress, language, and culture.

[§] *Okavango Delta.* Located in northern Botswana, this network of waterways and islands offers some of the most unspoiled game viewing in all of Africa.

6. *Miscellaneous.* This category includes odds and ends: clothing you buy under way, souvenirs you can't live without, toiletries, beverages, books, postcards, postage, and so on. Your estimate here is a matter of personal preference and available money. Whatever your estimate, add 25 percent. For this hypothetical trip, budget $180.

If you want to fine tune your budget, find out whether your own currency has grown significantly stronger or weaker since the information you're relying on was published. Banks and stockbrokers have this information. For current exchange rates, check the Currency Trading table in the third section of *The Wall Street Journal.* In recent years the weakness of the dollar has made Third World countries more attractive when contrasted with Europe.

To be even more conservative, add up all the categories and add 15 percent to the total to cover surprises and spontaneous splurges.

If the grand total is more money than you have, don't skip a beat. The purpose of your estimated budget is to simulate reality ahead of time to avoid surprises. Your estimate will put you on notice that you have to tighten your budget or redesign the trip a little. The estimates I've used above are relatively generous. Many travelers could easily make the same trip for 30 percent less.

In summary, avoid an absolutely bare bones budget if you can. Leave room for decent food and shelter, for small pleasures, treats, and special experiences. SAVE MONEY on big ticket items such as airfare and design lifelong memories into your budget.

Checklist: Budget

Predeparture Expenses
$_____passport, visas, and photos
$_____international student ID card
$_____guidebooks
$_____hostel membership
$_____camera, film, filters, other photo equipment
$_____luggage, daypack
$_____new clothes
$_____travel insurance
$_____gear (binoculars, money belt, etc.)
$_____health care (medicine and shots)
$_____toiletries
$_____reading material

Transportation
$_____air fares
$_____other (trains, buses, etc.)

Meals and Lodging
$_____en route
$_____daily lodging
$_____daily meals

Special Experiences
$_____safaris, scuba diving, glacier climbing, etc.
$_____entertainment (sightseeing, tours, etc.)

Miscellaneous
$_____souvenirs, gifts, tips, laundry, etc.

HOW TO MANAGE MONEY SUCCESSFULLY

In figuring out the cost of a trip as we did above, you learn how much money you'll spend before you leave and how much to take with you. Knowing that, you have choices to make about the *form* in which you take funds with you. Your choices include currency, personal check, travelers check, credit card, ATM card, and debit card.

Currency

Not so long ago, explorers and travelers carried their funds in truly hard currency; that is, in the form of precious metals or minerals. Everyone was relieved, although some were skeptical, when currency came along. Even though currency is convenient, it's still bulky, vulnerable to loss, and uninsurable. Given the options available today, it would be a major mistake to carry all the money you need in the form of currency. So why not forget it altogether and rely on travelers checks or one of the other substitutes? There are several good reasons and I'll touch on them in the sections that follow.

How Much and Which Currency?

I generally take currency equal to 10 to 25 percent of my estimated expenditures. For the hypothetical trip above, that would be between $250 and $700.

Some guidebooks recommend carrying more than one readily convertible currency, but I've never found that necessary. The few currencies accepted around the world for conversion into local money are the U.S. dollar, the German mark, the British pound, the Japanese yen, and, to a lesser extent, the Canadian dollar, French franc, and Swiss franc. Hotels, restaurants, and shops usually won't accept foreign currencies other than these. The U.S. dollar is the most widely accepted currency around the world, including on the black market.

Although carrying one dollar bills for gifts or tips makes sense, carrying change is pointless. Your coins are without value in most other countries. Tip someone with a quarter and it becomes worthless because the local bank won't give him anything for it unless he accumulates quite a few of them. Even then, the exchange rate is poor since banks don't want to transport heavy, bulky foreign coins (any more than you should).

You may want to carry a few personal checks since they're sometimes accepted in large cities or you may need them to get cash from AmEx. However, don't rely on cashing them along the way to finance your trip.

Travelers checks

Travelers checks are a safe way to transport money. They don't take up much room and you're protected in case of theft or loss. So why not take travelers checks and forget everything else? There are several good reasons:

- There may be nowhere to exchange a traveler's check for cash at the moment you need to pay for something (such as on a weekend when banks are closed). Further, many banks in less developed countries won't accept travelers checks at all. Sad to say, some merchants won't either. They've been burned by accepting checks that travelers then fraudulently reported as lost or stolen to get replacements. If the issuer invalidates the check before the merchant can redeem it, the merchant bears the loss.

- You may pay a fee when you buy travelers checks and again when you exchange them for local currency.

- You may get a less favorable exchange rate for travelers checks than for cash, although this is reversed where money exchange offices prefer to accept travelers checks so they don't have to guard stacks of hard currency.

- Travelers checks aren't accepted on the black market, so without cash you lose the opportunity for creative financing.

The Fee

Most issuers of travelers checks will try to charge a fee, usually 1 percent of the amount you want to purchase. Even if they imply that a fee is automatic, negotiate and you will SAVE MONEY. When buying checks from a bank, point out how long you've been a customer, promise to leave your account with them for a while, or persuade them you're on your way to becoming a tycoon who will do business with, or maybe even buy, their bank. Get that fee dropped. If you belong to an organization that dispenses travelers checks (such as the American Automobile Association), you won't be asked to pay a fee for converting your cash into travelers checks.

You can negotiate the fee for issuing traveler's checks.

Which Brands and What Denominations?

Carry only widely accepted brands of travelers checks such as AmEx, Thomas Cook, Citicorp, Barclays Bank, Visa, and BankAmerica. Some people recommend buying at least some travelers checks in foreign currency so you won't be stung by an unfavorable spread when you cash them overseas. I've never understood that since you're stung on the rate when you purchase them here.

If you want foreign currency travelers checks and your bank can't issue them, try AmEx, Thomas Cook (your travel agent can initiate the transaction online), or Ruesch International (800-424-2923). Using foreign currency checks saves you money when you convert to cash overseas, but watch the exchange rate when you buy them here.

In deciding what denominations of travelers checks to carry, the issue is bulk versus flexibility. Carrying packs of $10 checks gives you the greatest flexibility but chokes your money belt. If you take only $100 checks, you run the risk of being stuck with more local currency than you want as you're about to leave a country. I carry mostly $20s, a few $50s, and only enough $100s to pay for airline tickets and special events. If you use AmEx, you can leave home with some $500 checks and have them reissued in smaller denominations abroad. To minimize bulk, use a credit card to buy more checks as you travel.

What to Do in Case of Loss or Theft

The issuers of travelers checks promise they'll replace them if lost or stolen. And so they do, but you can make the process easier by knowing and following the rules. Sign travelers checks when you get them and sign only once. *Never* countersign a traveler's check until you're in front of the person accepting it. Most of them pay little attention, but if you draw one who does, your check won't be accepted if it's already countersigned. Further, if a check you've reported missing shows up bearing both your signature and counter-signature, you'll have some explaining to do.

When you purchase the checks ask how the replacement process works, request a booklet listing local representatives where you will be traveling, and get a telephone hotline number.

When you cash a traveler's check, record the number, amount, date, and place of the transaction. If you don't keep track, a clever thief could steal a few checks and you wouldn't discover it immediately. It's to his advantage for you to be long gone before you realize there's been a theft. You might even lose some checks yourself and fail to report them for replacement. Review your remaining checks once in a while to ensure that none are missing. If some are, you have to figure out whether you simply failed to record a transaction or they were lost or stolen.

To report a lost or stolen traveler's check abroad, contact the nearest office of the issuer. If you don't have the booklet with you, look up the number in a local telephone directory (under "travelers checks," "banks," or "travel agents") or ask a local merchant or bank that accepts the checks. If you have the original receipt, or a record of the check numbers and denominations purchased, as well as those that were lost or stolen, you can expect quick replacement. Without this information, expect to wait while it's obtained. You may only get partial replacement until enough time has passed for the issuer to be sure exactly which checks are missing.

Take the receipts on the trip but *keep them separate* from the checks. That sounds obvious, but I mention it because I've heard a couple of sad stories from people who lost both their checks and receipts at the same time. I also give a copy of the receipts to my travel partner and to someone at home. That's easier than steaming in Kuala Lumpur for a few days waiting for funds to arrive.

Credit Cards

What about credit cards? Can you forget travelers checks and just take plastic? Even though credit cards are accepted in Kathmandu, and you'll find ATM machines on street corners in Marrakesh, the answer still depends on where you are going. In many of the most fascinating parts of the world, credit cards are still unrecognized. And even if cards are accepted, you may not want to patronize the hotel or restaurant that will accept payment by charge card, especially when traveling on a modest budget. Still, in recent years the trend has been to rely on credit cards as the primary source of payment, at least where you can pay for almost everything with plastic, transforming travelers checks into a back-up source of payment.

> Back up your credit cards with alternate sources of funds.

The credit card, recognized and accepted in many far-flung places, has become an increasingly important travel tool. In a growing number of countries, including most of Europe, many expenses can be charged on Visa, MasterCard, American Express, and, to a lesser extent, Diner's Club and Discover. In fact, it may make sense to put everything you can on your credit card if you can do so without changing the nature of your trip (e.g., eating or staying in more expensive places than you would otherwise have chosen). And of course, if you pay off the balance as soon as you return. Since even the most experienced traveler can't calculate precisely the amount of money needed for a long trip, credit cards provide a cushion. However, even if credit cards are widely accepted at your destinations, back them up with an alternative source of funds.

Credit Card Benefits

Paying with a credit card has quite a few benefits. For example, you

- reduce the amount of cash you carry
- benefit from certain protections included in the terms of the credit card
- avoid some of the spread and commission charged when converting cash or travelers checks into local currency (but know *exactly* what your credit card charges for issuing cash)
- benefit from the exchange rate you get when using a credit card (the international corporate rate is more favorable to you than the rate you get from a local bank or currency dealer)
- have some protection should there be a problem with the purchase
- possibly earn frequent flyer mileage

More Benefits of Credit Cards

There's more. Credit card services go far beyond simply extending credit. As an example, I'll review some of the services of the lowest-fee American Express card (to confirm the current range of AmEx services, call 800-221-7282 for a copy of the *AmEx Traveler's Companion*).

1. *Cash.* Suppose you decide on a side trip to Irian Jaya,* or you've taken a few extra scuba dives or bungee jumps, or your money belt disappears from a shelf in the bathroom. In short, you need more money. What to do? Use your credit card to get a *cash advance.* Take your AmEx card to an overseas AmEx office or one of the almost 100,000 AmEx cash dispensing machines around the world. We'll discuss using a bank card in an automatic teller machine (ATM) a few pages later.

With an AmEx card, enroll in advance in the Express Cash program and get a personal identification number by calling (800) CASH NOW. Thereafter, you can withdraw up to $1,000 every seven days. There's a 2 percent fee per transaction (minimum fee, $2.50; maximum fee, $10). Express Cash also enables you to obtain travelers checks from American Express Dispensers and selected AmEx Travel Services offices.

2. *Check cashing.* With an AmEx card, you can cash your personal check at AmEx Travel Service Offices in more than 120 countries. You're limited to a maximum of $1,000 (up to $200 in cash, the balance in travelers checks) every 21 days. There's no fee for cashing a check other than a charge for the portion issued in travelers checks.

3. *Money transfer.* Using an AmEx Moneygram, someone at home can transfer up to $10,000 to you while you're traveling in any of 60 countries. Once you arrange the transaction, transfer takes only about ten minutes. You pick up the funds, usually in travelers checks, at an AmEx Travel Service Office. The catch is that fees are high. To send $10,000 by Moneygram, the sender would pay a 3½ percent fee; for $1000, the fee is 7 percent; for $100, the fee is 25 percent.

4. *Mail pick-up.* For card holders, the network of overseas AmEx offices will accept and hold mail for arrival. More on the mechanics of receiving mail in Chapter 20.

5. *Insurance benefits.* AmEx and other credit cards have certain no-extra-charge insurance benefits associated with use of the cards. AmEx provides $100,000 in accidental death and dismemberment coverage when you travel in a common carrier and have charged the tickets on your AmEx card. Benefits also include collision damage and theft insurance coverage for a rental car (up to a maximum of 15 days). This coverage usually applies when you decline the insurance option offered by the car rental company *and* charge the rental cost on your card. This useful benefit may permit you to avoid the exorbitant fees for collision damage and theft insurance that rental car companies attempt to charge. I say *may* because some car rental companies will

---

* *Irian Jaya.* Part of Indonesia, Irian Jaya shares an island with the country of Papua New Guinea.

not accept credit card policy coverage. However, credit card coverage is intended to be effective overseas while the insurance policy on your domestic vehicle is not. AmEx excludes some countries as well as some vehicles (such as Jeeps and RVs) and loss of luggage. Read the fine print.

It has become common practice for a rental car company to take an imprint of a credit card as security against possible uninsured damage to its rental car. They may then put a "hold" on part of the credit line you have available, meaning you no longer have access to that amount of credit. If that would be a problem, be certain you understand exactly what the rental car company intends to do and make your plans accordingly. Otherwise, you may be surprised at an inconvenient moment. See further discussion of rental car insurance in Chapter 16.

Purchases made with the AmEx card are covered for 90 days against theft and accidental damage up to $1,000, but only above other applicable insurance you have. This coverage includes shipment of items from overseas but does not include items stolen from a car. The basic AmEx card provides reimbursement up to $200 for expenses caused by delayed luggage and up to $500 in excess of the airline's liability if your checked bag is lost or damaged.

6. *Legal and medical assistance.* Card holders can call the AmEx Global Assist Hotline (202-554-2639) collect from overseas for the recommendation of a doctor or help in locating an English-speaking lawyer. Global Assist will keep your family and colleagues informed about your situation and assist in transferring bail payment. For information about Global Assist, call (800) 554-AMEX in the United States.

If your credit card doesn't provide legal/medical assistance, call the nearest consulate or embassy for the same information. Embassy staff will send messages home, file a protest if you are being mistreated, and receive money sent to you from home. They won't give you legal advice and usually can't get you out of jail. A pamphlet that deals well with these issues is *A Safe Trip Abroad* (send $1 to the Consumer Information Center, Department 154 X, Pueblo, CO 81009).

7. *Other benefits.* AmEx provides information on passport and visa require-ments, immunizations, and weather forecasts. It can also tell you how to replace lost documents and locate lost luggage. AmEx and some of the other cards offer free telephone translation services and will help you find a local interpreter, at your expense, if you need one. Also, check out the AmEx Geography Hotline at (800) 395-GLOBE.

If an AmEx card is lost, stolen, or destroyed, report it to the nearest AmEx Travel Service Office (which is easier if you're carrying the appropriate ad-dress pages from the AmEx Traveler's Companion directory). While abroad, report a loss by calling (919) 333-3211 collect. If you know your credit card number when reporting a loss, you may obtain an emergency replacement card within a day. However, since the emergency replacement card doesn't have a magnetic strip, you can't use it to get cash from an Express Cash machine.

Terms of the American Express card require that all charges be paid each month, so you might want to arrange to have this done at home. Otherwise, keep track of charges and send a check yourself. Similarly, if overseas charges, including possible purchase of airline tickets, approach the limit of a bank card, ask someone at home to make the minimum monthly payments needed to keep you below the limit, as well as to meet your card's minimum monthly payment requirement. The laws of some countries consider it fraud when a credit card holder makes a purchase that exceeds the card limit.

A final word on AmEx. If you travel frequently and/or in first or business class, the platinum card provides benefits that far outweigh its $300 annual fee.

I've used the American Express card as an example because it has an extensive overseas network and very useful services. However, the AmEx card is more expensive and more difficult to obtain than bank cards. Some vendors will not accept AmEx because charges to them are so high. MasterCard, Visa, Discover, and Diner's Club now offer many of the same services, such as (a) cash advances, (b) "extended protection," meaning double the manufacturer's warranty on products you purchase, (c) "pur-chase security," meaning that the issuer will replace, repair, or reimburse you (usually up to $500) for eligible items of personal property in the event of theft, fire, vandalism, weather, and so on (when bought with the credit card and claimed within 90 days), and (d) rental car collision and damage insurance.

If you'll be traveling with a credit card from an issuer other than AmEx, familiarize yourself with its features. For an outline of these features for Visa, call (800) 847-2911 (outside the United States, call 410-581-9994 collect). For Mastercard, call (800) 622-7747 (outside the United States, call 303-278-8000 collect).

Old meets new—
banker at overseas
ATM. Tangier,
Morocco.

Credit Card Tips

– If you will be away for a while, you may want to arrange for payments to be made on your credit card charges. The goals are to avoid a late charge for failure to pay the "minimum amount due," to avoid high interest charges, and to keep sufficient credit available as you travel on.

One option is to get your bank to debit you acccount when any credit card bills are presented by a friend you trust. Another way is to send one or more postdated checks to your credit card issuer. These checks can be made out to cover your projected spending or to cover the estimated minimum payment required. Most efficient is to sign a form from the credit card issuer that authorizes it to withdraw electronically from your money market fund or bank account. One way to find the best solution is to ask the issuer of the credit card for advice.

– When using a credit card, (a) read the entries carefully before signing the receipt and keep your copy to compare with the charge that later appears (if you can't prove that the figures were altered or incorrect, the credit card issuer probably will demand payment), (b) watch that a merchant doesn't slip two sets of forms into the handpress, and (c) take the carbon or watch it being destroyed. If your credit card disappears, you may be liable for only up to $50 as long as you report the loss at once. Any merchant who accepts the card can help you report its loss.

— Before using a credit card to get cash (especially from a human instead of an ATM), be sure you understand the fee. It can be high.

— Using a credit card does *not* free you from paying for an item if you are dissatisfied with it, if the goods turn out to be worth less than you thought, or the vendor ships you the wrong item. You do, however, have a right to complain to the credit card issuer and withhold payment while your claim is investigated. However, you must file your complaint within the time limit stated by the issuer of the card, usually 30 or 60 days. Moreover, when goods are defective the credit card usually provides protection only to a person who purchased the item *in their home state or within 100 miles of home.* In other words, they aren't required to investigate claims with respect to items you bought abroad. Although many issuers make at least an attempt to investigate the dispute, the facts are often impossible to determine so they rule against the debtor (the card holder). Laws abroad are usually tougher on the consumer than in the United States.

— If you're dissatisfied with the way American Express handled a dispute, you may contact the Federal Trade Commission (202-326-2222). In the case of Visa or MasterCard, contact the agency that regulates the issuer of the card. Order "Using Credit and Charge Cards Overseas," from Superintendent of Documents, Consumer Info Center, Dept. 365, Pueblo, CO 81009 (the cost is $.50).

— If you use a credit card to help finance your trip, *carry more than one card.* Don't let a technological glitch or plastic-eating machine bring your trip to a halt. Anticipate losing a card and have cash or travelers checks ready as back-up.

To sum up, whether a credit card should be a central source of finance or merely a potentially useful supplement depends on your budget and itinerary.

ATM Cash Cards

Automatic teller machines are eagerly waiting to put cash in your hand in many corners of the world, at least if you whisper your PIN in their ears. While the ATM card is reducing the need for traveler's checks, it should not become a crutch. The overseas ATM may have instructions you can't decipher, *it may not accept your card,* or it may be out of money. Or you may not be able to find one when you need it. By the way, if you plan to use ATM machines, carry a back-up card.

What You Need to Know:

- Exact locations of ATMs where you'll be traveling. The Cirrus (Master Card) and Plus (Visa) systems claim more than 250,000 locations each in almost 90 countries. Call (800) 999-5136 for a copy of MasterCard's *Shopping with Your ATM Card*. Call (800) 424-7787 for the Cirrus worldwide ATM locator service or ask your local bank for a Cirrus Location Directory. Call (800) VISA-911 to order the Visa Plus *International ATM Locator Guide* (check it out on the Internet at www.visa.com/visa/). From abroad, call (410) 581-9994 collect for Visa ATM machines.

- Whether your PIN is valid abroad. Foreign ATMs accept only numbers, not letters, and some require six numbers. Check with your bank.

- Whether overseas ATMs are open 24 hours a day (the fact that they usually don't sleep is a major benefit).

- Whether there is a daily limit on how much you can withdraw.

- What fees are charged for each transaction. Some cards (e.g. USAA) have no ATM fees; others do.

An ATM withdrawal will SAVE MONEY because it clears through your bank at the commercial rate of exchange, which is 3 to 5 percent better than the tourist rate you'd get at a local bank. There should be no commission nor, since you are drawing out your own money, will you pay interest. However, your home bank probably charges a transaction fee of $2 or $3 so it's worth asking. On balance, an ATM has become the most efficient source of cash in many countries.

Debit Cards

Visa is testing TravelMoney, a prepaid travel card similar to a debit card. You deposit a certain amount in advance with a Visa issuer and then use the card to withdraw cash from banks or ATMs until your deposit is tapped out. There probably will be no transaction fee and you won't be charged interest on withdrawals. You may be charged $1 if you use this card in an ATM but nothing if you use it in a bank. There's a fee for the card and, of course, you earn no interest on your deposited funds.

The European Union is now testing a debit card that permits disbursal of cash in several different European currencies. Machines are already in use in which a traveler can insert one currency, say dollars, and receive another, say marks. However, rates of exchange are typically below market. Nevertheless, diminishing national barriers and the spread of microchips are relieving monetary headaches for travelers.

Receiving Money Overseas

Suppose you're on the road and decide it's time for refueling from home. How do you get money from there to where you are? Here are some alternatives:

- Have someone send you a check payable in a foreign currency, say for 35 English pounds, from a U.S. bank. The typical bank will charge a fee of somewhere between $7.50 (Citibank) and $35 (Chase Manhattan), then it may charge you another $25 to wire the draft. That's quite a bit to pay just for getting less than $60 to England.

- Ask someone to buy a money order from, or take a bank money order to, Western Union who will then wire it to an overseas bank. The fees can be quite high. Furthermore, some banks abroad will insist on giving you your own money, which they received in hard currency, in local currency which may have no value beyond the border.

- Ask someone to have a travelers check issued in foreign currency (even if there's no fee for this, keep an eye on the exchange rate), fill in the payee, sign it, and send it to you overseas (perhaps by one of the express mail services such as Federal Express).

- Reusch International, based in Washington, DC, offers an economical solution. Call (800) 424-2923 and ask for the International Division. When you specify the foreign currency and the amount you need, they'll tell you the rate of exchange and the U.S. dollar equivalent. For $2, they'll mail you a bank draft payable in the foreign funds or, for $5, they'll mail that draft to someone overseas (or wire it for $15). If the exchange rate is right, that's the best deal in town.

Exchanging Your Money

Before we discuss where and how, let's discuss situations when you're better off not exchanging money for foreign currency. The first is where you have more bargaining power when you pay in U.S. dollars. Obviously, you SAVE MONEY then by using dollars. This situation is not uncommon in Third World countries. The second is where paying in U.S. dollars would cause you to pay a premium. I think of this situation as "dollar pricing." That's what occurs when the rate a vendor, let's say a hotel, quotes is much higher in dollars than it is in local currency. The two-tier pricing enables them to extract the maximum from tourists who don't know any better. Here's an example. When the Mexican peso cratered in 1995, many tourists called travel agents to book Mexican resort vacations. What a shock they got. Prices were as high as ever because major resorts quoted their prices in U.S. dollars. Thus, resort owners, not travelers or hotel cooks, benefited from the wounded peso. At the same time, prices were rock-bottom for independent travelers who stayed in hotels off the tourist trail, ate in local restaurants, and paid in pesos. It's an important lesson.

Before we explore the details, a quick word about the Euro. Eleven countries in Europe now use a common currency. During the transition period, ending January 1, 2002, there are no Euro notes or coins in circulation, but some noncash transactions will be in Euros. The good news for travelers in Europe: an end to changing money at every border—and an end to all those fees.

Where to Exchange Your Money

If you fly into a country, look for an exchange window in the airport. If you arrive by train, there will probably be an exchange window in the station nearest the border or in the first large city. If arriving on foot or by automobile, you should find an exchange desk just beyond the immigration office.

If you're arriving in a country between midnight and dawn when the money exchange office at your point of entry may be closed, you might be wise to have a little local currency in hand. For Europe that's not hard to do, but your bank at home is not likely to have kwatcha, pula, lempira, or shillingi for you to take with you. If it does, it will charge a hefty fee and give a poor exchange rate in the bargain. As an alternative, call Currency Rush (888-842-0880). In my experience, where no official money exchange is available, there are always informal bankers on the street.

The only times I've entered a country carrying any of its currency were when I had some left over from an earlier visit or had bought some from another traveler (which is, since it has become worth zero to him, an opportunity to get a great deal). Only once have I gone hungry for a couple of hours as a result of having no local currency.

A few countries require travelers to change a specified amount of money at the point of entry—at the official exchange rate. Countries with this requirement usually have an artificially inflated currency and, therefore, an active black market. By clipping travelers at the border, the government ensures that it gets at least some of your money at its pie-in-the-sky official rate. Tanzania border officials made me exchange U.S. $50 at the border at a rate of 191 shilling to $1. That was a little painful since the street rate in the nearest town was 280 to $1. Myanmar occasionally requires travelers to spend $300 to purchase local currency at a ridiculously low rate. Algeria mandates that a small amount of money be changed, but Sierra Leone sometimes requires travelers to change more money at the official rate than they'd intended to

> Wait to trade money until you know the fair exchange rate.

spend during their entire stay in the country. These requirements are rare and the amount is usually either a fairly modest fixed amount or an amount related to the number of days you'll be in the country.

Hustlers at borders, including the guys outside airports and train stations, try to con you into exchanging money with them before you know what rate you should get. Since exchange rates are always poor where travelers enter a country, change only the amount you need to get into town and pay for a night's lodging and a couple of meals.

If there's no human waiting to exchange your money, there may be a machine. Automatic currency exchange machines, which resemble an ATM and are named "MultiBank," or "MultiChange," or something similar, have joined the mechanical plague spreading around the world. Increasingly common in Europe, they make exchanges among as many as 15 currencies 24 hours a day. You feed the machine your currency and tell it what currency you want back. In some places, the machine's exchange rates are better than bank rates (taking bank commissions, fees, and stamps into account), but not always. Exchange the minimum amount you need until you can make a comparison. I have to admit, they're fun to play with, kind of like slot machines where you win every time.

In some countries, the only places you can exchange money are the banks. However, in Peru, Brazil, and Thailand, among others, government-sanctioned, privately owned currency exchange dealers operate in small offices along the main streets. Their rates differ from one another but are generally better than bank rates. Shop around.

Interestingly, some places in Europe post a notice offering a slightly better exchange rate if you show a student ID card. Even if there's no notice, it doesn't hurt to ask (a good rule to apply to all sorts of transactions).

The sellers of products or services, including hotels, restaurants, and souvenir shops, will almost always give you a poor exchange rate. Some will even zap you with a fee on top of that. Get your local money elsewhere.

How Much Local Currency Should You Buy?

I seldom travel with more than $50 to $100 in local currency unless I'm about to buy a ticket, pay a hotel bill, or anticipate some other large expense.

If you buy too much local currency, you waste money on the exchange transaction in both directions, buying and selling. Further, if you're stuck with the currency after you leave the country, it's probably a total loss. How much you need at a given moment depends on the day of the week and whether holidays are coming up. If you won't have ready access to an exchange window, exchange enough to avoid standing with an empty wallet in front of a closed bank on a holiday or weekend. You may find someone on the street who will exchange money, but if you're in a bind, you can bet the rate will reflect your situation.

To avoid winding up with excess local currency as they leave a country, partners need to keep each other current on how much local currency each is carrying.

Making the Exchange

Before you approach a currency exchange window, calculate roughly how much money you should receive in an exchange. Learn the rough relationship between your currency and theirs (e.g., you get three of theirs for one of yours), and the calculation becomes second nature. Among other things, it will keep you from being the victim of a misplaced decimal. It happens.

Things get a little complicated when you reach the window. Each foreign currency in which the dealer trades is listed, followed by several columns. The figure in the "Buying Cash" column is applicable when you are using your cash to *buy* the local currency *from* the dealer. In the "Selling Cash" column, applicable when you are *selling* local currency back *to* the dealer, there's a different figure. There will always be a difference, called the "spread," between the buying and the selling rates. The selling figure will be the higher of the two. In other words, you don't do as well when you cash out. For example, suppose you pay $10 to get 370 rupees (10 x 37). You don't use any of them, so you sell them back to the dealer. Instead of getting $10 back, you will get $9.49 (370 ÷ 39). This spread is like the house percentage in a casino, guaranteeing a profit to the dealer. Obviously, you don't want to pay that spread for any more A transaction fee money than you need. may be charged

The "Buying Travelers Checks" column shows the rate of when you buy exchange when you are buying local currency using your local currency. travelers checks. If the dealer's ratio differs significantly between cash or travelers checks, you will want to convert at the better rate (assuming you have both cash and checks to trade).

As you shop for the best exchange rate, keep an eye on the transaction fee often charged in addition to the spread. That fee may be based on (a) the total

Exchanging Indian Rupees

	Buying Cash	Selling Cash	Buying Trav. Checks	Selling Trav. Checks
US $	37.00	39.00	39.00	41.00
Yen	107.00	112.00	113.00	118.00
Mark	1.50	1.60	1.65	1.75
Pound	.65	.68	.68	.71

Notes: (a) At the exchange window above, you would get a better rate for traveler's checks than for cash. (b) In a restaurant or shop, you might receive 34 rupees for $1 (a poor rate).

amount of the transaction, (b) the *number* of travelers checks you cash (the worst case I've seen was a Viennese hotel that charged $6 to cash each traveler's check, no matter what the denomination), (c) the *amount* of the checks, or (d) whether you are exchanging cash or travelers checks. Even if it sounds confusing, it becomes easy with practice.

To calculate the net result of the numbers on the money changer's signs, say to each dealer, "How many (pesos) will you give me for a U.S. $50 traveler's check (or whatever you want to exchange)?" The answers give you net figures you can compare accurately with another dealer. If the difference between dealers is small, consider whether it's really worth walking back across town to chase a few pennies.

Unfortunately, travelers can't assume that all currency exchange clerks are honest. The amount given you may not just be incorrect—it may not even be close! Some clerks play little tricks on you. In Russia, the clerk may pass you a "doll." Named after the popular Russian stacking dolls, that's a packet of money in which the top and bottom bills are real and the ones in the middle are fake. That's just one of the reasons to always count the money before taking even one step away from the counter or window. Force yourself to ignore the people in line behind you. Count the money in plain view of the clerk. If it's correct, tuck it away out of sight before you leave the window. The money is at risk as long as it's in your hand or in an accessible pocket.

Speaking of getting correct change, I think of the clerk in the post office in Kathmandu who tossed my change, a wad of rupees, on the counter. I looked down at them, made no move to pick them up, then looked at him steadily, without expression. After a few moments, he noticed me still standing there, the money undisturbed. With no comment, but looking a little disgusted, he tossed a few more rupees on the pile. I glanced down, then back at him. Twice more our little drama repeated itself, after which he refused to look up. After his last contribution, I counted the money and found it correct. I left without a word, but with an inner smile.

In some countries in Central America, I've been almost startled to receive correct change when paying for something. The clerk or waiter often makes a small personal deduction from your change or gives you coins from a nearby country that are worth less (or worthless). I think of this practice as an informal self-help or foreign aid program.

In South America, India, and a few other places, merchants play an interesting game of monetary musical chairs. When a bank note becomes torn or worn, banks will no longer accept it—which means that merchants will not accept it from you. But, oh, will they try to *give* it to you! Take a look at your change, including money you receive in a currency exchange transaction. If there is a seriously battered bill, simply hand it back with a smile. They'll accept and replace it. No hard feelings; it was just a little test to see if you heard the music stop.

Currency Declaration/Exchange Forms

Many countries require you to fill in a currency declaration form as you enter, listing the amount of money you have in cash and travelers checks. In theory they want you to show, as you leave, that your remaining money, plus receipts for money changed legally, equals your original declaration. The idea is to prevent you from exchanging money at a more favorable rate on the black market (which would leave you with more money than you should have). I've heard of only one person whose money was physically counted on arrival, so it seems you wouldn't be at much risk if you "accidentally" declared more than you were carrying. Doing so would make it easier to balance if you used the black market and were checked on the way out.

If your official money exchange receipts were ludicrously insufficient to have paid for basic needs, it wouldn't take Sherlock Holmes to suspect some trading on the black market. I've never been clear about what would happen at that point. I suppose you could explain that you'd stayed with friends and spent next to nothing. If that didn't fly, there might be a fine or some unofficial solution.

Keep receipts you receive when you exchange money at sanctioned exchange offices because you may need them to sell unused local currency when you leave the country. This requirement is not always enforced, but if it is and you don't have receipts, your local currency becomes a souvenir.

Some people alter official bank receipts to indicate that they exchanged larger amounts than they actually did. Since that's evidence of clear intent to deceive, I think it is a very unwise solution.

What usually happens as you leave a country is . . . nothing. If your receipts are even asked for, they're dumped in a pile without review. I can't say there has never been a thorough check, but it's not the practice. Nevertheless, it seems wise to change a reasonable amount of money legally. Moderation in all things, eh?

The Black Market

Most guidebooks avoid discussing the black market or simply say you should avoid it. Certainly that's the safest course, but I *am* going to discuss the black market because many travelers encounter it and many use it—or want to. If you're one of those people, you should definitely know what you're doing. You won't have to look for the black market. It will find you—in forms ranging from a discreet, eyes-averted whisper to a growling proposal from a man grasping a wad of bills in each hand.

> You won't have to look for the black market—it will find you.

I've heard a couple of people object to trading on the black market, feeling that doing so is harmful to the local government. It's a complex issue and I've yet to hear the pros and cons articulated convincingly. On the other hand, I suppose conservative economists applaud the black market as an inevitable operation of the capitalistic system. I've also heard people justify it on the theory that a certain government is corrupt and *should* be ripped off. On balance, I don't see it as a moral issue.

What It Is and Why It Exists

Black markets come into being when a government insists on fixing the value of its currency higher than it would be in a free market. Besides making purchases more expensive for travelers, that makes the country's money unacceptable beyond its borders. Thus, its citizens can't travel abroad unless they somehow obtain hard currency. By hard currency, I mean coin or paper issued by a government and backed by resources adequate to redeem it at face value at any time. Its value is set by trading in the international market. In contrast, soft currency often lacks adequate backing. That's why you can't pay for a hard-money lunch in San Francisco with soft-money Indonesian rupiah. Local people also need hard currency to buy goods (from sewing machines to drugs to weapons) more cheaply in a neighboring country. Certain scarce goods may be sold only for hard currency, even within the country. The result is inevitable. To get your hard currency, local folk will give you more of their currency than you'd get at the official rate.

Of course, as we all know, not everyone is looking for money to buy a sewing machine. For many, exchanging money is their primary business and more than a few are not your most savory citizens. These black market traders profit by paying you one price for hard currency, then finding people who will eagerly pay them even more for your money.

Countries differ in how they deal with black market operations. In Brazil and Peru, for instance, most of the black market is officially tolerated. In neighboring Chile, it isn't. In Zimbabwe the government is so tough on local dealers that the black market has been forced underground (i.e., there are few street solicitors). On the bright side, if you can arrange a black market transaction in Zimbabwe it's likely to be free from shenanigans.

The reason travelers exchange money on the black market is no mystery. It's not uncommon to receive 30 percent more local money on the black market than you get when exchanging money at the official rate. The last time I was in Zimbabwe the street rate was 51 percent higher than the bank rate. In Bolivia, the black market rate has occasionally been 800 percent more than the official rate!

If the Myanmar government forces you to buy $300 worth of kyats at the airport at the official rate of six for $1, it would cost you about $150 for a cab into town. Later you can buy foreign exchange certificates (FEC) at a rate of, say, 100 kyat for $1. On the black market, you'll get 115 kyat for $1. Even where the spread is smaller, whether travel is very cheap or moderately expensive depends on how much you pay for your local currency.

Many of the major black market opportunities that previously existed in South America and Eastern Europe have diminished. However, substantial differences between the official rate and the black market rate (the spread) still exist in Algeria, Angola, China, Congo, India, Libya, Mozambique, Myanmar, Nepal, Romania, Rwanda, Surinam, Uganda, and Vietnam. There are other countries in which spreads are more modest, say 15 percent. If there's any risk in using a particular black market, I wouldn't consider it unless the bonus is more than 10 percent.

If you're going to a country with a black market and expect to use it, you may want to carry a higher percentage of your funds in cash. If you do, be especially watchful for thieves along the way.

Risks of Trading on the Black Market

Prepare for a black market exchange as you would for a legitimate exchange at a bank. Ask other travelers what rates they've been getting and where. Listen to offers, but make no deals until you have a good idea of the best rate. If someone offers you a below-market rate and won't raise it, smile pleasantly and walk off.

Prepare for black market exchanges as you would legitimate ones.

Here's a tip that's less obvious. If offered a rate considerably *above* the usual black market rate, don't even discuss it. Leave immediately because a rip-off is under way. The high rate is the bait and you've been cast in the role of fish. Because dealers operate within a narrow range of rates, an offer significantly above the range signals a transaction that, one way or another, is never going to close at that rate.

In evaluating risk, the first consideration is the potential legal penalty; where black market trading is against the law, you might get caught. An immigration official might conclude that you've been trading on the black market if your currency declaration form and official money exchange receipts don't explain your expenditures. They could ask questions, but it never seems to happen.

A police officer might witness a street transaction and arrest you. That's not pleasant to contemplate, but I've yet to hear of a traveler being confined for a black market currency exchange. For drugs or smuggling, sure, but it seems unlikely for a street trade.

The biggest risk is that you take a chance of getting ripped off yourself as you concentrate on beating the government exchange rate. In all the world, the risk of this is probably highest in Dar es Salaam, the capital of Tanzania. I estimate the chances of getting ripped off in Dar are at least seven out of ten.

Picture a traveler who has just arrived in Dar after a tiring trip. The heat and humidity, along with a couple of bitter, lukewarm beers beneath a drooping umbrella at the New Africa Hotel, have dulled his brain. As he steps out into the street, two young men smoothly slip alongside like pilot fish. In well-practiced English, they offer to help find a hotel, a taxi, a safari company, or whatever else he wants. No charge, of course. They are master directors, setting the stage for the play. Before long, this prologue leads to Act One in which the traveler agrees to change money with them. If he feels a little obligated, maybe even a little friendly, he won't even feel the hook go down.

Act Two can go several ways. In the midst of the transaction, just after he's handed over his money, a police officer rushes up. The traveler's new acquaintances start running and the cop goes after them. After standing there for a minute, the traveler says to himself something like, "Gee, those guys took off with my money." Or maybe the cop stays and threatens the traveler with jail . . . unless, of course, he prefers to pay a fine to the cop on the spot. He might even take the traveler to the police station. If that happens, he's well connected and the fine will be painful. How does $500 sound?

There's another variation. As the transaction gets under way with a dealer, several of his friends appear and simply take the money, using no more than implication of force.

Sometimes the dealer mixes small bills inside a stack of larger bills, includes a few outdated bills that have no value, or uses sleight of hand to give a short count. Maybe he slips in some currency from a country even more depressed than his own.

I talked with someone who had climbed into the back seat of a car parked on a busy street in Dar because it seemed a safe place for an exchange. Unexpectedly, the car drove away, putting the traveler at something of a disadvantage. A passenger in the front seat asked for the traveler's money to "check it for counterfeit." Oh, sure! At that point, the traveler noticed that there were no inside door handles. Thinking quickly as the car stopped at an intersection, he reached out the window, jerked the door handle, and hopped out. The car drove on and the only price he paid was a hot walk back to the center of town. It was a cheap lesson if he learned it. A traveler who comes away with anything at all from an exchange in Dar should immediately try his luck in Monte Carlo.

In summary, yes, there are risks. However, thousands of travelers successfully exchange money on the black market every day. Those who are repeatedly successful know what they're doing.

How to Do It Right

The best way to control black market risk is to exchange money with business people, especially restaurateurs, hotel managers, and shop owners, in their place of business. They'll be in the same place day after day. If they were to rip you off, they'd have to face you the next day. They'd rather make their money when they move your hard currency along in the system. As established merchants, they make arrangements to prevent unexpected official visits. To make it discreet, you may just pay your bill, using hard currency, at the black market rate.

Another relatively risk-free exchange is with a local person for whom it's an occasional transaction, a person doing it to serve a goal such as study or travel abroad. Since they want to keep their accumulation of hard currency quiet, there's not likely to be a problem.

In Kigali, Rwanda, a portly man on the street offered a rate of 115 Rwandan francs, compared with the bank rate of 77. When the traveler produced his money, the man offered his personal check in return. Personal check? It was the traveler's first week in Africa and it must have showed.

If you decide to deal with a street person, control risk by setting the ground rules yourself.

- Don't initiate the transaction and don't ask the rate. Let the offer come from the trader.

- Require that the exchange occur in a place you consider safe, such as your locked hotel room or a semipublic place that you choose.

- Don't let the other person see all your money, or even where you keep it. Count out the bills you'll exchange and put them, ahead of time, in a separate pocket.

- *Insist* that he hand his money to you or your partner to count first; not *vice versa* or even simultaneously. Never buy his line that since neither of you trusts the other the exchange should be simultaneous. You know you're not going to run off with his money but you don't know what he'll do. If he runs you won't catch him. Think about it: if he couldn't run faster than an outraged client, he wouldn't still be in business.

- Count the money carefully. Separate each bill from the next to avoid counting the bills he's folded in half as two bills. If he's up to something, he'll try to distract you, perhaps with conversation. Count the money again. After you've counted it, don't let him get it back from you on some pretext. If he gets his hands on it again, he has another chance for a switch. When you're satisfied, give him your money and watch his hands. He may try to palm one of your bills and claim he never received it.

When someone won't make the exchange on your terms, smile and take a hike. Trust your intuition. As Kenny Rogers preaches: "Know when to hold 'em, know when to fold 'em, know when to walk away, and know when to run."

In making a decision about trading on the black market, ask yourself what level of risk you are willing to tolerate? How much of your trip depends on getting the black market rate? Before you go ahead, assess the local situation. Talk with other travelers and consider the suggestions above. Never be greedy and never press your luck.

I have a fond recollection of a flight from India to Nepal. The flight attendant came to my seat and asked if my partner and I would like to join the captain in the cockpit. Surprised but pleased, we accepted instantly. Throughout the flight, the captain chatted away, identifying various Himalayan peaks, even standing the plane on one wing to point out Mount Everest. It was a fantastic experience. Only as we were on the final landing path into Kathmandu, runway racing up toward the cockpit windshield, did the long, slow curve break sharply over the plate. "I say," said the captain in that melodious Indian accent, "I wonder if you would like to change a few hundred dollars for rupees? Black market rate, of course."

Bargaining—When and How

Most Westerners are convinced they don't like bargaining, at least not "street" bargaining. Perhaps underlying a cultural hang-up is the belief that they don't know how to do it. Except for unhappy episodes when attempting to buy a car, most Westerners don't do much one-on-one bargaining.

A traveler should get ready for a change of pace because in most of the world bargaining is part of daily life. In the Third World, anyone who doesn't bargain is regarded as so foolish that he or she deserves to be charged a penalty. Even in Europe it's far more common than most Western tourists realize. It would be a shame to let inhibitions or cultural differences interfere with experiencing the art and sport of bargaining. Besides, if you use tips from this chapter you'll SAVE MONEY wherever you travel. It's a skill that can also help you SAVE MONEY when you return home.

In the Third World, prices in restaurants are usually fixed—but be prepared to bargain for almost everything else, including hotel rates, transportation, guides and treks, clothing, art, crafts, and souvenirs (even small ones). You may occasionally walk into a shop and see price tags on items, maybe even a sign that says "fixed prices." Occasionally prices really are fixed, but these signs are more likely the first move in bargaining chess.

Surely you can't bargain over air fare? Oh, but you can! The offices of most major airlines won't bargain, as far as I know, but many travel agencies abroad have some latitude in what they charge for a ticket. There's a spread between what they get from you and what they remit to the airline. Since you don't bargain with travel agents at home, you may feel reluctant but give it a try. You'll be surprised at how often the agent comes up with a previously unmentioned "special." You'll never get it without asking.

To begin the bargaining process, start with your own state of mind. Loosen up. Think of yourself as writing your own lines in an amusing play.

Ideally, you should decide what an item is worth to you before you start bargaining. That's easier said than done with spontaneous purchases, especially when it's something you've never seen or heard of before. Have you given much thought to how much an antique Peruvian coca pouch is worth to you? If there's a price tag on it, ignore it. If the merchant calls out a price, ignore it. Think for a moment what you would pay to have that particular object in your home. Only then should you investigate what the item is worth in the local market. Ask several people who've bought something similar. If you ask just one person, it may be someone who paid way too much.

Don't fall in love with something the first time you see it. Check out other shops. The colorful carved fish mobile that caught your eye in Ubud, Bali, has counterparts in a dozen shops—and they differ in quality as well as the shopkeeper's opinion of its value. Initial prices vary from merchant to merchant. Do some preliminary bargaining to get feedback from the market. After a few rounds of light sparring, you'll have an idea of the neighborhood of the outcome. More than anything, successful bargaining takes patience. As the process continues, you keep adding to your information.

See what local buyers pay for what you want. As you walk through the market, look over their shoulders. You may not get it for the same price, but you know what the merchant can sell it for and still make a profit. That's a big edge.

Recognize that the bargaining process begins earlier in a transaction than you think. While you're wandering around the shop, the vendor is sizing up your clothes and noting the amount of attention you give particular items. As she approaches, you'll hear: "You are from what country?" She may inquire about your occupation and where you're staying. Her bargaining strategy will be based on your responses, starting with the language in which you answer. As charming as she may be, her questions do not spring from friendly curiosity. They're part of a highly developed socioeconomic evaluation that would make Northwestern's Kellogg Graduate School of Management proud. Answering her questions would be like showing your hole card in the middle of a hand of poker. Instead, just smile, mumble, respond with a question of your own, or act as if you didn't understand her.

The bargaining process begins as you enter the shop.

It would be an expensive error to show enthusiasm for the thing you want, so bargain first for something else. Let your attention wander from one item to another, patiently letting the vendor guess what might interest you. The more time she invests, the greater her eagerness to conclude a sale at some price. I try to avoid bargaining in front of other shoppers since I don't know what affect their presence may have on the merchant.

She may try to hand you the item in which she thinks you have an interest. Just smile and nod, hands in pockets. If you accept it, you may have a difficult time getting her to take it back.

Don't hesitate to courteously criticize the item for which you're bargaining, pointing out real or imagined defects. Indicate aspects that aren't right for you or mention features of similar products elsewhere that this one doesn't have. However, I avoid implying that the shopkeeper or artisan is intentionally selling something undesirable or worthless. There's always some "face" involved and you do better by maintaining a courteous relationship. Keep the tone light, never angry. I cringe when a tourist bargains loudly and aggressively, heaping scorn on some object. Whatever the outcome, it's a disgraceful way for a visitor to behave. Similarly, if the vendor gets too aggressive, I'm out of there. I don't mind a skillful pitch, but I'm not there to be hassled. I am absolutely certain I do not want to carry an 8 x 10 carpet in my luggage, no matter how beautiful it is in the merchant's eyes. If I can't get her to stop trying to sell it to me, I leave.

Always let the merchant make the first offer. Don't respond when pressed for a counteroffer. Be cool. Keep looking around. See if the price will drop before you respond. The merchant's first price may be twice to ten times what will be accepted, so don't think of just knocking 10 or 20 percent off it. If you pay more than 60 percent of the asking price at the famous Sunday market in Chichicastenango,* the shopkeeper might light a candle in your memory. In other words, don't buy into the asking price as being somehow related to actual value. If interested, mention a figure you *might pay*; perhaps 20 percent of the reduced asking price. State your tentative counteroffer with reluctance and expect a response somewhere between incredulity and personal affront. In a rare case, your integrity or sanity may be challenged. Keep in mind that merchants are also actors with their own scripts.

If you have any expertise concerning an item, don't reveal it until you can use it to your advantage as you near the climax.

Tell the shopkeeper that you aren't a rich tourist and can't afford her price. If you're staying at an inexpensive hotel, say so. If what you say is consistent with how the shopkeeper has sized you up, perhaps a smaller profit will be more acceptable than loss of the sale.

Two people can be an effective team in a bargaining situation by playing a variation of the old "good guy, bad guy" routine. As one person bargains, the other begins to fidget, expresses disinterest in the item, checks the time, moves toward the door, and exerts pressure on the bargainer to come along. At that point, the prospective buyer mentions a price considerably lower than that at which the negotiation has stalled. The merchant, having only a few moments in which to make the deal, may yield a bit more.

If you're by yourself, suggest that you're going to leave and "look around," perhaps mentioning a competitor's prices, real or mythical. These are words that strike dread into the heart of any merchant. Once out the door, you're someone else's prey. Or say, "I'm going to see what my friend thinks." More grim words. Be sure to give the merchant a chance to make another "final"

Chichicastenango. This small town in Central Guatemala has winding streets, whitewashed houses with red tile roofs, and an Indian population in colorful traditional clothing.

A Curious Exchange

One of the most curious bargaining experiences I've had took place in New Delhi. I wanted to find a jacket to warm me at the high altitudes of Ladakh. After looking around, I spotted a coat with great character. The shop owner asked $35, a considerable sum in India. I looked dubious. He dropped the price to $30. I declined. We had tea and talked for an hour or so about politics. Then he said, "Okay, pay me $25, take the coat, bring it back, and I'll give you the money back." I was considering his unusual offer when he said, "No, never mind, just take the coat. Bring it back some day and tell me about Ladakh." And so, many weeks later, I told him my tales of the Kingdom of Ladakh.

offer. It shouldn't take long. If it doesn't come, step out the door. If a merchant won't drop the price any lower as you walk out, and doesn't follow you, you're close to a fair price.

If you've reached an impasse on something you really want, tell the seller you'll pay the price if some other widget you have an interest in is included.

If you're planning to buy several of one item, such as a sarong, first negotiate a price for a single item. Then introduce the possibility of buying several. Ask for a further discount of, say, 30 percent.

It sometimes helps to pull money out of your pocket and hold it in your hand. Psychologically, it may make the seller want to reach for it—by meeting your price. More than once I've put the amount of my target price in one pocket, pulling it out at the last moment and saying, "This is what I have." It sometimes works. If it doesn't and I still want to play, I check another pocket and discover a bit more money. Remember, timing is important—and she's been through this scene thousands of times.

In countries in which hard currency has special value, you may break an impasse by offering to pay your price, but in U.S. dollars.

Prices vary from season to season. In the tourist off-season, great deals are available, but when the market is pulsing with acquisitive tourists, you'll pay closer to the top of the range (but still less than the asking price). After all, the vendor knows there will be an innocent coming through the door right behind you, eager to be sheared.

It's easy to lose perspective during the bargaining process. You could find yourself getting hung up over $2, or even 50 cents. If you feel ambivalent about purchasing the item, hold firm or walk away. If it's something you want to own and walking off doesn't produce a last-minute concession, walk back and pay the shopkeeper's last price. Don't let your own "face" stand in your way. Why chastise yourself later over having left behind something you really wanted?

What if the asking price is so cheap that you're willing to pay it without discussion? If you're talking about a few cents, it's not worth your time to bargain. But if you want to make a contribution, why not choose an appropriate charity or a needy person? Why make a donation to a shopkeeper who, in that economy, is seldom one of the needier people?

If you accept something from the merchant, such as a cup of tea or a cold drink, be aware that her primary motive is to make you feel indebted and/or friendly. I'm not disparaging her motive, only saying that acceptance of a cup of tea creates no obligation on your part. If you don't reach agreement, leave with a courteous "thank you anyway." Under the rules of engagement, negotiating, no matter how lengthy, commits you to nothing. You're ethically free to walk away anytime. If you and the merchant place a different value on something and you can't resolve the difference, that's okay. However, when a merchant accepts a price you've offered, you should pay that price. It would be bad karma to walk away at that point.

As you bargain for anything, remember that your adversary is a pro, much more experienced at this than you are. She knows her costs and the quality of the item. She won't close a sale if she won't come out all right, so don't hesitate to do your best. Stay lighthearted and friendly. Since sitting all day in a market stall on a steamy day isn't anyone's idea of a great time, a good bargaining bout may be fun for the seller. However the deal goes, leave one another with a pleasant memory.

Remember that the shopkeeper is a pro at bargaining.

Here's a final thought about "after the sale." If it later appears that your purchase wasn't all that shrewd because of price or quality, learn what you can from the experience and forget self-recriminations. If somebody claims to have bought the same thing for less, think of it as a reminder of price elasticity that you can use to your advantage next time (and people have been known to shade the truth more than a little when discussing their own shrewd bargaining). All this may seem complicated at first, but it isn't in practice. In no time, you'll be improving on these strategies with your own flourishes.

More on bargaining in Chapter 11 (Lodging) and Chapter 21 (To Buy or Not to Buy).

7

Travel Gear

I had grown into my clothes, the way travelers do
who haven't looked into a mirror for weeks.
— Colin Thubron
Night in Vietnam

TRAVEL LIGHT!!!

That's so easy to say—and so hard to do. I hear of people who claim they can slide everything they need for a three-month trip under their plane seat every time. Or fit it all, plus the *Collected Works of Shakespeare,* into a daypack. But let's talk about normal human beings, people who want to travel with a good book, camera, shower shoes, maybe even a snorkel; people traveling to have fun. They too can travel light, but it takes some thought.

For my first long trip, I wanted to be prepared to dress (up) for any contingency. The predictable result: overload, a greenhorn's mistake. The fact is that local people are aesthetically understanding about travelers. If you look clean and smile, they don't expect high fashion. Randy Wayne White, whose excellent articles appear in *Outside* magazine, observed that inexperienced travelers take too much of what they don't need, and experienced travelers take too much of what they do need. Instead of throwing or giving it away, they lug the extra stuff mile after mile to be returned unused to the closet.

There's a better way. Don't include an item just because it *might* come in handy (the deadly "just in case" syndrome). You can almost always do without it. If not, you can probably find some local equivalent. Limit yourself to what you're willing to carry without complaint up a steep hill on a hot day. If you're traveling with a partner, travel light enough that either of you can carry all the luggage, leaving the other free to sprint ahead to find a room or good seats on a bus.

Try to hold your personal load to 25 pounds. Thirty to thirty-five is more likely, and still bearable. If you leave home with more than 50 pounds, I guarantee you'll cut down for the next trip. A few extra pounds may not seem to matter much at home, but they will on the road. Besides, international airlines may charge a penalty for everything above 44 pounds. Even if they waive the penalty, your back cannot.

Besides weight, consider the quality of your gear. There is no point wasting money buying trendy labels, but cutting corners could become expensive if something important fails on the road. Besides, the fancier the gear looks, or the more recognizable the brand name, the more it commends itself as a target for thieves. It's best to buy high-quality, durable, lightweight clothing and equipment, but don't let prices of the optimum gear keep you at home. Some people travel with the cheapest gear available and good fortune usually carries them through without a hitch.

When I tired of starting from scratch each time I prepared for a trip, I made a list of everything I'd taken on past trips and evaluated each item in terms of whether it had been needed. Then I made a list of everything that had been worthwhile. That list, tweaked to take climate and special activities into account, serves as the basis for every trip I take. It makes packing a snap.

Remember the guy who gave a speech that went on and on, boring his audience into slumber? At the end, he apologized, saying, "My speech would have been shorter if I'd had more time to prepare." Like giving a good speech, choosing the right travel gear also requires time and research. Proceeding in haste, an inexperienced traveler will always carry too much.

CHOOSING LUGGAGE

Choosing what to carry your gear in as you wander the world is an important decision. My criteria for luggage are transportability, durability, accessibility, and security. With these in mind, let's review the strengths and weaknesses of various types of luggage: hard-sided, soft-sided, duffel bags, backpacks, daypacks, and the accessories that go with them.

Hard-sided Luggage

After watching poor-quality, overstuffed luggage disintegrate in transit, baggage handlers recommend hard-sided luggage because of its durability. Of course, durability is important partly *because* of baggage handlers. However, I don't recommend a standard hard-sided suitcase for anything but a trip where you go to one place, stop, and return—a typical business trip. Weight is the major reason. A hard-sided suitcase adds an extra ten pounds or so beyond the weight of soft-sided luggage. Because it's dead weight dangling at the end of one arm, you'll be ready to abandon it after the first mile.

Soft-sided Luggage

My first choice, and that of many travelers, is to carry the weight on my back. Nevertheless, some people cannot or prefer not to carry a backpack. Maybe it's a back problem, maybe an image problem, maybe just habit. If that's the case, look for soft-sided luggage made of 1,000-denier Cordura nylon or polyester. If it has wheels, make sure they are wide and sturdy, partly recessed or protected by housings (dainty little wheels won't stand up to rough surfaces and long distances). A sturdy retractable handle is far preferable to a leash. Look for a waterproof pocket and compression straps inside (to keep your gear from shifting). Good construction is important. Rivets are more durable than D-rings or screws for connecting shoulder straps and handles. Seams are usually encased in plastic for water-resistance, but casings of leather, shell fabric, or wide woven tape resist abrasion better.

The Lark E-Z Traveler Soft Piggyback and the Samsonite Silhouette 5 Piggyback (call 800-262-8282 for both) have durable wheels, a retractable handle, and a strap. They're sturdy but expensive. The Lark, for example, costs around $425. An alternative is the Travelpro 727 Rollaboard (about $150), a soft-sided, roll-a-long bag small enough to be carried aboard. The Travelpro 777 (about $200) is a larger, check-in version. Although Travelpros are used by many airline crews, they have small wheels, which allow the bottom of the bag to scrape. If you'll be using the bag beyond the confines of plane and hotel, I'd consider something else.

Consumer Reports has given "Best Buy" status to the Airway Atlantic Concept (also $100), even though the shell is only 600-denier. They also liked the Atlantic Infinity (about $110). The TravelSmith Turbo Transit ($219) has something for everyone: 1000-denier Cordura, sturdy rubber wheels, a strong nylon strap for pulling, a leather handle, a pair of hidden shoulder straps so you can sling the whole thing onto your back, and a small pack that zips off the side for day trips. With the daypack zipped off, the Turbo Transit meets carry-on limits. Call (800) 950-1600 for the catalogue.

When you're shopping, picture yourself pulling the suitcase uphill on a winding lane in Greece. Are the wheels so thin they can't handle the cobblestones? Is the suitcase so high and narrow it will tip over every few feet? A suitcase that works fine for a European destination where it will be hoisted about by taxi drivers, porters, and bellmen (assuming you're willing to pay for their services) may be much less satisfactory where you are handling it yourself on subways and in bus stations. As you explore more deeply into the Third World, distances grow longer and the sun hotter.

Carefully examine brand name bags on sale in discount stores. Those bags are often inferior in quality to similar models sold in luggage shops. If you choose a shoddy bag and then stuff it to its limits, don't be surprised if it fails along the way. Improve the odds a bit by securing cheapo luggage with a couple of tough webbed luggage straps.

Another form of soft-sided luggage that may work well for some trips is a garment (hanging) bag. Since you will be carrying it, forget the wheels. Be certain it has a sturdy, padded, over-the-shoulder strap. Look for the quality described above and be sure all compartments can be locked.

Duffel Bags

A duffel bag with a broad shoulder strap works well for some people, although, because it has no frame, it offers little protection for the contents.

Consumer Reports gave a perfect rating to the L.L. Bean Sportsman ($120). It's made of 1,000-denier fabric and weighs only half as much (4.2 pounds) as most soft-sided luggage. Call (800) 221-4221.

Eagle Creek (800-874-9925) cargo duffels and cargo gear bags are much less expensive than a good pack. Made of Cordura nylon, they range in size from 2,000 cubic inches up to 12,100 cubic inches and come with a good shoulder strap. The Eagle Creek Toy Chest (5,850 cubic inches) has expandable side pockets, a comfortable shoulder strap, and lots of other goodies.

The BAD (Best American Duffel) Bag has the best workmanship I've seen in duffels. BAD Bags (call 800-424-2247 or see www.badbags.com) come in four sizes from 2,800 to 7,800 cubic inches. The 5,200-cubic-inch bag sells for $120. Made of 1,000 denier Cordura Plus with a one-ounce urethane coating for water resistance, BAD Bags have two inside pockets, an outside pocket, a leather handle, a seat-belt nylon shoulder strap, two grab loops, and heavy-duty hardware. BAD Bags look great and are built to handle hard wear on the road. One model was chosen by Will Steger for his seven-month dogsled trip across Antarctica in 1990. An *Outside* magazine writer wrote that "BAD Bags are the best all-around duffel bags available."

Because duffel bags hold so much, they can get very heavy. To address that problem, an interesting hybrid developed that has recessed rubber wheels on one end and a leash on the other (which, of course, makes them heavier still). If you go in this direction, I recommend getting one that has a shoulder strap. The Eddie Bauer textured nylon duffel bag with wheels has shoulder and waist straps (5,800 cubic inches, about $200; call 800-426-8020). The Briggs & Riley version looks very businesslike (about $180; 415-728-2000).

Backpacks

The days when backpacks were carried solely by hard-core hikers or hippies are long gone. They are now carried by travelers from across the economic spectrum. I've never grown fond of carrying a heavy weight on my back, but I consider a backpack the best choice for the type of travel I enjoy. It keeps me mobile and able to take my gear where I want to go without pulling my arm off. Using its harness, I can go farther, easier with a backpack than with any other form of luggage.

A good pack is made of tough fabric, provides easy access to its contents, can be locked up tight, and stands up to the rigors of any trip. For ten years, I had not one problem with my Kelty Kathmandu. When the main zipper finally failed, Kelty took the pack and replaced all the zippers and the back panel without charge. That's standing behind a product. To meet the criteria of durability, accessibility, security, and transportability, I recommend a convertible, interior frame backpack (sometimes called a "travel pack"). "Convertible" means that the harness suspension system can be zipped out of sight behind a zippered panel. In that mode, resembling normal luggage more than a backpack, you can walk into a hotel or a bureaucrat's office without being stereotyped as a backpacker. Oh, the concierge in a five-star hotel will probably notice, but if he's as good as he should be he'll never raise an eyebrow. Besides, who wants to plan a trip around the expectations of a concierge?

If you're going on a lengthy wilderness excursion over moderate terrain, you may prefer a backpack with an exterior metal frame to which a sleeping bag, climbing equipment, and other odds and ends can be attached. Otherwise, an interior frame pack is superior. It's lighter, less susceptible to damage, and unlikely to get hung up on an airport carousel.

just GO! magazine (which has evolved into *EcoTraveler*) gave the Eagle Creek Continental Journey pack its highest rating: sturdy construction, 3,900-cubic-inch capacity, Cordura Plus nylon, internal frame, lockable YKK zippers, and a zip-off daypack (4.3 pounds). The Eagle Creek Transport I backpack is very similar, except that it's a little heavier and more upscale in appearance. Another very popular Eagle Creek model is its smaller convertible called Solo Journey. Eagle Creek's most recent products are the Switchback and Switchback-Plus. The former is a convertible backpack with built-in rubber wheels and a pull-frame. The Plus version adds a zip-off daypack. *Consumer Reports* liked the L.L. Bean Travel Pack and the Jansport China Clipper. The Jansport Vagabond Travel Pack (6,240 cubic inches) also gets good reviews. Take a look at TravelSmith's Solution Bag (2,770 cubic inches), which includes a zip-off daypack and hidden pack straps. REI and Kelty packs also receive consistently good reviews from travelers.

Daypacks

In addition to one principal piece of luggage, I use a daypack to carry a book, journal, pens, maps, fruit, sunglasses, camera and film, medical supplies such as band aids and sunscreen, and, usually, a bottle of water—things to which I want easy access. I do *not* use it for carrying things that belong in my money belt. My daypack has one main compartment and two smaller ones, all with lockable zippers. It's a dark color and leaves home well treated with Scotchgard. Good models run from $25 (there's an excellent Jansport for $28) to $55. Apply the same standards of quality for a daypack as for a backpack. You'll rely on it for years, so go for quality.

Some women prefer, especially when traveling in Europe, a purse-equivalent to a daypack. If that's your choice, be sure it is sturdy and defensible, with a secure clasp and a tough strap. If you can do without a purse, you should.

That leads to the topic of a fanny pack. It should *never* be used as a storage place for valuables. It's probably better for carrying nonvaluables than a purse, but a thief may strike anyway since he won't know what you have in it. If you're interested in a fanny pack, they are sold everywhere. Some of the most ingenious are offered by L.L. Bean. To show how far uptown they've come, there are now modular system fanny packs with zip-off gear pouches,

Packs

I recommend that a pack have the following characteristics (many of which are equally applicable to suitcase, carry-on, or duffel bag):

- *Color.* Any pack gets dirty from spending time on train station platforms, the open deck of a boat, the roof of a bus, or as your seat in an ox-cart. A dark color makes the dirt less obvious.
- *Fabric.* Choose a durable fabric. One of the best materials is 1,000-denier Cordura nylon with a light urethane coating. Cordura is tough but not waterproof, so Scotchgard it before each trip. If your pack will be exposed to water, consider a rain cover (check the catalogues, $13 to $35). A large plastic trash bag provides protection and is less expensive.
- *Construction.* Look closely at the construction of luggage you are considering. On a pack, the seams should be double- or triple-stitched and reinforced at stress points. Inside seams should be taped or finished. Raw edges will soon begin to fray—and those little stringlets seek zippers like a Sidewinder missile seeks heat.
- *Handle.* It should be padded.
- *Shoulder strap.* It should be padded and wide.
- *Suspension harness.* It should be strong and easily adjustable. The stays should be aluminum so they can be fitted to the contour of your back.
- *Lumbar pad.* It should be large enough to provide a cushion where the pack rests against your lower back.
- *Waist belt.* It should be strong and padded.
- *Compression straps.* They keep the load from shifting around and reduce the size to meet airline baggage limits.
- *Zippers.* Plastic zippers seem to fail less frequently than metal and work more smoothly in very cold temperatures. Ensure that zippers are sturdy (such as #10 YKK) and well-sewn into the pack. Check that the zipper will reseat itself on its tracks if it splits open. There should be a flap over the zipper to keep rain out.
- *Compartments.* In single-compartment luggage, contents can become a hopeless jumble as you paw through. I prefer a large front-opening compartment plus several smaller, lockable compartments that let you separate contents on the basis of function. If a pack has just one compartment, use stuff bags of different colors to create mobile compartments and make things easier to find.

  Some people like packs with a zip-off compartment that can serve as a daypack, but I prefer a daypack designed solely to be a daypack.
- *Expansion.* Some packs have a soft bottom (and duffels an expandable end) that opens to increase capacity by up to 1,000 cubic centimeters. This feature is handy toward the end of your trip if purchases become irresistible, but it would be a great error to fill it up as you start the trip.

mesh water bottle holsters, urethane-coated packcloth for water-repellency, external tie-downs (for things like a wind shell), a padded back panel, and a Scotchlite reflective strip on the back. What would Daniel Boone think?

Baggage Limits

Not surprisingly, airlines limit the size and weight of luggage they permit passengers to check or carry aboard. Since luggage is more secure and protected from loss and rough handling if you carry it aboard, you need to know carry-on size limits. As airlines cram ever more humans into a finite space, they enforce carry-on limits much more strictly than in the past. Further, you need to know check-in limits so you aren't forced to leave a bag behind in some remote airport. This information should be one of the factors affecting your choice of luggage.

Because rules differ from airline to airline and change frequently, I can only give you guidelines. You need to know the rules applicable to your specific trip. Learning weight and size limitations will SAVE MONEY. If your luggage is overweight at the airport, a point at which you have little bargaining power, you may pay a stiff penalty. Penalties for excess baggage start at $45 per bag and increase from there.

As a general proposition, the cheaper your plane ticket (relative to other tickets for the same flight), the more strict are limits on weight, size, and number of pieces. In the United States, weight limits are seldom a problem, except on small planes taking you to small places. Most airlines will accept bags weighing up to 70 pounds. Typically, you are permitted to check two pieces of luggage and carry one aboard. Sometimes you're allowed to check a third piece in place of the carry-on. A briefcase, notebook computer, or collapsible luggage cart may be counted as part of your allowance. Reading material, 35mm cameras, binoculars, and similar items are not counted.

Check the airline's size and weight limits before you go.

There are no standardized international weight or size limits, but a maximum of 44 pounds is not unusual. For checked luggage, a total size of 62 inches (length + width + height) for one piece is common for economy class (with a total of 106 inches allowed for two pieces). Enforcement is erratic. In Bangkok, I've watched many passengers check four to six heavily strapped bags, each large enough to conceal a small water buffalo.

Carry-on luggage is often limited to a total of 45 inches for under-the-seat (9 + 14 + 22), 60 inches for overhead (10 + 14 + 36), and 72 inches for a garment bag (4 + 23 + 45). Some airlines have a simple test. They place a box near the check-in counter. If you can stuff your bag into it, you may carry it on board. If not, it doesn't go. I've listened to passengers scream in rage when told their bags full of fragile items were too large to be carried aboard. That was just before they received the bill for overweight luggage.

If you're about to get socked for an overweight penalty, be creative.

Reclaim your luggage. Unpack and wear as much as you need to (there is no limit on that yet). Load up your daypack. Ask someone to treat one of your bags as theirs (which they won't do if they're cautious). If nothing else works and the circumstances are right, leave a little currency in your ticket envelope (this is not recommended in the United States, Canada, and most of Europe).

Where to Buy Luggage

Where will you find the luggage you want? If you prefer a standard suitcase, visit department stores and luggage shops. If you're considering a duffel or backpack, start by reviewing catalogues, including L.L. Bean, Camp-Mor, Magellan's, Patagonia, REI, Eagle Creek, and TravelSmith. Scan outdoor and travel-oriented magazines. Educate yourself about what is available on the market and the price ranges. Don't forget discount stores such as Service Merchandise or Wal-Mart (it's amazing how quickly features of the best luggage are copied).

When you have a feeling for features and prices, stop by a local outdoor gear store or travel superstore to find packs with the features you want. By visiting a local store, you can see and touch the product, discuss fit, quality, and characteristics with a knowledgeable person, compare competing products, and get later help fixing any glitches.

Try on different packs with the assistance of a salesperson who knows how they should fit. Learn how to adjust the suspension harness properly for your body. When you've found a pack that feels right, examine its construction and features closely.

Resist the temptation to buy a pack that has too much volume for you. Given the compulsion to fill empty space, think about the maximum weight you want to carry and keep airline size limits in mind. One traveler I admire hasn't checked a piece of luggage for years. She travels for weeks with only a bag she can take on board and fit under the seat or in the overhead compartment. Besides eliminating the risk of losing her bag in transit, the smaller bag disciplines her to travel light.

Ask for recommendations from the sales person, especially if he or she is an experienced traveler. What are the strengths and weaknesses of the various types of luggage? Which ones have other customers liked the most? When you've made your choice, load it up and walk around the neighborhood so you know what to expect.

Shop for the best price for the luggage you want, but be cautious about buying something cheap. Quality matters. It's no bargain if you wind up with luggage that starts to disintegrate in the boonies. Good luggage will last a long time, so it's definitely a good value.

Locks

Luggage *must* be lockable. If there is only one zipper tab for an opening, there should be a ring to which it can be locked. If there are two zipper tabs, they should be designed so that one can be locked to the other. The zipper tab, which should be metal, typically has a large hole at the top and a small hole at the bottom. Buy a lock with a shackle small enough to fit through the *small* hole of the tab. If you lock the zippers using the large holes, the compartment can easily be opened enough to allow a hand to reach inside. Try it and you'll see what I mean.

Few little zipper locks are very strong, but avoid the cheapest ones. They're too easy to force or to pick. Small combination locks are even better since thieves are less familiar with them.

Some travelers use an electrical cable tie in place of a lock. When looped through the eyes of a zipper, a thief must cut it to gain entry—and you'll know he was there. Of course, you have to cut it yourself to get in. I prefer locks. At Radio Shack, a pack of thirty ties costs about $2.

A lightweight plastic-coated bicycle-locking cable makes it easy to secure your luggage to something immovable. Eagle Creek combines an ingenious 42-inch retractable cable with a combination lock (3 ounces, about $14). Any store that sells sailboats can cut a length of rigging wire and weld a loop into each end to receive a lock.

Even the best lock doesn't prevent someone from slashing your luggage, nor from stealing it, but it foils the opportunist, the sneak thief who has only a few seconds to get inside and doesn't want you to know he's been there. Locks signal an observer that you're aware of his presence. Like any wolf, he'll prey on the weakest in the flock—and that won't be you.

Luggage Tags

Buy sturdy luggage tags, perhaps ones that have a leather flap to hide the name and address from prying eyes. Otherwise, put a piece of paper (not a business card) bearing only your name in the window of the tag. Your address goes on the back to prevent passersby from knowing where your empty home is. Some travelers use an office address or a friend's name and address. Don't forget to include your country with the rest of the address.

Since baggage handling can detach any luggage tag, tape your name, address, and a friend's telephone number, to the inside of your luggage. I strongly recommend also tagging, or otherwise marking, your camera, daypack, and anything else from which you may become separated.

Use a distinctive mark on your luggage so it's easily identified.

When a lost bag is located, it is sent to the address on the tag. If that's your home, that might not be your first choice when you're in the middle of a trip. A recent innovation is a tag that asks the airline agent who locates your lost bag to read the enclosed itinerary and forward your bag to the appropriate destination. It's worth considering (Magellan's, $4.85 for two).

Unless your luggage is very distinctive in appearance, you might mark it with a strip of bright adhesive tape or a colorful ribbon. Besides being a signal to you, it keeps an inattentive fellow passenger from taking your luggage from the baggage carousel. It happens.

Most people get a kick out of airline check-in luggage tags from exotic places but it's better to pull them off as you go if you don't want your luggage to accidentally visit one of those places without you.

HOW TO PACK

For an extended trip, start assembling clothing and equipment weeks before departure, and, this is important, complete packing *at least three days* before you leave. Don't fudge on that date. Details, double-checking, and last-minute purchases can be stressful. By finishing early, you avoid mistakes and walk out of the house feeling comparatively peaceful. Laying things out early allows time to figure out what you can do without. Practice packing and you'll discover that not everything can make the trip. I urge you to leave with some room in your luggage, but no one ever does. Fortunately, it all settles after a while.

Packing Tips

- Clothes are like calories; they all add weight. After laying out all the clothes you think you need, let a few days pass. Then subtract one-fourth of the pile, maybe more.
- Use a list and check things off as you put them in the bag.
- Many travelers roll shirts, pants, underwear, everything, into cylinders, each secured with a stout rubber band. Rolling saves space and keeps clothes relatively unwrinkled (don't even think about lugging a travel iron along). When everything is rolled, searching for an elusive shirt doesn't scramble the contents of your bag. Some who don't roll their clothes wrap them in plastic bags from the cleaners to keep them separated.
- Pack no glass containers or containers with spout tops that open easily under pressure.
- Protect breakables, such as a camera, by surrounding them with cushions of clothing.
- Keep sharp edges away from luggage fabric to avoid a tear under pressure.
- To minimize shifting, put the heaviest things in the bottom.
- Stuff small items (socks, belt, etc.) inside shoes.
- Pack only small quantities of things, such as soap, that you'll consume as you travel. They're easy to replace so there's no reason to leave home with a supply for the whole trip.
- Figure out what you can share with a partner so you don't duplicate items.

- Leave home with your luggage partly empty so you have space for things acquired along the way. Of course, when you're disciplined enough to do this, you're a candidate for the Traveler's Hall of Fame.
- Put things in approximately the same places each time you repack on the road.
- Pack essential medications in carry-on luggage. The same goes for basic toiletries if you want to look spiffy as you de-plane after a transoceanic trip.
- Perhaps the most important packing tip concerns not "how" but "where." Valuables belong in your money belt, not in checked luggage. Semiprecious valuables, such as a journal, belong in carry-on luggage. The only exception may be film, which may have to be checked because it's so bulky.

CHOOSING CLOTHING

The following guidelines will reduce the weight of the clothing you take, help you stay clean and comfortable, and reduce potential problems on the road.

Equip Yourself for the Weather. It's obvious that a travel wardrobe should reflect the climate at your destinations. However, accomplishing that is not always simple since temperatures can differ quite a bit within a small area, often reflecting changes in altitude. It's not many miles from Mombasa on the coast of Kenya to the summit of Mount Kilimanjaro, but the temperature difference may be 70 degrees. A relatively short plane trip takes a traveler from midsummer in Indonesia to midwinter in New Zealand, another 60-degree temperature drop. Do the research necessary to find out what high and low temperatures (average temperatures are useless) and rainfall to expect. This information is available in some guidebooks, in libraries, from embassies, and from other travelers.

> "Your true traveler will not feel he has had his money's worth unless he brings back a few scars."
> —Lawrence Durrell

Layering. The strategy of layering can greatly reduce the bulk and weight of what you take on your trip when visiting cool or cold climates. Think of layering as dressing in three distinct layers. The inner layer is a thermal layer that also draws perspiration away from your skin, rather than trapping it, and allows it to evaporate. For this purpose, a synthetic material (e.g., Capilene or polypropylene) works very well. The middle layer is for insulation. Many materials work fine and need not be bulky. The outer layer is to protect you from rain, snow, and wind. It should be lightweight and breathable, and have pockets, a hood, and zippers for ventilation. I like some combination of a light synthetic undershirt or thermal underwear, a turtleneck, a warm canvas or corduroy shirt, maybe a down vest, and a Gore-Tex shell.

Dressing in layers makes it easy to adjust during the day to changes in exertion, temperature, precipitation, and wind. Best of all, layering helps you avoid lugging around a single heavy outer garment.

On a recent visit to New Zealand, which came after three months of traveling near the Equator, I found myself in the midst of their coldest winter in 30 years. Although I had no parka, layering provided plenty of warmth, even when I was scrambling across the glaciers. Each morning, I put on about half the clothes in my pack, including a Capilene undershirt, turtleneck, a long-sleeve canvas shirt, and a windproof shell. Rather than carry them all the way from home, I bought a sweater, gloves, and a wool cap within hours after arriving in Christchurch.* At night I was comfortable in a flannel nightshirt and thick socks. A lightweight poncho provided fine protection from rain. A good parka would have done the job, but I didn't want to carry one for a hundred days just to enjoy it for ten.

Timing. When you absolutely need bulky clothing for severe cold weather during part of a trip, try to arrange the trip so the need comes at the beginning. I'm referring to times such as high-altitude winter weather, or hiking that requires heavy boots and specialized gear. Use the heavy stuff, then ship it home inexpensively via sea freight.

Function over Fashion. Some travelers feel more secure if they are prepared to dress conventionally for any event that might come up. Since Europeans are more fashion conscious than the rest of the world, many travelers to Europe feel more comfortable with at least some dressy clothing. However, if most of a trip involves walking in central Africa, why worry about being a little underdressed if you drop into the famous Prague Spring Music Festival on your way home? If you go from the steamy canals of the Pantanal† to a fine restaurant in Rio, it's okay to be a little behind the fashion curve when the alternative is to carry a blue blazer through the rain forest. In other words, forget about packing clothes for every contingency.

Match the Pieces. Choose a color scheme so various items of clothing will match one another. One way to do that is to concentrate primarily on two colors. Take bottoms that will match well with several tops.

---

* *Christchurch.* The largest city on New Zealand's South Island is often described as the most English city in New Zealand. It is a departure point for the Southern Alps and some fine walks.

† *Pantanal.* One of the world's great wildlife preserves, much of this vast swampy region in southwest Brazil is accessible only by air or water.

Colors. Colors such as maroon, blue, red, black, and green don't show the grime and wounds of traveling as dramatically as light colors do. Taking much white clothing on anything other than a very warm weather or very urban trip would be a mistake. Even khaki shows dirt easily.

Avoid the Military Look. A potentially more serious mistake would be wearing clothing that looks as if it were military-issue, including olive drab or camouflage cloth. Why invite the authorities to question your mission?

Check for Good Condition. Examine all clothing you plan to take to be sure it's in good shape. Don't let a loose button or faulty seam make itself known at the most inopportune time. Nevertheless, your clothing may not be in great shape when you return. In many regions of Asia, for example, the cleaning process includes pounding clothes against a flat rock on a river bank. The laundry comes back clean but a little stressed.

Choose Easy-to-Clean Clothes. Choose clothes that resist wrinkling and are easy to care for. In the past, wool and 100 percent cotton were universally recommended, but synthetics have recently found more defenders. A wet cotton shirt or socks can stay cold and damp for much longer than polypropylene and synthetic blends. The latter are lighter weight, wash and dry more quickly, and look better after being rolled up in your pack. Leave at home anything that requires dry cleaning.

Check the price of laundry service before sending anything off. It's generally not as inexpensive as you might expect. Sometimes the charge is based on weight; more frequently it's based on the number and type of pieces. Wash small pieces yourself. Minimize expense, as well as wear and tear, by taking concentrated laundry detergent along.

Try to take clothes that will air-dry overnight and minimize those that can't be washed until you'll be in one place for several days. A Ziploc bag works well for transporting things that should have dried before some departure—but didn't. If you're trekking, fasten the Ziploc bag to the outside of your pack with a large safety pin.

Clothes wrinkle less if you shake them, roll them in a towel, and hang them up. If you hang rumpled clothes in the bathroom, steam from the shower eliminates most of the wrinkles.

Checklist: Clothing

The following list contemplates an informal trip of several weeks. Your adjustments should reflect personal tastes, the length of your trip, and anticipated climates and activities. As a general rule, keep clothing simple and modest. If you travel with a partner, don't duplicate any clothing you can share. And remember to count the clothes you'll be wearing as you walk out the door to the airport.

For Men

1. Shirts.

__ Two **short-sleeve outdoor shirts**. Consider 100 percent cotton mesh polo shirts with collars. They are cool, wash easily, and stand up well to travel stress.

__ Two **long-sleeve shirts** with collars (depending on the weather). My favorites are medium-weight cotton with front pockets that button. Smith & Hawken and Patagonia shirts are a good combination of quality and price. Depending on the trip, you may want one or two dressier, wrinkle-proof shirts.

__ Two or three cotton **T-shirts**. Buy more as souvenirs.

__ One long-sleeve **turtleneck** for cool weather. They're warm, look good, and travel well.

__ One **vest**. This is optional but can provide both warmth and a little dressiness.

2. Pants.

__ The number of pants needed depends on the trip; usually two pairs, seldom more than three. One pair should be a tough 100 percent cotton twill, suitable for rough parts of the trip. L.L. Bean offers these in several colors. If the weather will be very cold, I substitute 85 percent wool pants made by Woolrich. Smith & Hawken sells durable canvas pants in 8-ounce medium weight and $11^1/4$

For Women

1. Shirts.

__ Two T-shirts.

__ Three **shirts or blouses**, as dressy or basic as appropriate. Long sleeve or short sleeve, depending on the weather, but probably not **no** sleeve. Plunging necklines should be avoided. A **jogging top** can serve as a shirt, a swimming suit top, and even sleepwear.

__ Whether you bring a **wool shirt** depends on the weather; the same for a blue jean shirt. Either layers well over a blouse.

__ For cool weather, a **turtleneck** is very desirable.

__ Besides warmth and dressiness, a **vest** also provides an extra bit of modesty in conservative countries.

2. Pants.

__ One or two **lightweight** pairs of loose-fitting pants (possibly substituting one heavier pair, depending on expected weather). Buy casual pants on the road.

__ **One or two regular skirts** for slightly dressier wear. Skirts should fit loosely and skirt length should be below the knee. In some countries, especially the Arab world, women are expected to keep their legs covered,

For Men

2. Pants (continued)

ounce. "cast-iron" weight. The second pair should be **lighter weight** but very durable (again, 100 percent cotton). One useful style has legs that zip off at midthigh (creating a good pair of shorts for use when the sun rises high). The TravelSmith catalog (800-950-1600) offers two useful versions of these convertible pants. The third pair should be a potentially **dressy pair of khakis**. Patagonia sells khaki pants with a cotton outer sheath and polyester inner core that make them extremely durable. For European or big-city trips, add a pair of dress slacks.

Avoid pants in which the side or slash pockets do not swing freely, that is, ones in which the pockets are sewn to the pants leg. They dump change, keys, and everything else every time you put your feet up. For security, look for pockets that button, zip, or close with Velcro, or sew metal snaps into the tops of the pockets. In fact, some pants have sewn-on security pockets big enough to hold airline tickets.

__ One pair of **hiking or gym shorts**. To reduce weight, take shorts that can double as a swimming suit.

__ On the road, consider buying colorful, lightweight pants made in the local style. They're fun to wear even though they may begin to look a little weird or start to fall apart by the time they get home.

Contrary to expectations, blue jeans don't make great travel companions. They are heavy, have no dress-up potential, dry slowly, and can bind fiercely on a long bus trip.

For Women

2. Pants (continued)

so local standards of modesty should guide your choices. Some women prefer blue jean skirts.

__ Some women recommend a pair of sturdy **leotards** or **ballet tights** for warmth.

The comments I've heard about one-piece pants suits or body suits have been uniformly negative, referring either to lack of flexibility or incompatibility with using basic toilet facilities.

__ Bring at least one pair of modestly cut **shorts**.

For Men	For Women

3. Underwear.

__ Cotton or blended briefs in dark colors. Three pairs are plenty if you'll be able to wash them regularly. Taking nylon underwear, which doesn't breathe, to the tropics would be courting a fungal infection.

3. Underwear.

__ Three pairs of cotton or blended panties and one or two brassieres. Although silk underwear dries quickly, it's inappropriate for warm climates. There are many places where not wearing a brassiere would offend local mores and attract unwanted attention. Some women attach a runners key pouch to their bra as a hidden stash for emergency funds. You may also want a half-slip (Hidden Assets makes one with a money belt built in).

4. Socks.

__ Take three or four pairs of high-quality socks. You may want some wool socks (with a little nylon) heavy enough for hiking, as well as some that are lighter but still sturdy enough for sock-footed temple visits. Some argue that the best socks are made of hydrophobic (water-hating) synthetics that wick sweat away from the foot. Two favorites are the Wigwam Ultimax and the Thor-Lo hiking model. Various colors, even gym gray, conceal road grime better than white does. By the way, if you take several identical pairs of socks, you have less of a problem when one sock wears through or floats off down the Ganges. Depending on the trip, a man might want one pair of dress socks and a woman one pair of knee-high stockings (if appropriate for your shoes).

5. Shoes.

__ One pair of **sandals.** Cheap rubber sandals or plastic flip-flops are fine for showers and the beach, but you need sturdy sandals to cushion the feet and protect them from street debris when walking around town. Teva river sandals are a favorite, but similar brands work fine so long as they are well made and have an ankle strap and fairly thick soles. Wear sandals for a while before you leave so the straps won't rub raw patches on your feet when it matters.

I used to travel with hiking boots but seldom do so any more because they're heavy and space-consuming. Well-made, lightweight, low-cut **trail/ walking shoes** work well for all but strenuous hiking situations. Dark brown, gray, and black don't show dirt and look fairly dressy. Ordinary tennis shoes are okay, but they usually provide less arch and lateral support than good walking shoes do. If you're willing to spring for the cost of walking shoes, you'll prob- ably consider it a good investment. If cost is a problem, go with tennis shoes.

Rub in Sno-Seal to waterproof shoes. I've been told that the aerosol in at least some waterproofing sprays dissolves the glue between the sole and the upper (not to mention further stressing the atmosphere).

Whatever your choice in shoes, give them a good workout before you go. Don't get under way with a pair that doesn't fit. Your feet are your wheels; if you don't pamper them a little, you'll wish you had.

For women: My recommendations are the same as for men's shoes adding, perhaps, ballet-type slippers or light leather flats for dressier wear. They're light and compress well in a pack.

6. Belt.
___ Take one sturdy belt that fits the loops of all your pants.

7. Nightshirt.
___ You need some covering for hostels, overnight trains, and outdoor toilets, and to meet strict standards of modesty in some countries. A gym warm-up suit works fine but is bulkier than a nightshirt. In tropical countries, consider a **khanga, lava lava, lunghi, pareu, sarong**, or whatever it's called locally. It's a rectangular piece of cloth that you wrap around knee-to-waist or chest to provide modesty consistent with local custom. It also serves as a beach blanket or towel and only costs about $2.

8. Swimsuit.
___ On some beaches in the Third World, skimpy suits are not welcome. On others, suits are not necessary at all. If you bring a suit, it should be more modest than not and be made of quick-drying material.

9. Rain gear.
___ Consider a Gore-Tex **shell** or a waterproof **poncho.** The latter, which takes less room, should be long enough to cover a pack on the trail. Although hot and not very durable, a cheap raincoat or rain suit that stuffs into a pocket may be sufficient. Some efficient travelers use them as bathrobes and windbreakers as well. Samsonite offers an attractive raincoat with a hood (Magellan's, $16.85).

10. Extra warmth.
___ Light, warm synthetic is a good place to start. A lightweight **windbreaker,** which needn't be expensive or fancy, can be extremely useful. A polyester-cotton jacket or polypropylene pile works well. A **down vest** provides warmth in a small package. If you'll need a light sweater, it may be worth taking one along (but less often than you might think). Buy a heavy **sweater** when needed rather than carrying it all the way. Find warmth through layering or endure a little chill rather than lug a heavy jacket around the world. If it will be really chilly, take thermal underwear.

11. Towel.
___ Don't expect to be furnished a towel or washcloth very often in budget hotels. If you take a towel, it should be small and thin to save space and drying time.

12. Bandannas.

__ They make good sweat bands and are generally useful, especially for women. They're plentiful in local markets.

13. Scarves.

__ A nice scarf can dress up an otherwise road-weary outfit and a warm scarf makes you snug in raw weather. In certain cultures, women are expected to cover their heads with a scarf.

14. Hat/sun visor.

__ You should have one or the other. If you don't take one, you can easily buy it on the road.

15. Gloves.

__ If heading to a very cold climate, including high altitude, take a pair of insulated gloves. For less than bitter cold, a pair of wool knit gloves is fine. If you want to protect your hands and warmth isn't a factor, cheap cotton gloves are sufficient (e.g., paddling trips and in places such as Rwanda where gloves protect your hands from stinging nettles as you haul yourself up volcanic slopes to visit the mountain gorillas).

16. Tie.

__ If something comes up that makes you think you need a tie, buy it locally. If you can't, ties won't be the custom—so forget it.

17. Blazer.

__ If you expect to do some business or visit places where upscale dress is appropriate, tuck a wrinkle-proof blazer in the bottom of your bag. However, it's not worth carrying one on the off chance you *might* want it.

Checklist: Toiletries

Use a leak-proof, soft-sided toiletries kit (not a heavy leather kit). The see-through type works well. Unless you are on your way to Antarctica, you needn't take sufficient quantities of everything to last for your whole trip. Take small sizes and restock as you go.

__ **Band-Aids.**

__ **Comb** (and/or brush).

__ **Deodorant** (stick type preferable to aerosol).

__ **Dental care items:** including **toothbrush** (preferably a travel-type with its own storage container or cap), **tooth paste**, and **dental floss**.

__ **Insect repellent.** DEET is very effective, but since DEET is absorbed into the bloodstream, a 40 percent solution is preferable for use on a long trip. UltraThon ($6.85), a 33 percent DEET solution using a controlled-release polymer suspension, is becoming very popular. Permethrin clothing spray is also recommended (see Chapter 8).

__ **Laundry detergent** (more useful than you might imagine).

___ **Lip balm** (with sunscreen).

___ **Mirror** (metal if you believe in, or have, bad luck).

___ **Moleskin** (to prevent a blister from bringing your trip to a halt).

___ **Mosquito coils.**

___ **Nail clippers** (or emery boards).

___ **Panty liners** (if you will be doing a lot of trekking).

___ **Razor and blades** (ordinary soap or shampoo can serve as shaving lather). Many travelers aren't happy with a battery-powered electric razor on a long trip, but Braun makes a compact, eight-ounce version for under $30.

___ **Safety pins** (to pin keys in your pocket, pin a pocket closed, replace a button, etc.).

___ **Sanitary napkins or tampons** (*not* universally available, so you may want to take an adequate supply).

___ **Sewing kit.**

___ **Shampoo** (Johnson & Johnson Baby Shampoo can double as shaving lather and as laundry detergent).

___ **Soap** (small), in a plastic soap container.

___ **Sun screen** (waterproof; SPF 15 is popular, but there is a trend toward greater protection).

___ **Thermometer** (in a plastic case).

___ **Toilet paper** (take out the cardboard tube). "Don't leave home without it." Keep some in your daypack, more in your luggage. TP is for sale most places, but it's a rarity in Third World bathrooms or hotel rooms. Ignore this advice only if you intend to follow the local custom.

___ **Tweezers and scissors** (if not part of your Swiss Army knife).

Prescription and other medicines, as well as first aid supplies, are discussed in Chapter 8.

Checklist: Miscellaneous Gear

___ **Bags.** Take a couple sturdy plastic **garbage bags**, large enough to protect your pack from a downpour or salt spray, and a few sturdy, freezer-grade **Ziploc bags** (for leaky toiletries, a wet bathing suit, etc.). Plastic bags, such as dry-cleaning bags, keep muddy shoes from soiling their neighbors in your luggage. Light nylon camping **stuff sacks**, with drawstrings and cord locks, are useful for organizing small stuff.

___ **Camera gear.** Take more film than you think you'll need, a camera, zoom lens, extra camera battery, lens filters, and a lens cleaning kit. If you don't trust airport X-ray machines, carry film in lead-foil film bags (Sima Super FilmShield, $15).

___ **Clock.** Take an alarm clock that's durable and compact and ticks quietly—but has a loud, reliable alarm. I like one that also illuminates the face with a push of a button. You can find a very satisfactory clock with these characteristics for no more than $12. If you need an especially loud wake-up call and are willing to pay extra for it, consider the Braun, which has a built-in flashlight and increases in volume until it hits 82 dB (Magellan's, $37.85). Whatever your choice, start the trip with fresh batteries.

__ **Eyeglasses.** Remember sunglasses, prescription glasses, and contact lenses. Bring a decent-quality pair of sunglasses (with unbreakable lenses and UV protection) since many sunglasses for sale abroad provide little protection. BassPro AquaVision polarized glasses are good ($15, 800-227-7776). Whether it seems worthwhile to bring a second pair of prescription glasses depends on how much you rely on them. At least bring an up-to-date prescription in case you need a replacement. A **hard plastic travel** case keeps glasses from being crushed in your pack (TravelSmith offers a "bombproof" case for $9.50). Bring a retainer strap for glasses.

Dust and sand in the air sometimes cause problems for contact lens wearers. Since standard contact lens supplies are bulky and often unavailable on the road, some travelers have switched successfully to disposable contact lenses. Don't forget lens solution.

__ **Flashlight.** Take only a flashlight with a switch that can't turn on in your pack. One extra set of new batteries should be sufficient. **Batteries**, except for the lithium type used in high-tech cameras, are sold almost everywhere. A compact MiniMag or a key chain flashlight saves space, but I prefer an EverReady on which the case slides up to provide a lantern-like effect. Look for something waterproof.

There is even a combination AM/FM radio, clock, emergency siren, and flashlight. It's 8 x 2 x 2 inches and costs $20.

__ **Guidebooks** (or sections of them).

__ **Journal.** A five-by-eight-inch journal fits easily into a daypack.

__ **Locks.** For luggage, small sturdy locks are better than super-cheapies that can be picked in a second. Take enough for luggage and daypack zippers. Give a duplicate set of keys to your travel partner. Code each key to match the corresponding lock (with dots of paint or nail polish) to avoid frustrating fumbling. There are also locks that, when open, retain their keys (about $4/pair).

To avoid the problem of dealing with multiple keys, consider small combination locks. Using the first numbers of your zip code, your birthdate, or something else obvious, helps you recall the combinations. Three-number locks on which you set the combination yourself cost $5 at Sears, $3 at hardware stores, $13 for a pair from Magellan's.

For security in hotel rooms, some travelers carry a battery-powered doorstop alarm ($9.75), a wedge that fits under a hotel door. If the door moves, a shrill siren alarm goes off. A low-tech door wedge also works fine. A Travelock ($9.85) locks dresser drawers as well as hotel doors.

A Jammer is a device that sticks with a suction cup to the inside of a train or hotel sliding window. If someone tries to open the window, the Jammer is supposed to wedge in tightly to prevent entry.

___ **Maps.** Traveling without good maps is an unnecessary handicap. Some guidebook maps are good, but they're small. Buy large-scale maps to help in planning your trip and take them along to assist in rerouting. Travel bookstores and AAA are good sources (see Chapter 2). Tourist offices abroad have adequate maps.

___ **Money belt and wallet.** The traditional favorite money belt is a fairly flat ten-inch pocket designed to be worn around the waist under the clothes ($12 to $17). The better ones have two or three zippered pockets. For travelers who prefer something less bulky around the waist, consider shoulder-holster, hanging-from-the-neck, pin-on-the-bra, and around-the-calf styles. They provide good security, but their capacity may be too limited. For long trips, I like a hidden-pocket that hangs inside the front of the pants from a belt loop (about $10). It's much easier to reach than the around-the-waist type. Make sure it will hold all the things you must keep secure.

If you carry a wallet, Cordura may be preferable to leather because the rough Cordura surface makes it less likely to slip or be slipped out of a pocket. Some people prefer a trifold wallet that attaches to the belt with a light chain. They can be purchased in motorcycle shops and truck stops.

___ **Reading material.** Starting your trip with enough reading material for the entire journey means carrying a heavy burden. New books are often more expensive abroad than at home, but you'll find plenty of used book shops that will trade two of your books for one of theirs. At the excellent bookstore on the lake shore in Pokhara,* the very literate owner will sell you *The Snow Leopard* or some other book ideal for your trek to the Annapurna Sanctuary, then buy it back for half-price when you return. Readers recognize one another so it's also easy to trade with other travelers.

Reading the literature of a country as you travel through it—whether fiction, philosophy, history, art, architecture, or culture—brings greater depth of meaning to the words and to the trip. In terms of price, variety of contents, and weight, Norton Anthologies of short fiction, literature, essays, or poetry are an excellent value. Thousands of tissue-thin pages provide hundreds of hours of pleasure. See the Bibliography for many other suggestions.

___ **Rubber bands.** Take a dozen or two for rolling your clothes and all kinds of unexpected uses.

___ **Swiss Army knife.** A knife with a couple of blades is adequate, but it's the rest of the collection that makes Swiss Army knives indispensable. One version includes scissors, corkscrew, tweezers, can opener, bottle opener, and screwdriver. One caution: a knife may be confiscated by airport security if carried in your daypack or pocket.

---

* *Pokhara.* This colorful small town in central Nepal is a starting point for treks into the Himalayas.

___ **Wristwatch.** Desirable features include a display of the date and day, an alarm, a light for the face, and water-resistance. Whatever you wear, it shouldn't look expensive.

___ **Writing materials.** A couple of long yellow pads, plus a few ballpoint pens (which are easy to replace while traveling). If you have room, pens make nice gifts.

If some of the gear you want isn't available from your local outfitter, Magellan's (800-962-4943) has a catalogue filled with what they call "essentials for the international traveler." As travelers themselves, Magellan's telephone operators have used much of the equipment listed in the catalogue so they can discuss it accurately. Moreover, if you're looking for something they don't carry, they'll call you back when it turns up, even if it's a year later. That's good service.

REI, Camp-Mor, and Patagonia also publish very useful catalogues. Try also the Compleat Traveler (212-685-9007) for books and Traveler's Checklist (860-364-0144) for equipment.

Some of the best resources for a wide range of travel books, luggage, and equipment are TravelFest superstores, based in Austin, Texas (800-343-3378).

Checklist: Documents to Take Along

___ **Airline tickets** (and a copy).

___ **American Automobile Association membership card.** Foreign automobile associations may extend reciprocal benefits to AAA members, including maps and travel information. You may even get free road service if you've rented a vehicle.

___ **ATM card.** Take more than one.

___ **Certificate of Registration** (registration of expensive items with Customs on departure).

___ **Credit cards** (including a list of card numbers and telephone numbers for reporting a loss). Take more than one.

___ **Driver's license.** A normal driver's license serves as general identification and may be required to rent cars. In addition, the local American Automobile Association office sells an International Driver's License (for $10 and a passport-size photo). It is, at least in theory, required to drive in Japan, Indonesia, Thailand, Eastern Europe, and parts of Europe.

___ **Insurance.** Proof of insurance and your agent's telephone number.

___ **International Certificate of Vaccination** (yellow card).

___ **International Student ID card.** Widely accepted verification of student status.

___ **Itinerary.**

___ **Medical information.** Blood type, description of special medical conditions, allergies, personal physician's phone number, health insurance information.

___ **Names, addresses, and telephone and fax numbers.** People to be contacted in case of emergency and people to contact on the road and at home.

___ **Passport** (plus copies of the first two pages of the passport), extra passport photos, and separate proof of citizenship in case you must replace a lost passport.

___ **Permits** (trails, game watching, work).

___ **Photo ID** (for airport security).

___ **Prescriptions.** Extra copies of essential prescriptions.

___ **Reservations** (for hotels, etc.).

___ **Telephone charge card.**

___ **Travelers checks** (and a separate copy of check numbers).

___ **Visas.**

___ **Youth hostel membership card** (See Chapter 11).

Checklist: Optional Equipment

Everything on this list could add to the pleasure of your trip, and I've taken most of the items at one time or another. You could take them all at once if you want to—so long as you plan to travel with an elephant and bearers. The issues are weight, space, and simplicity.

___ **Binoculars.** Good ones are expensive—and attractive to thieves. They are essential for wild game viewing, but for most other purposes a zoom lens works well enough.

___ **Briefcase.** Eastern Mountain Sports, Eagle Creek, and others make a soft Cordura briefcase for keeping papers and documents collected inside your pack. These are surprisingly useful.

___ **Business cards** (or travel cards you've designed for the trip). Cards make a good impression on officials and are an easy way for travel friends to keep track of your name and number.

___ **Calculator.** For about $35, you can buy a Seiko SII. It's a calculator, currency converter, metric converter, and translator between English and a selected language (about 40,000 words, phrases, and idioms; most of the languages available are European). Although very small, it has sufficient memory to store travelers check numbers, flight information, telephone numbers, and so on. Simple solar-powered calculators sell for $2.

___ **Carabiners.** These small locking rings, used by climbers, are unexpectedly handy for avoiding losing things. No need to buy the high-quality type unless your life will be hanging from one.

___ **Cassette recorder/player.** There are times when familiar music is soothing, particularly when traveling alone. You may also want to record ethnic music to add magic to your memories. Some travelers use a recorder to dictate notes and record tour guides. Take only a few extra batteries (preferably the same size that fits your flashlight) and tapes since both are available on the road. If you're planning to write about your travel experiences and may be interviewing people, a recorder is a great help.

___ **Contraceptives.** They can be purchased abroad, but the brands may not be ones you recognize.

___ **Duct tape.** About three feet (wound around a piece of cardboard) is enough to fix a lot of what breaks on the road.

___ **Eating utensils.** A knife, fork, and spoon kit is nice when your hands are filthy or you don't feel like eating with them.

___ **Electrical gadgets.** Another reason, beyond weight, space, cost, and karma, not to take electrical appliances that have to be plugged in is that they may not work. For one thing, your plug may not fit in the local socket. If your trip is geographically limited, you may get away with one **adapter** plug ($3 to $5). Otherwise, consider an adapter plug set (Magellan's, $11.85). Note that a videocamera battery charger may need an adapter.

Since electric current in much of the world is different (220–240 volts) from that used in the United States (110–120 volts), you are likely to need a current **converter** as well. The type of converter depends on where you're going, the kind of equipment you will use (camcorder, razor, laptop computer, CD player, etc.), and how heavy your usage will be. Converters range from $15 to $28 and weigh up to 13 ounces. Magellan's catalogue tells you what converter you would need—but you have to decide whether you really need the appliance.

___ **Film shield.** A lead foil bag that protects 22 rolls of film (about $13).

___ **Immersion heater.** Plug one end of this device into a wall socket and dip the other in your tea or coffee cup, heating the water in minutes. It's lightweight, inexpensive ($12), and convenient, and it pays for itself quickly. Choose 220V or 110V depending on where you'll be traveling.

___ **Mace.** Be aware that carrying sprays such as Mace is forbidden on many airlines (more on security in Chapter 13).

___ **Mask and snorkel.** Although both are usually available for rent at dive sites, you can't always find a mask that fits well and has a clear lens. Fins available for rent are often weary and sized for people whose feet resemble fins less than mine do. Still, think twice before carrying bulky fins around the world. Scuba diving equipment is always available on site, but quality varies. Inspect it closely. If you doubt it, try elsewhere.

___ **Musical instruments.** Shared music is an instant introduction. I envied a Canadian with whom I traveled who had a wonderful time playing his fiddle with local bands. I carry a tenor recorder and a harmonica for my own amusement.

___ **Nylon clothesline.** Potentially useful, seldom necessary.

___ **Pillow, inflatable.** It sounds wimpy, but you'll love it on long overnighters on a bouncing bus. Consider a covered inflatable pillow (under $10), which tucks under your chin and curves around to rest on your shoulder. Some travel agents give inflatable pillows to good clients.

___ **Radio.** A shortwave radio, such as the Grundig Traveller II (13 ounces) or the Grundig YB 305 will pull in the BBC and music from around the world. If you're more interested in listening to local music and local language, a simple AM/FM radio will do.

___ **Sewing kit.** A small one, including a few safety pins, can be useful (no more than $3). On the other hand, it's easy and inexpensive to have sewing repairs done as you travel.

___ **Sheet sack.** Since beds in hostels don't come with linen, you must use a sheet sack. Some hostels rent them, but the cumulative expense would be fairly great for anyone staying in hostels frequently. Since a sheet sack takes up room in the pack, your decision should reflect how often you expect to sleep in hostels. You can make one, buy one from a hostel, or order one from Magellan's ($15 to $24).

___ **Sink stopper.** A flat rubber sink stopper can be handy, especially when washing clothes (one-half ounce, $2).

___ **Sleeping bag.** Seldom necessary; carry only if certain to use it.

___ **Sleeping pad.** You really have to need it to make it worth carrying for weeks or months. The Therm-a-Rest brand is tough and rolls up fairly compactly.

___ **Slippers.** If you want something other than socks or sandals for showers, down-the-hall toilet trips, or the beach, consider Ultra Soles. Partially net, they come in a pouch and weigh only four ounces. Magellan's ($7.85).

___ **Travel games.** When there's nothing going on and you're not creatively inspired, break out the **cards** and start a first-to-ten-thousand-points game of gin rummy. If you draw a curious crowd, use the opportunity to meet people and learn some of the local card games. **Chess, backgammon, and Scrabble** are available in miniature travel versions. Amuse yourself and others with any of the versions of **Trivial Pursuit** or its imitators (especially ones that focus on travel). A **Frisbee** is great for a playful spirit and a little exercise. A plastic jar of **soap bubble fluid** is an easy way to get involved with local kids.

___ **Umbrella.** I buy a cheapie on the road if I need one. If you'd rather start out with a good one, stick with an eight-inch compact version.

___ **Water bottle.** Choose a tough plastic bottle with a secure top (it's best if the top is attached to the bottle). It should hold no less than one liter, nor more than two liters (if bigger, it gets very heavy when full). TravelSmith offers an interesting collapsible canteen ($19) that holds two liters and fits easily in a pocket when empty. It's polyurethane inside and tough pack-cloth outside. A wineskin served me well for several months in South America. The reason I consider a water bottle only optional is that in most of the world disinfected water is sold in very serviceable plastic bottles.

Although a water bottle can ride happily in a daypack, Magellan's Bottle Bridle, an over-the-shoulder harness, is also useful ($9.85).

__ **Waterproof bags.** Seal Pak (800-531-9531) makes a waterproof bag that straps around your waist and goes into the water with you. It will hold a wallet, passport, or plane tickets. Similar is the five-by-seven-inch Water-Pocket from Watersafe ($13, call 800-355-1126). There is also a urethane-coated nylon Hydra-Pouch (about $10). It's a six-by-seven-inch neck pouch which keeps valuables dry. Basic Designs (707-575-1220) offers a bag with a screw top that will hold a small camera as well as valuables. It is made to be carried rather than worn.

__ **Whistle.** This could be useful for summoning help on a wilderness trek—or for security purposes.

Checklist: What Not to Take

- Breakable or leaky containers
- Electrical appliances
- Jewelry
- Illegal drugs
- Illegal drugs
- Illegal drugs
- Problems from home
- Anything you absolutely cannot stand to lose

These checklists will simplify your preparations and remind you of key items otherwise easy to overlook. Medicine and first aid items are covered in Chapter 8.

Jewelry

Wearing expensive jewelry conflicts with being a traveler. In addition, good jewelry and watches, including authentic-looking fakes, are a magnet for thieves. As I was checking into a small hotel on Ipanema Beach in Rio, a woman burst in through the front door, crying, blood streaming from her forehead and one elbow. A thief had knocked her to the sidewalk as he ripped a heavy gold necklace from her throat. She's wearing a gold necklace in Rio? Of course, the same thing would have happened had her necklace been only an expensive-looking fake. Dress yourself with local crafts. Buy inexpensive jewelry from local artists. Thieves know how little these things cost and leave them alone. If you buy expensive jewelry while traveling, keep it locked up.

Camping

For most travelers, carrying a full set of camping equipment is cumbersome and unnecessary. I've had no difficulty renting what I needed as I went along (inexpensively, at that). For whitewater trips, safaris, and similar events, equipment is available at the departure point. On most independent treks, there are villages along the way where you can find food and lodging so you needn't worry about a tent, foam pad, tarp, stove, and the rest. If you need cooking equipment, it's certainly better to rent it than carry it halfway around the world. In places where a hammock would be desirable, say on a boat chugging down a tributary of the Amazon, there are plenty for sale locally.

Sleeping bags are so heavy and bulky that I've never wanted to carry one around the world. If you do, synthetic is better than down if there's any chance the bag will get wet.

8

Keeping Healthy

I have traveled widely in my lifetime, having been struck
by the virus at an early age and having, as yet, developed
no antibodies to harden my resistance or immunity.
—Caskie Stinnett
Grand and Private Pleasures

Who hasn't heard stories about a vacation spent staring out the window at the beach while Montezuma exacted his revenge? More than 5,000 Australians canceled vacations to Bali after a report that one Swedish visitor died of encephalitis. Thousands of travelers canceled East African safari reservations after reading stories about the Ebola virus, even though the game reserves in Kenya and Tanzania are located halfway across the continent from where Ebola struck in the Congo.

Should international travelers be concerned about their health? Yes—at least enough that they learn what the issues are and take basic preventive measures. No—if that means exaggerating the risks and staying home.

Consumers Association in England, which probably conducts the most extensive travel health surveys in the world, recently announced that only about 15 percent of all travelers get sick, and only 4 percent become sick enough to seek medical attention. Moreover, even those small numbers were affected by higher percentages in destinations such as India and Africa.

At least as important as knowing the low rate of illness is realizing what affects those who do become ill. More than half have only stomach problems and diarrhea. Next in line are sunburn, coughs, colds, ear infections, and motion sickness. Of those who do get some bug, the overwhelming majority are over it by the time they get home; a very small price for the vast rewards of travel.

About one-quarter of traveler's deaths are related to injuries, not diseases, and often involve motor vehicles and alcohol. Another substantial percentage of deaths result from underlying medical problems, such as cardiovascular disease, and have nothing to do with travel. The risk of being affected by a major health problem while traveling is probably greater than the risk of being impaled by a unicorn, but it's certainly tolerable.

The potential health problems discussed below affect only an infinitesimally small number of travelers. For example, of more than 140,000 Peace Corps volunteers, only three died of tropical diseases in 34 years. With the exception of malaria, the other diseases seldom even appear on lists of potential hazards published by the World Health Organization.

I feel reluctant to devote so much space to health issues for fear it will make them seem daunting. I do it *only* because it is precisely this knowledge and preparation that can enable you to travel virtually anywhere without undue concern about getting sick. Knowledge reduces anxiety.

When it's so easy to stay healthy abroad, the behavior of some travelers amazes me. They assume they're bulletproof and won't get sick no matter what they do. They read an article on health risks, throw a couple of all-purpose antidotes in their toiletries kits, and never give another thought to health. Perhaps they believe that signing on with a tour group encloses them in a magic bubble. A few even convince themselves that the only way to truly experience a country is to live exactly as the locals do, eating street food and drinking tap water. These attitudes court disaster.

Good health depends on factors such as where you go, whether you take

Caveat

Since I'm not a doctor, what follows cannot be taken as medical advice. Even if I seem to state something definitively, I'm simply sharing with you the results of my research and the choices I make for myself. You must do your own research, at the time you're going to travel, applicable to the specific regions you expect to visit. I am not a substitute for your doctor. If you consult one or more doctors, ensure they are qualified to answer the questions you ask. A doctor may be expert in his or her field but inexperienced or behind the times concerning your foreign travel questions.

When I mention a product by brand name it's because I presently consider it to be the most effective choice. I have no interest in promoting any particular product. Any medicine mentioned in the text should be taken only by a person who is aware of its risks and possible interaction with other over the counter and prescription medicines. Be cautious about buying drugs over the counter abroad that are sold only by prescription in the United States. Ensure that you understand clearly what the possible side effects might be.

effective preventive measures, what care you exercise, what risks you take, and your state of health when you left home—plus your attitude and a little luck.

Prevention

I'm a naturally healthy person and have probably had good luck along the way, but simple preventive behavior has been the major factor in keeping me free from health problems on the road. Prevention is easy. It consists of doing a little research, exercising common sense, following a few guidelines, and getting check-ups before leaving for an extended period.

Start by considering honestly whether you have any disabilities or illnesses that should deter you from traveling independently to the countries you've selected. Evaluate the physical demands of the trip in the context of your general fitness. Keep in mind the style of travel you plan and the availability of health services. Discuss the trip with a doctor. Also remember that travel doesn't make people immune to things that make them sick at home, such as heart disease, upper respiratory infection, and chronic diseases like diabetes.

Instead of staying home or taking unnecessary risks, learn (1) which health hazards may exist on a particular trip, (2) what to do to avoid those hazards, and (3) what to do should a problem occur. This chapter is filled with that information.

Risk usually accompanies expansion of our horizons, but that didn't keep our ancestors at home and it shouldn't keep us at home either. I'll take Kenya anytime over fast foods and freeway driving.

Research

As soon as I have an itinerary, I contact the *Centers for Disease Control* (CDC) in Atlanta, Georgia. The CDC has current information on immunization requirements, malaria prevalence, and other travel-related diseases in every country. Call (404) 332-4559 for the international travelers voice hotline; (404) 332-4565 to order documents available by fax. Ask for disease outbreak bulletins, information on AIDS abroad, lists of useful publications, and so on. You'll be dealing with recorded messages, so be prepared to take notes. A typical call lasts five to ten minutes. Most of the same information is available on the Web at www.cdc.gov. Click on Traveler's Info. Check the blue sheets for current entrance requirements. You can even find sanitation reports on cruise ships.

Advice from a good *travel medicine clinic*, of which there are more than 500, is usually superior to advice from most general practitioners. To find a clinic, check the phone book for the subheadings Travel Medicine or Infectious Disease under the main listing for Physicians, or call a medical center or tropical medicine specialist. If you send a self-addressed nine-by-eleven-inch envelope with 98 cents postage to Dr. Leonard C. Marcus (Travelers Health and Immunization Service, 148 Highland Avenue, Newton, MA 02115), he will send you a list of more than 100 travel medicine clinics.

Prices vary considerably from clinic to clinic. Some charge a consultation fee ranging from $25 to $125 (which may include one or more vaccinations). A shot that costs $5 at one might cost $25 at another.

Most *local public health services* have exotic immunoglobulins and vaccines on hand (which doctors in private practice often do not). Their charges are reasonable and their nurses are expert at giving shots.

Among questions you should ask is whether any countries on your itinerary require visitors to have had specific vaccinations before entering. These requirements are listed in *Health Information for International Travel* published by the U.S. Public Health Service (available from the Superintendent of Documents, U.S. Government Printing Office (GPO), Washington, DC 20402, 202-783-3238). The GPO is an excellent source for overall travel medicine information.

If you'll be traveling to any place at all exotic, you'll probably need immunizations. Some immunizations consist of a series of two or three shots and some cannot be given at the same time as others. That means you can't wait until the last minute to get them. Tell the health service where you're going and which shots you want and they'll give you a schedule. Ask also about shots you should consider that are not necessarily related to travel, such as measles, mumps, chicken pox, diphtheria, tetanus, and influenza. If you're pregnant, ask whether each vaccine is safe for you. If you have the time, call three months before your planned departure. If you're in a hurry, a month may be enough.

Don't wait to get your immunization shots.

Travelers are occasionally stopped at some country's border and asked to provide proof they've had some immunization or another. An *International Certificate of Immunization* (known as the "yellow card" even though it's a booklet of several pages) is accepted as proof. If you don't have it, you may be turned back or required to get an inoculation on the spot under conditions that certainly would not be your first choice. Your local public health department, or whoever gives the inoculations, has the certificate and will list required vaccinations, other shots you've received, your blood type, allergies, and the person to notify in case of an emergency. The card lets you know how long each vaccine is effective. Since the yellow card is typically the only record of your shots, leave a copy at home.

If you have access to any of the major computer online services, log on for detailed international current health advisories.

I haven't suggested asking a doctor in private practice for information pertaining to international health issues because many don't have it. They usually weren't trained for these illnesses and don't encounter them with any regularity. You can't afford information that's out of date or just plain wrong.

Medical Help Abroad

The International Association for Medical Assistance to Travelers (IAMAT) provides a world directory of English- or French-speaking doctors abroad

> **Advice for Health Problems**
>
> If a significant health problem develops
> — ask for recommendations from a consulate (yours or anyone's)
> — contact a university medical center
> — call your credit card company if it offers medical assistance to travelers
> — consult your IAMAT list
> — check with volunteer organizations such as the Peace Corps
> — contact the State Department Overseas Citizens' Emergency Center
> — ask expatriates
> — get advice from other travelers
> — get assistance from local people
> — get to a big city where the standard of care is higher than it is in the countryside
> — hop on a plane for home

who meet its standards and have agreed to charge according to an established schedule of fees. IAMAT also provides a World Malaria Risk Chart, a booklet titled *How to Protect Yourself against Malaria*, and a World Immunization Chart. IAMAT even sells a freestanding mosquito net for beds. There is no charge for the information, but a donation of some amount is suggested (and needed). When you see the material, you'll feel like donating. Call (716) 754-4883.

Many credit cards have services that recommend hospitals and provide the names of English-speaking doctors to travelers abroad. They may even furnish an American doctor to consult with you or your foreign doctor.

Consider taking this chapter with you as you travel. If a problem develops, this information will help connect the symptoms with the probable disease—and thus with the appropriate medicine and other remedies.

THIRTEEN PRACTICAL TIPS

Even if some of the following tips seem obvious, I'm including them because I didn't understand them fully before I started traveling.

1. *Keep well rested.* Every traveler feels worn out once in a while from an overnight bus trip, several days of mountain trekking, or any number of things. Being immersed in a culture different from your own can be surprisingly wearing, especially early in a trip. You have daily tasks to do in a new environment, you're often in the midst of more people than you are at home, and you may be feeling a little homesick. All of this, plus a fast pace, can catch up with you physically and/or psychologically. If that happens, shut down for a day or two, or longer if that's what it takes. Being run-down makes you more susceptible to illness and undermines the positive attitude

that helps ward off oncoming disease. Taking time to rest is a trade-off, an investment in preventing future sick days. In planning an itinerary, schedule a few days on a beach or some other peaceful place after an especially demanding adventure.

Getting enough sleep usually isn't a problem on the road. There will be days when you're out at dawn to catch a bus or train or you stay up for late-night conversations and parties, but generally you turn in much earlier than at home. Away from cities, night life is pretty quiet. Where there is no electricity, yawns come early and most local people have to be in the fields or at the market at sunrise.

To ensure decent rest, find hotel rooms shielded from noise. Keep in mind that three sounds can penetrate the most determined slumber. The first is the sound of muezzins in long gray caftans standing on the balconies of minarets calling the faithful to dawn prayers. Even where a scratchy phonograph record and loudspeaker have replaced this classic figure, what has been lost in authenticity has more than been made up by an increase in decibels. The muezzin's command pierces a brick wall as if it were papier-mâché. Ask where the muezzin is and put some distance between his call and your bed. The second sound is ubiquitous. I used to think that roosters crowed only at dawn. They don't; they hold challenge matches all night long and it takes days to adapt to the raucous screeching. The third is the honking of impatient drivers in the early morning.

2. *Improve your fitness before you leave, then stay within your limits.* Work on physical conditioning before leaving home. Get into shape to walk three to five miles without discomfort. If your general health permits, lift weights for a few weeks to build upper-body strength. Extend your limits as the trip progresses, but don't try to do too much early on. It's easy to tear up a knee by plunging down a steep, rocky mountain trail before your thighs have strengthened to share the load.

3. *If you feel more than a little sick, get help.* Seems obvious doesn't it? Still, I keep meeting people like a German woman who fell ill in Nepal and stayed miserably, painfully sick for a month. When she finally went to a doctor, her dysentery was cured in a few days. Why suffer? Get help.

4. *Do not consume local water or food unless you are certain they are uncontaminated.* Assumptions aren't good enough, especially since they tend to be wishful thinking when you're thirsty or hungry. By following the guidelines in Chapter 12, you greatly improve the odds in your favor.

5. *Eat nutritiously, drink plenty of water, and take vitamins daily.* When making unusual demands on your body, eat well (even when it means eating unfamiliar foods) to keep up strength and resistance. If your diet becomes unbalanced, especially due to a shortage of greens, consider multivitamins

with minerals, and extra vitamins C and E. Acidophilus tablets are a good diarrhea preventive. Clean water is a necessary investment; drink plenty of it. Don't risk dehydration or a bladder infection.

6. *Keep clean.* Dress in combinations of clothes purchased in the last three countries you've visited, let your hair grow, do whatever helps you feel free— but get clean regularly. It's not for someone else or for the sake of convention, but because staying clean affects your health and state of mind. After a day in a gritty city, or coming off a dusty trail, a shower lifts the spirits. Opportunities to shower "later" evaporate all too often, so I've learned to take a shower when I have the chance.

Keeping your body clean helps keep cuts from getting infected or letting jungle rot get a foothold. No one really likes taking a cold shower in cold weather or washing out of a bucket, but it's worth gritting your teeth once in a while to get clean.

Because diseases communicated by touch are more common on the road, wash your hands much more frequently than at home. A good way to avoid accidental colds as well as fecal-oral transfer is to keep your fingers out of your mouth and avoid rubbing your eyes or nose. In public toilets, surfaces have been touched by many hands so don't touch anything you don't have to. Wash your hands in the morning, wash before eating, wash after visiting the bathroom. We may not wash as much as we should, but we can train ourselves to wash more than at home.

7. *Treat cuts and sores immediately.* The possibility of infection is higher when you're traveling, especially in the tropics. When skin is constantly moist, microbes flourish and small cuts and sores become infected quickly. When something needs first aid, tend to it right away.

8. *If you must receive a blood transfusion, exercise great caution.* Tainted blood supplies spread HIV and other diseases. If the need for a transfusion is foreseeable, consider flying, or being evacuated, to where the blood supply is safer. If that's not possible, call an embassy to see if it has a registry of screened donors. Make the medical facility aware of your concern. Insist on sterile needles and get someone trustworthy to supervise the process. The Blood Care Foundation in London can deliver fully tested blood by courier (if interested, write before you depart to P.O. Box 7, Sevenoaks, Kent TN13 2SZ, United Kingdom).

9. *Shield yourself from people coughing and sneezing near you.* During your travels, you'll be in crowds in train stations, on local buses, and on city streets. Even if you feel like a hypochondriac, protect yourself by turning away, moving away, or covering your mouth and nose. Those little droplets travel faster and farther than you would believe. Respiratory diseases are common, so being a little defensive is better than being a lot sick.

10. *Protect yourself from mosquitoes* (not to mention sand flies, black flies, ticks, mites and tsetse flies). This is one of the most important ways to protect your health. If biting insects are a problem, tuck your pants legs into your socks and wear a long-sleeve shirt. Stay away from stagnant bodies of water, rivers, and lakes around dawn and dusk when mosquitoes are most numerous.

Use an effective repellent. Although a persistent underground rumor suggests that Avon's Skin So Soft works as a repellent, recent tests do *not* indicate that it deters mosquitoes. Vaseline Intensive Care advertises a No Burn No Bite suntan oil, but apparently the slogan means only that it doesn't *attract* bugs. Anything based on DEET works best. However, DEET has some toxic quality and should be used with care, especially if use will be prolonged. For children, consider concentrations of as low as 10 percent (and ask a doctor before using on infants). Do not apply to a child's hands if the DEET could be transferred to the mouth. Consider applying over sunscreen to reduce absorption. Since pregnant women are generally advised to avoid insecticides, check first with a knowledgeable doctor. My personal preference is a concentration of 35 percent or less. I increase protection by spraying Permethrin on my clothing and mosquito net.

Some mosquito repellents will eat their way through your toilet kit if they spill, so transport them in a watertight container. When I look at the way they dissolve plastic, it makes me wonder what they do to skin.

Adjust the precautions you take according to the level of risk. Don't get spooked every time you hear a nasty whine, but do make an extra effort to avoid those little biters and suckers.

Since even the best prevention may not be successful 100 percent of the time, we'll discuss treatment for malaria later on in this chapter. Mosquito warfare is also discussed in Chapter 11 (Lodging).

11. *Carry good medical identification,* including notice of your blood type, allergies, and other special health characteristics (relevant medical or surgical history and names and doses of critical medication). List the name of a person to contact should you be in need. If you have medical insurance, carry evidence of it (though in some countries, medical facilities may still require payment in cash).

12. *First Aid.* The Red Cross offers a worthwhile first aid course and issues a useful first aid instruction card for travelers. They can also teach you how to perform cardiopulmonary resuscitation (CPR) and the Heimlich maneuver, important skills at home or abroad.

13. *Coming Home.* If you took malaria pills, remember to keep taking them for four weeks after leaving the malarial area. During your first weeks back, keep an eye on your health. If there's a problem, don't ignore it. Get a check up and tell the physician exactly where you've been (including time spent in rural areas or on the water) and whether you ate anything risky. If he or she is not knowledgeable about diseases in that area, find a specialist.

Minimize the effect of the relatively minor health problems on this list by washing frequently, dealing with a problem before it becomes serious, and using your head. Where I have mentioned medications, I've indicated whether the item is available over the counter (OTC) or by prescription only (P).

ALLERGIES

Even if not troubled by allergies at home, you might encounter something on the road that pushes an allergy button. Typical symptoms are sneezing, itchy eyes, nasal congestion, and headache. Antihistamines, such as Benadryl capsules (OTC) and Chlor-trimeton (OTC) could be helpful, but they have a sedative effect. Atarax (OTC) is less sedating than Benadryl. If you have a history of asthma, bring your medicine with you and don't let your travel schedule interfere with taking it regularly.

ALTITUDE SICKNESS

How to get it. Altitude sickness comes from ascending rapidly to altitudes where there is considerably less oxygen in the air than you're used to. For example, at 15,000 feet, there is only one-half as much oxygen in the atmosphere as there is when you're having dinner at the Top of the Mark in San Francisco. Symptoms of altitude sickness tend to occur in situations such as hiking in three or four days from the Tanzanian savannah at 5,000 feet to the 19,340-foot summit of Mount Kilimanjaro.

Sleeping at high altitude appears to be an important factor in causing altitude sickness. That's why mountaineers say: "Climb high, sleep low." In Nepal, a popular trekking destination, some trekkers are stricken when they ascend too quickly, sleep high, and cross 17,000-foot mountain passes before they become acclimatized. You also increase the chances of experiencing altitude sickness by overexerting yourself, getting dehydrated, and/or overconsuming alcohol soon after arrival at high altitude.

Physical fitness doesn't seem to protect against altitude sickness. To the contrary, the more fit the climber, the greater the likelihood of climbing too fast. Paradoxically, a recent medical study shows that climbers over age 60 are only half as likely to develop altitude sickness as people between ages 20 and 39.

Symptoms. At altitudes above 8,000 feet, about one out five people experiences shortness of breath, headache, loss of appetite, nausea, fatigue, and sleeplessness. Above 10,000 feet, the percentage may rise to 50 percent. These symptoms often indicate a mild case of altitude sickness. Symptoms appear during the first 18 to 48 hours, becoming more severe, depending on speed of ascent, then usually subsiding. If the symptoms become more severe and problems with balance develop, a severe case of altitude sickness may be developing. A dry, wracking cough can become a major problem, such as pulmonary edema. A friend of mine lost an opportunity to summit Mount Everest because his violent coughing fractured a rib.

Altitude sickness is no more than a minor problem for the great majority of people who experience it. However, it's important to be aware of the risk of *high-altitude pulmonary edema* (HAPE), which is fluid building up in the lungs and reducing the oxygen supply to the blood, and *high-altitude cerebral edema* (HACE), fluid building up in the brain.

Although pulmonary edema can occur as low as 8,000 feet, it is usually the result of rapid ascent, severe exertion, and sleeping at high altitude. A person who looks blue around the lips and develops chest congestion, wracking coughs, pink frothy sputum, rapid heart rate when resting, shortness of breath after very little exertion, persistent vomiting, serious loss of coordination, and extreme fatigue *must descend immediately*. With those symptoms, I don't think I'd argue. Symptoms of cerebral edema include severe headache, nausea, vomiting, hallucinations, difficulty maintaining balance, and bizarre behavior. To protect life, *descent must be immediate*.

How to avoid it. Ascending slowly is the best way to prevent altitude sickness. Take at least two days to get to 11,000 feet, then another week to reach 18,000 feet. Some experts recommend not increasing the altitude at which you sleep by more than 2,000 feet a day. This becomes more important the higher you go. If you ascend more rapidly, rest a day every 3,000 to 4,000 feet. As you ascend, you will naturally begin to breathe more deeply and, after a few days, your body will produce more oxygen-carrying red blood cells.

You can take acetazolamide (Diamox)(P), unless you have an allergy to sulfa, beginning a couple of days before starting your ascent and continuing throughout your stay at high altitude (although some climbers stop taking it once they have acclimated above 10,000 feet and are ascending slowly). By stimulating respiration and making the blood more efficient in delivering oxygen, it helps about 75 percent who take it. It also stimulates urination, so increase fluid intake, especially if your urine turns dark yellow.

When you exert yourself at high altitude, inhale bottled oxygen if it's available and get extra rest. Consume plenty of complex carbohydrates and go light on proteins and fats. Take in a little extra sugar, especially before you undertake strenuous exercise.

In the Andes, people drink *maté*, a tea made from coca leaves, in the belief that it provides some immunity to altitude sickness, perhaps by raising the rate of respiration. At the very least, it helps prevent *dolores de cabeza* (headache). The best evidence it works is that local people have continued drinking it for centuries. In general, however, tea, coffee, and alcohol are dehydrators and should be avoided. Instead, drink more water than you believe possible, increasing the amount as you ascend.

For people having trouble sleeping at high altitude, there's a temptation to take sleeping pills. The problem is that sleeping pills depress respiration and diminish the amount of oxygen being received. It's better to wait it out. If you must have a sleeping pill, consider Benadryl.

Treatment. If you develop a mild case of altitude sickness, take acetaminophen (Tylenol) or ibuprofen (Motrin) as well as Diamox. It would be wise to descend and see how you feel in a day or two. If you continue to ascend, be vigilant concerning your condition. Stop climbing if symptoms of a moderate case develop. Take Diamox and oxygen if available. If you don't get better, descend 1,500 to 3,000 feet and see if you improve.

If you develop symptoms of pulmonary or cerebral edema, descend immediately. Don't wait for help (or even daylight if descending at night is not ridiculously hazardous). Descend at least 3,000 feet; more is better. Get oxygen if you can. Don't try to tough it out. Pulmonary or cerebral edema can kill. Even if you feel better at the lower altitude, it would be better not to ascend again until an expert has evaluated your condition. For pulmonary edema, Nifedipine (P) is recommended. For cerebral edema, Dexamethasone (P). *If suffering from either, don't rely on medicine alone—get professional help.*

ATHLETE'S FOOT/FUNGAL INFECTIONS/BLISTERS

Keep your feet in good condition. Foot problems are frequent on the road and can put you out of action for days. Since high humidity and going barefoot in communal bathrooms contribute to getting foot fungus, wear shower shoes in and around the shower and dry your feet thoroughly. Don't let your socks get too grungy; change them every day if possible.

If your feet will be constantly wet, as they might be during an extended trek in Amazonia, coat them with Vaseline to ward off jungle rot. Sounds messy but it works.

If painful cracks develop between toes, treat them immediately. Tinactin (OTC), Desenex (OTC), or Monistat-Derm (OTC) as a powder or spray should work. If you're prone to problems with foot fungi, sprinkle Mexsana (OTC) powder in your shoes to absorb perspiration in which fungi thrive.

Wearing two pairs of socks helps prevent blisters. If you feel a blister developing, put on a band-aid with a patch of Moleskin (OTC) over it. If you pop a blister voluntarily, you're inviting infection, a bigger problem. If a blister pops by itself, treat it as you would a cut. Wash it often and, unless you're allergic to neomycin, try Neosporin (OTC) antibiotic. If you have that allergy, apply some other topical antibiotic. Cover the blister when you need to do so to keep it clean. The rest of the time, such as when you're in bed, leave it open to the air. Watch for infection. See if you can find and fix whatever caused the blister to form. It may have been something as simple as a rough spot on the inside of your shoe, or even a few grains of sand.

BIRTH CONTROL

The birth control method of your choice (if it's other than abstinence) may not be available as you travel, so you may want to take a supply with you. Both male and female travelers would be well advised to travel with condoms unless certain no new relationships will transcend the platonic. Be aware that high temperatures shorten the life span of most condoms.

The effectiveness of birth control pills may be diminished when a woman is taking oral antibiotics (including ampicillin and tetracycline). If a woman has continuing diarrhea, "the pill" may not be absorbed and she may not be protected. The stimulating experiences of travel have been known to cause some travelers to neglect their regular birth control routine. Since changing time zones may throw you off the once-every-24-hour dose required for maximum protection, it is recommended that you continue to take birth control on the schedule you used at home rather than shifting to local time.

It may be useful to know that disruption of circadian rhythms and hormonal imbalances that may occur during travel can disrupt a menstrual cycle, even causing one or two periods to be skipped.

BITES/PRICKLY HEAT

Most bug bites, excluding malarial mosquitoes, are little more than a temporary irritation. If there are dozens of bites, which may be the case if that nice-looking bungalow turned out to have bedbugs or you've run into a swarm of sand flies on the trail, it takes superhuman willpower not to scratch, even though you know scratching makes the situation worse. An application of Mexsana or Calamine (OTC) lotion helps hold down the itching.

If bites are in danger of becoming open sores that can become infected, try a 1 percent Hydrocortisone cream (OTC) or oral Benadryl (OTC) for three or four days. Hydrocortisone is a topical anti-inflammatory drug that doesn't cure anything but does help control the compulsion to scratch. Benadryl is an antihistamine tablet intended for temporary relief of upper-respiratory allergies, hay fever, and the common cold. In addition to their chemical effects, doing *something* to stop the itching helps control the psychological urge to scratch. If you do scratch a little, use something other than fingernails, something softer and less likely to transmit germs.

Spraying your clothes with Permethrin adds protection against pests like chiggers, mosquitoes, bedbugs, and ticks. One such spray is sold in sporting goods stores as Permanone Tick Repellent.

I've read about a dermatologist who recommends wearing dog tick and flea collars around your ankles to ward off sand flies and other insects. Until they do more for my dog, I'll pass on that idea.

Lice love to play in your hair but they don't mind making themselves at home elsewhere on your body as well. They'll come to your attention as you begin to itch or, the fates forbid, experience a kind of indefinable crawling sensation. There are plenty of shampoos available abroad that get rid of lice, so it's not worth taking anything with you. To make sure they're gone, wash your clothes thoroughly with hot water and detergent. The little devils like to hide in the seams, so scrub vigorously.

Keep an eye out for ticks. They seem to be the penance demanded in return for a great walk through the bush. In tick country, check your hair and skin each evening. If one has already burrowed into your skin and is gorging on your blood, you must remove it. If you leave the head behind it can cause an infection. Use the tip of a hot match, a spot of gasoline or alcohol, insect repellent, or iodine to make the tick want to let go. When the tick is gone, wash the site thoroughly with soap and perhaps apply an antibiotic cream (such as Neosporin). If you later notice a rash, swollen lymph nodes, or a fever, and no medical help is readily available, consider taking an antibiotic such as Amoxicillin or Doxycycline.

Who hasn't winced at the sight of Humphrey Bogart on the deck of the African Queen recoiling at the sight of leeches sucking his blood? We think of leeches in water but the land-based variety found in tropical rain forests is more common. Check your shoes and legs. If a leech has attached itself, use heat, iodine, or alcohol to remove it. Salt will also make one let go in a hurry. Wash the wound with soap and water. If it bleeds for a while because of the anticoagulant injected by the leech, apply pressure to stop the flow.

Fleas may await you in even the nicest-looking bed, but DEET will keep them away. If you don't have DEET, wad up the bedding, toss it into the hall, and hope the mattress is relatively uninfested.

Black flies, tsetse flies, mosquitoes, and sand flies spread unpleasant diseases though their bites. If the risk is significant, spray your clothing with Permethrin and use DEET on exposed skin. Reapply after swimming or sweating profusely. It may be better not to use extensive applications of DEET for more than a week at a time, but doing so seems better than picking up one of these insect-transmitted diseases.

Prickly heat, caused by sweat glands getting plugged, consists of a field of red bumps that itch like the devil. A common cause is clothing that doesn't let sweat evaporate into the air, especially in the sultry tropics. To avoid it, keep dry, wear loose cotton clothing, and apply talcum powder. Air conditioning should help (of course, you tend to get prickly heat where there isn't any AC).

There are a few other things that may take a bite out of a traveler. For example, it's best not to assume that all dogs are friendly. They are often guards rather than pets, which means they are very territorial and may move in for a nip if you intrude on their space (more on this subject under Rabies). If there's reason for concern, carry a stick or a handful of rocks. Monkeys are notorious biters and humans should stay clear of them. Snakes are more common in the Third World landscape than in your yard, but they'll do everything they can to avoid you. Just watch where you step. Contrary to the movies, most wild animals will flee from you (although hippos do attack humans and they take no small bites). If an animal does happen to take a bite, follow the recommendations in the section on Rabies later in this chapter.

BURNS

Immediately apply cold by means of a cool cloth or cloth-wrapped ice pack, or immerse the burned area in cool water. Remove clothing unless it is stuck to the burn and cover the burned area to keep it clean. Do not apply butter or other grease. There are good burn creams available locally, but when you need one, you need it immediately so it's worth carrying one along. Silvadene (OTC) is one of the best. Small burns will normally heal without further medical attention, but a large burn deserves medical help. By the way, it is the practice in some cultures to apply a poultice of dirt and dung over a burn. While I respect traditional medicine, I'd think twice about that particular remedy.

CHAPPED LIPS

The old favorites are Blistex (OTC), Vaseline (OTC), or Chapstick (OTC) in combination with an SPF 15 sunscreen.

COLDS AND COUGHS

Cold viruses live in the upper nasal passages and are usually spread from the nose to the hand of an infected person then to the hand and nose of the victim, often through intermediaries such as a doorknob or telephone receiver. Improve your odds of avoiding a cold by staying away from people with colds (easier said than done), washing your hands frequently, and keeping your hands away from your nose and eyes. You are more resistant to getting a cold if you keep rested and eat well.

We haven't done well at curing a cold, but there's plenty of help available to reduce symptoms such as a stuffy nose. Sudafed (OTC) tablets, Advil Cold & Flu (OTC) tablets, and Dristan nasal spray (OTC) are decongestants that shrink mucous membranes and open up nasal passages to make your nose run (the fluid takes the cold virus with it). Aspirin (OTC) or Tylenol (OTC) help with the headache. Note that aspirin is not advisable for small kids and Advil Cold & Flu may not be recommended for pregnant or lactating women.

For a congested cough that is interfering with sleep, consider Robitussin DM (OTC), which is both an expectorant and a cough suppressant. Robitussin AC (P) contains codeine, to which a significant number of people are allergic and it may also put you right to sleep. Guaifenesin (P) is the active ingrediant in Robitussin and Humibid LA (P). These expectorants are in tablet form. Water is also a very effective expectorant, as are hot beverages and soups. Cough lozenges of various types are available everywhere. If the congested cough is not interfering with sleep, concentrate on an expectorant only. For a dry, persistent cough, consider Benylin DM (OTC). In both cases, look for an alcohol-free product unless you want to knock yourself out.

Fever and thick green or yellow sputum accompanying a cough may be signs of bronchitis or pneumonia (discussed later).

CONSTIPATION

Drinking ample fluids and eating fruits (especially apples, dates, figs, and mangoes), veggies, and other fiber help prevent constipation. Should constipation not resolve itself naturally, try Colace capsules (OTC) or Senokot (OTC) for one or two days. Milk of Magnesia (OTC) is good but bulky to transport. Use constipation remedies for a short time only. Some are sufficiently addictive that after a while your bowels won't work properly without them.

When constipated, don't just lie around. Exercise is a strong stimulant to bowel activity. Suspend taking narcotic pain medicines (since they slow bowel activity).

CUTS

Have a doctor look at serious cuts or punctures. For the nicks that come with everyday living, start with a thorough washing with soap and clean water. Betadine (OTC) is a good antiseptic solution for the initial cleansing. Unless you're allergic to neomycin, apply Neosporin (OTC) ointment. The ointment will keep the dressing from sticking to the cut and will keep it moist. To keep a cut clean, cover it with a bandage during the day. Because exposure to air helps the healing process, leave the cut uncovered at night. By the way, mosquito repellent in a cut won't produce a smile.

If bleeding is severe, apply direct pressure (except to the head, neck, or torso), preferably with your hand on a thick clean compress—*without delay*. If no compress is available, use your bare hand. Raise the area of bleeding higher than the heart, but only if there is no fracture or neck injury. Apply a cold compress (ice wrapped in cloth). Apply pressure to pressure points in the groin and upper arms. Using a tourniquet on a limb may cause loss of that limb; so use only in an emergency. If a cut requires stitches, clean it, close it as much as possible (perhaps with a butterfly bandage), keep it moist, and get to a doctor within 24 hours. Start antibiotic treatment.

Since a cut, especially in the sweaty tropics, can be a magnet for infectious, change a dirty bandage right away. If an infection starts, you'll probably see red streaks around the cut. If the streaks run in the direction of the torso, Amoxicillin (P) is best, although Cipro (P) might work. The area will probably feel unnaturally warm, swollen, and tender, and you may run a low fever. If these symptoms appear, see a doctor at once.

Treat a minor abscess by puncturing it with a sterilized needle after sterilizing the area with alcohol or iodine. Wash it thoroughly and apply antibacterial ointment. Leave it open to the air part of the time and keep it clean.

You've probably heard that there is something different about coral cuts. Well, it's true. Infection probably comes from micro-organisms living on the coral or in the water. If you clean the cut immediately and thoroughly (alcohol or hydrogen peroxide, which bubble the coral fragments to the surface, are good), and treat it as a cut (e.g., with Neosporin) and not just a scratch, you should have no problem. If you don't treat it, infection is possible. Not long ago, I was with a friend who didn't tend to a coral nick on her knee. Within forty-eight hours, her knee became enormously swollen and so painful she couldn't sleep. It's worth being careful.

DEHYDRATION

Dehydration is insidious. You would expect it to be a problem in the Sahara, but it can happen anywhere, including at sea, at high altitude, and when you're sick. Prolonged diarrhea can lead to serious dehydration and even death. At home, drinking two or three pints of fluid each day may be enough, but during a hike in the tropics you could lose that much through perspiration in two hours. If you lose fluid equal to 5 percent of your body weight, you'll feel thirsty. Lose in the range of 6 to 10 percent and you'll experience headache and difficulty walking or performing any work. Lose more and you're heading for delirium, unconsciousness, and possible death. Put another way, an unacclimated person working outdoors in an extremely hot and humid or hot and dry climate should be drinking ten to sixteen pints of fluid a day. That's a lot! Most people fall far short and unknowingly risk the consequences.

Water, juices, broths, and colas are good. Coffee, tea, and alcohol are diuretics, which means that they tend to increase the discharge of urine. It may help your state of mind to bolt down a cold beer after a long day in the hot sun, but you need to follow it with nonalcoholic fluids. By the way, increasing salt intake helps retain fluids.

Even better is drinking clean water into which a packet of Oral Rehydration Salts (ORS) has been mixed. The ORS replace some of the electrolytes (or salts) that your body is losing. ORS packets are available throughout the Third World.

DIARRHEA

How to get it. Microbes that cause diarrhea are transferred from person to person by contact or they enter the system via contaminated food or water. The usual reason travelers are affected is that bacteria in the digestive systems of people at their destination are different from their familiar domestic bacteria. Not better or worse, just different. In addition, taking antibiotics tends to destroy friendly bacteria. This leads to diarrhea that should cease when you stop the medication.

Symptoms. Diarrhea is the symptom. The problem is actually gastroenteritis (inflammation of the digestive tract), which accompanies many diseases. Diarrhea's intensity varies and is usually self-limiting, meaning it will go away by itself. One person may feel a little queasy for a couple of days while another may have vomiting, stomach cramps, and mild fever. Simple diarrhea should clear up without treatment in two days to a week (only 10 percent lasts longer than one week). If it doesn't, stop in to see the doc.

How to avoid it. The best way to avoid diarrhea is to make a continuous effort to avoid contaminated food and water. Eat only peeled fresh fruits and veggies, eat well-cooked foods, and don't drink water that might be contaminated (see Chapter 12). Some of the pathogens that cause diarrhea will enter your system no matter what you do, but following precautions concerning food, drink, and cleanliness will greatly increase the odds in your favor.

To prevent diarrhea, some doctors suggest taking a prophylactic such as trimethoprim/sulfamethoxazole (Bactrim/Septra; P), Doxycycline, or iproflaxin (Cipro; P). However, in some cases they can cause an adverse reaction such as blood and liver disorder, photosensitivity, or a severe rash and may actually contribute to diarrhea. At the least, they help make invading pathogens more resistant to antibiotics. The majority of doctors I've talked to do not recommend preventive medicine for diarrhea.

A less intrusive preventive would include taking two bismuth subsalicylate tablets (the old standby, Pepto Bismol; OTC) four times a day. If you do so, don't be surprised if your tongue and stool turn black. If you also hear a ringing in your ears, take no more. It's better not to take Pepto Bismol and aspirin at the same time. Some people are convinced that acidophilus tablets also help prevent diarrhea.

If you are with a group and someone gets diarrhea, concentrate on your personal hygiene and avoid contact with the affected person.

Treatment. The best way to treat simple diarrhea is to take no medicine but drink plenty of clean water or other nonalcoholic (and, preferably, caffeine-free) fluids to avoid dehydration. Fruit juice and bananas replace lost potassium; honey and sugar replace lost glucose. Bottled soft drinks are fine, especially those that are caffeine-free, since they also replace glucose. To replace salts, add a little table salt to food, juice or soda. Alcohol is not recommended during a bout of diarrhea.

In many places throughout the world Oral Rehydration Salts (ORS) are readily available in pharmacies and general stores. Taken with clean water, they are an excellent replacement for lost salts, glucose, and minerals. You can make a rough equivalent as follows: three tablespoons of sugar (or honey), three-fourths teaspoon salt, one-half teaspoon baking soda, one cup of fruit juice, and enough water to make one liter. It's not too tasty, but it works.

Eat nondairy foods, especially carbohydrates, that are easy to digest. Take aspirin, rest, and let your system have a day or two (sometimes up to a week) to clean itself out. Keep fluids coming in, even beyond the point at which you stop being thirsty. The goal is replacement. As you tentatively start eating solid foods again, remember BRAT. The acronym stands for bananas, rice, apples, and toast. Your intestines will appreciate it.

Circumstances, such as an upcoming all-day bus trip, may make it temporarily preferable to prevent diarrhea from running its course, so to speak. For that purpose, Kaopectate (OTC) will give more body to the stool but it doesn't reduce other symptoms, like cramps, or reduce the frequency of the diarrhea events. For additional relief, there is Pepto Bismol. If you want *certainty* of relief from the primary symptom, the leading antimotility drug is Immodium (OTC). Lomotil (OTC) is equally effective but more likely to cause drowsiness and retention of urine. Either will contain the problem, but neither is a cure. To the contrary, both retard completion of the cycle, meaning they cause the body to retain the pathogens. Nevertheless, take Immodium along. When you need it, you definitely need it.

Another treatment for diarrhea is a general antibiotic such as ciprofloxacin (Cipro; P), ofloxacin (Floxin; P), or Bactrim/Septra (P). Some physicians feel it's better not to take antibiotics for diarrhea unless it is accompanied by fever. Those who do recommend antibiotics are divided on whether it's better to take antimotility drugs before taking antibiotics, or better to start with antibiotics, or take both together. There seems to be a small majority in favor of taking the antibiotic first, permitting the diarrhea to flush out your system.

Enterovioform and Mexaform are used to treat diarrhea in some other countries, but both are considered dangerous and neither is approved for use by the FDA.

Diarrhea accompanies quite a few illnesses, including dysentery. If the diarrhea doesn't disappear after a couple of weeks, or there are other symptoms (such as fever, severe cramps, blood or mucus in the stool, light sensitivity, or stiff neck), the cause may be more serious than unfamiliar bacteria. In such cases, do your best not to use the antimotility agents such as Immodium. Try Cipro or Bactrin and get medical attention.

Prolonged diarrhea may also indicate Giardia (discussed later). In that case, you might try metronidazole (Flagyl; P), but be aware that it causes nausea and vomiting in some people if they drink alcohol within several days of their last dose. Tinidazole (Fasigyn; P) is often used outside the United States.

FATIGUE/STRESS

Discomfort, ambiguity, concern about safety, and other stresses of travel burn considerable energy. The time a person can travel without feeling physically or mentally exhausted differs depending on personality, as well as physical and mental resilience. If you shed stress easily and have a light heart, you may coast through an entire trip without feeling fatigued. If you're less flexible, sleeping too little, or a little off your feed, daily demands can get to you. Weather can be a factor, too. A string of gray days causes most heads to droop.

Learn to recognize symptoms like crankiness, withdrawal, and lassitude for what they may indicate. Notice when little bumps in the road that would normally make you laugh don't seem amusing at all. A series of minor illnesses or accidents may be stress or fatigue related. You may find yourself thinking you should cut the trip a little short.

The remedy is simple. Stop! Chill out. Spend extra money for a while. Find a place to stay that's a notch or two up from your budgeted norm. Eat well. Play. Forget errands. Get shined up. After a few days, you'll probably be your high-spirited self again.

I've never gotten so fatigued that a good break didn't restore my energy, but if that happened I'd take a close look at my health and nutrition. I'd certainly try several remedies before calling it quits and going home early. Besides, I like to go home feeling strong, with that last burst of speed you summon at the end of a race.

By the way, if you recognize that fatigue or stress may affect your travel partner also, you'll be sought after as a person with whom to travel.

FEVER

Start with acetaminophen (Tylenol; OTC) or aspirin (OTC), except for small children, to lower body temperature. Remove excess clothing. Increase fluid intake. If you don't know what's causing the fever, consult a doctor. If that's not possible, and the fever is accompanied by headache, chills, and fatigue, and you are in a geographic area where malaria is a possibility, consider treating for malaria first (discussed later). If there is also bloody diarrhea, treat for bacterial dysentery (also discussed later). If your temperature increases to above 104 degrees, you must take stronger action: cool the body with water, ice, and moving air. Get a doctor.

FOOD POISONING

Symptoms are usually vomiting and diarrhea, sometimes with cramps. They may start within an hour after eating the contaminated food—but may take a day or more. Take ample fluids and symptoms should disappear within twenty-four hours. Contaminated seafood can make you more ill, including neurological symptoms and respiratory failure. Along with vomiting and diarrhea, you might experience a peppery or metallic taste in your mouth and loss of coordination. If that happens, get medical help.

FROSTBITE

Frostbite, which usually affects toes, fingers, and face, means that the tissue is freezing. It's caused when continued cold or inactivity reduces circulation of blood to the extremities. The affected area will probably look gray or white and feel taut or hard. As frostbite becomes more severe, the skin becomes insensitive to touch.

If frostbite occurs, warm the affected part quickly against warm flesh or in warm water. Do not warm it significantly above normal body temperature (that is, don't place it too close to a fire), and do *not* rub the affected skin. Either will aggravate the damage.

In case of severe frostbite, the area can be immersed in water up to 104 degrees until thawing occurs. However, partial thawing followed by refreezing can cause further damage, so it may be better not to attempt to thaw until the process can be completed without interruption.

HEADACHE

As a mild painkiller, many people choose acetaminophen (Tylenol; OTC). Aspirin (OTC) is an anti-inflammatory drug (i.e., it helps relieve inflammation and muscle aches) as well as a painkiller. Ibuprofen (Advil; OTC) has the same objectives but is stronger than, and does not contain, aspirin. Motrin is exactly the same as Advil, except stronger. You can achieve a Motrin-like result by increasing the dosage of Advil. Like Asprin, they have some risks for people suffering from ulcers and gastrointestinal bleeding. It is better not to take acetaminophen for pain relief while consuming alcohol or for a hangover because the combination may overtax your liver.

If a headache is accompanied by a distinctly stiff neck, fever, sensitivity to light, and a general feeling of malaise, the possibility of meningitis should be considered (discussed later) and medical attention sought immediately.

HEAT EXHAUSTION

It takes several days to acclimatize to an unusually hot, humid environment. Avoid exposure during the hottest part of the day. Wear a head cover. Cool down by wearing loose-fitting natural fabrics that enable perspiration to evaporate quickly. Light colors help reflect heat.

When working or exercising in the hot sun or in high humidity, make an effort to drink clean, nonalcoholic fluids and take in extra salt. If your urine turns darker yellow, it may be a sign you aren't drinking enough water.

When approaching heat exhaustion, you sweat heavily but your skin feels clammy and looks pale. You may feel nauseated or throw up. Your muscles may cramp and you may have a headache. Your heart rate is higher than normal but blood pressure may drop. At this point, your temperature may still be only slightly above normal. Stop what you're doing, get into the shade, rest, cool yourself, and drink as much fluid as you can hold (including ORS, if available).

If you respond properly, heat exhaustion shouldn't be a severe problem, but it can progress to heat *stroke,* which can be fatal (discussed later). I recall a huge sign on the pier at Agana, Guam, that read, "The Sun Is Hot In Guam!"

Tired of watching visitors keel over at midday, they were trying to put arriving travelers on notice.

HYPOTHERMIA

When a newspaper notes someone has died of exposure, it is reporting one of the greatest threats to outdoor travelers. What surprises people is that cold need not be excessive or even prolonged to cause hypothermia. I've seen hypothermia strike a person within 15 minutes of being dumped from a capsizing raft into Idaho's Yampa River in early summer. Hypothermia can begin when the core body temperature drops 2 percent or more. Most cases originate when air temperature is between 30 and 50 degrees.

As usual, knowledge helps prevent the problem. Wear layers of clothing (preferably synthetics or wool), cover head and hands, drink plenty of liquids, and eat high-energy foods. If you get soaked, forget your plans and head for cover, then watch one another for signs of early hypothermia: slurred speach, lethargy, loss of coordination, numbness, confusion or poor judgement, memory loss, or shivering. It's not unusual for a victim to deny he's in trouble. Don't believe him. If hypothermia is more serious—amnesia, inability to speak, jerky movements, irrationality (more than usual), muscular rigidity, drowsiness, even unconsciousness—no exertion should be permitted. Death is a possibility, so get help immediately.

Treat by removing the victim from the source of heat loss. Get him to a shelter and into some dry clothes. Cover his head and body and put him in a sleeping bag and provide warm body contact if possible. Get him to excercise if he feels up to it and symptoms are not severe. Build a fire. If he is able to eat, feed him carbohydrates. Try to keep him awake and *do not* give him alcoholic beverages. In more serious cases, put him in a prewarmed blanket or sleeping bag, and provide warm bare skin contact if possible.

INSOMNIA

When having trouble sleeping, some people take Benadryl (OTC). Although it's primarily an antihistamine, it will induce sleep, is nonaddicting, and is unlikely to conflict with other medicine you may be taking. I have also seen increasing recommendations in favor of taking Melatonin (OTC) for insomnia (see the discussion on Jet Lag).

If you choose to take a sleeping pill, there are many possibilities, including Restoril (P) and Ambien (P). None of these drugs should be taken in conjunction with alcohol, which is also a depressant. None should be taken without a doctor's approval or by anyone taking HIV medication. After a week or so, the body seems to develop an increasing tolerance to sleeping pills, meaning you have to increase dosage to achieve the desired effect. That, I am told, can become the path to addiction. Sleeping pills can also interfere with the normal stages of sleep, possibly leaving you poorly rested on awakening. Instead, some people recommend Hyland's Homeopathic Calms or Valerian.

Consider taking rubber or wax earplugs with you. They at least reduce the uproar in the street below your window to a tolerable level.

JET LAG

Jet lag is a kind of physical and mental disorientation that may disrupt your natural rhythms when you cross three or more time zones. Symptoms include inability to sleep, fatigue, and loss of appetite and mental sharpness. However, if it's any consolation, flying on a north-south axis without crossing time zones doesn't produce jet lag.

Some people recommend alternating feasting and fasting for three days before departure, getting extra sleep, and avoiding last-minute stress as a way of combating jet lag. Even if such a regimen works, it's not very consistent with the reality of getting under way on an extended trip.

In numerous articles written about jet lag, authors suggest eating lightly, drinking little or no alcohol, and getting extra sleep during the flight. That must explain why the airlines deliver a meal every few hours, serve free alcohol nonstop, and show movies all night.

For a long flight, set your watch to the current time at your destination and try to stake out three or four seats in the center section as nap space. Realizing it's already midnight at your destination makes it easier to convince yourself to catch some sleep, even at the cost of passing up those very forgettable movies. If you're a light sleeper, this is a fine time to break in your earplugs. If it's already daytime at your destination, minimize your sleep since you'll be going to bed there on local time.

Avoid caffeine during a long flight and don't arrive at a destination with an alcohol buzz. That's a time when you need your sharpest wits about you.

Despite your best efforts, your sleeping pattern may be out of sync with local time after a long flight. Your body wants to sleep when your eyes and brain say it's time to play. Given the physical and mental energy you burned getting ready for the trip, it should be no surprise if you're a little cranky.

Adjust your schedule to local time immediately. Plan a quiet first day but don't take a daytime nap. If you can't sleep easily for the first night or two, you might try a sleeping pill. Some research suggests that spending time in the sun may also help reset your biological clock.

Here's the good news: scientific tests (reported in the *British Medical Journal*, among other sources) show that taking readily available, inexpensive melatonin capsules effectively reduces the impact of jet lag. The premise is that proper functioning of our internal body clock is dependent on a natural hormone named melatonin (a derivative of the amino acid tryptophan), which is released by the pineal gland. At present, some recommend five to ten milligrams taken 30 to 90 minutes before bedtime on the day of your arrival and for as many nights thereafter as you feel any effects of jet lag. Lower dosage is needed for westbound travel since it's easier to stay up late than it is to go to bed at what your body thinks is noon. Melatonin is not magic, but it reduces the length and extent of jet lag and that's no small breakthrough. Side effects of synthetic melatonin can include headache, nausea, and a mild contraceptive effect in some women. Health food stores sell melatonin as a simple nutritional supplement for about 20 cents a capsule. However, these may vary in strength or purity. Drugstores sell it at half the price. The drug companies working on melatonin urge consumers to wait until melatonin, meaning their proprietary version, receives federal approval. They express concern about purity and standardization of dosage. In any case, consult your doctor.

The overall impact of extended air travel is more extensive than jet lag alone. In flight, the cabin is pressurized to the equivalent of an altitude of 4,000 to 8,000 feet. Therefore, passengers breathe air with a lower concentration of oxygen than they are used to. This alone can produce a slight headache, nausea, and fatigue. In addition, outside air coming into the plane is heated before being circulated in the cabin. In the process, it becomes very dry. To give you a comparison, relative humidity in the cabin of a transoceanic flight can get down to 10 percent, as opposed to 20 percent in the Sahara Desert. Since low humidity in the cabin causes your body to lose moisture, ask a cabin attendant to increase the humidity and drink extra fluids, especially water.

MENSTRUATION

Over the course of extended travel, it's not too unusual for menstrual cycles to become irregular or even stop for a while. That's one possible explanation if you miss one or more periods.

MOTION SICKNESS

Spending a week on Heron Island on Australia's Great Barrier Reef is a fine experience, but most people get there in a small boat that crosses 50 miles of rough water (the helicopter is much more expensive). There's a fabulous bus ride through the mountains of Sikkim, but it's like riding on a dragontail for eight hours. If trips like these challenge your tummy, you're susceptible to motion sickness. Despite what you may have heard, it's not all in your head. It occurs when there is a breakdown in the signal between the motion-sensing parts of the body (inner ear, eyes, and limbs) and the brain. However, your expectation of becoming sick from motion can increase the probability that you will. Motion sickness symptoms include lightheadedness, dizziness, sweat, pallor, nausea, and, as we know all too well, vomiting.

The solution is simple. Dimenhydrinate (Dramamine, OTC) or meclizine (Bonine, OTC) will stabilize your innards and your mind. Take one pill an hour or so before the onset of motion. Adults may prefer a Scopolamine patch (P) which, applied eight hours before any tummy twisting, remains effective for up to 72 hours. These medications can make you a bit sleepy, but that's a lot better than hanging over the rail or out the window. Some physicians recommend that these drugs be avoided by pregnant women, asthmatics, and anyone being treated for glaucoma.

On a more naturalistic level, try ginger root in the form of hard candy, gingerbread or, better yet, powdered ginger root capsules to settle your stomach. It works. Green olives, green apples, and crackers also help, as does Coca-Cola, and none of them make you drowsy. Many people swear by the effectiveness of a wristband based on the principle of acupressure. Its small beads pressing on the wrist do the job for many travelers. A German firm sells earrings with titanium electrodes that deliver a small electrical current to an acupressure point in the ear. Neither I nor the FDA can vouch for their effectiveness.

Whatever vehicle you're aboard, choose a seat that will have the least motion, usually somewhere in the middle. Get fresh air blowing in your face. Keep your eyes on a steady reference point, such as an object in the vehicle itself, rather than watching scenery rushing by to the side. You can't fool your inner ear, but there is no need to reinforce the sensations by watching endless switchbacks of a mountain road whiz by. If the vehicle stops, get off and walk around.

Perhaps most effective, other than medication, is diverting your mind (I know that's easier said than done). Make yourself as comfortable as possible and try to sleep. If you can't do that, focus your mind on something else or talk with the person next to you. Invite cigarette smokers to desist (pantomime the potential consequences if they don't). Watching someone else get sick is enough to put almost anyone over the edge.

If you toss your cookies, clean up as quickly as you can. Wash your face, brush your teeth, wash or put soda water on any soiled clothes. If someone else loses it, don't be upset with them. You know they would have preferred not to do it. Remind yourself that it will soon be over.

PARASITES

Worms tend to arrive in undercooked meats (especially pork) and fish. They're also quite at home in water. You probably won't see them, but their presence may be advertised by diarrhea, bloody urine, muscle pain, coughing, headache, and fever. Another sign may be rectal itching, most noticeable at night. Among the diseases they cause are amebiasis, American trypano-somiasis, Bilharzia (schistosomiasis), Chagas' disease, filariasis, giardiasis, leishmaniasis, malaria, and more. If you suspect a problem, have a laboratory test your blood and a stool sample to determine whether parasites are sharing your travels and, if so, what you should do. Correct treatment, which depends on the type of disease, is usually effective.

Since you can also pick up certain parasitic worms through your feet, resist the pleasures of going barefoot, especially on dirt. Keep shoes between you and those little augers. If you wear open sandals in Africa, wear socks as well.

As usual, the best prevention is good hygiene (especially handwashing before eating) and caution with food and water. Run-of-the-mill worms shouldn't cause much of a problem so long as you prevent reinfection, which you can do easily after returning home.

STRAINS/SPRAINS

A strain is an injury to a muscle, while a sprain is a tearing or stretching of the ligaments that hold bones together across a joint (as in a twisted ankle). Treat either by icing the area, preferably for at least a full day, and elevating it above your heart if practical. Wear an elastic bandage if you have one. Take an anti-inflammatory drug (such as Ibuprofen, OTC) to reduce swelling and pain and prepare to get some involuntary rest.

SUNBURN

Sunburn can bring a trip to a painful halt. I recently spent a full day snorkeling in a series of six spectacular bays on the island of Ko Tao.* To avoid sunburn, I wore a tank top and plenty of sunscreen. That night, I discovered I'd overlooked a couple of spots. Both of my Achilles tendons were inflamed and swollen, practically glowing. Along with the pain, severe blistering developed and there was considerable chance for infection. A friend wrapped ice cubes in a cloth and held them on the blisters to minimize the swelling. I immediately applied Aloe Vera and kept the burned area moist. Later, I treated the burns as if they were cuts, applied Neosporin, and took aspirin for the anti-inflammatory effect. Since I was returning to the mainland the next day the burns didn't interrupt my travel, but I wouldn't have been putting scuba boots on over those inflamed tendons any time soon. I learned my lesson.

Since one of my reasons for making a trip is to be outdoors, I don't expect to stay out of the sun while I travel. Nevertheless, I keep in mind that when the sun is high, a clear atmosphere lets through a lot of burning rays. On a boat or the beach, water reflecting the sun's rays multiplies the effect. The remedy: cut the time of exposure, cover up, wear a hat or a visor, and use a good sunscreen (rated SPF 15 or above). Even a waterproof sunscreen must be applied frequently—and use plenty of it. It's cheap compared to the alternatives.

---

* *Ko Tao.* This small island in the Gulf of Thailand has no cars, seven dive shops, and great restaurants on the beach. It's located on the suburbs of Heaven.

UPSET STOMACH

Unfamiliar foods, robust spices, poor sanitation, lack of refrigeration, stress, or even just bacteria new to your system may give you digestive problems. For effective relief, try Pepto Bismol (OTC). It comes in chewable tablets (anyone who puts a bottle of that pink liquid inside a pack deserves what will inevitably happen sometime during the trip). Pepto Bismol contains aspirin, which I mention because some people have ulcers or are allergic to aspirin. As an antacid, consider Maalox or Mylanta (OTC). Tagamet HB (OTC) is also popular although it can interact with other drugs.

If abdominal pain is severe, accompanied by vomiting and/or cramps and fever, stop eating and drink a little clean water. If there is a high fever, consider taking an antibiotic. Also check the right lower part of the abdomen. If it is very tender, appendicitis is a possibility. Severe abdominal pain can accompany several problems, some of which are surgical emergencies. Get medical help.

URINARY TRACT INFECTION

Bacterial urinary tract infection comes to your attention when urination produces a painful, burning sensation. Frequency and feelings of urgency increase. There may be some fever and back pain. To prevent urinary infection, drink plenty of fluids, including acidic drinks like cranberry juice, urinate frequently, minimize caffeine intake, and wear clean cotton underwear.

The indicated medications are usually Bactrim/Septra (P), Ampicillin (P), or Cipro (P). See a doctor, when you can, for precise diagnosis.

A similar burning sensation may also indicate the presence of a sexually transmitted disease or, in men, a prostate problem.

If you also have pain deep in the small of the back, accompanied by nausea and vomiting, it could be pyelonephritis, a serious kidney infection requiring prompt medical attention. If you're in the boonies, start the Cipro.

VAGINAL YEAST INFECTIONS

When a woman is taking antibiotics (such as doxycycline for malaria), especially in a hot, muggy climate, her chances of developing a vaginal yeast infection increase substantially. Contraceptive pills may also facilitate infection. The most common symptoms are rash, itching, and some discharge. A dilute vinegar or lemon juice douche may take care of it. If not, Miconazole (Monistat 3, OTC) vaginal suppositories used at bedtime for at least three consecutive nights, or clotrimazole vaginal suppositories are often recommended. Some women also recommend acidophilus tablets, citrus fruits, and decreasing the intake of sugar and alcohol.

Major medical problems referred to here include some from which you are generally sheltered at home but might encounter as you travel. **You don't want to experience them—and you don't have to if you make a reasonable effort.**

BRONCHITIS (and related respiratory diseases)

Bronchitis, an inflammation of air tubes between the throat and the lungs, is commonly caused by an infection (viral or bacterial), an allergy, or an irritation. If untreated, it may go away in a week or so—or it can lead to pneumonia.

How to get it. Usually by inhaling airborne bacteria or viruses.

Symptoms. Because airways have narrowed, the chest feels constricted. Green, yellow, or white sputum develops, but it's the fever and persistent wracking cough that get your attention.

How to avoid it. Good luck is the best ally, although general fitness helps by keeping immune levels high. Treat colds and flu early. Certain people have a predisposition to bronchitis: smokers, alcoholics, asthmatics, and people especially susceptible to allergies.

How to treat it. Bactrim/Septra (P) or Erythromycin (OTC) are the best bets if the cause is bacterial. If viral, antibiotics won't help. In either case, breathing hot vapors will help break up the sputum and reduce coughing. Keep a vaporizer or a tea kettle going if you can find one. Try Robitussin (OTC) and drink lots of water.

CHAGAS' DISEASE

This disease is a significant cause of death for inhabitants of Central and South America. It arrives via nocturnal insects (sometimes called "kissing" or "assassin" bugs) that emerge from hiding in the walls and ceilings of rural lodgings. Typically, they drop down from a thatch roof (or palm tree if you're sleeping outside). They bite, but it's their feces entering through eyes, mouth, or the wound caused by the bite that infect you. The first sign is a small red bump at the bite site, followed in a week or two by fever and a firm swelling at the spot. Chagas' Disease can result in congestive heart failure ten to twenty years after infection. The best defenses are insect repellent and mosquito nets. Nifurtimox or Benznidazole have been recommended as treatment. Although the disease rarely affects travelers, I mention it because the symptoms would be difficult for a general practitioner to diagnose.

CHOLERA

How to get it. Cholera, currently present in more than 40 countries, is caused by a toxin produced by a specific bacteria. Humans get it most frequently from contaminated water and food, especially raw seafood such as shellfish (in which the bacteria concentrate), or via infected food handlers who use inadequate hygiene. Fortunately, it is not spread by inhalation. Since it usually erupts as an epidemic, travelers hear about it and can easily avoid infected areas. In the absence of an outbreak, the risk of contracting cholera is very low. However, where cholera is endemic, there is still some risk of transmission by carriers not showing symptoms. Check with the Centers for Disease Control before you travel.

Symptoms. Cholera attacks the lining of the intestines and sucks vast quantities of fluid from the cells. The victim experiences copious diarrhea, often accompanied by vomiting and cramps. This massive loss of fluids and salts destroys the victim's electrolyte balance, prevents retention of nutrients, and causes collapse of the circulatory system. If untreated, death from dehydration is a possibility.

How to avoid it. The best protection is to stay away from current outbreaks. There is a vaccine against cholera, but it only lasts from three to six months and is thought to be no more than 50 percent effective. When I might be where cholera is present, I get this vaccine anyway. It comes in two doses, one to four weeks apart. Unhappily, there is a new strain of cholera in India and a few other Asian countries for which there is as yet no effective vaccine. However, the World Health Organization is now testing a new and inexpensive vaccine that is effective for up to one year.

Given the limited effectiveness of the present vaccine, follow hygienic precautions in any area where there are known cases of cholera. Don't drink untreated water and don't eat raw seafood (specifically shellfish), uncooked fruits and vegetables, or food prepared under unsanitary conditions.

How to treat it. See a doctor immediately and have a stool sample tested for cholera. Some cases of cholera clear up by themselves, but don't wait it out. Thousands of people die because they can't replace vital fluids. Because of small body size, children are especially vulnerable to severe dehydration. A victim should rest and take nothing by mouth except fluids (that's right, no food). After rehydration, starches are fine. It is *essential* to drink uncontaminated fluid and get sufficient rest. Water, broth, caffeine-free colas, and sugary juices are good. The real lifesaver is Oral Rehydration Salts (ORS) in clean water to replace salt, potassium, bicarbonate, and sugar. ORS are available from many health food stores and at many pharmacies abroad. If ORS are not available, follow the recipe in the section on diarrhea above. Clean water is important but may not be sufficient by itself. Avoid milk and drinks containing caffeine. Several antibiotics, such as Cipro (P) or Floxin (P), help reduce the length of a cholera attack, but they kill protective bacteria as well as the ones causing cholera. The drug of choice is tetracycline (P).

DENGUE FEVER

How to get it. The colloquial name, "breakbone fever," tells you right away that it's something you'd just as soon skip. Its most serious form is dengue hemorragic fever. It's found in tropical Asian countries, Africa, the Caribbean, Central America, and South America. North Americans don't hear a lot about it, but there have been epidemics in a dozen Latin American countries in the last ten years and it is a growing public health threat. It is brought into your life by a female mosquito who takes her nips and transmits the virus, usually during the day when you may not be expecting mosquitoes. Dengue-carrying mosquitoes hang out in urban areas and often venture indoors.

Symptoms. The symptoms may not show up for five to seven days. When they do, there are at least two stages. First, a fever develops, along with chills, headaches, and vomiting. These symptoms last three to five days before disappearing. They then return, accompanied by abdominal pains and wracking aches in joints and muscles. This round, which can remain in force for ten days, may be misdiagnosed as malaria until a diffuse rash appears on the trunk of the body, the palms of the hands, and the soles of the feet. Remission may be followed by a relapse and full recovery may take weeks. The good news is that it is seldom fatal.

How to avoid it. There is no preventive antibiotic or vaccine. The best defense is similar to that against malaria (except there are no prophylactics), but with increased vigilance during the day. Don't get bitten by those mosquitoes. If you hear of an outbreak of dengue fever, move on.

How to treat it. As a viral disease, neither antibiotic nor vaccine is known to cure it. Take acetaminophen (do not take aspirin or ibuprofen), keep taking fluids to avoid dehydration, and get plenty of rest. However, if you're not sure whether what you have is dengue or malaria, treat it as if it were malaria until you can get expert medical attention.

DIPHTHERIA

How to get it. Diphtheria, which causes inflammation and obstruction of the nose and throat, is spread primarily by contact with an infected person or his secretions. The mid-1990s outbreak of diphtheria in Russia, Ukraine, and other states of the former Soviet Union was the most severe in the developed world in 30 years.

How to avoid it. A diphtheria vaccine (usually combined with tetanus) provides a high degree of immunity. Almost everyone gets this vaccination as a child, but a booster is necessary every ten years. Because diphtheria germs are common, this immunization is important whether you travel or not.

DYSENTERY

How to get it. Amoebic dysentery (or amoebiasis) is caused by a protozoan, Entamoeba histolytica. Bacillary dysentery may be caused by Shigella. Both generally enter through one's mouth as a result of careless hygiene or through consuming contaminated food or water. Use of human waste as fertilizer and failure to wash one's hands after defecating contribute to contamination. Both types of dysentery can be spread by a food handler who doesn't wash his hands, by human contact, and by insects who have stepped in human waste before dropping by their favorite kitchen or outdoor market. The odds are you won't encounter dysentery if you are careful about sanitation and hygiene.

Symptoms. On the road, it is difficult to distinguish between amoebic and bacillary dysentery (in fact, it may be initially difficult to tell the difference between dysentery and simple diarrhea). Amoebic dysentery may produce mild abdominal discomfort and constipation with bouts of bloody diarrhea. Some Shigella infections are quite mild and have few definitive symptoms while others can be fatal. For a reliable diagnosis, the stool must be checked. The clues that point to dysentery rather than simple diarrhea are fever, and blood or pus in the stool.

In amoebic dysentery, abscesses may form in the liver, lungs, or brain. Not surprisingly, amoebic dysentery can be lethal, but with basic treatment there is little to fear. It is, however, a high price to pay for impulsively drinking tap water or being careless about personal hygiene.

How to avoid it. Choose with care the places you eat and drink. Wash your hands frequently and don't put your fingers in your mouth. Remember that dysentery can be spread from one person to another by touch. Avoid food that may have been in contact with insects.

How to treat it. If you're concerned by the symptoms, send a stool sample to a laboratory for analysis. If it is dysentery, take ORS and drink extra fluids to offset losses through diarrhea. If you have, or seriously suspect, amoebic dysentery, take Metronidazole (Flagyl, P), followed by Iodoquinol (P). Women in their first trimester of pregnancy should avoid Flagyl. Anyone taking it should also avoid alcohol for three days after the last dose. Tinidazole (Fasigyn, P) is used by many for killing amoebae in abscesses or the intestine, but it is not available in the United States.

Bacillary dysentery may go away in a week or so, even without treatment. Drink plenty of fluids to prevent dehydration. Rest, and eat light, nongreasy meals. Take Bactrim/Septra (P) or ciprofloxacin. If the strain has developed resistance to these antibiotics, drop into a hospital. Treated, the bacteria should be out of the body within several days. Untreated, a person could continue to shed bacteria in stools for several weeks.

GIARDIASIS

How to get it. When excreted by human or animal carriers, the Giardia parasite can survive for months, during which time it can easily wash into a water supply. That's one reason why even the apparently pristine rivers in the Sierra Madre mountains of California carry danger even downstream from the snowy wilderness. Besides being spread via feces in food or water, Giardia can spread from person to person via poor hygiene, which permits transfer of the infected feces.

Symptoms. Fewer than half the individuals who drink water heavily contaminated by Giardia develop infestations; most of those who do show no obvious symptoms. Whether one gets infected may be a function of the volume of the parasite consumed. The minority experience diarrhea, stomach cramps, excessive intestinal gas, and lack of energy. If the stool is foul smelling and the victim starts burping and experiencing a taste like rotten eggs, Giardia is a likely culprit. If diarrhea lasts for more than a couple of weeks, suspect giardiasis.

How to avoid it. Drink only clean water and eat hygienically prepared food.

How to treat it. Even if untreated, symptoms disappear in seven to ten days—but may recur. If treated, symptoms should disappear for good in about a week. If not treated, the victim may become a symptom-free carrier for years, capable of transmitting the disease to others.

Diagnosis is usually based on a test of the stool. The accuracy of the test depends on the number of cysts present at the time of the test, and the cyst count can vary hour to hour. Giardia can be treated with metronidazole (Flagyl; P), also used to combat amoebic dysentery. However, according to the CDC, Giardia has been increasing its resistance to metronidazole. In any case, it should not be taken by anyone who is in her first trimester of pregnancy, nor taken in conjunction with alcohol. If there is a relapse after treatment, consult a doctor.

HEAT STROKE

How to get it. Heatstroke (or sunstroke) is a risk when you spend too much time in the sun without replacing perspiration with fluid intake. Exercise or exertion contributes to the problem, especially in high humidity when sweat doesn't evaporate efficiently to cool the body. With heat stroke, the control system that regulates body temperature has stopped working. Temperature escalates, leading to possible kidney damage, brain damage, and death.

Symptoms. You feel feverish and confused and your skin is dry, flushed, and hot to the touch. Note: unlike with heat exhaustion, the victim has a high temperature and does not sweat. Pulse and breathing rate increase. Unconsciousness is possible.

How to avoid it. Drink plenty of fluids in conditions of intense sun and high temperature, especially when exercising. Reduce exercise when humidity is high and pay attention to your body. If your pulse becomes unusually rapid or you begin to feel faint, stop! Get out of the sun. Drink something and consume some salt.

How to treat it. Get the victim out of the sun immediately and lower the body temperature quickly. Undress the victim and put cold packs on groin, armpits, head, and neck; even immerse the victim in cool water if possible. Fan vigorously. Massage the limbs to assist circulation. Some recommend giving the victim a little to drink, very slowly. Others, to avoid the risks of vomiting or aspiration, prefer to give nothing. Best is an IV of saline solution administered in a hospital. When fever has subsided, cover the victim to prevent chilling and seek medical help. After the event, the victim should rest for several days, drink plenty of fluids, and, oh yes, avoid similar circumstances.

HEPATITIS

Although hepatitis is casually referred to as if it were a single disease, it comes in four versions: A, B, C, and E. All attack the liver, but they differ in how they're transmitted and in their effects. Those afflicted typically recover completely from types A and E, but B and C can become chronic and possibly fatal.

Hepatitis A

How to get it. Hepatitis A virus (infectious hepatitis), the least serious, is usually spread by consuming food or water contaminated with human or animal waste. Shellfish and raw fish are common sources. It's also transferred by contaminated needles and occasionally by sexual intimacy. The incubation period is two to seven weeks. Hep A is probably more common than all the more exotic diseases combined.

Symptoms. The symptoms are headache, nausea, and fatigue, similar to a case of flu that won't go away. Other symptoms include generalized aches and pains, fever, vomiting, lack of appetite, diarrhea, and upper abdominal pain. Urine becomes golden-orange. In most cases, jaundice ensues, meaning the skin and whites of the eyes turn a distinct yellow hue in five to ten days. This happens because the liver is under attack, failing to dispose of old red blood cells properly. At this point, the liver, located in the upper abdomen on the right side, is extremely tender to the touch. Lymph nodes also become distinctly enlarged. You're likely to feel sick for a couple of weeks and weak for one to three months. To check for hepatitis, get a blood test. Not everyone who gets hepatitis A, including children, shows the symptoms.

Any time you're not drinking enough water, especially if you're sweating heavily, your urine becomes more concentrated and may turn yellow. If that happens, drink several pints of fluid in a short time span. If the urine color doesn't become much lighter within a few hours, watch for other telltale symptoms of hepatitis A.

How to avoid it. For decades, many doctors have recommended receiving an immune globulin (IG) shot just prior to departure. This provides some protection but not immunity. The duration of the effectiveness of the shot depends to some extent on the dosage. A two milliliter dose is supposed to be effective for two or three months while a five milliliter dose lasts about five months. Health departments routinely give the smaller volume so if you want longer protection, ask for it.

In 1995, the FDA approved Havrix (or Varqta), a new vaccine already in wide use in more than 40 countries, which appears to give immunity for ten to twenty-five years. The first shot should be received four weeks before travel, followed by a booster six to twelve months later. Protection is estimated at 90 percent. If you'll be traveling to a high-risk area in less than four weeks, receive IG simultaneously with the vaccine. Since 100 percent immunity is seldom certain, continue to avoid food and water that may be contaminated. The CDC and the National Foundation for Infectious Diseases recommend this vaccine. Call (800) 437-2829 for an information brochure.

Avoidance of hepatitis A must become part of your daily routine on the road. Check out cleanliness when choosing a restaurant, drink only clean water, avoid ice, eat only thoroughly cooked foods, avoid raw shellfish, and wash your hands more frequently than you do at home. Even if food and water are not contaminated, the container they're in may be. By the way, if you hear a rumor that an alcoholic beverage will neutralize the hep A virus, it's wishful thinking.

How to treat it. If you're exposed to hepatitis A while traveling, but you're not yet showing symptoms, consider getting an IG shot immediately (but only if you can be certain the needle is clean). Antibiotics will not help; this is a virus. There is no known cure for hepatitis A, but it's self-limiting rather than chronic. Fatality need be of concern only to very elderly or chronically ill persons. If you get it, be as certain as you can that your sources of clean food and water are reliable thereafter. Then settle in for a good rest, eat well, drink lots of fluids (except alcohol until tests show your liver has recovered), and be careful not to pass it on to anyone else through contact.

Hepatitis B

How to get it. The hepatitis B virus is extremely infectious. The example sometimes given is that a single drop of hepatitis B–infected blood in a large swimming pool filled with unchlorinated water can infect a swimmer. Think of it as one hundred times more infectious than AIDS. The hepatitis B virus is transmitted most commonly in the same ways, and sometimes at the same time, as HIV: by sexual contact, contaminated blood, infected needles, or even from open sores on an infected person. It can also be transferred by infected blood products and oral-fecal contact. In parts of the Third World, transfusions and inoculations are risky because not all donated blood has been thoroughly tested for freedom from HIV, hepatitis B, malaria, and other diseases, and not all disposable needles are disposed of. High-risk areas include Southeast Asia, China, sub-Saharan Africa, the Amazon Basin, and several Caribbean islands.

Symptoms. The disease manifests itself from one to six months after exposure with gradual onset of abdominal pain and loss of appetite. Jaundice, similar to that with hepatitis A, occurs in about half of all cases of hepatitis B. Symptoms can last several months, but it's possible to have hepatitis B and show none of the usual symptoms.

How to avoid it. Newly developed vaccines Heptavax B, Recombivax-HB, and Engerix-B are effective against hepatitis B. The vaccine is given as a series of three shots over a period of six months, although they can be given within two or three months if need be. The opinion of the American Association of Pediatrics and other medical organizations seems to be that everyone should receive a vaccine. The National Foundation for Infectious Diseases has begun an education and vaccination campaign on college campuses. Others recommend the vaccine in connection with foreign travel only for health care workers and people who expect to have sexual contacts or stay for more than six months in areas such as Southeast Asia or sub-Saharan Africa where hepatitis B is endemic. The six months boundary seems a little arbitrary, so you might want to receive the vaccine even for shorter trips. The present cost is about $150, but protection may be worth it.

Avoid injections (including drugs, tattooing, and acupuncture), practice good hygiene, and avoid unprotected sexual contacts.

How to treat it. Receive hepatitis B immune globulin as soon as you know you've been exposed. You can eat anything, but you must avoid alcohol. Don't push yourself. Alpha interferon is said to help in some cases. There is a 95 percent probability of complete recovery and immunity, but if hepatitis B becomes chronic, as is not uncommon in Southeast Asia, it can be fatal. There is less than 10 percent chance that a victim will remain a carrier, but, if so, his risk of cancer or cirrhosis of the liver increases. Anyone with troubling symptoms after returning from a trip should mention the possibility of hepatitis B to the doctor.

Hepatitis C

Hepatitis C is widespread throughout the world, including the United States. Check with your local health department or travel doctor. It is transmitted in the same ways as hepatitis B and HIV (e.g., through infected needles or blood, and possibly through sex). The culpable virus was recently identified and tests have been developed to diagnose the disease and to screen infected blood products.

Hepatitis C is particularly dangerous because the virus is not killed in approximately 60 percent of the people infected. As a result, they remain carriers. A majority of them develop chronic active hepatitis. About 20 percent may also develop cirrhosis or scarring of the liver. The only treatment at present, alpha interferon, is not very successful and often is very hard on the patient. As always, it is best to avoid infection.

Hepatitis E

Hepatitis E is transmitted primarily by drinking contaminated water, but it can be spread in the same ways as hepatitis A. There is no vaccine against it and immune globulin probably offers no protection. The most important method of prevention is avoidance of contaminated water. Those infected generally recover from hepatitis E without any problems.

JAPANESE B ENCEPHALITIS

This mosquito-borne viral disease attacks the central nervous system. It is present in rural areas in Asia from China to Pakistan, especially in rice fields and pig farms, but it's extremely rare for an urban traveler to get it. Most infections are mild, but a severe case can cause brain damage and has a 25 percent chance of being fatal. A vaccine, approved by the FDA in 1992, administered in three doses over a four-week period, protects against the disease. It is recommended for anyone visiting an endemic area for four weeks or more. Check with the CDC with respect to countries you will visit.

LEISHMANIASIS

How to get it. Leishmaniasis is present in Central and South America, Africa, central Asia, the Middle East, and northern China. A quick nighttime nip from an infected female sand fly injects a tiny parasite that invades lymphoid cells in internal organs such as the spleen and liver, bone marrow, or mucus membranes.

Symptoms. Unfortunately, you may not even notice the bite until weeks or months later when it becomes a painful ulcer. Since it's difficult to distinguish Leishmaniasis from quite a few other diseases, it's important to realize that a skin ulcer may be a signal.

How to avoid it. Prevention being preferable to cure, take the usual precautions against sand fly bites, such as using insect repellent, wearing long pants, using fine mesh netting, and so on (see Malaria).

How to treat it. The problem is that most infected people wait several months before seeking treatment, and then they may consult a doctor who doesn't diagnose it properly because of lack of familiarity with the disease. Tell your physician that you've been traveling in exotic places, because, if left untreated, Leishmaniasis can be fatal. Treatment with Stibogluconate sodium (Pento-stam, P, available from the CDC drug service) should cure the problem. The type of Leishmaniasis that affects the skin creates lesions and boils, often on the face, backs of hands, forearms, and legs. These too can be treated with Pentostam. However, some disfigurement is possible if the parasites attack the mucus membranes of the mouth, nose, or throat.

MALARIA

Malaria is present in over 100 countries; almost 2 million people die from it each year, far more than die from AIDS. A child infected by one of the virulent strains of malaria can die within hours of showing the first symptoms. Of the 300 million people infected every year, only about 30,000 are travelers. To provide perspective, only .00003 of the 30 million U.S. travelers abroad last year got malaria. That's because with proper precautions, malaria is almost fully preventable. Amazingly, some travelers in known areas of risk ignore even the basic precautions of taking preventive tablets and following simple routines to avoid being bitten by mosquitoes, the carriers of the disease.

Although early treatment of malaria is usually effective, consequences can be very serious if treatment is delayed. People living in highly malarial areas may develop partial immunity after repeated attacks of malaria, but unprotected travelers are at risk.

According to the CDC, the risk is highest in tropical Africa, Amazonian South America, and parts of Central America, Mexico, India, the Caribbean, Southern Asia, Indonesia, and New Guinea.

Travelers to Africa should take malaria especially seriously for several reasons: it's a year-round problem, not just seasonal; travelers go to Africa specifically to spend time in rural areas, which is where mosquito infestation is most severe; and a higher percentage of mosquitoes in Africa than elsewhere carry the malaria parasites. For comparison, the odds against getting malaria are estimated as 2,000 times more in your favor in Latin America.

How to get it. Physicians used to believe there was something about the air in swamps and sewers that caused the disease. Hence the name "mal aria," or bad air. Turns out they weren't far off. We now know that it is the female anopheline (a Latin word meaning "the hurtful ones") mosquito, a lover of swamps and sewers, who delivers malaria to us. She is merely a carrier, picking up one-cell parasites from an infected person and transmitting them, via the saliva accompanying her pesky bite, to the next person. The parasites travel to the liver of the new host, multiply, and escape into the blood stream.

There, they invade red blood cells and multiply, causing the cells to burst and the parasites to flood the system like bloodthirsty pirates searching for more cells to invade.

Symptoms. Malaria symptoms usually appear between a week and a month after exposure but can take longer. The first round of symptoms includes chills that may last from 15 minutes to an hour, even up to eight hours. Chills are followed by several hours of high fever, then heavy sweating. These symptoms are usually accompanied by fatigue, severe headache, muscle pains, dizziness, and increasing weakness. When an attack of malaria subsides, the patient feels weary but much better (how could it be otherwise?). Symptoms may recur every one to three days, depending on which species of parasite is roaming around in the blood. The parasites can also damage the brain and kidneys (in the kidneys it's called Blackwater Fever because bursting red blood cells darken the urine), which can be lethal.

In only a minority of malaria cases is there any intestinal uproar, so a person who has some or all of the symptoms listed above plus nausea, vomiting, cramps, and/or diarrhea may have typhoid, cholera, dysentery, dengue fever, or hepatitis rather than malaria (now there are some great choices!). If you have an unexplained fever in an area in which malaria is common, get a blood test immediately.

How to avoid it. Prevention is the best answer. Don't get bitten. Before you leave home, review the *World Malaria Risk Chart* and *How to Protect Yourself against Malaria*, both available from IAMAT (716-754-4883). The IAMAT material is so helpful it's almost reckless not to use it. The CDC Malaria Branch publishes a useful booklet called *Recommendations for Prevention of Malaria among Travelers*. Call the Malaria Hotline at (404) 332-4555.

There are a number of ways to minimize the likelihood of feeling the mosquito's bites (I *don't* mean staying at home). Be more vigilant when mosquitoes are most active—during warm months and at dawn and dusk. Be wary of water, especially if it's slow-moving or stagnant. Strong scents and body odors attract mosquitoes, so a shower at the end of a hot day is practical as well as pleasurable. For anyone disposed to take hair spray, perfume, or perfumed cosmetics on their travels, the mosquito's keen nose is one more incentive to leave those things at home. Unfortunately, mosquitoes are even attracted by the CO_2 we exhale—and there's not much we can do about that.

Definitely use an insect repellent. Among those available, DEET is amazingly effective and no traveler should be without it in a malaria area. For years, DEET was greasy, could cause dermatitus and certain toxic reactions, and smelled bad. A new cream formulation is far better. It's much less toxic and lasts all day. The recommended concentration is 30 percent (10 percent for children) and it should be combined with sunscreen. In addition, spray Permethrin (sold as Permanone) on bed net and clothing. Permethrin does more than repel; it actually kills the mosquitoes. It's not toxic to humans, won't melt synthetic materials, and remains effective even after the clothing has been washed several times. Rub DEET on thoroughly and reapply it every few hours—more frequently if you sweat heavily or otherwise get wet. By the way, DEET on one part of your body does not deter mosquitoes from biting untreated skin nearby. Some people don't like the way DEET feels on their skin, and it does have a fairly distinctive, ahem, aroma, but these are minor considerations compared to a bout with malaria. Tuck your pants into your shoes, especially if ticks are a problem.

Ultrathon is an insect repellent that uses a polymer suspension to achieve controlled-release of a 33 percent DEET solution with very low absorption through the skin. It's supposed to keep mosquitoes, ticks, flies, chiggers, gnats, and fleas at bay for up to 12 hours, and it is resistant to water and perspiration. It leaves an oily feel but has a pleasing aroma. Whatever you select, use it. Not getting bitten is by far your most effective protection. We'll discuss this further in Chapter 11 (Lodging).

Clothing fends off mosquitoes fairly effectively, so at prime time in malaria-land, wear long pants and shirts with long sleeves. Protect your neck. Army surplus stores sell light, inexpensive hats with mosquito-proof mesh that covers head and neck (don't worry if you salute when an officer of the French Foreign Legion strides by).

Where mosquito nets are needed, you'll usually find them provided in your hotel room or for sale on the street. The most common type of net hangs from overhead, covering the entire bed. If there are holes or tears, tape them closed or tie the net around them into a small knot. If you can't seal the holes, ask the clerk for a better net. If you decide to take a net with you, there are some good nets available. The SleepScreen brand rests on the bed or ground and consists of a small dome over your face and a net that stretches down the bed. Weighing only 10 ounces, it costs about $30 (or 23 ounces and $40 for a double).

When mosquitoes are around, light mosquito coils at the head and the foot of the bed (some people prefer putting oil of citronella on themselves and the corners of the bed). After you're in, tuck the net under the mattress all around. Think of yourself as the favorite entrée on some mosquito's evening menu and act accordingly.

Virtually all knowledgeable travelers take a *malaria prophylactic* (I know you know that we're not talking about a condom here). Note that the word "prophylactic" means "to defend against," rather than "to prevent." At present, no drug regimen guarantees complete protection against malaria. What drugs do is suppress multiplication of the parasites in the liver, thus preventing their spread through the body to become full-scale malaria. However, even a person who's taken no antimalarial pills is unlikely to contract malaria from a single bite, so don't panic if one little dive bomber slips through. We seem to have at least a limited natural immunity but, since that immunity is minimal, protection remains very important.

Quinine protected Enrico Caruso when he sang grand opera 1,500 miles up the Amazon at the turn of the century and Dr. Livingstone as he trudged through the jungle trying to find the headwaters of the Congo, but it may not work for you. That's because malaria parasites have mutated, acquiring resistance. The areas in which these parasites are most resistant to chloroquine phosphate, the quinine-based drug everyone used to take, are the northern half of South America, virtually all of sub-Saharan Africa, and most of Asia from Afghanistan across to Papua New Guinea. Watch for a new quinine replacement named Artemether. However, it is a treatment, not a prophylaxis. The malaria parasites along the borders of Myanmar and Cambodia have become resistant to almost all drugs.

Some degree of chloroquine resistance has been reported everywhere malaria occurs except for Mexico, Haiti, the Dominican Republic, Central America north of Panama, and most of the Mideast. Not long ago, the CDC was suggesting that where parasites are resistant to chloroquine one ought to take Mefloquine (Lariam, P).

The CDC recommends Fansidar as a means of suppressing malaria symptoms long enough to reach proper medical treatment but doesn't recommend it as a prophylactic.

Some well-regarded antimalarial pills are not sold in certain countries. For a trip I took to central Africa, the most appropriate antimalarial drug appeared to be Proquanil (Paludrine). It wasn't sold in the United States but was available over-the-counter in England. I took a daily Proquanil and a weekly chloroquine pill and didn't get malaria. Of course, a friend relied on carefully selected Chinese herbs as antimalarial protection for the same trip and she didn't get malaria either. What can we conclude from that?

Since there may be some side effects with a malaria prophylactic, ask a doctor what to expect in connection with the one you choose. For example, some users have reported serious side effects from Lariam (e.g., nightmares and panic attacks). If my palms and the soles of my feet started scaling, I'd feel better if I knew it was just a side effect of Proquanil. If you take Lariam or Proquanil, it might be wise to start two weeks before your departure to see if side effects develop. Check also with the CDC International Traveler's Hotline (404-332-4555). Select information you want from document numbers they give you and enter your fax number, and they'll fax you right back with current vaccination and other recommendations. Here's a hot flash: **Ask about Malarone. When released by the FDA, it will be revolutionary. It is more effective and has fewer side effects than any other drug.**

I cannot recommend a specific antimalarial pill because that choice should be determined by where you're going, how much time you'll be spending in rural areas (where mosquitoes are most dense), and any drug allergies you have. You need current medical information to connect the best protection with your itinerary. Again, look at the IAMAT material and the CDC Web site.

The usual drill is to begin taking the pills two weeks before you enter an area where there's a malaria risk. As perhaps some slight evidence of global consciousness, almost every traveler I know who takes a weekly pill takes it on Sunday. To avoid an upset stomach, follow your pharmacist's directions (which is usually to take it after a meal). Continue taking the pills at prescribed intervals during your travels and for four weeks after you are last exposed to any risk of acquiring malaria. The objective is to kill any parasites that may still be lounging around your liver. If, for example, you're going to New Zealand after you leave the Philippines, the four-week period would begin the date you left the Philippines.

Women in their first trimester of pregnancy should be cautious of antimalarial drugs. Neither they nor young children should take these drugs without advice from a knowledgeable doctor.

A person who has taken any antimalarial drug is not permitted to donate blood for three years thereafter. The explanation I've heard is that the drug may mask the presence of the malaria parasite in the liver for many months. Since one might be hosting malaria parasites without knowing it, blood banks don't want to take the risk of passing them along in donated blood.

A few words about what does *not* work. Studies do not support the belief that Vitamin B1 is an effective mosquito repellent. Gadgets that project sound waves do not work. Avon's Skin So Soft acts as a temporary physical barrier because of its mineral oil, but is only about 50 percent effective as such and only if reapplied every ten minutes or so. As a Saint Joseph's Hospital (Atlanta) Travel Advisory put it, none of these alternatives will hurt you, but relying on any of them to prevent malaria "would border on lunacy."

How to treat it. In the 1700s, South American natives taught strangers how to use powder made from the bark of a certain tree to relieve malaria symptoms. That was good advice at the time, but if you believe you have the symptoms of malaria, see a doctor. If you must minister to yourself until you reach a doctor, take an increased dose of whatever prophylactic medicine you've been taking. The number of pills you should take depends on the dosage and contents of your tablets. When you buy the drug, ask "What dosage should I take if I experience symptoms of malaria?"

If you get malaria, a blood test will determine which type of parasite is involved. You then take a drug designed to kill that specific parasite and there should be no recurrence of the symptoms. In other words, malaria is curable. The danger is in failing to get treatment. Without treatment, one type of malaria parasite can be lethal. Other types are unlikely to be lethal but can cause recurrence of the symptoms and damage to assorted internal organs if untreated. The message should be clear.

If you see a doctor after you return from a trip during which you took antimalarial drugs, be sure to mention that fact. If you think you may have malaria, tell the doctor where you've traveled. Also ask him to consider the other diseases your research said might be out there. If you're concerned that your doctor may not be current on malaria and these other diseases, find a travel medicine or infectious disease specialist right away.

The bottom line: (a) with reasonable efforts, you can probably avoid mosquitoes and thus avoid malaria; (b) protective medicine greatly reduces the chances that full-scale malaria will develop; and (c) if you get malaria, proper treatment should cure it.

MENINGOCOCCAL MENINGITIS

In this disease, bacteria infect the membranes that line the spinal cord and brain. Because bacteria are spread by coughing and sneezing, people in crowds are most at risk. Fortunately, most adults have developed an immunity to meningococcal bacteria, but if a person is stricken, there is risk of brain damage or death.

There is a vaccine, effective for three years, that is often recommended for travel in sub-Saharan Africa, northern India, and Nepal. Symptoms include high fever, chills, headache, stiff neck, nausea and vomiting, and sensitivity to light. When meningitis is suspected, penicillin is often the recommended treatment.

POLIO

Polio, transmitted by oral-fecal contact or contaminated water, is common in underdeveloped countries and is still present in parts of Europe, especially around the Mediterranean.

If you've never had the polio vaccine, consider getting it before traveling in underdeveloped countries. Even if you have, consider a booster dose prior to travel. Ideally, you should start the course several months before your planned departure, but this can be cut a bit if necessary. Public health departments seem to recommend the Salk dead vaccine (received by inoculation) as slightly safer than the Sabin live vaccine (taken orally).

RABIES

Rabies (also known as hydrophobia) can cause prolonged suffering and death. It's present in most countries, including Europe and the United States. Rabies is found in raccoons, jackals, wolves, bats, cattle, cats, and dogs, among other animals.

Although symptoms usually appear within two to eight weeks, one nasty characteristic of rabies is that it can take up to seven years to show up—long after the victim has forgotten the incident that caused it (which could have been merely getting infected saliva in a wound). To be cautious, receive the Human Diploid Cell Merriaux Vaccine in three not particularly painful injections beginning a month before you travel.

As you travel, don't pet an animal that can bite you and get out of the way if you see an animal behaving strangely (erratic motions, howling bark, frothing mouth, and jaws fixed open). Rabid animals are fearless and will attack without provocation.

If bitten, or even licked on a wound by an infected animal (since the virus travels in the animal's saliva), wash the wound immediately with soap and clean water. Pour in some hydrogen peroxide. If no clean water is available, use alcohol, tea, or even carbonated soda. You are attempting to wash the virus from the wound, so wash vigorously and repeatedly. See a doctor to help decide whether to receive the vaccine (if you haven't had it) or an injection of rabies immune globulin at the bite site. The decision is much easier if the offending animal is caught and tested.

SCHISTOSOMIASIS (also known as Bilharzia)

More than 200 million people carry this parasite, which exists primarily in sub-Saharan Africa, the Middle East, Japan, China, the Philippines, Indonesia, Thailand, tropical South America, and the Caribbean islands. If you'll be traveling in one or more of these places, you should know the precautions to take.

How to get it. Schistosomiasis is caused by trematode parasites that live inside freshwater snails. After metamorphosis, they enter the water, seeking their next host (and humans are very hospitable). If these parasites are present, a person is at risk when swimming in, bathing in, drinking, or even just walking through water. Parasites can enter a host through the skin (a break in the skin, such as a cut, isn't required) or when ingested orally. They reproduce and attack the bowel, bladder, liver, and colon, ultimately appearing in the stool or urine. When parasite-contaminated excrement later enters the water source, the process begins again as the parasite seeks out the snail.

Symptoms. The first sign might be a brief rash where the parasite entered the body. Appearing three to ten weeks after infection, symptoms include abdominal pain, tender and enlarged spleen and liver, headache, chills, fever, diarrhea, blood in the stool or urine, nausea, aches, body rash, coughing, and loss of weight. Remission may occur two to eight weeks thereafter. In advanced cases, schisto has caused blindness, epilepsy, and even death. The diversity of symptoms makes it very hard to diagnose.

How to avoid it. Don't swim in rivers or lakes where schisto is a possibility, especially in stagnant water, immediately downstream from a city, or anywhere along the Nile. Even brief exposure can result in infection. If you must cross freshwater in a schisto-infected area, wear shoes and cover your ankles. If you get wet, rub your skin dry immediately; use alcohol if you have it. You want to remove or kill the parasite before it can penetrate the skin. Boil, filter, or treat water with iodine to disinfect it for drinking or bathing. If you can do nothing else, wash with soap. Prevention is important because schisto can do considerable damage before being detected.

How to treat it. You may need to be tested more than once because a test soon after having been exposed may be misleadingly negative. Schisto can be diagnosed by a urine or stool test and can be cured by a drug regimen, often using Praziquantel (Biltricide, P).

SEVERE PAIN (broken bones, kidney stone, etc.)

If you're going to be days away from outside medical help, take a heavy-duty painkiller along in case of serious injury. It won't cure anything, but it makes it easier to endure pain until reaching help. If you have an adverse reaction to codeine, consider Demerol (P). As a narcotic, Demerol should be treated with care and should not be taken in conjunction with alcohol. The bottle should be labeled to avoid any problem with customs. For lesser pain, ibuprofen (Advil, OTC) is an effective analgesic and anti-inflammatory drug.

SEXUALLY TRANSMITTED DISEASES

Acquired Immunodeficiency Syndrome (AIDS).

How to get it. AIDS, caused by the human immunodeficiency virus (HIV), is epidemic in at least ten African countries, India, Thailand, and the Philippines, and is a growing problem in many other countries. Good news: you do not contract AIDS just from being in certain places. Nor is it spread by casual contact, coughs or sneezes, food or water, toilets, or any of the usual suspects that cause many diseases. Whether you contract AIDS is determined primarily by your own behavior; it is not an inherent peril of being on the road.

AIDS is transmitted primarily by sexual intercourse or, euphemistically, by transfer of body fluids. It can be contracted during a single sexual contact. You get no free swings (so to speak). HIV infection can also be transmitted via a needle—while taking intravenous drugs, getting inoculations, getting a tattoo or an ear pierced, undergoing acupuncture or a blood transfusion, or when accidentally jabbed.

Symptoms. The symptoms are too complex—and well known—to bear repeating here.

How to avoid it. To avoid deterring tourists and business people, some governments low-ball the number of known HIV-positive cases in their countries. That means you should not rely on published information about the prevalence of AIDS in a given country. Unless you're skiing across Antarctica, assume HIV is present.

"Your next sexual partner could be that very special person. The one that gives you AIDS."
—Public Health Notice in Zimbabwe

The local people travelers meet most frequently are those who make their living on and around the tourist trail. Unfortunately for all concerned, this puts them in a high-risk group. Among those at highest risk are intravenous drug users, prostitutes, and guys who prowl the tourist trail hoping to seduce travelers. Keep in mind that other travelers who have sex with local people can, if infected, pass it on to you. You must not let blood, semen, or vaginal secretions from an infected person enter your body.

It's pathetic that your life may be on the line when you're considering a sexual relationship with an enchanting person as you travel—but that's the way it is. How many unexpected births must there be before we concede that condoms are scarcely fail-safe as protection. The odds overseas seem prohibitive to me unless both people have been tested and the relationship is exclusive.

If you haven't traveled extensively in faraway places, you may not be able to predict how you'll respond to the stimuli of romantic settings and attractive companions (about whom, unfortunately, you may not know a lot). A prospective partner may be unaware of, or unwilling to admit, his or her AIDS status. Or someone may even lie to you about their status or sexual behavior. If you are uncertain about what choices you might make as you travel, you would be well advised to take latex nonoxynol-9 spermicide condoms along. Although latex doesn't remain impervious to tropical heat for long, animal skin condoms are too porous.

Anyone who uses a questionable needle to inject recreational drugs or otherwise pierce one's skin in a foreign country has a death wish, one that may be accommodated. Stay away from tattoos and acupuncture unless you're certain the equipment is sterile (which is highly unlikely). If you require an inoculation, be certain that a new, still-in-the-package, disposable needle is used. Don't take anyone's word for it. *See* the package opened—or go elsewhere. Some travelers carry a syringe and needle along in case of injury in countries where AIDS is common.

A related issue is whether the blood supply available for transfusion is contaminated. Most underdeveloped and developing countries still can't ensure that their blood supply is free from hepatitis, AIDS, or other diseases, so travelers should do everything possible to avoid receiving a transfusion. In an emergency, consider the use of plasma extenders. If you're traveling with a partner, or a small group, you might compare your blood types and HIV status to determine who could be donors for whom should the need arise. If the need for a transfusion arises and you have the choice, buy a plane ticket. Fortunately, the odds against needing a transfusion at the moment you are in a high-risk AIDS country are massively in your favor.

How to treat it. There is no known vaccine for protection against AIDS, nor as yet any reliable cure.

Herpes

Since herpes is transmitted by direct contact with herpes sores on an infected person, the primary preventives for herpes are abstinence or use of a condom. Herpes manifests itself through small blisters on the lips or genitals which burst to form sores that last for a couple of weeks. If the herpes virus is already present, the blisters may be induced by exposure to intense sunlight or unusual stress.

There is presently no known cure for herpes. However, if herpes sores develop, treatment with acyclovir (Zovirax, P or Famciclovir, P) may reduce the severity of symptoms. It is available in ointment and capsule form, but dermatologists consider the capsules to be far more effective. Some dermatologists also recommend Ambesol Gel (OTC). Even Blistex (OTC) is said to have some effectiveness in reducing the symptoms of oral herpes. Do not touch the herpes sores and keep the area around them dry. Wash your hands often.

Syphilis, Gonorrhea, and Other Sexually Transmitted Diseases (STDs)

STDs are more prevalent in the Third World than in developed countries and they do not affect local people only. Nevertheless, more than a few travelers roll the dice, making an intimate decision based on a spontaneous evaluation of someone's personality or appearance. Abstinence is the best preventive medicine, followed by having sex only with a partner who has tested negative for sexually transmitted diseases. Condoms come in a distant third. If you decide to go forward, use a latex condom and a vaginal spermicide. In addition, check for sores or discharge, wash the genitals of a prospective partner with soap and water, and urinate after intercourse. Sounds pretty romantic, doesn't it?

Common STD symptoms include penile or vaginal discharge, urination that leaves a burning sensation, and lower abdominal pain. There may also be an ulcer, a rash, and fever. Men generally experience the first symptoms of gonorrhea within two to seven days, but it may be weeks before a woman feels symptoms—if ever. However, some STDs, especially gonorrhea in Asia, are asymptomatic. It would be prudent to assume that you might have been infected and practice safe sex until receiving negative results on blood tests. If you think you may have an STD, let partners know, avoid sexual contact, and start medication immediately.

Since gonorrhea has not become penicillin-resistant in many places (e.g., parts of southeast Asia and Africa and a few other places), consider ciprofloxacin (Cipro, P) or Ceftriaxone (Rocephin, P).

Treatment for chlamydia, which may be the leading cause of infertility, includes doxycycline, tetracycline, erythromycin, or ozithromycin.

Women may experience a pelvic inflammatory disease, often caused by gonorrhea or chlamydia. Treatment usually includes cipro, cefixine, and doxycycline (for nonpregnant women only).

Syphilis announces its presence ten to ninety days after infection with a sore on the genitals or the lips, fingers, or anus. Although the sore is painless, it is highly contagious. It disappears without treatment, but the disease continues to grow in the person affected. If untreated, syphilis may cause serious problems, including heart disease and insanity. When an unexplained sore appears in one of these areas two to ten weeks after sexual contact, get medical help (including penicillin).

Treatment for STDs can be complicated, so see a doctor as soon as you can.

SHOCK

Symptoms of shock include a weak, fast pulse, pale face, perspiration, fainting, clammy skin, dull eyes, and nausea. Shock often accompanies major trauma (e.g., a large burn, severe illness, extensive blood loss), but can occur even after relatively minor injuries or serious infections. Keep the victim lying down and, if injuries permit, elevate the legs higher than the head. Use blankets to conserve body heat. Giving the victim water or ORS (not alcohol), may help, but there is some risk of vomiting or aspiration. If the victim is unconscious, turn him on his side so he won't choke. Keep mouth and throat clear. Because blood is not flowing to vital organs, shock can kill. It is essential to get medical help immediately.

SLEEPING SICKNESS

Tsetse flies hang out around livestock, lakes, and river banks in central and most of sub-Saharan Africa. Bites become red and swollen and lymph glands become tender. DEET and Durathon are good repellents, and it apparently takes several bites to infect a human.

Symptoms include high temperature, sleeplessness, and sharp headaches. Drugs are available to treat sleeping sickness, but the choice depends on careful diagnosis. Failure to get treatment leads to lethargy, depression, and apathy (as in "sleeping")—and death.

SMALLPOX

Even though smallpox has been officially eradicated, a few countries in Africa still require evidence of a smallpox vaccination. If you'll be visiting one of them and have a smallpox vaccination entered on your yellow card, no problem. If you don't have or don't want the vaccination, ask your local public health department to give you a "certificate of contraindication," meaning you don't need the vaccine. That should get you past the border. In only two countries has anyone even asked to see my yellow card and in neither case were the entries examined with any care.

TETANUS

How to get it. Tetanus (sometimes called lockjaw) microorganisms are omnipresent and can infect someone through any break in the skin. Tetanus may invade through puncture wounds from splinters, thorns, and almost everything else. Remember your mom warning you not to step on a nail? It's a serious problem, but one that can largely be prevented through immunization.

How to avoid it. The Tetanus vaccine (usually combined with the diphtheria vaccine) provides a high degree of immunity. Almost everyone gets this vaccination as a child, but a booster is necessary every ten years (or within five years of your last immunization if you've had a dirty scrape, cut, or skin ulcer). Because tetanus germs are so common, this immunization is important whether you travel or not. Clean and cover any wound. If it's large, get medical attention.

TRAUMA

Trauma is a wound or shock produced by a physical injury. Travelers are more at risk of experiencing traumatic injury than of being affected by almost any of the exotic diseases on this list. Unfortunately, space doesn't permit inclusion of a complete course in first aid. It might be wise to take a first aid course before you travel—or read and take along one of the excellent small-format first aid booklets (see the bibliography). If a problem occurs that requires quick, effective first aid, a traveler can't count on outside help. Emotions or pain at the time of injury can create confusion. That's when knowledge and preparation pay off.

Traumatic injury can occur in many forms, but I have two suggestions that will provide some protection. First, be careful in traffic abroad because the traffic flow may be the reverse of what you're used to and the pedestrian seldom has the right of way. Look both ways before stepping into the street. Too often, drivers, especially drivers of big trucks, are careless of human life.

Second, if you're riding in a vehicle and the driver seems drunk, get out—or off. It's amazing how many canyons are littered with the remnants of buses because a cannonballing driver didn't see a curve in time. Don't assume, as you might at home, that the driver must know what he's doing and will get you safely to the barn. A high correlation between alcohol and accidents prevails around the world. Listen to your intuition.

I don't drive a car in Third World countries when I can avoid it. As much as I enjoy the convenience, it's like trying to dance when you don't know the steps.

If someone is injured in an accident, see if he or she is breathing, then check for a pulse. If CPR seems necessary, put to use those lessons you took before leaving home. If you think there's a broken bone, apply ice, immobilize the area with a splint, elevate it, and find a doctor. Be careful not to aggravate a neck or back injury by unnecessary movement. If movement is unavoidable, immobilize the injured area with a splint first. You can splint an arm by strapping it to the chest. Bind legs together. Use a tree limb, anything, to keep broken pieces from moving freely.

If there is serious bleeding, elevate and apply pressure to the wound or to the artery supplying blood to that extremity. If a person is unconscious and you can do nothing else, place the person on her side with her head lower than her chest so fluids can drain away from her lungs and exit her mouth. Call for help and be prepared to administer CPR.

TUBERCULOSIS

Tuberculosis (TB) has never ceased being a problem in underdeveloped countries. Recently, it's being spread by people who got it as a result of diminished immune systems due to AIDS. New forms of TB are increasingly resistant to standard drug treatment. There are three things you can do to reduce risk: keep yourself in good health, avoid letting people cough on you, and get a TB skin test if you may have been exposed. A vaccine, not presently available in the United States, may be considered by anyone who anticipates prolonged exposure to tuberculosis.

TYPHOID

How to get it. Consuming food and water contaminated by Salmonella typhi bacteria is usually how people contract typhoid. High-risk areas for typhoid, which is highly infectious, include areas of Africa, Asia, and Central and South America.

Symptoms. It begins like a cold or the flu and progresses to extreme fatigue, chills, high fever, coughs, bloody diarrhea, constipation, headaches, and loss of appetite. A telltale sign is that your pulse gets slower when your fever increases. After a week or so, there may be pink spots on the body and some delirium.

How to avoid it. Be alert to sanitation in places you eat and drink, especially in villages and rural areas. In 1994, the FDA approved Typhin Vi, a single-dose vaccine said to be effective with no side effects. The vaccine is received in two shots, four weeks apart, and then a booster is required every three years. A live oral vaccine, which provides a five-year immunity against typhoid, has been reported to be as effective as an injection and is, of course, painless. Typhoid is still common in underdeveloped countries so it's worth keeping this immunity current.

How to treat it. There should be no long-term complications if you get extended rest and take one of several antibiotics (Bactrim, Cipro, Floxin).

TYPHUS

How to get it. Bites or ingestion of contaminated feces from lice, fleas, mites, mice, and rats are the primary source of infection. Typhus exists mostly in the highland areas of Africa, Asia, the Middle East, Mexico, Peru, and Ecuador.

Symptoms. There may be days or weeks of fever, chills, severe headache, coughing, pains in the chest and back. There may also be a rash on the trunk of the body that lasts for up to a week. Typhus carried by lice and mites may progress to pneumonia after about a week. The severity of typhus depends on the specific bacteria involved.

How to avoid it. Watch out for lice, fleas, mites, ticks, and rats. Bathe frequently and wash your clothes in very hot water. Use insect repellents and a shampoo like Kwell (OTC). If you hear of an outbreak, go somewhere else.

How to treat it. Tetracycline (P) and Doxycycline (P) are considered effective.

YELLOW FEVER

How to get it. As with malaria, yellow fever is brought into your life by a mosquito. However, as with dengue fever, this one bites during the day.

Symptoms. Jaundice (yellow skin and eyes) gives this illness its name. There is an initial fever with rapid pulse. The fever ebbs, then returns with a slower pulse, perhaps accompanied by bleeding from the mouth and stomach, headache, loss of rationality, and possibly coma.

How to avoid it. Yellow fever is still present in most of Central and South America, Africa, and the Caribbean, especially in rural areas. If you may be in a yellow fever area, get a single shot of live virus vaccine before you go, then a booster every ten years. If a country requires evidence, as a condition of entry, that you've had this vaccination, you must have received it at least ten days prior to your arrival and had it entered on your Yellow Card. Countries that require evidence of the vaccination are all in central and west Africa, plus French Guiana. Note that the yellow fever vaccination must be separated from a cholera vaccination by at least three weeks. Check the CDC yellow and blue sheets for information.

How to treat it. There is no effective treatment, but medical assistance is necessary to provide IV fluids, monitor kidney functioning, and control gastrointestinal bleeding.

TRAVEL MEDICINE KIT

With this litany of unpleasantness in mind, it's obvious why a traveler is well advised to carry a thoughtfully prepared travel medicine kit. I'm no hypochondriac, but I carry more medicine when I leave the country than I ever keep on hand at home. I've never had to use even one of the major treatments and don't expect to.

If you don't take this chapter with you on your trip, consider taking at least the medical Checklists in the back of this book to help properly match the remedy with the problem.

You may have seen ready-made portable medicine kits for sale. Some may be okay for minor first aid, but I don't use or recommend them. Because

Medical clinic. San Pedro de Sula, Honduras.

they're designed for general use, they're incomplete and expensive. It's better to think carefully about what you might encounter and design your own kit.

If you prefer a kit, check the catalogues, outdoor stores, or call Medex Assistance (800-537-2029; kits at $35 and $100).

Medicine Kit Tips

— Transport medicine in a watertight case or sturdy Ziploc bag.

— Leave glass containers at home.

— Consider taking a brief first aid manual with you.

— When pills come in an unnecessarily large container, transfer them into a smaller one, along with the prescription information. Make sure all containers are clearly labeled.

— When you have a choice, take a capsule rather than a liquid. Even things that shouldn't spill sometimes do.

— Since medicines-of-choice change frequently, write on separate slips of paper what illness each medicine is intended for and its major symptoms. Put each slip in the appropriate container. Symptoms don't announce themselves with labels, so you have to be able to connect them with the appropriate remedy.

— Take copies of prescriptions and their generic names. If filled abroad, ensure that proper weights, presumably metric, are used. Have the pharmacist include the expiration date of each prescription medicine on the label so you'll know when it's time to throw something out.

— Don't rely on prescription medicine that is nearing its expiration date.

- Take most medicines along rather than planning to buy them while traveling. Otherwise, you might need a medicine where there is no source or when you have a problem communicating your need. In addition, some drugs sold abroad contain impurities. If you buy abroad, beware of brand name drugs being sold at absurdly low prices. Make sure the label looks authentic (misspellings, for example, don't inspire confidence).

- Take essential medications in your carry-on luggage (so they won't be lost if your checked bag is).

- Confer with your doctor before buying the components of a travel medicine kit. This is especially true for pregnant women; mothers who are breast-feeding; persons with asthma, glaucoma, diabetes, or hypertension; persons with kidney, heart, thyroid, or prostate disease; or persons with autoimmune or chronic disease. Review all drug doses and the circumstances in which you should take them with the doctor who prescribes them.

Checklist: Shots to Get before You Go

What shots you need depends on (a) where you're going, (b) the current status of your inoculations, and (c) the requirements of the countries you'll be visiting. Obtain annual information on the prevalence of specific diseases in specific countries, along with immunization requirements, from *Health Information for International Travel* (HIFIT). This information is available on a current basis in the semimonthly *Summary of Health Information for International Travelers* issued by the Centers for Disease Control. Call the CDC hotline at (404) 332-4559 for information. Also visit the CDC Web site at www.cdc.gov.

Because some shots interfere with others and some shots are given as a series, you can't drop into the health department at the last minute to get all shots at once. Besides, it's nice to have some time to recover from any adverse reaction. Although it would be ideal to receive the full series of immunizations over a four- to eight-week period, the pace can be accelerated if need be.

- **Cholera:** Vaccine four to six weeks before you leave. If practical, it should not be received at the same time as the yellow fever vaccine. Protection is only partial. Check with the CDC to determine whether a cholera certificate of vaccination is required to enter any country on your itinerary.

- **Diphtheria:** Vaccine six weeks before you leave. Booster every ten years.

- **Hepatitis A:** One week before you leave, take immune globulin to increase immunity. Since this is a blood-based product, it would be risky to get this shot in any country where blood is not screened and treated. Alternatively and substantially more expensive, there's Havrix, the newly approved hepatitis A vaccine. The first shot is taken two to four weeks prior to departure; the second, six to twelve months later.

- **Hepatitis B:** Ideally, the three-shot vaccine (Recombivax) takes six months.

- **Influenza:** Vaccine anytime. Especially important for people over 65.

- **Japanese B encephalitis:** Three shots over a four-week period. Since there is a possibility of severe reaction after each vaccination, the series should begin at least six weeks prior to departure.

- **Measles, mumps, rubella:** Vaccines six weeks before you leave. If born after 1956, it is recommended that you receive a measles vaccine even if you've had an earlier shot.

- **Meningococcal meningitis:** Vaccine two weeks before you leave.

- **Polio:** Even if you were vaccinated as a child, consider getting this injection several months before you leave.

- **Rabies:** Begin Human Diploid Cell Merriaux Vaccine series four to six weeks before you leave. It may be repeated every two years if indicated by a decrease in antibody levels.

- **Smallpox:** Vaccine eight weeks before you leave.

- **Tetanus:** Vaccine (combined with diphtheria vaccine) six weeks before you leave. Booster every ten years or after a puncture wound or major laceration.

- **Typhoid:** If you take the standard vaccine, get the first shot eight weeks before departure and the second shot four weeks later. The oral vaccine may be preferable but should be kept refrigerated and must be taken as directed. Booster every three years. Alternatively, take the newly FDA-approved single-shot vaccine, Typhin Vi.

- **Yellow fever:** Vaccine three weeks before you leave. Booster every ten years.

My public health service advises that yellow fever and immune serum globulin can safely be given at the same time, even though that isn't their first choice. The same is true for immune globulin and oral polio.

Enter each shot on your yellow card. Keep a copy in a safe place since it's probably the only record of what shots you've had and when.

If you are interested in studying potential health problems abroad in greater depth, I've included helpful resources in the Bibliography.

Health Reminder

If a health problem emerges after your return, including unexplained weight loss, which you suspect might be related to your travels, tell your doctor where you've been and your ideas about possible causes. If symptoms are severe, find a specialist.

9

When It's Time to Go

I travel not to go anywhere, but to go.
I travel for travel's sake. The great affair is to move.
—Robert Louis Stevenson

Just before I go—I decide not to go. There's too much to be done. I won't be ready in time. I'm very good at getting ready for a long trip, but I still can't avoid stress as my departure date grows imminent. Fortunately, I've gotten used to these feelings, so I get a grip and make the plane every time.

The trouble is that when you're stressed, you tend to forget things. Even when your checklists report that you've packed all your clothing and equipment, you still have to remember all your last-minute tasks and make arrangements for everything that someone else has to do for you while you're away. I've solved that problem by creating two checklists; one for me, one for my Guardian Angels.

Guardian Angels are what I call the relatives, friends, business associates, and significant others who pay my bills, care for my home, screen the mail, handle taxes, feed the animals, and do all the other tasks that keep my home life together while I'm away.

My absences can be a burden for my Guardian Angels. They have a lot of responsibility if a problem arises, especially since I seldom call home. For that reason, I shower them with postcards from far away. When I return, I bring them exotic presents and do whatever else is appropriate. I'll always be in their debt.

These checklists are intended to avoid that moment when, lying on the perfect beach on Bora Bora,* I sit up, snap my fingers, and say, "Damn, I forgot to . . ."

---

* *Bora Bora.* The most beautiful and magical of the Society Islands (of which Tahiti is the best known) in the South Pacific.

Checklist: Last-Minute Tasks

__ **Appliances.** Before you walk out the door, make sure you've turned off, set, or unplugged everything that runs on electricity (check whether your brand of refrigerator should be unplugged). Don't forget the computer. Don't let a power surge zap your tools and toys.

__ **Bills.** Pay everything outstanding. Open a special checking account with a Guardian Angel as a signatory, and put enough money in it to cover all foreseeable bills. Arrange to have incoming checks deposited. Sign and date checks for monthly rent or mortgage payments and put each in a separate stamped envelope to be mailed each month. Leave a petty cash fund so your Guardian Angel won't have to pay expenses out of his or her own pocket.

__ **Cable TV.** Depending on the length of your trip, you may SAVE MONEY by disconnecting cable service.

__ **Car.** Ask a Guardian Angel to start your car every week and roll it a foot or two to keep the tires happy. SAVE MONEY by transferring your car to "storage status" for insurance purposes (meaning you retain comprehensive but not liability coverage).

__ **Documents.** Give a Guardian Angel copies of important documents including: (a) the first two pages of your passport; traveler's check, credit card, and ATM numbers; reservations, airline tickets, and your itinerary; (b) a list of AmEx mail service offices along your route and approximate dates on which you expect to pass them; (c) telephone numbers of people to call if there's a problem at home for which repairmen might be needed, as well as telephone numbers for your attorney and accountant; and (d) access to insurance policies, stock certificates, mortgages, or other documents, if needed.

__ **Fax machine.** Consider using call forwarding to forward incoming faxes to someone else's machine or ask your Guardian Angel to check the output of your fax machine.

__ **Fireplace.** Close the flue with the damper.

__ **Freezing weather.** Ask your Guardian Angel to let the water faucets drip if freezing weather hits.

__ **Growing things.** Arrange for someone to cut and water the lawn and other green things. Lend indoor plants to people who will care for them. If you leave animals behind, obviously you'll arrange to keep food and water flowing, and leave the name of a veterinarian and authority to get care if needed.

__ **Keys.** Give house and car keys to people who need them. Hide a set outside and/or take one with you.

__ **Legal matters.** Consider giving someone a General Power of Attorney, enabling them to take action necessary on your behalf. Tell someone where your will is located.

___ **Mail.** File a change of address form with the post office, redirecting mail to a safe haven. There's no reason to discuss your impending absence with post office personnel nor to indicate a return date on the form. Ask the recipient of your mail to trash junk mail, set personal letters aside, forward bills to your designated bill-payer, and open the rest.

___ **Personal care.** Get travel clothes cleaned and mended. Consider a last-minute haircut.

___ **Security.** Lock all doors and windows. Use double-key dead-bolt locks and don't hide keys in obvious places. Make sure all accessible windows are locked or fastened by screws. Use several automatic timers with multiple on and off settings for the radio (perhaps the best justification for talk radio) and a light or two, perhaps including exterior lights. If the trip is a long one, a Guardian Angel might change the timer settings occasionally to conform to sunset and should reset everything after a power outage. Alternatively, consider the VersaTimer (about $80; call 800-835-1515). Plug it into your computer, install a simple program, and set up to three devices for as many as 672 weekly "power events." You can even change the schedule remotely via modem. It should work if a prospective burglar will just pay attention.

If you have a burglar alarm, let the operator know you'll be on a trip until further notice and tell them who to notify in the event of a signal.

Put new bulbs in the lights just before you leave (with spares nearby). Draw back side curtains but leave some open in front. Close some doors leading from one room to another. Leave enough clutter to make your home look lived in.

Tell your neighbors you'll be away and ask them to keep watch. Make sure no signs of absence are allowed to accumulate (including flyers, doorknob hangers, and shoppers newspapers that appear from time to time). Invite someone to park in your driveway once in a while.

People differ on whether to notify the police that they'll be away. I don't, nor do I let tradespeople know. I'm less worried that someone will guess that the house is unoccupied than I would be if strangers knew for certain. However, you can invite the police to come over and inspect your home and give you a safety checklist.

___ **Subscriptions.** Suspend newspaper and magazine subscriptions unless you really plan to plow through the pile on your return. The publisher is supposed to add the period of suspension to the end of your subscription period but you may have to follow up to make it happen. If you've forgotten to suspend any subscriptions, ask your Guardian Angel to suspend them as they arrive.

___ **Taxes.** If property taxes are your responsibility and will become due while you're away, arrange for payment rather than suffer a penalty. Arrange for an income tax extension if necessary.

___ **Telephone.** If your trip isn't too long and you anticipate nothing urgent, an answering machine may work. Otherwise, consider "call forwarding" to connect calls with some other number. If you subscribe to other special services (e.g., "call waiting"), SAVE MONEY by suspending them. Ask whoever receives your calls not to discuss your absence with callers unless it's someone known to them as a friend.

__ **Trash.** Anything not dumped could be a health hazard by the time you return.

__ **Utilities.** This is a great time to start over in the refrigerator and freezer. Give away what you can and store frozen food with someone else. Depending on manufacturer's recommendations, unplug them or turn settings to a high temperature. Those innocuous-looking boxes gulp electricity like a parched camel hitting a water hole.

Don't leave the water heater standing ready to provide steaming hot water on demand. Turn it off or set it to its lowest setting. Turn heating and air conditioning systems off unless the weather is likely to be extreme. If you leave them on, set the thermostat at a level that may leave the house uncomfortable but prevent extremes in temperature. Turn off inside water taps tightly but not the main valve at the street. In case of cold weather, you want your neighbor to be able to let the faucets drip for a while.

Make sure utility bills will be paid in your absence. Consider an automatic bill payment plan or leave money on deposit with the utility company.

__ **Valuables.** If you have valuables that should be safeguarded, hide them, store them with someone, or drop them into a safe deposit box. If concerned, store your computer, TV, and stereo with a neighbor. This is a good time to back up your computer hard drive and tuck disks away in a safe deposit box.

__ **Do you have everything?** Confirm that you've packed everything on your checklist. Double-check that you have packed tickets, passport, cash, credit cards, and travelers checks and that you've given copies to your Guardian Angels if appropriate. Does this sound too cautious? My partner on one trip to South America didn't discover until he got off the plane in Lima that he'd forgotten his travelers checks. I won't describe the repercussions except to say that investing a few extra minutes just before leaving is much better than wasting hours or days 10,000 miles from home.

Checklist: Guardian Angel

__ **Bills.** I've opened a special checking account (# _____ at _____ Bank) and you are a signatory. Please deposit incoming checks and pay incoming bills. Please mail, on the _____ of each month, one of the signed and dated checks for my monthly mortgage (or rent) payment. Pay the minimum amount due (or the full balance) on each credit card. I left extra money in this account for you to use as a source of petty cash for unforeseen expenses.

__ **Car.** Please start my car every week and roll it a foot or two to keep the tires happy. Since this car is in "storage status" for insurance purposes (meaning it has no liability coverage), it must not be driven.

__ **Documents.** I've given you (a) copies of the first two pages of my passport, reservations, airline tickets, and my itinerary and the numbers of my travelers checks, credit cards, and ATM card; (b) a list of AmEx mail service offices along my route showing the dates I expect to pass them; and (c) a list of telephone numbers of repairmen to call if there's a problem, as well as numbers for my lawyer and accountant. If you need information from my insurance policies, mortgages, and so on, they're located _____.

__ **Fax machine.** Please check incoming messages on my fax machine from time to time. If that's inconvenient, you can use my call forwarding to forward incoming faxes to another machine.

__ **Freezing weather.** Please let the water faucets drip if freezing weather hits.

__ **Growing things.** I've put my indoor plants in your care and have arranged for _____ (at _____) to cut and water the lawn and other green things. If there's a problem, please hire someone else to keep things looking well tended. Please fill food and water bowls for _____ each morning. I've left an adequate supply of food in the pantry. If _____ needs care, the vet is Dr. _____ (at _____). You have my full authority to obtain whatever care _____ needs.

__ **Keys.** I've given you two sets of my house and car keys.

__ **Legal matters.** I've given you a General Power of Attorney, which gives you authority to take any action necessary on my behalf. Should you need it, my will is located at _____.

__ **Mail.** Please trash junk mail, set personal letters aside, pay the bills, and open anything that looks as if it might deserve attention.

__ **Security.** Please occasionally change the settings on the three automatic timers to conform to sunset, and reset everything if there's a power outage. The burglar alarm is activated (please keep it on) and I've given you the code. If you need to reach the operator, the number is _____. Please replace any light bulbs that burn out on the lights on timers (spares are in the kitchen cabinet). I've left the doors and curtains as they are intentionally. Please make sure no signs of absence accumulate outside (like flyers, doorknob hangers, and shoppers newspapers). Feel free to park in my driveway.

__ **Subscriptions.** I think I've suspended all subscriptions, but if anything arrives please call and have it suspended.

__ **Taxes.** If I'm not back by_____, please mail the income tax extension I've given you. Please pay the property tax bills when due.

__ **Telephone.** If my answering machine memory fills up with calls, please empty it and make a list of calls received. If you receive a call for me, please don't discuss my absence unless it's someone you know well.

__ **Valuables.** I've stored my _____ with
_____, so don't be alarmed if you notice they're missing.

Last Minute

As the countdown reaches its end, remember to line up someone who can take you to the airport. Call the airline a day or two prior to departure to confirm your reservation, and call again a couple of hours before your flight to ensure the plane will depart as scheduled.

Lock the door on your way out!

Allow more time than usual to get to the airport. During periods when airport security is increased, airlines suggest that you check in an hour and a half before flight time. That requires quite an adjustment if arriving even 30 minutes early seems extravagant. Increased security means that cars arriving at the airport may be inspected by guards, parking lots nearby may be closed, and supersensitized metal detectors cause longer lines by detecting insignificant pieces of metal. No need to start a long trip with jangled nerves or, much worse, by missing a flight.

PART THREE

On the
Road
("Go!")

10

The Day You Get There

One of the gladdest moments in human life, methinks, is the
departure upon a distant journey into unknown lands. Shaking
off with one mighty effort the fetters of Habit, the leaden
weight of Routine, the cloak of many Cares and the
slavery of Home, man feels once more Happy.
— Sir Richard Francis Burton
Journal entry, December 2, 1856

Through the Airport

It's happening! Twenty hours and three connections after taking off, having ignored at least half of the prescriptions for preventing jet lag, you stagger off the plane, burning eyes squinting in the bright sunlight.

The immigration officer smiles pleasantly, examines your passport, and looks for a visa if one is required to enter the country. She may ask to see a ticket proving you have the means to move on, but that's rare. After a discreet glance down at her computer screen to see if you are on Interpol's "most wanted" list, she welcomes you to her country, nods to the next person in line, and you're on your way.

Your next stop is the customs counter. If you've filled in a customs declaration form, the official will take a look at it. If he hands it back, you're expected to keep it to show when you leave. Most countries are concerned about people secretly bringing in items they might sell to local citizens. Some countries also have absolute prohibitions against bringing in items such as alcohol, explosives, pornography, and anything that might carry a plant or animal disease. Unless smuggling is your game, don't enter a country without declaring weapons or unusual amounts of drugs, currency, or valuables. The customs officer may ask you to fill in a currency declaration form, especially if there's an active local black market. Most people are a little nervous about going through Customs, but it's generally painless. Before you know it, you're waved along with a smile.

Even if you can't read the signs, follow the crowd to the baggage area. In minutes you've claimed your gear and are ready to start on a few tasks. The first stop is the currency exchange counter, where you change just enough money to last for a day or two. If there's a tourist information counter, collect all the information that might be useful, including how to get into town. Then stop by the airline counter if you need to reconfirm a flight or do any other business.

Before long, you're ready to head for town. This is when you need to shift into "traveler's mode." You will seldom be as vulnerable to theft as you are at this moment. Your self-protective reflexes, soon to be fine-tuned and automatic, are still abstract and untested. Up shields!

The Ride into Town

The intense beehive hum you hear just outside the terminal comes from a zillion transport entrepreneurs seeking your patronage. And each one of those taxi drivers is hoping you have no idea of the fair price for a ride into town. Your job? Educate yourself on the correct price before you get to the curb. Ask people on the plane. Ask at Tourist Information. Ask a friendly local person. Before leaving the baggage claim area, try to line up a small group to ride together and split the fare.

If an airport has a system through which you buy taxi tickets at a booth inside the terminal, use it. Otherwise, a taxi driver will know he has a greenhorn who is about to help him pay for a new television set.

If there's an airport shuttle bus or local bus that stops near your destination, either will be much cheaper than a taxi. The local bus may cost less than one-tenth as much as a taxi. No matter where the bus drops you in town, the cost of transport from there to whatever hotel you choose will be far less than airport taxi rates. Ask at the airport about bus transportation.

At the curb, listen to what drivers are charging local people. Take advantage of competition. Get quotes from several drivers, then invite everyone to beat the best offer. Nine times out of ten, someone's self-interest will overcome the group's attempt to maintain a monopoly price. As you bargain, keep in mind that if the taxi driver doesn't get your business, he may have to drive back to town empty. When you get an acceptable price, climb in and enjoy the ride.

Some travelers relax the moment they see a meter. No bargaining, they think, just pay what the meter says. Things are seldom that simple when there's a taxi involved. First, the mere presence of a meter doesn't mean the driver intends to use it. He might prefer to start bargaining with you somewhere away from the airport. Second, if the meter is working, make sure it wasn't "accidentally" already running before you got in. Third, if the meter is "broken," there's a reason—and you won't like it. Strike a deal before the wheels roll. And last, even if the meter is flipped on as you get in, and it works, make sure you aren't charged a night rate for a day ride.

Some cities fix the rates taxi drivers can charge to take you to certain destinations. Those rates are supposed to be posted in the taxi. Unfortunately, some taxi drivers print their own official looking cards showing inflated fares to certain destinations. If a rate card looks homemade, climb right back out.

In a large airport where departure and arrival points are separate, try the area where *departing* passengers are dropped off. After dropping off a passenger, a taxi must go to the end of a long line waiting for arriving passengers to take back into town. Or, he can pick you up immediately—for a considerably discounted fare, of course.

As a final word on taxis, consider a couple of entreaties: (a) don't let yourself be separated from your bag before getting into your chosen taxi, and (b) never get into a taxi before you've settled on a fare.

Master this simple process of getting into town on a cost-effective basis and you'll SAVE MONEY for the rest of your travels.

Tourist Information

After you get to town, arrange lodging (more on this in the next chapter), then visit the local tourist information office. Its location is probably in your guidebook. If not, your desk clerk or a police officer or someone on the street will know where to find it. Watch for the international "I" or "?" symbol on street signs.

Someone in the tourist office is likely to speak some English and will gladly answer your questions. Even if no one speaks a language you know, you'll find brochures, posters, and maps—a gold mine of information. If you give the tourist officer a list of places you'd like to see, she can help organize your visits and suggest additions. She'll tell you about special events taking place while you're around, and she may even sell you tickets and arrange transportation. If the newspaper isn't in one of your languages, it's easy to miss what could be a fascinating experience. Friendly tourist information officers have told me about a ceremonial burial that was about to take place in a village in central Sulawesi,* an elegantly costumed

> "Afoot and light-hearted I take to the open road, Healthy, free, the world before me, The long brown path before me leading wherever I choose. Henceforth I ask not good fortune, I myself am good fortune, Henceforth I whimper no more, postpone no more, need nothing, Done with indoor complaints, libraries, querulous criticisms, Strong and content I travel the open road."
> —Walt Whitman, *Song of the Open Road*, 1856

---

* *Sulawesi.* This mountainous, K-shaped Indonesian island contains a remarkable blend of Islamic and animistic-Christian cultures. The ship-shaped architecture and death rituals of Toraja-land are unique.

dance performance celebrating the Hindu poet Rabindranath Tagore's birthday in Calcutta, a gathering of tribes performing ritual dances in northeast Botswana, and, in Prague, the best chamber music I've ever heard.

During your full first day, climb aboard one of those see-it-all-in-a-day tour buses. They're an inexpensive, efficient way to cover long distances in a new town to find what merits a visit. When you get tired of being herded, hop off. If you're lucky, you'll meet another traveler using the tour the same way.

Overcome the temptation to take taxis everywhere. They cut you off from local people and spontaneous experiences. Instead, learn to use local public transportation right away. Before long, you'll be flagging down brightly decorated *matatus* or *collectivos* or *jeepneys* or whatever the transit vehicles are called where you happen to be. Getting around the way local people do is definitely the way to go.

11

Lodging

> You fly off to a strange land, eagerly abandoning all the comforts
> of home, and then expend vast quantities of time and money
> in a largely futile effort to recapture the comforts that you
> wouldn't have lost if you hadn't left home in the first place.
> —Bill Bryson
> *Neither Here Nor There*

You never forget places where you lay your head as you travel. Some are wonderful, some make you laugh, and there are always a few that, well, make great stories. In this chapter, you'll learn how to find lodging that will suit you anywhere in the world.

I understand why new travelers feel uneasy about being able to find satisfactory places to stay as they venture abroad. As I began planning my first trip to Africa, I had little idea what to expect in terms of lodging. On arrival in Nairobi, surrounded by people offering shelter, I quickly learned how naive my concern had been. The reality is that providing lodging for hire is a leading means of economic survival in most of the world. Good lodging abounds and there is plenty of competition for your business.

In major cities and tourist centers anywhere in the world, you'll find upscale hotels that equal or exceed the opulence of those in your home country. Most are nationality-neutral and English is commonly spoken. You can't miss the logos of international hotel chains with their cookie-cutter amenities. They charge extraordinarily high prices because they provide a reassuring cocoon and know that most Western travelers, especially those on business or on tour, expect to pay high prices. These are "world" prices, usually in dollars, that have no relation at all to prices in the local economy.

Virtually everywhere you'll find pleasant, locally owned midscale hotels in which comfort and character outweigh occasional dings. Although their prices may be above the budgets of some independent travelers, they're very reasonable by North American and European standards.

Then there are the legions of lower-priced hotels with which many travelers become intimately familiar. They range from a concrete box ruled over by Quasimodo's ill-tempered brother to an architectural masterpiece gently supervised by an elderly couple whose mission in life is your daily happiness. At the lowest end of the rate scale, some hotels are best enjoyed with a measure of good humor and recognition of where you are. You may be pleased to know that shortcomings are more often in the nature of rickety furniture, or fixtures that don't work, rather than dirt or bugs.

Satisfaction with lodging depends in part on a good state of mind and realistic expectations. Here's an example: In the late seventies, when China had just reopened itself to strangers, tourist facilities were not highly developed. Our group (visitors then were required to travel as a group) stayed at the venerable Peking Hotel. Although it had a kind of Addams Family ambience, it was the best hotel in Beijing at that time and had an excellent location near the Imperial Palace. It turned out that there were a few, although generally small, holes in the walls. Some in the group were outraged by the holes and complained regularly. The rest hardly noticed and had a great time. It was a matter of state of mind.

Many North Americans leave home with a mental image of two queen-size beds, a private bath with operational tub and shower, air conditioning, good soundproofing, and reasonable prices, all in a large room with a view. Internationally, these expectations will be met and exceeded at the higher end of the price scale. Overall, however, expect some differences. For example, you'll find one large bed or two monastic singles, but seldom two large beds. Air conditioning is more the exception than the rule. Tubs become a distant memory. Soundproofing? Maybe if you block the window with a pillow. What you often get is character and an exciting new world just outside the front door.

"I dislike feeling at home when I'm abroad."
—George Bernard Shaw, English writer

Even if you start off with hotel reservations in hand, this chapter will be of benefit. After a few days on the road, you may decide to choose lodging that has more local character or better suits your pocketbook. Or you may find that the flexibility of traveling without reservations has become more important than it seemed at home.

HOW TO FIND GREAT PLACES TO SPEND THE NIGHT

How do you find lodging? No problem; it often finds you—through a tug on your sleeve. When you arrive in a new place, you're approached by *people representing low and midpriced hotels* (known as a *losman, ryokan, hospadaje, pension, residencial,* and many other names). If you're at the airport, touts spring forward to solicit your business, flashing photographs of hotels and their rooms. They may offer free transportation into town in return for your agreement to "just take a look" at the hotel. Ask questions. If a hotel sounds attractive and is located near where you want to stay, the offer is at least a good way to get into town and may result in a good room.

Your trusty *guidebook* is more reliable than the eager tout, at least as to quality. Providing information on hotel prices, amenities, and management is one of the ways a good guidebook justifies its price. It sometimes suggests real treasures and at least keeps you from running around town looking at dogs. On the other side of the ledger, guidebook favorites fill up early (and they will have raised their rates as soon as they were mentioned in the book).

Don't fall into the habit of thinking there are no alternatives to guidebook suggestions. Once you have your travel legs, you'll be perfectly capable of finding your own special places. Pretend you're writing a guidebook for a friend coming next year. Just go out and look around.

Ask *other travelers*. A strongly positive recommendation usually leads to a memorable stay. On only a few occasions have I reached a hotel someone raved about and wondered if the guy had been taking hallucinatory drugs. On the other hand, always pay attention to a warning about a specific hotel.

Many *tourist information booths* in or near airports, train stations, and bus depots offer a room-finding service. You may pay something for this service, either as a fee at the booth or in a slightly higher room rate, but it can be very helpful on a cold, drizzly night. Unfortunately, the least expensive lodgings in town are seldom on lists provided by these booths. However, the clerk may know about places that have yet to appear in any guidebook.

Ask a *hotel clerk*. If you've stopped into a place that has no vacancy or you just can't agree on price, tell the clerk what you're looking for. It's common to get helpful directions.

If you have several possibilities in mind, call to check for availability and prices. Crisscrossing town after a long day on the road is no one's idea of fun.

> "To awaken in a strange town is one of the pleasant sensations in the world. You are surrounded by adventure. You have no idea what is in store for you, but you will, if you are wise and know the art of travel, let yourself go on the stream of the unknown and accept whatever comes in the spirit in which the gods may offer it. The tourist travels in his own atmosphere like a snail in his shell and stands, as it were, on his own perambulating doorstep to look at the continents of the world. But if you discard all this, and sally forth with a blank and leisurely mind, there is no knowing what may happen to you."
> —Freya Stark, *Baghdad Sketches*

Telephoning is particularly useful if you're competing with a group of arriving passengers for scarce space in choice lodgings.

If no assistance materializes, it's no big deal. Find that special place *all by yourself.*

HOW TO CHOOSE LODGING THAT'S BEST FOR YOU

According to surveys, what most travelers look for in lodging is clean appearance, reasonable price, convenient location, good service, and security—in that order. After staying in a hotel, people are usually satisfied with location and price, but they remember dirt, lack of security, and noise forever.

Location

When you first arrive in a country, you may want to choose a hotel that has a reputation as an information node, a gathering place for travelers with interests similar to yours. These hotels are usually reasonably priced, but more important is the opportunity to learn quickly how the country works from people with current experience. Guidebooks sometimes note such hotels; if not, ask around.

If gathering information is not the primary objective, look for lodging located near some of the sights you'll be visiting, near public transportation routes, and within shouting distance of a restaurant.

Amenities

What amenities matter? Start with comfort and beauty. Memories grow from quiet courtyards and views of the Parthenon from your balcony. Of course, sometimes the only amenity that matters is a "vacancy" sign.

The level of amenities differs from continent to continent. Generally, Asia and South America offer better value, or at least more aesthetically pleasing rooms, than do Africa or Central America. Don't take specific amenities for granted:

- What's the *shower* situation? For openers, is there a shower at all? If so, is it in the room or is it down the hall? Is there a separate shower stall or does the whole bathroom become the shower stall? Since a private bath-

Five-dollar beach cabins. Ko Tao, Gulf of Thailand.

room can double the room rate, the more frequently you do without a shower in your room, the more you SAVE MONEY. Is there hot water? If you care, don't take anyone's word for it. Test the temperature. That will also tell you whether the water pressure is more than a symbolic drizzle. Don't assume that hot water is available 24 hours a day. In fact, it may be available for only six to eight hours a day. Forget to check these hours and icy water will greet you at a moment guaranteed to make you un-happy. When the plumbing doesn't work as represented, which is not uncommon, at least you'll hear some wonderfully inventive excuses.

When I checked my room at a lovely two-story stone lodge on the crest of a mountain ridge in Kalimpong,* no water flowed from the shower nozzle. However, the charming proprietress assured me that hot water would be available at 7 P.M. Given the chill Himalayan air, I watched the clock eagerly. Right at seven, the hot water arrived as prom-ised—at my door, in a bucket.

You may be startled to see water being heated by electric coils bolted loosely to the wall above the shower head. This arrangement seems a little dangerous, but I haven't heard of anyone being fried.

I've missed a few showers when I really wanted one and taken some in water that promised frostbite. Overall, though, there have always been enough showers at just the right times to make me remember showers on the road with pleasure.

---

* *Kalimpong.* Located in the foothills of the Himalayas in West Bengal, India, it is known for its orchids and access to Sikkim.

- What about the *beds*? Are they clean? Are they soft enough? Finding a firm bed is seldom a problem. Length? If you're tall, you learn to be comfortable in short beds.

- Is the room *secure*? Does it have sturdy locks on the doors and windows? For more on hotel security, see Chapter 13.

- Are the lobby and the room *clean*? Is there evidence that bugs might be a problem?

- Will the room be *quiet* enough for sleep? Don't trust the hotel clerk on this one. Either he's genuinely stopped hearing the racket or he's not going to tell you. It may be stone quiet when you check in at dusk. Then, about the time you're settling in, the disco next door roars to life for an all-nighter. Check out nearby bars, road traffic, muezzins, roosters, and thin walls—and hope there aren't too many noisy guests. If you suspect a problem, ask for a quieter room higher up or at the back of the building. Don't wait until 4 A.M. to discover the truck depot below your window.

- Any discussion of amenities must include *toilets*. I know one person who won't leave the United States because of her aversion to any toilet she believes to be inferior to what she's used to. Given the strength of her feeling, she's made the right choice. Fortunately, most people are more flexible.

  The toilet may be in your room, down the hall, or in a different building, and the price of the lodging will reflect the proximity of the toilet every time. Toilets come in quite a few forms. At the low end, so to speak, the toilet is a hole in the floor of a small room and waste drops into a fertilizer-collection room below. Squat toilets are common in Asia. On each side of a hole there's a place to put one foot, which may be a little ceramic footprint or nothing more than a plank worn smooth over the ages. They're easy to use. Well, maybe not the first time, but there's nothing to it once you learn to watch the relative position of your trousers.

  Western-style toilets have become increasingly common in hotels that cater to international travelers. Of course, in some of the least expensive places, toilet seats are sometimes missing and toilet paper is a rumor. If the room you're looking at has a Western-style toilet that's supposed to flush, see if it does. The flushing device may not be the familiar handle; look for a knob, a push button, a pull chain, a pedal, or even a bucket of water. If it doesn't flush, ask the clerk to help.

  Not all toilets are plumbed to accept paper. If there's a trash can nearby, that's where used paper should go. Otherwise, it will probably clog the pipes, distressing all involved. If toilet paper hasn't been provided, ask for it. The clerk may smile and say, "Sure," but you may have

Public Toilets

If you think a public toilet is hard to find in Los Angeles, wait until you look for one in Tangier or most of the rest of the world. Before a moment of supreme need, watch for facilities in museums, expensive hotels, and restaurants. It's the custom in some places to tip the public restroom attendant. Even if you are not used to tipping and can't see that the attendant has performed any service, leave a small tip with grace. We're guests.

to follow up. The majority of the world's population doesn't use toilet paper, which is the main reason you don't see people eating with their left hand. Your best bet is to carry your own supply of TP (including the high-quality stuff you borrowed from the upscale hotel where you stopped for a beer).

- When traveling through an area in which *malaria* is a problem, ensure there is some barrier between you and mosquitoes. This usually means screens on the windows or a mosquito net over the bed. If you take a mosquito net with you, buy one impregnated with Permethrin or spray it yourself. If there are neither screens nor a net, you may have to sleep with the windows closed. Although that turns a tolerable night in the tropics into a sweat bath, a hot night is a lot cooler than malarial fever.

  On tropical islands, windows are fitted only with rough hurricane shutters and no glass. That's part of the charm. About all you can do is fire up a green mosquito coil at both ends of your bed and sleep under a light sheet. I take a couple of packets of coils with me but they're brittle and hard to use when broken. When you're in mosquito-land, coils are generally available in the stores (if there are stores).

  Speaking of insects, hold your shoes upside down and shake them before putting them on. Give scorpions, spiders, or whatever a chance to live another day.

- Ask whether *breakfast* is included in the price and, if so, what it is. You're likely to find it surprisingly spare, usually of the bread and coffee variety. Find out where and when it's served. It's no fun to drop into the dining room with high expectations just after they've stopped serving. If breakfast doesn't appeal to you, perhaps you can negotiate a slightly lower room rate.

- I'm hooked on lodging that exemplifies an *ethnic architectural idiom.* I'm thinking of places like a *ryokan* in Japan with painted shoji screens and scented tatami mats, a *losman* in Bali with incense burning at Hindu shrines in manicured gardens, or a white-walled *posada* in Portugal nestled against the gray stones of a castle wall with views of red tile roofs and distant fields of corn.

- A *smiling, knowledgeable owner or clerk* who looks me in the eye and makes me feel welcome overcomes shortcomings elsewhere.

- My decisions about some amenities depend on the circumstances. *Air conditioning* is an example. It raises the room rent quite a bit and may seem a little decadent after you've been on the road for a while. On the other hand, when you're coming off a hot trek neither of those objections matter one whit. Air conditioning is not standard internationally, so if you're interested, be sure to ask.

  When the sun is high in tropical latitudes, a *ceiling fan* greatly aids a good night's sleep. Even a small oscillating table fan can make a humid night bearable. Besides cooling your body, the breeze from a fan keeps mosquitoes away.

  With the southern India solar furnace operating at full blast, I gratefully paid a premium to stay in the only hotel in Tiruchirapalli* that had a *swimming pool*.

  If it's not too hot, it's too cold. It was so cold one Christmas season in Ladakh, above 10,000 feet, that I rented a potbellied stove and had it set up in my room. It cost more than the room itself, but it was worth ten times what I paid. If a room heater isn't available, pile on blankets and hibernate.

- I love to waken to a *great view* out the window. When I can find a room with a balcony and a panoramic view, I pay extra every time.

Price

Lodging that ranges from satisfactory to terrific is available at reasonable prices almost anywhere. What do I mean by reasonable prices? The Residencial Las Mercedes in Arequipa, Peru, has a formal sitting room with a stately grandfather clock and a stylishly furnished wood-paneled dining room. Each morning I ate breakfast on a sunny flagstone patio with a view of two volcanoes. That double room cost $8 just a few years ago. In picturesque Ouro Preto, Brazil, there were plenty of rooms for $8. A room with a garden might cost $16. My room in the Colonial Palace in Cuzco, Peru, had a 15-foot vaulted ceiling with a skylight. It overlooked a courtyard containing a fountain and orange blossoms. All that for about $18.

---

* *Tiruchirapalli.* "Trichy" is located in the state of Tamil Nadu in southeast India. It is known for the Rock Fort Temple on a massive plateau that towers over the city and for the extensive temple complexes of Srirangam and Sri Jambukesjwara.

A lovely Balinese-style *losman* in Ubud, Bali, decorated with carved ceremonial masks and prints of scenes from the *Ramayana* cost $8, including a shower and breakfast. A private bungalow, just off the beach on the island of Ko Tao, had a bathroom, fan, verandah, and world-class view and cost $8 to $14 for a double. You could go all-the-way upscale with air conditioning and a pool for $20—or cheap-out for $2. Even better, some travelers were staying in those towns for half what I paid.

There's no shortage of pleasant, affordable lodging in South America and Asia. Much of it even has some style. Throughout most of Africa, lodging is more basic, less charming, but still very inexpensive. As a generalization, a decent double room might average $14 and there are plenty that are cheaper—much cheaper.

In Europe, the supply and variety are immense, but prices in large cities are similar to those in New York and Los Angeles; in other words, hotel rooms are expensive. However, a little searching will turn up affordable lodging even in Europe. The 350-unit Campanile chain charges about $57 for a double in France, $70 in the Netherlands, and $82 in Belgium. In Germany, a *zimmer frie* averages about $45 for a double. In Norway, you'll pay $75 to $150 for "budget" hotels. Still, in 1996 a determined budget traveler could often find adequate shelter for $25 to $50. Note that where hotel prices are high, food prices are high. How about $60 for a bottle of undistinguished whiskey in Norway?

There's a cardinal rule in renting a room: *see the room before you accept it.* For one thing, the reality may be very different from the clerk's description. For another, you can't bargain as effectively until you've seen the room. If you are traveling with a partner, one of you checks the room while the other watches the gear. If a clerk goes with you, she'll probably be carrying keys to more than one room. No matter what you've said you want, **See the room** the clerk will open the bidding by showing a Western trav- **before you** eler the hotel's most expensive room, the local equivalent of **accept it.** the Emperor's Suite. Even if tatty, it's sure to be huge. Although the air conditioner pumps out more noise than cool air and the radio has only one channel, that room will cost at least 500 percent more than the room you said you wanted. They know Westerners are crazy. No problem, just smile and ask to see other rooms.

Cheap rooms don't always start out cheap. The clerk states the room rate as if it were fixed, but that doesn't mean it is. Feel free to bargain on the rate:

- when you'll be staying three or more nights
- in off-season, or when something (bad weather, a riot, a coup) has curtailed tourism
- when you see a lot of room keys hanging on hooks behind the clerk
- maybe every time, unless clearly inappropriate.

The cost of lodging is a large part of your budget. If you bargain effectively on lodging prices, you'll definitely SAVE MONEY. If you don't, lodging will still be affordable, but you'll spend more than you need to.

When the clerk states a price, you say it's too expensive, that you'd like a room that costs no more than "x" francs or rupees, or whatever. Actually, you have even more leverage if you call ahead and say you'd like a room for "x" francs. At that point, the clerk has no chance for your business unless she agrees. Cite prices at a competitor's lodging. Ask for a special rate on grounds of being a student, a teacher, an archaeologist, an old person, a young person, or anything else you can think of. If you have a business card or a membership card, lay it on the counter. Reality doesn't matter; the desk clerk doesn't care. The point is to persuade her that you won't stay in her hotel unless you get a discount of some kind. Then give her a theoretical reason for granting it.

Try not to look too exhausted from the day's travel and never let your luggage go to a room until you've agreed on a price. As she calculates her offer, the desk clerk is evaluating whether you have enough energy to try another hotel. If she senses your energy waning, she'll become Gibraltar.

Be firm but pleasant, never argumentative. It's poor strategy to disparage the accommodations being offered. Why behave like a person the clerk wouldn't want under her roof? Further, the clerk probably lives in worse conditions than the room you're discussing.

If you can't get the room rate reduced, ask for a better room at the same price. If the clerk offers a lower rate but for a less desirable room, offer to pay the lower price for the room you really want.

If you're one of a group of people traveling together, occupying several rooms, insist on a group rate discount, all or none.

You should receive an almost automatic discount of 10 to 30 percent if you'll be staying at one place for three or more days.

If you've reached a temporary impasse, ask if the clerk "can do any better." Ask her for an alternative. If nothing happens and you're not satisfied, say you've decided to look around at other hotels, but leave slowly enough that she has a chance to make another offer. You're likely to hear a call from over your shoulder. On the other hand, if your bargaining doesn't achieve what you want, don't let pride send you away if you really want to stay there or if you'll collapse if you don't inhale an ice cold beer in the next 60 seconds.

Be certain you and the clerk agree on the final price.

Make sure that the room will be available to you for as long as you want it or at least until a certain date. Otherwise, you could be evicted unexpectedly.

In the end, be certain to agree with the clerk on a *total* price. Don't set yourself up for miscellaneous charges and taxes that were never mentioned. At the upper end of the price scale, it is becoming more the rule than the exception to add various luxury taxes and service charges. Ask the clerk to write down the total price on a piece of paper or enter it on the ledger,

Lodging. Lisboa, Portugal.

anything to ensure that no misunderstanding arises at checkout time. Be certain what time period is covered by the price (especially in India). Get it all straight on the front end so you can part friends when you leave.

When you've reached agreement, pick up a hotel business card. Some have a map on the back and all have the address in the local language—which is how you get home after you've forgotten the name of the hotel and how to get back to it. One night I took a series of buses across Beijing, guided through two transfers by a Chinese acquaintance who spoke a bit of English. She showed me where to get off to attend a performance by a famous troupe of acrobats and continued. When I emerged from the theater hours later, I realized I had no idea which bus to take, let alone how the transfers worked. If I hadn't had the hotel card, I'd probably still be circling Beijing like Charlie on the MTA.

A last thought: *always check behind before you check out*. Look under the bed, in the closets, on the shelves, everywhere. Did you leave anything drying on an outside line? Even if you find an about-to-be-forgotten piece only once every 20 times, it's worth checking. Do the same thing in a restaurant. As you're about to leave, take a quick check for daypack, camera, and journal. It's an easy routine. If you leave something behind, either you won't be able to get back for it or it won't be there when you do. Take the easier way.

OTHER INNOVATIVE CHOICES

Hostels and Elderhostels, YMCAs and YWCAs, the Gray Circuit, Back-packer Hotels, Formule 1, and Homestays were specifically designed to help you SAVE MONEY. They're also fine places to meet other travelers and local people.

Hostels

Hostels, especially in Europe, are the financial salvation of budget travelers. However, many people who can afford to pay more for lodging seek out hostels because of the ambience. They're good places to meet like-minded travelers, find a temporary traveling partner, and gather information.

Where will you find hostels? They're everywhere in Europe (slowly expanding into Eastern Europe) and you'll find some in northern Africa (Egypt, Sudan, Morocco, Tunisia and, if you're feeling adventuresome, Libya). In sub-Saharan Africa, there are a few hostels in Kenya, Zimbabwe, Lesotho, and South Africa. In the Middle East, there are hostels in Israel, Syria, and Saudi Arabia. Traveling east to Asia, look for scattered hostels in Pakistan, India, Nepal, Sri Lanka, Thailand, Malaysia, South Korea, and the Philippines. Although there are many hostels in Japan (more than 600), Australia, and New Zealand, there are comparatively few in the United States and hardly any in Central and South America.

How much do hostels cost? In the United States, you'll pay from $5 to $22. In Europe, hostels cost in the range of $10 to $25 a night. Prices are lower elsewhere and many hostels offer excellent family rates as well. Take a look at www.hostels.com.

Joining *Hostelling International—American Youth Hostels* (HI-AYH), a member of the International Youth Hostel Association, gives you access to almost 6,000 affiliated hostels in more than 70 countries. A twelve-month membership in HI-AYH costs $10 for a person 17 years or younger, $25 for a person 18 to 54, $15 for anyone over 55, and $35 for an entire family. A lifetime membership costs $250. Purchase membership at any hostel or from any HI-AYH office (the main office is located at 733 15th Street NW, Washington, DC 20005; 202-783-6161).

Here's the most important point. Despite the word "youth," there is *no maximum age limit* (except in Bavaria), and more than 10 percent of hostellers are over age 55. There is also no minimum age limit except that a person under 18 may be asked to provide parental permission and very small children may not be accepted by hostels that don't have appropriate facilities for them. All you have to be is young in spirit.

In the past, youth hostels had requirements such as getting in before curfew, being locked out most of the day, and doing some household tasks. In urban hostels, these limitations have largely disappeared, although guests are expected to clean up after themselves. In rural areas, some hostels still close during the day (since the manager may have a day job elsewhere) and residents are sometimes asked to sweep a room or take out the trash. Hostels may limit the length of stay to five days during busy seasons.

Hostels range from clean, basic shelter to architectural or cultural marvels. For example, you can stay in a castle in Altena, Germany, or aboard a three-masted sailing ship in Stockholm. In the United States, there's a Spanish Village built as a bohemian artists' community in Miami; an old Longshoremen's Hall in Seattle; a Greek revival farmhouse in Peninsula, Ohio; a turn-of-the-century home in Redwood National Park, Klamath, California; a lighthouse in Cape Vincent, New York; and a former lifeguard station in Nantucket, Massachusetts. *Historic Hostels*, which describes hostels in historic buildings, is available from HI-AYH for $3.

Hostels are a great way to meet fellow travelers.

Some hostels serve hearty, inexpensive meals, while others permit you to cook your own meals. Besides being a great way to SAVE MONEY, hanging out in the kitchen is a good way to meet other travelers. It's not unusual to find a pool table, a library full of well-worn books, or a piano with which to amuse yourself.

Traditionally, sleeping accommodations have been dormitory-style, segregated by sex, although the trend is toward rooms with four to six beds. The hostel furnishes blankets and pillows, but you need a sleep sheet, which you can bring, rent, or buy. Carrying a sheet is a small burden, but if you expect to stay in hostels frequently, renting would be expensive. Expect to pay $15 to $25 to buy a sleep sheet.

Making advance reservations at popular hostels may be a good idea during peak seasons in Europe. In most other places it usually isn't necessary. If you choose to book ahead, send a letter about six weeks before your arrival giving the date of arrival, number of beds (or private rooms) desired, and length of stay. Enclose a deposit for the first night's stay. Otherwise, you can call a day or two ahead of arrival, or even the same morning if you won't get there until later in the day. Some hostels provide reservation envelopes that you drop through the mail slot if the door is locked during the day. You can also make reservations abroad through any HI-AYH office. The majority of travelers just drop in with their fingers crossed.

By paying a slightly higher nightly rate (usually about $3 more), nonmembers may be permitted to stay in a hostel. If this extra charge applies to the membership fee and you stay a week or so in the same place, you pay for membership on the spot. Naturally, members receive priority over nonmembers for beds.

HI-AYH offers "discovery tours" to help people learn about different cultures, experience new environments, and make new friends. These groups usually consist of ten or fewer travelers. Since they sleep in youth hostels, prices are modest.

Two handbooks tell you what you need to know about hostels: *Europe and the Mediterranean Budget Accommodations* and *Africa, America, Asia, and Australasia Budget Accommodations*. The International Youth Hostel Federation in England (44-707-332487) publishes both. They can also be obtained from HI-AYH or any of its 38 regional offices. Good guidebooks also describe hostels, and tourist information offices usually have pamphlets published by local youth hostel associations.

Elderhostels

Elderhostel programs are for people over the age of 60 (who may be accompanied by a younger spouse or companion). These programs combine inexpensive lodging with classes at more than 1,900 universities and other educational institutions in the United States and 43 other countries. Participants stay in residence halls or nearby youth hostels. The emphasis is on studying interesting subjects and meeting like-minded people. Elderhostel has recently introduced Service Programs, through which participants provide volunteer service to worthwhile causes (such as Habitat for Humanity) around the world. Call (617) 426-7788 for a free Elderhostel catalogue.

YMCAs and YWCAs

The Ys offer travelers lodging in almost 3,000 locations in nearly 100 countries. They are often a little higher priced than most budget places but uniformly clean, pleasant, and friendly. Unlike hostels, cooking is seldom permitted. To find information about YMCA lodging around the world, obtain a copy of the *World Alliance Directory* ($14) by calling the YMCA Program Store at (800) 747-0089. Call the Y International at (212) 760-5869 for a catalog of YMCAs and YWCAs. Call (212) 614-2700 for the YWCA *Worldwide Directory* ($10).

The *U.S. and World Wide Travel Accommodations Guide* ($16.95 from the Campus Travel Service, 800-525-6633, P.O. Box 5486, Fullerton, CA 92635, and many campus and retail bookstores) includes information on YMCA lodging, home and farm stays, home exchange opportunities, more than 700 colleges worldwide that rent rooms (costing between $10 and $30 a night) when school is not in session, and more than 7,000 economy and moderate hotels and motels.

The Gray Circuit

For decades, security regulations required travelers to the former Soviet Union and Eastern European countries to stay in designated high-priced tourist hotels and restricted the flow of travelers to fit the number of hotel rooms available. When the borders opened, there were far too few hotel rooms to serve the flood of business and pleasure travelers so the entrepreneurial profit motive immediately spawned the "gray circuit."

When you arrive in Moscow, you're quickly contacted by representatives of the gray circuit, the unofficial housing service. Someone, probably claiming to be a student, will approach you and invite you to see a small apartment they represent. One way to tell if it's good, and cheap, is if it's already crowded with other travelers. Since these places are typically in large apartment blocks, staying in them is a good way to meet Russians.

In Eastern Europe, tourists commonly pay $200 to $300 for a hotel room with only basic amenities. However, because of the economic crunch and the rise of budding capitalists, renting a room in a family home has become increasingly common. Prices are much lower, although they are rising (partly because of utility costs). In Prague, for example, a room that went for $20 just after independence might be in the $50 to $70 range today. Top Tour (42-2-232-1077) and AVE (42-2-2422-3226) are agencies in Prague that find rooms in this range. On the other hand, people with space will approach you outside American Express, the post office, the train station, or as you're walking along the sidewalk. The situation is similar in Budapest, Bucharest, and other major cities. I've heard of nothing but good experiences from renting rooms in these unofficial places.

Backpacker Hotels

In New Zealand, even basic motels are moderately expensive. Youth hostels are a budget option but they aren't always easy to find. To fill the void, an extensive network of excellent backpacker hotels has sprung up, most of them old centrally located hotels that have been spruced up and given a few new amenities. They radiate charm and good vibes—and you can often stroll downstairs to a pub and restaurant. Rooms seldom cost more than $10 per person and you needn't arrive with a backpack. This sort of alternative is growing in Australia and elsewhere.

Formule 1

Formule 1 hotels, which style themselves the "McDonald's of the hotel industry," have become very popular with travelers in Europe. There are already about 450 of them (approximately 400 in France, the rest in Germany, Belgium, and the United Kingdom) and the concept is spreading quickly throughout Europe (and heading for Australia and South Africa). Since they are usually located on the periphery of cities and towns, they best serve people who have their own transportation.

You can check in at the front desk or by slipping your credit card into a slot in a reservation machine. Your credit card also opens your door, but only for as long as you reserved the room when checking in.

The private rooms are only eight by twelve feet with a double bed and full-size bunk bed, sink, desk, and color TV. Very clean bathrooms are down the hall. They don't offer much style or ambience, but at about $32 they are an affordable alternative to overpriced dumps.

Homestays

When you have an opportunity to stay with a family, whether for free or fee, take a chance. If you'd like to set up something before you hit the road, try one of the organizations described in Chapter 4 that specialize in arranging trips where the focal point is a homestay. If you haven't arranged anything in advance, ask around until you find a family who'll take you in for a while. Don't let uncertainty about what it might be like dissuade you from accepting a family's invitation. The odds are good that it will be an experience you'll remember with affection.

If an opportunity to stay with a family arises from hospitality rather than a commercial motive, be sensitive to what's needed to fit in. Despite its good intentions, the host family may not really be able to afford the food and drink it lavishes on you. Some travelers become sponges, accepting hospitality as though it were their due and overstaying their welcome. Instead, reciprocate by making some contribution. They probably need money, but it may feel awkward to offer it. If a gift seems okay, buy something such as groceries, cloth, or tools (a simple rice thresher costs only a few dollars in Indonesia but greatly eases a family's workload). In some situations, it may be better to do some tutoring or other useful work for the family. Ask others about the local customs concerning hospitality as a guide to what you should do. Without fail, send a card or letter to the family later in your trip or when you get home.

This discussion has been about choosing lodging that pleases you at a price you're willing to pay. If price doesn't matter or you feel an urge to splurge, arm yourself before you go with the results of polls that rate "the world's best" hotels (take a look at Traveler Online at http://www.cntraveler.com). Here are some of the best—and their rates: Claridge's (London, $405–466 for a double); Cliveden (Berkshire, $332–625); Hotel de Crillon (Paris, $653–714); Hotel Ritz (Paris, $714–851); Villa Cipriani (Asolo, Italy, $188–250); Hotel Hassler (Rome, $389–564); Hotel de Paris (Monte Carlo, $388–449); Mt. Kenya Safari Club (Kenya, $285–530); Bora Bora Lagoon Resort ($634–964); The Peninsula (Kowloon, $337–492); The Regent (Kowloon, $285–453); Four Seasons (Bali, $425–2,000); The Regent (Singapore, $245–260); Shangri-La (Bangkok, $211–279); and The Ritz-Carlton (Sydney, $194–233).

Turn About

When you meet people from faraway places traveling in your home country, remember the hospitality you received when you were on the road. Be sensitive to how expensive it is for most foreigners to travel in the West (think of the feeling you get when you price a new car—or new tennies for that matter). Be generous. Pick up that tab. Take them to see your local wonders. Provide a secure pillow when you can.

12

Eating and Drinking

> If you are lucky enough to have lived in Paris as a young man,
> then wherever you go for the rest of your life, it stays
> with you, for Paris is a moveable feast.
> —Ernest Hemingway
> *A Moveable Feast*

Pleased to see a sign advertising a Mexican restaurant, I dropped in for a meal. The first clue I wasn't in Acapulco came when the waiter urged me to "Try the enchilada with our special monkey gland sauce." That restaurant, in Bulawayo, Zimbabwe, was owned by a Maltese and a South African, neither of whom had been within 4,000 miles of Mexico.

Even though the local version of some dish isn't prepared the same as it is at home, can you find food you like as you travel? The answer is an emphatic *yes*. In fact, good food is one of the rewards of travel. Europe is renowned for culinary excellence, of course, but you'll easily find high-quality restaurants throughout the world. If local cuisine isn't to your taste, Chinese, Indian, and Italian food are almost universal. In one country after another, you'll discover a new symphony of tastes. Many local dishes are so delicious you'll seek them out when you return home. That's important to know because if you're worried about whether you'll find what you like to eat in some faraway place, you may not go. I've known that feeling.

HOW TO FIND FOOD YOU REALLY LIKE

Picture yourself walking into the little town of Pokhara, Nepal, after a three-week trek in the Kali Gandaki Gorge alongside towering Annapurna. You crave a pizza. What are the chances? Actually, they're great. A little place with a view of Lake Phewa serves a pizza that could hold its own in Chicago. Next door, travelers crowd in to chow down on water buffalo burgers. Take your choice.

A typical meal of rice and condiments. Myanmar.

Except in parts of Europe, good meals are also inexpensive. At your table on a balcony in a restaurant in Cuzco, lean back against the finely chiseled stones of an old Inca wall and listen to *El Condor Pasa* played on Andean flutes. A meal of delicately spiced grilled fish, several vegetables, whole-grain bread, and a large Cuzquena dark beer might cost $5. On the island of Roatán, off the north coast of Honduras, marinated tuna filet, French fried potatoes, salad, and a couple of Salva Vita beers, served on a deck extending over the moonlit Caribbean, could run $6.

For dining tips before departure, clip references from travel magazines. Once you're abroad, check your guidebook and ask other travelers. Hotel clerks and taxi drivers eagerly offer recommendations, but the kickback they get may be more appealing to them than the food. Glance through windows of places filled with smiling local diners. Most restaurants post their menus outside, making it easy to check out dishes and prices as you stroll.

"Street food," not common in the United States, consists of snacks, a single dish, or a simple meal that you buy from a streetside stall or cart. Often, the food is fried, grilled, or tumbled in a wok as you watch. Street food can be tasty, cheap, fast, convenient, and ethnically authentic. *It may also be hazardous to your health.* Although the high temperature of bubbling fat sterilizes the wok, food may sit on greasy plates in the sun for hours while flies feast. The hands that go with the smiling face may not have been washed all day.

Considering that the gastronomic pyramid ranges from street stalls with plumbing and a roof to establishments that serve the finest cuisine, I offer two cautions. Although some hotel food ranks among the finest in the world, too often you get only high prices and little character. Why stay cooped up in the hotel when you can have dinner aboard a teak sailing junk moored in Hong Kong Harbor or in a candlelit garden at the edge of a cascade of terraced rice paddies in Bali? Similarly, avoid restaurants that market themselves vigorously to tourists. Why settle for the same food and faces you find at home?

Shopping in local markets can provide good, cheap meals. If there are no posted prices, watch what local people pay for what you want. Don't be bothered by being charged a small premium, but avoid being badly ripped off. It could be a mistake to hold out a handful of money and invite the lady to take what she wants for her tomatoes. If you have no idea, hand her what you think might be right. If a little more is due, she'll ask. After you've stocked up, you're ready for a terrific picnic.

In New Zealand and quite a few other countries, lodging frequently includes common cooking facilities. It's fun to cook in a kitchen with other travelers, sharing tales of the road.

Finding food you like becomes easier as you add appropriate food words to your vocabulary. Draw on a phrase book, ask questions, and take notes.

How to Order

You've found the perfect restaurant, but the menu is in a language you can't read. Now what? The daily special is always popular and cheap, but until you're certain of your tummy's tolerance I'd review the ingredients before placing an order. If you see someone else eating a meal that looks appetizing, stroll over to their table. After a friendly greeting, ask what's on their plate. If there's a language problem but the food looks good, take a chance.

If communication is a problem, point to an item on the menu as you pronounce it. When you sense it's needed, use your fingers to show the waiter how many of an item you want to order. Be sure you and the waiter understand each other. If in doubt, ask that your order be repeated back to you.

Check prices carefully. They're usually clear but there are exceptions. The fish you order in that picturesque little cafe overlooking the Danube may seem affordable until you get a monumental bill. That's when you discover that the menu price was for a serving of 100 grams and you just enjoyed a very expensive 400-gram fish. Ouch!

Before you receive the bill, figure out roughly how much your meal should cost. You may be surprised at how frequently there are "mistakes" in the bill. Just in case the cashier assumes you are unfamiliar with the currency or are fabulously wealthy, count your change. No point in getting annoyed. It's part of the game.

Exotic Dishes

There aren't many foods my stomach can't handle, but I'll admit there are many local favorites my mind can't take. How about roasted locusts, toasted silkworms, stewed grasshoppers, dog kabob, roasted tarantulas, bull penis soup, stir-fried termites, newborn mice, deep-fried scorpions, broiled rat, roasted walrus, pig snout, anaconda head, yak lung, pan-fried palm grubs, and sea slugs? Makes chocolate-covered ants sound almost appetizing. Becoming a part-time vegetarian as you travel shields you from giving offense if you decline well-intentioned offers of food that you find too challenging.

HOW TO EAT HEALTHY

It's far better to return home raving about newly discovered spices and food preparations than to start raving on the road as a result of what you ate. Travelers find delicious-looking food almost everywhere in the world, yet as in the melancholy folk song about the lemon flower, not all is as edible as it appears. Fortunately, this paradox is easily resolved. If you understand the risks and know what to look for, eating will be a pleasure to remember. Be careless, even once, and you may be, as was that balladeer from the sixties, "a sadder man but wiser now."

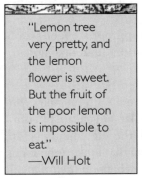

"Lemon tree very pretty, and the lemon flower is sweet. But the fruit of the poor lemon is impossible to eat."
—Will Holt

Outside of Europe, Australia, New Zealand, and a few other destinations, the rule is: *If it's not boiled, peeled, or cooked, forget it.* While that's easy to remember, it's also a little simplistic. It takes more than that to safeguard your health on the road. How cautious you should be varies greatly country to country. The fact is that outside of developed countries, you must limit your food choices. Virtually all travelers who follow a few basic rules come home in perfect health. The major issues to consider are preservation and sanitation.

Preservation

Restaurants should store perishable food at temperatures of less than 45 degrees or more than 140 degrees and keep dairy products refrigerated. However, in many countries, scant attention is given to proper preservation, sometimes even in upscale restaurants. Consequently, meat and fish spoil quickly, exposing unwary diners to parasites, dysentery, hepatitis, and other food-borne diseases. Because local people eat food not kept at proper temperatures, they often have the very problems you want to avoid.

Where proper refrigeration is improbable, seek very hot food such as vegetables stir-fried as you watch. Avoid any food that has been sitting around for more than a few minutes. If everything were cooked well-done and served immediately, most of the risk would be eliminated. Too often, that isn't what happens.

If you choose meat, be certain it's cooked well-done. Beef (or pork, buffalo, venison, etc.) may be a higher risk than chicken since the chicken may

Street market. Lisboa, Portugal.

at least have been killed on the same day it's served.

Seafood is typically sold soon after being caught or has been dried so thoroughly it looks like shoemaker's scraps. Either way, it's relatively safe. However, many travelers skip raw fish and shellfish because they are often associated with outbreaks of cholera. Perhaps it's a blessing that so much of the seafood around the world is served fried.

In Darjeeling, a German fellow told me that he'd been traveling in India for five months, eating street food and drinking tap water. He said it with some pride, asserting that he was experiencing the real India. I was impressed by his hearty constitution or his extraordinarily good luck and felt like a wimp for the care I'd been taking with what I ate. "You mean you never got sick?" I finally asked him. "Yeah, well, when I was in the hospital for malaria, they found out I had roundworms and Giardia. That was kind of a bummer." Maybe he was experiencing the real India, but I like my way better.

Sanitation

Poor sanitation practices are another health concern. In street stalls, there is seldom even a gesture toward sanitation (not too surprising since there's no running water), which raises the risk of contaminating serving utensils as well as the food. It's also hard to become comfortable with the sight of a stringy length of unidentifiable flesh dangling above a bloody counter, swinging from a rusty hook like a slow pendulum in the sun, a mobile buffet for flies.

Food handlers may themselves be transmitters of diseases, especially hepatitis. The farther away the source of clean water, the less likely it is that hands get washed during the course of a day.

Lakeside village restaurant. Lake Atitlan, Guatemala.

If a cook uses a knife to cut a raw fish then slices your potato, you may be about to ingest anything that was wrong with the fish. Similarly, if your tea is served in a cup used by someone else, then swirled around in a pail of murky wash water, you may be about to swallow someone else's problem. The solution: keep your eyes open and be impolite rather than becoming indisposed.

When I eat street food I choose my spots carefully, eating only well-cooked vegetarian food like vegetable tempura or boiled corn. Even though freshly deep-fried food is pretty well disinfected, I can't tell if fragments of meat or fish have been cooked clear through. Food can also become contaminated if it sits around on an open shelf for a while after being cooked. Keeping snacks such as fruit, bread, and nuts in your daypack helps avoid yielding to street-stall temptation.

Since a diner's hands can also transmit disease, they should be washed thoroughly before every meal. In a few countries, it is the custom to eat with your fingers. If you're comfortable with that custom, give your hands an extra scrubbing. Otherwise, ask for silverware. If it comes wet, dry it off or pour some hot tea over it. If you really don't want to do without silverware, carry a Scout-type metal set or plastic utensils. Whether you use silverware or not, in some countries it is the custom not to eat with one's left hand (see Chapter 17). If there is no napkin, you'll probably be given a bowl of water in which to dip your fingers at the end of the meal.

In most less-developed countries, do not eat fresh green salads. Except in Europe, avoid fruits and vegetables unless they have been peeled or cooked. They may have been fertilized with human or animal waste, or irrigated with contaminated water. Bacteria or pesticides that aggregate on the skin are no problem once the skin is removed. Thorough cooking kills the bacteria, but merely rinsing vegetables off with water does not eliminate the problem. If the rinse water is contaminated, it adds to the problem. Adding sufficient chlorine or iodine to the rinse water helps make food safe.

Ice cream, cheese, and other dairy products are on the forbidden list in most less-developed countries. The reason is use of unpasteurized milk and contaminated water. Travelers have reported health problems from ice cream even in Europe. Just because you see local people eating ice cream doesn't mean it's safe for you. Watch out for mayonnaise and cream sauces too.

> Generally, avoid dairy products in less-developed countries.

Fruit will become an important part of your diet. Luscious fruits with earthy, lascivious tastes are abundant in the tropics. You will enjoy some so much that you will miss them at home. Bananas and pineapples can keep you going over some long stretches.

Bread is generally a safe, tasty way to fill up—unless it bounced off the cart onto a Calcutta street on the way to your table. Yes, I saw that happen. Of course, you may have second thoughts after seeing a bare-chested deliveryman, sweating in the oppressive heat, walk into your restaurant with a load of pita bread tucked under his arm. Ever wonder why some pita tastes so salty?

By the way, adding fresh lime juice or lemon juice to your food may overcome minor contamination.

Just when your health should be at its best, you may be unbalancing your diet. Respond by eating lots of peeled fruits and well-cooked veggies. Consider starting vitamin supplements before your departure and taking vitamins as you travel.

The Bottom Line

Remember that, like the lemon flower, not everything is as desirable as it looks. There's no reason to be obsessed or overly concerned; just know and follow the basic rules. Knowing what to watch for and making thoughtful choices enables you to eat wonderful food around the world.

HOW TO DRINK HEALTHY

The moment you enter many countries, you are sentenced to carry a two- to three-pound weight with you every day. You're on the honor system, but it would be wise to abide by the terms of your sentence. The weight I'm talking about is a bottle of potable water.

You see labels that say water has been "boiled," or "treated with ozone," and others that claim "natural water from mineral springs" (meaning nothing was done to purify it because it came from a supposedly safe source). A label in Sulawesi, Indonesia, proudly declares that the bottle contains "Mississippi

Mountain Spring Water." If you've counted the mountains in Mississippi lately, you may not find that one too reassuring. But that's what they sell, so that's what I drink.

In most European countries, tap water is potable. Nevertheless, if you drink it you may feel queasy simply because the bacteria cocktail is new to your system. When I'm in Europe for a short time, I stick with bottled water. If I'll be there for a longer time, I drink local water and let my stomach adjust.

In hot, humid weather, especially when exerting yourself, your body needs much more water than you normally drink. Yet not having ready access to clean water and having to pay for bottled water leads too many travelers to cut back on consumption. That's a mistake. Cutting back can result in exhaustion, urinary tract problems, or even a kidney stone. One way or another, you'll get sick. If you stop urinating for several days, or your urine attains a golden hue, gulp down a quick liter or two of clean water and increase your daily intake.

Keep well hydrated when traveling.

If troubled by a minor bout of diarrhea, replace the fluids you're losing. If safe water isn't available, drink other nonalcoholic fluids. Keep in mind that alcohol, as in the cold beer that tastes so good, is a diuretic. In other words, your output will ultimately be greater than your intake.

Illness at home is often a well-tended inconvenience, maybe even a respite from your job, but illness on the road is unpleasant and expensive (in terms of risk and time). Your body needs water to function well, especially in hot climates. Pour it in and daydream about free, plentiful, pure water at home.

Learn to drink healthy and you can be a happy traveler.

Prevention

Some travelers say they drink water in restaurants, even tap water, with no ill effects. Maybe so, but isn't that like playing Russian roulette? Sooner or later, you're going to lose.

Don't assume that water served in restaurants, including expensive restaurants, is safe. In regions of the world where water safety is doubtful, ask for bottled water, bring your own, or drink something else. I've never noticed any restaurant staff appearing offended by someone drinking water they've brought with them (bought in a store for half the restaurant price).

Bottled water is better than tap water only if it's *not* just tap water. Some unscrupulous merchants take used bottles and refill them with unpurified water from the local spigot. In India, vendors invite you to sell empties back to them, one more reason to ensure that what you buy has a factory seal. Since they usually can't or don't reseal the bottles, make sure bottles you buy are firmly sealed. If you order bottled water in a restaurant, you should be the one to open it at the table. Ensure that the bottle is filled to the customary level, with an air space at the top. If it's filled all the way to the top, suspect a backroom refill. It's safer to drink carbonated bottled water since it's hard to replace the little bubbles at home. Drink contaminated water and you may spend a lot of time in one place.

Here's the cold truth: ice is water. When you order a drink, you must specify "without ice" (*sin hielo, en Español*). Otherwise you'll be leaving untouched drinks behind or figuring out how to discreetly dispose of the ice cubes you've hastily hauled out of your glass. If some ice has already melted in the drink, give it a pass. The bugs that can harm you aren't much bothered by having their environment reduced to zero degrees centigrade, and the alcohol in your drink will affect you much more than it will them. Further, your ice cubes may be little chips off a large block that was carted or dragged through the streets to the restaurant.

Prudent travelers brush their teeth with bottled water and don't drink shower water. Many avoid tap water even aboard an airplane.

In Ngorongoro Crater,* I met a Scottish couple on their honeymoon. They had just dragged in from Zaire where they'd spent a week lying sick in the back room of a nearly empty general store in a ramshackle village. Their temperatures and the temperature outside on the dusty road had both hovered around 104 degrees Fahrenheit. They ruefully acknowledged that they'd gotten careless about water. Not surprisingly, they'd made some resolutions.

How to Disinfect Contaminated Water

When planning to filter, boil, or chemically treat water drawn from natural sources, draw from the safest sources possible. Look for wells, springs, water upstream from human habitation, swiftly running water, clear water, or water running over a rocky or sandy bed. Avoid water that is stagnant; water downstream from human, industrial, or animal contamination; and water that is smelly, scummy, or muddy or contains decaying vegetation. Seems obvious, doesn't it?

---

*Ngorongoro Crater. This version of paradise is located in northern Tanzania, close to the Serengeti, Olduvai Gorge, and Lake Manyara. Wild game roams the crater floor of this extinct volcano (12 miles across and 2,000 feet deep). In the early part of the century, it was often called a "Garden of Eden."

Boiling

Suppose you're going to travel by dugout canoe in the Okavango Delta and you can't bring enough bottled water along for a two-week trip. One solution is to purify what you need by boiling. Boiling requires a container, time, and fuel and is somewhat dependent on weather and altitude, but it works so long as the water is brought to a rolling boil. When the surface of heated water begins to be disturbed and vapors rise, the water is not boiling and may not have reached the temperature lethal to the bacteria, viruses, and parasites that concern you. Although it consumes sometimes scarce fuel and water, let it boil for several minutes.

Filtering

Filtering is generally thought of as an alternative to boiling, but let's look at what we want to avoid in contaminated water:

- Suspended solids, such as decaying vegetation and mud, are usually not very harmful and are easily removed by a filter.

- Worms, larvae, and similar large organisms can be filtered out.

- Protozoa, single-cell organisms that cause illnesses such as amoebic dysentery and Giardiasis, can be removed by a fine filter.

- Chemical contaminants, which can make water unpleasant to taste and smell and are sometimes dangerous, can be removed by only some filters.

- Bacteria, small single-cell organisms that cause cholera, typhoid, bacillary dysentery, salmonella, and diarrhea, can be removed only by very fine filters.

- Viruses, including the type that causes Hepatitis A, are too small for even the finest filters to capture. They are, however, susceptible to boiling and chemical treatment.

The most basic kind of filtering might be called do-it-yourself. Merely pouring contaminated water through a finely woven cloth removes many large contaminants. If that's all you can do, do it. You can make your own rough filter by filling a container with clean sand and poking a few holes in the bottom. Pour water gently and slowly, discarding the first water through. Another approach is to let water sit undisturbed in a container for 48 hours or more. Some contaminants will settle to the bottom and others will die. Draw water from the surface without disturbing the sediment.

Portable water purifiers, available in catalogues and from outfitters, claim to filter out bacteria and parasites, but they do not remove the threat from viruses unless a lethal chemical ingredient has been added. Another limitation of filters has to do with capacity. If a manufacturer states that its filter is effective for 100 gallons, how do you know when that limit has been reached? To solve that problem, select a filter that clogs and can't be used when it's reached capacity.

Katadyn (call 800-950-0808) makes high-quality portable filters. The eight-ounce MINI is a ceramic microfilter (.02 microns) designed to remove bacteria and protozoa without using chemicals. It costs about $140 and needs a $60 replacement filter after 2,000 gallons.

The MSR (Mountain Safety Research) WaterWorks II (call 206-624-8573) filter uses a carbon/membrane microstrainer, weighs 18 ounces, and costs about $125. Replacement of its key components runs about $65. It is designed to remove bacteria, protozoa, and organic chemicals.

Recovery Engineering's Pur Explorer purifier (800-845-7873) combines a 1.0 micron filter with a tri-iodine resin matrix. It weighs 25 ounces and sells for about $130 (plus about $40 for the replacement cartridge needed after processing 500 gallons). Recovery Engineering also offers the Scout version for about $80 (replacement cartridge for about $40). It is designed to remove bacteria, protozoa, and viruses.

Basic Designs (707-575-1220) sells a ceramic filter designed to get rid of bacteria and protozoa. It costs about $30 (plus replacement filter after 500 gallons).

The General Ecology First Need filter costs about $60 (replacement filter needed after 100 gallons) and weighs about 16 ounces. It is designed to eliminate bacteria, protozoa, and organic chemicals.

The Timberline filter weighs only 6 ounces, will disinfect more than 400 liters before replacement, and costs about $20 (plus $14 for replacement). The filter can be used separately as a straw. The hitch is that the filter is 2.0 microns, so it doesn't remove bacteria or viruses (although it does take out Giardia and other protozoa).

Simpler and less expensive is the Water Tech purifier, a plastic cup weighing four ounces, with a clip to hook it onto your belt. It disinfects by use of a resin material impregnated with penta-iodine, represented as being lethal to all protozoa, bacteria, and viruses. The cup will process 100 gallons (3,000 cups) and disinfects much more quickly than iodine tablets. The disinfected water passes through a carbon stage to remove any taste and odor from the penta-iodine. At about $30, this cup is very satisfactory for low-volume use. The same company also makes the Oasis Portable Water Purification System, which resembles a bicycler's water squeeze bottle and uses similar technology. Good for about 100 gallons, it may be even better than the cup (about $30).

If you take a filter, remember that (a) weight and size matter, (b) you must follow instructions, including keeping it clean and not using it beyond its capacity, and (c) it can't protect you when you don't use it.

Iodine

Suppose it's the middle of the night and you've just checked into a hotel in Xi'an.* There's a container of water on the night stand but you have no idea whether it's been boiled. Even though you're very thirsty and have no filter, it wouldn't be good for international relations to build a fire in the middle of the floor. A 2 percent tincture of iodine solution from any pharmacy is one answer. It will kill parasites, bacteria, *and* viruses. Mix the iodine solution with the water and let it sit for ten to thirty minutes to ensure that disinfection has taken place. If the water is cloudy, let it sit long enough for most of the suspended particles to settle *before* adding your iodine. If the water is cloudy or cold, make the iodine solution up to twice as strong and let it stand twice as long. Even better, let the mixture sit overnight.

To eliminate the risk of spilling iodine solution in your pack, carry a bottle of 50 iodine tablets (Potable Aqua, about $6, in the United States, or Aquapur in other parts of the world). Give the tablets 20 to 30 minutes to do their job. Since the tablets deteriorate over time, toss them out after a year. There is also a crystalline iodine product called Polar Pure. A $10 bottle will disinfect about 2,000 quarts of water, so it's very economical. Both are available in camping goods stores and catalogs.

If anticipation of the taste of iodine gives you involuntary shivers, you'll be delighted to learn that Potable Aqua now sells PA Plus (about $10) that removes the yellow-brown color and singed-iron taste from iodine-treated water. PA Plus is made mostly of vitamin C, so you could substitute lemon juice or your own vitamins to remove the taste.

Think of iodine as back-up purification. If you are considering using it as your primary disinfectant for an extended trip, consult your doctor.

---

* *Xi'an.* The largest city in central China, Xi'an is one of the world's oldest populated areas (established in 6,000 B.C.) and is considered the cradle of Chinese civilization. It was the Chinese anchor of the Silk Road and is now visited by those eager to see the recently excavated terra-cotta figures from the tomb of Qin Shi Huang Di, the first emperor of unified China.

In the market. Sulawesi, Indonesia.

Chlorine

Chlorine (bleach) also disinfects water. Check the label for the percentage of chlorine contained in the solution. If it is 1 percent, add ten drops per quart of contaminated water. If it is 4 to 6 percent, add two drops per quart of water. If it's 7 to 10 percent chlorine, add one drop per quart of water. Let the mixture stand for 30 minutes before drinking.

Whether it's worth taking iodine tablets, chlorine, or a filter with you depends on what part of the planet you visit. When I'll be in remote country for a week or more, I take the purifier cup and a handful of iodine tablets. They're cheap and light and will handle anything I'm likely to encounter.

Problems are not limited to contaminated water. You may also have to give up *milk* in many countries. If you can't be certain that the milk has been properly pasteurized, assume it hasn't been. Even a legend on the container claiming that the milk has been pasteurized is less than conclusive in some countries. Why risk tuberculosis or brucellosis? If milk is brought to a boil before being served in tea or coffee, it should be safe. Unfortunately, restrictions on milk extend to milk products, including *cheese* and *ice cream*.

Beer, wine, soda, and *bottled soft drinks* are okay. You encounter an incredible variety of beers as you travel, often local brews in which people take great pride. Watch for brands such as Ohlsson's Lager in Botswana, Three Horse in Madagascar, Tusker in Kenya, Primus in Zaire, Cuzquena Malta in Peru, Brahma Chopp in Brazil, and Polar in Chile.

There are a couple of drawbacks to beer. Besides being a diuretic, it's often served warm (because there is no refrigeration and the ice melted two days ago). If a bottle of beer is served with a glass, chances are the glass has been swished through tepid contaminated water at best. You are better off drinking from the bottle after wiping its mouth. A straw is a good solution for some beverages, but it's hard to maintain your poise sitting in a bar drinking beer through a straw.

In less-developed countries, wine is much less common than beer, more expensive, and seldom memorable. At the Alcove Restaurant in Dar es Salaam, a headwaiter in a rumpled tux offered me their featured wine: Thunderbird.

Tea and coffee made from boiling water are safe. Highland nomads in western Nepal say, "Tea is the horse of the traveler." I agree and drink huge quantities of tea wherever I go. Loaded up with sugar, a few cups of tea will get you through the coldest morning. But remember, an otherwise safe liquid can be infected by a contaminated container or prolonged exposure to air. In practical terms, that means the tea is fine but the teacup may get you. Take your own cup, clean what's available, take a chance, or go without.

To summarize: use bottled water and break the seal on the bottle yourself. Otherwise, boil water, filter it, or drop in those little iodine tablets, and avoid containers that may be contaminated. It takes only a little thoughtfulness to be a healthy traveler.

13

Safety and Security

Toto, I've a feeling we're not
in Kansas anymore.
—Dorothy
from Frank Baum's *Wizard of Oz*

"**Y**ou've got to be crazy!" That's what I hear from friends when I say I'm heading for some distant place they perceive as dangerous. While it's normal to wonder how you'll be treated in Johannesburg, New Delhi, Santiago, or any other place you don't know much about, I've been met with overwhelming friendliness on every continent. People smile, call out greetings, offer to help, and want to talk. They welcome travelers to their country and their homes, proud of their culture and their kids. Friendliness is the rule.

Having said that, it's still true that traveling does present certain risks. However, it's important to know that risk abroad is very different from the drug-related crimes and armed robbery featured in our daily newspapers. In fact, the most frequent problems afflicting travelers abroad are stubbed or broken toes (apparently from stumbling around in dark hotel rooms), lost luggage, being bumped from an overbooked flight, and diarrhea acquired from contaminated water. These risks should deter no one from traveling.

Although physical assault is very rare, opportunistic nonviolent theft *should* be a concern. The traveler is an inviting target unless he or she knows what to expect and is prepared to avoid or respond to any problem. Many of the people you meet have seen the United States depicted on television as a land of unimaginable luxury. The fact that you're in their country tells them you have enough money to travel beyond horizons they'll never approach. As some associate you with what they've seen, you'll sense admiration—but perhaps a little envy too. The possessions you carry may be worth more than the average annual income in their country, so to a few people you represent an opportunity for a little informal redistribution of wealth.

A *Condé Nast Traveler* poll revealed that 42 perent of its readers who responded had money, clothing, or jewelry stolen while traveling (by the way, most of them were in Europe). Almost half of those who had lost something said it was taken from their hotel rooms; 26 percent experienced street theft (mostly by pickpockets); and almost 30 percent encountered some scam such as the basic taxi rip-off, a tricky currency exchange, or a slippery purchase. Virtually all of those losses could have been avoided with a little knowledge and preparation.

Since 33 percent of those who responded to the poll had been victims twice, that group must have included some slow learners or very unlucky folks. There's a clue in the fact that only 36 percent reported carrying their money in a money belt.

Being prepared reduces risk. Here's an example. Suppose I know that anyone who comes up to me on the street, says the word "baput," and counts to 100, will then demand that I hand over my money. What will I do if that scenario actually begins to unfold? Obviously, I'll leave the scene long before the count reaches 100. What if I also have a description of the kind of person who says "baput" and know where he's likely to approach me? The risk of that person surprising me would be pretty slim, wouldn't it? Well, that's what this discussion is about: knowledge, preparation, and good habits.

Knowledge and preparation reduce risks.

To a lurking thief, a traveler wandering down the street looking lost or preoccupied appears the way a limping gazelle does to a hungry lion. Now turn that image around. Picture a traveler walking with an air of self-assurance and purpose. I don't mean acting arrogant or "tough," just confident and alert, aware of his or her surroundings. Since that person doesn't look like easy prey, especially if in the company of others, the thief will look elsewhere.

Remember that old joke about two guys who are suddenly confronted on the trail by a grizzly bear? The grizzly rears up and roars, about to charge. Ben cries, "My gosh, what shall we do?" His partner Scott says, "I'm getting out of here!" "You're crazy," shouts Ben as the bear starts its rush, "you can't outrun that bear." "I don't have to," Scott calls back over his shoulder, "all I have to do is outrun you!" That's all each of us has to do as a traveler, simply make sure we're not the thief's first choice.

It's your job to know whether you need to be especially alert in the places you'll be visiting. Overseas, as at home, crime is most common in cities and where tourists congregate. High-risk areas include train and bus stations, streets around tourist hotels, and nightlife areas. There are also a few cities where it might be wise not to wander the streets at night under any circumstances. These include Bogotá, Dar es Salaam (Tanzania), Kinshasa (Congo), Moscow, and Rio.

Some guidebooks offer good advice concerning security risks at your destinations, but it's worth taking advantage of other resources as well. Review Consular Information Sheets or Travel Warnings (see the next section) and talk with experienced travelers before you leave home.

Talk with other travelers as you approach a country. Seek guidance from the desk clerk at your hotel. Question local people. Adjust your alertness based on what you hear and see. If a situation requires caution, be cautious. No lapses.

We don't worry much about certain risks at home because we know how to avoid them. Abroad, however, risks are more real for anyone who doesn't "know the territory." Unprepared tourists are right to worry—because they don't know how to protect themselves. Knowledge prevents problems. When the simple routines in these columns become automatic, you can travel the world without fear.

WHICH COUNTRIES TO SKIP

Are there countries you should skip? There certainly are and you should identify them while drafting your itinerary. However, since it's hard for reporters to get the facts, let alone evaluate them, disturbances in a distant country are frequently reported as being worse than they are. And, of course, a little sensationalism never hurts sales.

Unfortunately, when talking with returning tourists, we tend to hear from the one person who had a problem, not from the dozens who had none. By analogy, when someone has a bad meal in a restaurant, he's likely to talk about it, and the meal gets worse with each telling. Almost anyone who has traveled has succumbed to the temptation of telling, and embellishing, some adventure. After all, stories about a coup or riot sound pretty exciting when repeated at home. Nevertheless, even taking sensationalism and exaggerations into account, there are always a few places, changing year to year, that a traveler should leave off the itinerary.

How do you identify which countries to skip? Start with the countries the U.S. government forbids its citizens to visit. Beyond those, it's a matter of research and common sense. News reports, even if unnecessarily alarmist, signal places that deserve careful review before inclusion on your route.

U.S. Department of State *Consular Information Sheets* describe crime and security conditions, political disturbances, and areas of instability in every country. They also include addresses and emergency telephone numbers for U.S. embassies and consulates. If conditions in a country are considered particularly dangerous, or a major demonstration will occur on a specified date, the State Department also issues a *Travel Warning*. These publications tend to be extremely cautious because "hostage" is not a welcome word around the State Department. To get this information, call the State Department Citizens Emergency Center (202-647-5225 or 202-647-3000, or see travel.state.gov/travel_warnings.html on the Web) and follow the prompts you hear to have sheets or warnings faxed to you. Both operate 24 hours a day. If you prefer the computer/modem route, dial the Consular Affairs Bulletin Board at (202) 647-9225. You can also obtain them via CompuServe (GO STATE) or America Online (keyword TRAVEL). You can also contact your own embassies and consulates abroad. The State Department Bureau of Consular Affairs publishes *Tips for* . . . (name of country), which offer advice on travel to various countries. Ask a travel agent if there are any warnings applicable to your route.

If you ask the embassy of the country about local safety, keep in mind that their response may be subjective. If there's an internal problem, one government may want to keep foreigners away so they don't see it. Another, more dependent on tourism, may minimize danger so tourists won't cancel.

A recently returned traveler is a good source of information provided you can evaluate his frame of reference. Here's what I mean by frame of reference. A bunch of us were talking one evening in a Bangkok cafe as it bobbed gently on the Chao Phraya river. Those of us who had just arrived from South India saw Bangkok as intimidatingly modern and distressingly westernized. An Englishman, just arrived from vacationing in New Zealand, saw the same Bangkok as dirty, disorganized, and distressingly Asian. That's frame of reference, the eye of the beholder.

There are, however, real problems that have to do with civil war or terrorist attacks. Terrorists sometimes pressure a government by attacking places that attract tourists. If bombs are being set off in an airport or scenic destination, even occasionally, go elsewhere. If hostage taking is in a cycle of local popularity, it's a good idea for travelers not to attract attention by looking affluent or dressing in pseudomilitary clothing.

There are many wonderful places to visit that go through periods when they belong on no traveler's route. I'm thinking of parts of Angola, Colombia, India (Punjab, Jammu, Kashmir), Sudan, Sri Lanka, Uganda, the Kurdish section of eastern Turkey, the Philippines (northern Luzon, Mindanao), and various fragments of the former Yugoslavia. I'd skip Nigeria, Liberia, and North Korea for the foreseeable future and be cautious about traveling by train or private car in Cambodia.

On the other hand, some places have a fearsome reputation but feel very different when you're there. For example, Thailand's notorious Golden Triangle, long reported as the epicenter of battles among opium-trade warlords, seems disappointingly normal when you get there. In fact, it's now distinguished by a resort hotel where sweating tourists beam beneath a masonry arch while having their photograph taken with the muddy Mekong River in the background. You can hardly find a warlord anymore, unless you count the one who owns the resort.

There are a few precautions you should consider when traveling in a genuinely high-risk area. Tell people at home what they should do in case you find yourself in an emergency situation. Check in with your embassy on arrival. Don't discuss your itinerary with strangers. Leave nothing controversial in your hotel room. Watch for people who seem to be following you. Keep a mental note of potential safe havens and develop a plan of action should a dangerous situation arise. If shooting starts, take cover and don't pick up a weapon (forget Rambo!). Sit someplace out of sight and try to remember why you came.

The bottom line: some places should be off limits from time to time, left for another day. Do the research. Find out whether a place is as forbidding as it initially sounds. If it's a close call, trust your instincts. If you decide to go, get updates from other travelers when you arrive. In making decisions, the frequency of random violence and attacks directed toward tourists, and the attitude of the government, should be given considerable weight.

HOW TO PROTECT YOURSELF WITH A MAGIC CLOAK

Standing in a crowded bus station in San José, Costa Rica, I heard a tourist complain loudly that someone had just snatched his passport from his shirt pocket. He kept it in his shirt pocket? Anyone who does something like that must be brain dead. There's no reason to be a victim when thievery can be avoided so easily. Knowledge and preparation form a *magic cloak* that, when followed without exception, makes a traveler almost invulnerable.

Perhaps the most important part of the routine is a mindset you establish before you leave home. That is, deciding that you won't defend your dignity or property at risk of injury or life. Suppose you're walking along a street in Tangier and some guy standing in a doorway with his buddies makes a nasty comment about you, your partner, or your country. Fortunately, you've already decided not to be provoked by a meaningless, gratuitous insult. Does it make sense to play someone else's game on their home field? So you walk on without looking back.

In the serenity of an easy chair, it's easy to agree that the possessions you carry aren't worth trading your life to protect. It's more difficult to imbed that principle so deeply that you won't make a different decision in the heat of the moment or after several beers in some exotic port. That decision should become the first of your routines.

Money Belt Routines

Some of the most important routines concern your money belt.
– Keep all your valuables (passport, credit cards, driver's license, immunization record, airline tickets, and most of your cash and travelers checks) in a money belt. *Always.* It's a small hassle to get them out when you need them, but it keeps them from disappearing unexpectedly. A money belt can take many forms: a belt around your waist, a pocket hanging inside your pants from your belt loop, a pouch dangling from your neck, a shoulder holster, and so on.

– Whatever the form of your money belt, it must be *inside* your clothing, riding comfortably without signaling its presence. Although its fabric may be water-resistant, it won't keep out rain or the perspiration generated during a long hike, so keep the contents inside a Ziploc bag. Transporting valuables in a pouch outside your clothing, including the often-seen fanny pack, may be comfortable and convenient, but it puts them at great risk. Fanny packs can't be protected effectively and get clipped off every day. That's when the wearer realizes that carrying valuables in one was a mistake.

— Lock your money belt in your luggage at night unless you feel you're in a high-risk area. If you are, keep the belt with you while you sleep.

— You find lots of things on the beach—sea shells, a volleyball game, maybe even a new friend—but you can lose things too. When heading for the beach, leave your money belt in the hotel safe if you trust it. If you don't, lock it in your luggage in the hotel room. If you take it to the beach, ask a friend to wear it while you're swimming, or take it in with you in a waterproof pouch.

On a beach such as Copacabana in Rio only about 20 percent of the sharks are in the water. Don't even think of hiding your money belt under your towel or digging a hole for it. As an acquaintance put his money belt under his towel, I noticed a teenage guy stroll by. He eyed us obliquely and kept going. Several minutes later he eased down just behind us, only a few feet away. I watched in fascination as his foot slowly snaked across the sand until his toes could probe under my friend's towel. I yelled. He scrambled to his feet and tore off down the beach. My friend had underestimated the caliber of the competition.

— Keep a small amount of cash and travelers checks in your luggage to avoid being cleaned out if a thief were somehow to get your money belt. For the same reason, it's prudent for partners to split up cash, travelers checks, and credit cards between them.

Making the small effort to follow these simple routines will make your trip a happier one. Convince yourself that the very first time you're careless with your money belt, it will disappear. Why learn the hard way?

Wallet Routines

— Make it routine to put your wallet in a secure front pants pocket, a buttoned or Velcro-closed thigh pocket, or some other inaccessible place. Some travelers use a wallet attached by a loop to their belt. I grimace when I see a traveler stuff a wallet into a rear pants pocket, an inside jacket pocket, or a purse—all predictable places. When a thief knows where to look for your wallet, he's halfway to his goal.

I met a documentary filmmaker in Ternate* who had a special pocket sewn on the inside of his pants, opening at the waistband, in which he kept his wallet. It worked. Then he left his hotel room door unlocked in Sengiggi Beach, Lomboc, and someone walked off with his backpack. He forgot there's more than one routine to follow.

— If your wallet is vulnerable, make it "sticky" by wrapping it with rubber bands.

— Act as if the thief can get your wallet wherever you put it. On that assumption, keep only business cards, a few dollars, and a couple of travelers checks in it. Everything else belongs in your money belt. Sure, it's a little inconvenient, but it's a lot easier than canceling and replacing credit cards, wiring home for money, and suffering the anxiety of a major loss. Travel is supposed to be fun.

Luggage and Daypack Routines

The objective is to prevent anyone from opening your luggage and removing what he wants—or walking off with the whole thing. These routines can foil his plans.

— Keep your luggage locked most of the time. If you have something valuable in your daypack, such as your camera, lock it when in crowded places or when you check it at a museum.

— Bus and train stations and, to a lesser degree, airports, attract people who admire your possessions. While waiting, keep your hand or foot through your luggage strap, lean against it, or otherwise keep in physical touch with it.

David, an Israeli as hirsute and bulky as a bear, asked if I would watch his pack one afternoon at a bus station in Pisco, Peru. I agreed. When he locked his pack to my belt with a chain, I knew he was an experienced traveler. That was his not-so-subtle way of saying he expected me to watch his pack as closely as he would watch it himself.

— When you check your luggage, ask the agent for the letter designation of your destination. See, don't assume, that the right tag is attached. In addition to inadvertent errors, I heard of a ticket agent who purposely mistagged bags, sending them to another city where a

---

* *Ternate.* Portuguese and Dutch forts on this tiny volcanic island in northeastern Indonesia are a reminder of the glory days when Ternate was at the center of the spice trade (it was one of the world's few sources of cloves). Sir Frances Drake stopped by in 1579.

confederate waited to claim them. Clever, eh? Watch your luggage depart toward the plane and watch as it's loaded on a bus.

— If your bag gets lost in transit, you have to prove it was in the custody of the carrier. That's much easier if you have a baggage claim check (try getting one at a Guatemalan bus stop).

— Your luggage can go astray on arrival. Not all the folks watching the bags clunk around the carousel are passengers. Some are official porters who promote their services by snatching your bag and guarding it until you see it and come over. Then there is the unofficial porter who picks up your bag if it looks unattended. If you see it happen, he smiles and acts like a porter. If you don't, he's out the gate. I'm sure you've seen those warning signs that say, "Bags look alike." It must be true. To a thief, your bag looks like his.

Station yourself close to the point where bags enter the baggage claim area. That way you'll get first shot at your bag. If you're farther down the line, chatting with someone you met on the plane, your bag may leave the airport before you do.

At the airport in Trivandrum, India, I was waiting for my backpack to roll into sight when a slightly built young man swooped down like a fish eagle on the daypack at my feet. His boldness probably meant he had confederates nearby to whom he planned to pitch my pack on the run. As always in a crowd, I was standing with my size thirteen shoe firmly planted through the pack's strap. When the pack didn't come away in his hand as he expected, he slid sprawling across the floor. I'm sure he was back the next day.

— Vulnerability increases in crowded places such as a train station. After a long trip you're tired and a little disoriented, thinking about the town, talking about lodging, maybe looking for a friend, and you're not concentrating on the present. Zap! You've been stung. Theft may be nonviolent but that doesn't mean it's polite. Even if you see the person who raced by and grabbed your daypack out of your hand, you have little chance of catching him. Be alert in crowded places, watch the people around you, and keep in touch with your gear. Force the thief to look for an easier target.

— If you have much walking around to do, or you'll be waiting for hours, consider storing your bag in a locker or the "left luggage" room.

— Suppose you're in a public place and can't store your bag and can't stand taking it with you while you run errands. If you ask someone reputable-looking to watch it, set it clearly within their territory.

Reduce the risk by locking it to something with your bicycle lock. Make sure you are communicating with one another about how long the person will be there.

- If you sleep in a public place, lock your bag to something or use it for a pillow. Even lacing the straps through a bench or around a stanchion will foil someone running by.

- When traveling in a group, help one another. Leaving the train platform in Puno,* passengers are jammed together as they're funneled through a single exit gate, a perfect situation for thieves. The architect of that place must have been a member of the Pickpockets & Pack-Slashers Union. As our group of six approached the exit, we formed a circle, packs in the center. Does that sound overly cautious? Well, that train station has a terrible reputation—and our little merry-go-round formation didn't lose a thing.

- If you have a compartment on a train, keep the door locked when you're out of the room and lock your bag to the washstand or something else built in. If that won't work, lock two bags together. If you have an open berth on the aisle, use your bag as a cushion between yourself and the wall while you sleep, or lock it to something.

- Bus travel tests your vigilance. When your bag is traveling on the roof of a bus, secure it to a rail with a bicycle chain-lock. That keeps it from falling off on a curve or being pitched off into waiting hands.

- If you have your bag with you in the rest room, take it into the stall with you.

- A hotel room is not always a safe zone. As you're leaving the room, take a moment to lock up things you'd rather not contribute to the local economy.

- The locks on your hotel room door and windows won't help a bit unless you use them.

- Believing them easier targets for grab-and-run theft, thieves target women. A woman should wear her shoulder bag strap diagonally across her chest rather than hanging off one shoulder. When a man is walking with a woman, he should walk between her and the street to guard against someone making a grab for her shoulder bag.

---

* *Puno*. High, cold Puno is located in the southeastern corner of Peru on the shore of Lake Titicaca. It has a fine market for llama and alpaca wool articles and offers excursions to the floating reed islands and the island of Taquile (to see Inca ruins and fine textiles).

- If you have your daypack on your back in a crowded bus, beware of busy fingers trying to get inside. If you tend to carry it over one shoulder, be alert against a grab-and-run. Each time you set it down, keep in touch with it; keep your hand on it or your foot through a strap. Keep it out of reach of passing hands. If you put a camera in your daypack, be especially alert.

- Carry a local language newspaper prominently under your arm if it will help you pass as a local.

- Be alert when someone offers to help, especially when you didn't know you needed help. An offer needn't make you defensive, just alert. Similarly, don't be too quick to volunteer to help someone else. Don't suppress your friendly instincts, but take a moment to size up the situation.

The comments above are not meant to make travel seem daunting. It's just that knowing what to expect, following the simple routines I've described, and using the information in the rest of this chapter provides a magic cloak to guard your travels.

WHERE TROUBLE COMES FROM—AND HOW TO AVOID IT

We've talked about protecting your money belt, wallet, luggage, and day-pack from theft. Now we're ready to discuss other potential safety and security problems a traveler might encounter. You can learn to recognize and sidestep every one.

Political and Religious Discussions

As we all know, discussions of politics, sex, or religion can become very spirited. They are especially tempting topics on the road because a vigorous discussion can generate cultural insights you might otherwise have missed. The problem arises when what seems like stimulating give-and-take to you may be personal and confrontational to others. Tempers can flare even more when controversial subjects are combined with alcohol.

If you want to stir things up, try converting others to your way of thinking or insist that your country's political system is the only rational one. Voice your opinions about the merits and demerits of local persons of the opposite sex, and throw in a few complaints about the inconveniences you've encountered in their country. Then get ready for fireworks.

I'm not suggesting that you avoid discussions of politics, sex, or religion; I'm only suggesting that it's better to ask questions than to preach. Be open-minded and sensitive to the mood of the group. Keep it light and humorous. Should the mood sour, pay for a farewell drink for your new acquaintances, if appropriate, and bail out. The bottom line: there's no upside to getting into an argument in a bar.

Alcohol, Drugs, and Firearms

Alcohol

Alcohol is as much related to problems of safety and security when you're abroad as it is on highways at home. After a few drinks, you become a shade inattentive. You fail to recognize a problem developing or you take a risk you'd otherwise have avoided. Suddenly you're face-to-face with an unpleasant situation. If you gulp down a couple of beers after a hot afternoon of trudging through the temple grounds of Prambanan and Borobudur,* or add a cool bottle of white wine to your dinner in Rio, stay a little more alert to your surroundings than you might at home.

Drugs

I have one word of advice about drugs: DON'T! Don't buy them, don't sell them, don't use them, and don't transport them in or out. This isn't about morality. It's about safety and security. Using exposes you to impure drugs and can put your life on the line. Anyone who buys or sells drugs may be dealing with an informer or a cop. Sneaking illegal drugs through customs might work . . . except when it doesn't. More than one-third of all U.S. citizens incarcerated abroad for any crime are in on drug charges, many with very long mandatory sentences. Anyone busted on drug charges learns quickly how very different the legal process is and how much more severe penalties are in most foreign countries. Maybe you saw the movie *Midnight Express?*

Avoid drugs at all costs.

Some drug sales are setups from the beginning. The seller has tipped off the cops or is a cop. The buyer is arrested during or immediately after the deal goes down and the drugs are confiscated—probably for recycling. Naturally, the buyer's drug money disappears. Somewhere along the way to the police station, a large amount of money may be mentioned with the implication that its receipt might be related to the buyer's freedom. If not, the buyer may be held without trial for years. Under the legal systems of many countries, a person under arrest is considered guilty until innocence is proved. Perfunctory trials and harsh sentences are common. On bulletin boards in La Paz hotels, I've read pitiful notes posted on behalf of foreign prisoners begging for someone to contact a relative. Roadside billboards in Malaysia promise execution as the reward for trafficking in drugs!

---

* *Prambanan and Borobudur.* The Hindu temple complex at Prambanan on Java, built A.D. 700–900, is the largest in Indonesia. After being destroyed by earthquakes, restoration has been ongoing since the 1930s. The Buddhist temple at Borobudur, near Prambanan, is the largest ancient monument in the Southern Hemisphere. It is a five-story pyramid, over 400 feet on a side. Buried for 1,000 years by volcanic eruptions and tropical vegetation, it was discovered by chance in 1814. Its restoration, the largest such project since Abu Simbel in Egypt, began in 1973.

A traveler who expects the embassy to intervene, give them a good scolding, and put them on a plane for home should have a chat with the State Department ahead of time. Embassies have neither the ability nor willingness to do much more than provide a list of lawyers and notify next of kin.

If a new acquaintance asks you to take a package home as a favor, agree or not as it suits you, but don't actually accept it without opening and inspecting the contents carefully. Whatever reasons are given for not opening the package, they're not good enough. If it contains drugs or other illegal goods it is you who must answer to the law.

Sadly, drugs also mean that travelers must be thoughtful about accepting apparent hospitality. Whether you accept food or drink from someone should depend on the circumstances. If the offer is from someone you have reason to trust, no problem. If an offer comes from a new acquaintance or seems inappropriate in some way, be cautious. Bus and train stations are special-alert zones. If you have the slightest doubt about an offer, turn it down. You can decline on grounds of being a vegetarian, a nondrinker, having an upset stomach, or give no reason at all. Be polite, but put your own welfare first.

I recall a 22-year-old Japanese student who accepted an orange soda from a person he met in a bus station in Tanzania. He awakened 36 hours later in a hospital to which some kind passersby had taken him. After the drug wore off and his headache subsided, he asked about his backpack. The nurses shook their heads and shrugged their shoulders.

The State Department reports that no U.S. citizens have been arrested abroad in connection with prescription drugs they bought in the United States and took along for personal use in labeled containers. However, you can get into trouble by legally buying large amounts of certain drugs, such as tranquilizers and amphetamines, in one country and attempting to take them into other countries where they are illegal. The same goes for attempting to return with them to the United States if the quantity is such that Customs might suspect commercial intent.

Firearms

Sentences for illegal possession of firearms abroad can be very harsh, at least by U.S. standards. How does 30 years sound? Don't consider taking a weapon to another country without first obtaining a permit from its embassy. A little political instability can make border guards, police, and other officials convinced that your weapon indicates your intent to help the insurgents. What could follow would not be pretty.

Prohibited Photographs

Since we'll discuss this subject more thoroughly in Chapter 22, I'll mention only briefly that a traveler can get in trouble by taking photographs of forbidden objects. What's forbidden? Fortunately, there's a standard list: bridges, airports, harbors, military personnel and installations, and some temples. After watching me take a couple of photographs of Calcutta Harbor, an officer of the law gave me a sharp warning and definitely wasn't interested in whether I thought the regulation was reasonable. If there's the slightest doubt about who might be watching, skip the shot. I don't know what the actual penalties might be, but no harbor is that picturesque.

Encounters with the Law

Few people arrive in a foreign country intending to cross the law, but it can happen anyway, usually because of ignorance or carelessness. Buying, selling, using, or transporting drugs is by far the most effective strategy for winning a trip to jail. Other common problems involve visas, currency violations, fraud, theft, customs violations (bringing in or taking out something prohibited), being in a traffic accident, or violating a local statute, such as entering a restricted area. Being drunk or disorderly in public comes in second. Carrying a weapon may or may not protect you, but it will get you stopped at the border of every country in the world.

You are governed by the laws of the country you are in.

When visiting a country, you are governed by its laws and they may be based on principles of jurisprudence very different from those in your own country. The differences relate to the issue of whether an individual's rights or the government's rights have primacy. In most places, the government wins hands down. For example, detention for a week or more without being formally charged and with no showing of probable cause is common. There may not even be a right to immediately contact anyone outside jail. Bail may be denied and right to trial by jury is far from being universal. The best plan is to obey local laws.

When your path collides with officialdom, your behavior can make all the difference in how things turn out. Don't be disrespectful or show anger. That's easier said than done, but it's essential. There is a saying in Ghana that goes: "Once you have crossed the river, you can be rude to the crocodile." That wise counsel needs no explanation.

Suppose there's no question of guilt? You did what they say you did and you both know it. No matter how silly the regulation seems that you're being charged with breaching, don't criticize it. Express naive surprise. Apologize immediately. Promise that, now that you know the law, you'll never commit this offense again. However, if you did not commit any offense, I wouldn't say otherwise.

If detention is prolonged or the interpersonal dynamics are deteriorating (e.g., the guard is getting drunk or you're losing your cool), call for a superior officer. If appropriate, request a representative of your embassy or consulate. They probably won't get you out of jail, but someone from the consulate should visit you and put you in touch with a well-connected lawyer, preferably one who speaks your language (although maybe that won't matter if he's connected well enough). They will also notify your family and/or traveling partner, help get money transferred from home if you need it, and arrange for food and bedding (which usually doesn't come with the jail cell).

I've heard a couple of people say they responded to difficulty by offering a bribe. That's not a solution that comes naturally to me and it entails some risks. We'll discuss bribes at greater length in Chapter 17.

In India, it's fine to be persistent but if you decide to employ assertiveness or anger, brace yourself to encounter the full weight of an infinite bureaucracy. In Africa, the odds that your display of temper or threats will intimidate a 19-year-old private holding a submachine gun are infinitesimally low—off the board, I'd say. At the same time, the chances that your show of anger will escalate the situation to your disadvantage approach 100 percent. The slightest hint that you deserve special treatment *because* you are a foreigner will provoke special treatment all right, but perhaps not in your best interests.

It's important to keep such encounters in perspective. During one somewhat hectic three-month journey in Africa, I passed through a total of 54 immigration and customs stations and had not one problem. At almost every station, I was passed through with a friendly wave. At the others, I did as I was asked, which usually meant opening my pack to be searched. I asked and answered questions politely. Not wanting to appear nervous or say the wrong thing, I volunteered little information. When asked why I was there, I said, "To see this beautiful country." If you're calm and patient, you can out wait most problems.

At a police checkpoint in Tanzania, a guard ordered me to put my journal away. "No writing at this police station," he said. The police station in question was a card table in the paltry shade of a scraggly baobab tree. Curious, but not wanting to debate the wisdom of his requirement, I smiled and buried my journal in my daypack.

In Prague, I discovered I'd used up my multiple visa for Hungary. To return, I needed another visa. They told me at the Hungarian Consulate that they didn't issue visas on Saturdays, meaning I'd have to delay my trip for two or three days. Prague is a great place to spend a weekend but I was scheduled to catch a flight out of Budapest the following Monday. I calmly asked to see a higher official. After a long delay, a man appeared who coldly agreed to issue the visa but only if I paid a "special service" fee of $80. Swallowing my retort, I asked to see the most senior officer on duty. He turned out to be an erudite, sophisticated person who spoke fluent English. After a friendly conversation lasting over an hour, mostly about new business opportunities in free Hungary, he issued the visa, stamped "diplomatic courtesy," at no charge.

I am not advocating that you present yourself as a person who can be taken advantage of. That could be a mistake. Instead, try to establish some person-to-person contact with the official. Ask personal questions. Establish eye contact—difficult if the guy is wearing shades or one of those stiff army hats with a black visor. If you ask for his help or advice, he may transform himself into an individual human and show you how to solve the problem. Reasonable flattery works in every language.

As you travel you will interact with more officials than you normally do at home. Most will be pleasant human beings. Only a very few will be tight-lipped, self-important creeps. If one starts to give you a problem, it's your job to keep the situation under control. It's not difficult when you're prepared.

Disturbances

What do you do about disturbances that spring up while you're on the scene? Fortunately, most of them aren't nearly as dangerous as they appear from a distance. Take the 1985 coup in which the commanding general of the army deposed the president of Bolivia. The newspaper reports made La Paz, the capital, sound like the last place in the world you'd want to be. The militia fired a few machine-gun volleys into the air, imposed a curfew, and shut down transportation for three days. That was all there was to it—for me, at least. The outgoing president, on the other hand, was awarded a lifetime vacation in a remote village in the steamy lowland jungle. There weren't even any T-shirts commemorating the event.

Friends told me of watching a riot from their hotel room window in Caracas while seeing the same scenes televised on CNN.

I was in the Perinet* forest searching for lemurs while a military coup was attempted in Antananarivo, the capital of Madagascar. With radio and telephone shut down, news finally reached us along the railroad line. By the time we heard about the battle, the shouting, if there had been any, was over. No problem, except that it looked bad in newspapers at home. If friends and family know you're in an area in which a disturbance is taking place, they need your reassurance.

I recall one disturbance that didn't seem threatening until it suddenly burst out of control. As I stood in a shop doorway in a Chilean town talking with the shop owner, a street intersection a few yards away filled with students. Before long, they were shouting angrily as fiery speakers demanded that the government reveal the whereabouts of students who had "disappeared." Squads of heavily armored policemen arrived, looking menacing but not interfering. Without warning, someone threw a stone through a storefront plate glass window. As the glass shattered, so did détente. In an instant, clubs were swinging and rocks were flying in every direction. I ducked into

---

* *Perinet.* This forest reserve, located in central Madagascar between Antananarivo and Toamasina, is home to the rare Indri Lemur.

the shop just as the owner hauled down his steel mesh security curtain with a clang. If I hadn't made it, I'd have been trapped in the furious crowd. As it was, shots cracked a few feet away from where we crouched under the counter. I sometimes learn the hard way, but I don't recommend it. Since that day, I've kept my distance.

Whether it's a student protest meeting, police breaking up a strike, or an all-out coup attempt, no traveler should let curiosity lead him into the middle of it. The rule is simple: *stay away from trouble.* If there's a flare-up when you're around, don't go to watch. If you go anyway, thinking you'll keep your head down, you may too late find yourself caught in a mob. Stay in your hotel. If there's action in the street below, stay away from the windows. Pull the curtains or blinds to stop flying glass. Store some food and water if you have time. Just in case water is cut off, fill the bath tub or whatever containers you can find. Keep your flashlight nearby in case power goes off. Know where the fire escape is. If there's a curfew, obey it. An ice cold beer on a hot night isn't worth getting shot.

If it looks as if the situation may continue or deteriorate, ask the hotel manager to help you slip away. For a price, someone is ready to accommodate virtually any need.

Theft: Scams, Pickpockets, and Sneak Thieves

The vast majority of theft is so cunning it reminds me of the definition of true sarcasm: a blade so keen the victim doesn't know he's been struck until he turns to walk away and his head falls to the ground. Victims don't know the thief has struck until they discover something missing. I have grudging admiration for the creativity that thieves put into separating people from their belongings, but not enough to reward it. Having learned what to watch for, I'm prepared for them.

The magic cloak of routines we discussed at the beginning of this chapter is excellent protection against standard brands of theft. However, an elite group of thieves has concocted some especially clever ways to take possession of your valuables. When you're in their neighborhood, you can't afford even a short lapse of attention. However, when the simple routines we've discussed become automatic, anxiety disappears.

As you read the examples below, it may be hard to believe they could be real because they're so different from your daily experience. But they are, every single one of them. And there are dozens of variations in all languages. If you read and remember them, they'll remain nothing but amusing anecdotes to which you will add your own.

Scams

The variety of scams is as infinite as the imagination. A few scams have even achieved the status of classics, informally inducted into a Travelers Hall of Fame. Fagin would be proud of his successors. As a neophyte traveler begins to tell the story of what just happened to him, his more experienced listeners exchange wry smiles and nod their heads in recognition after the first few lines. It's like hearing a couple of bars of an old familiar song. Here are some of the scams out there.

People who want to do something for you. A smiling, always smiling, young man appears at your elbow offering to help load your luggage into a taxi, guide you to a hotel, find you a discount, get tickets for you, anything. If he's legitimate, he'll provide a helpful service and earn a small tip. Nothing wrong with that, but if he's not legitimate his offer may not be quite what it appears. A yellow caution light should go on when a stranger offers to help.

The first hustler you meet may be an official in an impressive looking uniform at the airport or the train station. He takes you in hand, guides you through the baggage-collection process and toward a car waiting at the curb. If you get into that car, you're signing up for an expensive ride—and will wind up at an expensive hotel. It has to be to cover his kickback. And, of course, he's no more an official than you are.

You're standing on a street corner in Athens, lost, looking for the Plaka district. Someone comes up and asks if you need help. "Oh, no problem, I'm going that way myself," she says. Somewhere along the way, it's your wallet that gets lost.

"Ten baht, ten baht," cries the smiling *tuk-tuk* driver. He's offering to drive you to three temples for a fare of ten baht (40 cents). What can you lose?—so you hop into his canopied three-wheeler and he chugs off to a nice temple. After seeing that temple, he stops in front of a large gem store, which he begs you to enter "for few minutes only." If you go inside, the store gives him a coupon valid for five liters of petrol plus a commission on anything you buy (which, of course, raises its price to you). As you leave the store, he takes you to another temple. When you come out, he's long gone, crying "ten baht" somewhere else. No big deal. You've gotten more than your ten baht worth.

Then there's the taxi driver who tells you that the Royal Palace, where you just asked him to take you, is closed today. Ever helpful, he offers to take you to the last day of the "Special Gem Exhibition." Guess what, the "special" exhibition runs forever, the taxi driver is hoping for a commission on what you purchase, and the Royal Palace is open.

Selling you something that isn't what it's represented as being. If it were ivory, a rhino horn, an elephant hide (anyone trying to buy any of these deserves to be swindled), gold, or jade, it would be a great buy at the price— a "steal," you might say. You would have done the impossible: outsmarted the local merchant. Of course, if it turns out to be plastic or cowhide, the price is pretty outrageous and your new treasure has zero resale value. How many times have you heard someone say, "If it sounds too good to be true, it probably is?" or "There's no free lunch?" Clichés, yes, and so true.

You can definitely buy satisfying souvenirs in foreign countries at prices far below anything comparable at home, if there were such things at home. You can even buy authentically valuable items at bargain prices. However, if something is represented as handmade, antique, rare, or as having unique value, and those qualities are *not* reflected in the price, STOP! Think "no free lunch!" Make sure the claims are true before you buy. If you can't, recognize the risk.

Let's go back to that gem store and suppose that a beautiful emerald catches your eye. The ever-so-soft-spoken salesperson whispers, "This small stone will be worth three times more in your country. Sell it there and pay for your trip." You smile evasively and think, Oh, sure. . . . But you wonder if it just might be true. With practiced timing, the salesperson goes on, "If you can't sell this stone for at least 100 percent more than you pay here, you can take it to our embassy in your country and they will give you a 50 percent profit. Same day. No questions. Just show them the sales slip." Well, now, you think, if that's true, I could really clean up with a more expensive stone. "How much is that one over there? The big one." To help set the hook, he produces a fancy Certificate of Guarantee. If your yellow caution light isn't glowing brightly by now, you're in big trouble—and not just in this gem store. Do I need to tell you that the embassy will greet you with a stonewall when you state your request for 50 percent profit, even though they've heard the same sad story many times and know you're about to hit the roof? Of course, by the time you're talking to the embassy, you've already found out what the Certificate of Guarantee is worth.

Watch the ball all the way into the basket. After you've made a purchase, keep your eye on it until you leave the store. Let's say you've just bought a piece of batik art. Try not to let it be taken out of your sight to be wrapped. If it is and you can't go with it, inspect the package before you leave the shop or at least the city. It's disheartening to discover a switch when you're thousands of miles away.

Nothing at all for your money. Read the Letters to the Editor columns in a few travel magazines. They're full of laments about goods received that weren't what was ordered and purchases that never arrived. If you're having things made and shipped, such as Indian furniture, Hong Kong suits, or a Tibetan rug, it's not unreasonable for the merchant to ask you to pay in full at the time of purchase. It's not unreasonable for you to decline. Compromise. Advance enough money to cover the merchant's costs. If that won't work, offer to leave the balance at a local bank with directions to release it on receipt of shipping papers. The best deal is to pay the shipper when you pick up the goods. The worst deal is to pay for something that never arrives—because it was never sent. Using a credit card may protect you if nothing arrives. See the credit card section in Chapter 6.

Every item I've taken to a post office myself, and everything I've had a merchant ship via sea freight, has made it home. Of course, two colorful rugs from the Tibetan Refugee Centre in Darjeeling didn't arrive until nine months after I did. On the other hand, I know a fellow who's still waiting for the brass and teak silverware he purchased. Well, it's only been four years.

If the purchase price seems small and you really want an item, why not take a risk? Be as satisfied as you can of the merchant's legitimacy and try to pay a balance on delivery.

Students. You'll meet a lot of students as you travel. They're curious about you and want to practice speaking your language. They may dream of visiting your country and would love to have a contact. They can be engaging and interesting and introduce you to local life. The only thing wrong is that some of them aren't students at all.

What they want from you is the trust engendered by their proclaimed status. After some conversational groundwork, they may ask for money to get them home to see their parents or to support some political refugee project. Perhaps they are reluctantly willing to part with their family's cherished antique opium pipe or sake set or seal ring or whatever. They assert student status to persuade you to drop your defenses, including your common sense. The bottom line: when approached by a self-proclaimed student, be as open as you usually are but be alert.

Can you help me? A smiling young man approaches you on the street and says, "Excuse me, sir. Do you speak English? Will you do me a great favor? At our shop, we have an important document that we have translated into English. Would you be so kind as to tell us whether it is grammatically correct? It will take only a moment." Being a considerate traveler, you agree to help. You are taken to his uncle's store and wind up spending the next hour being shown gems, carpets, or carvings while waiting for the document that may or may not appear. The whole thing is a ruse to get you into the store. Hardly the end of the world, just a little off-putting.

Another approach begins when a pleasant looking middle-aged man asks for help finding his way. He produces a map and asks you to take a look. Get deeply involved in his map and something you own may be taking a trip without you.

Morning price. You are offered a special "morning price" because you are someone's first potential sale of the day. In the past, it was considered good luck for a merchant to break the ice with an early sale, so they'd drop their price to make it. The superstition may be gone but the come-on lingers. No problem, as long as you don't really believe it's either a first sale or a special price just for you.

Times two. Somewhat less amusing is the "times two" hustle. The local vehicle driver (taxi, collectivo, rickshaw, whatever) agreed on a price to take you and your friend to the soccer match. When you arrive, he demands double the price you agreed to, insisting that the price quoted was for one. In your generosity, you may think there was a misunderstanding. There wasn't. To keep discussions like these on an even footing, always remove your gear from the vehicle before commencing the payment ritual. Sometimes it helps to take out paper and pen and ostentatiously take down the driver's license number. Mention the tourist police. Move the discussion off the street and into a store or hotel lobby. Whatever your style in handling matters like this, actually losing your temper could turn bystanders against you.

> Regardless of the circumstances, losing your temper is never a good idea.

Keep perspective. The small amount of money involved does not justify spoiling your day or risking escalation into a serious dispute. I'm not suggesting that you routinely give in; just that you acknowledge that taxi drivers (a) are not representative of the rest of the population, (b) live a pretty hard life, and (c) still don't earn very much. About the best you can do is try to reach clear agreement before you get into the vehicle, then stay calm if a disagreement arises. If you want help, ask a shopkeeper to call a police officer.

Post office. A particularly annoying form of petty theft occurs when a postal clerk accepts your postcards, planning all the while to steam off the uncancelled stamps and turn your postcards into wall decorations. This trick happens all over, but Kathmandu is notorious for it. What to do? Ask that the stamps be hand-canceled. Don't accept a promise; stand there until you see it happen. They know the reason for your request. It's part of the game.

Be reluctant to give a hotel desk clerk money in return for her promise to buy stamps and post your mail. I know better than to create such a temptation, yet recently did just that. Is six months too soon to expect postcards to arrive from Buenos Aires?

Pigeon drop. This threadbare hustle is alive and working around the world. Someone "finds" some money, a watch or anything else of value (in Rio, the favorite is a fat book of lottery tickets) on the street just as you pass by and calls it to your attention. Get ready: the curtain is going up. You are being invited to participate in a masterful performance. Before long, as a condition to sharing in some great benefit, you are asked to put up some "good faith" money. That may sound ridiculous as you read it, but for many people it somehow seems to make sense when the scam is under way. Go along for a while if you want some amusement and can stay in a public place, but be ready to fold the hand fast.

Take my picture, mister? The teenager walks up with a smile, hands his camera to you, then retreats a dozen yards away to stand in front of a tourist attraction. Always a good neighbor, you snap his picture. He not only doesn't come back for his camera, he sprints off into the distance. Puzzled, you turn around—to discover that his accomplice has slipped up behind you and disappeared with your daypack, camera, or whatever you set down to do the favor. After all, you were chosen precisely *because* you were carrying something you'd have to set down. His camera? It's defunct or a $10 cheapo.

I may write an entire book devoted to *Street Scams around the World*. Not only would it help travelers avoid problems, but it would reveal the true creativity of the human mind. As you have experiences you'd like to see in the book, I hope you'll let me know.

Pickpockets

Pickpockets abound the world around. Some are five-thumbed fumblers while others are such proficient artists they can score on anyone. Fortunately for travelers, Fagin's descendants tend to concentrate in predictable places and strike at predictable times. Like the bank robber Willie Sutton, pickpockets go where the money is. Knowing those places and times, you're better prepared to foil their quick hands. For example, travelers not alert for pickpockets in Rio, Tangier, and Saigon would do better to mail their money to a charity and stay home.

In Italy, several cute young girls approached four elderly tourists. The smallest youngster shyly held up a ragged piece of paper covered with drawings she said were hers. The tourists smiled, clucked approvingly, and leaned forward to admire her work. The other cute little girls, also very talented with their hands, busied themselves by picking the pockets and purses of the four art-lovers. Those thefts were not even discovered until the group got back to the hotel. A variation involves a group of kids who run up and start jabbing at you with rolled-up newspapers or sticks. It's a diversion to cover their sneak attack on your valuables.

One spring afternoon, strolling along the Vltava River in Prague, a man in a well-pressed suit with an expensive topcoat draped over his right arm walked up to me. Given his distinguished appearance, I was a little surprised when he said, "Sir, you would like to change money?" He named an exchange rate substantially above the normal black market rate. Since money-changers' rates stay within a fairly tight range, his offer immediately raised my guard. He stepped closer, speaking in a quiet, almost confidential tone. I never felt his right hand, concealed beneath his topcoat, as it slithered into the side pocket of my pants but, because I was expecting his move, I caught his wrist in a tight grip. We stared at one another. When I let go, he slowly backed off then walked briskly away. His gimmick was to distract me by arousing my greed, diverting my attention. Later that same afternoon, I was walking back along the river and spotted the same man standing close to a young woman. I yelled and ran toward them, calling out a warning. The man strode away looking disgusted. I imagine he still patrols the river every afternoon.

Pickpockets seek easy marks. Favorite targets include obvious greenhorns, people wearing or carrying something expensive, and anyone whose attention can be distracted or who's had too much to drink. Here are some examples of where they flourish.

- Walking through the colorful market, you stop in the midst of a jostling crowd to watch the camel auction. Later you start to pay for a carved bone necklace and . . . guess what? When in a crowd, especially when your attention is attracted to things around you, leave valuables behind or in your money belt. If you're carrying your daypack, keep it locked or in front of your body. Instead of carrying your camera or purse hanging off one shoulder, wear the strap diagonally across your chest. Keep your hand on it, not on the strap. If you're wearing a jacket, keep your purse under the jacket.

  A fanny pack extends the same invitation as a dangling purse. Since it's almost impossible to protect, it should never contain your valuables. If you wear a fanny pack, a thief doesn't know what's in it so it may serve as a lure anyway.

  No experienced traveler carries a wallet in an insecure back pants pocket unless it's a decoy to send a pickpocket on his way. A front shirt or pants pocket that can be buttoned, snapped, safety-pinned, or zippered is more secure. A Velcro closure helps but will yield to a determined hand. When I carry my wallet in a front pants pocket, I stick my comb into it or put several rubber bands around it, either of which make it more difficult to pull from the pocket. Whenever you take your wallet out of your pocket, it's vulnerable.

- Every time you pay for something, you show a pickpocket where you keep your money. That gives him a big edge—and gives you another reason to keep most of your cash separate from the money you need immediately. Keep telling yourself: if you put it where they can get it, they will get it.

- Some tourist destinations post a sign that warns tourists to be wary of pickpockets. The result is similar to what happened when Sherlock Holmes used an alarm of fire to trick a lady into revealing where she'd hidden a valuable letter. When she heard the alarm, she promptly ran to save the letter—and he had her. Upon reading the warning sign, most people touch their wallet to be sure it's still there. If it is, both they and the pickpocket now know it. Similarly, when someone shouts "Purse snatcher!" almost everyone will touch his or her valuables. Then the thief's accomplice begins his harvest.

- Taking your belongings becomes child's play, sometimes literally, through skillful use of diversions. Someone "accidentally" bumps you fairly hard, but a bystander is there to keep you from falling. The hands of one or the other are about to lighten your load. A drunk lurches into you, maybe drops a bottle at your feet; a deformed beggar clutches your clothes; a loud noise or a fight attracts the attention of the crowd. In the jostling as the crowd presses forward to see what's happening, wallets find a new home.

  As a group of colorfully dressed teenage girls runs up to several tourists, offering trinkets for sale, one drops her handful of coins to the cobblestones. Responding to her cry of alarm, the tourists obligingly start picking them up. As they help, they're stripped as quickly as if by piranhas.

  Sometimes it's a team effort. A person stands behind a card table on the sidewalk, demonstrating sleight-of-hand tricks. As the crowd watches his hands, the other half of the team, the real expert, explores their pockets.

  What should you do? Protect yourself from being a victim by accepting a very simple premise: a skilled pickpocket can get whatever you keep in your pockets or purse. Your response? Keep in your pockets only what you can afford to lose.

Sneak Thieves

- In many restaurants and bars, you're vulnerable to sneak thieves. You set your camera and daypack on the chair next to you and when you look again, they're gone. Instead, put your stuff on the table in front of you or on your lap. If you put your daypack and camera on the floor, put your foot through the straps. Use the chair next to you only if it's shielded by your body, out of reach of a snatch-and-run thief. If a couple of people sit near to you and begin to argue loudly, watch your gear.

- Many of us enter a semihypnotized state as we enter the fascinating experiences of the day in our journals or share experiences with our friends via postcards. In that stuporous condition, we're as defenseless as a deer on the road staring at oncoming headlights. You needn't abandon your literary efforts. Just tuck your goodies out of sight.

- When you're exchanging a large amount of money, write down the amount you want and show it to the clerk rather than announcing it to listening ears behind you. Put your money securely away before leaving the bank. Cornelia, a German botanist friend, exchanged her marks for Madagascar francs, which she stuffed into her breast pocket as she walked down the steps of the bank. Quick as a trout striking a lure, a guy reached over her shoulder from behind and left her poorer but wiser.

- In Lima, during a very early morning walk to catch a bus to Nazca, Peru, a middle-aged woman approached and pointed to my daypack. I looked over my shoulder and saw a patch of nasty-looking yellow goo on the side of the pack. She produced some toilet paper and offered to help me clean it off. Not wanting to miss the bus, I decided to wait and clean it off at the station. I thanked her and kept going. A block or two farther on, a stocky man caught up with me and pointed. He, too, offered toilet paper. This apparently coincidental profusion of toilet paper registered even on my sluggish early-morning mind. I stepped away from him, just as several young men emerged from the shadows and converged on me. As they neared, I bolted for a nearby church. They followed me inside but stopped short of the front pew where I was surrounded by people attending Mass. After a few minutes, the men drifted away to play their tricks elsewhere.

  I mention this experience as an example of diversion. The goo had been lathered on my pack by someone who was trying to get me to stop, take the daypack off my back, perhaps even hand it to the Good Samaritan to clean. Within seconds the wolves would have swooped down and that pack would have had a new owner. This particular trick and its sophisticated variations are on their way to achieving classic status around the world. A couple of years after it happened to me in Lima, local thugs, armed with mustard or ketchup, began using it at Kennedy Airport against Japanese tourists.

- Sneak thieves love trains. An old woman in an alpaca shawl stands outside your window offering a carved stone replica of an Inca figure. As soon as she has your attention, her accomplice runs down the aisle and scoops up your camera. Between cars, she tosses it to a buddy. From then on, you'll be buying picture postcards. You can prevent it so easily by knowing what to expect. You'll know you're a seasoned traveler if, when a distraction occurs to your right, you look first to your left.

- By the way, a sneak thief may have his eye on your carry-on luggage (especially that notebook computer). Be wary as you pass through the electronic security gate. If held up, don't be distracted. Watch your gear that has already passed through the x-ray machine.

The long list above may seem pretty complete—but it's not. As you travel, you'll come across variations or even something new. I hope you'll share them with me so I can pass them on to other travelers.

Muggers

Although theft encountered by tourists is almost always nonviolent, there are a few places in which theft by force is not uncommon. I'm thinking of Maputo (Mozambique), Kinshasa (Congo), Tangier, Lima, Bogotá, some beaches in Spain and, increasingly, Rio de Janeiro. Even in those places, I consider the risk low enough that I won't skip them—but I am extra careful.

How to Avoid the Problem

As always, preparation and common sense are your greatest protection. If you're new in town, ask the manager of your hotel about areas to avoid, or times of day when there might be increased risk. Don't make yourself a target by having too much to drink too far from your hotel, wearing an expensive watch or ring, flashing wads of cash, or hanging around where people make you feel creepy. Pay attention to your intuition. Don't walk down dark streets. Take a taxi if you feel uncomfortable.

Don't act bewildered or lost. In other words, don't behave like a first-day tourist. Any mugger is going to choose the easiest- and wealthiest-looking target, and that's not the person striding along with an air of confidence or the person drinking his nightcap at the hotel.

If you feel someone walking toward you looks suspicious, walk in another direction. Walk in the center of the sidewalk, away from alleyways and parked vehicles.

If a male traveler decides to woo a local woman he's met in a bar, he'd be wise to keep an eye on his drinks (among other things). Otherwise he may meet some new friends on the way home.

A recent study indicated that the chances of being mugged are reduced by 70 percent just by walking with one other person; by 90 percent if with two people. Makes sense to me.

How to React

If you're walking in a high-risk zone and are approached by someone seeking something (the time or whatever), step away and casually go to "yellow alert." That's a sad commentary on human relations, but a good way to avoid a problem.

Decide how you'll respond if confronted by someone who looks as if he's armed and/or willing to use force. Stay as calm as you can. Try to make the other person relax a little. Act self-possessed, but don't argue or show anger. Cooperate and disengage as quickly as possible. The idea is to escape without violence. Depending on the situation, it may be best to drop or throw your wallet or jewelry or whatever on the ground, then back away. If he stoops to pick it up, be ready to flee.

I've heard a suggestion to carry a second, or dummy, wallet with just a few dollars in it to surrender to a mugger. That may be a way to protect another wallet loaded with cash, but you shouldn't have that kind of money in a wallet anyway. Even if you did, would you want to risk your life to protect it?

If an assailant demands that you come with him, it's only to give him greater advantage. Do not go with him. Pretend you don't understand. Act like you think he's joking. If that doesn't work, yell, throw your wallet, and run in the opposite direction.

If you feel you must fight, use every weapon you have: keys spread between your knuckles, a pen, or a bottle; even a daypack loaded with books swings a lot of weight. Fight all out! Yell for help as loudly as you can. Shout "Fire!" Bite, pull, try to break a finger, go for the genitals (a grip is better than a knee). Act like you've gone crazy.

There are very few places where someone will threaten a traveler's personal safety unless the traveler

- takes foolish risks
- gets involved with people of a type he would avoid at home
- uses drugs or alcohol to excess in public
- doesn't do his basic research and puts himself in places he should have avoided
- loses his temper and provokes a confrontation
- values his possessions too highly, protecting them by risking his safety
- behaves in ways inappropriate to the culture.

Hotel Security

You can learn a lot about hotel security before you ever walk through the door. Hotels that have earned reputations for poor security are sometimes noted in the guidebooks. Ask other travelers about the hotel you're considering. Notice whether there are people hanging out in front of the hotel who you wouldn't want to pass after dark. A shabby lobby may be a clue that the owners make their money less by pleasing guests than by ripping them off.

Ask other travelers about a hotel's security.

While checking in, keep in touch with your gear. When you go to look at a room, take your bag along unless you're confident there's no risk in leaving it untended.

Since the hotel staff and other guests will see the register after you sign in, a woman may be well advised to use initials.

Don't let anyone see your valuables as you check in.

An ordinary door lock is almost worthless for security purposes. What television bad guys do to locked doors with a credit card also happens in real life. Even if it bars the general public, the lock on your door won't keep the hotel staff out. One security expert estimates that 85 percent of hotel room theft is committed by dishonest hotel employees. Besides, who knows how many room keys are floating around in the hands of former staff, or former guests for that matter?

If someone knocks on the door claiming to be a hotel employee, call the desk to confirm if you have the slightest reason to be concerned.

I assume that someone will be in my room while I'm out and that I can't outsmart anyone but a thief-in-training by hiding my valuables in some cranny. Therefore, I lock in my pack anything I'd rather not lose. When I have reason for concern, I lock the pack itself to something secure. Fortunately, most hotel staff members, baggage handlers, bus drivers, and the like don't have lock-picking skills. Even a tiny lock requires forcible entry, which you can spot immediately, and many people won't steal when they think you'll notice right away that you've been ripped off. Locks also communicate that you're not a goose passively waiting to be plucked.

> Assume someone will be in your room while you are out and prepare accordingly.

For effective security in a hotel room, you need a dead bolt or a chain-and-slide bolt. Even a hasp on which you can use a padlock will work. The Portabolt door lock (800-999-3030; $19.95) attaches easily between any door and its frame to provide security similar to a dead bolt.

Some travelers carry Travel Guard, a battery-operated alarm about the size of a pager that combines a detachable flashlight and alarm clock with a smoke detector and vibration sensor ($50 from Immcon; 800-829-5044). If the door moves while Travel Guard is hanging on a doorknob, an 85-decibel alarm goes off. When you pull a pin out of the Companion Personal Alarm (also from Immcon), a 110-decibel siren sounds.

Radio Shack sells a combination personal alarm/motion detector that has a built-in flashlight ($14.95). Safety Zone (800-999-3030) offers a wide variety of travel safety items. If you prefer low-tech, jam a simple plastic wedge under the door or brace a chair under the handle. If there's no way of securing the door, change rooms or hotels unless the circumstances convince you there is no risk at all.

A thief doesn't always politely enter a room from the hallway, so don't build a Maginot Line at the door only to forget the windows and balcony door. Can the windows be locked? Are there bars on them? Could anyone get into your room by climbing through the window? If an arm can reach through the bars, keep your gear well out of reach. Lock the windows when you leave. If the hotel rises higher than two stories, a room on the third to the sixth floor at least puts you above outside-entry thieves with a fear of heights.

Hotel smoke detectors are almost nonexistent in many parts of the world. If that concerns you, consider the Traveler Portable Smoke Detector, a palm-sized detector that emits an 85-decibel alarm (call 800-962-4943; $24.50). If you leave the key in the lock when you go to sleep, you won't have to search for it if there's a fire. If you hear a fire alarm, touch the door knob. If it's hot, call the desk or see if you can escape out the window. If trapped in your room, use a wet towel to block the space under the door, shut off fans or air conditioners, and try to signal from the window. If the knob is cool, take your money belt, lock the door behind you (if you recall the little boy who cried "Wolf!" you know there's not always fire where there's an alarm), and head for the fire exit. Don't try to use an elevator to escape from a fire. If there's smoke, crawl under it.

If there's a Do Not Disturb sign in the room, I may hang it on the door knob when I go out to mislead anyone wandering the hallway. I usually don't leave my room key with the desk clerk when I leave for the day. That won't keep the staff out of my room, but it does keep the presence of my key in the box from advertising to others that I'm away. It also keeps passersby from reaching across the counter and snatching the key in the clerk's absence. Key control is often a joke.

Make sure the safe truly is.

What about leaving your valuables in the hotel safe as you start on a ten-day trek in the tropical heat? Good idea, except that not everything called a safe is what you think of as a safe. Be sure the safe is someplace secure to which only the owner or manager has access. Otherwise, the "safe" might turn out to be a desk drawer or a space under the cash register drawer.

An Englishwoman in Zanzibar gave all her money to the obliging desk clerk to put in the hotel safe. When the day came to catch a boat back to the mainland, she went to reclaim her money. The clerk denied having received anything from her. The manager shrugged his shoulders. That's when she realized she had no receipt.

Present your valuables in a sealed envelope with your name written across the flap. A reliable safe-keeping operation should have a printed receipt form. If your hotel doesn't, get a written receipt from the manager or owner. If they try to evade giving you one, don't leave your valuables. Think twice about staying in the place at all.

Suppose you want to leave your bag behind while you take a trek through the rain forest or a side trip to the beach. Leave it with the hotel manager if you can, with instructions to release it only to you. Ask for a receipt. Find out if it will be locked up, rather than left behind the front desk day and night. Even in a storage room, I lock my bag to something with my bike chain lock. Since your belongings will be stored with those of other travelers, it's not impossible that something of yours might be picked up by someone else if it's not secured. When you return, check the contents. When the hotel staff sees that you are treating security of your bag seriously, they'll be more inclined to do so as well.

Being anxious about safety and security would be a waste of time and detract from the pleasure of your trip. Instead, don your magic cloak. The routines become automatic. I've never lost a single item to a thief as I've traveled and I believe most knowledgeable travelers can say the same.

LOSING YOUR VALUABLES

Lost Airline Ticket

Treat an airline ticket as carefully as if it were cash. If it leaves your possession unexpectedly, call or go to the nearest office of the issuing airline and submit a Lost Ticket Application. This process will be much easier if you know the ticket number, flight numbers and dates, and the amount of the fare. Since few of us memorize this stuff, it helps to have a copy of the ticket along. It will cost you time and money if you have to call home to your travel agent to get this information.

One U.S. airline states clearly on its ticket that it will give no refund for a lost ticket. Others charge a fee of $50 to determine whether your ticket has been used. If it has, you get nothing. If it hasn't, the ticket may be reinstated or you may get a credit for the price, minus the search fee, against the price of a ticket for some future flight. However, you may be asked to sign a form agreeing to pay for the replacement ticket if someone uses the lost original. The message here is to act fast before someone can use or exchange the stolen ticket. At best, airlines typically wait 90 days or more before issuing a refund.

If you lose your ticket while overseas, you'll probably have to buy a new ticket for the rest of your route. That would be very bad news because you would lose whatever discount you got on the original ticket (e.g., APEX, round trip).

To avoid the whole problem, keep that ticket safe in your money belt and keep a copy stashed somewhere else. Actually, the possibility of the loss is another reason to buy plane tickets as you go. You can't lose what you're not carrying.

Lost Credit Card/ATM Card

If a credit card disappears, call immediately to cancel it. The telephone numbers when calling from overseas are as follows: American Express (919) 668-5271; MasterCard (314) 275-6690; Visa (410) 581-9994; and Discover (801) 568-0205. When a card is stolen, report it to the police and get a copy of the report. If fraudulent charges show up on your bill later, you must notify the card issuer in writing within 60 days of receiving the bill to limit your loss to $50.

If your ATM card disappears, notify the issuing bank and get a new card. You are only liable for up to $50 for fraudulent use of your card if you report the loss within two days. Some banks will hold you liable for as much as $500 after that.

Lost Passport

According to *Money* magazine, only 3 out of every 1,000 travelers have their passports stolen. That doesn't count the ones who lose them in other creative ways. How to prevent it? Keep your passport in your money belt when it's not in use. If you have to let it out of your possession, such as when turning it over to a hotel clerk to register with the police, get a receipt. Never leave town without checking that you've tucked it safely away.

Since having a copy of the first two pages of the lost passport greatly speeds replacement, make three copies of the first two pages of your passport before leaving home. Put one in your money belt, put one in your luggage, and leave one with someone who can fax it to you.

If you lose your passport, get a police report and take it, along with four two-by-two-inch photographs, to your embassy or consulate. They will require a copy of your birth certificate. If you haven't brought it along but have left a copy with someone who can fax it you, you're in great shape. If you overlooked that detail, they may accept an affidavit from someone else (who must be able to prove their own American citizenship) vouching for your citizenship. The replacement passport will be good for only one year, but when you arrive home, you can trade it in for a new permanent passport.

Make copies of your passport to facilitate replacing it.

Lost Luggage

A traveler can lose luggage anywhere, but it's at the airport where we most often put it out of our sight and control, trusting that it will rejoin us thousands of miles away. And that's a reasonable expectation since, according to the National Institute for Aviation Research, only 1 out of every 200 bags checked with major U.S. airlines is reported lost. Whether you consider those odds acceptable may depend on whether you've ever been the "one."

Rather than focusing on ways to be reunited with your luggage after it's lost, follow a routine to keep it from getting away in the first place. Whether you're traveling by plane, train, or bus, check in well ahead of departure time, make sure your bag is marked for the correct destination, and remove any old destination tags. Take off the shoulder strap and zip away the backpack harness so the bag won't get hung up in baggage-moving mechanisms. Watch it as far as you can to ensure it is put on the right vehicle.

If you take a bag aboard a plane and there's no room for it, don't just hand it over to an attendant. Take out any valuables, then get a claim check for it. Be ready to collect it promptly at your destination.

Suppose it's not there. First in frustration and then with mounting concern, you search for it as other passengers drift away. Check the lobby area and baggage storage room in case your bag arrived before you did. If it's not there, fill in a form describing the bag and its contents. Put the form and a copy of your ticket and baggage claim check in the hands of the most senior person you can find. Get that person's name and keep a copy of the form. If you give up your claim check, get a receipt.

Tell them that your name and address are on a luggage tag securely attached to your bag and that your itinerary is inside. Let them know where to reach you while you're waiting for the bag and where to deliver it when they find it. Motivate the carrier to find that bag.

If the delay is more than a few hours, they should reimburse you for reasonable expenses, such as basic clothing and toiletries. If the carrier's representative doesn't offer to do so, ask for authorization before making purchases, but do so in a courteous tone that takes it for granted. Keep receipts as a basis for reimbursement. If the lost bag delays your onward progress, ask the carrier to pay for a hotel. After you leave the terminal, call with regular inquiries.

It's reasonable to think that if a carrier lost your bag and couldn't find it, they'd pay for it and its contents. Reasonable, yes; reality, no. Under regulations which the airlines were active in drafting, their liability to you is very limited. The maximum reimbursement is $1,250 (which may soon be raised to $1,850) on a domestic flight and $9.07 per pound for checked luggage ($400 for unchecked luggage) on an international flight. In practice, rather than record the weight of each bag, international airlines assume the maximum (30 kilos) and consider the limit of liability to be $640.

The airlines reimburse you on the basis of the *depreciated* value of your luggage and its contents, not replacement value (what it will cost you to replace what they lost). Then they unfurl a list of items excluded from coverage altogether: currency, cameras, camcorders, expensive jewelry, medication, and similar items. If that would be a problem, ask the airline in advance about Excess Valuation Insurance. The cost is from $1 to $2 per $100 of coverage up to $5,000. Note that these policies may exclude something you want to cover: breakables, antiques, musical instruments, art, and computers.

Your household insurance or personal effects policy may cover whatever loss is not covered by the airline's insurance. Further, that reimbursement may be based on replacement value, which is in your favor. See Travel and Health Insurance in Chapter 5.

Even when it's clear a bag has departed for luggage heaven, the airline may still take three to twelve weeks to reimburse you. In other words, carry your valuables in your money belt, your camera in your daypack, and nothing irreplaceable in your luggage.

14

Woman on Her Own

> All travel is a quest, conscious or
> unconscious searching for something
> that is lacking in our lives or ourselves.
> — Freya Stark

Who hasn't heard of a woman who was pinched on a bus in Rome or hassled in Morocco by some creep who just wouldn't get the picture? Fear of sexual harassment deters too many women from traveling on their own. It's a fear with some basis, but it shouldn't, in the opinion of many women travelers, keep anyone at home.

Thousands of women travel independently, and successfully, every year. Most travel in groups of two or three, but a great many travel solo. Since knowledge routs paranoia and controls risk, this chapter will discuss what a woman alone or with other women can expect and how she can minimize or eliminate potential problems.

Many women praise the benefits of traveling alone, most of which are the same as those treasured by any independent traveler. However, one benefit is unique. It's easy for a woman on her own to escape stereotypical male-female roles, including standard divisions of responsibilities. Responsible for coping, her self-confidence grows. The ways in which she interacts with people, locals as well as other travelers, are different from when she's in the company of a man.

The most common problem a woman may have to deal with is the hassle of low-grade sexual harassment. It doesn't happen everywhere, but there are certain countries in which a woman should be prepared for being hassled by local males. The hassling may consist of a suggestive comment, a call, a whistle, a touch, or more aggressive intimidation—anything to test the woman's interest. This problem seems most persistent in certain countries where there's a strong religious presence—places such as Spain, Morocco,

Italy, Sicily, Greece, Egypt, Turkey, Saudi Arabia, Oman, Yemen, Pakistan, and Mexico.

There seems to be a relationship between offensive male behavior and generally repressed, unrealistic attitudes about relationships with women. In some countries, men are raised with the idea that women are subordinate; women are expected to bend to the male will. Trash television has further shaped male attitudes about Western women, especially when they see foreign women act in ways that would result in anything from ostracism to stoning in their own society. Soap operas don't do female travelers any favors. With this background, some men feel it's their right to make advances, and they expect them to be welcomed. These attitudes are diminishing, but they're not gone yet.

And what of concerns of bodily harm? Statistics show that rape is far more common in industrialized nations, such as the United States, than in underdeveloped countries. Unfortunately, that's a little misleading. A female traveler is more visible than local women on whom the statistics are based, and she's likely to be penalized by attitudes of local men toward Western women. Further, when a woman is in an unfamiliar culture, she may be unaware of behavior that might be taken as provocative by local males. She's also likely to be less knowledgeable about dangerous areas she should avoid.

HOW TO TRAVEL SAFELY

A woman who hasn't traveled alone may ask, "Will I be safe?" The answer is "Yes!" or at least, "Yes, if . . ." Women travelers are not obliged to free men from their cultural ruts, but there are many things a woman can do to insulate herself from unwanted attention. Here are some suggestions, many from women who have traveled alone.

- Observe how local women dress and try to follow that pattern. In cultures that retain old traditions, a local woman covers most of her body with clothing and tends to stay out of public view. In that context, a female traveler who wears tight shorts and a provocative T-shirt will quickly become conscious of the effect she's having, attracting some observers and offending others. Loose-fitting clothing that covers arms and legs is usually appropriate. It's easy to copy local customs, even without wearing local-style clothes.
- Minimize eye contact with men. If a friendly smile can be misinterpreted, a wink can start a war. Dark sunglasses are an excellent way to avoid eye contact.
- Common courtesies such as thanking a man for opening a door for you can lead to being followed. An impassive nod may have to be sufficient.

- Pay your own way so that neither of you feels that one of you is indebted.
- Drinking alcohol or smoking cigarettes in public may be considered provocative. It's not a question of right or wrong; it's a case of "When in Rome . . ."
- Many women elect to hook up with other women travelers when passing through a zone of possible annoyance. Others ask a male to accompany them for a while, being up front about the reason. A little hand-holding in public goes a long way. A show of a relationship discourages unwelcome attention, even more so abroad than at home. Even an imaginary boyfriend or husband who is "on his way over" can help.
- Don't let a strange man touch you, except during a handshake or when giving help you've requested. Even an apparently neutral touch may be a way of testing your limits. In Europe, among other places, a man may take advantage of a crowded place to press against a woman in an offensive way. The consensus is that she should raise hell, pushing him away with a shout. At the same time, be prepared to accept being squashed in a crowd as part of travel.
- If a man forces his attentions on you, don't just shake your head, smile, or say "No, thank you." Rather than behaving in an apologetic way, respond immediately and directly, saying "No!" or "Stop!" loudly and firmly, preferably in the local language since you may not be understood in English. Frown fiercely and let bystanders know there's a problem, calling on them for help if necessary. Your plea should be addressed to one person (another woman is best) rather than to the crowd. Tears help to engage bystanders. Being firm and determined is better than being rough or violent.
- In a new town, ask the desk clerk, manager, or owner of your lodging to identify parts of town to avoid. Ask for suggestions of restaurants where a woman traveler will feel comfortable. At the same time, be cautious not to let a male member of the hotel staff think you are flirting.
- In restaurants, reading a book or writing in a journal helps discourage men from approaching.
- Keep your hotel room door locked. Otherwise, in some places, staff people with legitimate business walk right in. Be alert when a male member of the hotel staff enters your hotel room. Stand up. Let your body language show that you're on guard. Watch him. If a problem develops, call the front desk. If there's no phone, step into the hall and shout for help. Don't admit anyone until you're satisfied about who they are.

- Don't accept gifts from strangers. That sounds obvious, but some offers may be superficially appealing, such as taking you snorkeling, hiking, surfing, or on some other attractive local adventure.

  After two years in the Peace Corps in East Africa, Luanna met a young local man at a restaurant in a beach resort and accepted his offer to spend the day with him on his sailing dhow. She was cautious enough to insist that they not go alone. "No problem," he said. "My mother lives in a village just down the coast. We'll sail down and pick her up." No village. No mother. Bad trip! If you feel a need for a chaperone, start the trip with one. Don't be lured beyond the range of help.
- On trains, try to find a compartment occupied by a family or by several women.
- On buses, sit next to a woman rather than a man.
- Beaches tend to attract men who may become a problem.
- If something in the environment is making you feel uncomfortable, hire a taxi instead of walking.
- Some women travel with a fake wedding ring. If a conversation becomes overly personal, they refer to an imaginary husband, perhaps producing a photograph to back up the story. Note that wearing an expensive-looking ring could present temptation of a different kind.
- If a situation is becoming uncomfortable, mention that you have a specific communicable venereal disease.
- I've yet to meet anyone who has used Mace, but it may offer a feeling of security in an extreme situation.
- Don't be drawn into discussion of controversial topics, especially male/female relations.
- Be wary of any local lothario who prowls around tourist attractions. He's experienced in approaching foreign women and has had plenty of opportunities to develop his "line." He may say he wants a chance to practice his English, or he may pretend to be a guide—anything to get you into a conversation. If you don't want his attention, don't answer even the first question.
- Study self-defense before leaving home. The self-confidence you project as a result of this training sends a signal to many who might otherwise approach you.

Resources

As a starting point for learning the extent to which females may be hassled in any country, consult a guidebook and ask other travelers. *Women Travel: Adventures, Advice, and Experience*, edited by Miranda Davies and Natania Jansz, discusses comparative levels of potential sexual harassment in 70 countries. One of Thalia Zepatos' objectives in writing *A Journey of One's Own: Uncommon Advice for the Independent Woman Traveler* was to help women feel more confident about traveling on their own.

Other useful resources for women travelers include *Travelin' Woman*, a monthly newsletter intended to help prepare women to travel (call 800-871-6409); a newsletter called *Solo Travel International* (602-748-2092); *The Independent Woman's Guide to Europe* by Linda White; and *Traveler's Guide to Asian Customs and Manners* by Kevin Chambers. Look for *Women & Travel* at www.globecorner.com. American Express publishes a free guide entitled *Travel Smart for Women* (Women's Travel Booklet, American Express, 200 Vesey Street, New York, NY 10285).

The Bibliography contains many books by and about woman travelers.

Women's Wire, which commenced operation in 1994, is the first interactive computer network devoted to women's issues. In addition to a travel-related database and the opportunity to ask questions and exchange travel tips online, Women's Wire lists women interested in travel. Fifteen dollars a month entitles the subscriber to two hours online. Rates start at $2.50 per hour for usage beyond that. Call (415) 615-8989.

If a woman chooses not to be offended by stares, whistles, and comments in a few places, she can keep that part of her trip from being spoiled. It's a shame anyone should have to alter their behavior because of someone else's offensive actions, but a little caution prevents many problems. A few women travelers I know recall the exasperation and anger they felt at being made the center of attention when they wanted to be left alone. The majority, however, have felt safe and relaxed throughout their journeys.

15

Language

> The treachery of the phrase book . . . is that you
> cannot begin to follow the answer to the question
> you've pronounced so beautifully—and worse still,
> your auditor now assumes you're fluent in Swahili.
> — Pico Iyer

The Peugot taxi dropped me off in front of a new, but already shabby, shopping mall somewhere near the center of Gaborone, capital of Botswana. I looked around for the only hotel in town listed in the guidebook as charging less than 65 pula, about $40, per night (I like the fact that the name of the currency in Botswana, which is 85 percent desert, is also the word for "water"). No hotel in sight. Despite knowing how to say almost nothing in the Setswana language, I knew it was time to ask for help.

Using my phrase book and exchanging gestures with a helpful soldier, I deduced that the hotel I was looking for had been torn down to make room for the shopping mall. The soldier pointed vigorously down the road. Always hopeful, I decided that he might be indicating another hotel. Of course, he was also pointing toward South Africa. There being no public transportation in sight and no other source of information, I swung my pack onto my back and started down the road.

Twenty minutes later, I arrived at a sleazy roadhouse. That the "DISCO" sign dwarfed the "Rooms 70 pula" sign communicated the management's priorities. After some spirited sign language to convey the thought that I was more interested at the moment in sleeping than dancing the night away, and wasn't looking for a companion, I was taken to a room modeled after a Devil's Island original. I figured the mosquito coils and the aerosol bug spray cans in the room would probably be useful since the cow standing outside the window had pushed her head into the room through the screen. Nevertheless, I had overcome a language barrier.

HOW TO OVERCOME A LANGUAGE BARRIER

Many people worry, and I was one of them, about the so-called language barrier. As it turns out, there's no reason to be intimidated. Not being able to speak a local language causes difficulties, but nothing insurmountable. Learning to pronounce 20 to 100 words of vocabulary will get you through anywhere. Even a dozen words, an expressive face, and two hands go a long way. Okay, you could probably get along with nothing but English and your arms in a strait jacket.

In vast reaches of the world, you'll encounter English, Spanish, French, or Arabic. Even in Africa, with its multitude of local languages and dialects, you can communicate most places using one or another of those four languages, maybe adding a few words of Swahili. Given the limited language skills of many First World travelers, it's fortunate that the English planted their flag as widely as they did a few centuries ago. Since English is spoken in varying degrees around the world, at least for a few meters on either side of the tourist trails, you can often get by without learning anything else. But why do that? In return for a little effort, you make more friends and fewer mistakes. The first step is to overcome the embarrassment of stumbling in a language strange to your ears.

People like to hear you speaking their language. At least as important, you feel a part of the country and a sense of accomplishment when you master some of the basics of the language (well, "master" may be overstating it a bit).

No one need have language-related apprehension about traveling in Europe. If you studied a European language, no matter how long ago, you remember more than you think; at least your eyes will, if not your tongue. In metropolitan areas there may be a bit of a language gap in some budget hotels, restaurants, and taxis, but nothing troublesome. If you need help, drop into an upscale hotel. You encounter plenty of people who speak English when you need it. Even in the countryside, local folks who don't speak English have seen enough foreigners to know what their needs are. Picture a non-English-speaking person entering a restaurant in your country. One way or another, he or she would be served something pleasing. So will you.

People like to hear you speak their language.

How to Learn

If you're out of school, how do you get started learning a new language? Simple: join a regular class, enroll in a school language lab, or hire a tutor. Take yourself to study in places as pleasant as Paris, Madrid, Antigua (Guatemala), or San Miguel de Allende (Mexico). Check out international travel-study programs through the American Institute for Foreign Study (203-869-9090), explore immersion classes in the United States at the Language Schools (802-388-3711), or gather information from the National Registration Center for Study Abroad on schools abroad offering language classes (414-278-0631).

Teach yourself using one of the series of good language books I mentioned in Chapter 2. The Passport Books *Just Enough Series* is one of the best. Small dictionaries are good. Take a look at the very useful *BBC Phrase Books* (also Passport Books) that include built-in dictionaries. The better guidebooks include a section of basic vocabulary and phrases. Laminated cards (four-by-eight inches) provide frequently used words and phrases in a handy, practically weightless form. Don't forget handheld electronic translators. Besides being helpful, they endlessly entertain bystanders.

Dorrance Publishing Company (643 Smithfield Street, Pittsburgh, PA 15222; 800-788-7654) publishes the *Traveler's Pictorial Communication Guide* ($6.95) based on the principle of, as they put it, "One picture is worth ten thousand words." This book is packed with illustrations of clothing, menu items, lodging, transport, various services (e.g., barbers, medical help), and many other aspects of daily life. You point to the picture—and the idea gets across. *The Wordless Travel Book* (Ten Speed Press, 1996, $4.95) and a book titled *Point It* work the same way: just flip open the book, point at an icon—and you're communicating.

For a language in which pronunciation is difficult, reading alone may not be adequate. Hear the language spoken on cassettes, records, or videotapes. Let your computer help through CD-ROMs and foreign language software. Here are some of the better choices: Berlitz Think 'n' Talk (about $200), Learn to Speak 4.0 (about $180), PictureIt! (About $70), The Rosetta Stone (about $400), and Video Linguist (about $100).

It's easy to learn basic words by listening to daily conversation, pointing to things, and asking questions. Pronouncing words as you would in your own language may not be correct in another language. Listen carefully to how local people say things. If you use the same pronunciation, they'll have some meaning. Otherwise, you'll earn some blank looks.

Connect conversation with actions. Learn more than the basic five or ten words that most travelers learn. As soon as you enter a new country, make a list of useful words, the words of daily commerce. Practice that new vocabulary out loud without letting fear of mistakes slow you down. Don't get hung up on verb tenses.

What to Learn First

Here are some key words and phrases that every traveler needs to know. Rather than fumbling through a phrase book, write down or memorize these appropriate words and phrases.

- greetings and expressions of courtesy such as hello, good day, good-bye, please, thank you, pardon me, "my name is . . . ," and "what is your name?"

- yes and no
- directions (few phrases are as useful as "where is . . .")
- toilet (if you ask for the washroom, bathroom, rest room, or little boy's or girl's room, you may mystify the listener)
- food-related words (including, "May I have the bill, please?")
- lodging-related words ("Do you have a room with two beds?")
- transport words (including airport, bus station, train station, subway station, and gasoline)
- phrases for bargaining in the marketplace ("How much is . . ." and "That's too much.")
- personal pronouns
- numbers
- time of day
- the verbs "to be," "to have," and "to go," when combined with personal pronouns (I am, he is, etc.)
- pleas for help such as "I don't understand," "Please speak more slowly," "Stop!" "Help!" "Go away!" and "I need a doctor."

There are some sure tests to show whether you've become operational in a language. If the bus to your destination is leaving a busy station in ten minutes and you can buy a ticket and find the bus in time, you're a linguist. When you can make small jokes in a language, you're a linguist.

WHERE TO GET INFORMATION AND ASSISTANCE

If your trusty phrase book fails you, it's a setback, nothing more. It merely means it's time to get some help. That's easy if you know where to look.

- Look for young people, on the theory they might be students studying English.
- Expensive or Western clothing suggests that a person may be well educated or in business, either of which may mean some training in English.
- Many countries have excellent tourist information centers whose addresses are listed in good guidebooks. In most countries, someone on the staff speaks a little English.
- Talk with local travel agents to find out what's going on in the area and transportation options. Let them know what you want and ask for suggestions. It seems as if "for only $5 . . ." someone's cousin's son is always willing to give you a lift up to Portillo* the next morning.
- Your embassy or consulate can help. A considerate staff person in the

---

* *Portillo.* North of Santiago, Chile, Portillo offers the best skiing in South America.

English is not always the easiest language. Chiang Mai, Thailand.

Citizens Service Section of a consulate may give you useful information on a person-to-person basis.

- Drop into the local office of the United States Information Service (USIS), the overseas network of the USIA. The typical USIS office has travel advisories, summaries of international news, and a great library. The air-conditioned libraries of various USIS offices are fine sanctuaries from tropical heat.

- The staff at your hotel can provide helpful information, especially if you develop a friendly relationship with them. They can direct you to banks, shops, doctors, tourist attractions, and restaurants, or find you a cab, opera tickets, a boat for your snorkeling trip, or even a mountain guide. They can tell you fair prices for local transport, popular types of clothing, and almost anything else. Of course, price information should be taken with a grain of salt since it may be biased toward the home team. If your own hotel can't help, try an upscale or chain hotel. Either the staff will be able to communicate in your language or there will be a travel agent in-house who can.

- Draw on other travelers. When you meet someone who has recently visited a coming stop on your itinerary, ask about accommodations, restaurants, transport, exchange rates, everything. The guidebook I use in Indonesia highly recommended a small hotel on the island of Ternate. That's where I planned to stay until I talked with a Dane who had stayed there a week earlier. He said the hotel was as nice as the guidebook said, except that it was crawling with bedbugs. I was pleased to avoid learning that the hard way. A couple I met in Chobe National Park in northern Botswana was so enthusiastic about mighty sand dune formations deep in the Namib Desert in Namibia that I drove eight hours out of my way to find them. Not only was the drive through spectacular scenery but the couple had understated the beauty of the dunes.

The corollary to seeking assistance from others is that you should take time to give information to others. It's one of the karmic laws of traveling.

WHEN SPEAKING ENGLISH

Speaking English in countries in which it's not the primary language has made me more aware of its complex and confusing structure. If your local vocabulary isn't getting the job done and you need to try English, tailor it to the situation.

- It's not condescending to use short words when speaking English to someone for whom it is a second or third language. Pronounce words clearly and speak in short sentences. Make one point at a time. Gentle repetition is fine.
- Speak slowly but not so deliberately that it sounds patronizing. Speaking rapidly makes anyone hard to understand.
- If phrasing a sentence one way doesn't work, try it a different way.
- Use expressions in your language that are similar to ones used in the local language.
- Use plenty of gestures.
- Contractions, slang, idioms, jargon, and abbreviations don't translate well.
- Watch the listener's eyes to see if he or she is following what you're saying. Ask whether you are being understood.
- Avoid raising your voice as if speaking to a child who is hard-of-hearing, and avoid mimicking the accent of local people speaking English.
- Be polite and patient and take responsibility for your own shortcomings in speaking the local language.

HOW TO ASK QUESTIONS

When language is a problem, a traveler must learn the art of asking questions in ways that elicit helpful answers. Otherwise good-hearted people are likely to give you an answer intended to please you, even if they have to guess what that might be.

Approach with a smile. Hold your hands in sight, and let your body language convey a peaceful, friendly intent. Don't be aloof or demanding. If all this sounds obvious, remember that the other person may be smaller than you and uncertain of what to expect.

Begin a question by saying "Good day" or "Pardon me" rather than impolitely intruding with your desire to get an answer.

If you have no language in common, think of yourself as a preacher who has lost his tongue or a writer whose commandment is "show, don't tell." Use your hands, paper and pen, even the dust at your feet. *Perform* your question. Build a picture of what you want.

When Translation Isn't

As a reminder of the significance of nuance, here are a few of the many signs, apparently in English, that may make you smile as you travel.

- "Because of the impropriety of entertaining guests of the opposite sex in the bedroom, it is suggested that the lobby be used for this purpose." (Zurich hotel)
- "Ladies are requested not to have children in the bar." (Norwegian cocktail lounge)
- "Please leave your values at the front desk." (Paris hotel)
- "Please take advantage of the chambermaid." (Japanese hotel)
- "Our wines leave you nothing to hope for." (Swiss restaurant)
- "The manager has personally passed all the water served here." (Acapulco hotel)
- "If this is your first visit to the USSR, you are welcome to it."
- "Welcome! Don't enter!" (In Taiwan)
- "Specialist in women and other diseases." (Rome doctor)
- "Fur coats made for ladies from their own skin." (Swedish furrier)
- "Is forbidden to steal hotel towels please. If you are not a person to do such thing is easier not to read notis. Please do bathe inside the tub." (Tokyo hotel)
- "Drop your trousers here for the best results." (Bangkok laundry)
- "Ladies, leave your clothes here and spend the afternoon having a good time." (Rome laundry)
- "Order you summers suit. Because is big rush, we will execute customers in strict rotation." (Tailor shop in Rhodes)
- "In face of dog, please walk back with slow. This dog are friendly with you. Only bark. Never harm before you." (Thai garden)
- Then there's the sign in the lobby of the Jambo Inn in Dar es Salaam: "Women of immortal turpitude are strictly not allowed any room." I swear it's true. I saw it every evening as I headed upstairs.
- A breakfast menu in India offered me "stress lemin, juices tin, tasty cult lates, choice omelet, con flakes, paper poasted, solid curmel custid." On top of all that, they promised to bring "bad tea" to my room.

Avoid asking questions in which you imply the answer, especially when asking directions. Avoid questions that can be answered by "yes" or "no." Questions such as "Is the train station down that street?" or "Does the train leave at eight o'clock?" contain the seeds of disaster. The local person, only partially understanding, is likely to nod affirmatively or even say "Yes," when there may not even be a train. Instead, say "Where is the station?" and then, "What time does the train leave?"

If you lack confidence in an answer, follow up with a contradictory question. If a person has pointed to the left to indicate the direction of the train station, ask, "Is the train station that way (pointing some other direction)?" Whatever the next answer, it will tell you something.

A map does wonders to overcome pronunciation difficulties. If you have a guidebook or map that has the name of your destination in it, show it to the other person.

Always be patient. The person with whom you're talking doesn't exist merely to answer your questions. She wants to help and she's doing you a favor. She's not ignorant and speaks her language well. It's your language she's having trouble with or your pronunciation of her language. Let her answer in her own way, and never imply that the difficulty is somehow her fault.

The bottom line: the language "barrier" is only a speed bump.

16

Transportation

> Going from point to point in other countries,
> one follows a thin line of road, railway, or river,
> leaving wide tracts unexplored on either side.
> — Amelia Edwards
> *A Thousand Miles Up the Nile*

Picture yourself in Provence[*] drifting along a quiet river bordered by vineyards; aboard a scraggly, spitting camel lurching along the dusty road to the airport in Varanasi;[†] swaying toward a Thai hill tribe village balanced on a crusty elephant back; or crossing Calcutta in a tattered rickshaw. Imagine cramming yourself into an Indonesian minivan called a *bemo* or relaxing in a stately Austin Fairway taxi as you head for a gin and tonic in the faded luxury of Nairobi's Norfolk Hotel.

Fly into the heart of the Okavango Delta in a five-passenger Cessna, then transfer to a hollowed-out log canoe to glide along waterways lined with watching crocodiles. Perch on bulging sacks of grain as a water-buffalo cart carries you down dusty roads in sight of the Himalayas. Roll through the Indonesian hill-town of Tomohon in a two-wheeled surrey called a *bendi*, soothed by the cloppity-clop of hooves on cobblestones. Settle back in a 25-foot outrigger canoe sailing from Manado for a ten-mile voyage to some of the best snorkeling in the world.

---

[*] *Provence.* Provence is located in southern France, bisected by the Rhone River, and bordered on the south by the Mediterranean. It includes Marseilles and Avignon, the spectacular Gorges d'Ardeche, and Mount Ventoux. Bright and sunny, its extraordinary light attracted Cezanne, Van Gogh, and Picasso—and has attracted legions of tourists ever since.

[†] *Varanasi.* Misnamed Benares by the British, Varanasi is located in eastern central India. On the sacred Ganges River, it is one of the most important Hindu pilgrimage destinations. Bathing ghats (steps) and burning ghats line the river bank. This picturesque city has also been a center of learning for more than 2,000 years.

Here's a fundamental truth: transport in the rest of the world is very different from what we're used to at home. It's far more than just a means of getting from one place to another; it's part of the essence of travel.

Although Third World transport is often picturesque, it's not always comfortable. Travelers love to tell stories about agonizing overnighters on third-class, hard seat Indian trains. Then there's the local joke that goes, "What's the maximum capacity of a Guatemalan bus?" The smiling answer: "One more." On many local buses, blaring music, too little leg room, and animals pecking at your toes are pretty standard. If there's too much character and too little comfort, paying more will make any trip easier. Even in less-developed countries, there is always a veneer of upscale transport in which passengers are sheltered from the hurly-burly of the environment.

Taking local transport means talking with people, seeing the countryside close at hand, and discovering unexpected adventures. Even when things don't go quite right, it always works out, bumps and all, if you remember that "the trip is the trip." Travel is more than destinations, and transport is more than just a means of getting from one place to another.

> "Your road is everything that a road ought to be . . . and yet you will not stay on it for half a mile, for the reason that little, mysterious roads are always branching out from it on either hand, and as these curve sharply also and hide what is beyond, you cannot resist the temptation to desert your chosen road and explore them."
> —Mark Twain, American writer

TRAVELING BY BUS

The elite fly, the burghers take the train, and the people ride the bus. At home, buses come mostly in vanilla, but in the rest of the world there's a wide range of flavors. Even when the vehicle is sufficiently comfortable to pamper the most demanding traveler, traveling by bus is almost always an excellent way to SAVE MONEY while seeing the nitty-gritty of a country. For example, you can ride every mile of every bus route in the kingdom of Sikkim for less than $15.

Some trips combine spectacular scenery with luxury. The air-conditioned Scania superbus that cruises 1,200 miles from Santiago to Arica, Chile, has a bar, a bathroom, three movie screens, and a smiling hostess. As the sleek bus hums across the moonscape of the Atacama Desert, you spy huge boulders balanced on barren mountainsides. In most climates, rain and erosion would long ago have tumbled these hot air balloon–sized rocks into dry canyons below. In the desert stillness, they hang suspended for centuries. As heat waves shimmer outside the window, cool air breezes across your face and the hostess

Local transport—a taxibus. Antananarivo, Madagascar.

sets an ice-cold beer at your elbow. At night, your seat reclines to nearly horizontal, a leg rest pops out, and you're in bed. All that for about $40.

On the double-deck luxury bus from Windhoek,* Namibia, to Cape Town, South Africa, the attendant serves near-gourmet meals and fine South African wines. When the splendid landscape fades into dusk, she appears at your side with soft pillows and warm blankets.

Another fine double-decker travels the Garden Route along the south coast of Africa from Cape Town to Port Elizabeth (about $36). For 800 kilometers this bus passes through small towns and rainbow arches of blooming flowers crossing the road. Your partner sits across a table from you, sharing tea and conversation.

For rugged beauty, it's hard to top the two-day cliff-hanger in the Himalayas from Srinagar, Kashmir, to Leh,† or the seven-hour trip west from Gangtok§ to the foot of Mount Kanchenjunga,‡ or the nine-hour trip from the humid lowlands of Ujung Pandang up to the cool plateau of exotic Toraja-land.**

To be candid, I should mention that the buses on these last three routes are

---

* *Windhoek.* Clean and modern, the capital of Namibia could pass for Wichita, Kansas.

† *Leh.* This small town, capital of Ladakh in far northern India, was an important trading stop on the ancient Silk Road from China to Europe. Its many active monasteries and gentle Buddhist culture make Ladakh a fascinating place to visit. The road in from Kashmir and the flight across the Himalayas from New Delhi are "don't miss" experiences.

§ *Gangtok.* The capital of Sikkim, Gangtok has gorgeous views of the Kanchenjunga range.

‡ *Mount Kanchenjunga.* The world's third highest peak is located on the border of Sikkim and Nepal.

** *Toraja-land.* Located on the island of Sulawesi, Indonesia, this province is noted for its ship-shaped homes and unusual death rituals.

rolling wrecks. In fact, many Third World buses are rust-holed and thread-bare, seats torn and metal surfaces shiny from the momentary grips of a million hands. Either the windows won't open or they won't close, fans haven't worked in living memory, and overhead light fixtures are shadowy holes. Shock absorbers and springs don't. One thing that always works is the horn; shrill, penetrating, and every few seconds. Another piece of equipment that works is the boom box, usually the size of a suitcase. If you're lucky, you'll get local music. If not, you'll discover what happened to the worst U.S. rap and disco tapes. Desperation hits when you find that your earplugs are tucked away in your luggage instead of nearby in your daypack.

It may not be fair to say that all bus drivers are aggressive, but once I saw a bus driver, reflexes programmed to blast away at any obstacle, honk furiously at a speed bump in the road.

Nuts and Bolts of Bus Travel

Unlike train stations, few bus stations are architectural marvels. In fact, "yards" would be a more apt description. Picture dozens of buses parked helter-skelter in a dusty plaza. Travelers mill around, loaded with everything from briefcases to small animals to heaping baskets of fruit. Vendors weave though the crowd as conductors shout and engines race. The word cacophony captures the essence of this scene but doesn't begin to describe how captivating it is.

There's probably a relationship between where a bus is parked and where it's going, but, if so, few travelers are likely to figure it out. Most buses display their ultimate destination on a tattered piece of cardboard in the front window. Of course, if you're not going to the end of the line, or are transferring to some other bus along the way, it won't be your destination that's displayed. No problem. Stay calm and keep asking and you'll soon be directed to the right bus. Then ask the driver to be certain. Since it's easy to confuse place names in a language strange to your ears, write the name on a piece of paper and show it to the driver. If you already have a ticket, show that to him. When you start wondering where to get off, enlist the aid of your fellow passengers. You get so much help, you feel like a member of the family by the time you wave good-bye.

When buying a ticket, try for an express bus. On a short trip, it doesn't matter much, but a long-distance *local* bus sometimes lurches forward only a few hundred meters at a time, stopping to pick up anyone who waves from the roadside. If you buy your ticket anywhere other than from the bus driver, find out exactly where the bus departs. It may be right outside the ticket office, or somewhere across the bus yard, or even blocks away. Make an assumption and you may be making new plans.

Keep your ticket; it may be checked several times throughout the trip.

When you give the ticket to the driver or conductor, it will be torn or punched, or you'll get a receipt. Keep it. The ticket or receipt may be checked several times in the course of the trip and collected as you get out. Even though the driver may toss it out the window after you give it to him, he may not let you off without it.

The most pressing problem on a bus is leg room. A tall person's knees are driven into the seat ahead, scrunched up to his chin, or forced out into the aisle. That's when you find that your extended knee is a tempting place for someone to sit. For any trip over an hour, reserve a seat in the first row. If reservations aren't accepted, the driver may informally reserve a seat if you tell him about, or pantomime, the leg-room problem. If you can't reserve a seat, get to the door of the bus early and, when it opens, take no prisoners.

If you think your comfort level may differ from that of a high-altitude llama herder, get a window seat so you get first choice of whether the window is open or closed. Think about which side of the bus will be receiving the force of the sun and whether you want to be toasted.

The roof of a bus is sometimes preferred seating in terms of space, fresh air and electrifying views. Riding the roof also lets you keep an eye on your luggage and avoid watching the driver getting progressively drunk. So you can't be turned down, just climb to the roof without asking permission and snuggle out of sight amid packs and baskets. Speaking of electrifying, watch for wires hanging low over the road.

I know an experienced traveler who always talks to the driver—to test his sobriety. She then chooses a seat on the driver's side of the bus, on the theory that in an emergency the driver will protect his side of the bus.

No matter the time or temperature, few buses in the Third World willingly depart while even one seat is unoccupied. At the Yogyakarta (Java, Indonesia) station, for example, touts leap off incoming buses to solicit passengers with piercing cries, even trying to capture people who had no thought of going anywhere. When the driver gives up on filling every seat, he gets under way, accelerating like a race car, careening wildly around corners. The idea is to pass the bus that left just ahead of him, thereby getting first crack at prospective passengers along the road. Since stopping to pick up a passenger would leave a bus vulnerable to being overtaken by the bus speeding along behind it, the conductor hauls newcomers (often a mother with a baby and a basket of groceries) aboard as the bus slows to a fast roll. Anyone wanting off the bus is ejected as soon as the bus slows to a sprint.

Only when the bus is full does the driver relax. Of course, "full" has different meanings in different places. Usually it means that the aisle is packed with produce, baggage, livestock, and farm equipment and not one additional fare-paying life form can be leveraged into the vehicle.

People jammed together in the aisle edge over a millimeter at a time until they're almost on top of you. As you're settling in, the baby is handed to you by the woman perching on the back of your seat and an unseen fowl pecks at your shoelaces. Try to defend what you consider your personal space and your trip can be, shall we say, strenuous. If you see the humor and go with the flow, it will be memorable instead.

Except in Europe and Japan, a bus usually reaches a destination faster than a train—unless, of course, the bus breaks down, which happens frequently. Because of all the practice they get, drivers can repair virtually any mechanical failure on the spot. On the mountain road to Rumtek Monastery,* an explosion blew a ragged hole in the floorboard of our bus. An Israeli traveler in front of me turned calmly to his friend and said, "Car bomb!" It turned out that the rear tire of the bus had detonated with such force that a large chunk of rubber had blown through the floor. The driver nonchalantly parked on a steep uphill curve, replaced the tire and adjusted the clutch, all in 30 minutes. Of course, you still had to watch your step in the back of the bus or you'd become axle grease.

Since a bus may come to an unplanned, extended halt far from any human habitation, wise travelers carry a snack. Peanuts, fruit, bread, and a little water can help make a pit stop pleasant.

The price of a bus trip increases disproportionately if the bus crosses a national border. You will almost always SAVE MONEY by buying a ticket to the border, crossing on foot, and hopping on another bus on the other side. In some cases, because of time of day, remoteness of the border crossing, or a mismatch in schedules, attempting this could be a false economy.

Security

Near Chitwan,† an agile young man drops from a tree limb to the roof of a passing bus. After a furtive glance around, he grabs three of the many bags stored on the roof and tosses them off the back. As the bus slows for an uphill climb, he swings down to the back bumper, hops off, and sprints back to collect his loot. The question is: was one of those bags yours?

Let's face it, travel abroad requires a little more caution than is necessary in the United States. From Peru to the Philippines, it's up to you to make sure your luggage doesn't go astray.

Lock your bags when they're placed on a bus' roof.

If joining your bag on the roof isn't your idea of fun, lock it to a roof rail with a light, plastic-coated bicycle chain. This little chain also keeps it from sliding off as the bus rounds a curve. On a mountain road near Darjeeling, India, that thin chain saved my friend's pack from yielding to centrifugal force and becoming airborne over a 1,000-foot drop. On another trip, I met an American in Manuel Antonio Park, Costa Rica, whose backpack had bounced off the roof

---

* *Rumtek Monastery.* In eastern Sikkim, across the valley from Gangtok, this brightly restored monastery is the seat of the Kagyu-pa sect of Tibetan Buddhism.

† *Chitwan.* A game preserve in southern Nepal, famous for rhinos.

of a bus, taking with it his passport and travelers checks. How many mistakes can you count in that picture?

If rain is a probability and your bag is on the roof, make sure it's completely covered by a tarp or inside a waterproof pack cover or garbage bag. Once you're rolling, the driver is unlikely to stop to do this little chore.

As fast as the helpful driver shoves tourists' bags into the bus storage compartment that opens from both sides, someone may be pulling them out the other side. Now that's a bad way to start a trip. If someone is planning to snatch your pack, they're watching you—so you must be watchful too.

When the bus lets someone off, see that your pack doesn't go along. Get off to stretch your legs—and watch. When the bus stops for lunch or a toilet break, don't leave anything valuable aboard even if the driver says he'll lock the doors.

If you're likely to sleep along the way, keep your daypack strap looped around your foot and keep everything else between you and the side of the bus. If your luggage is overhead, lock it to the rack. Of course, your real valuables are—where?—around your waist. A friend puts her pack on her lap and rests her head on it to sleep (like an ersatz air bag). These precautions may seem a little excessive, but they quickly become part of a comfortable, even amusing, routine.

Bus Passes

With a bus pass, you pay a fixed amount for unlimited travel on a bus network for the duration of the pass. In a large country, a pass can be a major money-saver. While some passes must be purchased outside the country, most can be bought on the spot. A pass usually puts you on a comfortable coach run by an established company. In fact, upscale bus services in many countries abroad use Mercedes or Scania coaches that are considerably more luxurious than buses in the United States.

The U.S. Alternative

Though emphasizing U.S. routes, the Green Tortoise also offers wonderful trips in Central America. The Green Tortoise offers a nine-day loop through the southwestern desert ($249 + $61 for food), nine days in the Grand Canyon ($329 + $71), sixteen days though various western national parks ($499 + $121), and twenty-eight days in Alaska ($1,500 + $250). It has recently added trips from San Francisco to Antigua, Guatemala ($749+ $151; twenty-three days), Antigua to San José, Costa Rica ($699 + $151; twenty-one days), and other routes in Central America. Call (800) 227-4766 or visit www.greentortoise.com.

New Zealand favorites are the Magic Bus and the Kiwi Experience. After paying an initial fee based on your preferred route, you hop on and off the colorfully decorated buses at will as they cruise around the country connecting you with a network of backpacker hotels. When you're ready to move on, call a toll-free number and reserve your spot on the next bus through town. It's a great way to travel.

Try the Baz Bus in South Africa, another good value for backpackers.

Buses are an excellent way to see the countryside, meet people, and learn about local culture. You immerse yourself in conversations with local people of all ages, trying to ignore the driver chatting with the conductor as the bus leans around yet another curve in the sky. The way you know it was a truly great trip is if you swear, as you get off, never to ride a bus again.

TRAVELING BY TRAIN

In the Western world, trains have become an anachronism, remembered mostly by seamed-faced farmers who watched them puff across the prairies of their youth. In the rest of the world, trains are still woven into the fabric of daily life, aesthetically worn but still mechanically valiant.

On a train, you travel close to the land, slowly enough to absorb what's going on, with as much privacy or contact with people as you choose. You sleep wonderfully, rocking along to a soothing rhythm, waking to a new vista emerging with each dawn.

"Anything is possible on a train; a great meal, a binge, a visit from card players, an intrigue, a good night's sleep, and strangers' monologues framed like Russian short stories."
—Paul Theroux, *The Great Railway Bazaar: By Train Through Asia*

From a train window, the world is a visual banquet. I feel as if I'm stationary, watching a panorama of lives flow past. I remember a young woman watching from her kitchen window, leaning on her elbows, holding my eye until the train rounded the bend.

A train passes through time as well as space. The train north from Singapore leaves the city's futuristic mirrored-glass towers behind and within an hour is clacking through a Malaysian countryside little changed since man discovered he could plant and gather his food.

Throughout the world, there are thousands of routes along which travelers are transported in reasonable comfort. Of them, a dozen or more have trains worth a detour of many miles to ride. Writers in posh travel magazines rhapsodize about super-luxury trains, but my favorites are old-fashioned trains that maintain the style of a half-century past. I like trains that leave stations reeking of character (among other things) to pass first through inhabited areas that reveal how urban people live, then slowly through landscapes of mountains and forests, clear lakes, and curious faces.

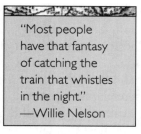

"Most people have that fantasy of catching the train that whistles in the night."
—Willie Nelson

I want to share with you a few very special train trips from around the world. Some are special because of stylish furnishings, but more often it's the landscape that makes these trips unique. When you anticipate a ride on such a train, ask someone knowledgeable whether it will be daylight when you pass the most spectacular scenery and on which side you should sit.

Chile. Chile's *Ferrocarril del Estado* serves the 700–mile Santiago to Puerto Montt run, passing through towns settled by groups as disparate as Temuco Indians and fifth-generation German immigrants. The compartments in the 60-year-old coaches are masterpieces of faded elegance: gold-brown velvet-nap seats, carved dark wood furnishings, and etched glass. The wash basin has a brass spout and porcelain handles decorated with tiny red and yellow painted flowers. Craggy Andean peaks and snowcapped crowns of volcanoes dominate the view to the east. The 22-hour overnight trip costs about $35 for a comfortable private seat and cozy upper berth with crisp linen.

Peru. In southern Peru, nine coaches painted orange with a broad horizontal yellow stripe are pulled across the high desert by a near-antique engine. Lonely tracks stretch from the "white city" of Arequipa* past mountains from which flow the birth waters of the Amazon River. Isolated shepherds' villages stand as sentinels on the high plains. Vast herds of sturdy brown and white alpaca warily lift their heads at the labored breathing of the passing machine. The conductor sways down the aisle carrying a black rubber balloon filled with oxygen for use if a passenger has difficulty breathing the thin air. Ten hours later, the train pulls into Puno on the shore of Lake Titicaca. When you've explored Lake Titicaca, the legendary birthplace of the first Inca, continue on by train to Cuzco, capital of the Inca empire.

Another Peruvian trip, lauded by train buffs as one of the seven wonders of the railway world, travels from Lima to Huancayo.† The train zigzags its way from coastal plain to mountain heights, crossing more than 60 viaducts spanning black-walled gorges and tunneling through the frozen hearts of the mountains. Where it can't cross over or bore through, it creeps along a track chiseled into a near-vertical precipice. Even the most intrepid passengers turn

---

*Arequipa. Located near the Chilean border at the foot of snowcapped Volcan Misti, 600 miles south of Lima, Peru. Arequipa is called the "white city" because so many of its buildings are constructed of pearly white volcanic material.

† Huancayo. Large city located at almost 11,000 feet altitude, east of Lima, Peru. It has a fine Indian market.

their heads from the edge. Climbing at an average of 50 feet a minute, it's not long before gasping passengers signal the conductor for a whiff of oxygen. Reaching 14,800 feet, this may be the highest passenger train in the world.

Mexico. In northwestern Mexico, board the *Chihuahua al Pacifico* for the comparatively short journey from Chihuahua through the Copper Canyon to Los Mochis, a small fishing resort in northwest Mexico. This has been called the most dramatic train ride in North America, a claim based on canyons carved more than 6,000 feet into the earth's surface. Passengers may visit Cuauhtemocto, a community of German-speaking Mennonite ranchers, and get off at Divisadero or Bahuichivo to hike down into the Copper Canyon. If you have a few extra days, take the opportunity to experience the unusual culture of the Tarahumara Indians, people renowned for their endurance as long-distance runners.

Morocco. A fine track loops from Tangier, down to Casablanca, Marrakesh, and back. On this trip, the attraction is as much the people you travel with as the destination. I shared a compartment with a woman who wore a deep blue gown, a gold-embroidered veil, heavy mesh stockings, and ornate gold rings on eight fingers. Her young daughter wore white leggings, pink T-shirt, a scarlet sweater, scuffed blue loafers, and a short-sleeved black leather jacket. Who could resist the Marrakesh Express?

Kenya. The train drops from Nairobi, on its mile-high inland plateau, into the sultry coastal heat of the ancient trading port of Mombasa. Although first class (about $19) costs twice as much as second, many visitors prefer it because, in second class, passengers are segregated by sex. As sometimes happens, "first" is relative. In some compartments, half the lights don't work, shades on the windows won't close, and the doors refuse to lock. Of course, the smiling train captain assures the passengers that everything will be fixed before the next trip—or at least "sometime." But the disheveled interior doesn't matter at all when the tracks enter Tsavo National Park, where ostriches, giraffes, elephants, and antelope graze against the backdrop of Mount Kilimanjaro's snowy summit. This trip is often the only way to see Tsavo since the park frequently closes as rangers battle the poachers.

Zimbabwe. A steward in a crisp, white shirt, gold cuff links, and a homey blue cardigan sweater settles you into a comfortable wood-and-leather compartment. Right on time, the ten-car train, pulled by a bright yellow engine, chugs out of the Bulawayo station bound for Victoria Falls (about $12). Homes in some villages along the way have grass thatch roofs; in others, homes resemble those in a typical Kansas town. Night falls as the train enters Hwange National Park, renowned lair of black leopards. In the morning, you are dropped off on the front lawn of the colonial-era Victoria Falls Hotel.

South Africa. From Port Elizabeth on the South African coast, this train sweeps northeast for 21 hours across Orange Free State and the Transvaal to the urban sprawl of Johannesburg. The price is extremely reasonable considering the linen and silver in the dining car, comfortable overnight accommodations, and the idyllic landscape. We added to the amenities by bringing a picnic lunch and bottles of excellent South African Columbard and Riesling.

The internationally famous *Blue Train* covers 1,001 miles from fashionable Cape Town to big-city Jo'burg in 26 hours and high style. However, the hand-painted china and sparkling crystal come at a fairly high price—$639 and up, way up—not to mention having to dress for dinner. When I was in Cape Town, the Blue Train was sold out for eight months.

The *Pride of Africa*, billed as the "world's most luxurious train," runs 287 miles (21 hours) from near Kruger National Park to Pretoria. Suites cost $566 to $707 and include all the chilled champagne you can drink.

Australia. The modern *Indian Pacific* crosses the Nullarbor desert (which means "no trees," if I remember my Latin) to connect the west coast city of Perth with Sydney, almost 2,700 miles (and 64 hours) away. A one-way economy ticket costs about $300 (economy berths are almost $600 in high season.) This is a comfortable trip, but it has none of the ethnic intensity and scenic variety found in Asia and Africa. You get an idea of the topography from the fact that one 297-mile stretch is the longest straight run of track in the world. Still, it's worth seeing the sunbaked nineteenth-century mining towns, the Australian outback, and the sun rising from the desert like an explosion of orange flame.

New Zealand. A thousand miles across the Tasman Sea, you roll south from Auckland* on the *Northerner* (previously the *Silver Fern*) past volcanoes, ski slopes, blue-green mirror lakes, and rivers bursting with trout. For most travelers, the destination is "Windy Welly"† on the Cook Strait, but you needn't stop there. The train boards the Picton Ferry, crosses the Strait, and continues 200 miles south to Christchurch. At that point, you can turn west and cross the mountainous spine of the South Island, alternating between spindly viaducts and pitch-black tunnels until you emerge in Greymouth on the rocky west coast. Or, if you'd rather, board the *Southerner* for a 400-mile trip to the tip of the South Island. The branch line from Invercargill to Bluff bills itself as the southernmost public railway in the world.

---

* *Auckland.* Located on the North Island of New Zealand. Surrounded by water and volcanic hills, Auckland's population is approaching 1 million (including the largest population of Polynesians in the world).

† *Windy Welly.* Wellington is located on the southern tip of the North Island of New Zealand. The capital of the country, it is swept by brisk (sometimes gale force) winds from the Cook Strait.

Eurostar

The mid-90s saw the inauguration of a dramatically modern way to cross the channel. It's a new train service through the "chunnel" known as *Eurostar*. Carrying up to 800 passengers, the coaches reach a speed of 160 miles per hour on the three-hour trip from the center of London to the center of Paris. Fares are $154 one way first class and $123 second class. The cheapest fare is the Discovery Special, $75 one way, second class. However, there are also discounts for advance purchase, trips over a Saturday, children (under age 12), youth (under age 26), and holders of certain rail passes. Eurostar is a major step in connecting several national high-speed train services into an international network.

Europe. Europe is a treasure chest full of fine train trips, although they're considerably more expensive than their counterparts in the Southern Hemisphere. Since 1883, except for an interruption or two, the royal blue coaches of the *Venice-Simplon Orient Express* (VSOE) have been bearing people across the European continent in luxury. Even before you add the cost of formal clothes (about half the men wear black tie), a one-way ticket from London to Venice costs over $1,500, double occupancy. If you start the trip in London, you cross the Channel to Boulogne, France, and drive on to Paris to board the elegant VSOE with its polished wood, Lalique crystal tulip lamps, Limoges and Wedgewood china, Irish linen, French soap, and gourmet meals. After sipping champagne in the bar car to the music of a tuxedoed pianist, you may dine on caviar, duck breast and foie gras, French cheeses, and wine. Mata Hari, Princess Grace, or Nikita Krushchev may have sat just where you're enjoying your Courvousier.

Other examples of excellent European routes are the *Chopin* (Vienna-Moscow), the *Nord-West Express* (London-Copenhagen), the *Ost-West Express* (London-Moscow), the *Sud-Express* (Paris-Lisbon), the *Remus* (Vienna-Rome), the *Lusitania* (Madrid-Lisbon), the *Britannia* (London-Munich), the *Rembrandt* (Amsterdam-Stuttgart), the *Citalia* (London-Rome), and the trip from Bergen to Oslo. And for a fabulous short trip, try the *Brunig Panoramic Express,* which passes through a magic land of lakes, forests, and alpine peaks from Interlaken to Lucerne, Switzerland.

Although political changes have opened rail-riding opportunities in Eastern Europe, coaches are worn and long stretches of landscape are industrialized and polluted. On the other hand, it's a chance to travel slowly in countries newly opened to the world. For an afternoon's amusement in Budapest, take a leisurely 12-kilometer trip through a peaceful forest aboard one of the red and silver cars of the *Pioneer Railway.* This little railroad is staffed by children dressed in formal blue uniforms bearing red epaulets.

Thailand. Many travelers enjoy the one-and-one-half-day, two-night train from Bangkok's Hualampong Station to Singapore (an ordinary berth costs about $85). The coaches are comfortable and the route traverses pleasant scenery. However, an alternative has emerged fairly recently. The Orient Express hotel chain refurbished the old green and yellow *Silver Fern* carriages (that used to run from Auckland to Christchurch) with teak, brass, crystal, silver, and fine fabrics, and christened the result the *Eastern & Oriental Express* (EOE). To travel the same 1,200-mile stretch of track I traveled for $85, passengers now have the option of paying $1,270 to $3,290 per person to ride on the EOE. Of course, they receive side trips to the River Kwai and Penang; premium tea from a silver pot is served in delicate china cups on the *Express*, while on my train tea was handed through the window in a clay tumbler.

Aboard the train from Bangkok to Chiang Mai in northern Thailand, crew and passengers frequently stand, salute, and sing the national anthem at major stops. Now that's something you don't see just anywhere.

China. Another luxury liner, the *Marco Polo Express*, made its debut in 1993. The nine-day, 2,000-mile trip runs from Beijing to Urumqi, a city farther from an ocean than any other city in the world. It tracks a portion of the ancient Silk Road on which Chinese silks were carried across Asia to Venice and Rome. A two-berth compartment, complete with mahogany writing table, a plump easy chair, and a heavy brass reading lamp, costs about $5,500 *per person*, plus another $1,000 or so for side trips and return by air to Beijing. Are the Chinese catching on to capitalism?

On standard Chinese trains, there are sometimes no reserved seats. To give foreigners a chance, the clerk allows them a running head start though the gate for the train. Seconds later, the local crowd bursts from behind the barriers like the first wave at the New York marathon. The cars are so crowded that you may have to climb out the window when it's time to get off.

India. The Indian train system has been described as "exhilarating anarchy." Its coaches, many pulled by the world's largest fleet of old-fashioned steam locomotives, carry more than 12 million passengers every day.

The Darjeeling-Himalayas train, known affectionately as the "toy train," click-clacks uphill from New Jalpaiguri in North Bengal to Darjeeling in the foothills of the Himalayas. Its miniature steam engine slowly pulls four reduced-scale passenger cars on narrow-gauge tracks through dozens of small towns and manicured tea plantations. After seven hours, passengers disembark in Darjeeling, a favorite hill station of the English raj. It's great fun even though the train is always crowded, has head and knee room suitable for Munchkins, and takes twice as long as the same journey by road.

The apogee of Indian train travel is the *Palace on Wheels*. Departing from New Delhi, *Palace on Wheels* visits some of India's most colorful cities, including Rajasthan's Jaipur, Udaipur, Jaisalmer, and Jodhpur, then turns east to Agra, Varanasi, Kathmandu, and finally back to New Delhi. Travel is at night so passengers can be taken to historical sights each day. The trips are for nine to seventeen days at a cost of around $300 per day. The burnished teak, polished brass fittings, velvets and brocades, crisp linens, fine food, constant service, and exotic itinerary make this trip a good investment for many. Another luxary train, the *Royal Orient*, offers ten day trips.

Other recommended long-distance trips in India: the *Rajdhani Express* (Delhi-Calcutta), the *Gitanjale Express* (Calcutta-Mumbai), the *Frontier Mail* (Amritsar-Mumbai), and the *Taj Express* (Delhi-Agra).

Russia. The eight-day, 6,000-mile trip aboard the *Trans-Siberian Express* (the correct name is the *Russia Express*) from Moscow to Vladivostok is by far the longest train trip in the world. I can't give you prices since Russian currency fluctuates so much, but it's generally cheaper to buy the ticket in China. While the Trans-Siberian has a certain *Dr. Zhivago* romantic appeal, a week is a lot of time to commit to counting millions of trees filing slowly past your window (at 40 miles per hour top speed, this is not the world's fastest train). At long intervals, the tracks pass gray industrial cities filled with concrete apartment towers standing mute in the vast silence. At least there's plenty of time to sip vodka and talk with Russian and international passengers. There's even time to hop off for some quick exercise during brief stops, except from November to March when the bone-numbing Siberian cold could turn you into a seasonal platform monument.

Nuts and Bolts of Train Travel

With all these exceptional train trips in mind, it's time to consider the practicalities of train travel.

Cost

In most countries, train travel is inexpensive, much cheaper than flying. A berth always costs more than a seat, but it's much more comfortable for overnight travel. How much more it costs depends on whether the berth is in a private compartment, a shared compartment, or lengthwise along the aisle. However, when you travel at night, the cost of transportation includes the cost of lodging.

It's seldom wise to buy the cheapest ticket available. Third-class, hard-seat trains are a rough way to travel in almost any country. Unless you're determined to see a country on $2 a day, are writing a book on ultimate hard-core travel, or practicing extreme self-mortification in contemplation of reincarnation, do yourself a favor: skip third class hard-seat. If you do try it, I'll wager it will only be once.

In a private compartment, which costs only a few dollars extra, you're comfortable and free from cigarette smoke if you choose to be, and your luggage is relatively secure. You may even reach your destination fairly well rested. If you forego a berth and sit up the whole way, you can save a few dollars, but that could be a foolish economy on a long trip. The downside is that if you travel in a two-person compartment you miss fine opportunities for conversation. When I'm in the mood for company, I travel in large compartments or in open seating. When I need solitude, I try for a small compartment.

Where to Buy Your Ticket

Don't expect a travel agent to tear a ticket with your name on it from a computer printer. That would be far too easy. More likely, you'll have to go to the train station to buy the ticket. That, by the way, requires finding the correct station. Don't learn too late that the city you're leaving has more than one station—and it's not the one where you're standing.

The Ticket Line

If you travel by train, you'll find yourself standing in line. Realizing that you haven't moved forward for ten minutes, you notice that people are joining the line ahead of you. Maybe they're relatives of people in line, members of the same cavalry unit, travel agents, who knows, but try to avoid expressing Western-style complaints about people who cut into lines. You'll probably be understood but neither appreciated nor helped. To avoid treading water, you can circle around and join the front of the line where it resembles a rugby scrum, or pleasantly ask someone for help. I was once taken out of the line by a fellow ticket-buyer directly to the office of the ticket master, who personally handled the transaction.

Buying Your Ticket

When you reach the ticket agent's window, be your usual courteous self. Greet him (it's almost always a "him") with a friendly smile and a cheerful "hello" or "good day." After all, he's been getting a lot of pressure all day. Make sure you know the name of your destination as spelled in the local language. Ask for the seat you want, which is surely a window seat, and specify whether you prefer a nonsmoking car (don't underestimate the impact of rolling clouds of unfiltered smoke on your lungs).

Before you leave the line, confirm that the ticket handed you is what you asked for, count your change, and, oh yes, be sure the guy pressing against you isn't picking your pocket. If all is okay, thank the clerk for helping you. Wouldn't you like him to tell his family at dinner about how courteous people from your country are? Maybe as a result of your courtesy, he'll help the next traveler who has no idea what's going on.

By the way, quite a few countries require that foreigners purchase first-class tickets with hard currency. If you want to SAVE MONEY, buy second-class tickets with local currency, then upgrade once on board, again using local currency.

The Tourist Quota

Getting a ticket may be more difficult than you expect. In fact, you may not get one unless you know about the special ticket lines and quotas set aside for foreign travelers. Suppose it's just under 100 degrees, so you ask for a seat in an air-conditioned car. The ticket agent snaps, "Finished" (which means "You must be crazy; air-con sold out 60 days ago"). A little grumpily, you decide to settle for a compartment with a fan. Again, "Finished." Okay, you think, I'll sit up and sweat all night—but those seats too are "finished."

You feel frustrated, but, as a knowledgeable traveler, you aren't even close to giving up. That's because you know that a "tourist quota" of tickets has been reserved with you in mind. If there were no quota, and you tried to buy tickets only a day or two ahead of departure, you might never get a ticket, especially in countries like India. The tourist quota may not get you into first class or air con, but it will probably assure you a berth if you want one and almost certainly a seat of some kind. So you stroll over to the information booth—there is some kind of information source in most train stations—and ask for the location of the "foreigners' window." That's where you'll find the clerk who dispenses tickets under the tourist quota.

In Chennai, India,[*] the foreigners' window is at the end of a line designated "VIP, handicapped, ladies, freedom fighters, and senior citizens." Because the train we wanted was sold out, we were sent upstairs to see if the "big man" could help. After two hours in a sweltering office, during which time we witnessed a flurry of fists between a ticket agent and a prospective passenger and sat through two black-outs due to power failures, the big man permitted us to buy tickets for a non–air conditioned, shared compartment.

Baksheesh

A bribe, or tip, has many names around the world. A common one is *baksheesh*. Beyond cultural reluctance to try it, there are practical questions of to whom and how much. Find the lowest-ranking person who can provide what you want, starting with the conductor. The lower the rank, the less the amount of *baksheesh* required. Start by saying, "Isn't there some other way to handle this?" or, "Isn't it possible to pay an extra fare?" These classic expressions translate into any language.

Sometimes a bribe can help find a previously "filled" seat.

---

[*] *Chennai.* Formerly Madras, this is the capital of Tamil Nadu in southeastern India. Although it's India's fourth-largest city, it's also one of the most pleasant. It is the point of departure for visiting the fabulous temples of South India.

The amount of *baksheesh* required is always a guess. Factor in the cost of the ticket, the standard of living in the country, and how much getting what you want is worth to you. One approach is to put a small amount of money in one pocket and a back-up amount in another. Empty the first pocket and, if that doesn't fly, pull out the back-up stash. Try to avoid getting out your wallet. If you offer too little, it may be ignored. More likely, you'll receive some clear, nonverbal signals that you need to up the ante. It works.

Confirming Your Space

If you buy your ticket ahead of time, find out when you are expected to confirm your reservation—and do it. If you don't confirm when you're supposed to, someone else's seat will be in yours.

Using a Rail Pass

The following information pertains to using a rail pass in Europe, although using a pass is similar in most countries. Plan to arrive at the train station at least 30 minutes ahead of departure time. You won't need that much time unless there's a problem, but if there is you may need every minute.

Before your first ride, validate your ticket at the ticket window in the train station, not with the conductor (who may charge you a penalty). From then on, skip past the ticket lines and hop on the train.

A rail pass allows you to board the train but is not a reservation. That is, it doesn't guarantee a seat, couchette, or sleeper. In Western Europe (except Austria, Benelux, and Germany), high-speed and premium trains require reservations. Reservations must also be made for sleeping accommodations and are recommended for trips lasting more than three hours and for TGV, ICE, EUROSTAR, and certain InterCity trains. Lines that require a reservation are clearly marked (with an "R") in the *Thomas Cook European Timetable*, in national rail timetables, and on departure sheets posted in stations. If you want to travel on EuroCity or international express trains over the weekend or on holidays, you risk disappointment if you don't make reservations.

At the height of the tourist season, some travelers purchase a reservation ($3 to $10) to ensure they won't have to stand. On the other hand, if you have to stand it's only until the next station. There, you simply out-hustle boarding locals to the vacated seats. When a reservation isn't required, most people don't bother.

If you plan to sleep on a train, you have four choices. You can sit up all night in a regular train seat and greet the morning with hollow eyes. You can try for a fold-out seat and hope there's room to fold it out. You can pay a little extra for a couchette. Or you can splurge on a sleeper. The couchette provides a bunk in a tiny six-bunk, co-ed dormitory room. It costs about $20 extra. The sleeper compartment contains two or three beds and a sink and costs an extra

$40 to $100. Sleeping aboard saves the cost and hassle of finding a hotel and frees the day for exploration.

While traveling, keep the rail pass safely tucked away to avoid loss or theft. If it's lost and you have a police report, you may be able to get a partial refund when you return home. In the meantime, you'll have to buy a replacement ticket. You can't get a refund after the ticket has been validated (stamped the first time) or beyond one year after the date of issuance, even if unused.

Wherever you're traveling, a good map lets you know where you are on a continuous basis. Beyond adding interest and showing you how place names are spelled in the country, a map prepares you to get off on arrival (some trains don't tarry long in a station).

Finding the Right Train

On the platform, don't rely on direction signs alone. Ask other passengers where the train you're about to board is going. If you have a general seating ticket, assure yourself that the car you board is going to your destination. Otherwise, you may be unexpectedly shunted onto a siding as the rest of the train continues on. When you hear an announcement over the loudspeaker that you don't understand, watch how others respond. If they all start packing up and moving toward another track, ask questions quickly.

Finding the Right Seat

If you have an assigned seat, its number should be printed or written on your ticket. If it's not, your name will be on a bulletin board near the proper track. Join the scores of other passengers searching for their names on one of the sheets of the passenger manifest, squinting at erasures, insertions, and cross-outs. The cross-outs, by the way, include those people who didn't believe it was really necessary to confirm their reservations.

Changing Seats

If you've been assigned a bad seat, say facing backwards or receiving the full blast of the sun, move to a better seat immediately. If someone appears with a legitimate claim, smile and move on.

Meals

If you'll be aboard long enough to become hungry, ask whether there is a dining car. There is often no food service on overnight trips, but stewards sometimes walk the aisles selling sandwiches and drinks. At unpredictable intervals, a porter may come around with inexpensive meals, usually on tin trays.

Local vendors may clamor below your window at every stop, but taste likely surpasses hygiene. To serve health and preferences, a wise traveler generally boards a train with ingredients for a picnic on wheels, including beverages.

TP

Assume that the train will have no toilet paper—or if it does, it will run out soon after you leave the station.

Security

With respect to security, you can't automatically trust the train crew or even your fellow passengers, so it would be a mistake to leave your daypack behind when you leave your seat. If you ask someone to watch your gear, make it someone you trust, not a passing acquaintance. Don't leave your luggage unlocked or your daypack accessible to anyone else at night. Lock both to something secure while you sleep. See Chapter 13 for more on security.

When you travel by train abroad, stations become part of the memory. Some are remarkable works of art, such as the soaring iron masterpieces of Gustave Eiffel. Others are massive, cold, and depressing. In some countries, they're a microcosm of the entire culture.

Walk into the New Delhi station just before midnight and there will be hundreds of people camped out, perhaps resembling the rear guard of Shah Jahan's army. Vendors cry the merits of their dosas and samosas, steaming mounds of dal, and assortments of unrecognizable fried . . . things. Extended families have made themselves at home on the long concrete platforms between trains, cooking meals on flaming braziers. Gold-thread saris and crimson tikas glow as women hover around the flames. Old men perch on burlap bales and baggage bound with twine; others squat on their heels, eating, talking, gesturing. There are Sikhs and Punjabis, Rajasthanis and Kashmiris, in turbans, beards, dhotis, and beautifully cut business suits. Cows wander at will, munching dinner leftovers and baggage. Stations like this are very much part of the trip.

Trains are one of my favorite ways to travel. I love the beat of the iron wheels clacking rhythmically across junctions in the track and the slow pace that allows me to recharge my batteries and center my thoughts. Train travel connects me with the mellowness of an earlier era. I have yet to be ready for a journey to end.

TRAVELING BY AIR

At home we can choose among airlines on the basis of ticket price, departure times, and destinations—even friendliness of passenger agents and on-board personnel. Flying in Europe is similar, but most of the rest of the world is quite different. Your planning should acknowledge the differences. There are far fewer choices and you may have to take whatever flight you can get. In most countries, airlines have few planes, customarily fly with all seats occupied, and visit some destinations only infrequently. They are definitely not always "ready when you are."

On the positive side, flights are so inexpensive in some places that you wonder how they pay for fuel. In Honduras, for example, you can fly most of the way across the country for $35.

How Safe Is It?

Most airlines keep their planes well maintained and provide great service; some do not. Flying on international airlines such as Thai Air, Air New Zealand, Varig, Swiss Air, and Singapore Air is a real treat. On an Air Madagascar flight from Antananarivo to Nairobi, the flight attendant appeared in the coach section bearing smoked kingfish, veal, Camembert and baguettes, a crisp white Bordeaux, and Taittinger champagne.

In contrast, on my first flight on CAAC, the Chinese national airline, the pilot cranked the engines and the passenger cabin immediately filled with dense blue-gray smoke. When the attendants didn't even take notice, I assumed it must be a common occurrence. In the early 1990s, the Chinese government licensed dozens of new airlines to serve newly mobile masses. The sharp increase in flights has resulted in high accident and hijacking rates (ten flights diverted to Taiwan in one year alone).

Aeroflot, once the largest airline in the world, never won a warm place in anyone's heart. Its fatal accident rate for the past 25 years was the worst of all major airlines. On flights that made it, service was atrocious. It's hard to believe, but the situation has deteriorated from there. Aeroflot has been split up among the former Soviet republics. As a result, maintenance and air traffic control systems are more stressed, planes are overloaded, and pilots are poorly trained. So many of the old Aeroflot planes are being operated beyond their guaranteed lifetime that the U.S. State Department has instructed its staff to avoid flying on domestic Russian airlines. A group of Russian aviation officials flew to a conference in the United States on a Finnish airline rather than risk their lives on Aeroflot.

In what may be a first, passengers on the Sahara India Airline flight from Mumbai (Bombay) to Delhi recently refused to board until an official from the Civil Aviation office inspected the plane and declared it safe to fly. Those passengers may have known that fatal airline accidents occur in India at ten times the rate in the rest of the world.

Many knowledgeable travelers avoid flights on Chinese, Russian, Indian, and Colombian airlines. Airlines from Belize, the Dominican Republic, Gambia, Ghana, Honduras, Nicaragua, Paraguay, Uruguay, and Zaire were banned from landing in the United States. Airlines from Bolivia, El Salvador, Guatemala, and the Netherlands Antilles are allowed to land but are on probation.

That's the bad news. To put it into perspective, the FAA reports the "death risk per flight" as 1 in 200,000 for Aeroflot, 1 in 1.5 million for Air Canada, 1 in 3 million for British Airways, 1 in 20 million for El Al, and zero for

Singapore Air. Compare these odds with findings at the University of California (Berkeley) that odds of death from a coast-to-coast automobile trip are 1 in 14,000, from a bicycle accident 1 in 88,000, and from lightning 1 in 1.9 million. In the United States, roughly 95 people are killed each year in plane crashes. Compare that with 112 people killed each *day* in auto accidents. Overall, the odds of death from a commercial airline accident are put at 1 in 10 million.

Nevertheless, it's worth paying attention to those monotonous instructions the flight attendants recite at the beginning of each flight, at least when they talk about where the nearest exits are. A smiling attendant for Southwest Airlines introduced the three attendants by name, then recited the familiar information. As usual, he was ignored. At the end he held up a $100 bill and said, "I'll give this to the first person who can tell me our first names." No one got that $100—but I'll bet every one of those passengers pays more attention to the instructions when they fly Southwest in the future.

Nuts and Bolts of Air Travel

To make air travel a happy experience, a traveler should follow a few basic routines.

Buying Your Ticket

- Make reservations further ahead of departure than you may be used to.
- Check your ticket to see that it is completely correct. It's risky to take accuracy for granted when the ticket includes several flights, countries, and airlines.
- Most airlines will assign seats up to 30 days in advance of the flight, so you're better off making an informed seat selection before arriving at the airport. For one thing, having an assigned seat reduces your vulnerability if the flight is overbooked. The next obvious reason is to get a seat that suits your preferences. If two people traveling together select an aisle seat and a window seat, there's a chance that the middle seat will not be assigned. If it is, it's easy to arrange a switch. On the other hand, if you book seats next to one another, leaving an aisle or a window vacant, it's likely to be assigned to someone else. Keeping that middle seat empty adds a lot of comfort to a long trip.

    If you crave a view, ask the agent to look at the seating configuration for the plane on which you'll be flying and assign you a window seat that is not over the wing. If the agent doesn't look at the configuration, he or she may be guessing and you may wind up staring at shiny sheet metal for several hours.

    On most planes, the best leg room comes with the front seats, just behind the bulkhead. Sometimes bulkhead seats are held for unexpected handicapped passengers, families with children, or airline personnel. If one is empty when the cabin door closes, I leap for it, sometimes after checking with the flight attendant. The trade-off is reduced storage space and a rather oblique view of the movie screen (the latter is seldom much of a loss). Seats in the midcabin exit row also have extra leg room and the seats in the row ahead may not recline, another blessing.

If being seated in the nonsmoking section is important, ask to be seated far from the transition row. Fortunately, there is an increasing trend for flights to be 100 percent nonsmoking.

— If you want special meals, such as vegetarian, diet, low-sodium, diabetic, religious, or children's, place your order when you buy the ticket. Avoid heavy meals.

— Ask about departure taxes you may encounter and in what currency you must pay them. If permitted, buy the tax stamp from the travel agent to save time.

— At home, we often think of being "wait listed" as nearly equivalent to having a reservation. Overseas, it's definitely not the same. A very low wait list number may have a fighting chance. If you're given a high number, forget it unless providence intervenes—but you may be able to give providence a jump start. If circumstances warrant, ask whether a small additional payment might help you move up the wait list. In Manila, I engaged a travel agent, for a small fee, who got me moved from number 37 on the wait list to a seat on the plane ten minutes before departure. He said he reminded the clerk that, as a foreigner, I would be paying in hard currency. Who knows, there may even have been a more personal, microeconomic explanation for my good fortune. Take it for granted that others on the wait list will also be invoking providence on their behalf.

When I decided to go to the Andaman Islands* to scuba dive, I got a reservation to depart Madras the following day. As I was leaving the travel agent's office, she mentioned casually that I was wait listed, not

---

* *Andaman Islands.* A group of islands in the Bay of Bengal, between India and Thailand. The Andaman Islands are noted for fine beaches and diving.

confirmed, for my requested return date. I was so eager to get to the Andamans that I barely remembered to ask, "What number am I on the wait list?" The answer was, "One hundred and fifty one. The first date we can confirm your return is, hmmmm, let's see, thirty-two days from now." It turned out that school holidays had begun earlier in the week and hundreds or thousands of Indian families had already flown to the Andamans. Even with my good travel luck, I decided not to toss those dice.

— Confirm and reconfirm flight reservations. Fail to confirm and your paid-for ticket will probably be canceled and someone else will sit in what you'd been thinking of as your seat. You may get your money back someday, but in the meantime you'll be standing on the ground growling as you watch the once-a-week flight leave without you. If the ticket doesn't tell you when to confirm, do so at least three days (72 hours) before the flight. It's sometimes worth dropping by the ticket office on the day of the flight before going to the airport to ensure that departure time hasn't changed—or that the flight hasn't been canceled. It happens.

— Ask airline clerks for a copy of their route maps and schedules to help with your on-the-road planning. There may only be one or two flights a week to remote destinations.

At the Overseas Airport

— Get to the airport on time. Airlines in Europe typically ask you to be at the airport an hour and a half ahead of scheduled departure time. In the Third World, it's more often two hours. You may feel this is unnecessary, and sometimes you would be right. In the United States, I roll in 15 minutes before departure. Overseas, I'm there two hours ahead of time. If you arrive later than the time indicated, you may lose your reservation.

Remember that the trip starts not at the airport, but at your hotel. Check out the night before if it's practical. If you're leaving from a large city, anticipate traffic accidents, breakdowns, and gridlock—expect the unpredictable. Allow twice as much time to get to the airport as you think you need. I have a friend whose taxi was immobilized in downtown Bangkok traffic for so long that the driver fell asleep. A bus to the Warsaw airport was halted for almost an hour by security forces accompanying a motorcade bearing Lech Walesa. In Gaborone, Botswana, the taxi driver who promised to pick me up at my hotel at 6:30 A.M. never showed. I barely made that flight by hitching a ride in the back of a pickup truck. In Calcutta, I walked out to the street at 7:30 A.M. with plenty of time to catch a taxi to Dum Dum Airport. That's when I discovered a general transportation strike had started at 7 A.M. I finally found a private "pirate car" willing to risk running a possible bus drivers' blockade, but his improvised fare schedule could have been drafted by Jean Laffitte.

Airport officials don't care at all when you *arrived* at the airport. They only care whether there is time for you to get through the process.

Airport officials don't care when you arrived, only if there is enough time to check you in. Plan for lines at the ticket counter, the currency exchange window, the tax stamp window, and customs. In some airports, officials stop accepting passengers a half-hour before flight time if it will take longer than that to clear customs. If you arrive at one of those airports 25 minutes before departure, you're out of luck. Because there are more airlines than check-in counter spaces at the Warsaw airport, the ticket agents for a departing flight yield their counter space to another airline 30 minutes before departure. Arrive after that and there's not even anyone with whom to plead your case.

Suppose you're running late and there's a long line at the check-in counter. If you wait in line, you'll miss your flight. Go to the front of the line and, as calmly as possible, explain the situation to the agent. Try to enlist the sympathy of the person next in line. If your karma is good, they may make space for you. If everyone in line is also anxiously hoping to board the same flight, sprint for the gate. Sometimes the agent on that end will check in your bag and have it carried directly to the plane.

As another motivation for early arrival, there is a strong positive correlation between luggage checked in close to flight departure time and lost luggage. If you check in late, your luggage may not make your flight but it will probably go *somewhere*. Rush the ticket agent and you're asking for a luggage tag that says SLC (Salt Lake City) instead of SCL (Santiago, Chile).

There is also a direct relationship between the time you check in and what your rights are, if any, if you get bumped because the flight was overbooked.

— Immediately after checking in, ensure that the agent pulled only the correct coupon. If he or she has accidentally taken two coupons, you will have an untimely problem somewhere down the line.

— Stay alert while waiting in the terminal for your flight to depart. The announcements that are so difficult to understand may be telling you that the departure gate has been changed. Ask around. Watch other passengers. Bury your head in a book and you may have more than enough time to finish it when you look up.

On Board

- Drink eight ounces of water each hour (coffee, alcohol, and carbonated drinks, dehydrating diuretics, don't count). You need to compensate for the extremely low humidity in the cabin.
- Contact lenses, especially the thin disposable kind, can adhere to the cornea in the low humidity. Have eyedrops available or consider leaving your lenses in their case during a long flight.
- If you have a cold or an allergy, changes in cabin pressure may cause ear or sinus problems. Consider using a decongestant an hour or so before departure. If your ears bother you, try chewing gum, yawning, or pinching your nose shut, closing your mouth, and blowing gently.
- Get some exercise during a long trip. Roll your head and shoulders, twist your body, reach over your head, tighten the muscles in your buttocks, lift your thighs and rotate your feet. Propping your feet up relieves pressure on the back of your thighs. Walk around the cabin and get off during layovers.
- Take a blanket and pillow from the overhead bin when you board. Otherwise, they may have been claimed by the time you feel a need.
- If you're airborne when you discover you may miss a connection, see if the attendant can fix the problem before you arrive. If it will help, ask the attendant to arrange transport to the another gate by electric cart or try to delay departure of the other flight. If the attendant cannot help, move near the exit so you'll be one of the first at the ticket counter. Be creative and determined, but always courteous with the customer service person (who is beginning hours of hell dealing with angry people demanding attention).

If there's a long line at the ticket counter, don't get buried there. Minutes matter. Head for other airline counters to find alternatives or for a telephone to call toll-free reservation numbers or your travel agent to get booked on the next best flight. The airline on which you were scheduled is more likely to help you than any other.

Even if it looks from the monitor as if it's too late to catch a flight, sprint for the gate anyway. You never know. If no alternative can be found, ask the ticket agent for a hotel room and meals at airline expense—in a way that implies that both of you take it for granted.

Overbooking, Delays, and Diversions

Airlines do not guarantee their schedules, nor does the law. In the event of delay or cancellation, your remedies are governed by airline policy, which means they're negotiable. If *cancellation* of a flight was not caused by a so-called act of god, an airline agent will offer to rebook you on another of their flights. Some may offer you a free coupon for a similar flight, but you may have to ask for it. If they divert your flight to an alternate destination, they may offer you a hotel room.

When a flight is *delayed,* an airline may provide meals and pay for telephone calls unless the delay was caused by bad weather, in which case you feed yourself. Airlines will not reimburse ticket holders for inconvenience, financial losses, or broken romances related to a delayed arrival.

Your rights are different in the case of *overbooking,* which is quite legal. If you don't want to get bumped, check in early. Being somewhere in line when they fill the last seat does you no good, nor does holding a boarding pass mean you'll be allowed to board. You must receive a boarding *assignment*; that is, you must be checked in.

If a flight is oversold, the clerk will call for volunteers to be bumped. If you're willing to trade your time for money, tell the clerk ahead of time that you'll agree to be bumped, but only if there is an alternative flight acceptable to you and they pay for meal, hotel, and phone call expenses. In addition to a free flight, they can also offer some combination of an upgrade, a temporary pass to a first-class lounge, and/or a cash payment in the range of $200 to $500. It's all negotiable.

Suppose you don't volunteer and they bump you anyway? For flights in and originating from the United States, the policy of U.S. airlines is that if they can put you on another flight that arrives at your destination within an hour of when you were originally scheduled to arrive, you receive no compensation. If you will arrive more than one hour late but less than two, you are entitled to a cash payment equal to the amount you paid for your one-way ticket or one-half the cost of your round-trip ticket, up to $200. If the delay is more than four hours on an international flight, the airline doubles the payment, up to $400. Plus, of course, the airline must still get you to your destination. The airline may try to get you to accept free air travel in the future in place of the cash payment. You may accept, but you don't have to.

Here's the joker. If you checked in *after* the deadline shown on your ticket jacket, you may receive no compensation at all. And, of course, late arrivers head the list of bumpees. Even for me, a chronic late arriver, the lesson is clear.

The policies of foreign carriers with respect to overbooking are consistent with European Community regulations, which are similar to U.S. regulations. The policies of U.S. carriers pertaining to flights originating outside the United States are, so far, inscrutable.

When the starboard engine on our Madrid-to-Atlanta flight failed over the Atlantic, the pilot dumped fuel and returned to Madrid. The airline put us up in a five-star hotel, wined and dined us royally, and doubled our frequent flyer miles. The next morning, I requested an upgrade to Business Class from a friendly clerk—and got it.

To summarize, reconfirm your ticket repeatedly and get to the airport early. Avoid stress and disappointment and take advantage of a little journal-writing time. If a problem comes up, being prepared will reduce its impact on your trip.

You'll find additional information on air travel in Chapters 5 and 6.

LOCAL TRANSPORT

As music reveals the character of a country, so do its small vehicles. In the same way taxis and subways reflect the nature of Manhattan, collectivos in Lima and motor scooters in Rarotonga capture the spirit of those places.

European public transportation systems are extensive and efficient. Since they're familiar to us, we use them with little hesitation. However, modern transportation systems have few equivalents in the Third World. Instead, small entrepreneurs take over—and their solutions are wondrous to behold. Local transport is inexpensive, often uncomfortable, and almost always fun.

Don't be intimidated by local transport.

Because it's unfamiliar to them, some travelers are initially intimidated by local transport. With a little experience, though, they soon hop aboard all kinds of vehicles with confidence and a smile. They're at home in a VW van decorated with colorful murals, a pickup truck with a striped metal awning above bottom-polished wooden benches, or a horse-drawn cart with a fringed roof and a honey jar filled with fresh flowers.

Local transport includes bemos, bendis, bicycles, camels, canal boats, collectivos, elephants, jeepneys, makoros, matatus, minivans, motor scooters, oplets, outrigger canoes, ox-carts, poda podas, pouse-pouses, taxi-brousses, tongas, and many more. Since they are so common around the world, I'll comment here on taxis, minivans, subways, and bicycles. The others will come as a series of happy surprises.

Taxis

In a taxi, you travel in comfort and with a reasonable likelihood of reaching your planned destination, sometimes paying a considerable premium for the convenience. Unfortunately, taxi drivers, as a group, seldom create a favorable impression. The problem is money. You have it and they want as much of it as they can get. Hope for a working meter or, from an airport, a fixed fee. Otherwise, bargain on the fare.

Since taxi drivers are experienced in dealing with travelers, you'll pay dearly unless you strike a bargain before the wheels roll. If you bargain in advance, you can ride for an hour and a half in a Madagascar taxi-brousse for 85 cents, even less in a rickshaw called a *pouse-pouse*. If you don't bargain, the sky's the limit. Bargaining with taxi drivers as an art form is discussed in Chapter 10.

River taxi on Chao Phraya River. Bangkok, Thailand.

When it's time to pay, first get your luggage out of the taxi, then give the driver the exact fare agreed on. That way, in the event of a difference of opinion, your luggage can't be held hostage. If you have only a large bill, state the amount of the fare before handing it over. Otherwise, with your bill in his pocket, he may claim that the fare was higher than you agreed. Regardless, he may claim he has no change, hoping you'll be in too much of a hurry to wait. With a little forethought, you can avoid this scenario.

Before your hotel clerk calls for a taxi, ask whether the call will result in an additional charge by the driver. In Athens, for instance, the charge for being summoned can exceed the charge for driving all the way to the airport. You may prefer to walk to the curb and handle it yourself.

Since it's not unusual for a taxi driver to levy a supplemental charge based on how many bags he puts in the trunk, keep at least small pieces of luggage in the car with you.

In many cities, rates increase dramatically at night. Local law may permit charging double the fare on the meter. Spare your blood pressure a peak experience by asking in advance.

Minivans

Picture yourself standing on the curb as a minivan skids to a brakes-locked stop in front of you. It has an end-of-the-line destination sign in its window, which is probably not the name of the place you want to go. You aren't sure what the fare is or what you're supposed to do next, and you have only seconds to decide whether to board. Confused, you step back and look for a taxi. After learning that taxi rides aren't exactly problem free and cost 20 times more than the "people's transport," you try again.

When you board the minivan, you find all seats occupied, the roof too low to permit standing upright, and 15 people looking at you. Since you have no idea what the 12-year-old fare collector is saying, you're reduced to holding out several coins. He takes what he wants. Fortunately, it's usually less than ten cents.

You had a general idea of the direction in which you wanted to go when you got in, but after ten minutes of turning corners you're not so sure. Seeing a street name that looks about right, you climb out, shoulder your daypack— and realize you're lost. It really doesn't matter; it's part of your adventure. You can't go very wrong. When you've looked around, you catch another minivan, craning your neck to see out the window, thinking surely you'll see something familiar. Maybe you do, maybe not. Either way, you get home, or somewhere.

Before long, you realize how willing other passengers are to help. If your destination is some distance from the minivan route, someone may even jump off and show you the way. Because systems are so similar, your new knowledge will serve you everywhere in the world.

In most cities, local minivans race endlessly like slot cars around their circuits. You summon one with a wave as it approaches. For transportation from one town to another, there are established, even if not marked, stations from which the minivans set out. If there's no schedule, minivans won't leave before their seats are full. Touts will try to steer you toward the van that employs them. They'll say they are just about to leave, that theirs is the only van going where you want to go, or anything else they think might work. They'll try to get you to take a seat and to pay for the trip in advance.

Since the driver expects foreigners to be impatient by nature, he may try to get you to convert his van into a private taxi by buying all unoccupied seats. If he asks if you would like to leave at a time when the van is still only half full, find out what the deal is. There is no free lunch.

You might expect that the van with the most passengers already in it would be the next to leave. Instead, it's common for a driver to get his buddies to sit in his van to pass the time, hoping that you'll see his van nearly full and choose

Right of Way

As you stroll to roadside to find a ride, repeat to yourself: PEDES-TRIANS DO NOT HAVE THE RIGHT OF WAY. Soft-shell humans must yield to trucks, buses, cars, ox-carts, camels, bicycles—everything. Not only will vehicles not stop, most won't even swerve. To make things more interesting, traffic moves on the "wrong," or driver's left side, of the road in many countries. As a rule of thumb, if a reasonable amount of English is spoken in a country, look to your *right* before you step into the roadway.

it. After a while, you notice that every time a real passenger climbs in, someone else gets off—and the van goes nowhere. If the vans are filling up fast, take a seat. Otherwise, think of it as an opportunity to stroll around nearby, perhaps finding someone to talk with, until you see a van actually getting ready to go.

Intercity minivans have set fees for local people, but the driver may ask you to pay whatever he thinks you're good for. If you've learned some vocabulary, ask another passenger what the fare is. Even better, watch what someone else pays, being aware they may not be going to your destination. If you're carrying luggage, you may have to pay an extra fare, certainly if it's taking up a passenger's space. Don't pay until the vehicle is about to leave. That way, if another cranks up to leave first, you're free to switch to it if you want or need to. As you start to get out, the driver may offer you a reduced fare. Let them bid for your business.

Since drivers' incomes depend solely on fares, they let everyone aboard who can cram themselves in, and then they drive as fast as they can for as many hours as they can stay, more or less, awake. Exhausted, driving without speedometers or any other dashboard indicators, sometimes buying off official or unofficial interference with bribes hurled out the window, it's no wonder that little problems crop up.

Minivans are ubiquitous, cheap, and almost always fun—and no traveler should fail to give them a try.

Subways

Many people travel to the great metropolitan areas of the world and never experience the metro, underground, or whatever the local subway system is called. That's understandable. If you don't travel by subway at home, a foreign system can appear pretty intimidating. However, because subways are fast, convenient, and inexpensive, it's worth overcoming any hesitation. Some subways, and Moscow's is a prime example, are even architectural or artistic marvels.

A route map, which you can get from a tourist office or from the ticket seller, makes riding subways a lot easier. Although the first map I saw in Paris looked like a plate of spaghetti, I figured it out and now feel confident on any subway system in the world. Let's see if I can explain how subway systems work.

There are two stages in navigating through subways. The first is when you look at the map and figure out which line or lines you need to ride and where the nearest station is. The second is in the subway station as you figure out where to go to board the right car. The second stage is made more interesting by the common need to transfer midride to another line.

The first stage is simple. On the map, locate where you are and the station at which you'll start your journey. Then locate your destination and note the names of the lines you'll ride. Each line is named for the *last* station at both ends of the line. For instance, a line you'll board might be named, in English,

Airport–City Hall. If it's not clear from the map, ask at your lodging, ask the ticket seller, ask another passenger, or just trust your intuition.

Let's say you want off at the "Art Museum," and that's the name of one of the stations listed on the Airport–City Hall line. Look for a sign in the subway station that directs you toward that track. As you near it, you decide from the map whether the art museum is in the direction of the "airport" or the "city hall." That decision determines on which side of the track you stand and, therefore, in which direction the car will be going. A map on the inside of the subway car shows all the stops, letting you know when the art museum stop is coming up. It's a lot harder to describe than it is to do.

If Art Museum isn't the name of one of the subway stations on the map, note the name of the nearest station and get off there.

Now, suppose the line you first board doesn't go past the art museum and you have to change lines to get there. It's not difficult since each line on the map is numbered or depicted in a distinctive color. Identify the station at which the line you're on and the line to which you want to transfer intersect. When you get off at that intersection, you'll see a sign directing you to the line you want and the right direction. When you change lines, you'll usually walk up or down a level in the station. On the platform, you have an opportunity to check the route map on the wall or confirm your plan with someone.

On the subway, as on many other types of public transportation, lots of folks are pressed together in a confined space so it's wise to keep part of your mind on security. Keep your daypack in front of you. If you have a camera, keep it out of sight or keep your hand on it. Carry nothing you care about in an insecure pocket.

Bicycles

Few means of local transportation provide the pleasure that comes from exploring on a bicycle. It's cheap, relatively safe, gives you great range, lets you see things at a gentle pace, and gets the kinks out of your legs. A few travelers sign up for a bike tour and some plan a bike trip on their own, but too many forget that renting bikes locally is an option.

In Europe and a few other places, you can rent bicycles as multigeared and lightweight as you want. Elsewhere, expect a single gear and a handlebar bell. In most cities around the world, it's not hard to find places that rent bikes. Ask around. If there's nothing organized, it's not hard to find some local person delighted to earn a little money by renting his bike.

Riding local transport produces some of the finest and funniest memories from any trip. Seek it out, the more exotic the better. Ride a yak or a camel or an elephant; listen to the sounds of the creaking leather harness of the pony cart late at night; stand at the rail of a freighter as the Andes glide by in the moonlight. Using local transport is a great way to SAVE MONEY, but it does much more. It helps transform a tourist into a traveler.

CAR RENTAL

In the United States, Europe, and Oceania, we rent a car without a second thought. In much of the rest of the world, doing so deserves several second thoughts. Make no mistake, renting and driving a car abroad can be a challenging and sometimes perilous experience.

In less-developed regions, rental cars are often very expensive, especially when you add in high-priced petrol, insurance, tax, theft protection, drop-off fee, airport location, and mysterious surcharges. Reflecting irregular maintenance, mechanical problems are not infrequent and breakdowns seldom occur at convenient places. Worse, driving may expose you to considerable liability, not to mention turning your nerves into banjo strings. Automobile accidents are one of the leading causes of injury or death for overseas travelers.

The flexibility of having your own car can be very appealing.

Why discuss car rental at all? First, because the flexibility and freedom of having your own transportation is very appealing. Second, sometimes you need to rent a car to get where you want to go. Third, a rental car makes it easier to stay in hotels far removed from expensive downtown hotels in Europe. Since some number of travelers will rent a car abroad, this chapter will help make it a successful experience.

Driver's License

Ask the rental agent, in advance, what kind of driver's license you need to rent their car. In most of Western Europe, your own state driver's license is sufficient. Among common tourist destinations, Spain, Hungary, Russia, Thailand, Japan, Argentina, Brazil, Chile, and Venezuela nominally require either an International Driving Permit (IDP), available from any AAA affiliate for about $10, or a translation of your license into the local language. However, many travel agents say that a passport and your own driver's license are sufficient. If you go without an IDP, and then decide to rent a car in one of the few countries that nominally requires one, it's likely you can make an "arrangement" that will cure the problem. In my experience, the IDP has become little more than a souvenir.

When to Rent

If you decide to rent from an *international company*, one way to SAVE MONEY (as much as 50 percent) is to reserve and pay for a car *before* you leave home. Talk with your travel agent. You may be able to get a deal on a car as part of a package with your airline ticket. If you walk up to an international car rental counter in Europe, expect to pay much more than if you'd made the arrangements at home. At that point, call home and make the deal there! You might get an even better rate from a small local company but, on your first trip to a distant destination, you may prefer the security and convenience of knowing there'll be a car waiting.

Several companies, including Kemwell, permit you to buy vouchers in the United States and choose your rental days after you arrive. Doing so adds flexibility while retaining the big savings over renting from the same companies locally.

Rental rates are higher in some countries than in others. For example, you could pay almost twice as much for a car in Italy or France as you would in the United Kingdom or Germany. If it fits your plans, rent the car before entering one of the more expensive countries.

When you reserve a car, the clerk will ask what time you'll pick it up. After you state a time, find out how long they'll hold the car if your arrival is delayed. Some companies flush your reservation after 30 minutes, others give you until closing time, and some will wait patiently for up to 24 hours. If a rental agency has your flight number, it should know if your flight is behind schedule. Nevertheless, if you'll arrive later than expected, let them know.

If you've made a reservation and find you won't be able to honor it, cancel as early as possible. Not only does your courtesy free the car for another traveler, but it may enable you to avoid a cancellation fee. Rental companies are beginning to charge no-shows a fee, often $25, but it could be as much as the entire amount of the rental contract.

From Whom to Rent

Can you afford a rental car on a modest budget? It's difficult if you rent from one of the heavily promoted international companies, but for convenience and out of habit, that's what most people do. If you plan to rent from an international company, SAVE MONEY by comparison shopping. Prices charged by car rental firms differ widely. For example, you can get substantially better rates from firms such as Auto Europe (which has more than 4,000 locations in Europe and claims to beat anyone else's rate; call 800-223-5555), Budget (800-527-0700), Europe by Car (800-223-1516), European Car Reservations (800-535-3303), or Kemwell (800-678-0678), than from companies such as Hertz or EuroDollar. In a 1995 *Condé Nast Traveler* readers poll, Kemwell was voted as having the best rental rates overseas.

The following examples are based on fact, but they are only for illustration since quoted rates fluctuate frequently. In England, you would have paid $189 for a subcompact for a week rented from Europe by Car compared with $303 for the same car and term from Hertz. In Germany, European Car Reservations charged $182 while EuroDollar charged $291. To rent a car for a week in the Czech Republic you could have paid $225 to AutoEurope or $580 to Avis. By the way, most Western Europe rental companies will not let you take their autos across a border into Eastern Europe.

SAVE MONEY by renting your automobile from the foreign equivalent of Rent-a-Wreck. What do you care about a few dents when you're driving across South Africa?

You almost always SAVE MONEY if you skip the car rental counters at the airport whose rates reflect the taxes and fees they pay the airport. If you don't see signs advertising away-from-the-airport rental agencies, try the yellow

Prices charged for car rentals vary, so shop around.

pages. They'll usually come for you. If not, go into town and rent from the bus driver's friend, a local rental company, or even a local travel agent.

Here's an obscure way to SAVE MONEY. Ask a local agent if it has a car to be returned to another location. If you appear responsible, you may get the car without charge, paying only for the gas. I did this in New Zealand and the agent even left a sack of freshly picked apples on the front seat for me. Some travelers routinely rent from car dealers at very low rates.

Anyone with a blemished driving record, especially by a recent DUI or accident, may not be allowed to rent a car from certain companies. Rather than learning about this restriction as you're trying to take delivery of the car, call ahead to find out what the policy is. Also, most agencies require a renter to be at least 18 years old, some 21, and some 25. Further, check to see if there's a maximum age.

The Terms of the Deal

Special rates. If you call because of a special rate you saw advertised, don't assume that the clerk at the reservation counter will offer you that rate. Since you may have to ask for it, perhaps even insist on it, it's good to have the ad with you or be able to cite the code number in it. Car rental agents also have a pocketful of deals they can offer on their own, but they won't do so unless you prompt them. Instead, they'll try to sell you extras and upgrades (including various insurance options).

Bargaining. SAVE MONEY by bargaining. Ask for a discount on the basis of your occupation, your membership in some organization (such as a corporation, automobile association, frequent flyer club, church group, or the Mouseketeers), your age, your credit card, anything you can think of. Bring up competitor's prices. State how much you're willing to pay. Ask about weekend, by-the-week, and other discounted rates. You can sometimes get a better deal simply by walking from one counter to the next in full view of all the agents. When you get a quote from one, invite another to beat it. It's a very competitive business, so they'll often take what they can get.

Price. Determine exactly what is included in the quoted price and what isn't. Don't let yourself be surprised by "extras" such as an airport pickup charge, state or city surcharge, late return charge, additional driver fee (which could be $5 for each additional driver per day), under-age surcharge, VAT (value added tax, which adds up to 18 percent in some European countries), extra equipment charge (e.g., a baby seat), one-way drop-off charge (which can be astronomical), collision/loss damage waiver (which runs $3 to $15 per day), theft protection (mandatory in some countries), charges for road service, and so on.

If asked for a deposit, use your credit card. If an agent demands a large cash deposit, you may return to discover it locked up or otherwise unavailable when you want it—and of course you're getting on a plane in a couple of hours.

Ask whether you get a price break when you're renting for a weekend or for five days or more. It can be less expensive to rent for six days than for four. Similarly, if you plan to use a car for more than 17 days, see whether the company has a lease option. If so, you'll SAVE MONEY over a straight rental.

Features. Don't assume that air conditioning and automatic transmission are standard; in many countries they are not. Nor are seat belts. If you care, ask whether the car has any of the new high-tech features. For example, the Avis computerized navigational device has a video screen that shows the car as a moving dot on a map; after the driver chooses a destination, the system gives verbal prompts. The Hertz system provides a detailed printout of directions.

If the car has antilock brakes, be sure to know how to use them properly before leaving the parking lot.

Before leaving the airport, get a map or directions to your first destinations and find out where to drop the car on your return. Be sure you know what time the rental office closes where you'll return the car.

If you rent a car in Europe, you might read *Motoeuropa* (Eric Bredesen, Box 1212, Dubuque, IA 52004), which provides country-by-country details about renting, driving, or buying a car. *Autorental Europe* (Bill Meier, Lansing Publications, Box 1887, Pleasanton, CA 94566) is another useful resource. There are also some good "driving itenerary" guides (e.g., Frommer).

Thrifty and National Interrent offer automated check-out and check-in systems that resemble ATMs. The machine scans your driver's license and credit card and spits out a rental agreement for your signature. Is this getting a little spooky?

Size. The size of car you choose is important. Ask how many passengers it can transport in comfort. Lower fuel efficiency (kilometers per gallon) in large cars means the petrol bill will be high. If an agent offers you a car larger than you need, be wary. That large car may be available precisely because it's a gas-guzzler. On the other hand, be cautious about renting a microcompact in Germany, Italy, or other places with high-speed highways where it may be blown away by drivers doing 200 kph. If you reserve a small car, as many people do, and the agency is out of that size when you arrive, it should either upgrade you to another of its cars or obtain a similar car from another company without charge to you.

Read the Contract

If there's a problem, *it does no good to claim ignorance of a provision in the rental contract*. Here are some things to look for:

— Does it define exactly what your responsibilities are?

— On the basis of the blank credit card slip you signed, does the company tie up part of your credit line as security for damage to the car? It may not be just the rental amount; it could be all or part of the value of the car. You need to know whether your credit line is about to be tapped out.

— How do they compute charges if you return the car before or after the end of the agreed-on rental period?

— Do you get unlimited free kilometers or is the rental fee based on the number of kilometers driven? If you pay more every time the little odometer numbers click, you may not feel free to explore as many mysterious detours.

— Does the rental agreement contain instructions about what to do if the car breaks down? Is there a phone number to call in case of a problem? If you feel compelled to make repairs before receiving authorization, get receipts to support your request for reimbursement. Who is responsible for routine maintenance?

— Are you required to return the tank full of fuel? If so and you fail to do so, you'll be charged at a rate substantially above market price. In some countries, rental companies deliver the car to you with the tank full and instruct you to return it completely empty (the so-called "fuel purchase option"). That's so they can charge you an inflated price for that first tank of petrol. Since it's a little perilous for most travelers speeding to catch a plane to skid into the parking lot on the last drop, the company gets the petrol left in the tank as a second bonus. Slick, eh?

— Are you permitted to drive the car into another country? Be alert to this one if you intend to drive from Western to Eastern Europe.

Insurance

The moment comes in every transaction when the clerk asks whether you want the collision insurance offered by the rental company, meaning an additional charge of $10 to $20 per day. This insurance covers only damage to the rental car, leaving you on your own as far as other liabilities. Further, it is littered with exceptions to the coverage. Reading one of the policies is scary. It is so overpriced and profitable to the rental company that the clerk has been trained to urge you to buy it. His compensation may depend on how successfully he peddles this product. Therefore, he may even insist that whatever alternative insurance coverage you offer is invalid.

To respond rationally, you must know ahead of time whether you already have insurance that covers damage to the rental car and whether this company, as opposed to what the clerk may say, accepts it. Because they don't know those answers, far too many travelers pay a high price for collision insurance they don't need.

Most *domestic automobile insurance policies* offer an option providing collision coverage for cars rented in the United States, but *not* for rental cars driven abroad. Call your auto insurance agent and specify where you expect to be driving. If there is coverage, ask whether (a) the amount of coverage is limited to the value of your personal car (which might be less that the value of the rental car), (b) additional drivers would be covered, (c) it covers unusual vehicles such as RVs or trucks, (d) there is a limit on how long coverage is valid overseas (e.g., 30 days), (e) your regular deductible applies, and (f) the policy provides liability coverage for injury to persons and property. If your domestic policy provides coverage, obtain acknowledgment from the car rental company in advance and carry evidence of the policy.

Ask your agent if there is coverage available for rental cars overseas.

If you intend to use the insurance protection of your credit card (see the discussion in Chapter 6), call the credit card issuer to be certain its coverage is in effect where you'll be traveling. Then ask the car rental reservations agent if the credit card coverage will be accepted where you pick up the car. Since it is not universally accepted, insist that they check with their *local* agent. Since a local agent may still tell you on arrival that your credit card coverage is not valid, verification in writing may come in handy. If they still balk, call a regional office for confirmation. If you were to pay for the collision damage waiver (CDW) at that point, it would probably cost even more than if you'd paid for it with your prepayment for the car. If you must pay for it to get the car, write on the contract that you are doing so at the clerk's insistence and seek a refund when you return home. If a country's laws require renters to purchase local insurance regardless of credit card coverage, you will have discovered it in advance.

Note that neither the car rental company's collision insurance nor your credit card collision coverage is liability insurance covering damage you may do to people or property. If you have domestic automobile liability insurance, read your policy or ask your agent whether it's effective when driving a rental car abroad. In the United States, state law requires car rental companies to carry various levels of liability insurance. Overseas, the situation varies.

If your own automobile liability insurance does not cover driving a rental car abroad, or you have no automobile liability insurance, investigate buying "nonowner" liability coverage. Alternatively, consider buying $1 million in liability coverage from the rental car company for the trip.

Some European border stations require that you present a "green card," proving you have third-party insurance coverage, before they'll let you drive a rental car into their country. Look for it in the glove box. Without it you'll be doing a U-turn at the border.

Insurance coverage may be invalidated when the driver (a) was not listed on the rental contract, (b) was intoxicated at the time of the accident, or (c) violated a geographical limitation in the rental contract, such as by taking the car across a border or on specified roads. The company will probably never know that you violated the limitation—unless you have a wreck in the forbidden zone. Then they'll know and you'll get the bill for damages.

Don't take any risks with insurance. Travel magazines are full of letters lamenting horrendous situations as a result of an accident for which the writers were not insured.

Inspect the Vehicle

My cardinal rule when renting a car anywhere other than a big city franchise situation: SEE THE VEHICLE before handing over any money. Otherwise, the shiny car parked nearby as a lure may not be the car in which you depart the next morning amid grinding gears and acrid smoke. If the agent tells you that "your" car isn't available for inspection at the moment, it may be off hauling a load of swine and turnips. Ask that it be brought to your hotel before you sign up. If the car promised isn't the one that shows up the next day, be insistent. They may discover something more suitable or drop the price as you drop your standards.

Inspect the car for damage *before* you leave the lot. In some countries, it may already look like the loser in a destruction derby. On the other hand, some European rental agencies are very picky and returning with a tiny dent or scratch could result in demand for payment on the spot. If there are dings, get a witness or have the agent note them on the contract. When you return, take a look at the car yourself. It's seldom the policy of a rental company to inspect at the moment you return, but you may want to have the clerk note on the contract that there is no damage. Damage "discovered" after you've left may be charged to your credit card and you will not have much of a defense.

Check the lights, air conditioning/heater, horn, windshield wiper, seatbelt, and brakes. Make sure there is a spare tire and jack. If the tires aren't safe, change tires, change cars, or change companies. While you're inspecting, make a note of the license number, make, model, and color of the car. If the car is stolen while in your custody or you misplace it in a crowded parking lot, you'll feel foolish if you can't identify it. If you'll be driving the car for an extended period, ask for an extra key. If one isn't forthcoming, consider having one

See the vehicle before handing over any money.

Author scrunched in a horse-drawn *bendi*. Tomohon, Sulawesi Indonesia.

made. Solving a lost key problem is much more time-consuming in Bulgaria than in Baltimore.

Before you roll away, be sure you understand how to operate all switches, knobs, gears, and repair equipment. Ask whether the car has an electronic antitheft device. If so, have it demonstrated. Otherwise, you may wind up with a car that won't start or whose shrieking alarm won't stop.

If the tank is supposed to be full, see that it is. By the way, if you drive in Europe you should be aware that gas stations charge for services such as cleaning the windshield or filling the tires. Of course, in the United States, you either get no service or it's built into the price of the gas.

While planning a trip from Victoria Falls, Zimbabwe, to Chobe National Park in northern Botswana, then on to Etosha National Park in Namibia, I found no evidence of public transportation along that stretch. I figured we could hitch from Vic Falls to Chobe and on to Katima Mulillo, a village at the northeastern tip of Namibia, but since the several hundred miles of sand and sagebrush beyond that point seemed uninhabited, hitching farther seemed impractical. Then my partner discovered that a small resort in Katima Mulillo was a lonely outpost of an international car rental agency. It had a grand total of one car for rent and we reserved it instantly. When we arrived at the resort months later (amazingly, on the date agreed), the owner was distressed to learn that we intended to take his little Toyota all the way to Windhoek, the capital. For all its sheltered life, his pet Toyota had been confined to short scenic excursions. Nevertheless, waving our reservation, we rented the Toyota and didn't see another car for the next eight hours. All told, we put about 2,000 hard kilometers on that little car before turning it in. I understand the resort abandoned its affiliation with the rental company soon afterward. Can't say I blame them.

Safety

For safety reasons, it's better not to stop if anyone other than a police officer tries to flag you down. The "good Samaritan" scam involves someone waving at you, apparently to alert you to a problem with your car. Perhaps another car pulls alongside and a passenger points at one of your tires with an expression of alarm. While you and the Samaritan check out the imaginary problem, his confederate empties your car.

If you are rear-ended, a favorite ploy in southern France, don't get out of your car if you have the slightest doubt about the situation. That little bump may be an informal introduction, the equivalent of "What's your sign." The thief wants to know you better. If you can, drive to a service station or some other well-lighted public place. Otherwise, stay in your locked car and wait for the police.

Someone who has access to your car, say in a service station, may start a slow leak in a tire. I've seen a hand-crafted blade that attaches to the toe of a shoe for exactly that purpose. When the tire goes flat later, someone will be there to help you out—and help himself. It's sad to say, but anytime you accept help, you or your partner should keep an eye on the helpers.

Be alert for thieves who may try to snatch something from your car when you stop at a traffic light. In Buenos Aires this has gotten to be such a problem that many drivers slow a bit, combine a quick sideways glance with a prayer, and cruise right through red lights. Keep those doors locked and, if circumstances warrant, windows up. In some places, it's better to keep your gear on the floor of the car than on the front seat. Don't leave a tempting target for a quick hand slipping in an open window.

Be alert when driving in an area that seems risky. If someone approaches your car, perhaps indicating he wants to ask directions, be prepared to drive away immediately. If caught off-guard by someone who demands your keys, consider tossing them to him—but missing. Escape as he retrieves the keys.

If an unmarked car with a flashing light signals you to stop, drive to a well-lighted place to do so. Unless you are certain it's the police, keep the car doors locked and roll the window down just far enough to show your license. Ask for identification. If you're not satisfied, refuse to get out of the car and ask to be escorted to a police station.

If you believe you are being followed, make a series of turns. If the other vehicle is still with you, look for a police station or a busy petrol station.

A rental car company sticker is an invitation to thieves, so ask for a car without one. If there is one on the car, remove it. Remember the glee you felt as a child when you saw Christmas presents under the tree? That's how a thief feels when he spots a rental car. It's a giant stocking stuffed with cameras and luggage.

Park in well-lighted areas and don't leave any belongings visible. Assume that a rental car will be broken into and never leave anything expensive in the car overnight. Think of it as wheels, not as a secure place to leave your gear. Locking something in the trunk is better than leaving it on the seat, but even that provides little real protection.

You may have an opportunity to make the car temporarily secure by engaging the services of a car guardian. In places such as Mexico City and Naples, the offer from scruffy adolescents to guard your car is straightforward blackmail. They're offering to guard it from themselves and, frankly, it's a good investment of a few pesos or lira or even a euro.

Driving conservatively is good practice since traffic can be quite chaotic, and foreign rules of the road, both official and informal, may be unfamiliar to you. Reading signs in a foreign language takes your attention off the road for a few extra seconds. Contact local auto clubs for rules of the road and general advice. Besides avoiding an accident, driving conservatively helps avoid a traffic ticket. If you get a ticket in Europe, you pay a fine on the spot (asking for a receipt early on may help keep the fine in line with the official schedule). In other parts of the world, when and how much you pay is more likely to be a matter of negotiation on a very uneven playing field. If the police photograph your car committing a violation, they will bill the car rental firm, which will add it to your credit card.

Besides slowing reflexes when they're needed the most, being intoxicated while driving can lead to jail. In Europe, penalties for driving under the influence are severe. Further, "influence" is defined as a blood alcohol level only one-half to one-quarter what it is in the United States. Roadblocks with Breathalyzer tests are not uncommon.

In almost a dozen countries, cars drive on the lefthand side of the road. You can learn to do it, but it will take a few hours (or more). So how do you avoid trashing the car during that time?

- Consider renting a car with an automatic transmission.
- Locate all the gadgets (horn, lights, wipers, signals) before leaving the rental lot (you'll wish you had if you need one of them halfway through a roundabout!).
- Take a practice spin in the rental lot or on some nearby bunny slope.
- Avoid starting off in rush hour.
- Take advantage of a partner who can handle the map, read street signs, and watch for bogies. Ask about signage and driving customs before you leave the lot.

In the end, driving on the "wrong" side of the road isn't the hard part. The hard part is the constant embarrassment of walking up to the wrong side of the car, then trying to pretend you're just there to check the tire pressure.

Stress

Monetary costs of car rental seem modest compared to the mental havoc some people experience when driving a car in less-developed countries.

Roads are jammed and the horn takes the place of the brake. If you aren't used to sharing a narrow road with massive trucks and with rattle-trap cars lurching along without benefit of headlights, and if you don't find pleasure in weaving through throngs of bicycles, rickshaws, horse carts, camels, and basket-laden pedestrians, forget it!

From Rwanda to Sri Lanka, I've rented cars that come with a driver. This is not an extravagance. The cost for the driver is, after a little bargaining, minimal when balanced against the guidance and tranquility he provides. At the end of the day, he helps find suitable lodging for you before curling up in the backseat of the car or a back room of the hotel. It's not unusual to hire car and driver from a nontraditional source, such as a travel agent or desk clerk, for considerably less than you'd pay for the vehicle alone from a heavily promoted car rental firm.

Traveling in Your Own Car

For people tempted to buy a vehicle in, or take a vehicle to, a foreign country, I'd mention several considerations. First, staying in your own vehicle can isolate you from local life as effectively as being on a regimented tour. Second, in many countries the roads are in such terrible condition they can reduce your vehicle to scrap. Third, the difficulty of finding spare parts and experienced mechanics is multiplied by the square of the distance from your auto's country of origin. Fourth, every time you cross a border you may have to buy a bond guaranteeing you won't sell your car while in the country. Fifth, to get your car across some borders you may have to pay significant bribes. Sixth, traveling a long distance with a fully loaded vehicle means accepting considerable risk of theft.

Despite all these objections, I bought a ten-year-old Citroen 2CV at the beginning of a two-month postgraduation trip in Europe. It was broken into once and run into twice but provided great flexibility and enormous fun—and I made $100 when I sold it to an arriving student.

If you'll be in Europe for a month or more and are determined to drive, a lease may be less expensive than a rental. Or, look into a purchase/repurchase deal (the rough equivalent of a lease) with one of the car rental companies. You pay for maintenance, fuel, repairs, and other "owner's" expenses, but you are not charged for mileage. At the end of the period, the rental company repurchases the vehicle for a price that makes the net cost to you less than rental.

TRAVELING BY WATER

Freighter Travel

One of the great freighter trips I've taken was aboard the *Evangelista*, sailing the Chilean "inside passage" between Puerto Montt and Puerto

Natales.* A tiny stateroom and three meals cost about $40 a day. In addition to incomparable views of the Andes and glaciers, the captain allowed me to take the helm for hours at a time. Navimag (phone 56-2-2035030 or 56-065-253318), which owns *Evangelista*, and a company named Transmarchilay offer comfortable, inexpensive trips from Puerto Montt to the island of Chiloe, the small towns of Chaiten and Chacabuco at the base of the Andes, glaciers spilling into Laguna San Rafael, and Puerto Natales. These trips take from one to six days.

Opportunities for freighter travel in the traditional sense have diminished substantially over the past several decades. That was due, in part, to regulations that require a doctor on board if there are more than 12 passengers. However, after hitting a low in the mid-1980s, capacity for passengers on freighters is again on the upswing. Increased mechanization has freed more officers' staterooms for passengers. And when cargo tonnage drops, shipping lines are delighted to earn revenue from passengers. Some of the more popular trips from the United States sail to East Africa (60 to 70 days), Australia (70 to 75 days), and South America (35 to 50 days).

Freighter travel isn't as cheap as it was in the past, but it's still possible to travel in a first-class freighter cabin for around $90 a day, considerably less than many cruise ships (and there are discounts for off-season travel). Some charge as little as $70 per day. Cabins are likely to be more spacious than those on cruise ships, and there are often accommodations for singles with no surcharge. Most are outside cabins with large windows, comfortable sitting areas, and private facilities. Because the best cabins go to those who reserve first, some travelers make plans a year or more in advance.

You will spend more time at sea in freighters than in cruise ships.

Wholesome meals, included in the price, are usually served in the officers' dining room. Depending on the carrier, these meals may be very ethnic, so make sure you know what to expect. There won't be a dance band or over-the-hill entertainers in shiny tuxedoes, but there will probably be a sun deck, VCR, library and, perhaps, a saltwater pool. The crew is there to work, so you'll have plenty of time to write the novel that's been waiting to spring to life.

Freighters travel slowly, providing more time at sea than you'd have on a cruise ship—and that's exactly what most freighter travelers are after. Because freighters are working ships, they may not adhere to their planned schedules. If you're kept at sea extra days because the ship detours to an unexpected port to capture a cargo, there's no extra charge.

Generations of young men have told fond stories of working their way around the world as deck hands on freighters. Sadly, there are no longer jobs

---

* *Puerto Natales.* This tiny port town in southern Chile is a departure point for trips to the Chilean fjords, Torres del Paines National Park, and Punta Arenas.

for U.S. citizens aboard foreign-flag freighters and long lines of professional merchant seamen stand idly in hiring halls waiting for scarce jobs aboard U.S. flag carriers. There's no room before the mast for adventuresome youths to holystone teak decks in return for passage.

I don't know how Joseph Conrad would feel about modern freighters, but they can be a fine way to travel if you're flexible and seek the ultimate in relaxation. To investigate a trip, try the following:

- *ABC Passenger Shipping Guide* provides detailed listings of ships, capacities, itineraries, fares, and sailing frequencies of passenger-carrying freighters all over the world (ABC International, Dunstable Beds, LU5 4HB, England).
- *Ford's Freighter Travel Guide* lists scheduled freighter trips ($14.95; 818-701-7414).
- *Freighter Travel News* is a well-established source of information about opportunities for freighter travel (3524 Harts Lake Road, Roy, WA 98580, $18/year).
- Freighter World Cruises represents 16 shipping lines and 20 different itineraries. It publishes *Freighter Space Advisory* biweekly (818-449-3106; $33 per year). Fares range from $75 to $125 per day and trips are generally from 30 to 75 days.
- *Pearl's Travel Tips* is a well-known agent specializing in freighter travel (813-393-2919).
- TravLtips Cruise and Freighter Travel Association provides information about freighter routes and publishes reports from freighter travelers. For a $12.50 annual membership fee, you receive *TravLtips*, a bimonthly newsletter. As a travel agency, it can book trips for you (800-872-8584).

Freighter lines that don't charge a single supplement include Bank Line, CAST Lines, Egon Oldendorff Line, Ivaran Lines, Mediterranean Great Lakes Line, Mediterranean Shipping Co., Mineral Shipping Co., and Reederi Bernhard Schulte. Also try Lykes, Columbus (212-432-1700), Pace, and Navaran Lines.

Ferries and Small Passenger Ships

Unfortunately, taking a ferry is not quite as carefree an adventure as it might sound. On modern, well-maintained ships, ferry travel is fun. Then there are all the other ferry lines, the ones that provide lifesaving gear for about one-quarter of the passengers and consider maintenance an extravagance. Maybe you've seen a few of those two-inch newspaper filler stories reporting ferries that rolled over, drowning 400 people.

After taking a long look at a ratty-looking, jammed-beyond-capacity ferry about to make an eight-hour rough water crossing from Dar Es Salaam to

Zanzibar, I let my instinct persuade me to skip it. That particular boat made it but another, about a month later, didn't. On the other hand, many other ferries, such as the one from Brindisi, Italy, across the Adriatic Sea to Corfu, or the one from Buenos Aires to Uruguay, are terrific. Give the ship a close look, locate the lifejackets, and sit near an exit.

The MV Ilala II is a 45-year-old ship that sails the length of Lake Malawi in central southern Africa. Although it carries more than 400 passengers in third class, most Westerners aboard for the entire six-day trip are happier in one of the six top-deck cabins. The scenery of distant mountains, tropical shoreline, and the walls of the Great Rift Valley is spectacular. The ship's motorboat putts ashore to visit villages and some of the resorts catering to European vacationers. The cost is about $400 plus meals. Contact the Malawi Tourist Office for more information.

Try the Bergen Line, whose steamers sail north from Bergen, Norway, every day all the way up the fantastic coast of Fjordland to Hammerfest above the Arctic Circle. Call (800) 323-7436.

Don't miss traveling the canals by boat in Venice, Bangkok, and Amsterdam, or the beautiful rivers of England, France, Germany, and Hungary. Of course, in modern Europe the Danube is blue only in song.

The Inside Passage in southeast Alaska is another premier trip with views of fjords, thousands of islands, and mountainous coastlines. Plenty of cruise ships make that run, but why not hop on one of the Alaska Marine Ferries? For a schedule, call Alaska Marine Highway at (800) 642-0066 (or 907-465-3941 in Juneau). The popular trip from Bellingham, Washington, to Skagway, Alaska, takes two and a half . Although these ferries have been known to run late or even break down once in a while, they are an excellent way to meet other travelers and the views are spectacular. Service extends far beyond the Inside Passage, even up to Dutch Harbor at the tip of the Alaska Peninsula.

Facilities aboard ferries and passenger ships in less-developed countries vary considerably. Assume that the trip will last longer than planned, and bring sufficient food and water aboard. Reserve space in the highest class accommodation your budget will allow. Lock your cabin door and window and lock your gear to something immobile. If conditions warrant, take a mosquito net and plenty of repellent. Expect a great experience—and that conditions will be inferior to what you hope for.

Cruises

The purpose of taking a cruise is not simply to be transported from one place to another, so the topic doesn't fit easily in this chapter. Still, because cruises are another way to touch the rest of the world, I want to provide some information about them.

Because the cruise industry advertises in every medium and travel agents love to book cruises, you'll have no difficulty obtaining information about cruise opportunities anywhere in the world. But while many brochures feature couples looking romantically into one another's champagne-glazed eyes, they're a little short of the kind of details you need to know about. When you find a cruise that seems to fit your objectives, ask for a copy of the contract and read it carefully.

Be sure you receive answers to the following questions:

- *Price.* What is the published price and precisely what does it include (for budgeting purposes, don't forget airfare and meals ashore)? Rates for cruises are similar to hotel rack rates in that there's no need to pay them. Try for a big discount by signing up early, or late, or because you can't afford the listed price, or for any other reason you think of. Like an airline seat, a cabin is a dead loss if it's empty when the ship sails. If the cruise operator can't fill it, you'll probably get a discount, but only if you ask for it. Give the operator a price to beat. Invite them to find a basis on which you qualify for a discount. If the price is inflexible and you're willing to pay it, ask for an upgrade at that price. Is there a single supplement charge—and will they waive it? Is cancellation insurance included in the price? If it's not, it may be worth considering if there is a reasonable possibility you might miss the sailing.

  Expect to pay extra for things such as laundry service, alcoholic drinks, tips, and on-shore excursions. Ask the operator for a list of expenses not included in the price. One common add-on is referred to as port fees/taxes/charges and can increase the cost considerably.

- *Cabin.* What is the size of the cabin and what does it include (e.g., bathroom, bunk beds, desk, window or porthole, view)? A cabin with a porthole or window may cost twice as much as an interior cabin. Since you pay for space, decide how much time you plan to spend in the cabin. Make sure it's not next to the bar, restaurant, or engines.

- *Shipmates.* What will be the ages and nationalities of your shipmates and how many will there be? If the group is too large, time ashore may be reduced and meal service slow. See if the cruise tends to cater to a particular age group and, if so, whether it's one with which you would be comfortable. Ask whether any large groups or organizations would be on the cruise. If so, might they set a tone for the trip that could make you unhappy?

- *Scheduled activities.* Are there any? Will lectures be in a language you understand?

Useful resources include *Berlitz Complete Guide to Cruising and Cruise Ships* (Douglas Ward. Macmillan, 1994. $17.95); *How to Book a Perfect Cruise, Cruising for the Handicapped Traveler,* and *Protecting Your Travel Dollar* (800-882-9000); *Answers to the Most Asked Questions about Cruises* (call Cruise

Discounted Cruises

If you're interested in a cruise, SAVE MONEY by contacting a discount cruise specialist. The following are a few of the many companies that sell cruises at a discount:

Cruise Line, Inc.	(800) 777-0707
Cruise Market Place	(800) 826-4333
Cruise Shoppe Operations	(800) 338-9051
Cruises of Distinction	(800) 634-3445
Cruiseworld	(800) 321-2784
CSAA Travel Agency	(415) 565-2141
Travel Company	(800) 367-6090
VIP Tours and Travel	(800) 847-4386
White Travel Service	(800) 547-4790
World Wide Cruises	(800) 882-9000
1-800-BEST CRUISE	(800) 237-8278

Lines International Association in New York City); and *Fodor's Cruises and Ports of Call: Choosing the Perfect Ship and Enjoying Your Time Ashore* (Andrew Collins, ed. Fodor Travel Publications. $18).

Sailing

Serving as crew for a transoceanic or Caribbean cruise sounds pretty romantic. After all, it's a free ride to exotic ports, isn't it? Yes and no. The volunteer crew may pay no money, but they will contribute plenty of work. Still, it can be a fine trade-off. Ship captains are looking for experienced sailors, but you may be accepted if you can cook, provide medical services, or record the trip on film or in writing.

One way to find a ride is to frequent marinas that cater to ocean-going yachts. Introduce yourself to owners and captains and mention your availability. Present yourself as a person who will be a pleasure to be with for several weeks in a very confined space. Put a notice on yacht club and marina bulletin boards and give your phone number to marina personnel. Watch local newspaper ads as well as those in boating magazines.

HITCHHIKING

There is so much public transport available around the world, and it's so much fun and so cheap, that hitchhiking should be avoided unless absolutely necessary. Where there's no public transport, there is often almost no private transport either and hitchhiking may become a necessity. If you don't accept rides with drivers who are drinking, hitchhiking may not be very risky—but who ever knows for sure?

Whitewater Rafting

I suppose whitewater adventure trips are not strictly considered transport, but I want to include a few words about them. Just because an outfitter is in business doesn't mean its staff knows what it's doing. Ask who the guides are and how much experience they have on the river you have in mind, as well as on others. Ask about safety equipment. Do they provide helmets? Are the life jackets in good condition? Will safety kayakers accompany the trip? Will the river be at a safe level? Are the rafts self-bailing? Do the rafts have foot cups? If wet suits are needed, will they be provided? By the way, a good outfitter should ask you some questions about your experience and physical condition.

The importance of the answers to these questions varies depending on how challenging the particular river is. If a river is ranked I, II, or III, there's little to worry about. If it has class IV or V rapids, you should be listening closely to the answers. If it's ranked VI, binoculars are all you need. If whitewater trips were completely safe they wouldn't be any fun. After all, you're in it for the thrill and the challenge. Still, if you are relying on the skill and equipment of an outfitter and its guides for your safety, don't take much for granted.

I've listed several books in the Bibliography that provide a keen sense of what river travel is about. Romanticize about the Amazon, Congo, Niger, Nile, Omo, and other great rivers, but know what you're getting into before you sign up for a week or more.

Hitchhiking can be educational. One summer day in southern Africa, I spent hours waiting in the shade of an acacia tree. Finally, a Toyota van appeared and the white passenger allowed her black driver to pick me up. In the course of conversation, I asked her how many people lived in her town. She said, "About a hundred." When I expressed surprise at how small it was, she added, "Oh well, there are about three thousand locals." I got the picture of how she saw the world.

On a trip from Botswana to Zimbabwe, two friendly middle-aged men picked me up. They had some difficulty squeezing my backpack into the trunk of their car because the trunk was already stuffed with appliances, tools, and several bulky, taped-up bags. When they told me that a sewing machine costs $400 in Botswana but $1,700 in Zimbabwe, I understood why they'd been shopping in Botswana. At the border, the driver took my passport, bypassed dozens of people waiting in line under the blazing sun at the customs house, and returned in two minutes with the proper stamps. When the car was waved through the barricade without inspection, I suspected I was in the company of a couple of pros.

Fifteen Tips for More Successful Hitchhiking

Hitchhiking can be fun or it can be frustrating. These road-proven tips should help speed you on your way.

- Early in the morning, when trucks start their journeys, is usually the best time to hitchhike. Stroll out after a leisurely breakfast and you may have missed the wave. Ask local people. Be hesitant about hitchhiking after the sun falls below the yardarm and alcohol flows more freely. Besides, you may not want to fall asleep with some stranger driving.

- Stores, petrol stations, border posts, restaurants, and other places at which drivers stop are ideal for picking up a ride. Local people can tell you whether there's an informal depot for hitchhikers in town or whether it's better to walk to an out-of-town intersection.

- If several people are waiting for a ride, it's the universal custom for the most recent arrival to take the position farthest down the road from approaching traffic. In other words, the early bird gets the Mercedes. A couple of times, I've been standing in the middle of an ad hoc line of local people waiting to catch a ride when a driver stopped and beckoned to me to get in. He may have wanted English conversation or believed that he could charge me a higher fare, but I won't cut in front of local people who've been waiting longer.

- If not waiting in a line, give the impression that you're walking, not just standing by the roadside. Drivers like to think you're making an effort to get somewhere on your own.

- In choosing a spot, make sure oncoming drivers can see you clearly and have a safe place to pull over. Stand far enough off the road that you can't be clipped by a load hanging off the side of a truck.

- As a car approaches, make eye contact with the driver (which means no dark glasses). Smile and look like someone a driver would like to talk with. Make your gear look clean and compact.

- There is no universally correct hitchhiking signal. The traditional closed fist with upraised thumb, so natural in most of the Western world, is an obscene gesture in some places. In Indonesia, you raise and lower your open palm, holding it face down and parallel to the road. In other places, point your index finger and shake it up and down at the place where you'd like the vehicle to stop. Some hitchhikers hold up a sign with their destination written on it (as spelled in the local language, which is not necessarily how the name is spelled on your map). Some prefer not to use a sign because it somewhat commits them to ride with a driver whose company they would rather do without.

— Some hitchhikers make an obscene gesture toward a vehicle that didn't pick them up. Not only is that offensive behavior by a guest, especially one seeking a favor, but it's a disservice to other hitchhikers. Giving a smile or a wave will work out better for you and for other travelers.

— I recommend against a single woman hitchhiking alone. She's likely to get picked up quickly, but then what? It's much safer to hitchhike with a companion. A male and female together will have good luck, especially if the woman stands at roadside and the man stands at a distance, approaching after the vehicle has stopped. I know it sounds a little deceptive . . . well, I guess it is.

— Be cautious about accepting a ride with more than two men. I'm not saying not to do it; just be careful.

— Some people won't accept a lift from anyone who speeds by and then turns around to offer a ride. Their eagerness may indicate a motive other than hospitality.

— Before getting in, ask the driver's destination before mentioning yours. If you have any reason for concern, courteously decline the ride. The world is not as gentle as it once was.

— If it's practical, keep your belongings next to you in the car. In the situation I described above, I felt vulnerable with my backpack in the trunk.

— The driver who picks you up may expect some pay, which is not unreasonable given relative economic circumstances. You might bring up the subject before you climb in, or at least early on, to make sure there's no disagreement later. If local people pay, there may be fairly standard fares for certain distances but a traveler will probably be asked to pay a small premium. I sometimes buy the driver a snack.

— Don't buy alcohol while under way. It's common for drivers to drink and it causes a lot of fatal smash-ups. If you feel you should depart, say you're sick or have to relieve yourself. Living is more important than courtesy.

17

Etiquette

Wherever you go, you will receive impressions
of the places you see and the people you meet.
Do not forget that those people will
receive impressions of you.
—Broughton Waddy,
A Word or Two Before You Go

Etiquette, tradition, and custom exist because they help make people comfortable in their relationships with other people. We know intuitively that to be welcomed as guests we have to know and observe local ground rules. Given the subtleties of the thousands of different ceremonies and rituals on this planet, can any traveler get up to speed? Actually, it's less of a problem than it seems. In this chapter, we'll focus on issues likely to be touchy in quite a few cultures.

Before starting your trip, read about customs in other countries. When you arrive, be especially alert to how local people behave in the key areas of eating, personal space, punctuality, sanitation, gestures, and relationships between genders.

Travelers of a few nationalities are held in "minimum high regard" (as they say in the U.S. Senate) around the world. They've earned criticism by their self-centered, jingoistic behavior and unwillingness to respect local culture. We can do much better than that.

Cultural intrusion of the West has already become incredibly far reaching. Gezing is a small town in the Sikkimese foothills of the Himalayas, just down the mountain from the venerated Pemayangtse Monastery. Strolling through town late at night, when fires had been banked and lanterns shuttered, I came across a dozen kids in a lopsided shack enthralled by a row of battery-run video games. Few of those kids will become educated monks of the monastery, or even remain in their home town much longer. Unlike Johnny Appleseed, we should avoid sewing seeds of our culture as we travel.

CUSTOMS

- *The language of courtesy.* As a nonlinguist, I'm proof that anyone can quickly command the few words necessary for basic courtesy. Learn the local words for hello, please, thank you, and excuse me, and use them often. Travelers too often begin an encounter by peremptorily barking a request, such as "Where is the Post Office?" It's far better to speak first in the other person's language even if all you can say is "good morning." It shows respect and has a positive effect on what happens next. Go out of your way to create a good impression as you travel.

- *Greetings.* In many countries, greetings are exchanged more frequently than in our country. It becomes fun to call out a greeting in the local language and exchange smiles. On the tiny island of Gili Trawangan,* as you head for the coral reef you say good morning to your neighbor with *Selamat pagi* (it's *Pagi-pagi* if it's very early, but I seldom had the opportunity to use that one). Everyone walking along Himalayan trails in Nepal smiles, makes eye contact, and sings out *Namaste*, saying, more or less, "I salute the spirit within you." Throughout the Arab world, you'll be greeted with *Salaam alaykum.* In Israel, *Shalom* is said both on arriving and departing. A respectful traveler has appropriate words ready to greet people.

"If an ass goes traveling, he'll not come home a horse."
—Thomas Fuller, English clergyman

In much of Asia, it's traditional to greet a person by bringing the palms together, fingertips anywhere from chest to eye level depending on the level of respect being conveyed, and inclining the head forward a little. In Thailand, this gesture is known as the *wai* and is still common in small towns and the countryside.

The handshake, ubiquitous in the West, is less common in the rest of the world. Follow the local person's lead. As a rule, don't extend your hand to a woman unless she initiates the gesture. Zambia and several other African countries add a nice touch: your left hand grips your own right wrist as you extend your hand. Primarily in Latin America, but in many other countries as well, be prepared to receive a hug and one or more kisses on the cheek, regardless of the gender of the other person. Respond in kind.

Remember that personal space is cultural and try not to feel invaded if the person you're talking with stands closer than you are used to.

---

* *Gili Trawangan.* This tiny island lies off the coast of Lomboc, Indonesia. It offers sunny beaches, snorkeling, and spectacular moonlight.

Rhodesia/Zimbabwe

A word about names. Call the country what its citizens call it. For example, Zaire has become Congo. Zimbabweans are not Rhodesians and Russians are not Soviets. Since independence, you'll please *Ken*-yans by not calling their country *Keen*-ya, the colonial British pronunciation.

Since people in other countries are more formal when first meeting than are people in the United States, be hesitant to address new acquaintances by their first name unless requested to do so. In fact, you may be expected to use an academic or honorary title with their last name. Unfortunately, it's not always easy to know what the last name is. For example, when you see a written name in China, the surname is first and the given name last. In Latin America, except Brazil, many names are a combination of the father's and mother's surnames. Thus, you would address Sr. Fidel Romero Santamaria as Senor Romero, using his father's surname. If uncertain, ask the other person how he or she would like you to address them rather than give offense unintentionally. Similarly, when a person says his name, ask that it be repeated until you have it right. You'll be respected for knowing, or wanting to learn, the custom.

- *Nuance.* When people for whom English is not the first language speak to you in English, they may not understand the exact nuances of what they're saying. For example, if someone calls out "Hey, you!" or "Hey, mama!" there is probably no intention to be rude. They are seeking your attention but have a limited vocabulary from which to draw. Keep this in mind and you're unlikely to be offended.

- *Be discreet when speaking to other travelers.* Don't offend someone or embarrass yourself by saying something inappropriate on the assumption that local people around you don't understand English, or whatever language you're using.

- *The national honor and other hot topics.* Citizens of most countries are very sensitive about their national honor. This feeling is intense in Latin America, as well as in countries governed by any form of monarchy (some African quasi-monarchs are more than a little touchy as well). Don't show disrespect for a national flag, criticize a national leader, or comment publicly about controversial aspects of the society. Avoid discussing religion, politics, and border conflicts. And I assure you that no one wants to be reminded that their country receives foreign aid from your country. As a guest, err on the side of discretion.

The author and giant tortoise on Galapogos Island

- *Hospitality.* In many cultures, and Arabic cultures are good examples, hospitality is taken very seriously. You risk giving offense if you don't accept a sincere offer of food, shelter, or assistance. Nevertheless, be very circumspect in the Arab world when talking to or about some-one else's wife. Hospitality does not extend that far and your comment could be taken more personally than you intend. Remind yourself of the penalty for thieves and extrapolate.

  On the other hand, be cautious about expressing excessive admiration for someone's property, say a gold watch. He may insist that you accept it as a gift. If you refuse, you risk giving offense—but you might be expected to reciprocate.

- *Dress in accordance with local custom.* Assuming you won't be dressing exactly as local people do, at least modify your normal dress to fit local standards. Not surprisingly, restrictions on dress affects women more than men (see Chapter 14). For women, local custom often means dressing in loose clothing and covering shoulders and legs. Watch local people. In many temples, head and legs must be covered and feet must be free of shoes. Even though toplessness, and some-times total nudity, are acceptable on quite a few European beaches and various isolated spots around the world, wearing a skimpy bathing suit is a poor idea unless you're certain it won't offend local sensibilities.

It's unusual to see local men or women wearing shorts in Asia or Latin America, but male travelers can wear shorts without giving offense (except that they may not be admitted into some temples). However, female travelers in shorts may attract unwanted attention anywhere. The double standard is international.

> If you're unsure about a particular custom, ask.

- *Left hand.* Because toilet paper is sometimes not readily available in non-Western countries, some local people use the left hand as a substitute (in conjunction with a bucket of water when it's available). Even assuming that you carry TP with you, make it a practice not to eat with your left hand. If you forget, your dining neighbors will consider you uncivilized, not to mention unclean.

- *Shoes.* It's common in the non-Western world to remove one's shoes prior to entering certain spaces, including homes and temples. Watch others. If in doubt, slip your shoes off at the door.

- *Feet.* In some places, such as Thailand, it is offensive to point the soles of your feet, with or without shoes on, toward another person. You may need to concentrate on this one for a while to avoid doing it without thinking. Speaking of your feet, don't step on the low sill at temple doorways; step over it because good spirits live under the sill.

- *Thank you.* In many countries you should arrive with candy or flowers or some other small gift if invited to dinner in someone's home. However, a gift of flowers demonstrates the complexity of local customs. In various places, you should not give an odd number of flowers, nor 13 flowers, nor chrysanthemums or purple flowers (both of which may be suitable only for funerals), nor roses (which may have an overly personal romantic connotation). How to know? Ask. When someone does you a favor, send a thank you note. Give them something tangible to let them know they didn't drop out of your thoughts the moment you left.

- *Punctuality.* Punctuality is less prized throughout Latin America than in Europe, but it's hard to generalize about punctuality in the rest of the world. Two tips will see you through. First, if you arrive at the scheduled time, you're unlikely to give offense. Second, if the other person arrives significantly later than you did, hold your tongue and temper since his arrival may be consistent with local protocol.

- *Eating.* In some countries, the custom is to finish everything on your plate. In others, you're expected to leave a bit, indicating that the host was so generous you couldn't finish. You please any host by sampling some of everything. If something doesn't look palatable, it is better not to ask what it is since the reply is unlikely to improve the situation. Beyond all else, don't eat anything that might jeopardize your health, not even to be courteous.

- *The elderly.* Elderly people are treated with special respect in non-Western countries. In a group, treat the oldest person as spokesperson for the group.

- *The head.* In some places, such as Thailand, the head is considered the seat of god in a person. Therefore, avoid touching anyone's head. If you do so accidentally, offer an immediate apology. In various places, including in temples and at religious ceremonies, a woman is expected to cover her head.

- *Monks.* A woman should not touch a Buddhist monk. Step aside if necessary to avoid doing so. It is polite to give your seat to a monk who's standing, although not all local people do so.

- *Public affection.* There is little public display of affection in many countries. With the modern tide inundating the world, this inhibition is diminishing, but travelers should respect the local custom. Holding hands is fine, whether from affection or as a self-defense strategy, but holding more than that may not be.

- *Servers.* Being demanding of a serving person in a restaurant is impolite. Besides, what seems like poor service may be consistent with a custom unfamiliar to you. For example, it may be customary to serve dishes in what seems an odd sequence. If you're polite, perhaps the server will point out the things on your plate that are garnishes, not intended for consumption. Otherwise, she'll just watch as you gulp them down with a grimace (yours, not hers).

- *Body language.* In parts of southeast Asia, standing with your hands on your hips as you address someone projects hostility. This is a good posture to avoid when dealing with an official.

- *Curiosity.* You're likely to be the object of considerable curiosity, often undisguised. I have a photo in which I'm walking down a narrow lane in Darjeeling in the midst of a group of striking tea workers carrying placards. The cause of the strike appears momentarily forgotten as every marcher stares at my 6'4" figure. Unusual height, blond hair, or anything different from local appearances may attract considerable curiosity. Learn to accept it graciously.

- *Business cards.* Business cards are taken more seriously in other countries than in the United States and are offered at even a cursory meeting. You can get along without them, but you'll gain status if you bring some along. They also help avoid errors in pronunciation and help new friends keep in touch with you.

- *Littering.* Whatever your habits at home, tossing litter, even a ciga-rette butt in some places, can result in arrest and a fine. Malaysia, Singapore, and Australia are some of the countries that do not regard themselves as an ashtray.

- *Face.* Publicly embarrassing a person can give grave offense, espe-cially in Asia. "Face" is taken seriously and offenses are not lightly forgiven. Public displays of temper should be avoided altogether.

- *Humor.* Few local people are amused by a traveler's jokes about local cuisine, government, and so on. What they might say among them-selves they resent hearing from an outsider, no matter how humorous the intent.

- *Home habits.* Since Europe is considerably more formal than the United States, habits that are acceptable, or at least accepted, in the United States may give offense. I'm thinking of things like chewing gum in public, interrupting when another is speaking, and slapping someone on the back.

- *Gestures.* Familiar gestures may not travel well. For example, the thumb and forefinger "OK" sign you flash in a friendly way in Chicago refers to an intimate part of the anatomy in Brazil. In Britain, giving someone a "V" sign with your palm facing inward is the equivalent of the middle-finger sign in the United States. To wave good-bye in France, hold your palm up facing the other person and wave your fingers up and down; wave your arm side-to-side, as in the United States, and you'd be saying "No." In Peru, as in Europe, pointing to the corner of an eye means "Be alert; keep your eyes open."

    If you thumb your nose at someone in Europe, be ready to step back. Beckoning someone by crooking your finger at them is an insult in Asia or the Middle East. In parts of South America and Europe, slapping the back of one fist with the other hand conveys your wish that the other person undertake an improbable activity. In Greece, an upward nod of the head means "No," whereas tilting the head to one side means "Yes." If you raise an open hand to refuse something offered to you in Greece, your gesture may be understood as "Go to hell." In that connection, be warned that a Greek may smile when angry. In India, emphatic wagging of the head side to side doesn't mean "No." It might mean "Yes," or any number of other things.

— *Religion.* Although it is just impressive architecture to you, it may be a holy place to someone else. If in doubt about the appropriateness of taking pictures, obtain permission or don't do it. Don't let your conversation interfere with someone else's worship. Activity in countries where Islamic customs prevail will come to a complete stop for prayers five times a day. While you're not expected to participate, you must not interrupt or show impatience.

Observing the customs I've described in this chapter will ease your way a great deal, but I can suggest two books that provide more comprehensive guidance. They are *Do's and Taboos Around the World* and *Do's and Taboos of International Trade*, both edited by Roger Axtell (John Wiley & Sons).

In addition, I recommend *Culturegrams*, published by the Kennedy Center for International Studies at Brigham Young University (call 800-528-6279 or 801-378-6528). The center publishes annually updated four-page culturegrams on at least 140 countries. Each provides a comprehensive background on a country and describes what to expect in terms of language, religions, attitudes, local food, tipping, holidays, customs and courtesies, and visa and inoculation requirements. You can buy them singly or buy a set covering all countries of a continent or all countries that speak a single language. Culturegrams are a bargain.

BEGGING

Beyond the borders of developed countries, travelers are often shocked and saddened by the number of excruciatingly poor people they see. Most are not beggars, just people struggling to survive. But in some places there are beggars, and they congregate, naturally, where there are tourists. Children are forced to beg because their parents have learned that children arouse tourists' compassion. Stories persist of parents or master beggars who cripple children horribly to make them more pathetic and therefore more successful as beggars.

As a traveler, you must come to terms emotionally with beggars and develop a mindset that permits you to be neither constantly depressed by their condition nor constantly annoyed by their appeals. At the same time, their existence should never come to seem acceptable.

Akha tribe family in the northern hill country. Thailand.

Since tourists like to give candy to children, small shops near scenic attractions sell candy for just that purpose. Some tourists who know better than to dispense candy feel okay about handing out pens, maybe on the idealistic theory that a pen will permit a poetic genius to emerge. Catching on quickly, kids ask for pens, then sell them.

It's probably impossible to assess the authenticity of a beggar's condition. A woman with a child on her hip came up to me on a Calcutta street. Asking not for money but for milk, she guided me a block or so to a small shop where I bought her a carton of milk. I left feeling that I'd made a good choice. Did she sell the milk back for cash as I turned the corner? I don't know. Should I care, or is it her right to use the best device she can to secure money for whatever she determines are her most pressing needs?

Some tourists use skepticism to mask inherent stinginess. Others give something to every supplicant for a while, then nothing to anyone. I have a friend who, each time she visits India, selects a reputable charity and makes a contribution, but doesn't give to individual beggars.

If you are moved to respond to the ubiquitous "Hey, mister" from a child tagging along behind you, one choice is to personalize the experience by giving a postcard that features your hometown. You might show photographs of your house or your significant other. I know a guy who carries an inflatable globe. He puffs it up and shows kids the world and their place on it. Another traveler plays tunes on his harmonica and lets kids experience the magic of his zoom lens and a magnifying glass he carries. Balloons, tops, and sleight-of-hand tricks draw a crowd in seconds. These things solve no fundamental problems, but they let kids be kids for a while in a hard world.

If you give to even one person while in public view, you are marked and memories are long. A generous person could probably return to Bombay after an absence of ten years and be remembered for her generosity.

Before you leave home, consult your feelings about responding to beggars. A traveler wants to be liked, but leaving a trail of trinkets behind scarcely enhances a person's image in the eyes of local people. We should face the reality that begging often changes values and lowers self-esteem. Of course, it may also keep a family alive. Whatever you decide, the reality of deformed, emaciated children will strike you like a stinging slap in the face.

TIPPING

Tipping protocol in Europe is similar to that in the United States. Travelers commonly tip airport baggage handlers, porters, room service waiters, waiters and wine stewards, tour guides, taxi drivers, and almost everyone associated with a cruise. The total of these tips can be substantial enough that you should include them in your budget. If you arrive in a country with none of its currency, don't worry. A $1 bill is readily accepted as a tip almost everywhere.

In many European countries a service charge is added to your bill. In France, for instance, the menu will probably say *Service Compris,* meaning they add a percentage, usually 15 percent, to your bill. In that case, the establishment expects you to tip no further. Of course, the waiter may still try for a tip from anyone whose travel clothes look fresh off the rack. Waiters used to tourists are likely to work them for a tip regardless of local custom and pressure them with evident displeasure if they don't get one.

When you tip, the chance of it reaching the intended recipient is much greater if it comes directly from your hand rather than being left on the table.

If you plan to tip after a service is provided, you might award part of it at the beginning to send a message and start good service flowing right away. On cruises, some experienced passengers tip half of the anticipated total on the first day or two, tip another half about halfway through, and award a sincere smile on the way down the gangplank.

Extremely low wages in most underdeveloped countries are a motivation to be generous in tipping, certainly by local standards. Along with a tip, I look the person in the eye and say, "Thank you for helping me."

In Russia, China, Scandinavia, some of the Pacific islands, parts of Asia and Southeast Asia, and most of Africa, tipping is discouraged except at upscale establishments that cater primarily to tourists. If you're unsure, check your guidebook and ask several people outside the tourist industry. If it's not the local custom to tip, don't impose a foreign custom.

BRIBES

Despite euphemisms such as *baksheesh, dash, wairo*, and *mordida* (the last means "little bite"), what we're going to talk about is, if I may be so indelicate as to call it by its true name, a bribe. Since bribery is not a custom most of us grew up with, it makes us nervous.

The first thing to know is that in many countries a bribe is not always considered improper, let alone illegal. It's often looked at as a just reward for having wiggled oneself into some minor, underpaid bureaucratic job from which a little leverage can occasionally be exerted. The problem is that once an official has learned that a few Westerners will pay extra for his services, he makes demands on all who follow. At the same time, in some other circumstance, offering a bribe could offend someone or lead to legal trouble.

In many countries, a bribe is considered proper.

Although I've probably missed a few subtle signals, only once has an official made it clear to me that he expected a bribe. That was at the U.S.-Mexican border and it involved getting permission to take my car into Mexico. I thought I had the upper hand and there was little risk to my safety, so I ignored his demand. He backed off and nothing happened.

Twice, a customs official has asked me to give him something from my backpack. The first asked for several film canisters, which he probably intended to sell. The other boldly asked for my camera. The first I pretended not to understand; the other I refused with a laugh as if we both knew he was joking. Nothing happened.

When I tried to buy a train ticket on the midnight special out of New Delhi, three clerks told me the tickets were "finished." Not willing to give up, I casually laid a few dollars on the desk of the senior ticket master. Giving my offering the briefest glance, he repeated that there was nothing he could do for me. As I was leaving, he called to my attention that I had left something on his desk, indicating the bills with a one-eyebrow-raised nod. Sheepishly, I picked them up, feeling as if I'd been caught with my hand in the cookie jar. Twenty minutes later, a Sikh acquaintance straightforwardly bribed a porter to let us board the train. A second bribe gained us icy-cold metal berths. I spent most of the night reading Shakespeare and drinking Indian Army rum to keep warm. We got to Udaipur in time to hear an Elvis Presley imitator perform at a New Year's Eve party at the famous Lake Palace Hotel. That was *baksheesh* well spent.

If an impasse develops between you and an official who won't do what you need unless you pay him, ask to see a superior official. If the first guy is trying shakedowns on his own, you may get help. If everyone is in on it, you may be stuck.

Obviously, there's no formula for calculating the amount required to make something happen. It seems to be related to the service you need, the grandeur of the official, and whether someone has sized you up as impatient or a wealthy pigeon. In one situation, you might offer a small amount to a low-ranking official right away. Another time, you might be better off going to the person in charge. If time permits, start with a small amount and then pull incremental amounts from different pockets as needed. The ultimate amount will reflect the relative value of money in the official's life and the urgency of your desire to make something happen.

When offering a bribe, be discreet. Use ambiguous words when making an offer. Ask if there "isn't some other way" to handle the problem. For example, perhaps you could pay a small "fine" to the official on the spot, or buy an unspecified "permit." If you do the deal in silence you can, as politicians put it, maintain deniability. Don't let other officials see money change hands and never let anyone see how much money you have.

DOING FAVORS

Someone may ask you to have an application form sent to him from a university in your country. Another may ask you to make a telephone call to her relative in the States or to send a copy of the photograph you took of her family at the dinner table. Since a traveler receives so much help while on the road, doing favors is essential to balance the scales. Further, the favor one traveler does for someone may motivate a kindness to some other traveler. Or it may just be the right thing to do. You don't have to agree to do everything anyone asks, but when you promise to do a favor, do at least what you promised and more if possible. By extension, when you meet a foreign traveler in need of assistance in your home country, you are honor-bound to help. It's part of the traveler's code of ethics.

18

Meeting People

> Travelers are often advised to take a long book
> on their journeys, but who would devote his attention
> to a book when he can turn the dog-eared pages of a
> total stranger whom he may never meet again.
> —Quentin Crisp
> "Riding with a Stiff Upper Lip," *The New York Times*

MEETING LOCAL FOLKS

Long after temples, dive spots, and mountain trails have merged in your mind, you remember the guide you talked to while walking through the rain forest, the family you stayed with in Oslo, and endless conversations on Indian trains. You remember the people and they remember you. They remember whether you liked their country, whether you were polite, and whether you were sincere. Meeting local people is the essence of independent travel.

Travelers too often base their opinions of local people on the few who make their living working the tourist trail, selling food, products, and services (including, unhappily, taxi drivers), relationships that are commercial, superficial, and sometimes adversarial. That's why it's worth the effort to meet normal people outside the areas frequented by tourists. Even if you feel inhibited by language or fear of rejection, it's worth doing. You learn about family life, politics, religion, cooking local specialties, symbolism in arts and crafts, their view of your country, and who knows what else. You may be permitted to witness special rituals or be taken to places you wouldn't otherwise have found. And you make genuine friends.

One easy way to meet local people is via an introduction from a friend, including the ever-helpful "friend of a friend," especially if they'll send a note in advance of your visit. Another way is to ask your alumni office whether any graduates of your high school or university live where you're going. Ask for a

Women in traditional dress. Cairo, Egypt.

letter of introduction from your place of worship to counterparts abroad with which it has relationships. Get names from professional associations (lawyers, florists, anything).

If your city has a sister-city abroad, the sister-city organization will have names and addresses of contacts. Overseas members of your local social and business clubs will be delighted when you look them up. I've seen Rotary, Kiwanis, and Lions signs in some pretty far out places. Your branch of the Friendship Force, the Council for International Visitors, Girl Scouts, and Boy Scouts can give you addresses of international visitors who have been in your hometown.

Make contact by joining in an athletic contest. Volleyball, soccer, table tennis, and badminton are enjoyed worldwide. Get out your Frisbee and invite someone to toss it with you. Attend local sporting events. Ride local transportation. Walk through residential neighborhoods. See if the local tourist office introduces travelers to local people.

It's not enough to return home and rave about how hospitable "they"—the locals—were. While still with them, leave favorable memories behind. You'll almost always have more money and time than they, so put both to good use.

MEETING OTHER TRAVELERS

When I first started traveling, it felt great to meet travelers for whom English was their first language. I felt comfortable with them, perhaps because we had so much in common. Over the years though, having become more at home away from my hearth, I've discovered the immense rewards of meeting travelers from distant lands, people with whom to share and from whom I learn. It's more than worth the struggle to communicate.

Travel is an opportunity to be more extroverted.

Although I understand, it saddens me now to see some travelers from certain countries relentlessly seek out fellow countrymen, forming a clique, creating an artificial home away from home. They miss so much.

Travel is an opportunity to be more extroverted, taking the initiative to meet other travelers. The potential for learning, a good conversation, or a long-term friendship makes stretching worthwhile. Here are just a few of the benefits you can expect from making friends with other travelers:

- *You collect information that improves your trip.* Travelers are like reliable, interactive up-to-date guidebooks, talking about trustworthy places to buy cheap airline tickets and where to find the best safari company. If a guidebook lists ten places to stay in Ubud, Bali, they'll be filled with people who've read that book. But from other travelers you'll get opinions about the other 65 places to stay in Ubud. The best information is on the travelers grapevine.

- *You may feel a sense of security from traveling with others.* For example, when trekking among the hill tribe villages in northern Thailand, you definitely feel more secure in a small group than wandering on your own.

- *You can negotiate better rates* for rooms, a vehicle, or a guide than one person can on her own.

- *You enjoy the refreshing equality of friendships formed on the road.* Since travelers are stripped to essentials, employment, possessions, and education are unknown and irrelevant—and they no longer determine status. In order to base my feelings about other travelers on the present, I avoid asking personal "background" questions that could lead to generalizations.

- *You're likely to have many shared values.* After all, you all made the effort to bring yourself to the distant place at which you've met. Having experienced similar obstacles and marvels along the way, you feel a special camaraderie and bond, a good foundation for friendship.

- *You have someone with whom to share tales of the open road.*

- Traveling on your own can get lonely and there are times when *companionship provides an emotional lift.*

Crowd and musicians making Andean music.

That leads to the issue of how to go about meeting other travelers. In most towns, there are areas notable for the density of accommodations for budget travelers. The Thamel section of Kathmandu is an example, as are Khaosan Road in Bangkok and Sudder Street in Calcutta. Walk around the Boul Mich in Paris, the Piazza San Marco in Venice, Jalan Sosrowijayan in Yogyakarta, and similar crossroads all over the world and you'll find as many travelers as you seek.

Sometimes the primary hangout is a specific place, like the well-known Iqbal Hotel and the Thorn Tree Cafe in Nairobi, or the Duck Inn in Maun, Botswana. Many are mentioned in guidebooks; others you find on your own. Travelers congregate in train and bus stations, airports, restaurants, and scenic attractions. All you need is a smile, a friendly greeting, and a ready question.

When traveling as a couple, you have to initiate conversations with other people. Otherwise, they'll tend to keep their distance. Older travelers may need to take the initiative as well. Why remain separate just because you're twenty-five years older than travelers around you when you can close the gap so easily?

Somewhere along the way, you may meet expatriates. Although the word expatriate has literal connotations of banishment and exile, most expats live voluntarily in a country other than their own. Some are military personnel who end their careers while stationed overseas. They've become accustomed to a pleasant lifestyle and may no longer have intimate ties at home. Ex-Peace Corps volunteers are known for developing attachments to "their" countries and remaining for years after their formal service ends. Many North American oil company workers retire in northern South America. Thousands of people who have long-term jobs with multinational corporations move from country to country like lonely satellites. Some people who work for humanitarian organizations become stateless, circling the globe for life. From Ecuador to Honduras to Malawi to Laos, missionaries remain away from home for decades, some of them helping local people obtain justice.

Relationships between expats and their adopted countries vary. Some expats involve themselves in local life while others live in near-isolation. Almost all know their way around the place in which you meet them, share a language with you, and can be a fine source of information. A traveler who accepts their hospitality should bring something to the table besides conversation. Buy the beer, help with the cooking, or fulfill a request to send something from home.

Two final thoughts about meeting other travelers. First, you'll inevitably meet people who have traveled longer and farther than you have. Learn what you can from them, but never let their exploits diminish your trip. Second, when sharing travel anecdotes, it's important to share air time as well. The other person has at least as much interest in sharing her experiences as you do in listening to yourself talk.

ROMANCE ON THE ROAD

Let's face it: travel can be an aphrodisiac. Not only is the trip a terrific high, but you're meeting other travelers with whom you share some important values. And you have time. In addition, there are all those exotic, attractive local people. Ah, if only life were so simple. The fact is that engaging in a relationship (okay, sex) on the road deserves some serious thought.

Your Partner's Feelings

If you're traveling with a partner, would your involvement with another person cause your partner a problem? How would you feel if your partner became involved with someone else? Could a third person join your partnership comfortably? Would your partner just as soon spend a little more time alone? A good traveling partner is not to be offended thoughtlessly. If there could be a problem, talk it over honestly early on, before you have to meet to split up the partnership's assets.

Other Travelers

Given all that time in sensual settings, romances on the road are hardly unknown. It's easy for travelers to get to know one another quickly through the candor and vulnerability that emerge in remote places. A relationship may develop that will bridge oceans and international datelines—or last at least until paths diverge.

In no case, however, does the magic of an exciting new relationship confer immunity to sexually transmitted diseases. Some of these afflictions are annoying, some are serious, some are fatal. You can't know your new friend's previous sexual history at home nor with travelers or local folk while on the road. Each of us must make his or her own decision about abstinence, but the imperatives of safe sex are worldwide. If you don't drink the water, does it make sense to carelessly take a risk of a much greater magnitude?

Local Contact

One of the reasons to travel is to meet local people. If your pace is slow and your senses tuned, you may be emotionally and physically attracted to a local person. That's the good part. The bad part is that in many countries sexually transmitted disease is widespread. That's especially true with respect to local people associated in some way with the tourist trail. At the very least, condoms and hygienic caution are a must.

There are many lovely people in the world and you may develop a genuine, loving relationship with one. If so, be aware that other cultures differ from yours so don't unintentionally create expectations that won't be met. For example, if you fall in love and the relationship is to continue, one of you will have to learn to live in a new culture. The ramifications deserve serious thought.

There can be a darker side to a relationship with a local person. No one has more than anecdotal information about the frequency with which travelers are seduced for reasons that are more mercenary than romantic, but it does happen. In other words, something other than love may be requested or taken.

19

How to Get the Most Out of Your Trip

> The journey not the arrival matters.
> —T. S. Eliot

At times on a trip I feel like Theodore Dreiser's leaf floating along on the surface of a stream, completely out of control. At other times, I have at least the illusion of being in control. Fortunately, there is one vital variable I can always affect, one that can make or break my trip. That's my state of mind.

STATE OF MIND

Days and nights are filled with new experiences: art, architecture, exotic and perhaps erotic dance, theater and music, magnificent landscapes, physical challenges, and new friends. What a great way to live!

At the same time, everything is different. Language and food may be difficult to digest. Everything has to be bargained for. Something set down unattended can disappear in the blink of an eye. Decisions must be made all day long. Travel is an excellent investment, but like most investments, it's not completely free from stress.

Any traveler who expects plans to work out as smoothly as they do at home, or is determined to force them through despite unexpected circumstances, will be unhappy. To enjoy the trip, give yourself permission to change course, to go with a better idea when it comes along. When it starts raining and the trail turns to mud, you have to be ready to find the humor. Feeling that the rain god has a personal grudge against you will only make the mud deeper.

You chose your destinations for the very reason that they are different from your country. Take pleasure in the differences. Leave generalizations, preconceptions, and stereotypes at home.

Patience

The airline insisted that passengers turn up two hours ahead of flight time, then didn't allow us on board until half an hour beyond the scheduled departure time. After baking on the sun-scorched runway for 30 minutes, we were told to climb back off the plane. Milling around under the blazing sun, we discovered that this was happening because someone forgot to load the lifejackets required for the flight. I'm human so I felt a little exasperated, but I've learned to look automatically for the humor in situations. Lifejackets? For a flight across Saudi Arabia?

I watched a traveler radiate exasperation as he turned from the clerk in a Jakarta hotel and snapped to his partner, "He doesn't even understand plain English." Sure, the traveler was hot and tired, but that didn't excuse his behavior. If he'd seen the clerk as a person he would have acknowledged that the young man wanted to help. It was the traveler who was falling short. He hadn't learned the basic utilitarian phrases in Bahasa Indonesian and didn't have a phrase book handy. When his request in English didn't communicate, he lost patience. To restore calm, his partner responded, "Be or be one." By that he meant, as they both knew, be patient or you'll soon be a patient.

Officialdom

If officialdom in the Third World had a family crest, it would feature a hand-stamp. When you need something from an official, whether you get it may depend on your state of mind. For example, if you convince yourself that a bureaucrat has intentionally singled you out to ignore, you may feel justified in becoming angry. On the other hand, if you understand that time is treated differently than in your country and that waiting is part of life for everyone, it's easier to remain a little detached. Visualize yourself as bamboo swaying in the wind. If there's something you can't change, go with the flow. Learning to accept things calmly conserves vast amounts of energy.

When I see a traveler leaning angrily over an official's desk, demanding some privilege on grounds of being a foreigner, I assume he must value self-indulgence over peace of mind or success.

When you can pass by an official anonymously, do so. If he's an obstacle, or you need assistance, try to make him *want* to bend a regulation. Look him in the eye, smile, make personal comments, and compliment his country, the weather, anything. If you can't persuade him to do what you want, ask him to suggest a solution himself. Realize that sometimes you just have to take "no" for an answer.

People Who Want to Sell You Something

State of mind makes a big difference when dealing with people selling things. Persistent peddlers can test your sanity unless you settle on a way of dealing with them. I was blissfully strolling across the sunny *plaza de armas* in Pisco* when a woman started following me, pestering me to buy one of her handwoven belts. Snapping at or ignoring her would have been unfair, not to mention abrasive. I tried to connect with her urgency by imagining that she was supporting a large family and remembering that for eight months of the year there are no tourists to whom she can sell anything. I still didn't want to buy another belt so I looked at her and said, pleasantly but firmly, "*No, gracias.*" She wouldn't go away. I stopped walking and said, "*No tengo dinero* (I have no money)." That discouraged without offending her. If a merchant just won't stop, I go about my business without getting annoyed.

Expectations about Time

Expectations about time will make a big difference in the serenity of your travels. Think of travel as resembling a marathon rather than a sprint. You have to pace yourself, even losing a little time here and there. Traveling too fast is a prescription for burnout.

Most of the world's population takes the longer view of life, not being too concerned when things don't happen precisely when scheduled. This attitude may be related to feelings of powerlessness. At home, you believe you can affect your environment and so you attempt to do so. In much of the world, people view themselves as objects on which the system acts as it will. If you're obsessive about punctuality, independent travel will either be a liberating experience or leave you a quivering heap. Your choice. Think of getting stressed as similar to getting sunburned. It can spoil your trip, so why not avoid it?

Persistence

I wanted to see the interior of an elegant theater in Oaxaca,† but the massive front doors were locked. I tried the doors on one side, then at the rear—both locked. It was a rainy, dreary day and I was about to give up and head for cover. Then I thought, I'll just take a look around that last corner. Sure enough there was an open door and a man with a peg leg, probably in his eighties, emerged to show me around. As he thumped along, he reminisced

---

* *Pisco.* The name of this port 145 miles south of Lima in southern Peru is known in bars around the world—for "pisco sours." The Bay of Paracas, just south of Pisco, is one of the best marine reserves in the world and a short boat trip takes you to the Ballestas Islands to visit sea lions and penguins.

† *Oaxaca.* Located 300 miles south of Mexico City, Oaxaca is noted for architecture and Indian culture. It's near Monte Alban, ancient captital of the Zapotec culture.

> **Inshallah**
>
> Mechanical malfunctions are so commonplace that people learn patience without anxiety. The one o'clock bus will leave when it leaves. If it breaks, it will be fixed when it's fixed. *Inshallah*, or "As God wills," is offered as an explanation for daily mysteries. The flow of life is a deep current, one against which travelers are well-advised not to struggle. Say *Inshallah* with a rueful smile. Saying something more vehement will change nothing.

about the past glories of the theater and then lapsed into whispery tales of the Aztecs, breathing life into the past. Since then, I've characterized persistence in terms of always turning one more corner. That means asking one more question, walking a little farther, seeing if there isn't some way to make something happen. I'm not talking about being obsessed or bullheaded. I mean that with just a little more effort, turning one more corner, you're likely to get more of what you want.

Context

Travel has helped me understand people's behavior in its own context, rather than in mine. Seeing hundreds of Chinese crouched beside a roadside using hand tools to break boulders into piles of pebbles, I felt critical of the government for not having provided a more mechanized way of doing the job. Miles farther down the road, I realized that machines would throw those hundreds of people, and perhaps millions more, into unemployment. That's what I mean by seeing things in context.

I've also learned not to generalize about an entire country because of an unfortunate experience with one person. That taxi driver was just a taxi driver, not a national symbol.

Attitude

I traveled with a partner who was so relentlessly positive she was almost otherworldly. She'd find the single ray of light in the gloomiest sky. When I asked how she was feeling after an incredibly hot, jolting all-day bus trip, she responded with praise for some beautifully-shaped trees she'd noticed along the way. She knows that happiness is not a destination, it's an attitude.

In many countries it's a serious loss of face to display anger. It follows that the hot temper of a traveler will be met with glacial resistance. Ralph Waldo Emerson advised us that a man should behave "so that, on whatever point soever of his doing your eye falls, it shall report truly of his character . . ."

It's no myth that there *are* obstacles in the road over which a traveler may stumble. A train you planned to catch has been discontinued, your bus misses a connection, a border post closes early. You're grounded when transportation workers strike in Sydney. The power blackout in Manila snuffs out the air conditioning for which you paid double room rent. Your snorkel snoozes in its stuff sack while a mystery bug scrambles your intestines. Things happen. Stifle that temptation to whine. Often, if you're unhappy people around you are too—and they certainly don't want to hear about your problems.

I prepare myself to accept, genuinely accept, discomforts as I travel. Temporary discomfort is part of the price of admission to the rest of the world. You can control how unhappy you want to be. In my opinion, the hard bed is softer to a relaxed body.

When there's a situation you just can't influence, take it in stride. Be open, not defensive. Follow your own path, not one that might meet someone else's approval. Act with intensity when you must, but let your trip be characterized by calm.

GIVE YOURSELF A TREAT

In their efforts to stay within a budget, some travelers live at a scruffier level than makes sense. Even though you've prepared yourself for a standard of living lower than at home, excessive frugality is not a virtue. If carried to an extreme, it may make you forget the reasons you decided to travel in the first place.

> "If you can keep your head when all about you are losing theirs ... wait and not be tired by waiting ... fill the unforgiving minute with sixty seconds worth of distance run, yours is the Earth and everything that's in it. ..."
> —Rudyard Kipling, If

On the island of Lamu, I met a young couple from Australia. They'd rented a single-room hut in the middle of the island reached by a long walk across rock-strewn fields. Their paradise had one lantern, a concrete-like mattress, an outdoor toilet and shower, and no protection from mosquitoes, and they had to fight off snapping dogs every time they put a foot out the door. They'd chosen that lovely cottage solely because it cost only $5 a night. On the other hand, I had a large room with attached bathroom, an overhead fan, and a balcony overlooking the sea and the social life of the village, for which I paid $9. I believe that couple had lost perspective.

There is usually some correlation between cost and sanitation. If paying $2 less rents you a crop of bedbugs or a mosquito net full of holes, it's time to remember why you're traveling.

Throughout these chapters, I've made suggestions on how to SAVE MONEY and how to connect with the world in which you are traveling. The idea of giving yourself a treat does not contradict these suggestions. My point is to avoid false economies, to avoid being "penny wise, pound foolish." Ask yourself which is the better choice: renting a cheap room directly across from the bus station and staying awake all night or finding a quieter place for a few more dollars? Would it be wiser to book a berth than sit up all night on a long train trip? Don't you deserve an air-conditioned room after a trek in the steamy jungle? Every once in a while, check to see if you're treating yourself well enough.

The Regent Hotel in Kowloon is a masterpiece of satiny black marble and gleaming brass. Beyond the soaring glass wall of the bar, a zillion lights twinkle from Victoria Peak, and yellow lanterns swing from bowsprits of hundreds of junks in the harbor. Standing at that bar, I imagined standing on the bridge of the Starship Enterprise looking into the galaxy. You owe yourself an evening in that bar even though a mai tai costs five times what it would a few blocks inland.

The old-fashioned Oriental Hotel on the bank of the Chao Phraya River in Bangkok ranks among the very best in the world. Treat yourself to afternoon tea at Noel Coward's favorite table. Listen for echoes of conversations between Somerset Maugham and an Oxford-educated Thai prince; imagine Joseph Conrad grumbling about the waiter too slow returning with a mug of rum.

In Nairobi, the venerable Norfolk Hotel was the scene of the wild social excesses of colonial Kenya. If you happen to see a party going on, watch for an evanescent Karen Blixen or Beryl Markham across the room. Perhaps the grizzled old man wearing the bush hat and pulling on an icy Tusker can tell you stories of guiding Scott Fitzgerald or Teddy Roosevelt on safari. When you hear Churchill's booming laugh behind you, you may have had one whiskey and soda too many.

Feast at the all-you-can-eat braai (barbecue) under the stars at the Victoria Falls Hotel in Zimbabwe. The thunder of falling water plays a million-year old bass behind the string dance band. It's a fine splurge after you've been minding your budget.

As a kid, I tried out for a Little League baseball team. Incredibly nervous my very first time at bat, I was relieved when the umpire called the first three pitches balls. The next two were strikes. Hoping I'd get on base with a walk, I let the last pitch go by without swinging. The umpire called it a strike and I walked away dragging my bat in the dust. I've never forgotten that experience and never let it happen again. I decided not to let life whiz by without taking a swing, a full swing. For me, that includes involving myself wholeheartedly in whatever appeals to me as I travel.

When it's time, bust that budget. After all, when planning your trip you built in a little surplus for that very purpose. Think about what turns you on. Tickets to the Bolshoi Ballet in Moscow? Front row seats for an outdoor performance of the "Ramayana" in the full-moon shadow of an ancient Hindu temple? A whitewater raft trip down the Zambezi? A helicopter landing on a New Zealand glacier? Since you can experience some things only when you're there, is the price really so high? How would you value the same amount of money at home? It may seem expensive at the moment, but don't let being on the road rob you of perspective. Treating yourself well creates lifelong memories.

20

How to Stay in Touch with Home Base

Travel sharpens the senses. Abroad, one feels,
sees, and hears things in an abnormal way.
—Paul Fussell
The Norton Book of Travel

The way Ken Kesey saw it, each of us is either "on the bus" or "off the bus." What he meant was that we either make a commitment or we don't; we can't have it both ways. You have to make choices, and one of mine is to be completely where I am, not halfway somewhere else. I've found that too much contact with home during a trip pulls me back down the steps of the bus. However, if you want to or need to be in touch with home, it's much easier if you understand the systems. That's what this chapter is about.

TELEPHONES

In parts of South America, it's a challenge to *find* a telephone, let alone use one. In Vietnam, you may have to make a reservation two days in advance to place your call. On the other hand, in tiny San Pedro La Laguna on the north shore of Lake Atitlan in Guatemala, an operator in a two-room adobe hut connected me with San Francisco in seconds. From a pay telephone in Te Anau, New Zealand, you hear your friend's voice in Atlanta as clearly as if she were a block away. Overall, improvements in communications technology make international calling much simpler than it used to be.

There's no need to be intimidated by a foreign telephone system. Even though it's different from the one at home, you can figure out how it works. If instructions on the wall of the booth are not in one of your languages, the illustrations should get you through. If there are neither instructions nor illustrations, look closely at the instrument. Are there buttons that invite you to push them? If necessary, ask a passerby to show you how it works.

The sound of the dial tone is not universal. It may be the sound you're used to, or it may be a sound you associate with a busy signal. Don't hang up; they're all dial tones.

In Europe, Japan, New Zealand, Australia, and an increasing number of other countries, debit phone cards are sold in post offices, hotels, gift shops, railroad stations, and similar places. Using them is quicker and cheaper than calling home collect. When you insert the card in the telephone box, a screen shows you the monetary value remaining on your card, then counts down as the amount is reduced. Some U.S. companies have begun to sell these debit cards for use in the United States and some other countries. These include: AT&T's "Teleticket;" World Telecom Group's "Amerivox;" Sprint's "Instant Foncard;" and Global Telecommunications Solutions' "Global Card." Since charges vary wildly, some are a bargain and others are not.

Here are several useful tips for using telephones overseas:

— To SAVE MONEY, a lot of it, avoid having a hotel operator place your call. If you feel disposed to make your call from a hotel anyway, find out in advance how much the surcharge will be. The hotel surcharge, referred to as a rip-off in traveler's circles, often adds 40 percent to the cost of the call and one London hotel routinely charges guests five times the actual cost of the call. By the way, watch out for substantial charges for local calls and even for access to calling card and 800 numbers. Don't lift that phone until you know the rules.

— A less expensive way to place a call is to find a public telephone booth. To place an international call, you need the international access code and the country code of the country you're calling. To that, add the area code and local number you want. Using a pile of local coins or a debit card is usually the cheapest method. Beware. Some pay phones are privately owned. If you place a collect call on one of these, the recipient may be billed $50 for a one-minute conversation.

With a phone card, you can use AT&T's *USA Direct* to reach the United States from about 150 countries. Simply dial (not through the hotel operator) the toll-free access number assigned to the country from which you are calling. It's listed on a card you get by calling (800) 331-1140. When connected with an English-speaking operator, give your AT&T Calling Card number or say you want to call collect. To phone someone in another country while abroad, use the same access number to call back to the United States. Your call is then rerouted to any of about 100 countries. As you might guess, the latter is an expensive service. For more information on how this works and the access telephone numbers for individual countries, contact AT&T at (800) 331-1140.

Here's an interesting option. Call (800) 628-8486 for information on the AT&T Language Line. For a reasonable fee, you hire an interpreter (from English into 140 languages) for your call. From overseas, you can access the Language Line via *USA Direct*.

An MCI call-home program, named *Call USA*, is operational in over 100 countries. *WorldPhone* is the MCI service for calling among about 30 foreign countries. For access codes and information, call MCI at (800) 444-3333. The MCI International Travel Guide is full of information and tips on saving money.

Sprint Express is operational in almost 80 countries; for information, call (800) 767-4625.

Most phone companies now have international calling plans into and out of the country. They are an excellent way to SAVE MONEY.

If you're in a country not served by your call-home program, you can call your program's access number in a nearby country and, essentially, call home from there. That will save the long-distance charge home and enable you to make the connection quickly.

Note that using one of the three cards above to call among foreign countries is not always the cheapest option. Before using a phone card, check the charges.

Check out the American Travel Network (ATN; call 800-477-9692), which is linked to the Computer-Assisted Variable International Automatic Redialer (CAVIAR) system. Dial in your calling card number and security code. Your card number tells CAVIAR what country you're from and you receive instructions in that language. The ATN card may or may not be cheaper when calling the United States from abroad, but it is often cheaper when calling within a country. Within the United States, ATN long-distance service offers a discounted rate for calls away from home. At the moment, ATN is cheaper than major carriers during prime time and about even during off-peak times.

— Many travelers call from a government international telephone office because there are no surcharges. It's often located near or within the central post office (often referred to as the PTT for Postal, Telephone & Telegraph). Your hotel clerk will know where it is. If you're out for a stroll when the urge to phone hits, look for a microwave tower on top of a building that doesn't have a lot of people in military uniforms standing around.

At the PTT, you give the clerk the telephone number you want and are assigned a booth while the clerk makes the connection. The length of your call is metered. If you left a deposit with a clerk, return after completing the call to pay the balance of the bill (although sometimes the connection is broken after the time you've paid for is up).

- SAVE MONEY by placing your call during hours when rates are lowest.

- I've found that the cheapest way to call home from Europe is on Voicenet.

- Forget the phone and step into a cybercafe. You'll get Internet access for about $5 per half-hour.

- Cell phones will not work abroad unless your company has a roaming agreement with a company at your destination. However, check out the Iridium system. It's a network of satellites that allow cell phone services to work internationally.

- Figure out local time at the place you're calling so you don't reach an answering machine or someone groggy with sleep.

- Calling collect, which is not always permitted, is very expensive. If that's the only choice you have, SAVE MONEY by making a one-minute call and having the other person call you back.

- If the call is about something specific, it helps to make a few notes ahead of time so you don't leave things out in the excitement.

- In countries where the government operates with a heavy hand, your call may be monitored, which should affect whether you criticize the country or the government.

If there's an emergency at home, your friend or relative can contact the Office of Overseas Citizens Services at the State Department (202-647-5225), which will relay a message to the appropriate U.S. embassy on your itinerary. Embassy personnel will attempt to locate you.

MAIL

The challenge is to enjoy the pleasure of sending and receiving mail without letting the process disrupt your trip. For some travelers, writing home frequently can draw too much attention from the present, so they write home in bursts, days or weeks apart. If you keep an informal log listing the date of the most recent burst, you'll know where to pick up geographic descriptions when you write next.

American Express

Many travelers use the American Express client letter service as a convenient way to receive mail (not packages, registered mail, or telephone calls). To pick up mail, you're supposed to have an AmEx card or AmEx travelers checks, and some identification. However, many offices will allow a traveler to pick up mail merely by paying a small fee.

When giving your itinerary to pen pals at home, include addresses of appropriate AmEx mail drops. A complete list of foreign offices is available from AmEx, but choose only those offices marked as mail drops. Since most of the offices also have fax machines, include those numbers too. A fax via AmEx is a fast, reliable way to reach a traveler in case of emergency at home.

Remind your correspondents that it takes two or three weeks for a letter to make its journey. Note on your itinerary the date by which a letter should be mailed to reach an AmEx office before you do. On the itinerary, type a reminder to CAPITALIZE your last name and underline it. To reduce the chance of misfiling, ask the writer not to include your middle name or initial.

When you stop in for mail, ask the clerk to check under the first letter of your last name AND under the first letter of your first name. If you're not sure you are communicating, write out your name. Since your eye is more likely than hers to recognize your name, lean over the clerk's shoulder if you can.

Rather than wasting a day or more or detouring for miles to check in with a mail pickup point, ask friends to send a copy of each letter to the next mail stop down the line on your itinerary. That will prevent regrets about a wonderful letter left behind.

If you arrive at a mail pickup point ahead of schedule, ask that mail for you arriving there later be forwarded to an office farther along your itinerary. They'll do it for a small fee. When you depart from the itinerary you left with friends at home, tell the AmEx office where to forward mail that might arrive in your wake. An office will usually hold your mail for 30 days.

I've used AmEx as an example, because I greatly prefer it over receiving mail via local general delivery. If you decide to use general delivery, advise your correspondents to address letters to your name, "c/o Poste Restante, General Post Office" in a specific city and country. No further address is needed.

By the way, give your cards and letters a fighting chance of getting home by starting them on their way from a city rather than from a village. Take your postcards and letters to the post office rather than leaving them in the hands of a hotel clerk.

FAX MACHINES AND ELECTRONIC MAIL

Fax Machines

The fax machine has circled the globe with the speed of rock music. You can send a fax from Nairobi to San Francisco even when Nairobi residents can't reach one another across town by telephone. Don't leave home without a list of fax numbers for people you may want to reach. If a friend at home doesn't have a fax, take the fax number of a nearby business office or quick-print office.

Where to find a fax machine? In international cities of any size, signs advertise fax services on almost every downtown block. The fax machine itself may be located in an upscale travel agency or in the back of a bakery next to a grandmother dozing with a lap full of knitting.

The owner of the fax pays a fee for use of the phone line, then charges you what competition will permit (meaning there may be room for a little bargaining). It usually works out to less than you'd spend on a long distance call. They also charge a minimal fee when you receive a fax. Include the fax number from which you are sending so the person you are contacting can reach you later.

The fax is a good way for home folks to reach you in case of emergency. They may send a fax to an AmEx mail drop office, your hotel, or through one of the fax services. For example, AlphaNet Telecom (619-736-7070) offers a service called FollowFax. In return for an initiation fee (about $20) and a monthly fee ($10 to $30), a traveler is assigned a permanent personal fax number. Any fax sent to that number is held in a confidential mailbox. You access the AlphaNet system from a local fax machine, enter your PIN, and download any waiting faxes.

Electronic Mail

E-mail is the hot news in international communications. Access is increasing rapidly, and, since it consists of local calls from network to network, it's inexpensive.

If they know your e-mail address, friends at home who have no idea where you are at the moment can leave a message in your e-mail box. You then access it at your leisure.

In contrast to a telephone call, you can send an e-mail message without worrying about what time it is at the destination.

All that is needed for e-mail is a computer and modem at both ends. If you travel with a notebook computer, you may, depending on the service you use, be able to e-mail at will. Since most travelers don't have a computer tucked under one arm, are they out of luck? Not at all. Some universities and businesses have been willing to let travelers use a computer for a few minutes. The best opportunity comes from the growing number of "cyber cafes." For a small fee, about the cost of a bottle of Guiness Stout, you use their computer to log on to send your messages and check your e-mail box. Nothing to it. Before long, the grandmother in the fax shop will be dozing next to a fourth-generation Pentium chip powerhouse.

21

To Buy or Not to Buy:
That *Is* the Question

But there is one priceless thing that I brought back from my trip
around the world, one that cost no money and on which I paid
no customs duty; humility, a humility born from watching other
peoples, other races, struggling bravely and hoping humbly
for the simplest things in life.
—Felix Martí-Ibanez
Journey around Myself

As I write this, I'm sitting in the midst of yak-wool pouches from Kashmir, Masai bead work, Peruvian flutes and textiles, jewelry from Tibet, and
more—all things I couldn't resist buying. Even though I'm no shopper, who
can resist magnificent craftsmanship, not to mention spur-of-the-moment
infatuations? And no one should miss the colors, sounds, and aromas of local
market days. Virtually everyone who travels comes home with mementos.
Although this chapter will be of greatest help to those who take shopping more
seriously, some points are relevant to anyone who buys anything abroad.

I have to confess my personal view that shopping is not traveling. I flinch
when casual acquaintances ask me to bring home "something wonderful" for
them. I resist the pressure of having to shop because I don't want to be concerned about theft or breakage, and I don't want to tote that extra weight. So
why is it that I arrive home from every trip laden like a trans-Saharan camel?

Note that I don't consider cost an inhibition to buying. Except in Europe,
prices usually are so reasonable in relation to the quality of products that
much of what you see seems very affordable. Travelers encounter art, crafts,
clothing, jewelry, carvings, precious metals, antiques—a mercantile smorgas-
bord for sale at very reasonable prices. Of course, the original cost may not be
the final cost. Consider how much you'll have to spend on your purchase after
you get home. For example, a professor friend paid $6 for lovely amber beads
in Moldova, then spent $120 in the United States to have them strung with

tiny gold beads. I bought a magnificent piece of batik fabric art in Yogyakarta for about $15 but spent more than $100 at home to have it properly mounted. Buy a jewel at a bargain price and you may pay much more to have it put into an appropriate setting. Bargains are bargains only if they're bargains after you've spent the additional money needed to use and enjoy them.

I remind myself of two things as a method for keeping purchases under control. First, it's possible and sometimes preferable to enjoy things for themselves rather than having to possess them. Second, many things look terrific in their own context but lose all appeal when transported to a domestic coffee table; ethnic hats become moth-eaten relics at home and the lederhosen bought in Munich mildew at the bottom of a drawer.

There are two kinds of travelers who, if they don't shop, won't consider their trips successful. The first is the knowledgeable collector. She's studied the symbolism of masks in Sierra Leone and wants to own some. The second is the compulsive shopper. Unlike diarrhea, compulsive shopping is not self-limiting.

The temptation to buy is at its most feverish when one first rolls into a country. Try a cold shower instead, then shop around, comparing quality and price. After a few hours, you'll notice substantial differences in workmanship that weren't evident at first. Buying during the last few days of a trip also minimizes problems of breakage, theft, and weight.

HOW TO PREPARE YOURSELF BEFORE BUYING

If you might shop, SAVE MONEY by beginning the process before you leave home. Make a list of clothing sizes of people for whom you plan to buy gifts. It helps to know sizes in inches or centimeters since size codes at home have little in common with those abroad. Think about whether gifts will relate to a holiday, birthday, wedding, love, friendship, or whatever. Decide how much you feel comfortable spending and build that amount into your budget.

If a country you'll be visiting is renowned for certain items, do the research needed to evaluate quality and prices. Take a list of what you're interested in and what it sells for at home. This research is especially important if you're considering buying jewels or electronic or photographic equipment. Travelers who fail to do advance research often wind up buying something that isn't quite what they wanted and paying more than they would have at home. But they do get to lug it around the world, then pay duty on it.

Bargaining, which we discussed in Chapter 6, should be in the forefront of your mind, especially if you intend to visit local market days when a cornucopia empties handcrafts from the countryside into town. The initial price quoted may be twice or up to ten times the price at which the merchant will eventually sell. It's up to you to get the price down.

As part of your preparation, decide *not* to buy certain things. For ethical and legal reasons, don't buy coral, wild bird feathers, marine mammal fur, endangered animal skins, ivory, live or stuffed birds, or sea turtle products. The U.S. Customs Service can provide a list. Further, if you arrive at the U.S. border with fresh fruit, endangered plants, or live animals, prepare for an exciting afternoon trying to avoid confiscation and/or a fine. A traveler discovered with an unapproved antiquity may be considered a thief, no matter what the obliging dealer said as he pocketed the cash.

HOW TO TELL IF IT'S THE REAL THING

There are bargains and there are ripoffs. High quality cannot be assumed. If you're thinking of buying something, inspect it more closely than you would at home because you won't be able to return it for a refund. For example, many people buy colorful clothing in Bali only to discover later that some of that lovely fabric is so thin it won't last long enough to be worn on the plane home. Cheap thread and careless stitching can result in unexpected vents at inconvenient moments. If you pay $6 for a pair of lightweight loose-fitting pants to wear for a couple of weeks, you probably won't care whether the patterns are machine-printed or will fade in the first wash. If you do care, take a closer look.

Inspect all purchases closely; you won't be able to return them for a refund.

Authenticity is always a question. Is it batik or print? Elephant hair or black plastic? Leading the list of substitutes are phony designer labels. Of course, when you see foreign track shoes labeled "Niko," it makes you wonder about the quality of the shoes. If an item is offered to you as an antique, be cautious. If you like it for what it is, fine; just don't pay the price for an antique that isn't.

Jewels are difficult purchases. Unless you can tell whether a gem is genuine and, if so, know what it would cost at home, you're just off the turnip truck in the showroom of the gem dealer. If a dealer offers to authenticate a jewel or some precious metal, take it for granted that he'll provide test results that will appear to prove his representation. If the price is substantial, get an outside expert. For high-ticket items, try to buy from a merchant for whom you have a positive reference, perhaps from someone at home. *Caveat emptor* was never more true than at your friendly jewelers.

Before snapping up a reminder of some faraway place, try to find out if it comes from where you think it does. One example: tourists who fly to Antarctica routinely buy souvenirs without realizing that what they bought arrived in Antarctica on the same flight they did.

According to *Condé Nast Traveler*, most complaints from readers about foreign purchases involve electronic equipment bought in Hong Kong, artwork in Italy, glassware in Venice, jewelry in Bangkok, and rugs in Turkey, Morocco, and India. That's good information to remember.

Guatemalan market.

HOW TO GET WHAT YOU BOUGHT

When you make a purchase, guard against a switch while it's being wrapped in the back room. Yucatán* hammocks are famous for their quality, but the one you examine in the front of the shop may be higher quality than the one later handed to you in a plastic bag. Either stick with your purchase or examine it before you leave the shop. If you don't do that, check it as soon as you're back in your hotel.

Before you pay for something, figure out how much change to expect and count what you receive. Watch out for coins from a neighboring country which have no value for you. If a merchant intends to pull a scam with the change, he'll also be doing something to divert your attention so you won't notice. Be alert.

Yucatán. A flat, humid, hot peninsula in southern Mexico, rich in Mayan sites. Chichen Itza, Uxmal, and Tulum are the best-known sites, but there are many more.

HOW TO GET IT HOME

The best way to get it home is to take it home with you. Especially true if it's fragile—or a rug. It's amazing how a silk rug can turn to cotton if shipped by the vendor. If you're not going to wrestle purchases all the way home, you'll have to figure out how to ship them. Choices include the merchant, the post office, courier and air express, freight forwarders, sea freight, your concierge, and homebound travelers. An established merchant, especially in Europe, can arrange for shipping by whatever means you specify. This is a helpful service but you're taking some risk if you've already paid in full. It might be time to consider insurance.

The local post office, the most common choice, is much less expensive than courier and air express services. In some countries, however, you must prepare your purchases for shipping. In India, I had to hire a tailor to wrap my purchases in burlap until they resembled a mummy. Only then would the New Delhi post office anoint them with its elegant red wax seals. A few helpful post offices sell packing materials to help you along.

Federal Express, DHL, and UPS offer fast, reliable service—at high prices. Another alternative is a local freight forwarder. Its representative will pick up your purchase from the vendor and pack and ship it. Its counterpart at the port of entry will handle customs and forward the item on to your home. This, too, can be an expensive service.

The charge for shipping by sea, usually based on size rather than weight, is reasonable, but delivery may take months. Look up shipping firms in the telephone book.

A knowledgeable concierge can handle shipping for you, but a $15 room usually doesn't come with a concierge.

On rare occasions, destiny delivers someone you can trust, heading toward your home and willing to carry your purchases. Sometimes you find that person by asking around. Whatever your choice, consider insurance if the cargo is particularly valuable.

VAT/GST REFUNDS

A value-added tax (VAT), the equivalent of a sales tax, is added to most of your purchases in Europe. In some other countries, such as Canada and New Zealand, it is called a goods and services tax (GST), but the effect is the same. Because the tax averages about 20 percent, and can be 33 percent, it's worth knowing the rules.

Since these taxes are intended to apply to national residents, travelers can obtain refunds on certain purchases. VAT/GST paid on goods and services purchased for consumption in the country, including meals, hotel rooms, and rental cars, are not refundable. However, you can usually get a refund on taxes you paid on items purchased to take out of the country—but only if you ask for it. Some countries allow you to avoid the VAT/GST if the merchant mails the purchase to you at your home.

There are a couple of common ways to obtain refunds. Ask for a tax-refund form from the merchant, have it stamped by the customs officer as you leave the country, and then mail it back to the store. The merchant then sends you a refund check or credits the amount to your credit card account. A refund check in the currency of the country where you made the purchase will be expensive to convert. Better, try to obtain a refund directly from customs as you leave the country.

If you make a purchase at a store with "tax free for tourists" signs, your purchase is sealed and you get a VAT/GST refund check immediately from the merchant. You can cash it at a service desk or window at most airports and train terminals (look for "Tax Free Shopping"). Of course, they charge a fee for this convenience.

One final complication: you usually have to make a minimum purchase, for each transaction, to be eligible for any refund at all. This minimum may range from $35 to $250 and is often about $100. No refunds are given on purchases below the minimum.

CUSTOMS

At most borders, you'll meet a customs official who wants to see what you're bringing in—and sometimes what you're taking out. Customs agents look for items acquired abroad on which duty is payable, and for items not allowed in their country at all. However, unless a traveler is intentionally smuggling or recklessly carrying firearms, illegal drugs, or the body parts of endangered animal species, passing through customs should mean no more than a slight delay.

Certificate of Registration

Outbound from your country, you can obtain a Certificate of Registration from customs confirming that your camera and other named expensive items are leaving the country with you. This certificate ensures that you won't have to pay duty on these items on your return. For expensive new camera equipment or jewelry, a certificate might be worthwhile. Otherwise, few travelers bother.

Searches

Searches are not nearly so random as one might believe. The agent sizes up people as they wait in line. Sometimes informers mingle with incoming passengers, hoping to pick up suspicious behavior. Anyone fitting a certain profile or behaving in an unusual way is in for a search. If an agent is getting an assist from a drug-sniffing dog, do not attempt to pat him (dog or agent).

If you're stopped by an agent, remain calm. Even if you think you may have committed a minor violation, don't hesitate to open any bag when asked. Volunteer no information and don't try to bluff your way through by blustering or threatening. An agent has been through this drill many times and won't be intimidated, but you can make one angry if you try. If a problem develops, ask what your rights are. Call a lawyer if necessary.

In some countries, customs agents have been known to steal from bags as they search them, so don't let your attention wander during the search.

Favors

If someone you don't know asks you to clear a bag through customs while he changes money or does some other chore, don't do it. Getting caught with illegal drugs can put you in the slammer for a long time. Don't wait until the dog starts barking before you realize your mistake. At that point, the person for whom you were doing the favor will be long gone.

I have several times met people who were about to fly home and practically begged them to take stuff home for me. I sent 70 rolls of film and several journals home with a guy I met scuba diving in Indonesia. We were both cautious. I gathered enough information so I could find him if delivery was delayed. He looked in my film canisters to be sure they contained nothing but film. When he did that, I knew he was an experienced traveler and would make the delivery.

Don't clear a stranger's bag through customs.

Duty

When returning home, you'll be asked to fill out a customs declaration listing your purchases. Misrepresentation or failure to declare something can result in penalties, seizure and forfeiture, and even imprisonment. Heck of a way to end a trip; who would give your slide show?

Customs agents have a pretty good idea of the market value of what they see. If one challenges your valuation, it's helpful to have a receipt. Of course, the concept of a receipt would make vendors in local markets shake their heads. If an inspector discovers an item not listed on your declaration, you may be given a chance to amend the declaration. If you decline, he can impose a fine and increase the duty. If an agent catches a traveler concealing something or using a falsified receipt, he can increase the duty up to 600 percent.

A returning traveler owes no duty on the first $400 worth of goods he or she brings home. This exemption can be used only once every 30 days. The goods must be for personal use and must be in your possession. This exemption increases to $600 when returning from about two dozen countries in Central America and the Caribbean. Duty kicks in at 10 percent on the first $1,000 above the $400 exemption. Above that, the amount of duty is determined by what the item is and where it came from.

Since special interests have made duty regulations look like Swiss cheese, I can only provide a broad outline. To generalize, items such as china tableware, leather goods, jewelry, and furs have been singled out for special treatment. You would pay 27.5 percent on silver jewelry, but only 6.5 percent on most other jewelry. Duty on cut jade is 2.1 percent while that on set jade is 21 percent; crystal ranges from 6 to 20 percent, and wool sweaters from 7.5 to 17 percent. If you expect to make expensive purchases abroad, ask the customs Service what duty percentages apply. Duty, which must be paid on your return home, can be paid by cash, personal check, or travelers check (in some of the larger ports of entry, a credit card is also acceptable).

The largest exception, called the Generalized System of Preferences (GSP), is granted for purchases made in less-developed countries. To help them export their goods, the United States permits many purchases made in about 125 countries to come in free of duty. If you'll be traveling in the Third World and plan to do considerable shopping, call the Customs Service for specifics or check with the American consulate on the spot. Ask for a leaflet named *GSP & The Traveler.*

You owe no duty on a gift you mail home if the value is less than $100 and you send it to someone other than yourself. Duty is owed if the addressee receives more than one gift a day. Write "unsolicited gift; value less than $100" on the package. A customs inspector may open these packages before they reach the recipient. Gifts that you carry back with you are subject to duty unless they fit within your exemption.

Unique works created by a professional artist are admitted free of duty. However, mass-produced items and the work of craftsmen are subject to duty.

An item must have been made at least 100 years ago to be considered an antique. If so, the good news is that it may be admitted free of duty. The bad news is that you may have violated the laws of a foreign country if you removed it without an export permit. If you purchase an authentic looking reproduction, obtain a written statement from the vendor confirming that it's

---

Duty Free

Have you thought about what "duty free" means? It only means that goods are being sold without addition of a local sales tax or import duty. That means low prices, right? Very seldom. In fact, duty-free shops often sell imported luxury goods at inflated prices. The absence of local tax is almost immaterial. These shops are traps for wealthy and/or inexperienced tourists. A duty-free purchase may make sense if you have foreign currency left that you can't exchange back before leaving the country. The fact that you bought something in a duty-free shop overseas has no effect at all on whether you owe duty on it when you return home.

a reproduction. That will help you get it out of the country but makes it subject to duty at home.

Items not permitted into the United States include plants (except that cut flowers carrying no bugs may be allowed through), fresh fruit, vegetables, meat, illegal narcotics, switchblades, poisonous items, and hazardous articles such as fireworks. Drugs and medical devices sold overseas but not approved by the FDA are not permitted to enter even though purchased legally. You can return with firearms so long as you can prove, by prior registration with customs or the Bureau of Alcohol, Tobacco and Firearms, that they are they same ones you left with. Otherwise, unless you are a licensed firearms importer, firearms will be confiscated.

Samples of or items made from ivory, tortoise shell, coral, leopard fur, hides, shells, and feathers or teeth of an endangered species are also prohibited and you may be fined for attempting to bring them in. Don't think that just because the vendor assured you there would be no problem that customs will permit you to keep them.

Copies of brand-name merchandise ("knock-offs") probably violate someone's patents or trademarks. If the customs agent spots a fake Rolex or pirated cassette tapes or computer programs, he's likely to confiscate and destroy them. All you can do is grin and bear it. After all, you only paid that guy on the beach $20 for the "Rolex."

If you contemplate returning home with a live animal, or any wildlife product, discuss the subject with customs or the U.S. Fish and Wildlife Service before you go or with an embassy or consulate overseas. Otherwise, you may run into an expensive quarantine.

For more information on customs regulations, including current duty rates, contact a customs official at one of the more than 40 district offices in the United States (check government listings in the telephone book under U.S. Department of Treasury, U.S. Customs Service, District Director). Also obtain a copy of *Know before You Go, Customs Hints for Returning Residents* from the U.S. Customs Service (P.O. Box 7407, Washington, DC 20044, or call 202-566-8195). Also helpful are *Your Trip Abroad* (#141Z, $1.25) and *Custom Tips for Travelers* (#454Z, $.50) from the Consumer Information Center, P.O. Box 100, Pueblo, CO 81002.

IMPORTING

"These are great," he says. "I could sell a million of them back in Chicago." He's looking at a papier-mâché box in Kashmir or maybe a commode in New Zealand that has half-flush and full-flush buttons to conserve water. Last week, he talked with another traveler who planned to pay for his entire trip by collecting old watches to sell in London.

Most travelers come across items for which there might be a market back home. Many never recognize the opportunities; others do, make notes in their journals, and never follow up. But a few are serious. They come home determined to import thousands of something or other and make a fortune. Well, it's been done and it can be done again, but being successful in the import business is no slam dunk.

This discussion isn't a course on starting an import business, but I can pose some questions that will reveal how serious you are. You could answer some of them before you go, but at that point your entrepreneurial spirit won't have yet become inflamed by some item that begs to be imported. However, answering them while you're still on the road will make your travel time more productive.

Basic Questions

- What do I want to achieve through importing?
- Why do I think I'll succeed?
- Am I an entrepreneur at heart? Am I willing to work hard enough to get a new business going?
- How much money am I prepared to put at risk?
- Do my skills match those needed by this business?
- Do I have the time?
- Do I have correct information about suppliers, a distribution system, prices, transportation, and financing?
- What's the competition?
- What are the demographics of potential buyers?
- What are the trends in the market I'd be entering?
- How many units can I sell? How many must I sell to make a profit?
- What is a reasonable rate of growth for sales?
- What governmental regulations will affect import and sale of the product?
- Can I get a trademark or patent to protect my product from competition?
- Do channels of distribution exist to get the product to market?
- If the product will require service, can I supply it?

Check the Importing section of the Bibliography for good resources, most of which are free. If you think you might be interested in importing, it would make sense to review some of them before you depart.

Determining Effective Demand for Your Product

The impulse to import strikes a surprisingly large number of travelers because they see so many appealing items they've never seen before and "they're so cheap!" They believe they know their home market, and being personally captivated by an item, they assume it will appeal to the general public. If that assumption turns out to be wishful thinking, the business is

Masks for sale. Chichicastenango, Guatemala.

about to become an expensive hobby. It takes good research as well as intuition to answer the question of whether there's a sufficient market for a product.

For demand to be effective, potential buyers must be willing and able to pay the price you have to charge to cover overhead and make a profit. The item you want to import may cost very little to purchase, but to that you must add your personal expenses, freight (land freight overseas, international air or sea freight, and domestic freight), freight forwarders' and customs brokers' fees, duty and bond charges, costs of financing, advertising, communications, insurance, and commissions to your sales representatives. When you add an acceptable profit, you have the price at which you can sell to a retail outlet. After the retailer doubles that price to the public, will your product sell in acceptable volume?

Run these numbers before making serious commitments. If they're acceptable, establish relationships with suppliers and commit to buy a small number of the product. When the product arrives, test the market to determine whether demand is as strong as you thought or whether you've just purchased your Christmas presents for the next 50 years.

Evaluating Suppliers

Importers sometimes fail to ensure that their suppliers can furnish the number of products desired while maintaining the required level of quality. People who live on the tiny island of Taquile on Lake Titicaca produce blouses of outstanding quality and design. At the low prices they charge for their fine work, you feel guaranteed of a profit when you resell the blouses at home—so you buy all the embroidered blouses on hand. You guessed right and there is an eager market. Confident you can sell ten times the quantity you bought the first time, you write the weavers in Taquile asking them to substantially increase their output. Perhaps they're delighted, send you more first-quality blouses, and everyone is happy. But, not being compulsively materialistic, they may decide instead not to increase production. Or they may try to increase output, but quality suffers and they wind up shipping you inferior blouses. You run the risk of having built market demand that you can't meet without delivering inferior quality. There goes the business.

Whatever the product, production shouldn't start until you and your suppliers are in agreement about standards of quality. Ability to maintain the original quality at increasing levels of demand is essential to success.

Until you identify reliable suppliers who consistently meet quality and quantity standards, plan to return with some frequency to the country in which your product is made. Alternatively, hire a local agent if you find one you trust and with whom you have good rapport. Someone on site helps overcome misunderstandings.

The next issue is delivery. Your imported blouses become such a hit that you land a big contract with a chain of women's boutiques, committing to deliver the blouses three months after signing the deal. Although it seemed an easy commitment to meet, it turns out that because of a drought some of the natural dyes are no longer available, or religious holidays interrupted production, or increased income enabled the weavers to award themselves more leisure time. For one reason or another, you miss the contract date. You can't do that very often and retain credibility, especially if your customers have been advertising the product. Be realistic in determining whether your suppliers can meet agreed-upon delivery dates.

Capital Required

Few suppliers are going to ship their products thousands of miles to you on consignment (i.e., letting you pay for them after you've sold them). Therefore, you have to pay for the goods in advance or on receipt. This creates the classic cash flow crunch. You can use your own money as initial capital, but more often importers arrange for a letter of credit to pay for goods. Banks charge a fee for this letter of credit and require that you have a good financial reputation. Later, after a year or two of reliable performance, suppliers may give you a short (e.g., 30-day) grace period after delivery before you must pay.

If an importer engages in wishful thinking when projecting the rate of sales, undercapitalization can lead to catastrophe. An otherwise sound business idea will fail because the company can't sustain itself until the rewards of success arrive. Be realistic and prepare for the long haul.

Learning the Business

The best time to learn the mechanics of importing is before you leave home. It's not essential, but you'll have a better idea of what information to gather and which contacts to make while abroad. It's a world of bills of lading and other shipping documents, customs forms and procedures, international financial arrangements, insurance, duties, and quotas. New terms and symbols, such as FAS, FOB, C&F, and CIF, must become part of your vocabulary. Success or failure of your business may depend on how well you learn the regulations that apply to your imports. For example, the amount of customs duty charged can depend on facts as minuscule as in what country care tags or buttons are sewed on. Happily, the U.S. Customs Service is helpful in explaining its regulations.

Other government organizations will help with importing, although they're considerably more enthusiastic if you're exporting, as will international trade departments of commercial banks. In addition, hundreds of world trade and import/export clubs provide information and hold regular meetings and seminars. Books, magazines, and newsletters on the subject are legion. Freight forwarders, the transportation experts who get your goods from there to here, are an excellent resource. Consultants and experienced friends can help. Then you learn by doing.

Years ago, most U.S. rugby clubs ordered their team jerseys at the beginning of each season from manufacturers in New Zealand or England. Since it took months for orders to be filled, many team members had to play in old sweatshirts. Seeing an opportunity, Rex, Tony, and I started Leather Balls, Ltd., to import Canterbury rugby jerseys from New Zealand. This was long before yuppie pseudo-jerseys clogged the catalogues. Because we maintained a large inventory and were able to deliver within a week of receiving an order, we soon dominated the rugby club market. As business expanded, we signed up a few trade reps ("Good morning, I'm the rep with Leather Balls.") and developed markets in ski shops and department stores. Although we were successful, I realize now that our lack of market research exposed us to much more risk than necessary.

Importing initially seems attractive because it provides a reason to return to a country you enjoy. Unfortunately, a business trip is very different from a pleasure trip. When doing business you're constantly rushing, bargaining, and unraveling red tape. There may be time for pleasure, but if pleasure comes first it could be a costly trip. Earning a profit from your travels is quite possible, but don't spend money on a romantic fantasy while believing it to be a business. Of course, if you *know* it's a romantic fantasy and you want to spend money on it, that's fine.

22

Remembering

Like all great travellers, I have seen more than I remember,
and remember more than I have seen.
—Benjamin Disraeli

No trip ever really ends. Memories can become faint glimmers over the years or they can remain vivid and rich. It's up to you.

By far the best way to gather memories is by being completely present where you are, immersing yourself in the experience, imprinting conversations, colors, sounds, and breathtaking views into your cells. Maps, handcrafts, coins, receipts, literature, and souvenirs all contribute to memories, but being 100 percent present is my highest priority. That requires not thinking about what's going on at home or what things will be like when I return. It means not reading international editions of magazines or newspapers as I travel. "News" usually isn't, and when I return, little of substance will have changed.

Being 100 percent present means stopping often to appreciate where I am—seeing more by seeing less. It means taking risks, making an effort, and reaching out to people. Being 100 percent present is not for spectators; it's for participants.

KEEPING A JOURNAL

Since memory is so fallible, mental images benefit from backup systems. One backup is a good journal. A journal also helps you share your experiences with friends, including those you won't meet for 20 years after the trip. A journal packed with reports of people, emotions, events, and ideas provides information and insights for years.

Accuracy and truth are requisites of a worthwhile journal. Accuracy is a matter of practice and paying attention. The truth is sometimes hard to write when dealing with issues close to the bone, such as when you didn't meet a challenge as well as you wanted to. Still, those are the very truths to record. It may be easier to explore emotions on paper if you intend for no one else to read your words. When traveling with a partner, journals should be explicitly confidential.

I keep track of observations by scribbling occasional notes on a piece of paper during the day. Otherwise, with so much sensory input, I'd lose a lot before I had time to record it all in my journal. When I miss a day or two of journal writing, daily notes help me catch up.

> "To lose a passport was the least of one's worries: to lose a notebook was a catastrophe."
> —Bruce Chatwin, The Songlines

Drawings capture details that might otherwise be missed. A trek across western Nepal became even more interesting after I sketched the subtle ways in which construction and design of buildings in each mountain village differed from those in neighboring villages, though separated by less than a mile.

Make observations about people you see or meet, record your feelings about what you did, and include changes in your perspective and plans for the future. Explore similarities and differences among cultures in terms of religion, architecture, art, agriculture, and language. Attempt to capture the spirit, as well as the form, of a temple, landscape, or person.

Someone said, "Ixion breakfasted with the Gods and remembered only the pattern of the tablecloth." That's how I feel when I record only facts. Dry reporting doesn't retain the flavors. Try to make that journal sing with impressions, reactions, and reflections.

I walked for a while with an older man I overtook on the Milford Track in New Zealand. Each time the trail turned a bend and a new panorama unfolded, he'd lift a small tape recorder to his lips and whisper, "Beautiful, beautiful," or "Spectacular," or something similar. Not once did he draw a verbal picture of what he saw, nothing from which to later recreate the beauty he was experiencing.

Are you interested in publishing articles related to your experiences? If so, read a book on travel writing (perhaps one of those in the Bibliography) before you leave to learn the type of information to collect as you travel. If you fail to collect what you need, you may regret a missed opportunity.

Here's another way to SAVE MONEY. If you write with publication in mind, you may be able to deduct some or all of your travel expenses on your income tax return. If that's a possibility, keep track of expenses to support the deductions you claim. The guidelines for deductibility are pretty straightforward. Ask a lawyer, accountant, or the IRS.

Giraffe in the Masai Mara Reserve. Kenya.

TAKING FINE PHOTOGRAPHS

Why do we bother taking photographs? After all, the right photographic equipment takes time to gather, adds weight, and takes up precious space in the bag. Equipment, film, and developing add significantly to the cost of the trip. You have to guard the equipment and care for the film. Finally, shooting pictures may change the nature of a trip, slowing its pace, perhaps even intruding between observer and experience. However, most of us brush these objections aside because we intend to return home with photo-memories.

That being the case, a little preparation can help ensure high-quality photographs. Here are a few preliminary tips:

— Be clear on the purpose of your photos. Will they accompany a story you plan to sell? Join a series of images gracing your walls? Reside in an album, waiting to be called on to stimulate your memory years in the future? Prove to your friends that you stood your ground within the leap of that black leopard? Having a clear purpose, or even more than one, gives your photos coherence.

— A photographer who simply snaps away each day is likely to discover, when she reviews newly developed prints or slides, that she's totally failed to capture the essence of a country or culture. Before you leave a place, consider what characteristics best represent it and see whether you have them on film.

- If your objective is to tell a story, think about the type of photographs required and keep your objective in mind all day. If you simply want fine individual photographs, your task is much easier because one shot need not be linked to another.

- If you plan to sell your photographs, contact newspapers, travel magazines, and special interest publications to find out whether they prefer (or insist on) black and white or color, slides or prints. Even if your photographs will be published in black and white, some publishers will accept color slides since new computer scanning equipment produces clear images (and has reduced the cost of the conversion process). In other words, shoot with your market in mind.

- Keep good notes about each photo. Don't lose a sale because you can't identify the subject matter or location.

- Imagine yourself at Versailles. One photographer after another stands in the footprints of those who came before, each snapping the obvious shot. If you want to record something pleasing for the bedroom wall, standing where everyone else does is fine. Similarly, if you're taking the shot to accompany a story, the editor probably wants a familiar image that readers can identify. If, however, your goal is personal interpretation, you must stand where others have not, or capture the image under unusual conditions. See the subject with sight unique to yourself.

- Sometimes the shot of the year requires incredible patience, waiting for perfect light or the ideal cloud formation. It can also be captured by a photographer who recognizes opportunity and knows the equipment well enough to take a well-composed shot on three seconds' notice. It rarely emerges from ignorance or luck. If you're not already experienced, consider a course on outdoor, or existing light, photography. Check out a good book on photography and practice.

- If you are thinking of buying photographic equipment overseas, research the item you want, including domestic prices, before you leave. Some overseas "bargain" prices aren't bargains. When buying photographic equipment abroad, be sure you get authentic, new equipment. Watch out for warranties that require the equipment to be returned to Hong Kong, Singapore, or some other faraway place for repair. If you wait to buy your trip camera abroad, you'll be depending on a camera with which you haven't practiced, and one that may turn out to be defective.

Equipment

If you're going to buy a camera for the trip, buy decent equipment, learn how it works, and *use it before leaving*. It's too common for someone to buy a new camera, toss it in the bag, and jump on the plane. Unless you're a masochist-in-training, read the manual, then shoot and critique a couple of training rolls before you leave. Solve problems at home where you can get advice easily. By the way, if you haven't used a camera for several months give it a trial run to check its mechanical integrity before leaving.

> "Many beautiful sights are impossible to transfer onto film; rather than intrude my camera into an experience for no purpose, I simply enjoy them."
> —Galen Rowell, *High and Wild*, 1983

Cameras

For easygoing photographers, an ultra light, fully *automatic camera* with a built-in flash, compact zoom lens, and autofocus is quite adequate. Although lack of manual control of lens speed and aperture and, therefore, of depth of field limits the effects that can be achieved, beautiful images are still possible. Nevertheless, these cameras can be fooled by light conditions and may not be appropriate for travelers seeking pictures of publishable quality. At least try to find one that has a backlight feature that compensates for a subject brightly lit from behind.

Serious photographers travel with at least two *35mm single lens reflex* (SLR) camera bodies and several interchangeable lenses. I've sometimes wished I had two cameras with me so I could be ready with both color and black and white film or film of different speeds, but never enough to lug that much weight around. Fortunately, Kodak and friends have come up with Advanced Photo System film. More about that in the Film section below.

One 35mm SLR camera that operates in both manual and automatic modes is quite sufficient for my purposes. Professional photographers seem to favor Canon, Nikon, Pentax, and Olympus, but there are so many fine cameras you can hardly go wrong if you keep weight, size, and durability in mind. Check consumer magazines and photographic trade publications for help evaluating the alternatives.

If you want to take photographs underwater, choices include an expensive *underwater camera* (such as a Nikonos), a midrange camera (such as a Vivitar), a cheap throwaway (which works fine for shallow snapshots), or a waterproof camera housing (EWA-Marine has a good series for SLRs and camcorders; call 800-257-7742).

Batteries

Superautomatic, multigizmo cameras are extremely dependent on batteries and suck energy like crazy. The biggest guzzlers are the auto-winder and autofocus features. Besides dramatically reducing battery life, they also make the camera vulnerable in especially cold temperatures. When it's really cold, it helps to keep your camera inside your jacket when practical, and to keep spare batteries comparatively warm.

The author feeling the extreme heat at a Mayan site. Mexico.

If your camera goes into an electronic coma in Europe, you can find a replacement battery within an hour. In much of the rest of the world, your camera might be disabled for quite a while. Further, the battery that costs $10 to $15 at home may sell for $50 in Kenya (and you'll have to pay it). Although many SLRs operate several manual shutter speeds without electric power, the lesson is clear: if your travels take you outside relatively modern cities or to very cold weather, always carry a couple of spare batteries.

Zoom Lens

Many photographers consider at least one zoom lens indispensable. When I see someone with a gigantic telephoto taking a close-up of the left eye of a rhino 200 yards away across the savannah, I tell myself they're on a tour, have three bearers to cart their camera gear, and are only seeing the world through a camera lens—and I'm still envious. I usually carry a 28–80mm, a 70–300mm, and a telextender. Consider a lens with macro capability for extreme close-ups (including bugs and plants).

Filters

I take two filters. The first is ultraviolet, whose principal purpose is to protect the lens from being scratched. Pros substitute an 81A filter that produces a slight warming effect. The second is a polarizing filter, needed only occasionally to cut glare and reflections and intensify colors. However, a polarizing filter cuts flexibility because it consumes about two f-stops of light, requiring a slower shutter speed to avoid losing depth of field. Further, if you don't align a polarizing filter properly with each shot, it actually makes the picture worse. Don't leave it on the lens when there's not a specific reason to use it. Using a polarizing filter in conjunction with a wide-angle lens may create dark areas on one side of the sky in your frame but not on the other (seldom a desired effect).

Lens Cover

Since a lens cover is an incorrigible escape-artist and difficult to replace on the road, attach it to the barrel of the lens with a "keeper," an elastic band designed for that purpose. You might even consider taking a spare.

Lens Hood

A collapsible rubber lens hood or a screw-on lens hood shields the lens from glaring sun, as does a well-placed hat or hand casting a shadow on the lens.

Flash

A flash is worthwhile for capturing places like interiors of temples or tombs, gloomy rain forests, and nightlife. If your camera doesn't have a built-in flash, the nature of your trip determines whether it's worth bringing one along.

Tripod

The steadiness with which you hold your camera, especially in dim light, affects the sharpness of your photographs. A tripod solves that problem, but if a full-scale tripod seems too cumbersome, consider an 18-ounce monopod with a ball head or a tripod about five inches tall with a C-clamp on one end. If you decide against a tripod, finding something to brace against, maybe cushioned with a shirt or bandanna, helps. For a particularly long exposure, try setting the camera on a stable surface and using the autotimer.

Cleaning Stuff

A simple brush, lens cleaning solution, and soft lens tissues help keep the lens spotless. Microfiber cloths sold in camera shops are excellent. Q-tips are good for cleaning the view finder and the perimeter of the lens. Avoid using your handkerchief to clean a lens.

Camera Bag

A camera bag is useful at home, but it's bulky and a target for sticky fingers when abroad. A stuff sack or army surplus shoulder bag keeps the camera out of sight and shielded from dust. Even a Ziploc plastic bag provides good temporary protection. Camera equipment should be protected from heat, cold, grit, and moisture (especially salt spray)—and rapid changes in temperature, which can cause condensation. When camera or lenses are riding in luggage, cushion them well with clothing.

Film

Slide or Print

You have a choice to make between slide film (transparency) and print film. Slide film is less expensive to develop, but you have to add in the cost of a screen, projector, and slide trays. Slides are noted for excellent color and sharpness, and it's exciting to see a life-size lion yawning in your living room. On the other hand, because slide film is less forgiving of incorrect exposure settings, shooting slides requires more skill than shooting prints. In addition, less can be done in the lab to improve incorrectly exposed slide film. If you shoot slides but want something to hang on the wall, you can have prints made from your slides (although the process is relatively expensive).

Color or Black and White

People shoot black and white either because it's for a publication that insists on it or because it's the best way to express a personal vision. If you're using black and white for a publication, they'll probably want you to submit prints, not negatives. If you don't do your own black and white processing, obtaining prints will either be expensive, if you pay someone for a custom job, or result in unremarkable images, if the drugstore does it on a machine. In other words, go with color unless you have a special purpose.

The new Advanced Photo System film developed by Kodak offers a very useful midroll interrupt feature. That means you can switch between film of different speeds, print or slide, black and white or color rolls easily, without losing a lot of unexposed film.

Brands

Different brands of film yield somewhat different color values. Fuji is known for emphasizing greens and blues, Agfa for yellows and oranges, and Kodachrome for reds. Any custom photo lab can show you comparisons to help choose what pleases your eye.

Kodachrome ISO 25 is said to be the sharpest and least grainy slide film easily available. The problem is that except on sunny days you have to shoot at slow shutter speeds and get little depth of field. ISO 50 provides more flexibility. I usually choose ISO 100 for outdoor photography, trading the ultimate in sharpness for greater flexibility. I also carry rolls of ISO 200 and 400 for lower light situations. Some people love Fujichrome Velvia (ISO 50) and others prefer Kodak Ektachrome Lumiere 100X. However, neither is ideal for photographing people because they do odd things with skin tones.

Black and white photography has become fairly rare, but it can convey mood hard to attain with color film. If you don't have access to a professional lab, you may want to shoot Ilford XP2 400 film that can be developed by color processing.

Kodak also offers a film specially designed for use underwater.

Number of Exposures

To cut down on bulk and frequency of reloading, carry rolls with 36 exposures. Even if you like to use every frame, make an exception when a particularly photogenic event is coming up. Sacrifice several unexposed frames and load a new roll ahead of time, especially if you can load in some sheltered spot instead of aboard a sailboat or in the midst of a camel race.

Where to Buy Film and Equipment

High-volume outlets sell film and cameras at prices local retail stores can't match. Check the back pages of Popular Photography or other photography magazines for advertisements. When ordering film from one of these outlets, ask about the expiration dates of the film they're offering. As film draws close to its expiration date, outlets sometimes cut the price in half. That's a great way to SAVE MONEY since you'll expose it within the next few weeks anyway. Whatever film you buy, store it in the refrigerator or freezer in Ziploc bags.

How Much to Buy

The amount of film to take depends on how much space you have and on your personal style. Do you fire away all day, hoping to capture a few wonderful images, or do you take a few carefully thought out shots? It also depends on where you travel, in that some places are much more scenic than others. On average, I take enough film to shoot one-half roll a day; a friend takes enough to shoot two rolls a week.

There are at least three good reasons to overstock: (1) exposing film is cheap compared to the cost of reaching some remote place; (2) film is less expensive at home than in remote places; and (3) film you buy abroad may not have been well cared for.

Film Care

Don't leave either camera or film sitting in direct sunlight or in a space likely to become very hot. When there's film in your luggage, follow the same rules. If necessary, wrap film to shelter it from extreme cold. When film is very cold, prevent condensation by warming it gradually before loading it into the camera.

The National Association of Photographic Manufacturers evaluated the

Buddhist temple.
Chiang Mai, Thailand.

effects of baggage X-ray machines on various types and speeds of film and concluded that the effects are negligible, even after film was exposed to the machine as many as 100 times (note: NAPM still suggests that you avoid putting films faster than ISO 400 through the machine). That conclusion may be reassuring in the United States, but when I go through an airport X-ray security station abroad, I pass my camera and the film in my daypack around the X-ray tunnel. Even if the attendant insists there's no danger, it makes me feel better. Do what some professional photographers do and insist that every roll of film be examined by hand. By the way, X rays have no effect on video cameras.

Film in baggage you check through is a different matter. Because luggage may be zapped by high-powered X-ray machines on the way to the belly of the plane, film (and even computer diskettes) can be damaged. Therefore I seldom leave film in luggage I'm checking through. If I must do so, I use a double-thick lead-laminated pouch to protect rolls of film. Pouches are available in several sizes from camera stores (Sima Super FilmShield, $15). I pack the pouch in the center of my luggage.

Developing

I have yet to have a single roll of film developed while I travel. Everything I've heard and seen persuades me that processing is of higher quality and is less expensive at home. Rather than drugstore processing, try one of the reputable mail-order labs for higher quality at much lower prices. I've successfully used several: Seattle Film Works (206-283-9074), Kodalux (800-354-6873), Fuji Tru Color (800-224-5227), and Mystic Color (800-367-6061).

My last comment may be one of the most important. Anytime you'll be away from where you store your film, *check to see that you have plenty of UNEXPOSED film in your pocket or pack.* Don't wait until you're face to face with a silverback gorilla before discovering you're out of film.

Tips for Taking Fine Photographs

A great photograph sometimes just happens, but it's rare. Even given good equipment and a fine subject, superior results come from skill and thought on the part of the photographer. In this section, we'll discuss ways to add to the quality of the shots you bring home.

- See the subject of your photograph for itself, independent of your momentary presence. Take time to look at it, to enjoy it. When you snap a hurried picture without really seeing the subject, that distance shows in the result.
- When you know the subject matter is wonderful, consider bracketing. That is, take the first picture at the exposure and shutter speed you or your camera think is correct. Then take a photograph at the next smaller f-stop and one at the next larger (or you can bracket by changing shutter speed instead). Of course, if your camera is fully automatic, it will neutralize your aperture change by changing the shutter speed. If you can, switch to manual. Bracketing is more important when shooting slides than prints. Sure, bracketing eats film but how many times will you see the Taj Mahal under the full moon?
- Look at the subject through the viewfinder with your camera horizontal, then with it vertical. The difference can substantially change the mood of a picture, as well as avoid clutter.
- The lens loves clouds and shadows and the gentle light of early morning and late afternoon. At noon on a clear day the light will be flat and results will lack drama.
- To avoid shooting cliché photographs, experiment by shooting from unusual angles to get different effects. If you're about to take a picture

that would look good on a postcard, change your angle (or forget it and buy the postcard). The most important photographic equipment is your legs. Get out of the vehicle. Climb up the hillside. Scout alternative points of view. See what the shot would look like from one knee or with your elbows on the ground. Avoid the common standing eye-level shot, but don't let the quest for an unusual angle lead you into taking foolish risks. Wild animals will charge—and it won't be a photo-fee!

— The closer you are to the subject, the better your photograph. In Darjeeling, India, a zoo guard (for a little baksheesh) let me inside the cages to photograph the wild animals. *That* was close.

At the other extreme, I reached Kaladeo Bird Sanctuary in Bharatpur, India, just as rare white Siberian cranes arrived at the end of their long migration. Excited, I fired off most of a roll as they glided onto the far bank of the marsh, soft late afternoon light illuminating their snowy backs. On another occasion, trudging in a steady downpour through Perinet forest in Madagascar, my guide pointed up at several catlike Indris lemurs high in the tree-top canopy. Snapping quickly to minimize raindrops on the lens, I got a half-dozen shots before being driven undercover. Can you guess what those two sets of photographs had in common? Both featured bland scenery against which you could see, if you looked closely, several white dots in one set and several brown dots in the other. Only the photographer could have the slightest idea why anyone had bothered to snap the shutter. The image you see in your mind's eye is not always what shows up on film. Move closer or zoom in.

> The closer you are to the subject, the better your photograph.

— Photographing wildlife is harder than it might seem. If the subjects don't virtually fill the frame, the photo may be disappointing. Timing is also critical. When animals see you, they get nervous and start to move away. If you're slow, what you get is a wastebasket full of discarded photos of hind ends. Approach as near as you safely can, preferably downwind from the animals, and settle in. Stay still, not looking directly at them. In a short time, they'll return to grazing or playing and you'll have your shot.

— Most beginning photographers center the subject in the viewfinder. It's called bull's-eye vision. There's another method, sometimes called the "rule of thirds." Imagine drawing a tic-tac-toe grid on your viewfinder, creating nine squares. Placing your subject at one of the four intersections on that grid may create a more interesting photograph.

— Placing the horizon in the middle of the frame produces a predictable picture. If the sky is your reason for taking the picture, place the horizon in the lower third of the frame to improve the effect.

- When composing a shot, try to do three things every time: (a) Look beyond your subject to examine the background for anything that would detract from the shot, such as electric wires, advertising signs, Western tourists, and anything else that conveys a mood different from the one you're after. Since the background can make or break the picture, keep it as uncluttered as you can; (b) Look at the subject directly, not through the viewfinder, with one eye closed to see if your composition changes. After all, the camera has just one eye; (c) Just before you shoot, take your eye away from the viewfinder to see whether something is about to move into the picture. This small precaution reduces the number of photos that include the front bumper of a bus or half of some pedestrian's face.

- Try framing a distant subject by using something in the foreground. Shoot through an arch or use a tree trunk and branch or anything else that's handy. The idea is to add a sense of scale and dimension to the shot.

- Choose action shots over posed shots. Catch people doing something. Capture excitement.

- To be ready to take a shot quickly when using manual focus, focus your camera ahead of time at a selected point. When your subject arrives at that point, all you'll have to do is bring the camera up and shoot. Similarly, when you want to take a shot unobserved, adjust the focus on some object that's about the same distance away from you as the real subject, but in a different direction. You can then turn and shoot instantly.

- There's no reason you can't take a good photograph while you're moving, such as when aboard a train. Choose a fast enough shutter speed to freeze the subject. For most situations, 1/500th of a second is fine. The odds against a blurred photo are better if you shoot while the subject is coming toward you or receding into the distance.

- Using a reflection can produce a superior photograph. On the other hand, reflections can be an obstacle. When shooting through glass, say a car window, try to get the sun behind you. Hold the camera close to the window but don't allow it to touch. If it does, vibrations from the vehicle may blur the picture. A polarizing filter can help eliminate reflections off glass.

- Try shooting unusual architecture from odd angles and extremely close-up.

- Many captivating prints or slides are of people, the closer the better. It's easy to photograph monuments, and they do help recall where you were, but they can quickly become boring in your living room. Photographs of local people keep a trip alive. Next best are slices of everyday life, the shots that capture the essence of what a place felt like as you walked along.

- Recording the subject and the camera setting of each shot as I take it would drive me crazy. Still, if you're shooting dozens of temples, monasteries, or pagodas, they tend to blend together. I compromise by taping a number to each film container. As I use one, I enter that number in the back of my journal, indicating locations where I started and finished the roll. Another solution is to photograph something easily identifiable, such as an historical marker, to serve as a fingerprint of the location.
- Good equipment and good technique help, but developing an eye for what constitutes a memorable photograph is essential. We learn from feedback, so study your own photographs and those in good travel books until you have a feel for what works. Develop your own style. Take photographs that capture your point of view, that capture an essence, or that contain a message. The more you study the art of photography, the better you'll do. Toward that end, I've included several fine books on photography in the general section of the Bibliography.
- And of course, keep that light source behind you.

When to Shoot and When Not To

How would you feel if an odd-looking person speaking a strange tongue suddenly pointed a camera at you? Some people are fearful of, or offended by, being photographed. For some, it's modesty; for others, it violates spiritual beliefs. Some may be embarrassed by their poverty, aware of the contrast between their society and yours. Almost everyone responds in one way or another to being photographed and that reaction appears in the picture. If someone objects, your slide will show a person holding up a hand, or half-turning from the camera with a displeased expression. It's better to ask permission. Most people don't object to having their picture taken if treated with respect and friendliness rather than as a trophy.

Try taking a photo or two near a person before approaching her directly. If she notices your interest, lower the camera, wave, and walk closer. If you look guilty and retreat, you communicate that you were doing something wrong. Make eye contact, nod, smile, and take an interest in the work she's doing; try to indicate that you see her as an individual, not a curiosity. Then ask permission. If she agrees to be photographed, you have time to get an honest result. If she says no, that's the end of it. If tempted to take a picture notwithstanding protestations, imagine yourself in the place of the subject. It's a matter of respect.

On the other hand, some people enjoy being photographed because it makes them feel special. They pose, smile, and shake your hand. There are

Temple. Khajuraho, India.

also people who enjoy it because they expect to be paid. If you don't mind paying, go ahead. The amount is almost always negotiable, at least before you take the picture. If you don't want to pay in that situation, don't take the picture.

I was sitting on a small hill in the Masai Mara Game Preserve watching some Cape Buffalo when a white Toyota minivan stuffed with tourists stopped nearby. The tourists were pointing excitedly toward a half-dozen Masai shepherds. Each of the elegantly tall Masai, resplendent in bead necklaces and animal skins, stood balanced on one leg gripping an iron-tipped spear. As the tourists slung their expensive equipment into position for a photographic orgy, the Masai clearly indicated they wanted to be paid. The tourists snapped away, ignoring increasingly vocal demands. Then the van started to move, photo-satiated tourists now indifferent to the Masai. In seconds, the Masai raced forward, surrounded the van, and repeatedly thrust their nine-foot spears into its body. The driver spun off down the gravel road, panicked tourists screaming. Those tourists have a story to tell—but did they understand the lesson?

There are also *things* you should not photograph. General prohibitions include airports, bridges, harbors, and military installations, but you must watch for specific situations. If you take a picture of those 50-year-old destroyers tied up across the Huang Po River from Shanghai, snap a shot of the decrepit harbor of Dar es Salaam, or record on film that old bridge crossing the Moskva River in Moscow, cross your fingers. Current relations between the country you're in and your own may determine whether you'll go straight to jail—or merely have your camera confiscated. That choice won't be yours. The "No Photographs" signs outside certain temples in the Royal Palace enclosure in Bangkok are draped with rolls of exposed film. Subtle, eh?

For local guidance, check your guidebook. Read local handouts. Watch for signs. Ask someone. If you're not being watched, you may get away with it. Of course, you may be betting your camera or your freedom.

Let common sense prevail with respect to photographing *events*. If in doubt, ask. If there is no one to ask, consult your sense of appropriateness. If you decide to go ahead, watch peoples' response. Your Ladakhi hosts may accept your presence as the funeral procession winds up the barren mountainside behind their village, but they will surely object to your taking pictures as the deceased is folded into the circular cairn in which she will rest.

Slide Shows

If you've accepted invitations to see friends' slides of their last trip somewhere, you know how mind-numbing and eye-glazing a truly amateur production can be. Even if you don't want to take the time to create a professional quality show, a few suggestions will result in a show that pleases your friends.

Start by editing ruthlessly. Cut slides that evoke memories for you but would be meaningless to a detached observer. Then arrange the slides into a sequence that flows rather than one that follows your exact itinerary. Concentrate on communicating information and creating an appealing visual impact rather than presenting a literal itinerary.

Pace is important. Plan for between five and fifteen seconds per slide. If you're courageous, put the slide advance remote in someone else's control while you give your commentary. If you lag or digress, they can increase your pace without a word (or yawn).

Some conscientious maestros take the time to add printed titles to slides. A more subtle way of identifying transitions between places is by taking an occasional photograph of an airport or a street sign. While visiting a series of remote Maya sites last summer, I knew it would be hard to tell one location from another so I asked my friend to photograph me as I identified each site by using my body to form the first letter of its name.

A written outline of your commentary aids in gathering significant facts and commenting accurately on the slides. It cuts rambling, too, especially after a glass of wine. Having a large map handy, or showing slides of maps, also helps keep viewer interest high.

If you've recorded some folk music or bought tape cassettes during the trip, use them to set the mood for the show. Otherwise, find something in the library, a local record shop, or your own collection that's ethnically related to your trip.

Plan a show that will last an hour at most, which means 350 to 450 slides. Keep another tray or two on stand-by just in case the audience is really hooked. Of course, the trick is to be sure it's not just you who's hooked.

Video Cameras

Video cameras have become light and easy to use, but improvements won't eliminate appallingly bad post-trip videos unless people learn how to use their new toy before they travel. That includes shooting a few test tapes at home, then critiquing the results. Almost any videotape requires severe editing before a public screening.

Bring with you all the blank tapes you plan to shoot. If you buy tapes abroad, you won't get a picture if the image registration system of the tape is different from your camera's system. As a case in point, the system in general use in Europe is PAL, which is different from the NTSC system in the United States. If you buy a tape abroad, be sure you're getting a match.

In many places, a substantial fee is charged for a permit to use a video camera, sometimes as much as ten times the fee for a still camera. Tourist attraction officials seem to assume that people with a video camera are either shooting film for commercial sale or are wealthy tourists.

Be cautious about substituting a video camera for a 35mm camera. Until you are expert with it, it is at best a supplement.

There is an affinity between shiny-new, high-tech video cameras and quick-handed thieves. Carry the camera with care and try not to get completely absorbed in the filming.

REMEMBERING PEOPLE AND PLACES

You meet a lot of people as you travel; people in whose homes you stay, people you travel with for a few days, or people who accompanied you diving. Some are casual acquaintances; some you come to know well.

Most travelers keep a list of names and addresses, but as time passes, a list alone may not be enough. To help keep each person fresh in mind, I add the date, location, something about the circumstances, and sometimes a brief physical description.

Near the end of a trip, with better perspective for comparisons, I list places that turned out to be extra special. This list also helps friends in planning their next trips.

Not long after I'm home, I reflect on how I feel about the trip, what I learned, what I'd do differently. This is actually the first step in planning my next adventure.

Each of us has his or her own ways of keeping images vivid for years. But even if I were to travel with neither camera nor journal, the images would stay alive so long as I'd been 100 percent present each day on the road.

PART FOUR

The
Finish Line
("And the
Winner Is . . .")

23

Home Again, Home Again

> A boat was leaving in about ten days and the
> knowledge that I would be on that boat had
> already brought the journey to an end.
> —Henry Miller
> *The Colossus of Maroussi*

It's easier to leave than to return. However frequently I travel, I forget how strange it feels to come home. I avoid being met at the airport because I don't want to stand around the baggage claim area trying to sum up for someone the feelings and experiences of weeks or months on the road.

I feel a little lonely as the cab crosses the city, but that's outweighed by my desire to greet the familiar feelings of home alone. I hang my weary khakis and well-worn canvas shirt on a corner of the door and pull a collar-to-ankle *djellaba* over my head. As I set my money belt on the bureau, the routine kicks in and I drop it out of sight in a drawer. I pause, realizing I won't wear it again for . . . who knows how long? I'll miss it in the morning; it's been next to me every day of the trip.

I turn on the hot water heater, build a fire in the fireplace, put on some ethnic music, open a bottle of wine, and start thumbing through the mail my neighbor piled on the piano bench. My eyes wander to mementos of earlier adventures: framed photographs covering the walls, a hand-braided belt from Taquile, a midnight blue and scarlet rug from the Tibetan Refugee Center, a silver pipe from Kashmir, and ceremonial masks from the Amazon.

I don't call anyone, sometimes not for days, because I'm not ready to be back, let alone to begin telling trip tales. I want to ease back into my old world at my own pace, extending my time to think about new commitments and changes in priorities. Habits and rituals will exert their grip all too soon.

I feel stressed for a while after a long trip. There's so much to catch up on and the pace of life is always faster than I remembered. I feel a reverse homesickness, missing being on the road, missing people I met along the way.

On the road I was unique, a foreigner, a person who stood out in a crowd, whose opinions were sought, who was from the wealthiest nation on earth. At home, I'm just one of a quarter of a billion people. It's hard not to notice the difference.

Having accepted the risks of the high seas and navigated safely back to home port, I return with new perspectives and knowledge. Physically, I'm fit and my spirit is revitalized. Yet before me is the daunting challenge of bringing to my everyday life the energy and spirit of adventure I felt during my travels. I must continue to seek the unknown, to take chances, to stretch my mind and body. Above all, I must reject ruts and the trap of the comfort zone. In other words, I have to align my behavior in daily life as much as I can with my behavior on the road. That is every traveler's challenge.

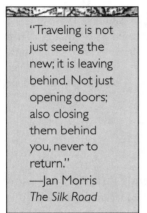

"Traveling is not just seeing the new; it is leaving behind. Not just opening doors; also closing them behind you, never to return."
—Jan Morris
The Silk Road

Although I'm different from the person who left colleagues and friends behind, those colleagues and friends don't see it. They comment on my tan, maybe mention I've lost a little weight. One may ask, "Where was it you went?" but, on hearing unfamiliar, almost alien, names, his eyes soon begin to glaze. Where I've been is so far away it's not quite real to him. If you understand that, you protect yourself from disappointment.

Seldom does anyone ask, "How are people reacting to freedom in Namibia (or Uzbekistan, Hungary, Chile, or anywhere)?" There's little chance of substantive questions about life on distant shores. You may return bursting with thoughts about how the world ought to operate and feelings about the wonder and tragedy of what you have seen, but you may not have many chances to share them. Speculate aloud about the heroic efforts to control AIDS in Rwanda, or the bloody tribal warfare between the Hutu and the Tutsi that has retarded that beautiful country for decades, and the most informed response will probably be some reminiscence about *Gorillas in the Mist*.

After you've been back a few months the trip is still resonating in your mind but your colleagues may have forgotten you were ever away. Remain too enthusiastic about your just-completed odyssey and you risk becoming a conversational black hole, the bane of hostesses. It's a reminder of how important it is to travel to satisfy your own goals, not the opinions of others.

When I feel a compelling need to share what I've experienced, I seek out other travelers. Like me, they're willing to watch anyone's slides from anywhere; they're eager to discuss politics and whitewater rivers, mountain treks and hanging out on remote beaches. Beyond that, I write, using word pictures to recreate the rumbling thunder of the mighty Zambezi River cascading over the ledge at Victoria Falls.

When I've been home about a month, I find myself reading articles and clipping stories from the newspaper. Without realizing it, I've begun planning my next adventure. As the Roman poet Martial said, "So, Posthumous, you'll live tomorrow, you say; too late, the wise lived yesterday."

"Here I am, safely returned over those peaks from a journey far more beautiful and strange than anything I had hoped for or imagined—how is it that this safe return brings such regret?"
—Peter Matthiessen, The Snow Leopard

When you return home, I urge you to write me about your trip. I'd love to hear about special places you found and anecdotes that illustrate points in this book. I'd also like to know what you found most helpful about *Traveler's Tool Kit*; about anything you feel I should have included or didn't get quite right. I'll be pleased to acknowledge your contribution in the next edition. Until then, may the wind be always at your back.

24

Rare Destinations

> Allah has laid out the earth for you like a vast carpet
> so that you will travel its endless roads.
> —*The Koran*

The more you know about special places waiting to give you pleasure, the more likely you are to get there. I invite you to join me on a magic carpet to visit some of the world's rare destinations. We'll stick with our magic carpet most of the way, but take local transport when that's more fun.

Before we leave, let me say what our trip is not. It's not a trip limited to well-known, "must see" places. Nor will we visit special places in Western or Eastern Europe, Russia and the former republics, the Middle East, the United States, or Canada—in fact, we'll visit very few places in the Northern Hemisphere. Our trip skips supermacho experiences such as plummeting down Mount Everest on one ski while blindfolded, or trekking solo across the Australian outback pushing an ice cream wagon—because that's not what most people do when they travel.

Instead, we'll concentrate on less-developed countries where our money will enable us to go farther and stay longer than it will in industrialized nations. Our magic carpet will visit rare destinations within the reach of almost everyone as far as physical effort. Most of them are perfectly suitable destinations for people new to international travel, although a few might be more fun with a trip or two under the belt. You needn't have been born with a backpack attached to your body to be able to visit these places. The information in *Traveler's Tool Kit* brings virtually any destination you dream of within your reach.

Let's leave our hometown behind, step aboard our magic carpet, and head for Africa, a continent almost one-third larger than North America. Although almost never the continent Westerners visit first, we start in Africa because it's a symbolic threshold for bold international travel. Because people know comparatively little about Africa, it seems distant, challenging, maybe even vaguely threatening. Yet Africa was home to some of our earliest civilizations, perhaps even the birthplace of humankind. In Africa, we see farthest into our past—as well as into our future. Either its enormous productive capacity or its profound human problems, or both, will bring Africa increasingly to our attention.

We stop first in Egypt. Even though its marvels seem familiar to us from photographs and films, reality surpasses expectation. Since the great pyramids of Giza are symbolic of Egypt, let's climb inside and clamber to their tops. Afterward, we sail up the Nile in a small *felucca* of ancient design. In Luxor, we walk through the temples of Karnak, the monumental cumulative effort of perhaps 17 dynasties. Awed, we fly farther up the Nile to Abu Simbel near the southern border with Sudan. Before us rise the mammoth sculptures erected by Rameses the Great to warn intruders from the south that his power was more awesome than they dared confront. After a stop in a desert oasis, we flee Egypt before the heat fries our temperaments.

We instruct our magic carpet to take us south the length of the continent to the desert country of Namibia, modern in some respects yet also home to Bushmen, Hereros, and other traditional cultures. We land in Etosha National Park, which consists of hundreds of square miles of desolate salt pan, barren for months but now exploding with life rehydrated by torrential rains. Free to wander on our own without guides or tour groups, we stake out one of the waterholes and watch herds and prides and flocks until our senses are satiated.

A short flight to the northeast and we're in Zimbabwe, the former Rhodesia. Our rubber raft slides into the Zambezi River just below Victoria Falls (locally named Mosi-oa-Tunya, or "smoke that thunders") to begin our descent of this world-class whitewater river. The experienced boatman makes it pretty certain we'll survive, but that doesn't detract from the pure excitement of running the raging rapids. Whitewater behind, we relax on the flagstone terrace of the moonlight-white Victoria Falls Hotel, one of the few remaining monuments to the era of Empire. The polished marble floors and staircases curving grandly to the mezzanine are a sharp contrast to our camp by the Zambezi where we fell asleep to the roar of the rapids.

In Hwange National Park, just down the road from Victoria Falls, we have the rare treat of seeing the elusive black leopard. Just before leaving Zimbabwe, we take a day-trip to Matopos National Park to see the unforgettable landscape of eroding boulders balanced in gravity-defying columns.

We cross the border to visit the Okavango Delta in Botswana, eager to visit this oasis of *afona matata* ("no problem" in the Setswana language) before it's overrun with visitors. We stop at the Duck Inn in the parched desert town of Maun on the eastern edge of the Delta. It's a traveler's crossroads where we ease into a conversation with some Peace Corps volunteers while savoring chilled beers on the screened porch. Refreshed, a five-passenger plane carries us above the lush wetlands of the Delta to Oddball's Palm Court Lodge. We pitch our tent near the open-air dining room nestled into a forest clearing.

Annual floodwaters flowing from the north have created a lacework pattern in the Delta, forcing the wild game onto hundreds of newly formed island habitats. With a local guide poling our dugout canoe (called a *makoro*), we slip silently into the labyrinth, gliding along narrow waterways bordered by tufted papyrus reeds. Swarms of butterflies and an occasional saddlebill stork come to see who's calling. Suddenly, a crocodile-shaped blur lunges explosively from its nest on the bank, diving darkly beneath our *makoro*. His massive corrugated mate watches us from the bank, her yellow eyes following us through narrow slits.

Several times a day, we climb ashore to stroll among curious giraffes, barking baboons, prowling lions, and ponderous elephants. One afternoon, we emerge from behind a termite mound and encounter a solitary Cape Buffalo bull less than 100 yards away. Spotting us, he leans our way, deciding whether to charge. His eyes narrow and he begins to lope in our direction, quickly reaching a speed faster than we can run in the tall grass. About 50 yards from us, he runs through a family of satiny brown antelope hidden in its grassy nest. They scatter and he curves off to his right, continuing into the forest. This unobstructed proximity to wild game is what makes the Okavango Delta one of the most appealing destinations in Africa. At night, we sit by a campfire sharing freshly roasted fish, vegetable curries, ginger snaps, and beer cooled in the floodwaters, and we talk of writing books about our adventures.

From Botswana our magic carpet takes us north up the spine of Africa to Rwanda where we head immediately for Volcano National Park. Surrounded by a ring of looming volcanoes, the park headquarters lies in ruins, bungalows collapsing, restaurant roofless, walls covered with graffiti denouncing the incumbent regime. It's a troubled time to be here. Before crawling into our tents, we take a short hike to villages occupied by pygmies wearing cast-off Western clothes. Just after dawn, we climb through bamboo forests, nettle fields, and lobelia plants to find the day's nesting place of a mountain gorilla family. Dian Fossey was murdered for her defense of these incredible primates, and we feel her spirit walking with us on the foggy slopes.

Crossing the border to the east, we stretch out on the grassy floor of Ngorongoro Crater in Tanzania. It takes little imagination to feel the rumble of volcanic eruptions, hear the echo of dinosaur screams, and envision our predecessors as they clumsily rose erect. In the present, lions, rhinos, and elephants watch us watching them.

Not far from the Ngorongoro Crater, Lake Manyara resembles a Rousseau painting, an earthly paradise for animals. The animals live together in harmony except when hunger intrudes. We see the famous tree-climbing lions lying motionless on shady limbs overhanging game trails . . . waiting.

A short distance away we stand on the rim of Olduvai Gorge where Louis Leakey searched under the scorching sun for 28 years before he discovered the skull of "homo habilis." Mary Leakey scratched the earth for twenty years more before finding the 3½ million-year-old footprints that demonstrate that man became a biped far earlier than we previously knew. We reflect and speculate in the silence.

The next leg of our trip takes us to Mount Kilimanjaro. Climbing to its volcanic lip, even when porters carry the food and heaviest gear, requires all of our strength and will. We need no climbing skills, but it's a long way up from the flat African savannah to Uhuru Peak at 19,340 feet. At the summit, we stand on the highest point of all Africa.

From Kilimanjaro, our magic carpet takes us east across the Mozambique Channel to Madagascar, where we hop on a train to Perinet Nature Reserve to seek the rare Indris lemur in the towering tree canopy. Furry, shadowy elves accompany us along the path under the full moon.

Next, north to Lamu, is a small island off the coast of Kenya. Its mud-walled structures are architecturally unchanged from centuries ago when Lamu was an Arab trading post. We snorkel, sail, stroll down narrow lanes in the company of Abyssinian asses, and toss back liters of Tusker beer at Petley's Inn after dusk. Lamu is an ideal place to rest after climbing Kilimanjaro.

"There is something about safari life that makes you forget your troubles and feel the whole time as if you had drunk half a bottle of champagne—bubbling over with heartfelt gratitude for being alive."
—Isak Dinesen

Our carpet takes us back to mainland Kenya to visit Masai Mara National Park, where sweeping savannah flows through bulky hills highlighted by thorn tree sentinels and flaming sunsets, home to vast populations of wild animals. Since Masai Mara is no secret, we're lucky to be here when it's not tourist season.

Not far away, we walk the paths of Amboseli National Park, fascinated by the incomparable sight of elephant families silhouetted against the snow-capped profile of Mount Kilimanjaro. Around the campfire, we talk with other travelers about everything from powder skiing to perestroika.

Before leaving Africa, we spend an evening in the bar of Nairobi's white stucco Norfolk Hotel, epicenter of the decadent turn-of-the-century white society of East Africa. Listening closely, we imagine conversations between Scott Fitzgerald and Ernest Hemingway after a hunt. Beryl Markham, an intrepid Kenya-based aviator who knew intimately everyone from Denys Finch-Hatton (played by Robert Redford in Out of Africa) to crowned heads of Europe, summed up Africa beautifully when she said, "Africa is never the same to anyone who leaves it and returns again. It is not a land of change, but it is a land of moods and its moods are numberless." With that insight in mind, we ask our carpet to take us east along the equator to Asia.

As if with a will of its own, our carpet turns north to India and its diverse and complex people. It's a country of contrasts: a modern industrial powerhouse astride hundreds of millions of impoverished people. In this home of nonviolence, great religions are locked in timeless combat. Tradition and chaos share the same space. Visiting India requires endurance and tolerance for ambiguity, but with a healthy sense of humor, we enjoy its rich rewards.

Our first stop in India is the famous Taj Mahal in Agra. Sure it's a major tourist stop, but we'd be crazy to miss it. Beyond aesthetic brilliance and fine craftsmanship, it embodies the romantic legend of Shah Jahan, his beautiful wife Mumtaz, and the Moghul Empire. After we've seen the Taj at sunrise and beneath the full moon, our knowledge of India begins to take shape.

Just down the road is the skeleton of a town called Fatepur Sikri, given life by an emperor following a mystic's counsel that building a new capital city would assure birth of a male heir. Its delicate minarets, high-ceilinged halls, and water-cooled bed chambers were sumptuous quarters for the royal court and the royal heir—but were suddenly abandoned. Centuries later no one knows why this beautiful city stands silent.

> "India reacts very strongly on people. Some loath it, some love it, most do both. . . . The place is very strong and often proves too strong for European nerves. . . . Everyone likes to talk about India whether they happen to be loving it or loathing it. . . . All the time I know myself to be on the back of this great animal of poverty and backwardness."
> —Ruth Prawer Jhabvala

Our carpet whisks us to Srinagar in the cool Vale of Kashmir in the northwest corner of India, where we treat ourselves to an evening on the verandah of a houseboat, sipping cardamom and cinnamon tea and gazing across a serene blue lake. Our 120-foot floating home has a carved dining table for eight, silk tapestries, brass lanterns, chandeliers, stained-glass windows, and downy beds with velvet spreads and hot water bags for our toes. After a couple of nights aboard the houseboat, we head to a nearby mountain village for some skiing. We leave Kashmir abruptly when crowds erupt into the streets over a religious dispute.

Heading east, our magic carpet trip to Leh, capital of the ancient Kingdom of Ladakh, is unmatched on this planet. We can almost touch the icy, wind-whipped summits of the Himalayas. Below us, the Indus River is only a thin, rocky stream giving no hint of the immensely powerful river it will become in Pakistan. Under the increasing influence of visitors, the Tibetan Buddhist culture of Ladakh is yielding to Westernization but its monasteries are still bustling with activity. Monks move briskly as they perform ancient rituals in the pure light of dawn. Twisting wreaths of smoke from pitch torches, generations of prayers, and eons of idols fill the cavernous stone chambers of the Hemis, Sheh, and Thikse monasteries.

East again and we're in Kathmandu, Nepal, a flask that may hold your personal genie. Because of its gentle people and breathtaking views, a trip to Nepal is a success even without climbing Chomolungma, Mother Goddess of the Snows (Mount Everest). Some say that if you were going to see only one sunrise in your life it ought to be from the village of Dhulikel on the southern ridge of the Kathmandu Valley. Impressed, we shiver all night on a stone bench, rising once in a while to stir the fire, eager for the sun to rise over the Himalayas. When it does, it is so spectacular that the chill is forgotten and no one speaks.

We travel overland west to Pokhara, then trek to the inspiring peaks of Annapurna, passing beneath towering Dhaulagiri and its stony friends. Our walk takes us high along the slopes of Kali Gandaki Gorge, called by some the deepest valley in the world (not to be confused with Colca Canyon in Peru, which may be the deepest canyon). We visit Ghandrung, Ghorepani, and Muktinath, picturesque villages finely constructed from the scales of the mountain. Since our lungs and legs are holding up, we walk on to Jomsom and the long-ago kingdom of Mustang. We step gingerly across swinging bridges, dodging ponies with brass bells around their necks and red plumes rising from their harnesses. We talk with sturdy old Gurkha soldiers dressed in tattered uniforms, grip cups of hot tea with near-numb fingers, and listen to the raspy sound of our breath when we reach the crest of a hard-won pass. Back in Pokhara, we rest in a flower-filled garden near the lake, sunshine on our faces, looking up through the clouds at the vertical fin of Machhupuchhare and reliving the footsteps of our trek.

From Pokhara, we whisk ourselves down to Chitwan National Park in southern Nepal to ride high on an elephant's back through cool dark forests and across fields of golden mustard blossoms. Our traveler's luck holds and we see a one-horned rhino and two Bengal tigers.

Next, we ask our magic carpet to fly us across the mountains to Quilin, China, and the Li River, where fantastic karst (limestone) mountain spires show the ethereal artistry of nature. As our small boat drifts along the Li toward the panorama of Seven Horse Mountain, we try to ignore chickens squawking as they sacrifice their lives to become our water-borne lunch.

We arrive next at the excavation site of the terra-cotta warriors outside Xi'an, where hundreds of finely-modeled soldiers stand patiently row upon row. Although they are a legacy to us from one of China's most progressive rulers, I wonder how many of the originals lost their lives willingly to build this monument to the emperor.

The Forbidden City, home of emperors, is well worth enduring the crowds. After almost a full day of wandering its paths, we rent a bike for a ride though the life of modern Beijing. Standing in front of the Great Wall, with its serpentine coils embracing steep hillsides, I think of the enormous effort and intrinsic folly involved in building it. In the end, as is so often the case, the fatal danger to the emperors came from forces already within their wall. We don't stay long because, at the points most accessible to visitors, the Wall is so crowded it might be Disneyland Far East.

Hong Kong, resting on China's edge, has its feet firmly planted in two distinct, even adversarial, cultures. Millions of people pack the city, urgently seeking success or survival in this former star of the British Empire. At the same time, we can almost hear the patient breathing of Hong Kong's billion Chinese neighbors. Brilliantly lighted skyscrapers broadcast the power of the economy, even if it rests on quicksand. Rio is close in grandeur, as are San Francisco, Sydney, and New York, but Hong Kong remains queen.

Leaving China reluctantly, we fly southwest down to Thailand. Because visiting Thailand is so easy, inexpensive, and rewarding, we immediately encounter swarms of travelers. In northern Thailand, we hire a guide in Chiang Mai and set off into the hill country, sleeping in bamboo and thatch houses in villages of different tribes. These tribes, who fled Burma or Laos decades ago, retain their original language and culture and resist assimilation into Thailand. The people dress in bright colors, harvest opium poppies during the day, and gather around our fire in the evening, open in their curiosity. We ride elephants from one village to another and pole along placid streams on crude rafts of bamboo poles lashed together with vines.

Our final flight in Thailand takes us to the tiny island of Ko Tao (Turtle Island) in the Gulf of Thailand. The presence of 16 dive shops confirms that scuba diving and snorkeling are excellent. Ko Tao has fine beaches, good restaurants, and a laid-back atmosphere. We spend about $10 for a private bungalow with a porch, toilet, and fan. Ko Tao may be close to paradise.

We reboard our magic carpet for a short flight to the south to Indonesia where we find diversity in culture, food, architecture, and art matched by few other countries. We ride a double-outrigger canoe out of Manado Bay, at the northeast tip of Sulawesi, to the small volcanic islands of Manado Tua and Bunaken to enjoy some of the best snorkeling and diving in the world. The coral is pristine and vigorous and ours is the only boat. When a massive fish rises from the 2,000–meter depths and swims toward us, it's time to continue our trip elsewhere.

Still on the island of Sulawesi, we visit mile-high Toraja-land and its picture-perfect rice paddies. Fields the radiant green of a van Gogh canvas are accented by gray-black boulders either too massive or too aesthetically perfect to move. Homes cluster at the edge of the manicured fields, the roof of each shaped to resemble the upswept bow of a ship poised to return to the ancestral homeland in Southeast Asia. In Toraja-land, the dead reside in narrow caverns carved into cliff faces. Tau-taus, fully costumed three-foot effigies of the deceased, watch us from balconies wedged into natural crevasses near the base of the cliffs.

From Sulawesi we fly to Bali to enjoy its renowned artistic culture, then move on to Papua New Guinea. On this half-an-island (shared with Irian Jaya), we visit remote valleys between slopes of towering volcanoes to meet some of the most primitive tribes in the world. Before World War II, large numbers of Papua New Guineans had no idea that an "outside" world existed. Since then, war, missionaries, commerce, and tourism have eroded that innocence. When the tribes gather at Mount Hagen for a "sing-sing" in elaborate costumes, customs of mountain life come alive. We're lucky to be here before the unique character of PNG is lost.

Flying into Oceania from Papua New Guinea risks serious culture shock. In Australia and New Zealand we return to Western societies and customs. In New Zealand we stop first on the North Island, visiting sunny bays in the pseudo-tropical north, boiling geysers and snowcapped volcanoes in its midriff, and the windswept piers of Wellington on its southern tip. For adventure we go on to the South Island. The forested mountain ridges, stony islands, and hidden coves of the Marlborough Sounds, followed by the art colony of Nelson nestled in the midst of apple orchards and vineyards, don't prepare us for the stormy west coast. Behind the blue-white Fox and Franz Josef Glaciers cascading into the Tasman Sea, we see the peaks of the majestic Southern Alps. We spend four days hiking the Milford Track, christened by National Geographic as the "finest walk in the world." That's so much fun, we walk the Routeburn, Heaphy, and Abel Tasman trails as well, even stopping once in a while to take one of the short walks that begin at roadside trailheads and lead off through the bush to emerald lakes or mountain passes.

We enjoy the Shotover jet boat out of Queenstown but add the longer jet boat trip up the pristine Dart River. From Queenstown we visit Milford Sound and Doubtful Sound, the best-known of the glacier-carved fiords. Before we leave, we take a few runs on the Coronet Peak ski slopes above Queens-town. Our last evening is spent, of course, in a pub full of friendly people and hearty beer.

Our last stop in Oceania is the Great Barrier Reef, the longest reef in any ocean. It's still a world-class attraction, despite damage at the hands of starfish and humans. The vast continent of Australia deserves more of our time, but we have to hurry along to reach Antarctica during its brief "warm" season.

We step off our magic carpet in Ushuaia, Argentina, and board a small passenger ship to sail across the Drake Passage to the Antarctic Peninsula. The shoreline is a seamless white glacier, white without features, white that is less a description of color than a blank between ocean and overcast sky. Twice each day, a Zodiac inflatable boat takes us ashore to wander among dozens of Elephant and Weddell seals and millions of Adelie, Gentoo, Macaroni, and Chinstrap penguins. Wandering albatrosses watch with cocked heads far overhead. We spend one morning in Hope Bay, the site of one of the largest penguin rookeries in the world. The next afternoon we drop anchor off Cuverville Island, probably no larger than 200 acres and consisting primarily of one steep, snow-covered mountain. Its magnificent bay is patrolled by wind-sculpted icebergs. Small wood huts shelter three female scientists from the Scott Polar Research Institute at Cambridge.

At Paradise Bay, one of the most beautiful harbors in the world, a black rock cliff face is brightened by streaks of blue-green copper ore, orange lichen, and emerald green moss. Bergie bits in the bay are manned by crews of seals and penguins. We celebrate Christmas Eve with a party on the fantail of our ship, singing Christmas carols and exchanging toasts with champagne and hot spiced wine as ancient glaciers glow under the midnight sun. Even though not nearly the end of our magic carpet trip, Paradise Bay truly feels like the "end of the world."

The landscape of Antarctica is unique. Seeing it is like being permitted to visit the Ice Age—comfortably. It radiates immense power, vastness, and indifference. If left unprotected, there would be no hope. There are billions of krill (shrimp-like food for whales), millions of penguins, huge numbers of seals and seabirds, a few whales—and not much else. Since there are no trees, no bushes, and no weeds, even tiny growths of lichen, algae, and moss are celebrated. Antarctica is a spectacular visual treat, but before long we yearn for diversity. It's time to leave for the abundant flora and fauna of South America.

Our magic carpet takes us to Punta Arenas on the southern tip of Chile, across the channel from Tierra del Fuego. A half-day overland we arrive in Paine National Park to trek along the Grey Glacier, accompanied by guanacos and scrutinized by condors. It would be hard to feel more distant from normal life than when sitting on the shore of a pristine glacial lake surrounded by vertical granite crags. Our next adventure in Chile is paddling the Bio Bio and the Futaleufu, rivers unequaled for beauty and danger.

From there, north to Puerto Montt, the starting point for a trip by small boat and bus across the Lake Country to the ski slopes of San Carlos de Bariloche in Argentina. The view always includes a lake, a mountain, or a forest—and often all three. Back in Puerto Montt, we board the S.S. *Evangelista* to glide serenely among the islands of Chile's "fiordland" (a term shared with Norway and New Zealand) down Last Hope Sound to Puerto Natales. Glaciers glow blue-white on the port beam while, thousands of feet above us, the Andes rise like jagged teeth in the cloudless sky.

Having been entertained by natural scenery for a while, we fly northeast across the Andes to another of the world's great cities. Rio de Janeiro, Brazil, where we're instantly swept into the life of the *cariocas* (as Rio's residents call themselves). The foul water in the bay doesn't attract us to swim, but Copacabana and Ipanema beaches are made memorable by thousands of beautiful people, most wearing revealing "thong" bathing suits. We join a boisterous beach volleyball game, one of perhaps a hundred along the beach, and play until dusk. Energized by the physical setting, which ranks in splendor with Hong Kong, San Francisco, and Cape Town, we throw ourselves into the intense night life. Money flows, voices are raised, future lovers are recognized, and tomorrow's labor has no reality. In the mornings, though, we're aware of hundreds of thousands of poor people living in the shadows whose daily struggle for survival leaves little time for contemplation of beauty.

In a remote village outside Salvador,* we visit a condomble, or religious-magic ceremony, sitting for hours in the midst of more than a hundred local people in a dimly lit room whose boundaries are lost in shadows. Chanting trance-dancers whirl mindlessly, flinging sweat-spray over the crowd. While white-gowned healers minister to the faithful with clouds of ceremonial cigar smoke, a relentless booming drum sets the beat of our hearts.

We cannot fully experience Brazil without visiting the Amazon. Villages are interesting, but few remain free of influence from the industrialized world. The rain forest, on the other hand, still retains unimaginable diversity and majesty. After threading our way through the forest we understand emotionally, not just intellectually, its role at the heart of our global ecosystem and the impact of its loss on the future of our species.

We fly above the forest canopy to the state of Mato Grosso to see the Pantanal, the largest natural wetland in the world. A guide with a small boat helps us explore this vast swamp that shelters millions of birds, mammals, and reptiles.

Our magic carpet takes us on up the Amazon to Iquitos, just inside the Peruvian border, where we hire guides for another trek into the Amazonian forest. We camp with Quechua Indians, wander quiet paths, build rafts to cross rivers along the way, and play catch with kids in river bluff villages.

Wanting to learn more about the rain forest in Peru, we use Explorer's Inn on the bank of the Tambopata River as a base. On our first hike into the forest, we stumble onto a dugout canoe on the shore of an oxbow lake and paddle slowly for hours, playing hide-and-seek with giant river otters. Dozens of butterflies cover our bodies, nibbling bits of salt.

It's only a short flight from the Tambopata to Cuzco, one of the world's more agreeable towns. Most visitors pass through quickly on a whirlwind tour to Machu Picchu and the sacred valley of the Urubamba, but we settle in

---

* *Salvador.* This port city in northeast Brazil is the capital of Bahia. It is noted for *Capoeira,* a foot-fighting dance, and *condomble,* religious-magic ceremonies.

for a while, becoming part of daily life. We talk with vest-makers and weavers of belts and women who mop the steps of the cathedral. A professor from the the Inca outpost of Machu Picchu, no matter where we are we'll summon a vision of that mysterious stone settlement on a narrow ridge in an ocean of peaks . . . and wonder.

We head south to see the amazing Nazca Lines. The huge figures carved into the dry coastal plain may have served as astronomical aids to farmers or landing signals to extraterrestrials (as Erik von Daniken thought), or they may have served some purpose we've yet to imagine. Whatever the lines were for, their existence confirms the intelligence of their creators.

Next, south to the "white city" of Arequipa and up to the altiplano (high plain) to the village of Chivay where Inca heritage lives in the faces of the villagers. We sit on a stone wall, the border of a terraced field first furrowed a half-millennium ago, that runs to the very edge of the 10,000–foot deep Colca Canyon. Our senses relax and time slows as condors glide across the silent sky.

It's time to leave South America, but we have time for just a few more stops before returning home. Having gotten to know the Inca, it's time to meet the Maya.

Flying thousands of miles north, we cross the equator and settle in the Maya city of Copan on the western border of Honduras. Spreading canopies of towering trees rooted in the heart of the ruins shelter the past from the blazing sun. As we watch, archeologists lift the shrouds from a 1,200-year-old society.

Just a short distance north in Guatemala, we drop in on Livingston, a Caribbean coastal town inaccessible by road (but easily reached by magic carpet) to cruise up the Rio Dulce in the company of manatees, toucans, and the seldom-seen quetzal. Continuing west, still in Guatemala, we reach incredibly beautiful, mile-high Lake Atitlan in the central highlands. Atitlan winds for more than ten miles in the shadow of terraced mountainsides and volcanic cones. Along the shore of the lake, which Jacques Cousteau calculated to be almost 3,000 feet deep, we visit a dozen villages in which traditional dress and customs still prevail.

Our last stop in Guatemala is Tikal. Rising above the far northern jungle, the pyramids and temples of Tikal are the most impressive of all Maya sites. We climb to the top of Temple IV to watch the sun set over a vanished empire. Our last stops before heading home are in Mexico at three of the most impressive of the Maya city-states, Palenque, Uxmal, and Chichen Itza. The Yucatán peninsula is a great place

> "I cannot rest from travel; I will drink Life to the lees; all times have I enjoyed Greatly, have suffered greatly, both with those That loved me, and alone; I am become a name; For always roaming with a hungry heart Much have I seen and known . . ."
> —Alfred Lord Tennyson, *Ulysses*

to relax and reminisce about our tour of some of the world's rare destinations. Thanks for coming along. I enjoyed traveling with you.

By the way, when not traveling by magic carpet, one of my personal special places is a window seat on an airplane. I love views, so I always ask ticket agents which side of the plane has the best views and which seats aren't over the wing. Some of the finest views from airplanes are on flights from Punta Arenas north along the Andes and past Mount Aconcagua's icy cone before settling into Santiago; north from Lima across Ecuador along the Andes; a Society Islands puddle-jumper from Tahiti to Huahine, Raitea, and Bora Bora; the flight from New Delhi into Kathmandu, watching the panorama of the Himalayas unfold ahead; flights winding among the Southern Alps of New Zealand and setting down on a glacier snow field; and almost any interisland flight in Indonesia with views of coral reefs and fuming volcanoes.

Looking back at our tour of special places, I could easily have included Angkor Wat, the temples of Pagan, the ancient cities of Petra and Sana'a, the Potala in Lhasa, Baltoro Glacier, Aswan, Ellora and Ajanta, and any number of other places. What about trips along the Silk Road from Xi'an to Venice, the Salt Road from Fez to the Haggar Mountains in the Sahara, the Burma Road from Rangoon to Kunming, the road from St. Petersburg to Yalta, and the length of the Pan American Highway? And what about a horse trek across Mongolia or hikes in the Italian Dolomites, the Zagoria region of northern Greece, the Brooks Range, or Glacier National Park? What about fishing for salmon in Russia's Ponoi River, for steelhead in the lower Dean River in British Columbia, or fly fishing in Patagonia? What about canoeing Lake Titicaca, sea kayaking around Ellesmere Island in the Arctic or along Hawaii's Na Pali coast or in Glacier Bay Alaska, or sailing the Turkish coast between Gocek and Marmaris? Yes, they're all special places—and that makes my point. The number of special places is very large indeed and they're all out there waiting for you. It's time to go.

CHECKLISTS

Travel Information Form

(Leave a copy at home and take one with you.)

1. Credit card numbers: _____

2. Driver's license number: _____

3. Travelers check numbers: _____
    _____

4. Contacts abroad: _____
    _____
    _____
    _____
    _____
    _____

5. Medical information: _____

6. Airline ticket information: _____
    _____

7. Address of bank: _____

8. Travel/medical insurance policy

9. Copies of first two pages of passport

10. Copy of itinerary

Checklist: Budget

Predeparture Expenses

$_____ passport, visas, and photos
_____ international student ID card
_____ guidebooks
_____ hostel membership
_____ camera, film, filters, other photo equipment
_____ luggage, daypack
_____ new clothes
_____ travel insurance
_____ gear (money belt, etc.)
_____ health care (medicine and shots)
_____ toiletries
_____ reading material

Transportation

_____ air fares
_____ other fares (trains, buses, etc.)

Meals and Lodging

_____ en route
_____ daily lodging
_____ daily meals

Special Experiences

_____ entertainment (sightseeing, tours, etc.)
_____ safaris, scuba diving, glacier climbing, etc.

Miscellaneous

_____ souvenirs, gifts, tips, laundry, etc.

Checklists: Clothing

The following list contemplates an informal, lightweight trip. Your choices will reflect personal tastes, the length of your trip, and anticipated climates and activities.

For Men

1. Shirts

_____ Two short-sleeve outdoor shirts
_____ Two long-sleeve shirts with collars
_____ Two or three 100 percent cotton T-shirts
_____ One long-sleeve turtleneck

2. Pants

_____ One pair tough 100 percent cotton twill or canvas (or 85 percent wool), one lightweight pair, one dressy pair of khakis (optional: pair of dress slacks)
_____ One pair of hiking or gym shorts

3. Underwear

_____ Three pairs of cotton briefs

For Women

1. Shirts

_____ T-shirts plus two or three shirts or blouses, a jogging top, turtleneck, vest

2. Pants

_____ One or two lightweight pairs of pants (possibly substituting one heavier pair, depending on expected weather)
_____ One or two skirts (optional: pair of panty hose or ballet tights)
_____ One pair of shorts

3. Underwear

_____ 100 percent cotton panties, brassieres

Checklists: Clothing (continued)

For men

4. Socks

_____ Three or four pairs of high-quality socks (optional: one pair of dress socks)

5. Shoes

_____ One pair of sandals

_____ One pair of lightweight, low-cut trail/walking shoes (optional: hiking boots or tennis shoes)

For women

4. Socks

_____ Three or four pairs of high-quality socks (optional: one pair of knee-high hose)

5. Shoes

_____ One pair of sandals

_____ One pair of lightweight, low-cut trail/walking shoes (optional: hiking boots, tennis shoes, ballet-type slipper)

For men and women

6. Belt

_____ One sturdy belt

7. Nightwear

_____ One nightshirt (optional: warm-up suit, sarong)

8. Swimsuit

_____ One quick-drying swimsuit

9. Rain gear

_____ Gore-Tex shell (optional: waterproof poncho, light rain suit)

10. Extra warmth

_____ One lightweight windbreaker (optional: jacket of polyester/cotton or polypro pile, down vest, light sweater, thermal underwear)

_____ One good scarf

11. Towel

_____ One light towel

12. Miscellaneous

_____ Bandannas

_____ Hat/sun visor

_____ Gloves

_____ Tie

_____ Blue blazer

Checklist: Toiletries

_____ Band-Aids
_____ comb (and/or brush)
_____ deodorant
_____ dental floss
_____ insect repellent (DEET, Ultra-Thon, Permethrin clothing spray)
_____ laundry detergent
_____ leak-proof toiletries kit
_____ lip balm (with sunscreen)
_____ mirror
_____ moleskin
_____ mosquito coils
_____ nail clippers (or emery boards)
_____ panty liners

_____ razor blades and shaving lather
_____ safety pins
_____ sanitary napkins
_____ sewing kit
_____ shampoo
_____ soap; soap container
_____ sunscreen
_____ thermometer
_____ toilet paper
_____ toothbrush (with storage container or cap)
_____ toothpaste
_____ tweezers and scissors

Checklist: Miscellaneous Gear

_____ Bags (garbage bags, Ziploc bags, stuff sacks)
_____ Bicycle locking cable
_____ Camera gear (film, camera, zoom lens, extra camera battery, lens filters, lens cleaning kit, lead-foil film bags)
_____ Clock (and batteries)
_____ Doorstop alarm (or Travelock or Jammer)
_____ Eyeglasses (sunglasses, prescription glasses and prescription, contact lenses, lens solution, hard plastic travel case, retainer strap)

_____ Flashlight (and new alkaline batteries)
_____ Guidebooks
_____ Journal
_____ Locks (luggage and daypack)
_____ Maps
_____ Money belt
_____ Reading material
_____ Rubber bands
_____ Swiss Army knife
_____ Wallet
_____ Wristwatch
_____ Writing materials (pads, pens)

Checklist: Documents to Take Along

____ Airline and other tickets (and copies)
____ American Automobile Association membership card
____ ATM card
____ Certificate of Registration
____ Credit cards (including card numbers and telephone numbers for reporting a loss)
____ Driver's license (optional: international driver's license)
____ Insurance (proof of insurance, agent's telephone number)
____ International Association for Medical Assistance to Travelers (IAMAT) card
____ International Certificate of Vaccination (yellow card)
____ International student ID card
____ Itinerary
____ Medical information (blood type, special medical conditions, allergies, personal physician's phone number, health insurance information)
____ Names, addresses, and telephone and fax numbers
____ Passport (plus copies of the first two pages of the passport), extra passport photos, separate proof of citizenship
____ Permits (trekking, game watching, work)
____ Prescriptions
____ Reservations (hotels, cars, etc.)
____ Telephone charge card
____ Travelers checks (and separate copy of check numbers)
____ Visas
____ Youth Hostel membership card

Checklist: Optional Equipment

____ Binoculars
____ Briefcase
____ Business cards
____ Calculator
____ Cassette recorder/player
____ Contraceptives
____ Duct tape
____ Eating utensils
____ Electrical items (adapter plug, converter)
____ Film shield
____ Immersion heater
____ Inflatable pillow
____ Mace
____ Mask and snorkel
____ Musical instruments
____ Nylon clothesline
____ Sewing kit
____ Sheet sack
____ Sink stopper
____ Sleeping bag
____ Sleeping pad
____ Slippers
____ Travel games
____ Umbrella
____ Water bottle
____ Waterproof bags
____ Whistle

Checklist: Shots to Get before You Go

What shots you need depends on (a) where you're going, (b) the current status of your inoculations, and (c) the requirements of the countries you'll be visiting. Obtain annual information on the prevalence of specific diseases in specific countries, along with immunization requirements, from *Health Information for International Travel* (HIFIT). This information is available on a current basis in the semimonthly *Summary of Health Information for International Travelers* issued by the Centers for Disease Control. Call the CDC hotline at (404) 332-4559 for information.

Because some shots interfere with others and some shots are given as a series, you can't drop into the health department at the last minute to get all shots at once. Besides, it's nice to have some time to recover from any adverse reaction. Although it would be ideal to receive the full series of immunizations over a four- to eight-week period, the pace can be accelerated if need be.

- **Cholera:** Vaccine four to six weeks before you leave. If practical, it should not be received at the same time as the yellow fever vaccine. Check with the CDC to determine whether a cholera certificate of vaccination is required to enter any country on your itinerary.

- **Diphtheria:** Vaccine six weeks before you leave. Booster every ten years.

- **Hepatitis A:** One week before you leave, take immune globulin to increase immunity. Since this is a blood-based product, it would be risky to get this shot in any country where blood is not screened and treated. Alternatively and substantially more expensive, there's Havrix, the newly approved hepatitis A vaccine. The first shot is taken two to four weeks prior to departure; the second is taken six to twelve months later.

- **Hepatitis B:** Ideally, the three-shot vaccine (Recombivax) takes six months.

- **Influenza:** Vaccine anytime. Especially important for people over 65.

- **Japanese B Encephalitis:** Three shots over a three-week period. Since there is a possibility of severe reaction after each vaccination, the series should begin at least six weeks prior to departure.

- **Measles, mumps, rubella:** Vaccines six weeks before you leave. If you were born after 1956, it is recommended that you receive a measles vaccine even if you've had an earlier shot.

- **Meningococcal meningitis:** Vaccine five weeks before you leave.

- **Polio:** Even if you were vaccinated as a child consider getting this oral vaccine several months before you leave.

- **Rabies:** Begin Human Diploid Cell Merriaux Vaccine series four to six weeks before you leave. It may be repeated every two years if desired.
- **Smallpox:** Vaccine eight weeks before you leave.
- **Tetanus** (combine with diphtheria vaccine): Vaccines six weeks before you leave. Booster every ten years or after a puncture wound or major laceration.
- **Typhoid:** If you take the standard vaccine, get the first shot eight weeks before departure and the second shot four weeks later. The oral vaccine may be preferable but should be kept refrigerated and must be taken as directed. Booster every three years. Alternatively, take the newly FDA-approved, single-shot vaccine, Typhin Vi.
- **Yellow Fever:** Vaccine three weeks before you leave. Booster every ten years.

My public health service advises that yellow fever and immune serum globulin can safely be given at the same time, even though that isn't their first choice. The same is true for immune globulin and oral polio.

Enter each shot on your yellow card. Keep a copy in a safe place since it's probably the only record of what you've had and when.

Checklist: Matching Medicines with Minor Annoyances

_____ Aches, sunburn, headache: aspirin, acetaminophen, ibuprofen
_____ Acid stomach: Maalox, Mylanta, or Gelusil
_____ Allergies, poison ivy, rash, etc.: hydrocortisone cream, diphenhydramine (Benadryl), chlorpheniramine (Chlor-Trimeton), Hismanal
_____ Altitude sickness: acetazolamide (Diamox)—do *not* take if allergic to sulfa drugs; dexamethasone (for severe symptoms); ibuprofen; acetaminophen
_____ Athlete's foot: tolnaftate (Tinactin powder), clotrimazole (Lotrimin AF), undecylenic acid (Desenex), Mexsana, Lotrisone
_____ Birth control: birth control pills, nonoxynol-9 condoms, other personal choices
_____ Blisters: moleskin, Band-Aids
_____ Burns: Silvadene
_____ Chapped lips: Blistex, Vaseline, or Chapstick
_____ Colds: Advil Cold & Flu for chest congestion; pseudophedrine (Sudafed), Benzedrex Dry Inhaler, Afrin, or Dristan; acetaminophen
_____ Constipation: docusate (Colace), bran tablets or natural bran
_____ Contaminated water: iodine tablets

Checklist: Matching Medicines with Minor Annoyances

_____ Cough: Robitussin DM syrup (or Guaifenesin capsules), or Naldecon DX (expectorants in tablet form); cough lozenges

_____ Cuts, blisters: Neosporin, Betadine (liquid antiseptic), or aloe vera gel; Cipro for infections; Band-Aids, gauze squares, adhesive tape, wound closure strips

_____ Diarrhea: Pepto Bismol (bismuth subsalicylate), Kaopectate, Lomotil, or Immodium; Oralyte (oral rehydration salts)

_____ Eye problems: eye drops; for contact lens wearers, contact lens solution and Sulamyd antibiotic eye drops

_____ Fever: acetaminophen, aspirin; thermometer

_____ Headache and general cold symptoms: aspirin, acetaminophen, or ibuprofen

_____ Herpes sores: Ambesol gel; acyclovir (Zovirax)

_____ Infection: Neosporin antibacterial ointment

_____ Insect bites: 1 percent hydrocortisone cream, Benadryl

_____ Motion sickness: Dramamine, Bonine, Phenergan, or Scopolamine patches; acupressure wrist bands

_____ Sleeplessness: Benadryl, Serax, Melatonin

_____ Strains and sprains: Ace bandage

_____ Sunburn and other minor burns: SPF 15 (or higher) waterproof sunscreen and aloe vera; Silvadene; Neosporin; ibuprofen

_____ Toothache: eugenol (oil of cloves)

_____ Unbalanced diet: vitamins

_____ Upset stomach: Pepto Bismol tablets

_____ Urinary tract infections: ciprofloxacin (Cipro), Ampicillin, or cotrimoxazole (Bactrim/Septra)

_____ Vaginal yeast infection: Nystatin vaginal tablets, vaginal suppositories

Checklist: Matching Medicines with More Serious Problems

_____ Bronchitis: Amoxicillin (avoid if allergic to penicillin), cotrimoxazole (Bactrim/Septra), erythromycin, ciprofloxacin (Cipro)

_____ Dehydration: oral rehydration salts

_____ Dysentery: metronidazole (Flagyl), ciprofloxacin (Cipro), cotrimoxazole (Bactrim/Septra)

_____ Giardia: metronidazole (Flagyl)

_____ Malaria: Mefloquine (Lariam), sulfadoxine (Fansidar), chloroquine phosphate, doxycycline, DEET, Ultrathon, Permethrin (one version is sold as Permanone Tick Repellent), mosquito coils. NOTE: It is essential that your malaria-related regimen be based on the places you visit and resistance patterns at that time

_____ Severe pain: Demerol; ibuprofen or acetaminophen for lesser pain

_____ Sexually transmitted diseases: condoms with nonoxynol-9, disposable needles

_____ Typhus: Tetracycline

BIBLIOGRAPHY

This bibliography contains periodicals and books I have found particularly enjoyable or helpful. I have marked with a # sign those books that may be hard to find but are too good not to bring to your attention. The dates given are of the most recent edition of which I am aware (i.e., not the copyright date, which may be much earlier). When there was a choice, I listed the paperback edition because it's cheaper and lighter.

PERIODICALS

— *Access to Travel*. Published by the Society for the Advancement of Travel for the Handicapped. Call (212) 447-7284. $13 for 4 quarterly issues. It serves travelers who have a broad range of disabilities.
— *Best Fares Discount Travel Magazine*. P.O. Box 171212, Arlington, TX 76003. Call (800) 880-1234. $50 for 12 monthly issues. Discount rates for airlines, hotels, car rentals, and cruises.
— *Condé Nast Traveler*. P.O. Box 57018, Boulder, CO 80322. Call (800) 777-0700. $18. Good all-around travel magazine, but with a tilt toward the upscale traveler.
— *Consumer Reports on Travel*. Call (800) 234-1970. $39 per year. Objective critical evaluations of the travel industry in the tradition of *Consumer Reports*.
— *Diabetic Traveler*. P.O. Box 8223, Stamford, CT 06905; call (203) 327-5832.
— *EcoTraveler*. Skies America. Call (503) 520-1955. $11.95 for 6 issues.
— *Escape*. P.O. Box 5159, Santa Monica, CA 90409. Call (800) 738-5571. $18 for 6 issues. Emphasis on adventurous journeys, foreign cultures, and the "thrill of escape."
— *Explorers Journal, The*. Quarterly publication of the Explorers Club (46 East 70th Street, New York City, NY 10021). Reports on expeditions, scientific discoveries, and exploits of hard-core travelers.
— *Going Solo: The Newsletter for People Traveling Alone*. P.O. Box 123, Apalachicola, FL 32329. $29 per year.
— *International Living*. 824 E. Baltimore Street, Baltimore, MD 21298. $29 per year.
— *International Travel News*. 2120 28th Street, Sacramento, CA 95818. Call (916) 457-3643. $18 for 12 issues. Down-to-earth reports by contemporary travelers. Strong on practical, current information. Great value!

— *Islands*. P.O. Box 51303, Boulder, CO 80321. $19.95 for 6 issues. Each issue is a "wish list" for island travel.

— *Journal 'n Footnotes*. Quarterly newsletter published by Wonder Women, a travel and adventure network for women over 40. Membership is $29 per year. For a sample copy of the newsletter, send $1 to 136 N. Grand Avenue, #237, West Covina, CA 91791.

— *Journeywoman Newsletter*. 50 Prince Arthur Avenue, Toronto, Ontario, Canada M5R 1B5. Call (416) 929-7654. $20 per year. Information on female-friendly destinations and travel tips for women.

— *Latin American Traveler*. P.O. Box 62921, Phoenix, AZ 85082. Call (602) 957-3741. $15 bimonthly plus excellent personal services for prospective travelers.

— *National Geographic*. National Geographic Society, P.O. Box 2895, Washington, DC 20077. $21 for 12 issues. Not much on "how to," but they don't get any better than National Geo on "where to." Its stories and photographs have probably gotten more people on the road than any other publication in history (except maybe draft notices).

— *The Natural Traveler*. P.O. Box 50400, Reno, NV 89513. Call (702) 786-7419. $29.95 per year. Solid information and bargains for travelers.

— *Outside*. P.O. Box 54729, Boulder, CO 80322. Call (800) 678-1131. $18 per year. Fascinating information about our planet as well as reports on the exploits of people who seek the ultimate in outdoor challenges.

— *South American Explorer*. P.O. Box 18327, Denver, CO 80206. Quarterly publication specializing in Latin America with in-depth stories about trips, explorations, and historical events. Well suited to independent travelers. With a $25 annual membership, you receive the magazine, use of the clubhouses in Lima and Quito, and access to thousands of trip reports.

— *Thrifty Traveler*. P.O. Box 8168, Clearwater, FL 34618. Call (800) 532-5731. $28 per year. This eight-page newsletter reports on events, health, saving money, and other issues of interest to travelers.

— *Transitions Abroad*. P.O. Box 344, Amherst, MA 01004. $19.95 for 5 issues plus an Educational Travel Resources Guide. Call (800) 293-0373. Articles on alternative traveling, living, working, and studying abroad.

— *Travel Books Review*. Mark Baffert (call 404-634-5874). A 16-page quarterly review of travel books and publishers. $19.95 per year.

— *Travel Companions*. P.O. Box 833, Amityville, NY 11701. Call (516) 454-0880. $36 per year for a monthly newsletter filled with travel tips and bargains for solo travelers. For an additional fee, join Travel Companions Exchange and receive hundreds of listings of males and females interested in finding travel companions.

— *Travelin' Woman*. Nancy Mills Communications, 855 Moraga Drive, #14, Los Angeles, CA 90049. $48 per year. Call (800) 871-6409. This ten-page monthly newsletter, written by an ardent traveler is a "know before you go" guide for women travelers.

— *Traveling Healthy*. 108-48 70th Road, Forest Hills, NY 11375. $29 per year. Call (718) 268-7290. Bimonthly newsletter covering general health topics.

— *Walkabout*. Box 5143, Portsmouth, NH 03802. $12 for 6 issues. Mostly reader-written newsletter for independent travelers.

— *We're Accessible: News for Disabled Travelers*. 32-1675 Cypress Street, Vancouver, BC, Canada. $15. Call (604) 731-2197. Newsletter for travelers with disabilities.

CATALOGUES

— *Camp-Mor*. Call (800) 526-4784 to order a catalogue. Wide variety and good prices.

— *Christine Colombus*. Call (800) 280-4775 or www.christinecolombus.com. Catalogue of clothing, luggage, and travel accessories specifically for women.

— *Eddie Bauer*. Call (800) 426-6253 to order a catalogue. Reliable outdoor clothing.

— *L.L. Bean*. Call (800) 221-4221 to order a catalogue. Fair prices for a wide range of reliable outdoor clothing and equipment.

— *Literate Traveler, The*. An excellent catalogue of the finest in travel literature. Call (800) 850-2665.

— *Magellan's*. Call (800) 962-4943 to order a catalogue. Describes its products as being "for more comfortable, safe, and rewarding travel."

— *Patagonia*. Call (800) 426-4737 to order a catalogue. Durable sports-related clothing and equipment.

— *Smith & Hawken*. Call (800) 776-5558 to order a catalogue. High-quality outdoor clothing.

— *47th Street Photo*. Call (800) 221-7774 to order a catalogue. Excellent selection of film and cameras at very competitive prices.

GENERAL

— *Aviation Consumer Action Project. Facts and Advice for Airline Passengers*. 1992. P.O. Box 19029, Washington, DC 20036.

— Axtell, Roger E., ed. *Do's and Taboos around the World: A Guide to International Behavior*. Compiled by Parker Pen Co., 1993.

— Biddlecombs, Peter. *Travels with My Briefcase*. 1996. Travels from a humorous businessman's point of view.

— Biestman, Margot S. *Travel for Two: The Art of Compromise*. 1986.

— Bond, Marybeth. *Gutsy Women: Travel Tips and Wisdom for the Road*. 1996.

— Bond, Marybeth. *Traveler's Tales: A Woman's World.* 1995. An anthology by women travelers.

— Bueler, William. *Mountains of the World: A Handbook for Climbers and Hikers,* 1970. A quick review of the best-known and the most difficult climbs around the world. #

— Cahill, Tim. *Pecked to Death by Ducks.* 1993. One of the best contemporary travel writers tells tales of Kuwait, Baja California, Guatemala, and Australia. Humorous and perceptive.

— Chatwin, Bruce. *What Am I Doing Here.* Penguin Books, 1990. A collection of stories, profiles, and travelogues from Nepal, Afghanistan, Hong Kong, Algeria, China, Chile, and more.

— Davidson, Robyn. *Tracks.* Pantheon, 1983. Excellent descriptions but perhaps insufficient to inspire many to duplicate her trip across Australia by camel.

— Dennis, Lisl. *How to Take Better Travel Photos.* #

— Department of Transportation. *Fly Rights: A Guide to Air Travel in the U.S.* Consumer Information Center, Dept. 131Z, Pueblo, CO 81009. Fifty-eight-page pamphlet full of useful tips for those who travel by air.

— Dickerman, Pat. *Adventure Travel Abroad.* H. Holt, 1986. A description of trips to 350 out-of-the-way locations. Good information for independent travelers. #

— Dickerman, Pat. *Eco Tours and Nature Getaways.* Crown Publishing Group. Call (800) 733-5000. Lists tour operators and trips around the world, with an emphasis on nature.

— Fisher, Frederick. *Successful Travelling Abroad.* Culture Shock series. Emphasis on trip planning and budgeting.

— Garfinkel, Perry. *Travel Writing for Profit and Pleasure.* Penguin Books, 1989.

— Gould, Jean. *Season of Adventure: Travelling Tales and Outdoor Journeys of Women over 50.* A collection of stories proving that age needn't diminish joy in living.

— Gray, William R. *Great Highways of the World.* Rand McNally, 1996. Journeys on 25 ancient and modern routes.

— Gray, William R. *Voyages to Paradise: Exploring in the Wake of Captain Cook,* 1981.

— Greenburg, Laura and Jonathan. *If You Can't Remember Your Last Vacation, You Need This Book.* Thunder Publications, 1993. Lists of outfitters for ballooning, fly fishing, photo expeditions, safaris, sailing, bicycling, kayaking, heli-skiing, etc.

— Grotta, Daniel, and Sally J. Grotta. *The Green Travel Sourcebook: A Guide for the Physically Active, the Intellectually Curious, and the Socially Aware.* Wiley, 1992. Descriptions of eco-tours available (less helpful for independent travelers).

— Heilman, Joan R. *Unbelievably Good Deals and Great Adventures That You Absolutely Can't Get Unless You're Over Fifty.* Contemporary Books, 1996. Discounts on airfare, hotels, car rentals, and other aspects of travel. It also suggests adventure trips, tours, and cruises for those over 50.

— Iyer, Pico. *Falling Off the Map: Some Lonely Places of the World.* Knopf, 1993.

— Iyer, Pico. *Video Night in Kathmandu: And Other Reports from the Not-So-Far East.* Random House, 1989.

— Jansz, Natalia, and Miranda Davies, eds. *More Women Travel.* Viking Penguin, 1995.

— Jansz, Natalia, and Miranda Davies, eds. *Women Travel: Adventures, Advice and Experience.* Penguin Books, 1993. Among other topics, this book discusses potential for sexual harassment in more than 70 countries.

— Lansing, Alfred. *Endurance: Shackleton's Incredible Voyage.* Carroll & Graf, 1986. Portrayal, drawn from the diaries of Sir Ernest Shackleton's Trans-Antarctic Expedition.

— Leocha, Charles. *Travel Rights.* World Leisure Corp., 1994. Good outline of the rights of credit-card holders, car rental clients, and airline passengers.

— Lewis, Norman. *A Dragon Apparent.* Eland Books, 1993. Travels in Vietnam, Laos, and Cambodia almost half a century ago by a sensitive, discerning traveler who is also a fine writer. His *Golden Earth* captures the spirit of Burma. Lewis is a traveler's traveler: intrepid, living unobtrusively like a local, always open to new experiences. His name is, as you might have noticed, an anagram of "New is normal."

— Malott, Gene and Adele. *Mature Traveler's Book of Deals.* Gem Publishing, 1997. Good, solid advice

— McMenamin, Paul. *The Ultimate Adventure Sourcebook: A Complete Resource for Adventure and Sports Travel.* Turner Publishing, 1997.

— Mead, Margaret. *Coming of Age in Samoa.* Morrow, 1971. Study of youth in a primitive society. How many times has this book been recommended over the years?

— Melchett, Sonia. *Passionate Quests: Five Modern Women Travelers.* Faber & Faber. Insights into the experiences and motivations of five extraordinary travelers/travel writers.

— Morris, Jan. *Journeys.* Oxford University Press, 1984.

— Morris, Mary. *Maiden Voyages.* McKay, 1993. Excellent collection of travel stories by female authors.

— Morris, Mary. *Nothing to Declare: Memoirs of a Woman Traveling Alone.* Penguin, 1989. Her examination of the cultures of Mexico, Honduras, Guatemala, and the Caribbean.

— Morris, Mary. *Wall to Wall: From Beijing to Berlin by Rail.* Penguin, 1992. Traveling on the Trans-Siberian Express toward her Ukranian heritage.

— Murphy, Dervla. *Cameroon with Egbert*. Overlook Press, 1992. A report on her trip around Cameroon with a horse (and daughter), usually walking.

— Murphy, Dervla. *Full Tilt: Ireland to India with a Bicycle*. Overlook Press, 1987. Imagine the courage and spirit it took to make this trip solo on a bicycle. To hear her tell it, she did it as a lark.

— Murphy, Dervla. *Muddling Through in Madagascar*. Overlook Press, 1990. Dervla Murphy can inspire any procrastinating traveler.

— Neumann, Karl (Dr.), and Maury Rosenbaum. *The Business Traveler's Guide to Good Health on the Road*. Chronimed Publishing. 1994. Travel medicine and more.

— Newby, Eric. *Short Walk in the Hindu Kush*. Penguin Books, 1987.

— Newman, Steven M. *Worldwalk*. Avon, 1990.

— *1995 Alternative Travel Directory*. Transitions Abroad Publishing, 1995. Eclectic collection of topics pertaining to living and traveling abroad.

— *Norton Introduction to Literature*. W.W. Norton & Co. The Norton series includes fiction, poetry, essays, drama, and so on. These paperbacks, which run 1,500 tissue-thin pages or more, are, pound-for-pound, the best value I've found for a long trip. They're fulfilling and stick with you.

— Parsons, Tom. *Inside Travel Secrets*. 1996. Emphasis on finding travel discounts plus other useful tips.

— Preston-Mafham, Ken. *Practical Wildlife Photography*. For committed photographers interested in botany and wildlife. #

— Rand-McNally. *Almanac of Adventure*. Descriptions of more than 50 adventures, many suitable for independent travelers.

— Robinson, Jane. *Wayward Women: A Guide to Women Travelers*. Oxford University Press. Reviews travels of 400 women through 16 centuries. Great bibliography.

— Rowell, Galen. *Vision: The Art of Adventure Photography*. Sierra Club Books, 1993. Explanations of how he produces outstanding outdoor photography.

— Rowlands, Peter. *The Underwater Photographer's Handbook*. Includes a guide to dive spots around the world. #

— St. Aubin de Teran, Lisa. *Indiscreet Journeys: Stories of Women on the Road*. Faber & Faber, 1991. Tales by 26 women about travels on six continents during two centuries.

— Savage, Barbara. *Miles from Nowhere: A Round-the-World Bicycle Adventure*. The Mountaineers, 1985. Story of her two-year, 23,000-mile bicycle trip.

— Schmidt, Gary. *Fly for Less: The Only Complete Guide to Selecting Reliable Consolidators and Wholesalers Who Offer Bargain Airfares*. Travel Publishing. At some bookstores or call (800) 241-9299. Great guide to consolidators.

— Schwartz, Brian M. *A World of Villages*. 1986. Interesting account of his six-year trip through Africa, India, Nepal, Indonesia, China, Tibet, and the Middle East. #

— Sereny, Gail Rubin. *Ms. Adventures: Worldwide Travelguide for Independent Women*. Guide for women traveling solo. #

— da Silva, Rachel, ed. *Leading Out: Women Climbers Reaching for the Top*. Seal Press, 1992. Excellent stories by and about unique female climbers.

— Simmons, James C. *The Big Book of Adventure Travel: 500 Great Escapes*. 1990. #

— *Smart Travel*. Ziff-Davis Press, 1995. Use computer-accessible resources to plan your trip. The book comes with a CD-ROM disk and $15 worth of online time.

— *Specialty Travel Index*. Alpine Hansen. Call (800) 442-4942. Published twice a year, the *Index* lists over 600 tour operators who emphasize adventure travel (cross-indexed by activity and destination).

— Speight, Phyllis. *The Traveller's Guide to Homeopathy*. Beekman Pub., 1990. Alternative suggestions for maintenance of health on the road.

— Teison, Herbert, and Nancy Dunnan. *Travel Smarts: Getting the Most for Your Travel Dollar*. Globe Pequot Press, 1995. From Travel Smart newsletters. Emphasis on domestic and European travel.

— Theroux, Paul. *The Great Railway Bazaar*. Ballantine, 1995.

— Theroux, Paul. *The Mosquito Coast*. Avon, 1983.

— Theroux, Paul. *The Old Patagonian Express: By Train through the Americas*. Houghton Mifflin, 1997.

— Theroux, Paul. *Sunrise with Seamonsters*. Houghton Mifflin, 1986. Consists of short stories and essays written during a 20-year period, including stories set in Africa and India.

— *Travel Buying Guide*. Consumer Reports. Typically informative; each chapter a compilation of articles from *Consumer Reports Travel Letters*.

— *Travel for the Disabled: A Handbook of Travel Resources and 500 Worldwide Access Guides*. The Disability Bookshop; call (800) 637-2256. Excellent tips for travel by disabled persons, plus lists of accommodations free of barriers.

— Twain, Mark. *Following the Equator*. 1997. Memoirs of a sharp tongue cruising from British Columbia through the South Seas to Australia and New Zealand.

— *Ultimate Adventure Sourcebook*. Turner Publishing. Detailed listing of many of the best action-sport experiences and destinations around the world.

— Waugh, Evelyn. *Remote People*. Ecco Press, 1990.

— Waugh, Evelyn. *When the Going Was Good*. Little, 1985. Ironical excerpts from the best of Waugh's travel books.

— Weaver, Frances. *This Year I Plan to Go Elsewhere (Last Year I Went Around the World)*. Fulcrum Publishing, 1989. Journey by a (self-described) midlife woman traveler.

— Williams, Anita, and Merrimac Dillon. *The 50+ Travelers' Guidebook: Where to Go, Where to Stay, What to Do*. St. Martin's, 1991.

— Windsor, Natalie. *The Safe Tourist*. Corkscrew Press, 1995. Mostly for domestic travel but many tips are useful for international travel.

— *Without a Guide: Contemporary Women's Travel Adventures*. Hungry Mind Press, 1996. Seventeen female writers recounting memorable adventures.

— Zepatos, Thalia. *Adventures in Good Company*. Eighth Mountain Press, 1994. Fine guide to women's tours and adventure trips.

— Zepatos, Thalia. *A Journey of One's Own*. Eighth Mountain Press, 1996. Does a fine job of providing practical information to encourage women to travel independently.

— Zobel, Louise. *Travel Writer's Handbook: How to Write and Sell Your Travel Experiences*. Surrey Books, 1992. If you're an aspiring travel writer, don't miss this one.

AFRICA

— Barboza, Steven. *Door of No Return: The Legend of Goree Island*. Cobblehill, 1994.

— Bowles, Paul. *Midnight Mass*. Black Sparrow, 1991. Collection of short stories.

— Bowles, Paul. *Points in Time*. Ecco Press, 1984. Vivid portrayal of Moroccan landscape and people.

— Bowles, Paul. *Sheltering Sky*. Random House. 1991. Bizarre physical and psychological journey in the Sahara.

— Boyle, T. Coraghessan. *Water Music*. Little Brown, 1981. Adventures of Mungo Park as he explored the Niger river. Fine insight into an earlier Africa.

— Brandenburg, Jim. *Sand and Fog: Adventures in Southern Africa*. Walker, 1994.

— Chatwin, Bruce. *Far Journeys: Photographs and Notebooks*. Viking. Photographs and journal jottings from travels in East Africa and Afghanistan.

— Conrad, Joseph. *Heart of Darkness*. Warner Books, 1995. Immerses the reader in the essence of the African experience.

— Dinesen, Isak. *Letters from Africa, 1914–1931*. Univ. of Chicago Press, 1984. First-hand descriptions of decadent European society in Kenya early in the twentieth century.

— Dinesen, Isak. *Out of Africa*. Random House, 1989. Memoirs of Baroness Karen Blixen's life on a coffee plantation early in the 20th century. $10.95.

— Fage, J. D. *A History of Africa*. Unwin, 1995. Outstanding one-volume narrative history.

— Fitzgerald, Mary Anne. *Nomad: One Woman's Journey into the Heart of Africa*. Viking. Insightful discussions of politics in sub-Saharan Africa.

— Flaubert, Gustave. *Flaubert in Egypt*. Flaubert's bawdy and humorous report of his 1849 trip along the Nile.

— Forbath, Peter. *The Last Hero*. Warner Books, 1990. A fictionalized version of Stanley's rescue of Emin Pasha.

— Forbath, Peter. *The River Congo*. Simon & Schuster, 1995. Excellent account of the grim history of the Congo, told with a journalist's flair. #

— Fossey, Dian. *Gorillas in the Mist*. Houghton Mifflin, 1983. Her report of 13 years among mountain gorillas in the rain forest.

— Gide, André. *Amyntas*. Ecco Press, 1988. Report of his five years in Tunis and Algiers.

— Gordimer, Nadine. *The Essential Gesture: Writing, Politics, Places*. Knopf, 1988. Reflections on South Africa and apartheid. Ms. Gordimer has also written fine novels about Africa in general and South Africa in particular.

— Gordimer, Nadine. *Livingstone's Companions*. Viking, 1970. Excellent short stories about Africa.

— de Gramont, Sanche. *The Strong Brown God*. Houghton Mifflin, 1975. Stories of the obsessed explorers who revealed the mysteries of the Niger River. #

— Harden, Blaine. *Africa: Dispatches from a Fragile Continent*. Houghton Mifflin, 1991. A *Washington Post* reporter's essays on six countries in "the Nth World."

— Harris, Eddy L. *Native Stranger: A Black American's Journey into the Heart of Africa*. Viking, 1994.

— Heminway, John. *Africa Journeys: A Personal Guidebook*. Warner Books, 1990.

— Heminway, John. *The Imminent Rains*. Little, Brown, 1968. Unhurried conversations with old-timers in the bush. #

— Hibbert, Christopher. *Africa Explored: Europeans in the Dark Continent, 1769–1889*. Norton, 1982. He walks with Mungo Park, Speke, Stanley, Livingstone, and others.

— Hudson, Mark. *Our Grandmothers' Drums*. Grove Weidenfeld, 1990. Study of the lives of African women in an isolated village.

— Huxley, Elspeth, ed. *Nine Faces of Kenya*. Viking, 1991. An anthology of Hemingway, Churchill, Dinesen, and others. Huxley's own writings, *Murder on Safari, Flame Trees of Thika,* and *Out in the Midday Sun* are vibrant descriptions of East African life.

— Lamb, David. *The Africans*. Vintage, 1985. Excellent combination of travelogue and contemporary history by a *Los Angeles Times* correspondent.

— Lamb, David. *The Arabs: Beyond the Mirage*. Random House, 1988.

— Markham, Beryl. *West with the Night*. North Point Press. Memoir of her remarkable life in East Africa. She was a flyer in every sense.

— Marshall, Richard. *Strange, Amazing, and Mysterious Places*. Smithmark. Mystic places of the earth linked as inspiration to the spirit.

— Matthiessen, Peter. *The Tree Where Man Was Born: The African Experience*. Dutton, 1983. Impressions from Sudan to Tanzania.

— Mazrui, Ali. *The Africans: A Triple Heritage.* Little, 1986. Discussion of Africa as a transmitter of Islamic, Western, and indigenous cultures.

— Michener, James. *The Covenant.* Fawcett, 1987. Five hundred years of South African history told from African, Afrikaans, and English perspectives. It helps explain the intensity of the struggle in South Africa.

— Naipal, V. S. *A Bend in the River.* Random House, 1989.

— Naipal, V. S. *India: A Million Mutinies Now.* Viking Penguin, 1992.

— Nolting, Mark. *Africa's Top Wildlife Countries.* Globe Travel, 1990. Lists top ten countries for wildlife, with maps, photos, safaris, and other practical information.

— Paton, Alan. *Ah, But Your Land Is Beautiful.* Scribner, 1982. Social protests against apartheid.

— Paton, Alan. *Cry, The Beloved Country.*

— Stengel, Richard. *January Sun: One Day, Three Lives, A South African Town.* Simon & Schuster, 1990. Fascinating story of three disparate lives through the course of a single day.

— Turnbull, Colin. *The Forest People.* Simon & Schuster, 1987. Turnbull describes the lives of pygmies in Zaire (now the Congo).

— Van Der Post, Laurens. *The Heart of the Hunter.* Harcourt Brace, 1980. Excellent description of the Bushmen's way of life—and apartheid.

— Van Der Post, Laurens. *The Lost World of the Kalahari.* Harcourt Brace, 1977.

— Winternitz, Helen. *East along the Equator.* Grove-Atlantic, 1987. Fine report of the infamous river trip from Kinshasa up the Zaire River to Kisangani, then overland to Goma on Lake Kivu.

ANTARCTICA

— Amundsen, Roald. *My Life as an Explorer.* Doubleday, 1927. The hero of the Antarctic. #

— Beaglehole, J. C., ed. *The Journals of Captain James Cook on His Voyages of Discovery: The Voyage of the Resolution and Adventure, 1772–1775.* Cambridge University Press, 1961.

— Campbell, David G. *The Crystal Desert.* Houghton Mifflin, 1992. This biologist makes science poetic. He describes the evolution of the continent, seabirds, penguins, seals, plankton, krill, whales, the weather—and throws in tales of early explorers. Possibly the best modern book on Antarctica.

— Chapman, Walker, ed. *Antarctic Conquest: The Great Explorers in Their Own Words.* Bobbs Merrill, 1965. A fine anthology. #

— Cherry-Garrard, Apsley. *The Worst Journey in the World: Antarctic 1910–1913.* Carroll & Graf. Personal account of heroism and determination on Capt. Scott's polar expedition as well as a trip between Cape Crozier and McMurdo Sound. A classic.

— Huntford, Roland. *Scott and Amundsen.* G.P. Putnam's Sons, 1980. A comparative biography of the men engaged in the great race for the South Pole.
— Lansing, Alfred. *Endurance, Shackleton's Incredible Voyage.* McGraw Hill, 1959. Excellent story of Shackleton's two-year ordeal. #
— May, John. *The Greenpeace Book of Antarctica.* Macmillan of Canada, 1988.
— Naveen, Ron, inter alia. *Wild Ice: Antarctic Journeys.* Smithsonian Press, 1990. Excellent photographs of the continent.
— Quigg, Philip W. *A Pole Apart: The Emerging Issue of Antarctica.* McGraw Hill, 1983. A review of political and scientific issues.
— Parfit, Michael. *South Light.* Ulverscroft, 1992. Discussion of the U.S. Antarctic program.
— Porter, Eliot. *Antarctica.* E.P. Dutton, 1978. Splendid photographs.
— Pyne, Stephen J. *The Ice: A Journey to Antarctica.* University of Iowa Press, 1988.
— Scott, Robert Falcon. *Scott's Last Expedition.* Carroll & Graf, 1996.
— Shapley, Deborah. *The Seventh Continent: Antarctica in a Resource Age.* Resources for the Future, 1986.
— Simpson, George G. *Penguins, Past and Present, Here and There.* Parmer Books, 1976.
— Steger, Will, and Jon Bowermaster. *Crossing Antarctica.* Dell Publishing, 1991. An incredible 220-day dogsled trip across 3,700 miles. Six determined men from different countries emphasize the unique international nature of the continent.
— Weddell, James. *A Voyage toward the South Pole Performed in the Years 1922–24.* David and Charles Reprints, 1827. #

ASIA

— Akutagawa, Ryunosuke. *Rashomon.* Liverwright, 1970. Japanese short stories. #
— Blum, Arlene. *Annapurna: A Woman's Place.* Sierra Club, 1983. Candid description of a successful, but tragic, women's expedition on Annapurna.
— Bohnaker, William. *The Hollow Doll: A Little Box of Japanese Shocks.* Ballantine, 1990. Negative impressions of modern Japan.
— Bonavia, David. *The Chinese.* Viking Penguin, 1993. The *New York Times* correspondent reviews what he calls "the most forthrightly materialistic value system in the history of mankind."
— Bonnington, Chris. *Everest: The Unclimbed Ridge.* Heartbreaking story, by one of the great climbers, of a disastrous Everest attempt in 1982. #
— Bonnington, Chris. *I Chose to Climb.* Ulverscroft, 1985.
— Braganti, Nancy, and Elizabeth Devine. *The Traveler's Guide to Asian Customs and Manners.* St. Martin's Press, 1986.

— Buck, Pearl S. *The Good Earth*. Oxford University Press, 1982. A Pulitzer Prize–winning description of China in an earlier era. One of the best.
— Cameron, Roderick. *Australia: History and Horizons*. Columbia University Press, 1971. Australia in the eighteenth and nineteenth centuries.
— Chambers, Kevin A. *A Traveler's Guide to Asian Culture*. John Muir, 1989.
— David-Neel, Alexandra. *My Journey to Lhasa*. Beacon Press, 1988. This remarkable French citizen was the first European woman to enter the forbidden city.
— DeGaury, Gerald and H. V. F. Winstone. *An Anthology of Writings on Asia*. Macmillan, 1982. Travel writing by the best.
— Dingle, Graeme, and Peter Hillary. *First Across the Roof of the World*. Have you been waiting for the right time to walk the length of the Himalayas? Too late—it's been done. These two were apparently the first. #
— Fleming, Peter. *Bayonets to Lhasa*. Oxford University Press, 1986. Fleming's travels on the Silk Road from Peking to Turkistan. #
— Fleming, Peter. *News from Tartary*. Tarcher, 1982.
— Forster, E. M. *A Passage to India*. Knopf, 1992. Insight into the Indian psyche; best read in India.
— Gandhi, Mohandas K. *An Autobiography*. Greenleaf Books, 1984. Look into the mind and values of one of the more evolved humans in history.
— Harrer, Heinrich. *Return to Tibet*. Schocken, 1985.
— Harrer, Heinrich. *Seven Years in Tibet*. Tarcher, 1982. Harrer, imprisoned in India at the outbreak of World War II, escaped, crossed the Himalayas, and became a confidant of the Dalai Lama. Excellent report of Tibetan life before the arrival of Chinese forces.
— Herzog, Maurice. *Annapurna*. Dutton, 1952. First ascent by the leader of the French team.#
— Hulme, Keri. *The Bone People*. Louisiana State University Press, 1985. Insights into the Maori culture.
— Iyer, Pico. *The Lady and the Monk*. 1991. Report on Kyoto, Zen, and passion.
— Jenkins, Peter. *Across China*. Fawcett, 1988.
— Jhabvala, Ruth Prawer. *Heat and Dust*. Harper Row, 1987.
— Jhabvala, Ruth Prawer. *Out of India: Selected Stories*. Simon & Schuster, 1987. Fifteen short stories.
— Johnson, Tracy. *Shooting the Boh: A Woman's Voyage down the Wildest River in Borneo*. Vintage. She faced a cobra-infested river—and middle age.
— Lee, C. Y. *China Saga*. Weidenfeld, 1987. Family saga from the Boxer Rebellion through the Cultural Revolution.
— Lewis, Norman. *An Empire of the East*. Henry Holt, 1994. Tribal war games, Stone Age agricultural practices, and the consequences of multinational copper mining in Sumatra, East Timor, and Irian Jaya.
— Maraini, Fosco. *Karakoram: The Ascent of Gasherbrum IV*. #

— Matthiessen, Peter. *Snow Leopard*. Penguin, 1987. Adventure and anthropology in the context of George Shaller's search for the seldom-seen snow leopard. See also Matthiessen's *East of Lo Monthang*.
— Miller, Luree. *On Top of the World: Five Women Explorers in Tibet*. Mountaineers, 1984. Great stories of five intrepid women who explored Tibet in the 1800s.
— Mirante, Edith T. *Burmese Looking Glass: Human Rights Adventure and a Jungle Revolution*. Grove Press. Beauty and horror of modern Burma.
— Morrow, Patrick. *Beyond Everest: Quest for Seven Summits*. Firefly Books, 1986.
— Naipal, V. S. *Among the Believers: An Islamic Journey*. Random House, 1982.
— Naipal, V. S. *India: A Million Mutinies Now*. Viking, 1991. Great guide to understanding castes and political parties.
— Narayan, R. K. *The Ramayana*. Viking, 1972. Modern version of the great Indian epic.
— Natwar-Singh, K., ed. *Tales from Modern India*. 1966. Twenty fine stories by some of India's best writers. #
— O'Hanlon, Redmond. *In Trouble Again*. Random House, 1990.
— O'Hanlon, Redmond. *Into the Heart of Borneo*. Random House, 1987. Trip up the Baleh River and to the summit of Mount Batu Tiban.
— Portway, Christopher. *Indian Odyssey: Around the Subcontinent by Public Transport*. Impact, 1993.
— Roberts, Joe. *Three-Quarters of a Footprint*. Bantam, 1994.
— Roberts, Paul William. *Empire of the Soul: Modern Travels in Ancient India*. Stoddart, 1994.
— Ronay, Gabriel. *The Tartar Khan's Englishman*. 1978. The story of an English diplomat-adventurer on whom the grandson of Genghis Khan was dependent as he hurled Mongol armies against Christian Europe. # A good companion piece is *The Travels* written by Marco Polo in 1298. #
— Spence, Jonathan D. *The Death of the Woman Wang*. Penguin, 1979.
— Spence, Jonathan D. *The Search for Modern China*. Norton, 1990. Four hundred years of history leading up to the violence in Tiananmen Square.
— Thubron, Colin. *Behind the Wall: A Journey through China*. Atlantic Monthly Press, 1988. Mandarin-speaking author writes of the small places.
— Wintle, Justin. *Romancing Vietnam: Inside the Boat Country*. Pantheon, 1991. Insights into a country, now at peace, striving to develop an identity.
— Wolpert, Stanley. *India*. University of California Press, 1991. Superbly written synopsis of Indian civilization.

MIDDLE EAST

— Bar-Zohar, Michael. *Facing A Cruel Mirror: Israel's Moment of Truth*. Scribner, 1990. Israeli politics and society from 1967 to the Intifada through the eyes of a member of the Knesset.

— Browning, Robert. *The Byzantine Empire*. Scribner, 1980. History of 1,000 years of empire.
— Burton, Sir Richard. *The Arabian Nights*. Regal Pub., 1992.
— Burton, Sir Richard. *Personal Narrative of a Pilgrimage to Al-Madinah and Mecca*, 2 volumes. Dover, 1893. Burton traveled in disguise to holy cities in Arabia forbidden to non-Muslims under pain of death.
— Durrell, Lawrence. *The Alexandria Quartet*. Dutton, 1957–60.
— Edwards, Amelia B. *A Thousand Miles up the Nile*. Tarcher, 1993. Classic tale of an Englishwoman's nineteenth-century trip up the Nile in high style.
— Elon, Amos. *Jerusalem: City of Mirrors*. Little Brown, 1989. Modern Jerusalem from the perspectives of various religions.
— Friedman, Thomas L. *From Beirut to Jerusalem*. Doubleday, 1990. Short history of the Middle East, especially helpful to understanding the complexity of conflicts among various religious factions.
— Goldschmidt, Arthur J. *A Concise History of the Middle East*. Westview Press, 1987. Conversational history from seventh to twentieth century.
— Heude, William. *A Voyage up the Persian Gulf and a Journey Overland from India to England in 1817*. Garnet, 1993.
— Holden, David, and Richard Johns. *The House of Saud*. 1981. The history of the rise and rule of the most powerful dynasty in the Arab world. #
— Lamb, David. *The Arabs: Journeys beyond the Mirage*. Random House, 1988. Excellent review of human aspects of Arab culture and history.
— Lawrence, T. E. *Seven Pillars of Wisdom*. Doubleday, 1991. Journal of an Englishman deeply involved in a revolution in Arabia against the Turks. Philosophy and anthropology written with great style.
— Manley, Deborah. *The Nile: A Traveller's Anthology*. Sterling, 1991. Journeys along the Nile by more than 80 authors.
— Mansfield, Peter. *The Arabs*. Penguin, 1985. Social and political history from nomadic times to the present.
— Michener, James A. *The Source*. Fawcett, 1986. An archaeological dig in Israel serves as the basis for recreating the history of Israel and Judaism.
— Nightingale, Florence. *Letters from Egypt: A Journey on the Nile*. Grove-Atlantic, 1988. Beautiful writing by an inquisitive traveler.
— Stark, Freya. *Baghdad Sketches*. Marlboro Press, 1992.
— Stark, Freya. *A Peak in Darien*. Transatlantic Press, 1977.
— Stark, Freya. *Valley of the Assassins*. Tarcher, 1983. A report of her travels across Syria, Iraq, and Iran through a world of castles, treasures, and murderers. #
— Thesiger, Wilfred. *Arabian Sands*. Viking Penguin, 1985. For 40 years Thesiger crisscrossed the deserts of Arabia, Iran, Iraq, Ethiopia, and Yemen with a will so fierce that his companions were left behind in the sand. "I have had a hard life," Thesiger said. "This was from choice. It was also an inexpensive one; this was essential."

— Thesiger, Wilfred. *The Last Nomad*. #

— Thesiger, Wilfred. *The Marsh Arabs*. #

— Uris, Leon. *Exodus*. Doubleday, 1958. History of Palestine and Zionism from the 1940s.

SOUTH AMERICA AND CENTRAL AMERICA

— Allende, Isabel. *House of Spirits*. Knopf, 1985. Chilean saga from the early twentieth century through the overthrow of Allende in 1973.

— Allende, Isabel. *Of Love and Shadows*. Knopf, 1987.

— Alvarado, Elvia. *Don't Be Afraid, Gringo*. 1987. A campesina's view of why the Honduran farmers fight and how they've learned to work the system. ("The foreigners love to fund women's projects. So the campesino groups respond by creating women's projects.") #

— Borges, Jorge L. *Borges: A Reader*. Dutton, 1981. Excellent survey of the writing of one of South America's finest authors.

— Bradt, George N. *South America: River Trips*. Description of some of the best river trips on the continent and how to prepare for them. Bradt also publishes a useful series of guidebooks for various South American and African countries.

— Branston, Brian. *The Last Great Journey on Earth*. 1970. Journey up the Rio Negro from Manaus, across a 200-mile natural channel to the Orinoco, and over dangerous rapids to the Venezuelan coast. Discusses parallels between treatment of indigenous people in Brazil and the United States.

— Chaplin, Gordon. *The Fever Coast Log*. HarperCollins, 1992.

— Chatwin, Bruce. *In Patagonia*. Viking Penguin, 1988. A classic in which Chatwin describes his close-to-the-ground travel across Patagonia. Nice report of his conversation with Borges.

— *The Cloud Forest*. Penguin, 1987. The high point is the section on running the Pongo de Mainique rapids of the Rio Urubamba. #

— Coe, Michael D. *The Maya*. Thames & Hudson, 1993. This book is a leader in archaeological investigations.

— Elder, Norman. *This Thing of Darkness: Amazon Notebook*. 1979. Tale of a Canadian explorer's experiences with two tribes of Indians in the Amazon basin. #

— Fleming, Peter. *Brazilian Adventure*. Tarcher, 1988. Fine writing. #

— Garcia Marquez, Gabriel. *One Hundred Years of Solitude*. Harper and Row, 1970. Seven generation family saga set in Colombia—except that nothing is quite as it seems. His whole body of work merits review.

— Greene, Graham. *The Power and the Glory*. Penguin, 1977. Priest on the run from an avenging army.

— Guillermoprieto, Alma. *Samba*. Vintage Books. Life in a Brazilian favela, carnival, and the samba.

— Kandell, Jonathan. *Passage through El Dorado: The Conquest of the World's Last Great Wilderness.* Avon, 1991. Detailed description of how lust for profits from rubber, gold, and cocaine ("cocadollars and corruption") in the Amazon basin led to exploitation of Indians.

— Kane, Joe. *Running the Amazon.* Knopf, 1990. A 4,000-mile boat trip from source to mouth of the Amazon. Ten started, four finished.

— LaFeber, Walter. *Inevitable Revolutions: The United States in Central America.* Norton, 1983. Essential to understanding the past and present of Central America: why it is so violent and how commercial interests created the system of dependency.

— LaFeber, Walter. *The Panama Canal: The Crisis in Historical Perspective.* Oxford University Press, 1990.

— Lawrence, D. H. *The Plumed Serpent.* Random House, 1955. Study of the Aztec culture.

— Lewis, Oscar. *The Children of Sanchez.* Vintage, 1979. Biography of a proud, desperate laborer and his more modern children as they survive in Mexico City's slums.

— Marnham, Patrick. *So Far from God: A Journey to Central America.* Transaction Pub., 1987. Fine description of travel in contemporary Central America.

— Matthiessen, Peter. *At Play in the Fields of the Lord.* 1965. The book is much better than the movie.

— McGuire, Stryker. *Streets with No Names: A Journey into Central & South America.* Atlantic Monthly Press, 1990. Human reality of life as seen during a 20,000-mile trip.

— Moore, J. H. *Tears of the Sun God.* 1965. Unusual story of botanists' trip through the savannah and jungles of Guiana, then via various tributaries to the Rio Negro to Manaus, Brazil, followed by some challenging climbs in Ecuador and Bolivia. Very tough trip. #

— Murphy, Dervla. *Eight Feet in the Andes.* Overlook Press, 1986. Adventuresome woman following Pizarro's route through the Andes.

— Nott, David. *Angels 4.* 1972. Eight-day ascent of 3,282-foot Angel Falls in Venezuela. Oddly, the waterfall was named for Jimmy Angel, a pilot who crash-landed on the plateau from which it originates. #

— O'Hanlon, Redmond. *In Trouble Again: A Journey between the Orinoco and the Amazon.* Atlantic Monthly Press, 1989. Four-month trip up the Orinoco and across the Amazon Basin. Entertaining, perceptive writing.

— Parris, Matthew. *Inka-Cola: Traveller's Tale of Peru.* Ulverscroft Books, 1992.

— Paz, Octavio. *The Labyrinth of Solitude.* Grove, 1983. Brilliant analysis of Mexican life and thought.

— Peters, Daniel. *Tikal: A Novel about the Maya.* Random House, 1983. Hypothesis for the abandonment of the greatest capital city.

— Plotkin, Mark. *Tales of a Shaman's Apprentice: An Ethnobiologist Searches for New Medicines in the Amazon Rain Forest.* Viking, 1993.

— Reed, John. *Insurgent Mexico.* International Publishers. Better known for his adventures in Russia, Reed's account of his days with Pancho Villa's army during the Mexican Revolution reveals the common clay and the convictions of the revolutionaries.

— Simpson, Joe. *Touching the Void.* Harper Collins, 1990. Incredible story of a catastrophic fall during a climb in the Cordillera Blanca of the Peruvian Andes. This story embodies enormous courage and generosity of spirit.

— Stephens, John L. *Incidents of Travel in Yucatán,* 2 volumes. Dover, 1843. Classic travel tale of systematic exploration of Mayan sites in the Yucatán.

— *Stolen Continents: The Americas through Indian Eyes since 1492.* Houghton Mifflin, 1993.

— *Time among the Maya: Travels in Belize, Guatemala, and Mexico.* Henry Holt, 1991.

— Vargas Llosa, Mario. *The War at the End of the World.* Farrar, Straus, & Giroux, 1984. Turn of the century revolution in northern Brazil.

— Wilson, Jason. *Traveller's Literary Companion to Central and South America.* In Print, 1993.

— Woodward, Ralph Lee. *Central America: A Nation Divided.* Oxford Univ. Press, 1985. One of the best Central American histories written in English.

— Wright, Ronald. *Cut Stones and Crossroads.* Penguin Travel, 1984. Trip from the Cordillera Blanca to Lake Titicaca, tracing the Inca and the history of Peru. #

HEALTH

— *Altitude Illness: Prevention and Treatment.* The Mountaineers Books, 1995. An 80-page pocket guide on preventing, diagnosing, and treating altitude sickness. Call (800) 553-4453.

— American Red Cross. *Standard First Aid and Safety.*

— Benenson, Abram S., ed. *Control of Communicable Diseases in Man.* American Public Health Association, 1990.

— Bezruchka, Dr. Stephen. *The Pocket Doctor: Your Ticket to Good Health while Traveling.* The Mountaineers Books, 1992. This light, small-format guide is packed with useful reminders of how to treat yourself when underway and when to seek help.

— Bryson, Dr. Lawrence. *The Travel Health Clinic: A Pocket Guide to Healthy Travel.* Silvercat, 1996. Review of far more than you're likely to encounter.

— Dawood, Richard. *Travelers' Health: How to Stay Healthy All Over the World.* Random House. Excellent reference although a bit hefty for a backpack at over 600 pages.

— *Diabetic Traveler.* Quarterly newsletter. Call (203) 327-5832.

— *Emergency Medical Procedures for the Outdoors*. Menasha Ridge Press. Excellent information on lifesaving procedures and treating medical complaints and injuries. Good book to learn from or take with you. Call (800) 247-9437.

— *First Aid: Quick Information for Mountaineering and Backcountry Use*. Mountaineers, 1997. Excellent, easy-to-carry first aid guide.

— Forgey, Dr. William W. *Travelers' Medical Resource: A Guide to Health and Safety Worldwide*. ICS Books, 1990.

— *Health Information for International Travel (HIFIT)*. Centers for Disease Control or U.S. Government Printing Office, Washington, D.C. 20402.

— Howarth, Dr. Jane W. *Bugs, Bites and Bowels*. Sensible information delivered in an entertaining tone (maybe the title gave that away).

— *Physicians Desk Reference*. Medical Economics Co.

— Rose, Dr. Stuart R. *International Travel Health Guide*. Travel Medicine, Inc. About half of this book is devoted to a review of health risks in individual countries. It's too comprehensive to carry in your luggage but contains very helpful pretrip material.

— Rubin, M. R., and B. L. Dessery. *The Medical Guide for Third World Travelers*. KWP Publications. #

— Schroeder, Dirk. *Staying Healthy in Asia, Africa, and Latin America*. Moon Pub., 1993.

— Sullivan, Donald L. *A Senior's Guide to Healthy Travel*. Career Press, 1995.

— *Travel Medicine Catalogue*. Contains hundreds of products designed to protect travelers from disease-causing insects, contaminated water, and medical emergencies. A valuable resource. Call (800) 872-8633.

— *Travel Medicine Specialist Directory*. Travel Directory, Connaught Laboratories, Dept TC, 1645 Oak Street, Lakewood, NJ 08701. Free listing of physicians who specialize in travel medicine and offer health care before and after international travel.

— *Travelers Health: How to Stay Healthy All Over the World*. Random House. Sixty-six physicians opine on every imaginable health hazard.

— *Travelin' Talk Newsletter and Network*. For handicapped travelers. Call (615) 552-6670. The Society for the Advancement of Travel for the Handicapped also publishes a quarterly newsletter. Call (212) 447-7284.

IMPORTING/EXPORTING

— *Basic Guide to Exporting*. Superintendent of Documents, U.S. Government Printing Office, Washington, D.C. 20229. Call (202) 783-3238.

— *Business America*. U.S. Department of Commerce. Monthly, $60 per year.

— *Commercial Agency: A Guide for Drawing Up of Contracts*. ICC Pub. Call (212) 206-1150.

— *Directory of Latin American Importers and Exporters*. Centro Internacional de Promocion Industrial, P.O. Box 73, Centro Colon, San Jose, Costa Rica. Call 33-86-97.

— *Encyclopedia of Business Information Sources*. Gale Research Company, Book Tower, Detroit, MI 48226. Ask for information related to the area of trade in which you are interested.

— *Export Marketing for Smaller Firms*. U.S. Deptartment of Commerce. Available from the U.S. Government Printing Office.

— *Foreign Business Practices*. U.S. Deptartment of Commerce. Available from the U.S. Government Printing Office. Emphasizes legal aspects of international trade.

— Green, Mary. *How to Be an Importer and Pay for Your World Travel*. Ten Speed Press, 1993.

— *A Guide to Export Documentation*. Educational Development for International Trade. Call (513) 276-5995.

— *Guide to Incoterms*. ICC Pub. Definitions of shipping terms.

— *Handbook on International Trade/Shipping Digest*. Call (212) 689-4411.

— *How to Make a Fortune in Import/Export*. Reston Pub. Written for individuals starting out in international trade. Call (201) 767-5054.

— *Importing into the United States*. U.S. Customs Service. Available from the U.S. Government Printing Office.

— *Network*. World Trade Institute, One World Trade Center, New York, NY 10048. Call (212) 435-8284.

— *Sourcebook*. Unz & Co. Good description of documents used in international trade. Call (800) 631-3098.

INDEX

Medex (evacuation service), 111
Medic Alert tag, 111
Medical issues. *See* Health issues
Medical kit, contents of, 251-53
MedPass, 111
Meeting people, 405-10
  expatriates, 408-9
  local, 405
  other travelers, 407-9
  romance in, 409-10
Melatonin, for jet lag, 224-25
Memories. *See also* Photography
  journal keeping for, 437-38
  of people and places, 453-54
  of travel, 12
Meningococcal meningitis, 243, 254
Menstruation, 225
Mexico
  sights in, 471-72
  train travel in, 352
Michelin Green Guides, 40
Michelin Red Guides, 40
Microsoft Network, travel web site of, 113
Milk, cautions about, 295
Minivans, for local travel, 370-72
Miscellaneous Change Order (MCO), 98
Missing person situations, 65
Modified American Plan (MAP), 78
Mombasa, Kenya, 24
Moment's Notice, 128
Money, 150
  ATM cards, 158-59, 325
  bargaining, 170-74
  black market, 30, 165-70
  change scams with, 426
  credit cards. *See* Credit cards
  debit cards, 159-60, 418
  declaration forms for, 165
  Euro currency, 161
  exchanging, 160-65, 317-18
    rate for, 29
    theft during, 318-19
  money belt for, 195, 301-2
  receiving from home, 154, 160
  saving. *See* Cost cutting
  travelers checks, 150-52
Moneygram, American Express, 154
Monkeys, 215
Monks, etiquette toward, 398
Moon Publications, 42-43
Morocco, train travel in, 352
Mosquitoes, diseases transmitted by
  dengue fever, 231
  Japanese B encephalitis, 237
  malaria, 238-43
  protection against, 210, 273
  yellow fever, 251

Motion sickness, 225-26
Motoeuropa, 377
Mount Kanchenjunga, 345
Mountain Travel/Sobek, 70, 85
MSN online service, 47
Muggers, 321-22
MultiBank currency exchange machine, 162
Multi-country trip, 20-21
Multiple-entry visa, 99

Namibia, sights of, 462
National Geographic maps, 56
National honor, respecting, 395
National Registration Center for Study
    Abroad, 336-37
National tourist offices, 25, 54
National Weather Service reports, 25
Nepal, sights of, 466
New Guinea, sights of, 468
New Zealand
  sights of, 468
  train travel in, 353
News for Solo Travelers, 64
Newsletters, travel-related, 55-56
Newspapers
  airline specials ads in, 136
  work opportunities in, 104
Ngorongoro Crater, Tanzania, 291, 463
No frills carriers, 127, 128
Noise, in lodging, 272
Nord-West Express, 354
North American Travel Guide (maps), 56
Northerner train, 353
NTC Passport Books' Handbooks of the World,
    43

OAG Electronic Edition Travel Services, 55
Oaxaca, Mexico, 413
Office of Overseas Citizens Services, 420
Official Airline Guide, 36, 38
Official Frequent Flyer Guidebook, The, 133
Official Tour Directory (OTD), 38
Officials, dealing with, 309-11
Okavango Delta, Botswana, 148, 462-63
On Track, 145
Online services, 47
Oral rehydration salts, 218, 219, 230
Organized tours. *See* Tour(s)
Orient Express, 354
Ost-West Express, 354
Outdoor Adventure River Specialists, 85-86
Outdoor Vacations for Women over 40, 83
Overbooked flights, 137, 367-68
Overland tours, 83-84
Overseas Adventure Travel, 83

Pacific Air Pass, 129

Reader Survey

Your comments can make future editions of *Traveler's Tool Kit* more useful to other travelers, so please take a few moments to answer the following questions, or just send some of your thoughts and/or experiences to:

Traveler's Tool Kit Reader Survey
P.O. Box 43673
Bimingham, AL 35243

Name (optional): _____

Hometown:_____ State: _____

Your age:_____ Gender: M   F

Where did you travel: _____

Dates of your visit: _____

We'd also like your comments to these questions::
1. Comments about transportation?
2. Comments about lodging?
3. Comments about your luggage?
4. Comments about food or restaurants?
5. Was language a problem? How did you handle it?
6. Were you on a modest budget? moderate? no limit?
7. Was theft a problem?
8. Did you experience any threats to your safety?
9. If you took a tour, what were its good and bad points?
10. Did you travel solo or in a group? Would you change this next time?
11. Where have you most enjoyed traveling?
12. Can you recommend any great adventures?
13. What has been your most amusing experience
14. What surprised you the most while on the road?
15. How have your travels affected your "normal" life?
16. How was Traveler's Tool Kit most useful?
17. What could be included in Traveler's Tool Kit to make it more helpful?

Ordering Information

I hope you'll consider making a gift of *Traveler's Tool Kit* to anyone who just needs some encouragement to get them on the road. If *Traveler's Tool Kit* is not available where you are—or if you would like to order several copies—write to:

Menasha Ridge Press
P.O. Box 43673
Birmingham, AL 35243

Phone: (800) 247-9437 or (205) 322-0439
Fax: (205) 326-1012

To communicate with the author, visit the *Traveler's Tool Kit* homepage site on the World Wide Web. The address is http://www.travelers-tool-kit.com

Future editions of this book will benefit immeasurably from your contributions. If you have an anecdote that supports a point, have spotted an error, or would like information on some area not covered, send a note to me via the publisher. I'd also love to hear how you've used information in the book.

Let the publisher know if you'd like a complete list of its books as well.